Global Insights on Women Empowerment and Leadership

Malika Haoucha
University Hassan II of Casablanca, Morocco

A volume in the Advances in Educational Marketing, Administration, and Leadership (AEMAL) Book Series

Published in the United States of America by
IGI Global
Information Science Reference (an imprint of IGI Global)
701 E. Chocolate Avenue
Hershey PA, USA 17033
Tel: 717-533-8845
Fax: 717-533-8661
E-mail: cust@igi-global.com
Web site: http://www.igi-global.com

Copyright © 2024 by IGI Global. All rights reserved. No part of this publication may be reproduced, stored or distributed in any form or by any means, electronic or mechanical, including photocopying, without written permission from the publisher. Product or company names used in this set are for identification purposes only. Inclusion of the names of the products or companies does not indicate a claim of ownership by IGI Global of the trademark or registered trademark.
Library of Congress Cataloging-in-Publication Data

CIP DATA PROCESSING

2024 Information Science Reference

ISBN(hc) 9798369328064 | ISBN(sc) 9798369349601 | eISBN 9798369328071

This book is published in the IGI Global book series Advances in Educational Marketing, Administration, and Leadership (AEMAL) (ISSN: 2326-9022; eISSN: 2326-9030)

British Cataloguing in Publication Data
A Cataloguing in Publication record for this book is available from the British Library.

All work contributed to this book is new, previously-unpublished material. The views expressed in this book are those of the authors, but not necessarily of the publisher.

For electronic access to this publication, please contact: eresources@igi-global.com.

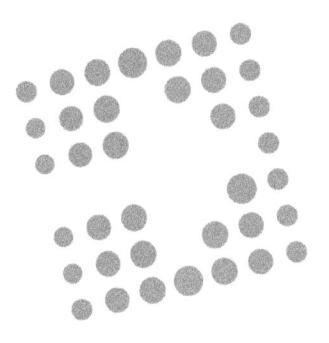

Advances in Educational Marketing, Administration, and Leadership (AEMAL) Book Series

Siran Mukerji
IGNOU, India
Purnendu Tripathi
IGNOU, India

ISSN:2326-9022
EISSN:2326-9030

Mission

With more educational institutions entering into public, higher, and professional education, the educational environment has grown increasingly competitive. With this increase in competitiveness has come the need for a greater focus on leadership within the institutions, on administrative handling of educational matters, and on the marketing of the services offered.

The **Advances in Educational Marketing, Administration, & Leadership (AEMAL) Book Series** strives to provide publications that address all these areas and present trending, current research to assist professionals, administrators, and others involved in the education sector in making their decisions.

Coverage

- Advertising and Promotion of Academic Programs and Institutions
- Enrollment Management
- Educational Leadership
- Educational Marketing Campaigns
- Educational Management
- Direct marketing of educational programs
- Faculty Administration and Management
- Academic Administration
- Consumer Behavior
- Governance in P-12 and Higher Education

IGI Global is currently accepting manuscripts for publication within this series. To submit a proposal for a volume in this series, please contact our Acquisition Editors at Acquisitions@igi-global.com or visit: http://www.igi-global.com/publish/.

The Advances in Educational Marketing, Administration, and Leadership (AEMAL) Book Series (ISSN 2326-9022) is published by IGI Global, 701 E. Chocolate Avenue, Hershey, PA 17033-1240, USA, www.igi-global.com. This series is composed of titles available for purchase individually; each title is edited to be contextually exclusive from any other title within the series. For pricing and ordering information please visit http://www.igi-global.com/book-series/advances-educational-marketing-administration-leadership/73677. Postmaster: Send all address changes to above address. Copyright © 2024 IGI Global. All rights, including translation in other languages reserved by the publisher. No part of this series may be reproduced or used in any form or by any means – graphics, electronic, or mechanical, including photocopying, recording, taping, or information and retrieval systems – without written permission from the publisher, except for non commercial, educational use, including classroom teaching purposes. The views expressed in this series are those of the authors, but not necessarily of IGI Global.

Titles in this Series

For a list of additional titles in this series, please visit: http://www.igi-global.com/book-series/advances-educational-marketing-administration-leadership/73677

Transformative Intercultural Global Education
Isabel María Gómez Barreto (Universidad de Castilla-La Mancha, Spain) and Gorka Roman Etxebarrieta (Universidad del Pais Vasco, Spain)
Information Science Reference • © 2024 • 457pp • H/C (ISBN: 9798369320570) • US $245.00

Challenging Bias and Promoting Transformative Education in Public Schooling Through Critical Literacy
Lyndsey Aubin Benharris (Fitchburg State University, USA) and Katharine Covino (Fitchburg State University, USA)
Information Science Reference • © 2024 • 207pp • H/C (ISBN: 9781668496701) • US $230.00

Decolonizing Inclusive Education Centering Heartwork, Care, and Listening
Erin Keith (St. Francis Xavier University, Canada)
Information Science Reference • © 2024 • 280pp • H/C (ISBN: 9798369318706) • US $235.00

Transformative Leadership and Change Initiative Implementation for P-12 and Higher Education
Tracy Mulvaney (Monmouth University, USA) William O. George (Monmouth University, USA) Jason Fitzgerald (Monmouth University, USA) and Wendy Morales (Monmouth University, USA)
Information Science Reference • © 2024 • 386pp • H/C (ISBN: 9781668499047) • US $290.00

Resilience of Educators in Extraordinary Circumstances War, Disaster, and Emergencies
Enakshi Sengupta (Borders Without Barbed Wires, India) Arni Thor Arnthorsson (American University of Afghanistan, Afghanistan) and M. Bashir Mobasher (American University, USA)
Information Science Reference • © 2024 • 305pp • H/C (ISBN: 9798369314838) • US $240.00

Impact of Gun Violence in School Systems
Jeffrey Herron (Campbellsville University, USA) and Sharon R. Sartin (Campbellsville University, USA)
Information Science Reference • © 2024 • 292pp • H/C (ISBN: 9798369317068) • US $245.00

Narratives and Strategies of Effective Leadership in Community Colleges
Stephen Damian Nacco (Danville Area Community College, USA)
Information Science Reference • © 2024 • 281pp • H/C (ISBN: 9798369317907) • US $245.00

IGI Global
PUBLISHER of TIMELY KNOWLEDGE

701 East Chocolate Avenue, Hershey, PA 17033, USA
Tel: 717-533-8845 x100 • Fax: 717-533-8661
E-Mail: cust@igi-global.com • www.igi-global.com

Table of Contents

Foreword xiv

Preface xv

Chapter 1
Unveiling the Challenges: Exploring Barriers to Women's Empowerment and Leadership 1
    Maneesha Nagabandi, Adler University, USA
    Riley Aris Kowalski, Adler University, USA
    Kailey G. Pickhardt, Adler University, USA
    Courtney Lyn Groenendyk, Adler University, USA

Chapter 2
Systemic Barriers and Challenges Impeding Women's Financial Independence, Empowerment, and Career Growth 17
    Zuberia Aminah Hosanoo, Edinburgh Napier University, UK
    Melina Doargajudhur, Edinburgh Napier University, UK
    Yarti Deonaran, Curtin Mauritius, Mauritius

Chapter 3
Illuminating Paths: Empowerment Through Education and Mentorship 42
    Kritika, Independent Researcher, India

Chapter 4
Empowered Women and Political Leadership 62
    Sureyya Yigit, New Vision University, Georgia

Chapter 5
Moving From Refugee to Entrepreneur in the US: A Feminine Perspective 82
    M. Gail Hickey, Purdue University, Fort Wayne, USA (Emerita)

Chapter 6
The Impact of Climate-Induced Livelihood, Health, and Migration on Women and Girls: A Review.. 100
    Laxmi Kant Bhardwaj, Amity University, Noida, India
    Prangya Rath, Amity University, Noida, India
    Harshita Jain, Amity University, Noida, India
    Sanju Purohit, Akamai University, USA
    Poornima Yadav, Fair Quality Institute, India
    Vartika Singh, Amity University, Noida, India

Chapter 7
An In-Depth Analysis of Women's Social Capital in Abu-Shouk Camp: A Quantitative Assessment.. 119
    Mawa Abdelbagi Osman Mohamed, University of Milano-Bicocca, Italy
    Eslam ElBahlawan, University of Milano-Bicocca, Italy
    Leila Omer Adam Ahmed, Independent Researcher, Sudan

Chapter 8
Empowering Moroccan Women Through Social Entrepreneurship: An Inclusive Approach............ 151
    Malika Haoucha, University Hassan II of Casablanca, Morocco
    Fadila Jehhad, University Hassan II of Casablanca, Morocco

Chapter 9
Women's Land Ownership in Morocco: An Empowerment Initiative... 173
    Malika Haoucha, University Hassan II of Casablanca, Morocco
    Fadila Jehhad, University Hassan II of Casablanca, Morocco
    Karima Ragouba, University Hassan II of Casablanca, Morocco

Chapter 10
Empresses of Legacy: Unveiling the Tapestry of Historical Triumphs in Indian Women's Empowerment 188
    Aparna Rao Yerramilli, GVP College of Engineering, India

Chapter 11
Statistical Analysis of the Empowerment of Women In India... 206
    Jothi Sagar Patil, Shahaji Law College, Kolhapur, India
    Sagar Dnyandev Patil, Sharad Institute of Technology College of Engineering, Yadrav, India
    Moula C. Sheikh, Shahaji Law College, Kolhapur, India

Chapter 12
The Relationship Between Premenstrual Syndrome and Menstrual Attitude: Women's Life
Quality in Deharadun City 217
    S. Srinivasan, Department of Humanities and Social Sciences, Graphic Era University
        (deemed), Dehradun, India
    Somya Rawat, Department of Humanities and Social Sciences, Graphic Era University
        (deemed), Dehradun, India
    Kanchan Yadav, Department of Humanities and Social Sciences, Graphic Era University
        (deemed), Dehradun, India

Chapter 13
The 360-Degree Gender Sphere and the Six Strategies to Create Resilience 259
    Dawn Adams-Harmon, Kean University, USA

Compilation of References 271

About the Contributors 308

Index 313

Detailed Table of Contents

Foreword xiv

Preface xv

Chapter 1
Unveiling the Challenges: Exploring Barriers to Women's Empowerment and Leadership 1
    Maneesha Nagabandi, Adler University, USA
    Riley Aris Kowalski, Adler University, USA
    Kailey G. Pickhardt, Adler University, USA
    Courtney Lyn Groenendyk, Adler University, USA

Women across the world face numerous challenges in obtaining leadership opportunities and economic empowerment. This chapter will focus on a number of these barriers, including gender biases and stereotypes imposed on individuals who identify as women, the impact of microaggressions on individuals in a larger system, economic impediments, and self-imposed biases from internalized identities. Biases and stereotypes are embedded and reinforced in society as early as the developmental years; they are maintained through differing institutions and practices such as the media and microaggressive language. Not only does this impact the expectations placed on women by others, but it also ensures that women may unknowingly minimize their own goals and experiences by internalizing these assumptions. Furthermore, the legal, cultural, and educational hurdles within economic barriers are collectively entwined. Women's empowerment and impediments are complex and salient topics consisting of many related factors, which will be further explored in this chapter.

Chapter 2
Systemic Barriers and Challenges Impeding Women's Financial Independence, Empowerment, and Career Growth 17
    Zuberia Aminah Hosanoo, Edinburgh Napier University, UK
    Melina Doargajudhur, Edinburgh Napier University, UK
    Yarti Deonaran, Curtin Mauritius, Mauritius

The contribution of women has been significant and incremental for decades. Despite enormous efforts of feminists on women's emancipation in the 21st century, women are nevertheless victims of the patriarchal society. Since eras, women in all cultures and societies globally subjected to wide-ranging societal pressure, constraining their role in society, and in their household - limited to bearing and rearing children, household chores, and family maintenance. With education, few women started earning and contributing financially to the household income. Their role in the work spheres have long been limited to low level jobs and career advancement to senior leadership positions have been slow and they are globally under-represented. Empowerment of women occurs through their financial independence and wellbeing. The chapter will be guided by the theories of planned behaviour, self-determination theory and the self-efficacy theory to assess the systemic barriers to women's career progress and propose some valuable recommendations.

Chapter 3
Illuminating Paths: Empowerment Through Education and Mentorship 42
   Kritika, Independent Researcher, India

Expanding access to quality education and mentorship are pivotal yet underutilized strategies for empowering women and girls globally. This chapter examines persistent barriers like poverty, cultural norms, and lack of female teachers inhibiting girls' education access. It highlights interventions including cash transfers, infrastructure improvements, and vocational training that have successfully boosted girls' school participation. However, gender disparities in secondary and higher education remain pervasive, limiting women's opportunities and leadership. The chapter also explores how curricula typically reinforce gender stereotypes rather than building agency,, and advocates approaches promoting skills like entrepreneurship. It emphasizes the benefits of mentors providing guidance, networking, and inspiration as women navigate career challenges, such as the shortage of female role models across sectors. Formal programs, virtual mentoring, and cross-national initiatives expand access amid mentor scarcity.

Chapter 4
Empowered Women and Political Leadership 62
   Sureyya Yigit, New Vision University, Georgia

When referring to empowerment, one focuses on women's greater autonomy, recognition, and the visibility of their contributions. Empowering women involves their full participation in all sectors and at all levels of economic activity to build strong economies, establish more stable and just societies, achieve development, sustainability, and human rights goals, and improve the quality of life of women. Women's access to and control of economic and financial resources is decisive for achieving gender equality, women's empowerment, and the economic growth of all countries. This chapter highlights the challenges and progress that women's empowerment has experienced in the past few decades.

Chapter 5
Moving From Refugee to Entrepreneur in the US: A Feminine Perspective.. 82
   M. Gail Hickey, Purdue University, Fort Wayne, USA (Emerita)

The US refugee population has grown exponentially. More migrants than native-born US residents decide to become entrepreneurs. More than one-third US entrepreneurs are women, yet the scholarship on women entrepreneurs is scarce. This chapter explores the pre- and post-migration experiences and perspectives of a Southeast Asian female refugee entrepreneur residing in the Midwestern United States. The interviewee owns and manages a hair salon. Collected data include recorded oral history interview and transcript, participant observation at the entrepreneur's business, field notes, and a variety of social media sources. Data analysis yielded four emergent themes: memories of growing up/ethnic culture, importance of family and family support, learning the business, and resiliency.

Chapter 6
The Impact of Climate-Induced Livelihood, Health, and Migration on Women and Girls: A Review.. 100
    Laxmi Kant Bhardwaj, Amity University, Noida, India
    Prangya Rath, Amity University, Noida, India
    Harshita Jain, Amity University, Noida, India
    Sanju Purohit, Akamai University, USA
    Poornima Yadav, Fair Quality Institute, India
    Vartika Singh, Amity University, Noida, India

Climate change is among the most well-known issues that the world's communities are currently dealing with in the 21st century. It calls into question basic assumptions about what objectives are suitable for socioeconomic policy, including the relationship between equity, growth, prosperity, and sustainable development. Globally, there is a general perception that the long-term resilience of societies and communities is threatened by climate change. The Earth's climate is changing as a result of greenhouse gas emissions brought on by human activity. Particularly impacted are women and girls, who eventually migrate as a result of food scarcity and social gender division. There are few studies on gender and migration brought on by climate change. An overview of the induced effects of climate change on women and girls' migration, health, and means of subsistence is given in this study. The objective of this article would greatly contribute to our comprehension of the existing connections between migration, patterns of displacement, and the effects of climate change.

Chapter 7
An In-Depth Analysis of Women's Social Capital in Abu-Shouk Camp: A Quantitative Assessment... 119
    Mawa Abdelbagi Osman Mohamed, University of Milano-Bicocca, Italy
    Eslam ElBahlawan, University of Milano-Bicocca, Italy
    Leila Omer Adam Ahmed, Independent Researcher, Sudan

This study explores the complex social bonds among women in the Abu-Shouk camp, an internally displaced person camp in Darfur, Western Sudan, against the backdrop of the prolonged Darfur conflict. Social bonds are essential for women in the Abu-Shouk camp as they provide emotional support, practical assistance, and a sense of community amidst the hardships of displacement. These bonds help them collectively guide daily challenges, fostering resilience and solidarity in the face of adversity. To examine these bonds, a robust research design was employed, including surveys to comprehensively assess various aspects of women's lives, including demographics, trust, solidarity, and women's empowerment. Findings reveal that trust plays a pivotal role, in influencing social relationships within the camp, as women show caution in various relationships. Moreover, education and age impact gift-giving behaviors, indicating potential avenues for stabilizing social ties. The study contributes valuable insights into the lives of women amidst conflict and displacement, emphasizing the centrality of trust and social bonds, and offering important implications for targeted interventions aimed at empowering women and promoting equitable decision-making within challenging contexts.

Chapter 8
Empowering Moroccan Women Through Social Entrepreneurship: An Inclusive Approach............ 151
    Malika Haoucha, University Hassan II of Casablanca, Morocco
    Fadila Jehhad, University Hassan II of Casablanca, Morocco

This chapter explores how social entrepreneurship empowers women in Morocco through an inclusive approach towards disabled women by advancing their economic, social, and political empowerment. The chapter moves progressively by providing a historical context of women's status in Morocco, conceptual frameworks, and impact assessments, with a view to depicting the significant role of social entrepreneurship in driving women empowerment, with a special focus on including women with disabilities. The chapter underscores the importance of collaborative efforts and supportive policies in fostering an enabling environment for sustainable change. It focuses on the significant impact of social entrepreneurship on women's empowerment and calls for continued support and investment in women-led initiatives to create a more inclusive, equitable, and empowered future.

Chapter 9
Women's Land Ownership in Morocco: An Empowerment Initiative... 173
    Malika Haoucha, University Hassan II of Casablanca, Morocco
    Fadila Jehhad, University Hassan II of Casablanca, Morocco
    Karima Ragouba, University Hassan II of Casablanca, Morocco

The present research endeavor consists of a preliminary documentary investigation which paves the way towards a larger future study focusing on Moroccan women who have benefited from government initiatives like the "Centre D'inclusion des Femmes au Foncier" (CIFF) and the Millennium Challenge Corporation (MCC) in empowering them, more specifically, through land ownership. Hence, this chapter provides background information in relation to women empowerment through land ownership and aims to highlight the achievements of the Moroccan government and CIFF in meeting predefined objectives. It's part of a broader vision to address legal, social, and customary barriers hindering women's access to land and to promote their active involvement in land governance.

Chapter 10
Empresses of Legacy: Unveiling the Tapestry of Historical Triumphs in Indian Women's
Empowerment 188
    Aparna Rao Yerramilli, GVP College of Engineering, India

The proposed chapter aims to shed light on Indian Stories of Historical Women's extraordinary courage and achievements which contributed to the empowerment of women in India. Examples of iconic women like Rani Padmini, Rani Lakshmibai, and Savitribai Phule will be discussed so as to illustrate their iconic roles in shaping India's socio-political and educational landscapes. The chapter will also delve into the contributions of these women in giving a direction to the movement of women empowerment in India. Hence, the focus on the women who played a pivotal role in social reforms, revolutionary movements, and political pioneers, freedom fighters, educationists who paved the way for inspiring the future generations to come, in a diverse and vast landscape as India.

Chapter 11
Statistical Analysis of the Empowerment of Women In India 206
    Jothi Sagar Patil, Shahaji Law College, Kolhapur, India
    Sagar Dnyandev Patil, Sharad Institute of Technology College of Engineering, Yadrav, India
    Moula C. Sheikh, Shahaji Law College, Kolhapur, India

In this study, various metrics derived from secondary data are used to assess the extent of women's empowerment in India. As evidenced by the survey, women in India continue to have less status and influence than men, despite multiple government attempts. The number of people who can obtain jobs and education varies based on gender. Depending on factors like age, education level, and employment, women's freedom of movement and decision-making power in the home differ significantly. Women are still accepting gender norms that are not equitable in society, it has been found. The final say in how they are paid has gotten less for women. Women receive less media attention than males do as well. It is more common for rural women than urban ones to experience domestic abuse. The gender gap in political participation is also very noticeable. According to the study's conclusion, achieving the goal of empowerment mostly depends on people's views towards gender equality, even though access to employment and education are only enabling factors.

Chapter 12
The Relationship Between Premenstrual Syndrome and Menstrual Attitude: Women's Life
Quality in Deharadun City 217
    S. Srinivasan, Department of Humanities and Social Sciences, Graphic Era University
        (deemed), Dehradun, India
    Somya Rawat, Department of Humanities and Social Sciences, Graphic Era University
        (deemed), Dehradun, India
    Kanchan Yadav, Department of Humanities and Social Sciences, Graphic Era University
        (deemed), Dehradun, India

The lives of women are characterized by honor and numerous responsibilities, including navigating biological complexities and cultural dynamics. Adjusting daily routines to accommodate menstruation is crucial. This study examines premenstrual syndrome (PMS), menstrual attitude (MA), and quality of life (QoL) for women, aiming to understand their experiences and perspectives on the menstrual cycle. Conducted with 124 female participants aged 18 to 35 in Dehradun, it highlights the significant challenges posed by PMS and MA, particularly for working women and college students, compared to men. Addressing these challenges empowers women and enhances their community. The research underscores the importance of socioeconomic background, revealing greater difficulties faced by women of lower economic status during menstruation. Overall, the study contributes valuable insights into the multidimensional impact of PMS on women's lives and emphasizes the need for supportive attitudes and behaviors towards menstruation.

Chapter 13
The 360-Degree Gender Sphere and the Six Strategies to Create Resilience 259
Dawn Adams-Harmon, Kean University, USA

Women in the bioscience sector continue to be under-represented at higher organizational levels. Only ten percent of the biopharmaceutical industry has female CEOs, and only one company had a board where women outnumbered men. Further, one female CEO exists within the largest pharmaceutical companies: Emma Walmsley of GlaxoSmithKline, and Reshma Kewelramani of Vertex joined in 2020. The bioscience sector is extremely lucrative, where the average female CEO pay is $5.2 million versus the average male earnings of $5.7 million. Diversity at high organizational levels within the bioscience sector is essential. Having women represented at higher organizational levels brings customer perspectives to the strategic decision-making process, provides mentors and sponsors for other women in the organization, and contributes to innovation and creativity. This chapter includes findings from previous research, which showed the barriers encountered "360-Degree Gender Sphere" and the strategies used "Six Strategies to Create Resilience" during career progression by women. There are three modules of this work. The first is an awareness program of the barriers women encounter while ascending in the bioscience sector the 360-degee gender sphere. The second section assesses and accentuates which barriers are most troublesome; and the last segment is "The Six Strategies to Create Resilience Action Plans". These programs assist females in understanding the barriers they may encounter and the necessary strategies one must take to overcome the peripheral "360-Degree Gender Sphere" and create resilience. The 360-degree gender sphere and the six strategies to create resilience conveys decades of knowledge from successful executives in the healthcare industry.

Compilation of References 271

About the Contributors 308

Index 313

Foreword

Global Insights on Women Empowerment and Leadership is a book that explores the transformative journey of women's empowerment and leadership, highlighting the diverse narratives, challenges, and triumphs that shape the landscape of women's empowerment worldwide. The book is not just an assembly of academic theories or statistics, but a heartfelt testament to the indomitable spirit of women who have risen to lead, inspire, and effect change in their communities and beyond. It delves into the multifaceted dimensions of empowerment, shedding light on the intricate interplay between cultural, social, economic, and political factors that influence women's roles and opportunities.

Through insightful fieldwork-based research, case studies, and personal accounts, the book offers a panoramic view of the global struggle for gender equality and the remarkable strides made by women leaders across different sectors and regions. As we navigate the complexities of the 21st century, the imperative to harness the full potential of half the world's population has never been more pressing. The book invites readers to engage in a thoughtful dialogue, challenging conventional wisdom and inspiring innovative approaches to accelerate progress towards gender parity.

The choices we make today will shape the world our daughters and granddaughters inherit. *Global Insights on Women Empowerment and Leadership* is a timely reminder of the resilience, courage, and transformative power of women everywhere, and a compelling reminder that their empowerment is not just a women's issue but a fundamental human right and a shared global responsibility.

Abbadi Idriss
University Hassan II of Casablanca, Morocco

Preface

Before tackling the different parts of the preface to the book: *Global Insights on Women Empowerment and Leadership,* it is worth stopping at the key words which form its title. **"Global Insights"** is a phrase that announces the aim of the whole book which is to provide a global view of the topic. This has been, indeed, achieved through the plethora of contributions through the 25 chapters coming from different authors representing four continents and providing a multitude of perspectives in dealing with the topic. Contributions came from Africa, Asia, America and Europe. The Second term which needs to be defined is "empowerment".

The meaning of the word **"Empowerment"** according to Cambridge Dictionary is "the process of gaining freedom and power to do what you want or to control what happens to you"[1]. In the literature, the word has been used to describe a wide range of concepts and a multitude of outcomes. Empowerment has been employed to depict various ideas and to delineate a multitude of results. Advocating for women's empowerment as a developmental objective is founded on a twofold rationale: asserting that social justice is a crucial facet of human well-being and is inherently valuable to pursue, and positing that women's empowerment serves as a pathway to achieving other objectives (Mehta & Sharma, 2014)[2]. However, despite all the efforts deployed by different countries, at varying degrees, to reach the goals in relation to sustainable development as outlined in the UN "2030 Agenda for Sustainable Development", out of the 17 defined goals, the "Progress towards achieving the gender equality goal has been slow and insufficient. The distance to equal is long and time is short. The world is currently not on track to achieve gender equality by 2030" [3]. Some progress has been achieved when it comes to women in political decision-making posts but a large gap is still persistent, according to the UN report on Women in Politics: 2023 [4]. Another term that requires some attention in the title is **"Leadership"**. It comes after empowerment and that is for a purpose. It is quite evident that in order to lead, one has to be given the authority and power to do so.

When it comes to women leadership, despite notable advancements achieved through strenuous efforts, women's representation is not progressing at an adequate rate. This observation is underscored by the 2023 findings from the Women in the Workplace report by McKinsey, conducted in collaboration with LeanIn.Org [5]. According to the same findings, women belonging to ethnic minority groups continue to be inadequately represented across all levels of corporate hierarchy. Nevertheless, there is a promising trend emerging in senior leadership in comparison with the sluggish progress for women at the manager and director levels.

In *Global Insights on Women Empowerment and Leadership,* we embark on a profound journey into the complexities, challenges, and triumphs of women's empowerment across the globe. Through a collection of 25 chapters, we delve into diverse contexts, from the barriers hindering women's access to leadership roles to the transformative initiatives driving change in communities worldwide.

The book begins by peeling back the layers of systemic obstacles faced by women, including gender biases, stereotypes, and institutional norms. From examining the multifaceted challenges impeding women's career progression to exploring the enduring hurdles obstructing their leadership advancement, our contributors shed light on the intricate nature of women's empowerment and the urgent need for collaborative action to dismantle systemic barriers.

Throughout the book, we journey through diverse landscapes, from the entrepreneurial arenas of Morocco to the political landscapes of Turkey and the economic realities of migrant workers in India. We uncover the transformative power of social entrepreneurship, the potential of mobile internet access to empower rural women, the resilience of refugee women entrepreneurs in the US, and the challenges faced by unorganized women migrant workers, offering insights into the intersections of gender, migration, and economic empowerment worldwide.

Additionally, we explore the impact of climate change on women's livelihoods, the role of social capital in conflict settings, and the historical triumphs of women leaders who shaped nations' socio-political landscapes. Through empirical studies, theoretical frameworks, and personal narratives, each chapter offers a unique perspective on the journey towards women's empowerment and leadership.

ORGANIZATION OF THE BOOK

This book consists of 13 chapters which offer global insights into the topic of women empowerment and leadership. A brief description of each chapter follows:

Unveiling the Challenges: Exploring Barriers to Women's Empowerment and Leadership

This chapter examines the multifaceted challenges hindering women's access to leadership roles and economic empowerment worldwide. It identifies various barriers, including gender biases, stereotypes, microaggressions, economic obstacles, and self-imposed biases stemming from internalized identities. These barriers are deeply entrenched in society from early developmental stages and are perpetuated through institutional practices such as media representation and subtle forms of discrimination. They not only shape societal expectations of women but also lead women to undermine their own ambitions and experiences by internalizing these assumptions. Additionally, legal, cultural, and educational hurdles compound economic challenges for women. The chapter underscores the intricate nature of women's empowerment and the pervasive obstacles they face, with a commitment to further exploration of these issues.

Systemic Barriers and Challenges Impeding Women's Financial Independence, Empowerment and Career Growth

The chapter underscores the ongoing struggle for women's empowerment despite advancements. It highlights how societal norms confine women to domestic roles, limiting their opportunities for career advancement. While some women achieve financial independence through education and employment,

Preface

they often face barriers in reaching senior leadership positions. The chapter aims to explore these systemic obstacles using theories such as planned behavior and self-determination. It will offer recommendations to address these challenges and promote women's empowerment through financial autonomy and overall well-being.

Illuminating Paths: Empowerment through Education and Mentorship

The chapter discusses the significance of education and mentorship in empowering women and girls globally. It identifies barriers such as poverty, cultural norms, and the lack of female teachers hindering girls' access to education. Successful interventions like cash transfers and vocational training have increased girls' school participation, but gender disparities persist in higher education and leadership roles. The chapter advocates for curricula that promote agency and skills like entrepreneurship. It highlights the importance of mentorship in navigating career challenges and suggests formal programs and virtual mentoring platforms to address the shortage of female role models.

Empowered Women and Political Leadership

When discussing empowerment, the emphasis lies on enhancing women's autonomy, acknowledgment, and the visibility of their contributions. Empowering women entails enabling their full engagement across various economic sectors and levels to bolster economies, foster fairer and more stable societies, accomplish developmental, sustainable, and human rights objectives, and enhance women's quality of life. Women's access to and management of economic and financial resources play a crucial role in realizing gender equality, women's empowerment, and the economic advancement of nations worldwide. This chapter highlights both the obstacles and advancements in women's empowerment over recent decades.

Moving from Refugee to Entrepreneur in the US: A Feminine Perspective

The chapter focuses on the experiences of a Southeast Asian female refugee entrepreneur in the Midwest United States. Despite a significant increase in the US refugee population, there is limited research on women entrepreneurs, who represent a substantial portion of the entrepreneurial community. The entrepreneur owns and manages a hair salon, and data collection involved oral history interviews, participant observations, field notes, and social media sources. Analysis revealed four main themes: memories of upbringing and ethnic culture, the importance of family support, learning the business, and resilience.

The Impact of Climate-Induced Livelihood, Health and Migration on Women and Girls: A Review

The text discusses the prominent issue of climate change in the 21st century and its implications for socioeconomic policies, emphasizing the interconnectedness of equity, growth, prosperity, and sustainable development. It highlights the global perception that climate change poses a significant threat to the resilience of societies and communities due to human-induced greenhouse gas emissions. Particularly affected are women and girls, who often face migration due to food scarcity and gender-based social divisions, yet research on this intersection remains limited. The text aims to provide an overview of the impacts of climate change on women and girls, focusing on migration, health, and livelihoods, with the goal of enhancing understanding of the complex relationships between migration patterns, displacement, and climate change effects.

An In-Depth Analysis of Women's Social Capital in Abu-Shouk Camp: A Quantitative Assessment

This study investigates the social dynamics among women in the Abu-Shouk camp, located in Darfur, Western Sudan, amidst the prolonged conflict in the region. Surveys were conducted to explore various aspects of women's lives, such as demographics, trust, solidarity, and empowerment. The findings highlight the crucial role of trust in shaping social relationships within the camp, with women exercising caution in their interactions. Additionally, education and age influence gift-giving behaviors, suggesting potential strategies for strengthening social connections. Overall, the study provides valuable insights into women's experiences in conflict and displacement contexts, emphasizing the importance of trust and social bonds while offering implications for empowering women and promoting fair decision-making.

Empowering Moroccan Women Through Social Entrepreneurship: An Inclusive Approach

This chapter delves into how social entrepreneurship in Morocco is empowering women, particularly those with disabilities, through an inclusive approach that advances their economic, social, and political standing. It progresses by offering insights into the historical context of women's status in Morocco, introducing conceptual frameworks, and conducting impact assessments. Its primary aim is to highlight the pivotal role of social entrepreneurship in promoting women's empowerment, with a specific emphasis on the inclusion of disabled women. Additionally, it stresses the importance of collaborative efforts and supportive policies in cultivating an environment conducive to sustainable change. The chapter underscores the significant influence of social entrepreneurship on women's empowerment and advocates for continued support and investment in initiatives led by women to foster a future that is more inclusive, equitable, and empowered.

Women's Land Ownership in Morocco: An Empowerment Initiative

This research project comprises an initial documentary investigation that sets the stage for a larger forthcoming study focusing on Moroccan women who have been empowered through government initiatives such as the "Centre D'inclusion des Femmes au Foncier" (CIFF) and the Millennium Challenge Corporation (MCC), particularly in terms of land ownership. The chapter provides background information on women's empowerment through land ownership and highlights the achievements of the Moroccan government and CIFF in reaching predetermined objectives. It is part of a broader effort to address legal, social, and customary barriers hindering women's access to land and to promote their active engagement in land governance.

Preface

Empresses of Legacy: Unveiling the Tapestry of Historical Triumphs in Indian Women's Empowerment

The proposed chapter aims to explore the remarkable courage and achievements of historical Indian women, highlighting their contributions to women's empowerment in India. It will examine iconic figures such as Rani Padmini, Rani Lakshmibai, and Savitribai Phule, illustrating their influential roles in shaping India's socio-political and educational landscapes. Additionally, the chapter will discuss how these women contributed to the advancement of women's empowerment in India, focusing on their involvement in social reforms, revolutionary movements, and political pioneering. By showcasing these inspiring individuals, the chapter seeks to inspire future generations in the diverse and expansive context of India.

Statistical Analysis of the Empowerment of Women in India

This study examines the level of women's empowerment in India through secondary data analysis. Despite governmental initiatives, women still lag behind men in terms of status and influence. Disparities persist in employment and educational opportunities based on gender, with various factors like age, education, and employment status playing significant roles. Women's autonomy within households varies significantly based on these factors. Gender norms continue to shape women's empowerment, affecting their financial control and media visibility. Rural women face higher rates of domestic violence, and there is a significant gender gap in political participation. Ultimately, the study concludes that achieving women's empowerment hinges largely on societal attitudes towards gender equality, with access to education and employment serving as crucial enabling factors.

The Relationship Between Premenstrual Syndrome and Menstrual Attitude: Women's Life Quality in Deharadun City

This chapter examines the experiences of women regarding Premenstrual Syndrome (PMS), Menstrual Attitude (MA), and Quality of Life (QoL). Conducted with 124 female participants aged 18 to 35 in Dehradun, it highlights the challenges posed by PMS and MA, particularly for working women and college students compared to men. The research emphasizes the importance of addressing these challenges to empower women and improve the community. Additionally, it underscores the impact of socioeconomic background, revealing greater difficulties faced by women from lower economic strata during menstruation. Overall, the study provides valuable insights into the multidimensional impact of PMS on women's lives and emphasizes the need for supportive attitudes and behaviors towards menstruation.

The 360-Degree Gender Sphere and the Six Strategies to Create Resilience

Chapter 13 addresses the under-representation of women in higher organizational levels within the bioscience sector and emphasizes the importance of diversity at these levels. It incorporates findings from previous research, which identified barriers faced by women in advancing their careers in biosciences, as well as strategies used to overcome these barriers. The chapter is divided into three modules: an awareness program highlighting barriers in the bioscience sector, assessments to identify the most challenging barriers, and action plans based on "The Six Strategies to Create Resilience." These strategies draw on the experiences of successful female executives in healthcare, with the aim of sharing essential knowledge with readers.

With its strengths and weaknesses, this book, through the plethora of research findings, narratives, reflections, and all the human effort invested in it, by both male and female contributors, the hope is for it contribute another building block to the architecture already established in the literature of women empowerment and leadership worldwide.

As the editor of the book, I extend my heartfelt gratitude to all the contributors whose expertise and passion have enriched this volume. I hope their voices will continue to resonate far and wide and their work will serve as a catalyst for dialogue, action, and progress in the ongoing pursuit of gender equality and the empowerment of women worldwide.

Malika HAOUCHA
FSJES, University Hassan II of Casablanca, Morocco

ENDNOTES

[1] https://dictionary.cambridge.org/dictionary/english/empowerment

[2] Mehta, P., Sharma, K. 2021. Leadership: Determinant of Women Empowerment. SCMS Journal of Indian Management, April - June, 2014

[3] https://www.unwomen.org/en/what-we-do/2030-agenda-for-sustainable-development

[4] https://www.unwomen.org/en/digital-library/publications/2023/03/women-in-politics-map-2023

[5] https://www.mckinsey.com/featured-insights/diversity-and-inclusion/women-in-the-workplace#/

Chapter 1
Unveiling the Challenges:
Exploring Barriers to Women's Empowerment and Leadership

Maneesha Nagabandi
https://orcid.org/0009-0003-5404-6434
Adler University, USA

Riley Aris Kowalski
https://orcid.org/0009-0002-9238-8462
Adler University, USA

Kailey G. Pickhardt
Adler University, USA

Courtney Lyn Groenendyk
Adler University, USA

ABSTRACT

Women across the world face numerous challenges in obtaining leadership opportunities and economic empowerment. This chapter will focus on a number of these barriers, including gender biases and stereotypes imposed on individuals who identify as women, the impact of microaggressions on individuals in a larger system, economic impediments, and self-imposed biases from internalized identities. Biases and stereotypes are embedded and reinforced in society as early as the developmental years; they are maintained through differing institutions and practices such as the media and microaggressive language. Not only does this impact the expectations placed on women by others, but it also ensures that women may unknowingly minimize their own goals and experiences by internalizing these assumptions. Furthermore, the legal, cultural, and educational hurdles within economic barriers are collectively entwined. Women's empowerment and impediments are complex and salient topics consisting of many related factors, which will be further explored in this chapter.

DOI: 10.4018/979-8-3693-2806-4.ch001

INTRODUCTION

Despite growing awareness of women's empowerment in recent years, several barriers remain to accomplishing an overall sense of power or equality. Barriers[1] are impediments or obstacles that prevent the movement and achievement of a process. Identifying such barriers to women's empowerment is crucial in addressing the structural and societal difficulties women face to promote and foster a sense of inclusivity and power, specifically within the leadership space. Reducing the obstructions to women's empowerment and leadership improves economic stability, health outcomes, and improves the well-being of women everywhere (Kooser, 2017). This chapter will discuss different barriers and their impact on women and their ability to enter and thrive in leadership.

BIASES AND STEREOTYPES

Although biases and stereotypes are related, they are distinct in that one's biases or assumptions can lead to generalizations or stereotypes. In a bidirectional fashion, these stereotypes can also lead to biases. Biases[2] are defined as "tendencies to favor or dislike a person or thing, especially as a result of a preconceived opinion" (Oxford University Press, n.d.). These biases can be created by an individual's background, culture, or personal experiences within a said group. Biases can be either implicit or explicit in nature, differentiated by the level of consciousness to both the presence and influence of preconceived notions of a group of people. Implicit biases[3] are those unconscious or unknown to the individual and entail their own challenges in addressing, specifically the lack of awareness of the presence of these biases and the subsequent harm they may cause to individuals within those groups. One may tend to gravitate toward a particular group, and when engaging in this bias, one may start to define these groups by overarching traits via stereotyping. Stereotypes[4] are defined as "a set of beliefs about the characteristics of a social group or category, where members of that category are assumed to have certain characteristics, based on membership of that group" (King, 2021). They are comprised of generalizations about a particular group of individuals, and although may be true for one individual, these labels and assumptions are not valid for the rest. Stereotyping may also lead to biases in that believing certain traits or aspects about a particular group can shape an individual's tendencies or actions towards that group or individuals within that group. In this chapter, we will focus on the biases and stereotypes geared towards women and the continual impact they have on women's advancement in leadership.

There are numerous types of differing gender stereotypes. The three types include (a) masculine and feminine stereotypes which describe differences in personality or behavioral traits; (b) male and female occupational stereotypes, which include how work is seen differently between the genders; (c) stereotypes associated with family and professional roles which describe a prototypical division (Mollaeva, 2017). Traits commonly deemed masculine include agentive, assertive, or self-protective. People described in such ways can be defined as "go-getters" who may be seen as willing to do anything it takes to get what they want or gain power or status. They may also be seen as more able to protect themselves and more independent. Traits often deemed feminine include considerations of being more communal, selfless, or concerned for others (Stein, 1992). As such, women are commonly perceived as having tendencies that focus on the well-being of others and are expected to put themselves last. They are seen as more likely to focus on community and be less "self-centered" than their male counterparts. Similarly, women in power are generally thought of as being weaker than their male counterparts, whether that be physically and/or mentally. They are often considered "too emotional," an attribute deemed to be both a negative quality and overtly detrimental in leadership or when considering a position of power. Women are often seen as not having the "strength" to withstand the intricacies of cutthroat work environments and leadership positions. Being prescribed these traits suggests that women in leadership are not willing to take risks and advocate for themselves and their subordinates, leading to a more passive depiction in a role necessitating a capacity for assertion and advocacy.

The Role of Biases and Stereotypes During Development

These biases and stereotypes are embedded and enforced in society through various systems and are often influenced and maintained by experiences during critical developmental years. As children grow up, their parents and the essential figures around them teach and demonstrate behavior through modeling. Though there is no concrete harm in growing up in a household with specific gender roles, learning that a specific lifestyle is obligatory and necessary can lead to the development of gender stereotypes. Learning from parents or other adults that men must behave in one way and women must behave in another way can lead a child to adopt those preconceived notions and subsequently assume that this is how the world works. Evidence shows that individuals first begin to perceive cultural stereotypes, specifically gender and race, and then begin to prefer peers of the same gender between the ages of two and three years old (King, 2021). Although most individuals prefer those identifying in a group similar to theirs, having an additional negative perception of other groups often leads to harmful stereotypes and biases. In a later section of this chapter, we will discuss the impact such assumptions can have on the individual within the group. These gender expectations are also taught within common culture through mechanisms such as media, peer interactions, and teachers. For example, it has been a long-standing idea that boys are better in mathematics than girls, when in fact there is no significant difference when looking at grades (Else-Quest, 2010). These notions can lead to an increase in academic anxiety and a decrease in academic motivation and progression among females. This not only poses a challenge for women in academia but also for those individuals aiming for a career in leadership as their male counterparts are likely to be seen as more intelligent or focused on their career.

Media

Media has played an instrumental role in both the development and maintenance of stereotypes. Female characters in media often exhibit the "typical" gender characteristics, such as caring "too much" about their appearance and being weak, emotional, caring, and nurturing (Fernandez, 2022) Not only does the media often reflect the assumptions perpetuated by society, but it continues to teach and establish these values and ideas to young minds. Another analysis found that 58 percent of doll commercials feature only girls, while 87 percent of transportation and construction toy commercials feature only boys (Ward, 2020). Not only does this broadcast the stereotype of what toys specific genders play with, but it can also lead to a bigger picture of how girls view their capabilities for the future. Although boys play with dolls, these dolls are often more masculine and include superheroes, military, and warriors, while girls typically have baby dolls or cooking sets. These commercials further promote the stereotype that women must care for the family and are gentler and more caring by nature.

Stereotypes and Gender Roles

Pertaining to occupational stereotypes, there are specific assumptions in many career paths regarding the gender of individuals in that profession. For example, doctors are typically thought of as male, as is much of the medical and scientific fields, while nurses are typically thought of as female. Careers such as doctors require more schooling and education compared to other fields of study, and women are seen as not intelligent or capable enough for occupying such a position. This automatic assumption minimizes the opportunities available for women to rise to leadership within the occupational area of functioning.

There are also generalizations that women should stay at home and take care of their family while men are the breadwinners and the individuals who work (Lee, 2020). Though historically a division of roles in this manner was common, the Industrial Revolution brought about a change in the dynamics of the workplace and the subsequent legal abilities of women to hold roles in different occupational spaces (Stanfors, 2017); due to the elevated necessity for manual labor from a boom in the economy, women were suddenly able to procure employment in factory-level positions. While the international population as a whole better understood that women were in fact capable of holding jobs, the norm became riddled with the expectation that women must concurrently manage home and work responsibilities and thus were unable to handle their careers as well as their male counterparts could. Today, this assumed division of roles poses a serious problem as individuals, irrespective of gender, should be able to choose their paths, whether it be a doctor or a homemaker, and these biases toward women impede their ability to progress in leadership in the manner a male individual can.

While these assumptions may be true for individuals, the problem is rooted in human nature to assume and expect the same behavior and perspective from all individuals within the group. Not all stereotypes around women are overtly harmful such as the idea that women are more caring, kind, and warm; though they become overtly detrimental to these individuals when these ideas or values become expected of them. Although some gender-related features may be genuine for specific individuals, the overemphasis and generalization of differences between these genders discredit both the differences and accomplishments among women such as obtaining higher positions in their occupations, advocating for their rights, or being able to be financially independent, like purchasing a house. When we apply these stereotypes, we assume specific attributes for all women, when that is not always the case, and hold expectations as to how one should behave. Women subsequently face unfavorable consequences when these societal expectations are not met, despite the relevance to the individual in question.

There are many areas of functioning in which biases and stereotypes have affected women in leadership. One such space is work performance; those who identify as women often receive lower evaluations or promotions compared to those who identify as men (Blau, 2006). Companies are less likely to hire women, which can be based on multiple reasons including stereotypes such as the automatic assumption that most women want to have children and the subsequent assumption that this desire will negatively impact their ability to work and an extra need for time off. It was found that women's applications were given less priority than men's and were at even more of a disadvantage when the women were mothers (González, 2019). The study found that a highly skilled woman without children had a 12.4 percent chance of receiving a call back while a woman with children with the same skill level had a 7.9 percent chance. In comparison, men without children continued to receive more priority, with a 13.6 percent chance of callback, as did men with children with, at a 12.6 percent chance; demonstrating the immense impact stereotypes can have on women empowerment in leadership, setting them back in employment opportunities before they begin. Even fitting the stereotype of being a mother can set women back in employment opportunities. Although these results depend on the occupation and the employers, women in the workspace continue to be a topic of evaluation.

Exposure at a young age to these stereotypical role definitions and expectations is applied to the roles and occupations of women throughout life. As individuals grow up, these biases and stereotypes are maintained through more diverse and direct interactions with the world. These stereotypes have even come into play in the discussion revolving around systemic issues, such as voting and equal opportunities, and in current-day reproductive rights and political roles. Not only do women learn these gender roles and stereotypes from those around them, but these expectations continue to be perpetuated via larger systems such as the media. These stereotypes and biases are often created and maintained by a lack of information, and although they may not necessarily be present in the conscious awareness of people, they can create lasting effects on women. The first step to addressing such assumptions is acknowledging the bias one holds as an individual. Continuing to learn about stereotypes and their impacts can have a large cascading effect on the ability of individuals within groups to accomplish their goals and, in this context, the ability of women to ascertain roles in leadership and an overall sense of empowerment.

Case Example

The following is a case example highlighting the impact of stereotypes in the workplace.

In the Supreme Court case of Price Waterhouse vs Hopkins, Ann Hopkins sued her employer, Price Waterhouse, an accounting firm, due to discriminatory decisions based on her sex. She reported that she was postponed a partnership role due to sex stereotypes because she did not present as "feminine enough" (Fiske, 1991). She was seen as more aggressive and assertive and was told to portray more feminine traits, such as walking and talking more femininely and wearing makeup. Hopkins defied the gender stereotypes placed on her and the perceived dissonance that negatively impacted her ability to pursue her career. This case demonstrates the complexity of stereotypes and their harmful nature when women do not meet the expectations set forth on them by others, specifically in the workforce and institutional settings. Although this case did end up in Hopkins' favor due to the Civil Rights Act, it demonstrates the harm stereotyping and expectations can have in the leadership space.

Microaggressions

In the landscape of impediments to women's empowerment and leadership, subtle yet impactful phenomena known as microaggressions play a significant role. These microaggressions manifest in various forms, encompassing microassaults, microinsults, and microinvalidations. Microassaults are explicit derogations marked by verbal or nonverbal attacks meant to inflict harm through name-calling, avoidant behavior, or purposeful discriminatory actions (Sue, 2007). For example, questioning an individual's competence or leadership abilities solely based on their gender, constitutes microassaults that hinder women's progress in the workplace. Microinsults, on the other hand, involve communications conveying rudeness and insensitivity, often undermining a person's identity via underlying messages (Sue, 2007). An example of a microinsult could be a colleague making subtle derogatory comments about a woman's ethnic background during a team meeting, thereby demeaning her identity. Additionally, microinvalidations consist of communications that exclude, negate, or nullify the psychological thoughts, feelings, or experiential reality of individuals from nondominant societal groups (Sue, 2007). For instance, a woman may encounter microinvalidations when her contributions in a meeting are consistently overlooked, negating her valuable input.

Microaggressions are operationalized to include being interpreted negatively by most if not all nondominant group members, reflect implicitly prejudicial motives, and harm the recipients' mental health (Lilienfield 2017). Nondominant groups, particularly women, frequently find themselves navigating professional relationships with colleagues or supervisors who express bias through microaggressions. These daily occurrences, whether intentional or unintentional, constitute brief indignities that communicate hostile slights and insults toward nondominant groups. Such experiences extend across various life domains, including occupational settings. A female executive consistently facing avoidant behavior from her male counterparts during collaborative projects hinders her ability to lead effectively.

The ambiguous nature of microaggressions poses challenges for individuals as they grapple with understanding the events and their meanings, potentially disrupting ongoing cognitive processes (Sue 2007). Moreover, microaggressions can have profound impacts on individuals' well-being and performance; targets of microaggressions may experience decreased sleep quality, heightened negative affect, and even depression (Fattoracci & King, 2022). These psychological disturbances play a strong role in overall well-being and thus greatly impact productivity, sense of accomplishment, feelings of empowerment, and more. The internalization of these negative perspectives conveyed through microaggressions about one's social group can further erode self-efficacy, ultimately diminishing performance outcomes (Fattoracci & King, 2022). For example, a woman constantly subjected to microaggressions questioning her competence in a seemingly subtle manner may eventually internalize these doubts, impacting her overall confidence and work performance.

Furthermore, these microaggressions are often viewed as insignificant to members of the dominant group or those in power, posing a notable difficulty in making a change. Microaggressions are subtle and often unintentional as they are fueled by implicit bias that the individuals are unaware of. Societal norms and cultural contexts often normalize these biases, making it harder for individuals of dominant groups to identify microaggressions. This difficulty is further impacted by a lack of awareness, the intentional nature of the impact, a lack of accountability, and a general lack of acknowledgment of the power dynamics at play. Moreover, individuals with less power often host a fear of confrontation regarding microaggressive language and are likely to be apprehensive of being perceived as overly sensitive or an inconvenience. These difficulties in identifying and addressing microaggressions serve as barriers to ensuring an inclusive work environment and subsequently act as impediments to women's empowerment and leadership.

Researchers have suggested that individuals facing microaggressions can employ self-protective strategies and engage in collective resistance efforts to disarm such occurrences fostering resilience. Recognizing the need for interventions in the workplace, efforts should focus on both effective victim-response strategies and altering perpetrator behavior (Fattoracci & King, 2022). Creating organizational climates intolerant of microaggressions is paramount. Similar to workshops addressing sexual harassment, there is a call for empirically informed interventions to educate employees about microaggressions. An example of such an intervention could be a workshop where employees learn to recognize and address microaggressions in the workplace, fostering a more inclusive and respectful environment. By understanding and acknowledging that microaggressions are unacceptable and unprofessional behaviors, irrespective of intent, organizations can take significant strides in eliminating subtly interpersonal biases at work.

The concept of death by a thousand cuts metaphorically describes the cumulative impact of seemingly small, incremental challenges and obstacles that collectively have a profound effect. In the context of women's empowerment and leadership, these seemingly minute occurrences and challenges, such as gender bias, stereotyping, discrimination, microaggressions, and more, accumulate to chip away at women's well-being and empowerment over time, subsequently hindering their ability to attain leadership positions. Communities and institutions must work together to challenge these barriers, create inclusive environments that empower the individuals within them, and foster both well-being and professional success.

ECONOMIC FACTORS IMPACTING WOMEN'S SUCCESS

Economic Barriers on the Macro Level

Women across the world face numerous challenges in obtaining leadership opportunities and economic empowerment. This is a vital area of exploration in understanding women's empowerment, for the fact that international economies continue to bar women from occupational and financial prosperity. Economic success perspective has the ability to provide women with a wider range of opportunities for leadership and empowerment in other aspects of their lives. Economic barriers are just one macro-level factor that impacts women's achievement of leadership opportunities. However, to better understand how economic barriers impede women from achieving executive success, it is imperative to analyze the micro-level factors that impact gender-based economic disparities. Globally, women face more legal, educational, and cultural constraints than men, which obstructs them from entering the workforce or obtaining jobs that provide upward mobility opportunities (Lemmon & Vogelstein, 2017). The result is an astounding gap in the number of women employed as compared to men and the pay differences between them. Because this is a common occurrence throughout the world, it logically follows that women struggle to achieve leadership opportunities when they are not compensated fairly or able to get their foot in the door to start.

The scope of economic disparities impacting women is pervasive and deeply rooted in systemic obstacles related to gender biases, stereotypes, and discrimination which lend to identity issues cross-culturally for women seeking economic empowerment. Although widespread recognition that policy change is needed to further capitalize on women's participation in economic endeavors, international economic leaders have continued to undervalue women's contributions to the workforce and broader global economies (Lemmon & Vogelstein, 2017). However, multilateral bodies such as Group of Twenty (G20) and the Asia-Pacific Economic Cooperation (APEC) forum have made commitments to stimulate economic growth by advancing women in the economy throughout African and Asian countries. Similar agreements have led to economic reformation in various countries which has increased women's ability to contribute to and benefit from their economies. Despite these modest developments, structural and cultural barriers based on gender continue to inhibit women's access to higher-wage occupations as well as perpetuate gender-wage gaps across the globe.

In an attempt to evade inequality in American labor markets, increasing numbers of women have begun choosing small-business ownership over larger enterprise endeavors (Losocco & Robinson, 1991). These small-business arenas tend to be in niches that men are uninterested in and converge within traditionally female-typed fields. Although women may feel drawn to small-business ownership, the same institutional disadvantages follow them into the small-business sector as well. While some research has indicated that owning a small business is a mechanism for upward mobility, the literature has suggested otherwise. For example, in societies with advanced capitalism, as it exists in the United States, small businesses occupy lower-ranked positions in the economy and experience higher rates of economic failure resulting in the persistence of labor market discrimination (Losocco & Robinson, 1991).

Micro-Level Factors Impeding Economic Success

The pipeline for women to achieve leadership opportunities and economic prosperity also requires adequate access to education, training, and mentoring. Many of the same micro-level barriers that impact women's economic achievement prevent them from receiving or affording education, further hindering women's advancement. While there has been an increase in women's presentation in higher education and positions of power in the United States, the disparities persist. Further still, legal and cultural boundaries exist internationally that obstruct women's educational empowerment and subsequent occupational advancement.

Entrepreneurship

Globally, women have shown an increasing interest in entrepreneurship resulting in the establishment of more female-owned and led businesses. As of 2016, the South African government has placed high importance on promoting entrepreneurship and business development for women to bolster economic prosperity (Meyer & Mostert, 2016). It has been observed that women carrying out entrepreneurial endeavors within their communities have made a recognizable impact on the innovation, employment, and wealth dispersion experienced in local economies (Popal & Langley, 2021). Following the COVID-19 pandemic, Syrian women who were working informally found creative ways to support themselves and other community members who were impacted by economic hardships, which aided in alleviating pressures on the labor market (Revel, 2020). Despite moderate improvements, South Africa and numerous other countries continue to lag in the creation of women's entrepreneurship programming.

Female entrepreneurs in the Middle Eastern and North African (MENA) regions are frequently shut out of credit markets and according to the International Finance Corporation (IFC), there is a nearly "$16 billion gap between the amount of credit they need and [what] they actually receive," (Popal & Langley, 2021). Meaning, the economic barriers facing women are extensive regardless of entrepreneurship opportunities. The World Bank analyzed ten years' worth of data to determine the impact legal discrimination has on women's employment and entrepreneurial undertakings. Results showed that most global economies award women three-quarters of the legal rights men have, meanwhile, women in MENA economies have less than half that of men (Popal & Langley, 2021). The support of entrepreneurship has the ability to promote innovation and bolster both local and national economies. A 2016 report on economic recovery and revitalization discovered that the creation of ten new enterprises led to nearly $1.5 billion in new revenue and roughly 2,500 new jobs (Popal & Langley, 2021). Because women face disproportionate discrimination in entrepreneurship, specifically within the MENA region, increased support for women's success can further enhance local and national economies.

Leadership

Although women have made significant strides in obtaining leadership and managerial opportunities, the "glass ceiling"[11] has continued to block women from occupational and economic equality (Ballenger, 2010). Former president of Harvard University, Larry Summers, is infamous for stating that women

Unveiling the Challenges

are "under-represented at the top of science and engineering because such leadership positions require a level of commitment that they are not ready to make," (Larry Summers, 2005, as cited in Cahyati et al., 2021). However, there are two major opposing theories for why women face difficulty in obtaining leadership positions: social role theory and expectation rates theory (Ballenger, 2010). Social role theory posits that female leaders are judged on a biased spectrum due to discriminatory beliefs about women and their ability to lead. Expectation rates theory goes a step further to describe how gender stereotypes and the perceived lower status of women lead to bias in the evaluation of female leaders (Ballenger 2010).

Additional barriers preventing women from high-power positions include education systems that are not providing the workforce skills essential to leadership. For example, case studies examining Jordan, Tunisia, and Oman have shown inadequate skills training in management, teamwork, leadership, and communication for women as compared to men (Popal & Langley, 2021). Furthermore, girls are at an increased risk of dropping out of school entirely, a potentially massive detriment to future economic prospects. Women tend to dominate in civil society and social work fields but are "underrepresented in decision-making positions worldwide," (Popal and Langley, 2021 p.6). Thus the resulting policy decisions being made regarding women's opportunities are not created by women, nor are they consulted in any part of the process.

An examination of over 300 Indonesian individuals in leadership positions (i.e., executives, directors, and CEOs) found that when comparing managerial and leadership qualities, women outperformed men when it came to appointing employees, developing staff, and organizing others' work (Cahyati et al., 2021). Women also outperformed their male counterparts in leadership skills such as expressing visions, setting high standards of performance, and maintaining responsibilities.

Mentorship

Women's career development is impaired by the disproportionate number of mentoring opportunities available for them compared to men. In addition to formal mentorship differences between men and women, there are informal partnerships that form as well and disadvantage women's success. The "good old boy network" as a concept in which male managers create circles where women are uninvited and unwelcome, leading to exclusion from occupational decision-making as a result (Ballenger, 2010). However, the implementation and expansion of mentoring for women has the potential to assist women in overcoming barriers and breaking down the glass ceiling.

Mentorship programs for women have found the most benefits to come from multiple mentors as well as different types of mentoring relationships (Ballenger, 2010). A diverse mentoring experience has the potential to address the mentee's self-confidence, provide career advice, offer friendship, and provide emotional support. Mentoring and being mentored is an essential step in creating greater equality within educational and occupational settings to support women in achieving leadership roles. Group mentoring opportunities may provide particular benefits for women from disadvantaged communities (Boddy, 2009). Group mentoring has the potential to become a useful tool in promoting positive engagement between women and encouraging career expansion, educational pursuit, and improved identity development.

CULTURAL AND LEGAL CONSTRAINTS

Cross-culturally, women encounter various barriers related to their cultural identity and legal restraints. Land ownership is one such factor impacting women across the world, and within the MENA region is one of the greatest legal barriers women face in obtaining economic empowerment (Popal & Langley, 2021). Women in this region make up only five percent of property owners and the land that female individuals do own tends to be smaller and lower quality than the land held by men. Middle Eastern and North African women have the potential to quadruple their income when given the ability to own and inherit land, leading to greater economic stability. Land ownership can also be used as collateral when establishing credit or requesting loans, both of which are often required for starting a business (Popal & Langley, 2021). Furthermore, many African countries prohibit women from opening bank accounts without the permission of a male relative, perpetuating gender-based discrepancies. Although women make up almost half of the agricultural workforce globally and produce nearly 80 percent of the food in developing countries, only one in five landowners are female (Halonen, 2023).

Worldwide, there are nearly 950 gender-based disparities that legally inhibit women's economic opportunity (Popal & Langley, 2021). Additional statistics show that 90 percent of the world's economies have at least one law inhibiting economic participation from women, an additional year of schooling could increase a woman's wage by up to 20 percent, and that 75 percent of the world's unpaid work is completed by women (Lemmon & Vogelstein, 2017). Although moderate improvements have been made nationally, progress is slow-moving and disparities persist that continue to inhibit women's empowerment. In many cultures, women may be discriminated against based on job type and sector as well as legal barriers regulating women's rights. Although many of these legal constraints exist in developing countries, women in Russia also are prohibited from working 456 kinds of jobs, and women in France are prohibited from any jobs that require the lifting of 55 pounds or more (Lemmon & Vogelstein, 2017). Furthermore, 65 percent of the countries in the MENA region find it inappropriate for women to have jobs outside of the home which may be legally or culturally enforced, further limiting women's access to economic opportunities (Popal & Langley, 2021).

Bidirectionality Between Women's Empowerment and Economic Success

In addition to the micro-level factors that impact economic prosperity for women, it is crucial to recognize the bidirectional relationship between female leadership and economic accomplishment. This is an important relationship to consider in demonstrating the value and success that empowering women can provide local and world-wide economies. Research focused on "women-friendly" companies, or those with women on their executive boards, experience a 42 percent greater return on sales and a 66 percent higher return on invested capital when compared to companies lacking gender diversity (Popal & Langley, 2021). Women's procurement of leadership positions is associated with political empowerment as well as more inclusive and effective policy making which effectively targets gender-based discrimination in economic empowerment. Gender diversity on occupational boards is also associated with greater contributions to philanthropy and reductions in employee layoffs. Generally, women tend to devote a larger part of their income to "their children's humane capital (nutrition, health, and education) and thereby indirectly to their nation's income growth," (Africa Partnership Forum, 2007, p. 12). Women also are more likely to send both their sons and daughters to school which encourages future economic success and occupational opportunities for the children while further stimulating the economic growth of the community as a whole.

Gender equality has been shown to promote economic prosperity and diversification while reducing income inequality, and yet women still face challenges in obtaining occupational empowerment. Lemmon & Vogelstein, 2017 described the following:

When women and girls systematically lack access to the education and training necessary to enter a profession or when barriers prevent them from advancing within a workplace, entire industries suffer from a lack of access to the best talent and economies are more likely to be homogenous. (p. 9)

Investing in women's occupational empowerment has the profound potential to bolster economic gain in companies and businesses, and yet global perceptions of women's capabilities interfere. The economic barriers that impede women's empowerment are comprised of legal, cultural, and educational hurdles that are collectively entwined.

Internalized Biases and Identities

Some of the most pervasive barriers to women attaining leadership positions that are often unnoticed are women's self-biases and identities. In addition to the structural and societal impediments to women's empowerment, women may also contribute by underestimating their own–and other women's–abilities, over-identifying with stereotypes and microaggressions, and placing undue burdens onto themselves. It appears that there are two main components: women both identify themselves as having fewer leadership qualities than men do, and they believe that it is their responsibility to be tasked with the bulk of domestic work, thus interfering with their ability to be promoted in the workplace.

Studies have shown that women may believe themselves individually to be less assertive and leadership-competent than they perceive women as a whole (Hentschel et al., 2019). This issue, also outlined by the Harvard Business Review, is not that women do not say or do the right things to get the positions they desire, but instead that they may be lacking the confidence to metaphorically fill space in a room full of men (Ibarra et al., 2013). Men are often taught to be the authority, especially in workplaces, and therefore have internalized more confidence in their abilities to both work and lead others. This confidence allows men to be outspoken, participate in workplace debates, feel comfortable as the center of attention, and value their own time. A related example of this phenomenon can be found when walking on city streets. While women tend to step aside when men are impeding upon their path, men are often noticed to continue walking in the same straight line, eventually making physical contact with the women in their path. Men are socialized to believe that their space and time are important in a way that allows them to take up both physical and metaphorical volume, consequently reinforcing the narrative that they should be put in leadership positions. Contrastingly, women are socialized to be quieter than their male counterparts and to be more agreeable, which similarly becomes ingrained in how we see ourselves, and therefore how we act and take up space in the workplace. This inevitably becomes a problem when women are seeking leadership positions because executives, who are typically male, tend to seek out candidates with similar qualities to themselves (*Pyramid: Women*, 2023). These executives will look to hire a candidate who is not only exceptionally skilled but also outspoken, authoritative, and confident; in doing so, their applicant pool becomes disproportionately male.

A similar self-bias that many women hold can be best illustrated through the presidential campaign of Hillary Clinton. In putting politics aside, nearly all women in the United States are familiar with the rhetoric that Clinton, and women as a whole, are "too emotional" to have access to the "nuclear button," as it is commonly called. The belief shared among a fraction of both men and women in the United States is that women, especially during menstruation, are unable to exhibit emotional control and, in acting as President, would consequently start a nuclear war. Although men have effectively caused nearly every war in history, women are depicted as untrustworthy at the helm (Slim, 2018). A recent study proves that this idea is not specific to those who identify as male. In 2023, Pew Research Center polled both men and women in the United States regarding their opinion on which tasks a female president would perform better than a male president. The study found that while 52 percent of women believed a female president would perform better than a male counterpart in the area of education policy, only 23 percent of women believed a female president would perform better than a man in handling issues of national security or defense (Horowitz & Goddard, 2023). This study illustrates how women tend to sell themselves, and other women, short on their ability to manage conflict or other emotion-inducing situations. In examining when and for whom emotion is appropriate in the workplace, it becomes evident that men are often viewed as simply passionate when displaying inappropriate emotions in their place of work. One such example can be seen during sports events wherein players become frustrated or impassioned in the heat of the game, and subsequently yell at either their coaches or teammates. Instead of being told their emotion is affecting their ability to think clearly, make calls or shots, and perform, they are understood as being "just competitive." In both high and low-stakes situations and workplaces, women are disproportionately judged for their emotionality and convinced that this makes them ineffective as leaders, which is then internalized and eventually becomes a barrier when applying for certain roles or fields.

Both organizations and individuals can overcome these biases; first by becoming informed as to the obstacles women face, and later by introducing policies that counteract the biases. While diverse hiring practices are paramount in ensuring women's participation in leadership roles, it is also necessary that women are made to feel comfortable speaking up at work. Some techniques that may assist in this goal include asking women their perspective on workplace conversations, encouraging them to continue speaking when interrupted, and even waiting to speak until someone with less authority has done so first. In empowering women to speak up in meetings or debates, they are encouraged to become more confident and, therefore, to fit the leader archetype. The second most important factor in empowering women to participate in leadership is avoiding microaggressive language. Becoming aware of harmful stereotypes such as "emotional" or "hormonal" allows both individual women and the companies that hire them to empower women to utilize their passion in a healthy manner instead of avoiding their feelings altogether.

Similarly, the identities and expectations women harbor may impact how they spend their time or energy, thus affecting their ability to go above and beyond for their jobs in the same ways as a male colleague might. This can be best evidenced by the societal expectation that women perform a disproportionate amount of domestic work compared to their male counterparts (Kan et al., 2011; Park et al., 2008). Many times, in conjunction with their professional work, women are tasked with the bulk of cooking, cleaning, shopping, and childrearing. The load of domestic work continues to fall onto women disproportionately regardless of their income or time spent at work. Reasons as to why this is the case are largely boiled down to socialization. Much like the previous example of young girls playing with baby dolls and toy kitchens, girls are taught to cook and clean, and are often tasked with babysitting or caretaking their siblings, beginning at a young age. As the old adage goes, "practice makes perfect," so by adulthood, women are often better at performing domestic labor tasks than men. The issue here

Unveiling the Challenges

becomes twofold in that both men and women believe that women are better at completing these tasks. When women recognize that they are "better" at domestic labor, they often prefer the job to be done "correctly" and subsequently prevent their male partners from participating or improving upon their skills. Similarly, when men see that women are "better" at domestic labor, they weaponize this incompetency by saying things like "you do it better" or "I'm not as good at…" thus placing the burden of completing such tasks back onto their female partner. As a result, the cycle continues by perpetuating the notion that women are "better" at household chores when the reality is that they have simply had more practice. This phenomenon, on both societal and individual levels, limits the amount of time and energy women can practically spend on their careers, and therefore prevents them from achieving leadership positions. After spending much of the day working, women are tasked with expending more energy when they return home and consequently feel too tired to do things like get to work early, give their best effort throughout the day, and concentrate during meetings. Male coworkers go to work and often come home to someone else rearing their children and cooking their dinner, allowing for an opportunity to "recharge" that women rarely receive. How, then, are women able to become similarly reinvigorated? The answer is simple: letting their partners do things "incorrectly." In allowing male partners to make mistakes while contributing to domestic labor, they practice their skills, become more efficient, and eventually lose the expectation that somebody else will take care of these chores on their behalf. Pushing back on this need to maintain the perfect house and children allows women to de-emphasize this domesticated identity that they often possess unknowingly, thus empowering them to substitute their hours of unpaid labor for their careers and goals instead. This is, of course, not to say that women are at fault for any lack of advancement in their fields or should be neglecting their home and families, but that women tend to de-prioritize themselves, especially in the context of a romantic partnership and family, and should therefore be encouraged to maintain their commitment to themselves and their personal (or professional) goals.

Women's own biases and identities significantly impact their abilities to both seek and attain leadership positions. As a whole, women tend to underestimate their efficacy and abilities, thus worsening outside perceptions of their capabilities. Stereotypes regarding women's emotional control exacerbate an already delicate situation by promoting the idea that some jobs or fields are entirely ill-suited for their personalities or hormones. The notion that women are more suited or "better" at domestic labor than their male counterparts is an additional barrier that women uphold due to a lifetime of socialization which has led them to believe that their worth is directly tied to how well they keep a home and how successful their children are. In de-emphasizing these beliefs and roles, women are significantly more likely to respect their own time and authority thus empowering them to attain leadership positions.

CONCLUSION

The challenges women in leadership face in achieving empowerment are numerous. This chapter outlined several barriers such as biases and stereotypes against women, the microaggressions women face, economic impediments, and their self-imposed biases and identities. These persistent barriers to women empowerment serve to maintain the status quo and benefit a governing class that is largely composed of men. The benefits of empowering women in leadership are countless, though some examples include economic advantages, public health, and education (Kooser, 2017). When women are provided with resources to attain an education, they make more money and, in turn, spend more money, thus, positively influencing national economies and benefiting entire communities and countries. Furthermore, empowering women benefits health and safety on both micro and macro levels. On an individual level, empowerment to attain education and leadership opportunities decreases both mother and infant mortality rates by encouraging women to utilize both prenatal care and "skilled birth attendants," as stated by Kooser (2017). Additional benefits of promoting women's empowerment for public health include decreased rates of common causes of death globally such as malaria, HIV, and pneumonia. When women are educated and empowered to make decisions, they are more likely to both seek and afford medical care for themselves and their children, consequently reducing the burden on public health systems. Finally, emboldening women to pursue education and attain leadership positions cultivates a more diverse array of research, thus promoting development in the vast majority of fields and technologies. As the value of women's empowerment is overtly significant, identifying and addressing the barriers, specifically in the realm of leadership, is an essential step towards mitigating their detrimental impacts and encouraging overall well-being, professional success, and a sense of empowerment.

REFERENCES

Africa Partnership Forum. (2007). *Gender and economic empowerment in Africa*. 8th Meeting of the Africa Partnership Forum, Berlin, Germany. https://www.oecd.org/dac/gender-development/38829148.pdf

Ballenger, J. (2010). *Women's access to higher education leadership: Cultural and structural barriers*. Forum on Public Policy. https://files.eric.ed.gov/fulltext/EJ913023.pdf

Blau, F., & DeVaro, J. (2006). New evidence on gender difference in promotion rates: An empirical analysis of a sample of new hires. *Industrial Relations, 46*(3), 511–550. doi:10.1111/j.1468-232X.2007.00479.x

Boddy, J. (2009). Challenging gender role stereotypes and creating pathways for goal achievement. *Qualitative Social Work: Research and Practice, 8*(4), 489–508. doi:10.1177/1473325009346527

Cahyati, D., & Hariri, H. Sowiyah, & Karwan, D. H. (2021). Women's leadership in higher education: Barriers and opportunities in Indonesia. *International Journal of Education Policy & Leadership, 17*(9). https://files.eric.ed.gov/fulltext/EJ1319884.pdf

Center, P. R. (2023). *Views of having a woman president*. Pew Research Center's Social & Demographic Trends Project. https://www.pewresearch.org/social-trends/2023/09/27/views-of-having-a-woman-president/#:~:text=Women%20(21%25)%20are%20more

Else-Quest, N. M., Hyde, J. S., & Linn, M. C. (2010). Cross-national patterns of gender differences in mathematics: A meta-analysis. *Psychological Bulletin, 136*(1), 103–127. doi:10.1037/a0018053 PMID:20063928

Fattoracci, E. S. M., & King, D. D. (2022). The need for understanding and addressing microaggressions in the workplace. *Perspectives on Psychological Science, 18*(4), 174569162211338. doi:10.1177/17456916221133825 PMID:36379041

Fernandez, M., & Menon, M. (2022). Media influences on gender stereotypes. *The International Journal of Social Sciences (Islamabad), 10*(2), 121–125.

Fiske, S. T., Bersoff, D. N., Borgida, E., Deaux, K., & Heilman, M. (1991). Social science research on trial: Use of sex stereotyping research in Price Waterhouse v. Hopkins. *The American Psychologist*, *46*(10), 1049–1060. doi:10.1037/0003-066X.46.10.1049

González, M. J., Cortina, C., & Rodríguez, J. (2019). The role of gender stereotypes in hiring: A field experiment. *European Sociological Review*, *35*(2), 187–204. doi:10.1093/esr/jcy055

Halonen, T. (2023). *Securing women's land rights for increased gender equality, food security and economic empowerment*. United Nations. https://www.un.org/en/un-chronicle/securing-women%E2%80%99s-land-rights-increased-gender-equality-food-security-and-economic

Hentschel, T., Heilman, M. E., & Peus, C. V. (2019). The multiple dimensions of gender stereotypes: A current look at men's and women's characterizations of others and themselves. *Frontiers in Psychology*, *10*(11), 11. doi:10.3389/fpsyg.2019.00011 PMID:30761032

Ibarra, H., Ely, R., & Kolb, D. (2013). Women rising: The unseen barriers. *Harvard Business Review*. https://hbr.org/2013/09/women-rising-the-unseen-barriers

Kan, M. Y., Sullivan, O., & Gershuny, J. (2011). Gender convergence in domestic work: Discerning the effects of interactional and institutional barriers from large-scale data. *Sociology*, *45*(2), 234–251. doi:10.1177/0038038510394014

King, T. L., Scovelle, A. J., Meehl, A., Milner, A. J., & Priest, N. (2021). Gender stereotypes and biases in early childhood: A systematic review. *Australasian Journal of Early Childhood*, *46*(2), 112–125. doi:10.1177/1836939121999849

Kooser, A. (2021). Empowered women change the world. *Opportunity International*. https://opportunity.org/news/blog/2017/03/empowered-women-change-the-world

Lee, I.-C., Hu, F., & Li, W.-Q. (2020). Cultural factors facilitating or inhibiting the support for traditional household gender roles. *Journal of Cross-Cultural Psychology*, *51*(5), 333–352. doi:10.1177/0022022120929089

Lemmon, G. T., & Vogelstein, R. (2017). *Building inclusive economies: How women's economic advancement promotes sustainable growth*. Council On Foreign Relations, Inc. https://cdn.cfr.org/sites/default/files/report_pdf/Discussion_Paper_Lemmon_Vogelstein_Women_Economies_OR.pdf

Lilienfeld, S. O. (2017). Microaggressions: Strong claims, inadequate evidence. *Perspectives on Psychological Science*, *12*(1), 138–169. doi:10.1177/1745691616659391 PMID:28073337

Losocco, K. A., & Robinson, J. (1991). Barriers to women's small-business success in the United States. *Gender & Society*, *5*(4). https://www.jstor.org/stable/190098

Meyer, N., & Mostert, C. (2016). Perceived barriers and success factors of female entrepreneurs enrolled in an entrepreneurial programme. *International Journal of Social Sciences and Humanity Studies*, *8*(1).

Mollaeva, E. A. (2017). Gender stereotypes and the role of women in higher education (Azerbaijan case study). *Education and Urban Society*, *50*(8), 747–763. doi:10.1177/0013124517713613

Oxford University Press. (n.d.). Bias. In Oxford English Dictionary (3rd ed.). Oxford University Press.

Park, B., Smith, J. A., & Correll, J. (2008). "Having it all" or "doing it all"? Perceived trait attributes and behavioral obligations as a function of workload, parenthood, and gender. *European Journal of Social Psychology, 38*(7), 1156–1164. doi:10.1002/ejsp.535

Popal, F., & Langley, B. (2021). *Women's leadership & economic empowerment: A solution for the economies of the middle east & north africa*. GWB Center. http://gwbcenter.imgix.net/Publications/Resources/gwbi-_2021_CIPE_paper.pdf

Pyramid: Women in the United States workforce [Infographic]. (2023, February 7). Catalyst

Revel, B. (2020, June 5). *How to maximize Syrian refugee economic inclusion in Turkey*. Atlantic Council. https://www.atlanticcouncil.org/blogs/turkeysource/how-to-maximize-syrian-refugee-economic-inclusion-in-turkey/

Slim, H. (2018, March 15). *Masculinity and war–let's talk about it more*. Humanitarian Law & Policy Blog. https://blogs.icrc.org/law-and-policy/2018/03/15/masculinity-and-war-let-s-talk-about-it-more/

Stanfors, M., & Goldscheider, F. (2017). The forest and the trees: Industrialization, demographic change, and the ongoing gender revolution in Sweden and the United States, 1870-2010. *Demographic Research, 36*, 173–226. doi:10.4054/DemRes.2017.36.6

Stein, J. A., Newcomb, M. D., & Bentler, P. M. (1992). The effect of agency and communality on self-esteem: Gender differences in longitudinal data. *Sex Roles, 26*(11-12), 465–483. doi:10.1007/BF00289869

Sue, D. W., Capodilupo, C. M., Torino, G. C., Bucceri, J. M., Holder, A. M. B., Nadal, K. L., & Esquilin, M. (2007). Racial microaggressions in everyday life: Implications for clinical Practice. *The American Psychologist, 62*(4), 271–286. doi:10.1037/0003-066X.62.4.271 PMID:17516773

Ward, L. M., & Grower, P. (2020). Media and the development of gender role stereotypes. *Annual Review of Developmental Psychology, 2*(1), 177–199. doi:10.1146/annurev-devpsych-051120-010630

Chapter 2
Systemic Barriers and Challenges Impeding Women's Financial Independence, Empowerment, and Career Growth

Zuberia Aminah Hosanoo
https://orcid.org/0000-0002-9583-9268
Edinburgh Napier University, UK

Melina Doargajudhur
https://orcid.org/0000-0002-0287-9691
Edinburgh Napier University, UK

Yarti Deonaran
https://orcid.org/0000-0001-7568-9744
Curtin Mauritius, Mauritius

ABSTRACT

The contribution of women has been significant and incremental for decades. Despite enormous efforts of feminists on women's emancipation in the 21st century, women are nevertheless victims of the patriarchal society. Since eras, women in all cultures and societies globally subjected to wide-ranging societal pressure, constraining their role in society, and in their household - limited to bearing and rearing children, household chores, and family maintenance. With education, few women started earning and contributing financially to the household income. Their role in the work spheres have long been limited to low level jobs and career advancement to senior leadership positions have been slow and they are globally under-represented. Empowerment of women occurs through their financial independence and wellbeing. The chapter will be guided by the theories of planned behaviour, self-determination theory and the self-efficacy theory to assess the systemic barriers to women's career progress and propose some valuable recommendations.

DOI: 10.4018/979-8-3693-2806-4.ch002

INTRODUCTION

Women's contribution in the formal paid workforce has significantly changed in the last era, with an increasing proportion of women in leadership positions. Yet, women continue to face discrimination on a global scale in a variety of contexts, including the family, community, workplace, economic, and political arenas. In comparison to men, women perform three times as much unpaid labour; of those over the age of 15, half work for pay, whilst over 75% of men do the same (Tyson & Klugman, 2017). Empowerment is "the process of raising others' self-efficacy perceptions" (Chen et al., 2003, p. 248). Therefore, empowering women entails providing them with the opportunity to recognize and act on their own individual abilities and self-motivation. Empowerment of women occurs through their financial independence and wellbeing. Financial independence is defined as an individual's ability to manage and sustain the latter's expenses self-sufficiently (Bea & Yi, 2019; Rughoobur-Seetah et al., 2022). Empowered women can make a difference to the economy at the micro, meso and macro level. At the micro level, personal empowerment occurs where women are able to enjoy higher wellbeing through a change in the personal beliefs and actions; at the meso level relational empowerment pertaining to beliefs and actions linked with others occurs; whilst the macro level is associated with broader social context leading to social empowerment, (Huis et al., 2017). Empowered women can make a significant difference and lead to an increase in productivity and economic progress. Financial literacy and career growth are fundamental tools to unlock women's potential and uplift their contribution in both financial and economic decision making. Conversely, career growth as a powerful means to empowerment of women is deeply challenged by the systemic barriers and the conscious and unconscious gender biases to advancement of women to senior leadership positions in the formal work spheres (Nikolaou, 2017; Madsen & Andrade, 2018).

Women in leadership, especially in the upper echelon, C-Suite leadership, has a significant role in gender equality, and organisational performance (Galsanjigmed & Sekiguchi, 2023). Women convey unique experiences and perspectives to leadership positions, resulting in greater innovation, better decision-making, and a positive work environment (Wu et al., 2022). Women in leadership positions being more inclusive and collaborative in their method, generate a productive and positive work environment (Cook et al., 2014). Yet, women face significant hurdles in reaching leadership positions, which include bias, gender stereotyping, institutional and cultural challenges, and a lack of advancement opportunities which will be discussed.

This chapter delves into the career advancement of women, empowerment and gender in leadership by unveiling the systemic barriers women face in reaching leadership positions and further introduces some enablers of women empowerment and upward career progression to leadership positions. Barriers can be described as events, factors or phenomena, preventing or controlling individuals' access to advancement, and barriers can be tangible and intangible (Saadin et al., 2016). To be able to overcome the challenges that women face, it is essential to understand those barriers preventing women from exploiting their potential and identify strategies to overcome those systemic barriers.

Gender, Gender Representation, and Gender Gap in Leadership

Top level leaders in institutions, government and business world formulate meaningful and wide-ranging decisions affecting countless aspects of society. Yet, figures are stark, as blatantly few of these influential positions are occupied by women. Despite noteworthy access to education, and significant progression in

Systemic Barriers and Challenges Impeding Women's Financial Independence

all professions, women nonetheless stand underrepresented and marginalised at all layers of leadership in politics, across organisations and industries globally (Hill *et al.*, 2016; Lutz *et al.*, 2023).

The drive for broader diversity persists amidst constant pressure from all stakeholders, including investors, employees and other groups. The S&P 500 Directors' report noted a considerable increase of 77% over a 10-year period, with 46% of new female directors in America, as shown in Figure 1.

Figure 1. S&P 500 directors' report of women in leadership position
Source: SpencerStuart 2022

NEW S&P 500 DIRECTORS: ONE, FIVE AND 10-YEAR BREAKDOWN BY GENDER AND RACE/ETHNICITY

	2022	2021	2017	2012	5-Yr % change	10-Yr % change
New directors	395	456	397	291	-0.5%	36%
% women	46%	43%	36%	26%	28%	77%
% Underrepresented racial/ethnic groups (Black/African American, Asian, Hispanic/Latino/a, American Indian/Alaska Native, Native Hawaiian/Pacific Islander or two or more races)	46%	47%	21%	12%	119%	283%
% female	20%	18%	6%	4%	233%	400%
% male	26%	29%	14%	8%	86%	225%
% new directors from historically underrepresented groups (women and/or Black/African American, Asian, Hispanic/Latino, American Indian/Alaska Native, Native Hawaiian/Pacific Islander or multiracial men and/or LGBTQ+ when disclosed)	72%	72%	64%	35%	13%	106%

Matter-of-factly, leadership prospects for women of colour and ethnic minorities are even more elusive. Ethnic discrimination is markedly prominent in the recruitment of senior positions in the corporate world (Adamovic & Leibbrandt, 2023). For instance, the SpencerStuart (2022) report unveils that only 20% of those leaders are from ethnic minority groups in America.

The World Economic Forum's Global Gender Gap Index data computes the share of men and women in professional and technical occupations as well as senior managerial roles. A steady global increase is noted in women's share of senior and leadership positions over the last five years (2017-2022), and the global gender parity for this category has stretched to 42.7%, which is the highest gender parity score thus far in history (World Economic Forum, 2023). Additionally, to complement the data, high-frequency analytics from LinkedIn data for 155 countries have provided evidence of gender parity in leadership roles in the year 2022, as illustrated in the Figure 2, which diagrammatically represents some of the highest and lowest female representation.

Figure 2. Female representation in leadership roles
Source: Compiled from World Economic Forum (2023)

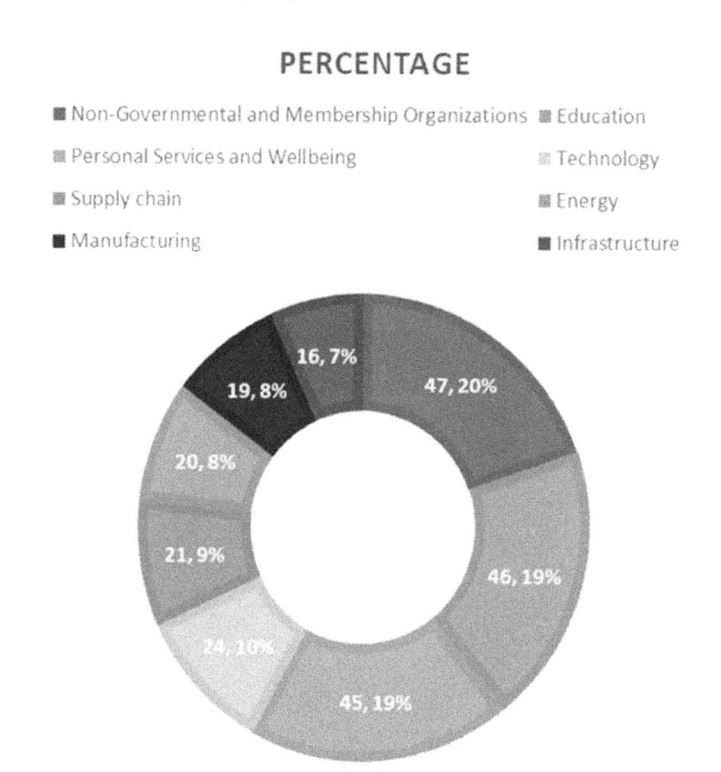

PERCENTAGE

- Non-Governmental and Membership Organizations
- Education
- Personal Services and Wellbeing
- Technology
- Supply chain
- Energy
- Manufacturing
- Infrastructure

16, 7%
19, 8%
20, 8%
21, 9%
24, 10%
45, 19%
46, 19%
47, 20%

Women are considerably less likely than men to be deemed leaders, in all sectors of activities, but more acutely in the upper echelon leadership in the corporate world (Kurtaran *et al.*, 2024). A slight acceleration in hiring of women into leadership roles have been noted in the Energy, Technology and Supply Chain and Transportation sector. It is further noteworthy to stress the presence of gender gap in leadership roles, in sectors dominated by female representation in the workforce. For instance, while women represent 62% of the total workforce in the personal services and Wellbeing industry, only 45% women hold leadership roles in the sector (World Economic Forum, 2023).

The *Global Gender Gap Report 2022* classifies states into eight regions: Europe, North America, Latin American and the Caribbean, Central Asia, South Asia, East Asia and the Pacific, Middle East and North Africa, and Sub-Saharan Africa. From the gathered data, North America has the most progression in gender gap closure, at 76.9% (Figure 3). European countries have further achieved 76.6% of gender gap closure, followed by Latin America and the Caribbean region, which has reconciled at 72.6%. East Asia and the Pacific together with Central Asia trail at an average of 69%. The Sub-Saharan Africa accounts a measure of 67.8% gender parity while the Sub-Saharan Africa is Middle East and North Africa region has reached 63.4% of its gender gap. Last of all, South Asia registers the smallest performance of all regions globally, with a gender parity degree of 62.4%.

Systemic Barriers and Challenges Impeding Women's Financial Independence

Figure 3. Global gender gap report on gender gap closure
Source: Global Gender Gap Report 2022

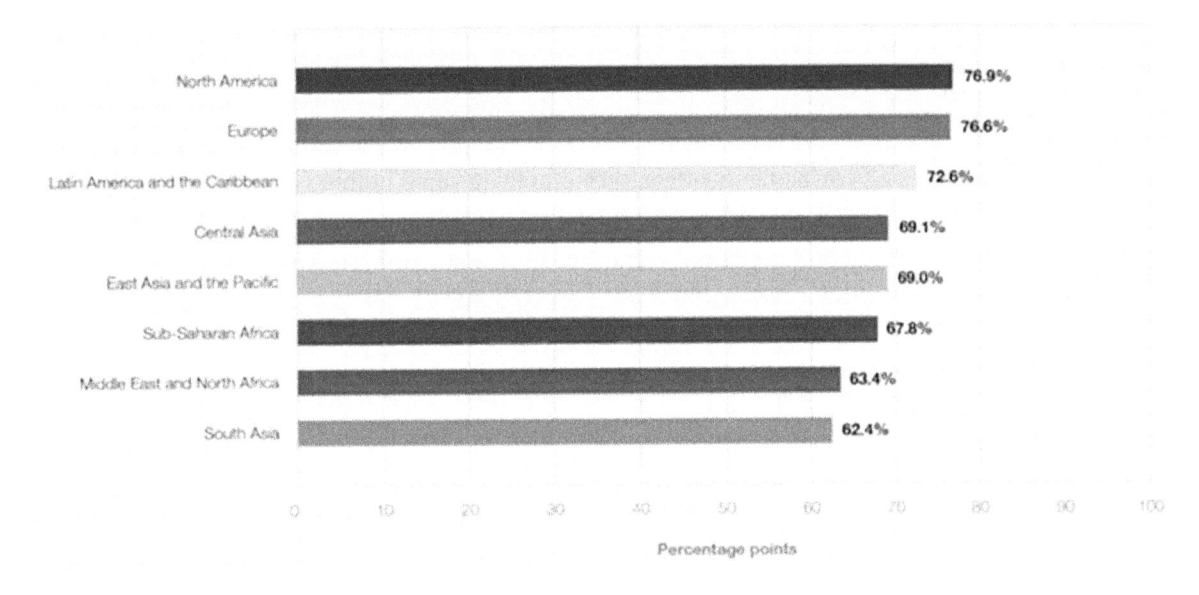

Region	Percentage
North America	76.9%
Europe	76.6%
Latin America and the Caribbean	72.6%
Central Asia	69.1%
East Asia and the Pacific	69.0%
Sub-Saharan Africa	67.8%
Middle East and North Africa	63.4%
South Asia	62.4%

Empowerment and gender equality, is an essential goal representing the United Nation's Sustainable Development Goals (SDG) 5: Gender Equality (UN, 2023) which focuses on: violence and exploitation against women; the eradication of discrimination against girl child and women; social practices and harmful practices against women; shared household responsibilities; the comparably equal involvement and opportunities for women in decision making in all context and life spheres; equivalent rights to economic resources; access to technology; and most importantly the reinforcement of enforceable legislations to uplift empowerment and gender equality of all girls and women (UN, 2023). Women's economic independence has since been acknowledged by research as one of the key drivers of gender equality and economic growth. Empowering women economically allows them to make more decisions about their families, which in turn leads to increased investment in healthcare and education and faster economic growth. Agenda's Sustainable Development Goal (SDG) 5 of 2030 has expanded the coverage to "achieve gender equality and empower all women and girls" in response to MDG 3's narrow focus and growing evidence of the positive impact of women's economic empowerment on a number of development outcomes. The scope encompasses women's access to information technology, safe and decent work environments, social security, financial services, productive employment, responsive public policies and regulations, paid family leave and domestic work, and political participation that advances women's empowerment and gender parity. Gender inequality is expected to change as a result of global pressure from development experts and governments to reduce inequality in order to meet SDG5 by 2030 (Roy & Xiaoling, 2022).

Women Leadership in Developed and Developing Countries Statistics

There has been a notable increase in the number of women employed and they play an essential role for economic expansion and the development of jobs, especially in emerging nations (Welsh *et al.*, 2018). Women make up about half of the working population, yet they are underrepresented in several fields of the workforce such as technology, science, engineering. Literature has reported that women's participation in these countries is more important than ever (De Vita *et al.*, 2014; Correa *et al.*, 2022). However, women still face discrimination in the workplace, low pay, unfavourable working conditions, and little prospects for professional growth. Gender bias is prevalent in most works, with women receiving lower pay than men despite performing comparable and equally important tasks. They hold a comparatively small percentage of high-level corporate and governmental positions when compared to men. Moreover, there are very few businesses owned by women, they employ a small number of people, and they have little room for future development and expansion. (Roy & Xiaoling, 2022). Despite global advancements in the promotion of women in leadership roles, there still exist large gaps between developed and developing nations. Women's leadership styles can vary greatly due to a range of factors, such as societal structures, gender equality levels, economic conditions, and cultural norms as discussed below.

Our literature search revealed that women's leadership may be better supported by cultural norms in many developed countries, where progress has been made towards gender equality. Nonetheless, prejudices and stereotypes related to gender persist, albeit in differing degrees. On the other hand, gender norms and patriarchy may pose serious obstacles to women assuming leadership positions in many developing nations. Cultural norms that restrict women's access to leadership positions and place a higher priority on family obligations than professional growth may also affect women (Fauzi *et al.*, 2023; Mahajan, 2019). According to Jha *et al.* (2018), there exists a disparity and notable distinction in the treatment of women despite their contribution to economic progress. One such difference is that females receive lower earnings that men do. In developing and emerging economies, women are still predominantly linked to domestic duties and family obligations such as raising children, tending to the sick and elderly, and cleaning the house (Jha *et al.*, 2018; Yousafzai *et al.*, 2015). Although women's socioeconomic condition has improved over the years, there are still concerns with social fairness and equality, discrimination, sexual harassment, atrocities, and violence against women in those nations. This may be due to the disparity in the legal and regulatory frameworks supporting gender equality which appear to be weaker in developing economies.

In a similar vein, developed countries typically provide women with greater economic options, such as access to jobs, education, and entrepreneurship. This can give women the tools and training required for leadership positions. However, in developing countries, their ability to pursue leadership roles can be hampered by economic issues like poverty, restricted access to education, and gender differences in work prospects (Mahajan, 2019). Literature has reported that in developing countries, within a patriarchal society, men typically hold power over women (Xheneti *et al.*, 2019; Zeb & Ihsan, 2020). For instance, it is not acceptable for women to engage in business or lead companies since their main responsibility is to take care of their families while men go to work. Thus, in today's modern culture, getting a job or starting a business presents a significant obstacle for women (Essers *et al.*, 2021) due to barriers such as work-family conflict, capital difficulties, gender discrimination, a lack of resources and infrastructure, and an unstable political and economic climate (Panda, 2018; De Clercq & Brieger, 2021).

Furthermore, developed countries typically have greater access to healthcare and education, which can help women in leadership roles by giving them more chances to grow as professionals, feel more empowered, and have better health and wellbeing. Conversely, the lack of infrastructure, cultural norms, and poverty are some of the obstacles that prevent women from pursuing leadership roles in many developing nations, making it difficult for them to receive healthcare and education (Fauzi *et al.*, 2023).

Our search process also indicated that women in developed economies tend to be more represented in politics, enjoy greater access to political rights, take part in governance, and are represented in groups that make decisions, whereas they are likely to encounter substantial legal, cultural, and structural hurdles to political involvement in many emerging nations (De Clercq & Brieger, 2021; Fauzi *et al.*, 2023).

It can therefore be argued that women are motivated to take on leadership roles based on push and pull factors. Push factors are associated with poor compensation and job satisfaction, but pull factors are motivated by autonomy, social standing, independence, and personal control. Both internal and external factors contribute to the difficulties that women encounter in both developed and developing nations (Isaga, 2019). For instance, work-family conflict, budgetary limitations, inadequate training, infrastructure, and the political and economic climate are among the difficulties faced by women (Panda, 2018).

THEORETICAL FOUNDATION

Social Learning Theory

Social Learning Theory (SLT) postulates that individuals gather knowledge and learn through observation, imitation and modelling each other (Bandura, 1971), and further stems from the symbolic role models such as sports or movie persona (Gichuhi & Mwangi, 2021). Rumjaun and Narod (2020) explain that the SLT is a confluence between behaviourist and cognitive behaviourist theories, emphasizing that a person's cognitive processes support the learning and imitation of some behaviour adopted by the latter. According to the propositions of the SLT, the majority of a person's behaviour is acquired either deliberately or unconsciously through modelling, and observation. People learn through the observation of others' behaviors. Their cognitive operations and behaviour establish and regulate the decision to mimic the perceived behaviour. According to Gichuhi and Mwangi (2021), an observed behaviour is learnt through four stages: attention, retention, reproduction, and motivation. A person's level of motivation is vital in inducing learning and modelling (Kurt, 2019), such as knowledge obtained from the latter's social experiences and observation of significant others (Head, 2015).

The SLT has been linked to women empowerment and the career motivation and success of women in multiple research (e.g. Khamis, 2022; Rametse *et al.*, 2021). Women make career decisions based on their learning and knowledge obtained from significant others, such as parents and through their socialisation process. Parents as socialising agents are influential in shaping the practices, values and attitudes throughout their children's existence (Salumintao et al., 2019). Women acquire empowerment drive and career aspiration from their interaction with their relatives, peers, colleagues, organisational culture and symbolic models in their personal and professional surroundings.

Theory of Planned Behaviour

The Theory of Reasoned Action (TRA) was developed in 1975 by Fishbein and Ajzen to foresee and explain behaviour. It paved the way to the Theory of Planned Behaviour (TPB) which was further developed by Ajzen in 1985. According to TPB, the intention to act in a certain way determines a person's behaviour. Intention relates to the motives to accomplish a given task and indicates how hard they are willing to try and make an effort to engage in a behaviour. Intention is determined by: Firstly, attitude in terms of how someone is feeling in terms of positive or negative emotions when a task is done. Secondly, social pressure in terms of subjective norms related to perceptions of people in the person's environment, termed as behavioural intentions. Third, the extent to which a person believes that behaviour can be controlled, termed as perceived behavioural control. Women leadership aspirations thus rhythm with the individual internal factors captured by attitudes and perceived behavioural control and external factors represented by the perception of others in society, (Boatwright & Egidio, 2003).

Self-Determination

Self-Determination Theory (SDT) is a comprehensive theory of human motivation that has been effectively implemented in several disciplines such as job motivation and management, parenting, education, healthcare, sports and physical exercise, psychotherapy, and virtual worlds (Deci & Ryan, 2013; Ryan & Deci, 2017). SDT explicitly states that an employee's motivation for their work activities has an impact on both their well-being and performance. As a result, SDT distinguishes between many motivational kinds and upholds that these motivational types have distinct catalysts, concurrents, and outcomes that act differently.

According to the SDT, each individual has three fundamental psychological needs: autonomy, competence, and relatedness, that influence their decision to act or not act in a social setting (Ryan & Deci, 2000). This theory is centered on intrinsic motivation and the elements that uphold people's fundamental desires for relatedness, competence, and autonomy. According to SDT, motivation and wellbeing are mostly driven by autonomy, or the capacity for free will and volition. When granted autonomy in decision-making and behaviour, women are more likely to make choices about career paths, feel empowered, and driven to lead successfully in the field of leadership. SDT also emphasises how important it is for people to feel capable and competent in their pursuits. In a similar vein, if women in leadership roles have access to mentorship, training, and skill development opportunities, this can boost their self-confidence. The third psychological need, relatedness, relates to having a sense of community and connection to others. The societal factors and stereotypes that affect women in leadership jobs might present special problems. In order for women leaders to succeed, it is crucial that they build networks of support, mentorship ties, and inclusivity.

Self-Efficacy

An individual's confidence, belief, and self-conviction to accomplish a behaviour is termed as Self-Efficacy as put forward in 1977 by Albert Bandura. Self-efficacy refers to the feeling that one is able to control how one functions as well as events that might impact one's life. This makes the person feel motivated, determined and serves as a form of cognitive power, Kolbe (2009). Therefore, Self-efficacy can play a critical role when it comes to women empowerment. Bandura (1977) advanced that Self-efficacy may be generated through four pathways. Firstly, a person can develop a sense of mastery when he takes a new challenge and is successful in accomplishing it. Success convinces people that they can complete new tasks, develop new abilities, and enhance their performance. Success allows the person to believe that he is capable of completing a task effectively. The second channel occurs when a person observes experiences of social role models. When a person sees other individuals completing tasks via consistent efforts, they are convinced that they too have the ability to master comparable activities to succeed. These positive self-beliefs are internalised and contribute to their success. The third source is through social persuasion, a person who receives positive feedback is convinced that he or she has the skills and capabilities to be successful. The fourth source of self-efficacy comes from the emotional, physical, and psychological well being of a person which determines how they feel about their personal abilities. The perception and interpretation of emotional and physical reactions is considered more important compared to the intensity of these reactions, (Bandura, 1977). Thus, women can improve their self-efficacy by learning how to manage anxiety and enhance positive feelings.

METHODOLOGY

The first step in a literature review is to locate pertinent scholarly works using electronic databases in order to gather primary material that discusses the research topic of interest. A variety of sources, including academic studies and industry publications, have been studied to examine the literature on women's leadership, financial independence, empowerment, and career advancement. Using Webster & Watson's (2002) structured literature review approach, the authors started their review of the literature. Quality academic databases including Google Scholar, SpringerLink, ACM Digital 17 Library, EBSCOhost, IEEE Xplore, ScienceDirect, Emerald, and ProQuest have all been searched and information on the subject has been gathered using key words and phrases. Numerous search terms were used for this research, ranging from one single word to a combination of words. Examples of search terms include 'Women Leadership', 'Women Empowerment', 'Women and Financial Independence', 'Women and Career Growth', 'Previous studies on Women in Leadership Position', 'Women in developed countries', 'Women in developing countries' and 'Barriers to Women Leadership'.

This resulted in a number of reports, articles, and conference papers that were carefully examined to make sure they were pertinent to the current research by looking at the title, abstract, and keywords. Only the most recent and relevant publications that were focused on our issue were taken into consideration, with some irrelevant articles being eliminated from the analysis.

Furthermore, a rigorous methodological approach was used to address potential publishing biases and take publication years into account in order to achieve a balanced representation of the literature. In light of this, quality assessment tools were employed in order to enhance the validity and reliability of the selected research. This necessitated examining elements such as sample size, data gathering techniques, research design, methodological approach, and statistical analysis applied in each study.

BARRIERS AND CHALLENGES TO WOMEN IN SENIOR LEADERSHIP

Disparity in Financial Education

Empowerment occurs when an individual's ability to undertake "strategic life choices" is broadened (Kabeer, 2003). Women empowerment consists of equipping women with the right toolkit to enable them to excel in various areas of life. An essential tool in the kit is financial literacy which has been defined by the Organisation for Economic Co-operation and Development (OECD) in 2022 as a combination of ''financial awareness, knowledge, skills, attitudes, and behaviours necessary to make sound financial decisions''. The ability to process economic information to make decisions with regards financial planning, wealth accumulation, debt and pensions has been termed as financial literacy, (Lusardi & Mitchell, 2014). Thus, Financial literacy has been recognised as the capacity to make informed judgements and effective decisions with regards to the use and management of money by the Australian Securities and Investments Commission, (Ali *et al.*, 2014).

According to Carpena & Zia (2011) financial literacy has a significant impact on three distinct dimensions of financial knowledge namely numeracy skills, basic financial awareness, and attitudes towards financial decisions. The authors advanced that first and foremost, financial literacy increases awareness and brings a change in attitudes towards financial products. It subsequently increases the ability to engage in numerical computations which helps to make comparisons between different financial options, and ultimately bring a change in financial behaviour. Therefore, Financial Literacy provides the relevant financial knowledge that informs individuals of different financial instruments that allows them to know what, how, where, why, and when they should take certain financial actions (Yap, Komalasari, & Hadiansah, 2018).

However, there are various barriers that contribute to the gender gap in financial literacy. There is a lot of disparity in terms of financial literacy across different countries, income earning brackets and gender. According to Klapper & Lusardi (2020), at a global level only one out of three adults are financially literate and can correctly answer three out of four questions on specific financial concepts. The authors advanced that around 3.5 billion adults, mostly from developing countries, lack basic financial knowledge. Even worse, the poor, women and lower educated respondents have less financial knowledge. Women display lower financial knowledge compared to men (Lusardi & Mitchell, 2008; Fonseca *et al.*, 2012; Gudjonsson *et al.*, 2022). The situation of women is actually more dire, since more than two third of illiterate adults in the world are women (Sharma & Johri, 2014) and lack of education has been shown to be positively associated with lack of financial knowledge (Singh & Singh, 2023; Kadoya & Khan,2020). In many developing countries girls continue to be deprived from education (Alderman *et al.*, 1996).

Household and Society's Norms

Women face discrimination due to society's rules, norms, customs, and character, (Andriamahery & Qamruzzaman, 2022). Social norms constrain the choice of occupation and tenure of jobs that women undertake; some labour markets are not readily accessible to women whilst family issues like childbearing impact on women's career. This is at times exacerbated in countries where women are paid lower salaries compared to men. Cumulation of the above factors lead to lower savings by women (Hung *et al.*, 2012).

Women are less financially literate due to intra household dynamics. In certain societies men are regarded as the Head of household and thus are responsible to make all major financial decisions. According to Hsu (2011), even in advanced economies like the United States, men are the financial managers of the family. This limits women's exposure to financial products and keeps them away from experiences that help them learn-by-doing through opportunities to acquire financial knowledge through experience, (Hung *et al.*, 2012).

Financial Inclusion

Beyond the family context, women's access to financial products is lower compared to men. Access to beneficial and reasonably priced financial instruments has been defined as financial inclusion (Kebede *et al.*, 2024). The gender gap in financial inclusion has improved over years with access to mobile money (Demirgüç-Kunt, *et al.*, 2022), however it is still prevalent especially among women in countries like South Africa, Eswatini, Kenya and the DRC (Njanike & Mpofu, 2024). According to Muravyev, Talavera *et al.* (2009), firms managed by women are less likely to obtain bank loans and more likely to face higher interest rates upon contracting borrowings. Discrimination in the grant of loans to women entrepreneurs (Agier & Szafarz, 2010) stuns women progress and advancement towards leadership aspirations within the business context. Lack of access to funds results in women having recourse to informal lenders to meet their financial obligations. Money lenders from the informal sector however charge the highest level of interest rates (Malapit, 2012) which results in women facing higher costs of contracting debts.

Financial Wellbeing

The ultimate aim of being financial literacy is to be able to attain a general positive feeling of financial wellbeing. The OECD has recognised that financial wellbeing can be attained through financial literacy. Financial wellbeing has been defined as *'a state of being wherein a person can fully meet current and ongoing financial obligations, can feel secure in their financial future, and is able to make choices that allow enjoyment of life'* (The Consumer Financial Protection Bureau (CFPB), 2015). In a study conducted amongst working women in Pakistan, Haque & Zulfiqar, (2016) showed that financial literacy, financial attitude, and financial wellbeing are positively and significantly associated with economic empowerment of women. However, the financial wellbeing of women is also impacted by specific factors like motherhood, gender pay gap and even incidents of violence as identified by Gonçalves et al., (2021). The latter identified various elements that impact on the financial wellbeing of women as depicted in the figure 5 below:

Figure 4. Elements impacting on financial wellbeing
Source: Gonçalves et al. (2021)

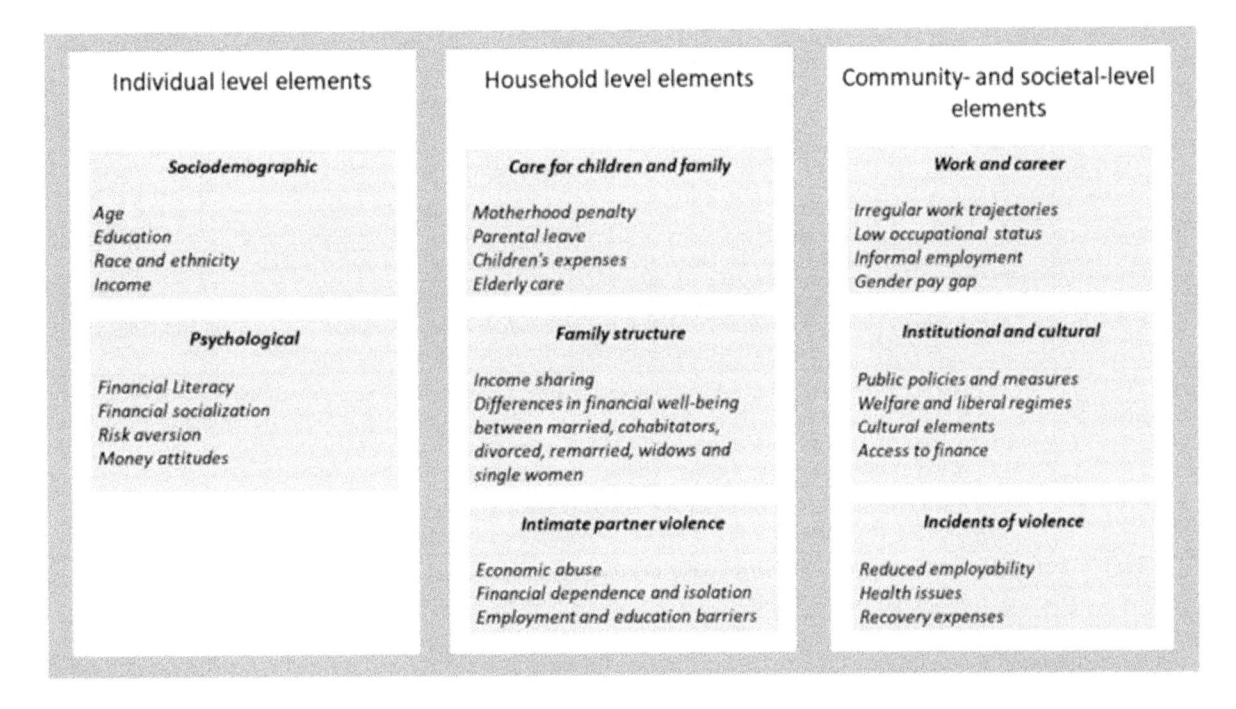

Individual level elements	Household level elements	Community- and societal-level elements
Sociodemographic Age Education Race and ethnicity Income **Psychological** Financial Literacy Financial socialization Risk aversion Money attitudes	**Care for children and family** Motherhood penalty Parental leave Children's expenses Elderly care **Family structure** Income sharing Differences in financial well-being between married, cohabitators, divorced, remarried, widows and single women **Intimate partner violence** Economic abuse Financial dependence and isolation Employment and education barriers	**Work and career** Irregular work trajectories Low occupational status Informal employment Gender pay gap **Institutional and cultural** Public policies and measures Welfare and liberal regimes Cultural elements Access to finance **Incidents of violence** Reduced employability Health issues Recovery expenses

Once women have sufficient financial knowledge and awareness of how to manage their finances, there may be catalytic growth in various aspects of their wellbeing. Financial literacy is a key tool for promoting social justice and enhancing women empowerment (Arini, 2018).

Biases

"Gender bias and gender stereotypes are so deeply entrenched in our culture that people of all genders fall into gender pitfalls" (Corbett, 2022). Today's workplaces are highly gendered, despite the evolution in gender roles. Biases and stereotypes in the workplace can be explicit, implicit, conscious, unconscious, or epistemic (Hutchison, 2020; Greenwald *et al.*, 2009).

Most of our social behaviours are unconscious and implicit. Implicit biases refer to one's mental associations beyond the conscious awareness that shape one's relational exchange with others (Greenwald & Banaji 1995). A person's implicit biases are moulded by the environment in which the individual evolves, live, and are now significantly linked to one's conscious beliefs and attitudes. Notably, implicit biases are related to an individual's behaviours in a socially sensitive environment (Greenwald *et al.*, 2009). Research has established implicit bias associated to ageism (Cullen *et al.*, 2009), masculine vs. feminine occupational discrimination (Cartwright *et al.*, 2017) linked to women working in science, technology, engineering, and math (STEM) and occupations such as medical or academic (Fleming *et al.*, 2020; Hutchison, 2020), and hiring and career development decisions (Rice & Barth, 2017; Erkal *et al.*, 2022). Males and females are framed with gendered expectations. Each gender acts concurring to their expected traits (Hoover *et al.*, 2019). As leading obstacles to women's leadership, barriers and biases originate in diverse shapes and sources. The biases that lead to the gendered workplaces and systemic biases can be succinctly summarised in Table 1:

Table 1. Types of biases

Type of Bias	Explanation
Affinity bias	Affinity bias instigates men to favour hiring, working with and socialising with other men. Despite that affinity bias often involves unconscious rather than conscious discriminatory intention, it systematically demerits women guilelessly since they are not "like" the other men who constitute the significant majority of leaders globally.
Gender bias	Gender bias triggers organisations and individuals to value men in high profile C-Suite leadership roles, while disregarding or underrating women's contributions. Both men and women unconsciously or consciously embrace gender stereotypes, deeply embedded in their values and perceptions.
Out-group bias	Out-group bias steers men to disregard women from unofficial, career-enhancing networks, and is mostly conveyed through exclusion (intentional or unintentional), discourtesy, harassment, microaggressions and microinequity. In-group members often display in-group favouritism (affinity bias) toward other in-group members without necessarily bearing negative feelings about out-group members. Women are often characterised as the out-group due to affinity biases.
Status quo bias	Status quo bias articulates a penchant for the familiar. People's degree of openness and aversion to change vary, but status quo bias is a dominant drive of resistance to organisational practices aimed at lessening gender inequality.
Epistemic injustice	Epistemic injustice ensues when stereotyping unjustly deforms judgements about a person's individual's expertise. Such stereotypes can undermine trust, credibility, and authority, all of which are essential to any profession

Sources: (Forbes, 2022, Hutchison, 2020)

According to Forbes (2022), numerous workplaces are ruled by males and function conforming to masculine values, norms, and expectations. Resultantly, women usually find it challenging to advance

Systemic Barriers and Challenges Impeding Women's Financial Independence

their careers as opposed to men, hence fewer women proceed to high-level leadership roles than men, despite the progressive shift toward equitable organisational policies. Biases and stereotypes are weighty barriers constantly striking women's role and progress in the workplace, hence explaining leadership gaps present in organisations (Hill *et al.*, 2026; Lutz *et al.*, 2023).

Stereotypes and Glass Ceiling

Gender stereotype refers to the generalisations of men's and women's attributes collectively shared in a society/culture. The generalisations include descriptive components (i.e., describing how women and men are) and prescriptive components (i.e., prescribing how women and men should or should not be (Heilman, 2012). Gender stereotype is a widespread prejudice about the characteristics or attributes that should be possessed by men and women or the roles that should be played by men and women. Moreover, gender stereotyping is the process of attributing to an individual woman or man specific traits, features, or roles due to their membership in the social group of men or women. At its core, gender stereotyping is the belief that triggers the holder of that specific belief to craft assumptions about fellows of the subject group (UNHR, 2014).

According to gender stereotypes, women are perceived as less agentic (i.e., active, assertive, and strong), and more communal (i.e., supportive, understanding, and caring), than men (Heilman, 2012; Hoyt & Simon, 2024). Female leaders repeatedly discover themselves in a double bind. While extremely communal women are backlashed for being flawed leaders, and highly agentic women experience criticism for not being female and feminine enough (Eagly *et al.*, 2014). Double-bind occurs when women leaders who display feminine traits are perceived as having substandard leadership capabilities, while women exhibiting masculine traits are perceived as mean, unfeminine and unlikeable, and even more so by female colleagues.

Despite collective initiatives to lessen overt bias through the establishment of legislations and institutional frameworks globally, implicit biases and stereotypes continue to impact the workplace globally (Hoyt & Simon, 2024; Braddy *et al.*, 2020), and there is persistent troubling inequity regarding women in senior leadership roles and lead to glass ceiling.

Glass Ceiling

In their employment cycle, women have the empowerment prospect and to escalate the leadership ladder but encounter many obstacles. Gender stereotypes and biases are widespread in their career progression, and women often face the glass ceiling phenomenon in male-dominated workspaces. Glass ceiling as a global phenomenon, denotes multiple hurdles that women confront, or have faced, in organisations preventing them to fulfill their aspiration to join the highest leadership roles in the corporate world (Zhang & Basha, 2023). The glass ceiling concept is a metaphor designating an invisible ambush blocking women and people from minority groups from career advancement. The obstacles are most often not in written form, meaning that women are more likely to be restricted from forward moving through accepted norms and implicit preconceptions rather than in a procedurally accepted manner. This point allows major glass ceilings to societal context like cultural elements, however organisational and individual contexts are also associated with women's success or failure to climb the hierarchical ladder (Gruneau, 2021).

Additionally, the glass ceiling, principally due to women's perceived incongruity with leadership positions, is a daunting hindrance that hampers women's career progression (Galsanjigmed & Sekiguchi,

2023). As women advance in the organisational hierarchy, they face biases such as out-group bias, as generally women have fewer significant networks than their male counterparts due to their initial segregation from managerial roles, cemented at lower managerial echelons. Likewise, women's segregation from the colloquial male networks in the office causes them to oversee the possibility to exercise leadership. Hence, this exclusion strengthens the glass ceiling within organisations, sternly hindering women from exercising their skills at the higher managerial levels (Zhang & Basha, 2023; Poltera & Schreiner, 2019).

The comparatively low percentage of women in the C-Suite leadership category is not only due to organisational factors but can also be linked to a general biological gender barrier, and further a socially constructed gender challenge (Heilman, 2012). Once a senior leadership position attained, women have an arduous struggle to have their authority maintained. Despite noteworthy evolution, the stereotypical attitudes in the society undoubtedly obstruct women's career selections when the work arena is controlled by masculine counterparts and cultures (Zhang &Basha 2023).

Organisational Barriers to Women Career Progression

From an organisational perspective, intricate organisational processes, practices, and systems thwart women's progression into the upper echelon leadership role categories. The organisational level hurdles range from hiring, career development, negotiation process, mentoring opportunities, networking structures, and gendered ageism (Ito & Bligh, 2024). The existing structural and systematic organisational practices such as distinctive arrangement for men to mentoring and networking opportunities, as well as professional job appointment opportunities are the undermining causes of the glass ceiling. Women have restricted access or no admission to mentoring opportunities essential for career advancement. Furthermore, women's under-representation in the C-suite leadership position entails that most of their senior mentors are mainly men (Khodijah *et al.*, 2024).

Deeply entrenched gendered organisational practices shift the resilience and learning challenge on women to change rather than organisation's shifting their status quo. While organisational policies are present in most workplaces, Williamson & Colley (2018) rightly opined that often the intent of those gender equality policies does not infiltrate the lower levels of organizations and decision-making process to reduce discriminatory organisational practices. Moreover, women face uncertainty, lack of resources and unclear career pathways negatively swaying on how women evolve as leaders (O'Brien *et al.*, 2023; Galea *et al.*, 2020). Moreover, De Pater *et al.*, (2010) advanced that women are generally less likely than men to be allocated stimulating tasks, thus depriving women from self-development, leadership and career development opportunities and this is further perpetuated by and also perpetuating entrenched gender inequalities in organisational social practices. is that bosses tend to assign more challenging tasks to male subordinates than to female subordinates. The findings support the idea that women are deprived of important opportunities for development by their bosses, which may further perpetuate gender inequalities in social practices within organizations. Because challenging experiences are critical to employee learning, growth, and career advancement, fewer opportunities for self-development for women compared to men can limit career advancement opportunities and hinder overall career development. Giving leadership development opportunities to women would produce better outcomes (Galsanjigmed & Sekiguchi, 2023).

Societal and Family Barriers to Women Empowerment and Leadership

The contribution of women has been significant and incremental for decades. Women's career trajectories and growth involve complex choices and constraints, and are often subject to cultural and societal norms. Despite enormous efforts of feminists on women's emancipation in the 21st century, women are nevertheless victims of the patriarchal society (Sultana *et al.*, 2018). Since eras, women in all cultures and societies globally have been subjected to wide-ranging societal pressure, constraining their role in society, and in their household - limited to bearing and rearing of children, household chores and family maintenance. With education, few women started earning and contributing financially to the household income. However, their role in the work spheres have long been limited to low level jobs and career advancement to senior leadership positions have been slow and they are globally under-represented (Nikolaou, 2017). The barrier to women empowerment and evolution in the business world are more rampant in the under-developed societies (Frola *et al.*, 2024).With deeply grounded patriarchal societies in third-world and developing countries (Panda, 2018), women in those economies have been facing several hurdles concerning their financial independence, and empowerment. The barriers to women empowerment are persistently widespread in the developing and underdeveloped economies according to researchers (Mensah & Derera, 2023).

In many societies, the girl child is sacrificed to marriage rather than access to secondary and tertiary education, seriously disempowering them and their access to managerial roles. For instance, many scholars have highlighted that early marriage is often linked with lack of access to education, disempowerment, poor school results and school retention for the girls (e.g. Marchetta & Sahn, 2016, Yorke *et al.*, 2022). With greater access to education and employment opportunities, there is a tendency to fading traditional gender roles and expectations. Still, the male breadwinner and female homemaker family model still prevail in many regions and families globally (Yu, 2015). Moreover, regardless of the advantages of women's increased career growth globally, gender stereotypes of heterosexual couples are highly prescriptive. Men are traditionally ascribed as the breadwinner of their family and holding higher status roles in society, while women are expected to be the homemaker and holding lower status roles (Haines *et al.*, 2016). Vink *et al.*, (2022) further purport that women's augmented social status can have damaging results for their relationship experiences (as a couple) once they have transcended their male partner in status.

Besides cultural and family dynamics, the prevalence of male-dominated workplace culture negatively influences women's career development, since several women voluntarily opt out of male-dominated jobs, or leadership positions even when qualified (Ceci *et al.*, 2014). Additionally, women do not have the determination to partake in challenging tasks because of their lack of self-esteem and self-perception of lower self-competence in comparison to their male colleagues (de Pater *et al.*, 2010). Some further workplace practices reinforcing a male-dominated work culture comprise of trusting male's work quality and leadership potential more than women's (Lekchiri *et al.*, 2019), gender-biased recruitment (Scholten & Witmer, 2017), long hours and labelling work– family matters as 'female problems' (Taser-Erdogan, 2022), and lastly adverse workplace attitudes of males toward female colleagues (Adisa *et al.*, 2019).

RECOMMENDATIONS

Globally, women's leadership has advanced, although there are still large gaps between developed and developing nations. To enable women empowerment and career advancement to senior leadership positions, women should overcome barriers and challenges. Based on our above discussion and findings, we propose the following enabling factors, as illustrated in Figure 6.

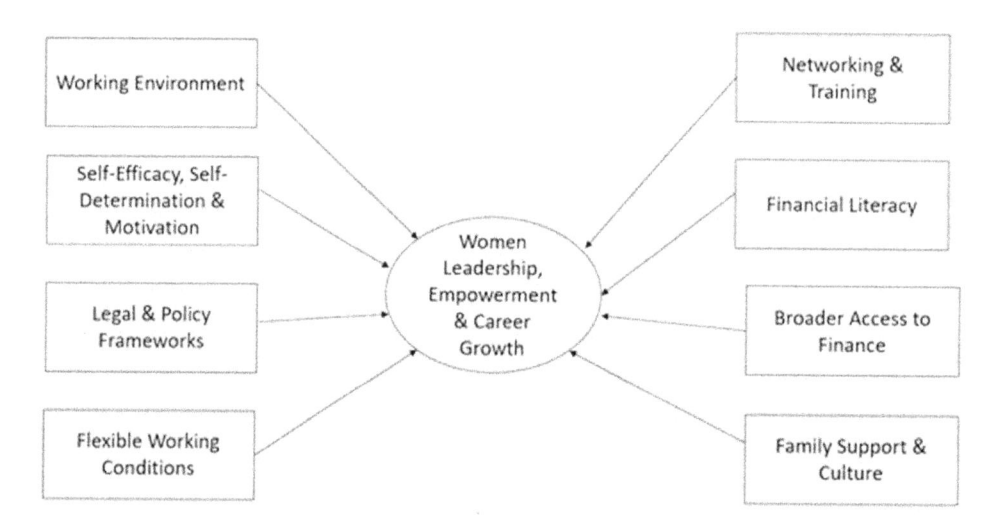

Figure 5. Enabling factors to women in leadership position

In order to address these gaps, extensive efforts must be made to subvert cultural norms, advance gender equality, increase economic possibilities, and fortify frameworks of laws and policies that support women in leadership roles in all circumstances. Society at large and organisation should recognise the worth of women in senior leadership positions and the empowerment of women and actively and collaboratively oeuvre to eliminate gender prejudices and stereotypes. This endeavour embraces defying conventional gender roles and fostering the awareness that leadership is not bounded to one gender. We therefore suggest the following recommendations:

1. Create enabling working environments for women leadership

Women's leadership must be fostered by providing an environment that is supportive, where policies, procedures, structures and other elements encourage and promote their active involvement in and progress in their leadership positions. Organisations should adopt gender-inclusive policies and gender-sensitive culture to implement fair and equitable policies, inclusive of women in the workplace. Women should in no way be perceived as different in organisational decision-making process, empowerment and participation. In a similar vein, the foundation of promoting women's leadership is ensuring equal compensation for equal labour, as well as fair benefits and chances for professional growth. To achieve pay equity, it is imperative to address long standing gender wage discrepancies and advance openness and fairness in compensation systems, across hierarchical levels in the organisation.

2. Developing self-efficacy, self-determination and self-motivation

On a broader scope, countries should boost their existing education system to ensure equal access to education opportunities, irrespective of gender. By funding literacy campaigns, women's education, economic opportunities and vocational and skill-training programmes, women can be provided with the information, and further enhance their skills, confidence, and independence they need to take up leadership positions and advance their communities. Through this initiative, women's self-efficacy, self-determination and motivation will be uplifted for them to compete for C-Suite leadership positions. This reasoning aligns with the aforementioned self-determination and self-efficacy theory described above.

3. Strengthen the legal and policy frameworks that safeguard women's rights and advance gender equality

It is crucial to set laws (e.g. anti-discrimination; equal opportunity; gender representation) into place that support gender equality and remove structural obstacles to women in leadership roles. Women's representation in government bodies and in the corporate world can be addressed by affirmative action policies like quotas and reserved seats, which can assist in closing the gender gap in political leadership, and gender representation in the top management team in organisations. Furthermore, women's voices and influence in decision-making processes can be amplified by encouraging their involvement in community organising, grassroots movements, and advocacy activities.

4. Offering flexible work arrangements

Women are better able to manage their personal and professional obligations when flexible work options are available to them, such as telecommuting, flexible scheduling, and parental leave. Hence, one way to lessen the difficulties women encounter in balancing leadership responsibilities with caring duties is through flexible employment arrangements, fairly applicable for both men and women. Equitable workplace policies and culture will empower both genders to advanced leadership positions, while striking a good work-life balance. This recommendation is consistent with the tenets of one of the theories discussed above, the self-determination theory, which posits that women can successfully ascend to C-suite positions when granted the independence in leveraging their competencies and pursuing their career goals.

5. Networking and training opportunities

Women leaders, both aspiring and established, can benefit greatly from the establishment of mentorship programmes and networking events designed exclusively for them to enable their leadership career development. Equal access to formal and informal networking events would decrease the gender stereotyping and out-group bias women usually face. These training and mentoring events can offer invaluable contacts, support, and direction. Mentors, irrespective of gender, can help women overcome the obstacles of leadership jobs by providing guidance, exchanging experiences, and offering support.

6. Financial Literacy

To address the gender gap in financial literacy, financial regulatory authorities, educational institutions and financial institutions should work together for the mass delivery of targeted financial literacy workshops to uplift the financial situation of women. The stakeholders should recognise the dormant silent force that can be unleashed once women are financially literate and start participating fully in the financial and organisational system. Women have the power to propel the economy to new heights once they are empowered.

7. Broader access to Finance

There have been several initiatives undertaken to help women financially especially with microfinance opportunities. However, their financial wellbeing, especially in developing countries, still lag. There is thus a need for broader access to finance in these countries, which can be furthered by equipping women with tools such as mobile phones, through which they can access their bank accounts. This could be achieved by funding sourced from large capitalised financial banks and institutions from the developed world through their Economic Social Governance initiatives. There should be a broader dissemination of banking and finance options available to boost their access and empowerment. Their financial independence permits them to explore and fund access to higher education opportunities, thereby boosting their self-confidence and motivation to pursue leadership roles. This reasoning corroborates with the self-determination theory which postulates that women can confidently aspire to higher career goals with greater accessibility to finance options.

8. Family support and culture

For women to evolve in their career, they should have the support from spouse and other family members for their homemaking and childcare duties. Similarly, the success of women leaders relies on the family support even in times of uncertainty for the husband who might have a lower-level job position. Society and culture should evolve to permit women to have higher roles than their husband and also provide girls the opportunity to equal access to higher educational levels. In the same vein, it can be argued that husbands play a significant role in influencing and shaping their wives' thinking so that they can aspire to become leaders in the corporate world.

CONCLUSION

Achieving gender parity and women empowerment is a feasible deal, which requires the steadfast pledge of all stakeholders and their conviction that the organisational area can benefit from ending the systemic gender inequality. Essentially, this requires the intentionally binding engagement of all parties to promote the diversity and inclusion of women in all spheres and levels of the organisation. There is the crucial need for men to proactively be willing to undertake domestic responsibilities to alleviate the homemaker burden of women so that women can pursue career objectives and progression in all fields. Furthermore, employers should transform their operational and organisational practices to a flexible workplace, to allow employees, irrespective of gender, to balance their career, family, and personal ambitions.

REFERENCES

Adamovic, M., & Leibbrandt, A. (2023). Is there a glass ceiling for ethnic minorities to enter leadership positions? Evidence from a field experiment with over 12,000 job applications. *The Leadership Quarterly*, 34(2), 101655. doi:10.1016/j.leaqua.2022.101655

Adisa, T., Cooke, F. L., & Iwowo, V. (2019). Mind Your Attitude: The Impact of Patriarchy on Women's Workplace Behaviour. *Career Development International*, 25(2), 146–164. doi:10.1108/CDI-07-2019-0183

AgierI.SzafarzA. (2010). Credit to women entrepreneurs: The curse of the trustworthier sex. *Available at SSRN 1718574*. doi:10.2139/ssrn.1718574

Agrawal, A., Gandhi, P., & Khare, P. (2023). Women empowerment through entrepreneurship: Case study of a social entrepreneurial intervention in rural India. *The International Journal of Organizational Analysis*, 31(4), 1122–1142. doi:10.1108/IJOA-03-2021-2659

Alderman, H., Behrman, J. R., Ross, D. R., & Sabot, R. (1996). Decomposing the gender gap in cognitive skills in a poor rural economy. *The Journal of Human Resources*, 31(1), 229–254. doi:10.2307/146049

Ali, P., Anderson, M. E., McRae, C. H., & Ramsay, I. (2014). The financial literacy of young Australians: An empirical study and implications for consumer protection and ASIC's National Financial Literacy Strategy. *Company and Securities Law Journal*, 32(5), 334–352.

Andriamahery, A., & Qamruzzaman, M. (2022). Do access to finance, technical know-how, and financial literacy offer women empowerment through women's entrepreneurial development? *Frontiers in Psychology*, 12, 776844. doi:10.3389/fpsyg.2021.776844 PMID:35058847

Arini, F. D. (2018, March). Financial Literacy in Women Empowerment. In *2018 Annual Conference of Asian Association for Public Administration:" Reinventing Public Administration in a Globalized World: A Non-Western Perspective"(AAPA 2018)* (pp. 635-643). Atlantis Press.

Bandura, A. (1977). Self-efficacy: Toward a unifying theory of behavioral change. *Psychological Review*, 84(2), 191–215. doi:10.1037/0033-295X.84.2.191 PMID:847061

Bea, M. D., & Yi, Y. (2019). Leaving the financial nest: Connecting young adults' financial independence to financial security. *Journal of Marriage and Family*, 81(2), 397–414. doi:10.1111/jomf.12553

Berg, A., Ostry, J. D., Tsangarides, C. G., & Yakhshilikov, Y. (2018). Redistribution, inequality, and growth: New evidence. *Journal of Economic Growth*, 23(3), 259–305. doi:10.1007/s10887-017-9150-2

Boatwright, K. J., & Egidio, R. K. (2003). Psychological predictors of college women's leadership aspirations. *Journal of College Student Development*, 44(5), 653–669. doi:10.1353/csd.2003.0048

Braddy, P. W., Sturm, R. E., Atwater, L., Taylor, S. N., & McKee, R. A. (2020). Gender bias still plagues the workplace: Looking at derailment risk and performance with self–other ratings. *Group & Organization Management*, 45(3), 315–350. doi:10.1177/1059601119867780

Bureau, C. F. P. (2015). *Financial Well-Being: The Goal of Financial Education*. Consumer Financial Protection Bureau.

Carpena, F., Cole, S. A., Shapiro, J., & Zia, B. (2011). *Unpacking the causal chain of financial literacy.* (World Bank Policy Research Working Paper, (5798)).

Cartwright, A., Hussey, I., Roche, B., Dunne, J., & Muphy, C. (2017). An investigation into the relationship between the gender binary and occupational discrimination using the implicit relational assessment procedure. *The Psychological Record, 67*(1), 121–130. doi:10.1007/s40732-016-0212-1

Ceci, S. J., Ginther, D. K., Kahn, S., & Williams, W. M. (2014). Women in academic science: A changing landscape. *Psychological Science in the Public Interest, 15*(3), 75–141. doi:10.1177/1529100614541236 PMID:26172066

Chen, G., Kark, R., Shamir, B. (2003). *The Two Faces of Transformational Leadership: Empowerment and Dependency.* 246-254.

Cook, A., & Glass, C. (2014). Women and top leadership positions: Towards an institutional analysis. *Gender, Work and Organization, 21*(1), 91–103. doi:10.1111/gwao.12018

Corbett, H. (2022). *Forbes. *How To #BreakTheBias At Work On International Women's Day.* And Every Day.

Cornwall, A., & Rivas, A.-M. (2015). From 'gender equality and 'women's empowerment' to global justice: Reclaiming a transformative agenda for gender and development. *Third World Quarterly, 36*(2), 396–415. doi:10.1080/01436597.2015.1013341

Corrêa, V. S., Brito, F. R. D. S., Lima, R. M. D., & Queiroz, M. M. (2022). Female entrepreneurship in emerging and developing countries: A systematic literature review. *International Journal of Gender and Entrepreneurship, 14*(3), 300–322. doi:10.1108/IJGE-08-2021-0142

Cullen, C., Barnes-Holmes, D., Barnes-Holmes, Y., & Stewart, I. (2009). The Implicit Relational Assessment Procedure (IRAP) and the malleability of ageist attitudes. *The Psychological Record, 59*(4), 591–620. doi:10.1007/BF03395683

De Clercq, D., & Brieger, S. A. (2022). When discrimination is worse, autonomy is key: How women entrepreneurs leverage job autonomy resources to find work–life balance. *Journal of Business Ethics, 177*(3), 665–682. doi:10.1007/s10551-021-04735-1

De Vita, L., Mari, M., & Poggesi, S. (2014). Women entrepreneurs in and from developing countries: Evidences from the literature. *European Management Journal, 32*(3), 451–460. doi:10.1016/j.emj.2013.07.009

Deci, E. L., & Ryan, R. M. (2013). *Intrinsic motivation and self-determination in human behavior.* Springer Science & Business Media.

Demirgüç-Kunt, A., Klapper, L., Singer, D., & Ansar, S. (2022). *The Global Findex Database 2021: Financial inclusion, digital payments, and resilience in the age of COVID-19.* World Bank Publications. doi:10.1596/978-1-4648-1897-4

Diehl, A. B., Stephenson, A. L., Dzubinski, L. M., & Wang, D. C. (2020). Measuring the invisible: Development and multi-industry validation of the Gender Bias Scale for Women Leaders. *Human Resource Development Quarterly, 31*(3), 249–280. doi:10.1002/hrdq.21389

Eagly, A. H., Gartzia, L. L., & Carli, L. (2014). Female advantage: revisited S. Kumra, R. Simpson, R. Burke (Eds.), The Oxford handbook of gender in organizations. Oxford University Press, New York.

Erkal, N., Gangadharan, L., & Xiao, E. (2022). Leadership selection: Can changing the default break the glass ceiling? *The Leadership Quarterly*, *33*(2), 101563. doi:10.1016/j.leaqua.2021.101563

Essers, C., Pio, E., Verduijn, K., & Bensliman, N. (2021). Navigating belonging as a Muslim Moroccan female entrepreneur. *Journal of Small Business Management*, *59*(6), 1250–1278. doi:10.1080/00472778.2020.1769989

Fauzi, M. A., Sapuan, N. M., & Zainudin, N. M. (2023). Women and female entrepreneurship: Past, present, and future trends in developing countries. *Entrepreneurial Business and Economics Review*, *11*(3), 57–75. doi:10.15678/EBER.2023.110304

Fleming, K., Foody, M., & Murphy, C. (2020). Using the implicit relational assessment procedure (IRAP) to examine implicit gender stereotypes in science, technology, engineering and maths (STEM). *The Psychological Record*, *70*(3), 459–469. doi:10.1007/s40732-020-00401-6

Fonseca, R., Mullen, K. J., Zamarro, G., & Zissimopoulos, J. (2012). What explains the gender gap in financial literacy? The role of household decision making. *The Journal of Consumer Affairs*, *46*(1), 90–106. doi:10.1111/j.1745-6606.2011.01221.x PMID:23049140

Forbes. (2022). Bias Holds Women Back. *Forbes*. https://www.forbes.com/sites/andiekramer/2022/02/24/bias-holds-women-back/?sh=6d0f775d3f09

Frola, A., Delprato, M., & Chudgar, A. (2024). Lack of educational access, women's empowerment and spatial education inequality for the Eastern and Western Africa regions. *International Journal of Educational Development*, *104*, 102939. doi:10.1016/j.ijedudev.2023.102939

Galsanjigmed, E., & Sekiguchi, T. (2023). Challenges Women Experience in Leadership Careers: An Integrative Review. *Merits*, *3*(2), 366–389. doi:10.3390/merits3020021

Gonçalves, V. N., Ponchio, M. C., & Basílio, R. G. (2021). Women's financial well-being: A systematic literature review and directions for future research. *International Journal of Consumer Studies*, *45*(4), 824–843. doi:10.1111/ijcs.12673

Greenwald, A. G., & Banaji, M. R. (1995). Implicit social cognition: Attitudes, self-esteem, and stereotypes. *Psychological Review*, *102*(1), 4–27. doi:10.1037/0033-295X.102.1.4 PMID:7878162

Greenwald, A. G., Poehlman, T. A., Uhlmann, E. L., & Banaji, M. R. (2009). Understanding and using the Implicit Association Test: III. Meta-analysis of predictive validity. *Journal of Personality and Social Psychology*, *97*(1), 17–41. doi:10.1037/a0015575 PMID:19586237

Gruneau, M. F. (2021). The persistence of social norms, family formation, and gender balance in politics. *Politics & Gender*, *18*(3), 1–33.

Gudjonsson, S., Kristinsson, K., & Minelgaite, I. (2022). Follow us, not? Gender differences in financial literacy within the global leader of gender equality. *Entrepreneurship and Sustainability Issues*, *10*(2), 351–361. doi:10.9770/jesi.2022.10.2(21)

Haque, A., & Zulfiqar, M. (2016). Women's economic empowerment through financial literacy, financial attitude and financial wellbeing. *International Journal of Business and Social Science, 7*(3), 78–88.

Heilman, M. E., Caleo, S., & Manzi, F. (2024). Women at work: Pathways from gender stereotypes to gender bias and discrimination. *Annual Review of Organizational Psychology and Organizational Behavior, 11*(1), 165–192. doi:10.1146/annurev-orgpsych-110721-034105

Hill, C., Miller, K., Benson, K., & Handley, G. (2016). *Barriers and Bias: The Status of Women in Leadership*. American Association of University Women.

Hoyt, C. L., & Simon, S. (2024). Social psychological approaches to women and leadership theory. In *Handbook of research on gender and leadership* (pp. 65–83). Edward Elgar Publishing. doi:10.4337/9781035306893.00015

Huis, M. A., Hansen, N., Otten, S., & Lensink, R. (2017). A three-dimensional model of women's empowerment: Implications in the field of microfinance and future directions. *Frontiers in Psychology, 8*, 1678. doi:10.3389/fpsyg.2017.01678 PMID:29033873

Hung, A., Yoong, J., & Brown, E. (2012). *Empowering women through financial awareness and education*.

Hutchison, K. (2020). Four types of gender bias affecting women surgeons and their cumulative impact. *Journal of Medical Ethics, 46*(4), 236–241. doi:10.1136/medethics-2019-105552 PMID:32229595

Isaga, N. (2018). Start-up motives and challenges facing female entrepreneurs in Tanzania. *International Journal of Gender and Entrepreneurship, 11*(2), 102–119. doi:10.1108/IJGE-02-2018-0010

Ito, A., & Bligh, M. (2024). Organizational processes and systems that affect women in leadership. In *Handbook of Research on Gender and Leadership* (pp. 292–311). Edward Elgar Publishing. doi:10.4337/9781035306893.00030

Jha, P., Makkad, M., & Mittal, S. (2018). Performance-oriented factors for women entrepreneurs–a scale development perspective. *Journal of Entrepreneurship in Emerging Economies, 10*(2), 329–360. doi:10.1108/JEEE-08-2017-0053

Kabeer, N. (2003). *Gender Mainstreaming in Poverty Eradication and the Millennium Development Goals: A handbook for policy-makers and other stakeholders*. Commonwealth Secretariat. doi:10.14217/9781848598133-en

Kadoya, Y., & Khan, M. S. R. (2020). What determines financial literacy in Japan? *Journal of Pension Economics and Finance, 19*(3), 353–371. doi:10.1017/S1474747218000379

Kebede, J., Selvanathan, S., & Naranpanawa, A. (2024). Financial inclusion and monetary policy effectiveness in a monetary union: Heterogenous panel approach. *Economics of Transition and Institutional Change*, ecot.12402. doi:10.1111/ecot.12402

Khamis, Z. K. (2022). The Social Learning Theory and Gender Representations in Leadership Positions. A case of Health Sector in Tanzania. *Journal of Social and Development Sciences, 13*(4 (S)), 24–33. doi:10.22610/jsds.v13i4(S).3318

Khodijah, A. S., Pekerti, R. D., Wara, A. A., & Rahmayanti, A. J. M. H. (2024). Women's Perceptions of Glass Ceiling In The Accounting Profession In Indonesia. *Journal of accounting Science/jas. umsida. ac. id/index. php/jas January, 8*(1), 58.

Kolbe, K. (2009). Self-Efficacy Results from Exercising Control over Personal Conative Strengths. Wisdom of the Ages.

Kurtaran, A. T., Aydin, A., & Yeşildağ, A. Y. (2024). Glass Ceiling Syndrome: A Perspective of Women Working in Health Institutions. *Ege Academic Review, 24*(1), 71–84.

Lusardi, A., & Mitchell, O. S. (2008). Planning and financial literacy: How do women fare? *The American Economic Review, 98*(2), 413–417. doi:10.1257/aer.98.2.413

Lusardi, A., & Mitchell, O. S. (2014). The economic importance of financial literacy: Theory and evidence. American Economic Journal. *Journal of Economic Literature, 52*(1), 5–44. doi:10.1257/jel.52.1.5 PMID:28579637

Lutz, H. L., Re, T. C., Brandt, J. A. A., & Garcia, R. (2023). Gender Bias toward Supervisors' Empowering Leadership Behavior. *Behavior and Social Issues*, 1-16.

Madsen, S. R., & Andrade, M. S. (2018). Unconscious gender bias: Implications for women's leadership development. *Journal of Leadership Studies, 12*(1), 62–67. doi:10.1002/jls.21566

MahajanP. (2019). Women in Leadership: Comparing Developed (The UK) and the Developing (India) Corporate Economy. SSRN 3444165. doi:10.2139/ssrn.3444165

Malapit, H. J. L. (2012). Are women more likely to be credit constrained? Evidence from low-income urban households in the Philippines. *Feminist Economics, 18*(3), 81–108. doi:10.1080/13545701.2012.716161

Mensah, M. S. B., & Derera, E. (2023). "Analysis of Ghana's and South Africa's women's entrepreneurship policies." *Women's Entrepreneurship Policy: A Global Perspective*: 214.

Mensah, M. S. B., & Derera, E. (2023). Feminist Critique of Ghana's Women's Entrepreneurship Policies. *JWEE*, (1-2), 1–31. doi:10.28934/jwee23.12.pp1-31

Muravyev, A., Talavera, O., & Schäfer, D. (2009). Entrepreneurs' gender and financial constraints: Evidence from international data. *Journal of Comparative Economics, 37*(2), 270–286. doi:10.1016/j.jce.2008.12.001

Nikolaou, A. (2017). *Barriers and Biases: A case study of women's experiences of underrepresentation at senior management levels.*

Njanike, K., & Mpofu, R. T. (2024). Factors Influencing Financial Inclusion for Social Inclusion in Selected African Countries. *Insight on Africa, 16*(1), 93–112. doi:10.1177/09750878231194558

Panda, S. (2018). Constraints faced by women entrepreneurs in developing countries: Review and ranking. *Gender in Management, 33*(4), 315–331. doi:10.1108/GM-01-2017-0003

Rametse, N., Weerakoon, C., & Moremomg-Nganunu, T. (2021). Parental role models' influence on entrepreneurial aspirations of Botswana female students. *Journal of Developing Areas*, *55*(1). doi:10.1353/jda.2021.0000

Rice, L., & Barth, J. M. (2017). A tale of two gender roles: The effects of implicit and explicit gender role traditionalism and occupational stereotype on hiring decisions. *Gender Issues*, *34*(1), 86–102. doi:10.1007/s12147-016-9175-4

Risman, B. J., & Davis, G. (2013). From sex roles to gender structure. *Current Sociology*, *61*(5-6), 733–755. doi:10.1177/0011392113479315

Roy, C. K., & Xiaoling, H. (2022). Achieving SDG 5, gender equality and empower all women and girls, in developing countries: How aid for trade can help? *International Journal of Social Economics*, *49*(6), 930–959. doi:10.1108/IJSE-12-2020-0813

Rughoobur-Seetah, S., Hosanoo, Z., & Balla Soupramanien, L. D. (2023). Financial independence of women–the impact of social factors on women empowerment in small island developing states (SIDS). *The International Journal of Organizational Analysis*, *31*(6), 2383–2408. doi:10.1108/IJOA-10-2021-2980

Rutherford, S. (2011). *Women's work, men's cultures: overcoming resistance and changing organizational cultures*. Palgrave Macmillan. doi:10.1057/9780230307476

Ryan, R. M., & Deci, E. L. (2000). Self-determination theory and the facilitation of intrinsic motivation, social development, and well-being. *The American Psychologist*, *55*(1), 68–78. doi:10.1037/0003-066X.55.1.68 PMID:11392867

Ryan, R. M., & Deci, E. L. (2017). *Self-determination theory: Basic psychological needs in motivation, development, and wellness*. Guilford publications. doi:10.1521/978.14625/28806

Saadin, I., Ramli, K., Johari, H., & Harin, N. A. (2016). Women and barriers for upward career advancement–a survey at Perak state secretariat, Ipoh, Perak. *Procedia Economics and Finance*, *35*, 574–581. doi:10.1016/S2212-5671(16)00070-8

Samie, S. F., Johnson, A. J., Huffman, A. M., & Hillyer, S. J. (2015). Voices of empowerment: Women from the Global South re/negotiating empowerment and the global sports mentoring programme. *Sport in Society*, *18*(8), 923–937. doi:10.1080/17430437.2014.997582

Sharma, A., & Johri, A. (2014). Learning and empowerment: Designing a financial literacy tool to teach long-term investing to illiterate women in rural India. *Learning, Culture and Social Interaction*, *3*(1), 21–33. doi:10.1016/j.lcsi.2013.10.003

Singh, B., & Singh, M. (2023). Financial literacy and its determinants among the schedule tribes: Evidences from India. *International Journal of Social Economics*, *50*(12), 1804–1817. doi:10.1108/IJSE-01-2023-0008

SpencerStuart. (2022). *2022 S&P 500 Board Diversity Snapshot*. Spencer Stuart. https://www.spencerstuart.com/-/media/2022/june/diversitysnapshot/sp500_board_diversity_snapshot_2022.pdf

Sultana, S., Guimbretière, F., Sengers, P., & Dell, N. (2018). Design within a patriarchal society: Opportunities and challenges in designing for rural women in bangladesh. In *Proceedings of the 2018 CHI Conference on Human Factors in Computing Systems*, (pp. 1-13). ACM. 10.1145/3173574.3174110

Tyson, L. D., & Klugman, J. (2017). *Women's economic empowerment is the smart thing to do. What's stopping us?* World Economic Forum. https://www. weforum. org/agenda/2017/01/womens-economic-empowerment-is-the-smart-and-right-thing-to-do-whats-stopping-us/

UNHR. (2014). *Gender stereotypes and Stereotyping and women's rights*. UNHR. https://www.ohchr.org/sites/default/files/Documents/Issues/Women/WRGS/OnePagers/Gender_stereotyping.pdf

United Nations. (2023). *Sustainable Development Goals. Goal 5: Achieve gender equality and empower all women and girls*. United Nations. https://sdgs.un.org/goals/goal5/

Webster, J., & Watson, R. T. (2002). Analyzing the past to prepare for the future: Writing 253 a literature review. *Management Information Systems Quarterly*, 26(2).

Welsh, D. H., Kaciak, E., Trimi, S., & Mainardes, E. W. (2018). Women entrepreneurs and family firm heterogeneity: Evidence from an emerging economy. *Group Decision and Negotiation*, 27(3), 445–465. doi:10.1007/s10726-017-9544-8

World Economic Forum. (2023). *Gender Equality: Global Annual Results Report 2022*. WEF.

Wu, J., Richard, O. C., Triana, M. D. C., & Zhang, X. (2022). The performance impact of gender diversity in the top management team and board of directors: A multiteam systems approach. *Human Resource Management*, 61(2), 157–180. doi:10.1002/hrm.22086

Xheneti, M., Karki, S. T., & Madden, A. (2021). Negotiating business and family demands within a patriarchal society–the case of women entrepreneurs in the Nepalese context. In *Understanding Women's Entrepreneurship in a Gendered Context* (pp. 93–112). Routledge. doi:10.4324/9781003139454-7

Yap, R. J. C., Komalasari, F., & Hadiansah, I. (2018). The effect of financial literacy and attitude on financial management behavior and satisfaction. *BISNIS & BIROKRASI: Jurnal Ilmu Administrasi dan Organisasi*, 23(3), 4.

Yousafzai, S. Y., Saeed, S., & Muffatto, M. (2015). Institutional theory and contextual embeddedness of women's entrepreneurial leadership: Evidence from 92 countries. *Journal of Small Business Management*, 53(3), 587–604. doi:10.1111/jsbm.12179

Zeb, A., & Ihsan, A. (2020, March). Innovation and the entrepreneurial performance in women-owned small and medium-sized enterprises in Pakistan. []. Pergamon.]. *Women's Studies International Forum*, 79, 102342. doi:10.1016/j.wsif.2020.102342

Zhang, C., & Basha, D. (2023). Women as leaders: The glass ceiling effect on women's leadership success in public bureaucracies. *Gender in Management*, 38(4), 489–503. doi:10.1108/GM-09-2021-0283

Chapter 3
Illuminating Paths:
Empowerment Through Education and Mentorship

Kritika
https://orcid.org/0000-0002-1186-6032
Independent Researcher, India

ABSTRACT

Expanding access to quality education and mentorship are pivotal yet underutilized strategies for empowering women and girls globally. This chapter examines persistent barriers like poverty, cultural norms, and lack of female teachers inhibiting girls' education access. It highlights interventions including cash transfers, infrastructure improvements, and vocational training that have successfully boosted girls' school participation. However, gender disparities in secondary and higher education remain pervasive, limiting women's opportunities and leadership. The chapter also explores how curricula typically reinforce gender stereotypes rather than building agency,, and advocates approaches promoting skills like entrepreneurship. It emphasizes the benefits of mentors providing guidance, networking, and inspiration as women navigate career challenges, such as the shortage of female role models across sectors. Formal programs, virtual mentoring, and cross-national initiatives expand access amid mentor scarcity.

INTRODUCTION

Across cultures and continents, education and mentorship serve as two integral yet oft-overlooked keys to unlocking women's empowerment. From the schoolhouses of rural villages to the boardrooms of multinational corporations, expanding access to impactful learning opportunities and strong role models provides women and girls the tools and guidance to reach their fullest potential as leaders. However, despite global progress towards gender equity over recent decades, women worldwide continue facing steep barriers to education access from a young age. Compounding these obstacles, women remain starkly underrepresented in leadership roles across sectors, depriving aspiring female professionals of

DOI: 10.4018/979-8-3693-2806-4.ch003

mentorship from those who have come before them. Bridging these gaps in education and mentorship is imperative for elevating women into positions of influence and authority.

The far-reaching benefits of educating girls have become increasingly clear. Studies show that educating girls leads to increased economic productivity, improved child and maternal health, and higher wages that lift households out of poverty (Psacharopoulos & Patrinos, 2018). Education also empowers girls to make decisions about their own lives and futures, fostering independence and self-efficacy (Sanders, 2017). However, entrenched gender roles and norms in many societies continue restricting girls' access. Poverty is a major driver, causing families to favor educating sons who will inherit the household over daughters who will one day marry out (Hill & King, 1995). Other barriers include child marriage and early pregnancy, gender-based violence at or on the way to school, lack of sanitation facilities, and long travel distances without safe transport (Mlama et al., 2019). Cultural attitudes devaluing girls' education also persist in certain contexts (Kumar & Sahoo, 2024).

While global enrollment in primary education has improved to near-parity between girls and boys, disparities widen at higher levels. Across sub-Saharan Africa and parts of Asia, girls' secondary school participation lags nearly 10 percentage points behind boys (UNESCO, 2016). Tertiary education gaps are even more severe, with global female enrollment at universities just 1.5 women for every 2 men (UNESCO Institute for Statistics, 2022). Even when girls are formally enrolled, quality issues from lack of female teachers to curricula reinforcing traditional gender roles inhibit the empowering potential of education (Jayaweera, 1997). Tailoring learning opportunities to equip girls with leadership, critical thinking, and vocational skills is essential to set more women on paths to achievement (Lloyd et al., 2016).

Equally important is providing girls and women at all career stages access to knowledgeable mentors who can provide guidance, support, and inspiration. Studies consistently demonstrate that mentorship accelerates women's professional advancement, conferring benefits like increased confidence, improved skills, and greater career fulfillment (Allen et al., 2004). Mentors provide insider information about advancing in particular fields, assist with networking, give candid feedback on performance, and serve as living examples that success is achievable (Ehrich, 1995). They help women navigate cultural norms, gender bias, and other specific obstacles faced (Darwin & Palmer, 2009).

Yet a lack of gender diversity in senior management, academia, politics, and other realms results in too few female mentors for the number of women coming up the ranks seeking role models (Novakovic & Fouad, 2012). This scarcity often leaves young women struggling to find mentors with shared experiences to provide them career direction tailored to the challenges they face (Patton, 2009). Even when senior female mentors are available, women report difficulty establishing effective mentoring relationships relative to men (Ragins & Cotton, 1991). Tapping networks outside immediate domains and embracing innovative virtual mentoring can help bridge these gaps (Murphy, 2011).

Realizing the full potential of education and mentorship to catapult more women into positions of leadership will require resolute efforts across institutions. Governments must prioritize increasing access to high-quality, empowering education for girls and incentives to steer their progress into higher education (Unterhalter et al., 2014). Corporations should strengthen recruitment, promotion and retention of senior female leaders, cultivating in-house mentors (Smith et al., 2016). Non-profits play critical roles in reaching women overlooked by public and private sectors (Teasdale et al., 2011). Families and communities sharing progressive gender norms and high aspirations for daughters and female youth boost success (Jejeebhoy, 1995).

Through collective action rooted in research on the multifaceted barriers women face, the world can break down limitations on girls' learning and women's leadership. Fulfilling every woman's right to education and mentorship, regardless of her circumstances, is imperative to ushering in a future of empowerment without boundaries. The paths are illuminated, now the journey lies before us. With women mentoring the next generation to soar even higher, the possibilities are boundless.

EXPANDING ACCESS TO EDUCATION FOR WOMEN'S EMPOWERMENT

Education is a fundamental human right and powerful driver of development. However, girls worldwide continue to face barriers restricting their access to quality learning opportunities. This chapter explores persistent obstacles inhibiting girls' education, interventions attempting to expand access, progress made, and recommendations to advance gender equality in education.

Barriers to Girls' Education

Poverty is arguably the most pervasive obstacle to girls' education globally, especially in rural regions. School fees, materials, uniforms and transport costs are prohibitive for impoverished families who often must choose to educate sons over daughters (Baah-Ennumh et al., 2020). Girls' domestic labor sustaining households further limits school participation, with chores alone accounting for 10% lower attendance (Alam et al., 2017). Child marriage affects 12 million girls annually, forcing them to drop out once wed (UNICEF, 2021).

Socio-cultural norms also depress girls' enrollment and retention. In patriarchal societies sons are prioritized as future household providers. Menstruation taboos stigmatize pubescent girls (Sumpter & Torondel, 2013). Gender-based violence at or en route to school creates unsafe environments prompting girls' withdrawal (Parkes et al., 2017). Low returns anticipated on girls' education steer households towards investing in sons instead (Psacharopoulos & Patrinos, 2018). Discriminatory attitudes make schools unwelcoming places for girls in certain contexts.

Interventions Boosting Girls' Participation

Against this backdrop of obstacles, targeted interventions have effectively increased girls' access and retention. Conditional cash transfers (CCTs) offer payment to households linked to girls' school attendance and progression, implemented broadly in Latin America and Asia (Soares et al., 2016). Transport provision via bicycles or safe transit systems facilitates access for remote areas (Muralidharan & Prakash, 2017). School feeding programs supply meals incentivizing attendance and enabling focus. Recruiting local female teachers and mentors provides relatable role models and support (Shah & Shah, 2012).

Scholarships offset costs most prohibitive for impoverished families. BRAC's Secondary School Scholarship Program for girls in Bangladesh increased enrollment 11% and reduced dropouts (Asadullah & Chaudhury, 2015). Infrastructural upgrades including lights, private toilets, and sanitary facilities alleviate safety concerns. Provision of menstrual products reduces absenteeism (Montgomery et al., 2016). Public awareness campaigns tackle norms undervaluing girls' education. Such multifaceted initiatives demonstrate that targeted, context-specific approaches can successfully surmount barriers.

Progress and Remaining Gaps

While tremendous strides have been made towards gender parity in primary education, gaps widen for adolescent girls. At the secondary level, a 10 percentage point divide persists between girls' and boys' enrollment across developing nations (UNESCO, 2016). Tertiary education inequities emerge from this shaky foundation, with fields like STEM exhibiting some of the widest imbalances. Updating curricula, improving infrastructure, recruiting diverse teachers, and financial support are key to strengthening girls' secondary and post-secondary participation (Tan & Barton, 2018).

Barriers intersecting at the household, community, and system levels continue undercutting girls' access to empowering education globally:

- Alleviating school expenses through affordable tuition, cash transfers, and eliminating ancillary fees (Soares et al., 2016).
- Improving infrastructure – girls' toilets, lights, safe transit and menstrual products (Sumpter & Torondel, 2013).
- Recruiting and training more female teachers and mentors (Shah & Shah, 2012).
- Preventing child marriage and supporting adolescent mothers' education (UNICEF, 2021).
- Modernizing curricula to build skills and open opportunities like STEM (Tan & Barton, 2018).
- Targeted efforts across sectors are still needed to achieve gender equality in education and its manifold benefits for girls as individuals and societies as a whole.

TAILORING EDUCATION TO EMPOWER WOMEN

While expanding girls' access to schooling is essential, the quality and content of education shapes its empowerment potential. Curricula often reinforce gender stereotypes rather than building girls' agency and skills.

Curricula Promoting Leadership Skills for Girls

Traditional education models focused on rote memorization tend to stifle creative thinking and leadership abilities. Teaching styles emphasizing conformity over critical analysis also discourage girls from envisioning themselves as leaders and change-makers (Stromquist, 2017). Transforming rigid, outdated learning approaches is key to nurturing future women leaders.

Leadership training and mentoring programs integrated into education provide vital support structures. Initiatives like the African Girls' Leadership Initiative equip girls to lead through workshops on public speaking, self-confidence, goal setting, and teamwork (Thomas et al., 2020). Embedding leadership development within schools guides girls to recognize their potential early on. Camfed's "My Better World" curriculum aims to instill agency in female students through leadership, entrepreneurship and life skills modules. Delivered via interactive workshops, it has reached over 5,000 schools across sub-Saharan Africa (Camfed, 2020).

Extracurricular activities including sports, clubs and committees allow girls to practice leadership skills. A study in India found that giving girls leadership roles in local sports teams increased their confidence speaking publicly and voicing opinions compared to peers (Girls First Fund, 2020). Model

United Nations helps students develop persuasive public speaking, debating, and negotiation abilities prized in leadership roles. Student governments and clubs offer hands-on management experience.

Academic content and pedagogical strategies should also consciously foster leadership readiness in girls. Teaching methods emphasizing critical thinking and questioning norms spur creative analysis key to leadership (Stromquist, 2018). Project-based learning where students address real community issues builds problem-solving and teamwork skills while discussing women leaders through history provides inspiration and schools can train teachers themselves on leadership development approaches to instill in female students.

Ultimately effective leadership education empowers girls to recognize their worth and potential to create change. This critical foundation enables women to ultimately shatter glass ceilings and pioneer as leaders across spheres.

STEM Education for Women as a Path to Opportunity

Science, technology, engineering and mathematics (STEM) fields offer immense potential for girls' empowerment. STEM careers provide economic stability and reward creative thinking. However, persisting gender gaps in STEM education constrain opportunities for women. Tailoring STEM learning to engage girls' interests is critical to expanding participation.

Stereotypes of scientists and engineers as male remain pervasive, signaling to girls a lack of belonging in STEM from a young age (Wang & Degol, 2017). Gender gaps in confidence regarding STEM abilities emerge early, undermining girls' persistence. However, hands-on, inquiry-based approaches spark curiosity and enjoyment in STEM for both genders. A robotic curriculum for Zimbabwean high school girls increased technology self-efficacy and interest (Vanderbilt University, 2021). Offering creative outlets like computing summer camps builds passion for STEM outside intimidating classroom environments (Google, 2022).

Access to female mentors and role models counteracts stereotypes, providing living proof that girls can excel and lead in STEM fields. A global research study found that female physics students with woman mentors reported greater confidence and belonging than peers without mentors (Lunsford et al., 2018). STEM teacher training programs recruiting more women provide in-class mentors guiding girls. TechWomen cultivates STEM leadership skills in emerging women across Africa, Central Asia, and the Middle East via mentorship and professional networks.

Strengthening girls' confidence plays a pivotal role driving STEM success. Growth mindset training emphasizing learning through effort over innate brilliance boosts motivation and achievement (Paunesku et al., 2015). Social-belonging interventions conveying peers' shared struggles in challenging majors alleviate discouragement (Walton & Carr, 2012). Career awareness exposing girls to diverse STEM professionals illustrates paths forward. Such initiatives help girls persist in demanding but rewarding STEM disciplines.

Tailoring STEM education to engage girls' interests and ambitions provides a gateway to advancement. With supportive mentors, strength-based instruction, and gender-inclusive learning environments, STEM fields can propel women to the forefront of innovation and progress.

Venture Capital and Career Education

Women who receive an education in entrepreneurship are more able to become financially independent and to hold leadership positions in the business world. Girls can prepare for fulfilling professions in in-demand industries with vocational training. By including these programmes in official schooling, women's opportunities are increased.

More and more programmes are offering entrepreneurship education with a focus on women and girls. Women entrepreneurs in 56 countries can get company management training, networking opportunities, and mentorship through Goldman Sachs' 10,000 Women project (Goldman Sachs, 2022). In Ethiopia, the Women's entrepreneurial Development programme combines start-up funding and support with entrepreneurial education. More than 90% of graduates have started profitable businesses (UNIDO, 2021).

Developing financial literacy, marketing techniques, record keeping, and operations management empowers women to achieve their business visions. Teaching effective negotiation trains women to confidently advocate for resources and fair deals, an area where gender gaps persist (Babcock & Laschever, 2009). Successful women entrepreneurs guest lecturing provide inspiration through real-world stories. Hands-on experience running school shops, cafeterias or agricultural plots allows girls to practice skills.

Vocational training equipping girls with qualifications for skilled trades and technical fields also expands opportunity. Hospitality, manufacturing, construction, cosmetology, healthcare, and technology offer viable careers. Preparing women for "non-traditional" occupations counters gender occupational segregation while increasing earnings potential (Adams & Gamage, 2008). Bangladesh's successful Secondary Education and Access to Skilled Employment program partners secondary schools with local industries. Students receive targeted vocational instruction combined with apprenticeships, fostering successful transitions into formal sector jobs (World Bank, 2022).

Entrepreneurship and vocational education empower women to achieve economic independence and secure family livelihoods. Integrating such programs into school curricula or offering parallel training provides vital skills beyond academics alone. As women utilize these capabilities to succeed in business and technical careers, they pave the way for future female leaders and innovators.

THE POWER OF MENTORSHIP

Women's progress in both personal and professional domains has historically been hampered by a lack of access to direction and support. But mentoring shows up as a potent instrument to close this gap. Mentorship promotes development, self-assurance, and success by pairing women with knowledgeable people who can provide guidance, motivation, and encouragement.

Women's Mentoring Programmes, Both Official and Informal: Embracing Diverse Pathways

There are many different ways in which mentoring might appear, from formal programmes to natural connections. Understanding these differences enables customised strategies to match women with the best mentors. Table 1 represents the benefits of mentorship.

Formal Programmes:

- Workplace initiatives: Companies are beginning to provide women with senior leaders or subject matter experts through formal mentoring programmes (Ragins & Kram, 2000). These programmes usually include specific objectives, mentor and mentee training, and frequent meetings and activities.
- Professional associations: A lot of associations for professionals run mentoring programmes that link women from different industries and phases of their careers. Peer-to-peer learning and assistance are encouraged by these programmes' expanded networks and varied viewpoints (Stasulovic & Mehta, 2019).
- Community-based initiatives: Community centres and nonprofits frequently provide mentorship programmes, especially for young women or those looking to change careers. Particularly for women who are up against more obstacles, these programmes can offer insightful advice and a network of support (Mott Foundation, 2019).

Informal Mentoring:

- Personal connections: People might actively look for mentors in their own networks by getting in touch with esteemed coworkers, relatives, or local authorities. These connections can promote trust and long-lasting relationships by providing a combination of professional and personal assistance.
- Peer mentoring: Developing connections with peers, especially those who possess similar abilities or backgrounds, can provide invaluable assistance and information sharing. According to Kram (1985), peer mentoring promotes community, shared learning, and cooperation.
- Virtual mentoring: Social media groups and online platforms link women with mentors who live far away, providing access to a wider range of viewpoints and areas of expertise. Although social media groups can help to foster natural mentoring ties, platforms such as "Mentor Match" and "Lean In Circles" provide structured virtual interactions.

Table 1. Benefits of mentorship

Benefit	Role played
For mentees	
Job Advancement	Mentors can help mentees find worthwhile opportunities, handle workplace dynamics, and offer professional advice
Talent Development	Mentors can provide advice on developing talents, impart industry knowledge, and assist mentees in finding training options.
Boosting Confidence	Mentors can assist mentees develop self-belief and overcome obstacles with higher self-efficacy by providing them with support and constructive criticism
Networking Opportunities	By introducing mentees to their network, mentors can help mentees gain new contacts in the business world and access various opportunities
For mentors	
Personal Development	Mentoring gives mentors the chance to think back on their own experiences, hone their leadership abilities, and acquire new insights
Enhanced Engagement	Mentoring helps companies create a feeling of community and purpose, which increases employee retention
Giving Back	Through mentoring, people can impart their skills and knowledge, helping others succeed and making a good difference
For organisations	
Varied and inclusive workforce	A more varied and inclusive workforce can be fostered through mentoring programmes, which can assist in luring and keeping women in traditionally male-dominated sectors.
Enhanced employee satisfaction	Mentoring programmes promote employee engagement, loyalty, and contentment, which in turn improves organisational performance.
Information transformation	Mentoring ensures institutional memory, promotes innovation, and helps transfer information between generations.

Effective Practices and Models for Successful Mentoring

To fully realise the benefits of mentorship, careful preparation and continuous assistance are needed. Building healthy relationships depends on important behaviours and a variety of models that address the requirements and objectives of each people. Table 2 represents diverse mentoring models.

Fitting With Accuracy

Cultural competency training: According to Earley and Mosakowski (2004), this is essential for developing cross-cultural mentoring relationships since it promotes successful communication and understanding.

Algorithms and matching platforms: These can help find matches that are successful and efficient, particularly in large-scale initiatives. Nonetheless, it's critical to take into account algorithms' limits.

Building a Strong Foundation

Clearly defining objectives and expectations from the start guarantees that all parties are aware of the relationship's purpose and intended results (Kram, 1983). This could entail talking about preferred communication styles and creating SMART goals—specific, measurable, achievable, relevant, and time-bound. Frequent meetings and communication: According to Eby et al. (2008), holding regular meetings and promoting constant communication keeps the connection going strong and promotes trust and accountability. Individual requirements and preferences can be taken into account when determining the frequency and nature of these contacts.

Flexibility and adaptability: Encouraging individual needs and promoting a more natural and meaningful relationship can be achieved by allowing for flexibility in goals, meeting frequency, and communication styles. This could be modifying the subject of conversations, adding virtual options, or modifying meeting timings in accordance with schedules.

Fostering Growth

Feedback and active listening: To promote development and reciprocal improvement, mentors and mentees should both engage in active listening and offer helpful criticism (Fletcher, 2013). Asking clarifying questions, summarising important information, and listening intently are all components of active listening. Feedback that is constructive should be given with empathy and respect, be precise, and be actionable. Establishing objectives, creating plans of action, and monitoring results together guarantee that the mentee is making progress towards the intended results (Eby et al., 2008). This could entail identifying the resources and assistance required to reach the bigger goals and breaking them down into smaller, more manageable tasks.

Challenge and support: To assist mentees in overcoming barriers and gaining confidence, mentors should assign difficult but doable tasks and offer continuous assistance (Cherrington, 2015).

Sponsorship and advocacy: By highlighting their mentees' abilities and accomplishments in their personal networks, mentors can go above and beyond providing assistance (Thomas, 2010). This could entail writing recommendations, giving uplifting testimonies, or exposing mentees to prospective prospects.

Table 2. Diverse mentoring models

Model	Description
Development model	Developmental model: This approach emphasises long-term professional growth, with the mentor helping the mentee along the way by offering advice, coaching, and support (Kram, 1983). Mentees looking for ongoing mentoring and career coaching can benefit greatly from this arrangement..
Psychosocial model	This approach places a strong emphasis on identity formation and emotional support to assist mentees in overcoming obstacles at work and gaining self-assurance (Kram, 1985). This strategy can help mentees who need help navigating the complexities of the workplace and developing their self-confidence.
Group mentoring	It is a paradigm that Clutterbuck and Megginson (2005) describe as pairing a group of mentees with one or more mentors in order to promote peer-to-peer learning, collaboration, and a sense of community. Mentees who appreciate learning from peers and do well in collaborative settings will find great success with this methodology.
Reverse mentoring	This approach reverses the conventional dynamic by having mentees share their technological or social media know-how with more senior mentors. This promotes understanding between generations and reciprocal learning (Stasulovic & Mehta, 2019). This strategy encourages information sharing and intergenerational understanding, which can be advantageous for mentors as well as mentees.

MENTORSHIP NEED ACROSS VARIOUS SECTORS

Mentorship provides invaluable guidance, support, and inspiration as women navigate career challenges and obstacles. However, many fields suffer from a lack of senior female mentors to nurture up-and-coming women professionals. Targeted efforts to recruit diverse mentors and implement formal programs are helping fill these gaps across academia, government, business, and more.

Mentorship in Academia

Higher education is pivotal for empowering women through knowledge and qualifications. Yet academia has long suffered from a shortage of female faculty to mentor young women. Women comprise just 21% of full professors at American universities. In fields like physics and engineering, fewer than 10% of senior faculty are women (Vitores, 2016). The lack of mentorship and role models contributes to female student attrition. Women earning bachelor's degrees outpace men, but men outnumber women earning PhDs by 12% (National Science Foundation, 2021).

To retain diverse talent, institutions are implementing mentoring initiatives and policies. Formal assignment of faculty mentors provides guidance navigating academia's unwritten rules. Peer mentoring among students creates communities of support countering isolation. Identity-based groups like the Association for Women in Mathematics provide mentoring at conferences. Virtual mentoring opens connections between institutions. Family leave and tenure extension policies help retain women faculty through parenting transitions while advancing careers.

Diversifying faculty is critical to long-term mentor capacity. Inclusive hiring initiatives target outstanding female candidates. Leadership training grooms women faculty for senior roles. Awards recognizing outstanding mentors motivate service. Academic mentorship helps catalyze women's pursuits of research, scholarship and education globally.

Mentorship in Government and Policy

Politics remains male-dominated across nations, creating a pressing need for women's leadership mentors in government and policy. As of 2022, women comprise just 26% of national parliamentarians globally (Inter-Parliamentary Union, 2022). The lack of female representation and precedents establishes politics as an insiders' game challenging for outsiders to infiltrate without guidance.

Groups like EMILY's List have successfully cultivated rising women policy stars in the US through mentorship and donor networks. Pairing less experienced candidates with elected officials provides campaign advice and political capital. Local politicos groom grassroots diverse women leaders to run for school boards and city councils, establishing foundations for higher office. Internships in legislative offices mentor new generations.

Parties actively recruiting and mentoring promising women leaders expedite progress. Public leadership training programs, like Vision 2020 in Turkey, provide critical skills and contacts. Once elected, peer mentoring cohorts help women officials navigate environments often inhospitable to newcomers. Mentorship is indispensable for dismantling boys' club political networks and clearing pathways for women to lead.

Mentorship in Business

Women entering the business world encounter manifold barriers to advancement. Ample research highlights the career benefits women gain from mentorship, including higher pay, faster promotion and increased satisfaction (Catalyst, 2004). But female leaders remain underrepresented across industries. Women hold just 5% of Fortune 500 CEO roles and 21% of executive/senior positions (Warner & Corley, 2017).

Structural disparities in access to senior mentors motivate formalized corporate programs. Mentorship requirements in manager training ensures participation. Affinity groups like Women in Finance provide guidance tapering isolation. Some firms institute mandatory "sponsorship" pairing rising women with executives advocating for their advancement. Cross-company groups like Chief expand networks.

Effective programs track participation and outcomes - pay, promotion, satisfaction - to gauge impact. Successful initiatives actively recruit senior managers as mentors and clearly define expectations. Women gain insider wisdom on positioning for leadership roles from mentors who have walked the path before them. Expanding mentorship access and networks empowers more women to attain corporate leadership.

Myriad sectors suffer from a dearth of senior female mentors for aspiring women. Yet well-designed initiatives are cultivating diverse mentoring relationships and capacity across academia, government, business, and beyond. Mentorship is not a panacea, but rather a vital component of multifaceted efforts required to achieve women's empowerment across occupations and industries. When women help each other navigate career challenges through mentorship, they collectively chip away at glass ceilings obstructing advancement worldwide.

GLOBAL MODELS OF MENTORSHIP FOR WOMEN

While mentorship needs persist across sectors, innovative programs worldwide are expanding access to guidance and support for women leaders globally. This chapter explores established cross-national initiatives, regionally tailored approaches, and virtual networking platforms that enable mentor connections transcending geography.

Cross-National Mentorship Initiatives

Groups like Vital Voices have successfully trained women leaders across borders through global mentorship models. Since beginning as a US government initiative in 1997, Vital Voices has grown into an influential NGO serving women in 182 countries (Vital Voices, 2022). Flagship programs like the Global Ambassadors Program and VV GROW connect emerging women leaders with experienced mentors and skill training. Nearly 15,000 women have participated to date, launching impactful new enterprises and organizations.

The Fortune Most Powerful Women network also runs a global mentorship program pairing female executives. Google's #IamRemarkable initiative encourages women to self-promote by sharing their accomplishments peer-to-peer. Multinational corporations can sponsor employee mentorship exchanges across international offices to build diversity and inclusion. UN agencies like UN Women facilitate South-South mentorship between developing countries to strengthen women's leadership while adapting global rights frameworks locally (UN Women, 2020).

Illuminating Paths

Effective global initiatives recognize regional variations in women's empowerment needs. Local partners help tailor programs to priorities like economic inclusion, preventing child marriage, pursuing elected office, or closing educational gaps. Exchange across borders spreads awareness of successful models. Consistent program evaluation ensures relevance. Global networks empower women to learn diverse strategies transcending cultural limitations.

Region-Specific Models

While global connections expand perspectives, regionally targeted approaches allow nuanced support attuned to local contexts. In East Asia, the Asia Society's Women Leaders of New Asia initiative convenes high-profile women from business, policy, and academia for peer mentorship and skills training focused on priorities like increasing women in leadership, supporting entrepreneurs, and improving work-family policies (Asia Society, 2022).

Groups like the African Women's Development Fund offer mentorship, leadership development, and funding tailored for African women promoting democracy, rights and social justice in their nations. In Latin America Redala provides virtual business mentorship by successful women entrepreneurs to assist peers in scaling their enterprises across the region (Redala, 2022). Such locally rooted initiatives understand social dynamics and policy environments, allowing responsive mentorship. They act as regional pipelines for women's leadership.

Even within countries, community-based mentoring for marginalized girls and women is key. Canada's Indspire connects Indigenous female youth with professionals as role models and guidance navigating education systems. Afghanistan's Women for Afghan Women provides mentors supporting women rebuilding lives and livelihoods amid ongoing crisis (WAW, 2022). Localized mentoring builds skills and hope.

Virtual Mentoring's Global Reach

Online platforms enable mentoring relationships unconstrained by geography. Sites like MentorcliQ match women seeking guidance with experienced leaders worldwide for virtual coaching sessions on topics like career planning, work-life balance, negotiating raises, and pitching ideas (MentorcliQ, 2022). IGNITE Worldwide's e-mentoring connects university students across India, Malaysia, Singapore and beyond with industry experts abroad for skills advice through email and messaging.

Such flexible digital options help women access mentors' expertise anywhere. However, challenges persist in forming deep relationships virtually. Programs incorporating opportunities to periodically meet at conferences, immersive retreats, or regional hub events for supplementary in-person interactions smooth the disconnect. Blended approaches optimize online convenience and offline community.

Shared platforms also foster peer mentorship on mass scale. Through the Female Wave of Change Facebook group, over 75,000 women across 175 countries participate in discussions, collaborations, advice sharing, and inspiration exchanges in service of gender equality and inclusion worldwide (Female Wave of Change, 2022). Technology enables both targeted and collective mentoring.

Programs worldwide illuminate innovative models to expand mentorship access, tailored to community needs while connecting across borders. NGOs, governments, corporations and institutions all play important roles designing initiatives to nurture women leaders. When women help each other navigate diverse barriers obstructing advancement in each society, they collectively chip away at gender inequality. Mentorship empowers women's progress in all corners of the world.

ADVANCING EDUCATION AND MENTORSHIP FOR WOMEN'S EMPOWERMENT

While substantial progress has been made towards gender equality globally, persisting gaps in girls' education access and women's leadership representation underline the need for continued action. This concluding chapter synthesizes recommendations to expand empowering education and mentorship for women and girls worldwide.

Recommendations for Improving Girls' Education

Government policies must eliminate school fees and increase education budgets to lower costs. This involves both abolishing tuition fees where they still exist, as well as expanding stipends to cover additional expenses like textbooks, uniforms, and transport that prohibit the poorest families from sending girls to school.

Cash transfer programs conditioned on school attendance help address poverty barriers. These CCTs have proven highly effective across regions like Latin America and Asia. Governments should expand successful models.

Communities can construct necessary infrastructure like girls' bathrooms, lighting, safe transit options, and provide menstrual hygiene products to establish accommodating learning environments. Local leaders should assess conditions at schools and identify priority upgrades enabling participation.

Awareness campaigns utilizing diverse media should counter norms undervaluing girls' education across all levels. Thoughtfully engaging male leaders as allies helps reshape restrictive patriarchal attitudes about appropriate roles for girls and women.

Teacher training initiatives focused on gender-inclusive practices are imperative, alongside concerted recruitment of more women instructors to serve as relatable role models and mentors for female students. This addresses biases that alienate girls in schools(Chisamya et al., 2012).

Modernizing curricula to build critical thinking, leadership skills, and technical abilities better equips girls for professional advancement. Moving beyond rote memorization models towards participatory, empowering learning is key.

Scaling Women's Mentorship Worldwide

Mentorship should be embedded into professional pipelines from student through executive levels via formal programs. This helps normalize guidance relationships in career journeys rather than leaving access to chance.

Companies must measure mentorship engagement and link participation to metrics like pay, promotion, and retention to motivate involvement across hierarchical levels. This conveys institutional priorities.

Virtual platforms provide flexible mentoring access unconstrained by geography, especially helpful for women in developing regions or remote areas lacking proximal leaders as role models. Blended virtual and in-person events optimize these tools.

Training more senior women to become competent mentors and sponsors addresses shortages faced by younger women entering fields still lacking gender diversity at higher levels. Mentorship readiness should be an integrated expectation and requirement for advancement into leadership roles.

Promising small-scale mentorship initiatives require evidence-based replication and scaling through partnerships to widen impact beyond isolated cases. NGOs piloting new approaches can collaborate with governments and businesses to maximize reach(Ensher et al., 2001).

The Vital Role of Government

Governments should pass and enforce laws mandating universal secondary education for girls and boys, alongside increasing budgets to improve school infrastructure, teacher salaries and curricula quality. Removing tuition barriers is vital.

Legislation and funding incentives should accelerate women's political representation through measures like gender quotas for parliament and supporting women's campaigns/leadership training.

Leading expansive public awareness campaigns via media, community forums, workshops, and activist mobilization can help change restrictive gender role attitudes that limit girls' and women's potential.

Providing social protection policies like childcare support and parental leave enables greater women's labor force participation. Affordable quality childcare also facilitates adolescent mothers continuing education if interested.

Leadership by the Private Sector

Businesses should invest in girls' education and leadership development programs which help level the playing field for future women employees and customers. Partnerships with nonprofits expand reach (Warner & Corley, 2017).

Companies must institute mentoring, sponsorship, networking groups, and leadership training to propel more women into management and executive positions. Tracking participation can gauge impact.

Covering education costs and providing career guidance/coaching for low-income female employees fosters workplace equality and talent retention. This strengthens women's economic security.

Donating funds or employee volunteers to support community girls' education nonprofits creates collective impact and builds future pipelines.

The Irreplaceable Role of Civil Society

Grassroots advocates provide vital supplementary or alternative education where public systems underserve marginalized girls due to poverty, culture, or conflict. They fill critical gaps.

Women-led NGOs act as mentoring and development pipelines for overlooked groups like rural, minority, and refugee women who lack access through mainstream initiatives.

Community partnerships where local advocates collaborate with schools/governments facilitate participatory solutions tailored to addressing barriers facing female students.

Activist organizations globally shine light on needs, pilot innovative models, and mobilize public pressure to enact policies that tangibly uplift women and girls. They lead the way that institutions often follow.

While governments, businesses, and non-profits all contribute unique resources and capabilities advancing gender equality in education and leadership, collective coordinated action across sectors is required for transformative impact at scale. When women have access to quality education and guidance from mentors who walked before them, they are empowered to become leaders shaping a more just and equitable world for all.

POTENTIAL BARRIERS ENCOUNTERED BY WOMEN ENTREPRENEURS

In their quest for business success, women entrepreneurs frequently encounter challenges that entrepreneurship presents a wealth of chances for both professional and personal development, women often face obstacles specific to their gender that might stand in the way of their advancement and prevent them from realising their full potential. Women may better prepare themselves to traverse the business landscape and open the door for empowerment through mentorship and education by identifying and removing these hurdles.

Stereotypes & Gender Bias: The entrepreneurial environment is still rife with persistent societal biases and stereotypes, despite notable advancements in the gender equality movement. In traditionally male-dominated industries, women entrepreneurs frequently face deeply ingrained biases and misconceptions about their capacity for competence, leadership, and decision-making (Brush et al., 2018). These prejudices can show themselves in a number of ways, including restricted access to capital, lowered self-esteem, and scepticism regarding their capacity as entrepreneurs.

Lack of Access to Networks and Mentors: Women entrepreneurs may find it especially difficult to establish strong professional networks and locate mentors who are a good fit. Women find it challenging to establish meaningful connections and obtain access to insightful advice because males predominate in many of the networks and mentorship programmes already in place (Brush et al., 2014). Women's capacity to obtain the information, abilities, and resources needed to successfully traverse the entrepreneurial landscape may be hampered by this lack of support and representation.

Challenges with Work-Life Balance: In addition to their professional obligations, women entrepreneurs sometimes take on the majority of household and caregiving responsibilities. Because women typically juggle numerous roles and confront cultural expectations surrounding their domestic commitments, striking a balance between entrepreneurial endeavours and personal responsibilities can be a demanding challenge (Jennings & McDougald, 2007). This may result in more stress, exhaustion, and possibly a compromise in their quest of their own business.

Limited Financial Resources: Compared to their male colleagues, women entrepreneurs sometimes encounter more obstacles when trying to obtain funding for their businesses. Investor reluctance to support women-led firms might result from gender prejudices and stereotypes influencing investment decisions (Brush et al., 2018). Women could also have less collateral or personal financial resources, which makes it harder for them to get the money they need for their entrepreneurial endeavours.

Lack of Confidence and Risk Aversion: Some women entrepreneurs may suffer from a lack of self-confidence and risk aversion due to societal conditioning and deeply set gender standards. A certain amount of confidence and a willingness to take measured risks are necessary to navigate the unpredictable and competitive world of business (Díaz-García & Brush, 2012). Women who internalise society norms or who are not exposed to successful female role models may find it difficult to acquire the requisite self-assurance and willingness to take risks.

Managing Business and Family Responsibilities: Women entrepreneurs frequently struggle to balance their business endeavours with their family responsibilities. The demands of operating a business can conflict with expectations of caring and domestic duties, as well as traditional gender roles (Brush et al.,

2009). It can be emotionally and physically exhausting to balance these conflicting goals, which may make it more difficult for women to commit the time and attention needed to their business endeavours.

It is imperative to take proactive measures to address these obstacles in order to illuminate the way towards empowerment through mentorship and education. Giving female entrepreneurs access to focused educational programmes, mentorship programmes, and encouraging networks can provide them the information, abilities, and direction they need to move past these challenges. Women can acquire more self-assurance, access to resources, and the capacity to overcome the particular obstacles they encounter by cultivating an accepting and encouraging entrepreneurial ecosystem. A more equal entrepreneurial environment can also be achieved by supporting gender-inclusive regulations, dispelling myths, and motivating male allies to stand by and support female entrepreneurs. Women entrepreneurs may illuminate their routes to success, empowerment, and sustainable entrepreneurial endeavours by taking on these obstacles head-on and making the most of mentorship and education.

THE ROAD AHEAD

The following recommendations can contribute to creating a more inclusive and supportive entrepreneurial ecosystem, empowering women to overcome challenges and realize their full potential:

Create Tailored Educational Programmes: Create and carry out instructional initiatives that are especially suited to the requirements and difficulties encountered by female entrepreneurs. A variety of subjects should be covered in these courses, such as financial literacy, corporate strategy, negotiating techniques, leadership development, and personal development. These programmes can help women develop resilience, confidence, and practical tools for navigating the entrepreneurial landscape by providing them with the knowledge and skills they need (Brush et al., 2014).

Create Mentorship Initiatives: Put in place formal mentorship programmes that pair up aspiring and beginning female business owners with seasoned and successful mentors. These mentors can share their experiences and lessons acquired while offering insightful advice, encouragement, and support. In addition to helping women entrepreneurs overcome isolation and take use of collective expertise, mentoring connections can also make it easier for them to access professional networks and resources (Baughn et al., 2006).

Promote Inclusive Communities and Networks: Promote the establishment and expansion of professional communities and networks that are inclusive, recognise women entrepreneurs, and offer support to one another. These networks can act as forums for idea sharing, cooperation, and experience sharing. According to Brush et al. (2018), women can develop meaningful relationships, share knowledge, and obtain opportunities by creating a secure and encouraging environment.

Encourage the Adoption of Gender-Inclusive Policies and Practices: Push for the integration of gender-inclusive practices and policies into the entrepreneurial ecosystem. This can involve putting in place gender-neutral investment standards, advocating for diversity and inclusivity in incubators and accelerator programmes, and enticing male allies to actively assist and advocate female entrepreneurs. According to Brush et al. (2019), women can have better access to resources, money, and assistance by eliminating structural inequalities and levelling the playing field.

Promote Role Models and Visibility: Raise the profile of accomplished women business owners in the entrepreneurial community by showcasing and honouring them as role models. These role models can motivate and inspire prospective women entrepreneurs by sharing their stories and showing their accomplishments, enabling them to see their own potential for success (Ahl & Nelson, 2015).

Offer Childcare and Family Guidance: Acknowledge the particular difficulties women encounter in juggling their desire for entrepreneurship with their familial obligations. To lessen the load and empower women entrepreneurs to commit their time and energy to their businesses without sacrificing their personal life, provide childcare help, flexible work schedules, and family-friendly policies (Jennings & McDougald, 2007).

Promote Cross-Sector Collaborations: To establish an all-encompassing support network for female entrepreneurs, promote cooperation between academic institutions, governmental bodies, commercial enterprises, and nonprofit organisations. A more robust and inclusive entrepreneurial ecosystem can be created by utilising the resources and strengths of all stakeholders, tackling the various obstacles that women experience (Brush et al., 2018).

Women entrepreneurs can illuminate their route to education and mentorship by putting these suggestions into practice and through focused educational initiatives, inclusive networks, mentorship programmes, and supporting policies and practices, women can acquire the skills, resources, and confidence needed to overcome challenges and realise their full potential as entrepreneurs.

REFERENCES

Ahl, H., & Nelson, T. (2015). How policy positions women entrepreneurs: A comparative analysis of state discourse in Sweden and the United States. *Journal of Business Venturing*, *30*(2), 273–291. doi:10.1016/j.jbusvent.2014.08.002

Allen, T. D., Eby, L. T., Poteet, M. L., Lentz, E., & Lima, L. (2004). Career benefits associated with mentoring for protégés: A meta-analysis. *The Journal of Applied Psychology*, *89*(1), 127–136. doi:10.1037/0021-9010.89.1.127 PMID:14769125

Asia Society. (2022). *Women Leaders of New Asia*. Asia Society. https://asiasociety.org/women-leaders

Baughn, C. C., Chua, B. L., & Neupert, K. E. (2006). The normative context for women's participation in entrepreneruship: A multicountry study. *Entrepreneurship Theory and Practice*, *30*(5), 687–708. doi:10.1111/j.1540-6520.2006.00142.x

Brush, C., de Bruin, A., & Welter, F. (2009). A gender-aware framework for women's entrepreneurship. *International Journal of Gender and Entrepreneurship*, *1*(1), 8–24. doi:10.1108/17566260910942318

Brush, C., de Bruin, A., & Welter, F. (2014). Advancing theory development in venture creation: Signposts for scholars. In A. C. Corbett, J. A. Katz, & A. McKenzie (Eds.), *Entrepreneurial Resourcefulness: Competing with Constraints* (pp. 111–132). Emerald Group Publishing Limited.

Brush, C., Edelman, L. F., Manolova, T., & Welter, F. (2019). A gendered look at entrepreneurship ecosystems. *Small Business Economics*, *53*(2), 393–408. doi:10.1007/s11187-018-9992-9

Brush, C., Greene, P., Balachandra, L., & Davis, A. (2018). The gender gap in venture capital: Progress, problems, and perspectives. *Venture Capital*, *20*(2), 115–136. doi:10.1080/13691066.2017.1349266

Brush, C. G., de Bruin, A., & Welter, F. (2014). Advancing theory development in venture creation: Signposts for scholars. In A. C. Corbett, J. A. Katz, & A. McKenzie (Eds.), *Entrepreneurial Resourcefulness: Competing with Constraints* (pp. 111–132). Emerald Group Publishing Limited.

Catalyst, inc. (2004). *Advancing African-American women in the workplace: What managers need to know*. Catalyst.

Catherine Ehrich, L. (1995). Professional mentorship for women educators in government schools. *Journal of Educational Administration*, *33*(2), 69–83. doi:10.1108/09578239510081318

Chisamya, G., DeJaeghere, J., Kendall, N., & Khan, M. A. (2012). Gender and education for all: Progress and problems in achieving gender equity. *International Journal of Educational Development*, *32*(6), 743–755. doi:10.1016/j.ijedudev.2011.10.004

Darwin, A., & Palmer, E. (2009). Mentoring circles in higher education. *Higher Education Research & Development*, *28*(2), 125–136. doi:10.1080/07294360902725017

Díaz-García, M. C., & Brush, C. G. (2012). Gender and business ownership: Questioning "what" and "why". *International Journal of Entrepreneurial Behaviour & Research*, *18*(1), 4–27. doi:10.1108/13552551211201358

Ensher, E. A., Grant-Vallone, E. J., & Donaldson, S. I. (2001). Effects of perceived discrimination on job satisfaction, organizational commitment, organizational citizenship behavior, and grievances. *Human Resource Development Quarterly*, *12*(1), 53–72. doi:10.1002/1532-1096(200101/02)12:1<53::AID-HRDQ5>3.0.CO;2-G

Female Wave of Change. (2022). *Female Wave of Change: Equality*. https://www.facebook.com/groups/femalewaveofchange

Inter-Parliamentary Union. (2022). *Women & Politics, 2022*. IPU. https://data.ipu.org/women-ranking?month=3&year=2022

Jayaweera, S. (1997). Higher education and the economic and social empowerment of women—The Asian experience. *Compare: A Journal of Comparative Education*, *27*(3), 245–261. doi:10.1080/0305792970270302 PMID:12348990

Jennings, J. E., & McDougald, M. S. (2007). Work-family interface experiences and coping strategies: Implications for entrepreneurship research and practice. *Academy of Management Review*, *32*(3), 747–760. doi:10.5465/amr.2007.25275510

Kumar, A., & Sahoo, S. (2024). Caste, gender, and intersectionality in stream choice: Evidence from higher secondary education in India. *Education Economics*, *32*(1), 20–46. doi:10.1080/09645292.2023.2170983

Lloyd, C. B., Mensch, B. S., & Clark, W. H. (2000). The effects of primary school quality on school dropout among Kenyan girls and boys. *Comparative Education Review*, *44*(2), 113–147. doi:10.1086/447600

Lunsford, L. G., Crisp, G., Dolan, E. L., & Wuetherick, B. (2017). Mentoring in higher education. The SAGE handbook of mentoring, 20, 316-334.

Mentorcli, Q. (2022). *Women's Mentorship Program*. Mentor Clinic. https://mentorcliq.com/women-leadership-program

Muralidharan, K., & Prakash, N. (2017). Cycling to school: Increasing secondary school enrollment for girls in India. *American Economic Journal. Applied Economics*, *9*(3), 321–350. doi:10.1257/app.20160004

National Science Foundation. (2021). *Women, Minorities and Persons with Disabilities in Science and Engineering*. NSF. https://ncses.nsf.gov/pubs/nsf21321

Novakovic, A., & Fouad, N. A. (2013). Background, personal, and environmental influences on the career planning of adolescent girls. *Journal of Career Development*, *40*(3), 223–244. doi:10.1177/0894845312449380

Paunesku, D., Walton, G. M., Romero, C., Smith, E. N., Yeager, D. S., & Dweck, C. S. (2015). Mind-set interventions are a scalable treatment for academic underachievement. *Psychological Science*, *26*(6), 784–793. doi:10.1177/0956797615571017 PMID:25862544

Psacharopoulos, G., & Patrinos, H. A. (2018). Returns to investment in education: A decennial review of the global literature. *Education Economics*, *26*(5), 445–458. doi:10.1080/09645292.2018.1484426

Redala - Red de Empresarias Latinoamericanas. (2022). *Quienes Somos*. ReDala. https://www.redala.org/nosotras

Stromquist, N. P. (2018). *The global status of teachers and the teaching profession*. Education International.

UNIDO. (2021). *Women's Entrepreneurship Development Programme. United Nations Industrial Development Organization*. UNIDO. https://www.unido.org/our-focus-cross-cutting-services/women-and-youth/womens-entrepreneurship-development

Unterhalter, E., North, A., Arnot, M., Lloyd, C., Moletsane, L., Murphy-Graham, E., & Saito, M. (2014). Girls Education and Gender Equality. *International Journal of Educational Development*.

Vanderbilt University. (2021). *MOTIV: Fostering girls' interest in technology careers through robotics*. Vanderbilt University. https://my.vanderbilt.edu/motiv/

Vital Voices. (2022). *Our History*. Vital Voices. https://www.vitalvoices.org/about-us/our-history/

Vitores, A., & Gil-Juárez, A. (2016). The trouble with 'women in computing': A critical examination of the deployment of research on the gender gap in computer science. *Journal of Gender Studies*, *25*(6), 666–680. doi:10.1080/09589236.2015.1087309

Wang, M. T., & Degol, J. L. (2017). Gender gap in science, technology, engineering, and mathematics (STEM): Current knowledge, implications for practice, policy, and future directions. *Educational Psychology Review*, *29*(1), 119–140. doi:10.1007/s10648-015-9355-x PMID:28458499

Warner, J., & Corley, D. (2017). *The Women's Leadership Gap*. Centre for American Progress.

Women, U. N. (2020). The Power of Women Leading Change in the Americas and the Caribbean. https://lac.unwomen.org/en/digiteca/publicaciones/2020/12/el-poder-de-las-mujeres

Women for Afghan Women. (2022). *Our Programs*. Women for Afghan Women. https://www.women-forafghanwomen.org/programs

World Bank. (2017). *What triggered the increase in girls' education in Mali in the 2000s?* World Bank. https://openknowledge.worldbank.org/handle/10986/28853

World Bank. (2022). *SEAES Providing Pathways for Bangladesh's Girls and Women*. World Bank. https://www.worldbank.org/en/news/feature/2022/03/08/seaes-providing-pathways-for-bangladesh-girls-and-women

Chapter 4
Empowered Women and Political Leadership

Sureyya Yigit

https://orcid.org/0000-0002-8025-5147

New Vision University, Georgia

ABSTRACT

When referring to empowerment, one focuses on women's greater autonomy, recognition, and the visibility of their contributions. Empowering women involves their full participation in all sectors and at all levels of economic activity to build strong economies, establish more stable and just societies, achieve development, sustainability, and human rights goals, and improve the quality of life of women. Women's access to and control of economic and financial resources is decisive for achieving gender equality, women's empowerment, and the economic growth of all countries. This chapter highlights the challenges and progress that women's empowerment has experienced in the past few decades.

INTRODUCTION

Raising our girls with the ability to defend and protect the highest interests of the homeland and nation should be a priority in national education. And it is essential to provide intellectual competence to our girls. There is no doubt that Turkish women are essentially geniuses. Turkish women have expressed their desire to be included in the political group that manages the fate of the country on behalf of the nation. Therefore, we cannot keep our women away from any civic duty. Because all rights arise from duties.

Kemal Ataturk *3 February 1931*

Women in politics and gender equality policy generally have a parallel relationship with ongoing development history. For this reason, scientific research in this area is an exciting segment of equality policy. The roots of the permanent anchoring of women in politics lie in the 1960s. During this period, equality policy also became more solidified. The reason for this lies in far-reaching changes in society. Thinking that was subsequently reflected in political action. A long economic phase supported these developments,

DOI: 10.4018/979-8-3693-2806-4.ch004

resulting in prosperity. These social, political and economic conditions have led to women with strong personalities being included in the male world of politics.

They were feared to have invaded – as a "conquest" - a male domain which was perhaps seen by many as revolutionary for the 1960s. However, in the fast pace of history, it is a decisive factor for a growing share of women in politics. As in all other areas of life, the first female politicians faced inequality and disadvantages. Through active participation in all political areas, for the first time, women could have a say in many laws and, thus, their special needs for everyday and professional life. This meant that the 1960s was the beginning of equality between women and men, for the independence of women and a self-determined life for women in work and family. The foundation in the 1960s then became another in the 1970s, leading to an even broader implementation of women-relevant concerns in the legal landscape. Western European governments were then able to implement majority ratios and improvements for equality for women. The 1960s were the most important decade for equality for women in Europe.

Daily political decisions are converted into scientific findings, which politicians ignore due to ideological interests and decisions that cannot be objectively justified. Politics does not make decisions based on "common sense" but relies on it exclusively based on expert reports. There are criticisms of such ways to deal with politics and science. Both areas should complement each other, create synergies for solutions, and release decisions with positive social, economic and social impacts.

Any area which is a desert island leads to isolation and, therefore, prejudices towards others. In this context, it is worth looking at the permeability between switching between science and politics, which means looking at the number of people who move from employment to political work. The path into politics can also be done through practical activity with the scientific profession, subject to strict rules and regulations. In contrast, an effective entry requirement exists for the politician - if this is even a profession - which is not mandatory or legally regulated. Of course, it makes sense for a minister of economics, for example, to receive training in economics or business administration, a finance minister has tax law has basic knowledge, and a justice minister knows the basics of the legal system; however, this is not a prerequisite for practising a profession as a politician.

A key difference between science and politics is the connection between the activity (Kelsen, 1951). Scientists are free as they can propose these. Freely choose and edit scientific analysis; the research in this area, and no limits are set. Scientists, therefore, also have the opportunity - freedom – to give the answers to the questions that they think are right. Also, in politics, the concept of a free mandate is theoretical. However, in reality, this is not the case. The case is that politicians are usually party members, belong to a faction, or are government members. This creates a lot of obligations and constraints. Even the simple Members of Parliament, who occupy one of the lower seats in Parliament, are on the line of the Party-bound – as this is about achieving voting majorities and enforcing decisions.

Hence, speaking about the relationship between politics, science and mass media, scientists communicate via specialist magazines which are predominantly aimed at a specialist audience interested in the subject matter to be read; their activities are, therefore, hardly under the control of the general public, as is the case with politicians who depend on their daily presence in the media. The same sentence that comes out of the mouth of the scientist's pen does not move much, not a whiff of wind, whereas a sentence from a leading politician often leads to a political whirlwind. The scientist's criticisms in the media can be relatively unimportant; for the politician, it can be the end of his/her political life.

This selection of comparative examples between science and politics could give the impression that science is in a brighter light than politics. However, such a conclusion is too simple: Light and shadow are not distributed one-sidedly. As proof, one may assert that more scientists enter politics than politicians switch to science. One need not justify the bigger problems that the switch from politics to science entails, but there is considerable attractiveness of politics for scientists.

It can be the desire to break out of a familiar routine and start something new. Scientific papers and political content are developed, but scientists are fundamentally opposed to similar problems. Scientists can answer political topics freely. However, there is a tension between neutral objectivity and one-sided subjectivity, the danger that the work will become scientifically worthless when party politics is adopted, and those excerpts from the work that bring a political ideology into the concept fit in and are published as scientific knowledge.

It is important for academia to analyse the arguments put forward critically and answer the questions using strict scientific criteria. This can ensure that scientists avoid falling into ideological boxes that can be categorised, which is what this chapter aims to accomplish.

LITERATURE REVIEW

Duflo focuses on the relationship between women's empowerment and economic development, arguing that the two are closely connected and acknowledging that development initiatives are crucial in reducing the inequality between men and women (Duflo, 2012). While empowering women can profoundly impact development outcomes, it is not entirely clear whether focusing on just one of these factors will create a self-sustaining cycle of progress towards gender equality. The central argument features continuous efforts to promote equality being key to achieving lasting progress towards gender equality. While development can lead to women's empowerment, and women's empowerment can drive development, it is not guaranteed that these efforts will create a mutually reinforcing cycle of progress towards gender equality. To achieve a self-sustaining cycle of progress towards gender equality, one needs to focus on promoting equality in all development initiatives, from education and healthcare to economic empowerment and political participation. Moreover, one must also recognise that gender inequality is a complex issue that requires a multi-dimensional approach, which includes addressing discriminatory laws and policies, challenging gender stereotypes and norms, and fostering a supportive environment for women's empowerment. Duflo provides a detailed analysis of the empowerment-development connection and highlights the need for continuous efforts to promote equality, concluding that much work still needs to be done.

Denmark focuses on examining leaders through the lens of their followers, though there is a need for more comprehensive research to explore how subordinates perceive leaders as empowering (Denmark, 1993). The central argument concerns that female leaders tend to face stereotypes from male and female subordinates, with a leader's ability to be empowering depending on their status. The higher the status of the leader, the more empowering they are perceived to be, regardless of gender. Given that significantly more men than women are in higher-level positions, it is challenging to assess leadership and empowerment accurately. Hence, having more women in high-level positions across various fields, such as politics, business, psychological associations, and academia, is vital. However, it is equally essential that these women are feminists who can empower and support other women. Feminist leaders are crucial to furthering the feminist agenda and promoting shared leadership with other feminists.

Mandal asserts that it was not until the "Women's Decade" declaration in 1975 that the concept of women's empowerment became deeply ingrained in government policies and programs (Mandal, 2013). Even though the Indian government granted the franchise to all its citizens regardless of their caste, creed, sex, and colour immediately after independence, the majority of women remained powerless until the last decade of the previous century. Due to their low socio-economic status, scholars, bureaucrats, and governments emphasised empowering women. However, due to India's feudal society, women's advancement would have been faster. Mandal addresses the challenges and realities of this situation, calling for the government, political decision-makers, NGOs, and other actors to come forward and ensure the all-round development of women to make India a developed country.

Given that women's empowerment is essential for positive change and transformation of the existing unequal society and that women's roles as mothers, homemakers, wives, and sisters are well known, their role in shifting the power relations of an entire country is a modern concept. She acknowledges that John Stuart Mill was the first person to attempt to establish equality between men and women, and after more than two centuries since the beginning of the struggle for women's empowerment and equality, the majority of women are still backward, and little progress has been made in their overall status and position in society. Lastly, it is pointed out that it is untrue that women in the Western world enjoy far better status and equality in society, politics, education, and the economy than Asian women. The problems and sufferings of women are almost the same in developed and underdeveloped countries - from Africa to Europe and from Asia to America.

Andriamahery and Qamruzzaman discuss the findings of a study that aimed to measure the impact of access to finance, technical knowledge, and financial literacy on women's empowerment through entrepreneurship, attempting to gauge a positive correlation between women's entrepreneurship sustainability and women's empowerment (Andriamahery & Qamruzzaman, 2022). They identify the mediating effects contributing to women's empowerment, highlighting the importance of effective policies surrounding financing accessibility, technical knowledge expansion, and financial understanding in promoting women's entrepreneurship sustainability and empowerment. Utilising Network Affiliation theory suggests that social relations and connections between aspiring entrepreneurs, assets, and opportunities influence entrepreneurship. The theory argues that the existence or absence of professional relations affects the entrepreneur's performance, and network availability is crucial in impacting business people's exhibitions. Since women entrepreneurs have better interpersonal networks than men, their overall performance in entrepreneurial activities remains exceptional. However, women's need for family assistance often overshadows their entrepreneurial capacity. They provide policy suggestions to ensure entrepreneurship sustainable development and women's empowerment in the economy:

They recommend that financial institutions develop novel loan products and marketing campaigns to expand their women's client base. Training bank employees on the unique requirements of women clients also help expand their services.

i. Women entrepreneurs should be provided with leasing options since they often struggle to deposit collateral to get loans from formal institutions.
ii. Women-owned companies may benefit from the financial performance of services supplied by the government, NGOs, and other interest groups.
iii. Women entrepreneurs could improve their financial literacy skills by attending seminars and courses on financial literacy and reading about money.

The research conducted by Le and Nguyen provides crucial insights into the relationship between education and women's empowerment (Le & Nguyen, 2021). Their study examines this relationship across 70 developing countries, utilising the variation in educational attainment between biological sisters. Their findings reveal that education is positively associated with women's intra-household decision-making authority in financial and non-financial domains. Additionally, education acts as a buffer against relational friction, particularly in reducing women's exposure to psychological abuse. Their analysis suggests that these improvements can be attributed to enhanced access to information, assortative matching, and improved labour market outcomes.

Their study's contribution is threefold. Firstly, it analysed the non-pecuniary effects of education on an important yet understudied aspect of economic development - women's empowerment. Secondly, the study evaluated the impacts of education on women's empowerment in the relational dimension, indicated by intra-household decision-making power and relational friction. This contrasts with most existing studies that focus on the returns of education from the financial or human capital domains. Finally, their study covers a wide range of 70 developing countries from 1992 to 2018, providing external validity to the estimates.

Their research examines potential mechanisms through which education empowers women, finding that education enhances access to information, which helps women make more informed decisions and increases their ability to negotiate with their partners. Education also facilitates assortative matching, which results in more equitable and satisfying relationships. Additionally, education improves labour market outcomes, which increases women's bargaining power and reduces their dependency on their partners.

The findings have significant implications for women's empowerment and sustainable development. The study indicates that education enhances women's decision-making authority within households, spanning financial and non-financial domains. These findings align with bargaining theory and are supported by numerous subsequent studies. Importantly, the results also highlight the adverse effects of female education on relational friction, as measured by women's exposure to psychological abuse. This insight adds to the existing literature on the relationship between female education and domestic violence.

Given women's pivotal role in all 17 Sustainable Development Goals, the findings underscore the importance of female education in achieving sustainable development. By expanding access to education for women, we can not only advance SDG-5 (Gender Equality) but also make significant strides in other goals. Female education is critical for promoting economic growth, reducing poverty, and achieving sustainable development, making it an essential policy goal for governments and international organisations.

The Triple Role: Women

Moser has carried out the GAD approach (Gender and Development) operational framework for the implementation of development programs and projects (Gender Planning) with a focus on the structure and dynamics of gender relations as well as on the different needs of men and women in developing countries (Moser, 2021). Since the 1970s, the "Women in Development" (WID) approach has paid more attention to the role of women in development processes (Koczberski, 1998). However, Moser nevertheless criticises the lack of sensitivity towards the oppression of women in the context of power and gender relations in economic, political as well as socio-cultural areas (Moser, 2005). Gender relations are seen as central to social processes and organisation and, therefore, to development, which is defined as a complex process involving the social, economic, political and cultural betterment of individuals in society itself. Regarding the GAD approach, it is important to examine gender relations - the relationships and interactions of women and men - at different social levels, especially at the family, household and community levels. The aim is to develop a greater awareness of the importance of the social construction of gender and gender hierarchies to explicitly address the structure and composition of the labour market, the household or the informal economy. In this one, the connection comes before everything; the gender-specific division of labour is problematised, which produces unequal socio-economic conditions based on biological divergences between men and women and social role attributions. This means, on the one hand, that women and men perform different tasks in society and, on the other hand, that divergent areas of responsibility create unequal conditions for access to and control over resources. In many low-income households in developing countries, women are under a "triple burden" because, in addition to the reproductive work in the household and family as well as volunteer activities in the community, they also pursue productive work as an employed person in order to ensure the survival of the family (Zuo & Zuo, 2016). These various activities of women in the household and the community are often assessed as "natural" or "natural" work of women, as housewives and mothers, and are therefore given less attention.

In contrast, male employment is paid more attention because it is recognised as a "productive" activity. On the one hand, this occurs directly through receiving wages, and on the other hand, indirectly through social status and political power in society. Above all, in developing cooperation, it is essential to describe the different areas of work and tasks of the genders in detail to predict better and assess the effects of development measures.

The following list of productive, reproductive and communal work is intended to provide a more sensitive perspective regarding the "triple role of women" and the gender-specific division of labour - especially about the socio-economic position of women and gender relations in the household and family as well as on the labour market. In this regard, particular attention must be paid to the growing workload on women if, on the one hand, the organisation of community work in the sense of a socialist social ideology largely falls into the female sphere of responsibility. On the other hand, socio-economic crises and the decline in state social benefits shape their everyday lives.

a) Productive work refers to work performed against payment (in money or kind) and market and subsistence production with effective or potential exchange value. In many regions worldwide, men and women do productive work, but this work area is also structured along ideologically determined gender asymmetry. Gender inequality shows itself in the Labour market, in the formal And informal sectors, as well as in urban and rural production, perpetuating women's subordinate position.

b) Reproductive work refers to tasks necessary for physical and psychological reproduction and maintenance of labour power. These include, for example, biological reproduction, childcare, various household activities, and caring for the elderly and sick. Women often carry out these activities. Since they are defined as "natural," it comes from a disdain for the "invisibility" of these works.

c) Community work: This task becomes, in the senses, the extension of the productive role at the community level, predominantly carried out by women, and it characterises its activities for the probably and receipt the community service should. Most cases involve voluntary or unpaid work, valued less than male-dominated community work. In order to show the prevailing inequality between the genders, Caroline Moser differentiates between "community management" and "community leadership". "Community leadership" refers to formal community politics, which men usually carry out. Apart from direct pay, these activities are associated with social and political prestige and power. "Community management" refers to providing services to the community (childcare, education, health, water supply.). Accepted women will largely do this work and point to the opposite of social acceptance. Male tasks have little to no social recognition.

Gender Interests: Strategic and Practical

The division into productive, reproductive and communal work, linked with the problematisation of a more gender-specific division of labour and social role attribution, is an important terminological basis for studying power and gender relations nationally. About the question of the emancipation or empowerment of women, the investigation of the divergent interests of women, focusing on their indirect and immediate personal needs, also plays a major role in this context. Moser's development planning instruments of practical and strategic needs build on Molyneux's feminist approach to practical and strategic gender interests, which will be explained in more detail below (Molyneux, 2005). The differentiation of women's interests or gender interests is intended to form an additional theoretical level for the investigation of the empowerment of women, which is intended to shed more light on the power relationship between the genders as well as the strategies and goals of the actors involved.

In her study of the impact of the Sandinista revolution on the situation of Nicaraguan women, Molyneux argues that women's interests must always be analysed in all their complexity: the forms of oppression reflect diverse causes and run along special structures and mechanisms, which, depending on place and time can occur differently (Molyneux & Molyneux, 2001). Although Molyneux sees women's interests as historically and culturally determined and politically and discursively constructed, she criticises the general assumption that the social situation and the specific priorities of various women's groups reduce these interests.

This allowed for the possibility of questioning how interests are formulated and the uses to which women put interest arguments and those seeking to mobilise them. In this context, Molyneux is primarily concerned with the conception and articulation of women's interests - on the part of the women themselves, the mobilising organisations or movements and within the framework of the state's promotion of women. In order to avoid a homogenisation or generalisation of universally applicable women's interests in the future, Molyneux is expanding the spectrum of her theoretical approach with the category of gender interests which are those interests that arise directly from gender relations and whose specific power constellations concerning men and women are based on their social position and gender-specific features (Molyneux, 2002). This differentiation should be made possible between the general/specific "women's interests" claimed by many women's organisations and those to distinguish between interests related to concrete gender-specific concerns. As a result, Molyneux differentiates between two forms of expression of "gender interests": practical and strategic gender interests, each being derived differently and each involving different implications for women's subjectivity.

Strategic Gender Interests

Strategic gender interests arise deductively from the analysis of women's oppression and aim to overcome gender hierarchies while formulating alternatives. Strategic gender interests imply transforming social relationships to improve women's social position and sustainably secure their repositioning in the gender order. These ethical and theoretical criteria promote the formulation of strategic ideas and goals. How is it possible, for example, the abolition of the gender-specific division of labour, the removal of domestic burdens (household, raising children, care), the dissolution of more institutionalised discrimination, the acquisition of political equality, sexual and physical freedom, as well as the adoption of effective means against male violence and control over women?

Practical Gender Interests

According to Molyneux, practical gender interests emerge inductively - from the desire to satisfy concrete needs that arise for women from the gender-specific division of labour (Molyneux, 2000). In comparison to the strategic, the practical gender interests are formulated by the women who are concerned for themselves and are not determined from the outside. As a rule, they are considered a response to something directly perceived. Needs and tracking are sometimes only strategic Goals. How, for example, women's emancipation or gender equality. Pursuing practical gender interests can improve women's living conditions and social status, but it should refrain from questioning structural inequality, such as gender hierarchies.

In her study, Molyneux addresses the sometimes contradictory relationship between women and the two forms of "gender interests". It would be the persecution of strategic gender interests, how equal rights, control over resources and more independence from men are not always in the interests of all women. Some women develop a negative attitude towards strategic gender interests because it could hinder the pursuit of practical interests and mean the loss of previous security and support systems or social privileges. In this context, from Molyneux's point of view, it is essential to include these conflicting practical gender interests of women when formulating strategic gender interests.

Here, interweaving the categories "Gender" and "Class" has one important role. Because women's interests are often determined to a large extent by class interests - according to Molyneux, a general agreement on gender interests cannot be assumed. For this reason, the formulation of practical interests cannot be treated separately from women's class membership. Historical records document that class conflict and divergent factors such as race, ethnicity and nationality challenge the assumed unity among women. In Molyneux's view, this becomes particularly clear in the case of a revolutionary upheaval - for example, when the issue of women's oppression is "overshadowed" by class conflicts. That means that, although women perceive gender-specific oppression, class affiliation is affected differently. However, this fact is not intended to convey that, although gender interests represent an insufficient basis for women's willingness to reach consensus in class polarisation, they disappear completely. Instead, there can be a redefinition - depending on social class affiliation. The claim that a state promotes the emancipation of women and gender equality could, in Molyneux's opinion, not be sufficiently proven or substantiated by the mere recognition of the existence of practical and class interests (Molyneux, 1979).

According to Molyneux, the differentiation between practical and strategic gender interests is particularly important because it documents the different types of argumentation and conclusions regarding the prevailing gender relations. The formulation of practical interests implies the assumption that there is a certain agreement or conformity towards the existing gender order. In contrast, when dealing with strategic interests, there is an explicit questioning of this social order and the women who maintain it through their behaviour.

The distinction between women's interests is also interesting in order to look behind the ambitions and goals of the mobilising forces - women's movements, development organisations, the state and to be able to analyse them more closely. How are women's interests formulated by these actors, and in what form are they implemented? What initiatives and strategies are being developed, and what opportunities for participation are given to women to help shape the conception and implementation? What positive and negative socio-political consequences arise from this? In many developing countries, especially in socialist states, practical gender interests are achieved within the framework of comprehensive structural reforms in the education, health, agricultural or housing sectors or through expanding services and social support programs.

However, it is precisely here that a gender-sensitive perspective must be adopted in order to break through socially perpetuated norms and rules. From a feminist perspective, it is argued that although the fulfilment of practical gender interests positively changes the everyday situation of many women and their families, gender-specific oppression and discrimination in many social areas and institutions - family, household, labour market, politics. There is a failure to consciously question the asymmetrical power relationships and traditional values, which would promote the achievement of strategic gender interests.

Empowerment: Origins and Developments

Empowerment is a widely used and discussed term that differs in definition and usage depending on its geographical and historical origin. Most often, empowerment is treated both at the academic level and in practice in connection with analysing power and power relations in tension between divergent actors on the macro and micro levels and in the context of political and socio-economic processes. In a variety of scientific disciplines such as the humanities and social sciences (sociology, anthropology, politics), regional development theory, psychology, women's and gender studies, but also education and economics, empowerment is considered an important object of study and a category of analysis. Apart from that, the term is used in adult education, health, and social work, as well as in the opposite areas of corporate and human resources management. This example shows empowerment's multidimensional character and complexity and illustrates the ambivalences and contradictions concerning the broad spectrum of applications and definitions. However, the frequent and varied use carries the risk that the term itself loses significant content and value and remains an empty shell. Feminists from the South, in particular, complain about the appropriation of the term by conservative political ideologies and neoliberal economic systems over the last decade.

In this regard, the Indian sociologist Batliwala emphasises the resulting instrumentalisation and legitimation potential of empowerment, which she sees as being due to its imprecise definition as it is one of the most loosely used terms in the development lexicon, meaning different things to different people – or, more dangerously, all things to all people (Batliwala, 2007). Especially since the 1990s, the term has become a buzzword within international development policy and development cooperation, as both civil society organisations (social movements, non-governmental organisations (NGOs), grassroots organisations) and nation-state organisations Institutions, as well as international development agencies, made empowerment the mainstream concept of their development policy programs and projects. In international development cooperation, the term was applied to existing development concepts transmitted and awarded new strategies and objectives, which are one appropriate basis of legitimacy. Empowerment has developed increasingly into one so-called "buzzword" as a panacea for development. Cornwall and Brock argue that keywords such as "empowerment", "participation", and "poverty reduction" before everything in the jargon of international organisations such as the World Bank and the UN can be used to give their development concepts a positive and universal character, a one-size-fits-all (Cornwall & Brock, 2005).

Using a brief historical review, Batliwala traces the origins and developments of the term and identifies - depending on the regional and contextual environment - different actors and their basic ideological and political assumptions about empowerment (Batliwala, 2007). In her opinion, one of the earliest forms of empowerment was the Protestant Reformation movement in Europe in the 16th and 17th centuries, and subsequent social movements and civil rights can be traced. According to Batliwala, it came specifically in the second half of the 20th century, during the formulation of the liberation theology in Latin America, the "Black Power" movement and increasingly feminist movements towards revitalising empowerment as a primary political concept.

In the 1970s, especially in Latin America, a stronger connection emerged between feminist-style empowerment approaches and those of the Brazilian educator Freire. His model of "Consciousness Raising" using "Popular education" follows the opinion that poor, out-of-marginalised people need to develop an independent critical consciousness (make themselves an acting "subject") in order to gain more power and control over their own life decisions (Cardona & Hamel-Roy, 2023). The prerequisite for this is a process of collective identity formation based on the shared experience of marginalisation. Although Freire's concept represented an important component in the feminist discussion of empowerment and, as a "bottom-up" approach, offered an alternative to the previous "community development" concept, the category "gender", which is essential for the feminist discussion, and a more precise analysis were missing gender-specific mechanisms of oppression. Despite these differences, numerous feminist movements drew on consciousness-raising as a source. They added elements such as gender oppression and the social construction of gender roles to provide a multidimensional approach to women's and social liberation to create change. Furthermore, revolutionised approaches, such as the theories of the social construction of gender and especially postcolonial theories, shaped the feminist empowerment discourse.

As part of the second wave of the women's movement in the 1980s, feminists developed different approaches to power and empowerment in Latin America and Asia depending on the regional and sociocultural context. It showed that the preoccupation with empowerment had shaped feminist discourses to the same extent as social movements or scientific studies. The approaches of Paulo Freire, Antonio Gramsci and Michel Foucault regarding power in social relationships and its historical and social conditioning have significantly influenced feminist theorists and activists (Fernández-Aballí Altamirano, 2016).

Connected against the background of the expansion of the neoliberal economic order with the rapidly advancing information and technology transfers on the one hand and the massive increase in poverty and impoverishment, especially in developing countries, on the other, empowerment is increasingly becoming the key concept for feminists and activists from the south. In their criticism, postcolonial feminist theorists such as Mohanty were primarily directed against the homogenised and stereotypical image of the Third World woman as a "powerless victim", the assumptions of European and North American feminists shaped by colonial and Eurocentric prejudices, and against development policy concepts from Western mainstream development agencies, such as the "Women in Development" (WID) approach (Mohanty, 1988). This focuses primarily on the mere integration of women in development processes, following the understanding of the development of the industrialised countries and externally induced "top-down" approaches such as "Equity", "Anti-Poverty", and "Efficiency Approach". WID was defined as criticising the one-dimensional or undifferentiated perspective of liberal feminists from the West, who neglected the interdependent connections between the micro and multi-acro levels as well as global developments and the concentration on economic and political-legal issues empowerment, the view on the deeper socio-cultural problem- and areas of conflict such as gender roles, class and race, especially in the local context were disguised.

The political manifesto by Sen and Grown, laid an important foundation for formulating an alternative concept of development (Sen & Grown, 2013). Third World women's perspective as representatives of the "Development Alternatives for Women in a New Era" (DAWN) network, was presented at the UN World Conference on Women in Nairobi in 1985. The DAWN manifesto attempts to demonstrate their individual and collective survival strategies by summarising women's active forms of resistance and organisation in global economic and political crises - debt, militarism, violence and fundamentalism

(Tambe & Trotz, 2010). DAWN takes a clear stance against victimisation and the uniform image of the passive, needy Third World woman and advocates for an independent, self-reliant woman and self-determined action by affected women from the south. The collective is concerned with new, alternative strategies and visions for building a better world and new approaches to "development" in which the perspective of poor women is crucial. In this regard, empowerment is defined as a provocative political approach that primarily addresses the question of the political, economic and social power relationships in which women find themselves - not only between the genders but also along social categories such as ethnicity, class and race. In order to avoid a stereotypical and one-dimensional view of women in developing countries in the future, different experiences are examined from the oppression of women.

In this one, the connection comes before everything, highlighting the transformation potential of feminism as a political movement. Feminism emerges from different forms of oppression and reflects the formulation of diverging needs and interests. In this regard, a dynamic and heterogeneous understanding of feminism emerges, which has the power to question the status quo as a political project.

Diverging Views of Power

After a brief outline of empowerment's different origins and areas of application and its contradictions, the basic essence of empowerment—"power"—will be examined below. As already mentioned, empowerment is often applied unreflectively and unquestioningly - without taking power and power structures in the social context into account, its users tend to assume that the appropriate meaning will be understood without explanation. It is used by people representing a wide range of political and philosophical perspectives, from the World Bank to feminist perspectives. A one-sided view of empowerment, based on the understanding of power as "power over" or "delegating power", which has become particularly popular in Western development discourse and the approaches of international development agencies, can be extremely problematic, especially for women's empowerment. It propagates that women must be integrated and "empowered" into the development process exclusively with the help of external forces (e.g., the WID approach) in order to be able to participate in political and economic decisions. Rowlands warns that power "given" or "transferred" to a person/group can also be taken away from them (Rowlands, 2016). This process does not initiate any deeper structural changes and will, therefore, not produce lasting improvements for the particular affected women.

Many feminist theorists criticise using a neutral and undifferentiated model of power and see it as essential to include the power relationship between the genders and between classes or races in the analysis. Wong focuses on the four interdependent forms of power directed, namely: "power over", "power to", "power with", and "power from within ", the possibility of showing the multidimensional nature of power at personal, collective, regional, national and international levels (Wong, 2014). Although diverging views also exist in feminist empowerment discourse, particularly regarding the meaning of "power from within" and the inclusion of male perspectives, the key factor in feminist theorising is understanding power as a relational concept.

As already stated, Rowlands, in her local study of women's empowerment in Honduras, based on the reflections of Lukes, refers in detail to these four forms of power, which, in her view, are reflected in empowerment and disempowerment (Rowlands, 1998). Since power has always been an important category of analysis in social science discourse and is seen as the root of empowerment, Rowlands sheds light on various areas in which power relations between genders and women differ. The opinion from Radtke and Stam can expand, on the one hand, as the root or cause of oppression when it is misused and, on the other hand, as a source of emancipation when it is used (Radtke & Stam, 2016). The four forms of power do not exist separately from each other - they complement each other and influence each other. This means that different forms of power can coexist at a specific time and place. Since the feminist framework model of power is not only linked to feminist analyses or gender analyses but also deals with power relations in social relationships, It is possible to examine factors such as class, race, age and ethnicity in parallel with gender. The four forms of power will then be worked out in order to clarify their location in the social context and later to be able to specifically work out the empowerment of women and the development of empowerment strategies in the area of tension between diverging spheres of power.

Power Over

Power over is the form of power in which one person/group exercises power over another person/group and thereby forces that person to do something against their will. It is probably the most well-known form of power and, in most cases, reflects oppression and control. Jo Rowlands defines "power over" as controlling power, which may be responded to with compliance, resistance or manipulation. This power can be localised at different levels, in the private and domestic sphere, at the national and international legal level, and in political decision-making processes. In this respect, it becomes "Power over" exercised by politically, economically, socially or culturally dominant groups over excluded sections of the population. In this regard, Rowlands understands "power" as "finite supply" – when some people have more of their own, while others have fewer (Rowlands, 1997). This is called the expansion from power for one person/group and can mean loss of power for another person/group – this is referred to as "zero-sum". Such power could be described as 'zero-sum`: the more power one person has, the less the other has. In this context, the understanding of power as "power over" gender relations and the empowerment of women can lead to fear of a loss of control and power on the part of men.

Men often perceive the change in power relations as dangerous, usually met with resistance and conflict. Although the empowerment of women does not automatically result in a loss of power for men, in many societies, it is seen as a danger in the form of oppressive power "power over". that women interpret about men. Batliwala puts men's fear of women's empowerment into perspective and sees more freedom during social change processes, as men in many societies view women's gains in power as threatening (Batliwala, 2012).

Power over can occur through the threat of violence, or it can follow perpetuated social patterns, with the weaker following the will of the stronger. Rowlands speaks of internalised oppression which is primarily used as a pure survival strategy but subsequently internalised by the person/group so that the resulting consequences result in a changed social reality - values, norms, social roles (Rowlands,1998). If control over a person by this has already become so internalised, is the exercise of power not more necessary? In this context, Rowlands refers to Steven Lukes unobservable conflict - invisible/unobservable conflict. (Rowlands, 1997). Lukes argues that power can be recognised in the visible or perceptible areas of conflict and invisible conflicts (Lukes, 2021). Lukes asserts the most effective and insidious use of power is to prevent conflict from arising in the first place. In this way, potential conflicts can be prevented in advance by making it impossible for the group/person concerned to think of anything other than believing in the prevailing status quo. According to Rowlands, it is particularly important from a feminist perspective to consider the dynamics when interpreting "power over" to understand oppression, specifically internalised oppression. Women, in particular, are often found to be suffering from "internalised oppression" (e.g. psychological and physical violence). When asked about it, they are unable to comment on it or recognise it as an act of oppression and violence.

Power To

In contrast to "power over", power to is not necessarily expressed in oppression and domination. It can take various forms that can contribute to the development of empowerment. Power is the power that empowerment refers to, which is achieved by increasing one's ability to resist and challenge power. "Power to" refers to a person's ability or capacity to make personal decisions, formulate goals, and act accordingly. This power relates to having decision-making authority; the power to solve problems can be creative and enabling. The main difference to "power over" is, on the one hand, that "power to" is free of conflicts of interest and, on the other hand, does not represent "zero-sum" since the seizure of power by one person does not have to mean the loss of power by another person.

Power With

Power with is the ability to achieve something with others that one could not have achieved alone. This power involves people organising with a common purpose or understanding to achieve collective goals. "Power with" is evident in social mobilisation and forming coalitions and alliances. For Rowlands, it is not only a capacity but an awareness, a sense of the whole being greater than the sum of the individuals, especially when a group tackles problems together (Rowlands, 2016). In the course of "power to" and "power with", a process is set in motion in which people become aware of their interests and combine them with the interests of others in order to achieve a stronger position in the collective or to make decisions influenced. One person standing up against an unjust law is unlikely to achieve much on their own; many people working together, however, are more likely to provoke a change.

Power From Within

Power from within arises from recognising that one is not helpless, not the source of all one's problems, and that structures outside oneself partially restrict one. "Power from within" characterises a person's mental and spiritual strength based on characteristics such as self-consciousness and self-esteem. This relates not only to acceptance of oneself but, above all, to respect for other people. Kabeer emphasises that "power from within" is not from outside induced or that one person "given" becomes a can, but rather, one himself needs to be developed (Kabeer, 2015). She is convinced that "power from within ", in particular, is essential for the development of empowerment as a necessary adjunct to improving their ability to control resources to determine and make decisions.

From Power to Empowerment

Rowlands argues that the feminist interpretation of power enables a multi-layered understanding of empowerment because it goes beyond the formal or institutional definition of power – and corresponds to the concept of "personal as political" (Jeanes, 2013). Viewed from this perspective, one moves away from the understanding of power in the sense of "power over". Moreover, formulating an empowerment strategy represents a mere "integration" of people into political and economic decision-making processes.

In this context, Rowlands emphasises that in these cases, one exercise of power in shape from "power over" and the dynamics of oppression and its internalisation must be considered (Rowlands, 1995). Because although power is not always visible, it is constantly produced and reproduced in discourse. Control over power is not exclusively through economic or physical exercise of force but also through socialisation processes and social practice. Parts of the feminist debate relate to these considerations of the theoretical assumptions of French philosopher Michel Foucault on power in social relationships.

The application of a more complex understanding of power, which integrates forms such as "power with", "power to", and "power from within ", can better reflect social interactions and dynamics and thus become a helpful analytical category for recording empowerment -processes. According to Rowlands, the feminist view of empowerment makes recognising the wide range of human abilities and potential possible. Empowerment has to be in this breakthrough of the negative forms of social construction and categorisation so that people recognise their capacities and align their actions and decisions accordingly.

In their study about women's empowerment strategies in Honduras, she develops a three-part, interlocking dimensional model, which she uses to analyse the divergent manifestations of empowerment. Differentiating the three dimensions of empowerment—personal, collective, and relational—should help deal with empowerment processes and facilitate conceptualisation regarding organisation and planning in practice.

Personal Empowerment

According to Rowlands, the empowerment process for women is a very personal and unique experience. This dimension includes the development of self-confidence and the recognition of one own capacity to act – this should overcome lead to internalised oppression. Personal empowerment further involves a sense of agency through which a woman can interact with her surroundings and cause things to happen.

Collective Empowerment

The collective dimension of empowerment refers to women's collective or shared experiences. It illustrates how a person influences a decision through collective action within a group.

Relational Empowerment

The third dimension of empowerment refers to women's close relationships with other family members, for example as a husband/partner, children, parents or parents-in-law. This level characterises the development of negotiation skills in one relationship, and the decision made within this relationship is to influence within. This means that individual abilities or capacities are related to the environment. In Rowland's view, empowerment is most difficult to achieve at this level, as the woman alone has to stand up for and defend herself and her decisions. For this reason, a certain degree of personal empowerment is required. In this context, the question arises about the connection between personal or individual and collective empowerment, which will be discussed in more detail in the next part of the work.

Looking back at the results of her study, Rowlands states that the three-dimensional model of empowerment can be used to determine in which areas and at what levels empowerment is experienced and exercised, but it falls far short of the complex interactions and dynamics of empowerment processes and the diverging forms of power and power relations in more detail (Huis, Hansen, Otten & Lensink, 2017).

The complexity of the interlocking relationships and interactions of different elements becomes apparent in the empowerment process. For this reason, she would suggest a more dynamic and fluid model for a more detailed analysis. Rowlands divides the different aspects of empowerment into three categories: the "contextual" or "material" aspect, the "structural" related to the structure of the organisation and its activities, as well as the "inner psychological" or "psychosocial" aspect of empowerment.

The Indian social scientist Kabeer explores the analysis of women in development processes; she also deals with the multidimensionality of power in a social context. Women's decision-making power means that this should not be analysed in a space devoid of power and without reference to the environment since women are exposed to an asymmetrical gender ratio in both public and private spheres. According to Kabeer, these gender-specific power hierarchies, as part of social norms and rules, significantly influence the choices and options available to individuals (Kabeer, 1997). In this context, social institutions, such as the state, the market, and the household, take control of women's choices in everyday life. In the course of these findings, Kabeer developed a multidimensional concept of power based on the power analysis by Lukes, around power not only on the micro level - interpersonal relations: family, partnership - but also at the institutional meso level. An institutional, rather than purely interpersonal, analysis of male power draws attention to the gender biases implicit within the rules and practices of different social institutions.

Kabeer defines empowerment - the ability to make choices - in connection with disempowerment (Kabeer, 1999). Only individuals who cannot make decisions or are denied it can be described as "disempowered". In their view, the ability to choose depends on certain preconditions or resources. As part of the empowerment process, people develop the ability to make or influence a decision. The framework for the development of empowerment is based on three interdependent dimensions: resources (prerequisites/resources: material, human and social resources), agency (the ability to define one's own goals and act accordingly, using "power to", "power from within" but also "power over") and achievements (results/results). She describes empowerment as expanding people's ability to make strategic life choices in a context where this ability was previously denied to them.

According to Kabeer, empowerment is a complex phenomenon with many dimensions. Everyone's empowerment process is unique and influenced by divergent factors and actors. Concerning the analysis of women's empowerment, it has already been mentioned that not only gender relations play an important role, but factors such as class, race, nationality, age, and sexual preferences - individual and collective experiences. These factors move in one political, economic and socio-cultural context. This means that women do not feel alone in one place either. Empowerment process condition: On the micro level are actors. How are the family, the community, grassroots or local organisations involved, and national or international development agencies, states, and financial institutions at the macro level? In this regard, Kabeer points out the need for empowerment to extend beyond the project level to the legislative level if it is to be sustainable and cause structural changes (Kabeer, 2017). State, civil society, economic and political activities influence women's lives daily, and all change processes occur in the tension between these forces.

In collaboration with numerous feminist grassroots organisations, leading Feminists, as well as development organisations out of South Asia, Batwiala provided a detailed inventory of those involved actors' conceptual and strategic empowerment understanding (Batliwala, 1994). This becomes empowerment as well as a process, and as a result, one process is defined as the change in the power relations between individuals and social groups. Since empowerment was widely used, especially in feminist movements, the transformation of asymmetrical gender relations within and across social categories was set as an indispensable requirement. The empowerment process, therefore, shifts social power in three crucial areas: by questioning those ideologies that justify or legitimise social inequality (gender, caste, religion), using the change prevailing pattern concerning the access and control over raw materials, economic (labour, land, water, money, credit), and intellectual (information, knowledge, ideas) resources, as well as through the transformation of the institutions and systems that consolidate the existing power structures (family, state, media, market). This chapter emphasises that changing ideological and institutional structures is crucial for sustainable empowerment and social change.

CONCLUSION

Women came into the focus of development policy quite late. First, Boserup asserted that previous measures have neither considered nor promoted women's economic contribution to development (Boserup, Kanji, Tan & Toulmin, 2013). On the contrary, under the prevailing modernist development paradigm, which expected positive social effects, the trickle-down effect from industrialization and, as a result, economic growth, women's economic and social position had deteriorated. In the following years, given the growing poverty in the Third World and the increasing insight into the importance of the role of women in development, women's promotion inclusion in the programs and projects of national and international development organizations.

This liberal feminist approach made women visible in a double sense: on the one hand, by researching their life situation and, on the other hand, by demonstrating their productive role in the development process. WID thereby intended to promote the integration of women into productive, i.e. market-based, employment in the development process in order to give them access to development resources and to ensure their economic independence and thus her subordinate social position - in the double sense - to cancel.

A different view of feminist development policy emerged in the second half of the 1970s. The criticism was sparked, among other things, by the following central WID thesis: The equality of women and men is achieved through equal participation in the economic process - according to Visvanathan, a typical modernization theory assumption that postulates individuals as the catalysts for social change and does not provide for structural change in the system in which women are to be included (Visvanathan, 1997). This explicit emphasis on the social sphere of employment as a place of emancipation, social progress and, therefore, the decisive space of power; these goals coincided with a series of implementation strategies that dominated women's advancement policy until the 1980s (Yigit, 2023). These include the equity approach, which is about the equality of women and men; the anti-poverty approach through income-promoting projects for women targeted; and finally, the so-called efficiency approach, the focus of which is the efficiency and effectiveness of development projects as well as the promotion of women's employment to be designed according to this standard. The welfare approach is equivalent to the more general development policy paradigms.

In the early days of development policy, the modernization strategy was discussed; in the 1970s, the poverty-oriented basic needs strategy was the centre of interest. In the 1980s, the Neoliberal economic policy in the guise of structural adjustment programs for developing countries was pushed through, bringing up two aspects of development policy in the late 1980s (Yigit, 2021). A paradigm shift was initiated from women to gender as an analysis category or analytical concept formation and from integration to empowerment as a transformation strategy. The latter claimed a "power-critical" analysis of gender relations with the subordination embedded therein and oppressive relations - subordination - whose repeal through empowerment should be achieved by gaining creative power.

The empowerment approach, developed by feminist researchers and activists from the Third World, has had a significant influence on the feminist development discussion and international development policy. It addresses the substantial change in women's social power, emphasizing the right to dispose of resources, make decisions, and shape society without deriving domination over others from this power. This approach has been instrumental in shifting the focus of development policy towards empowering women.

DAWN insisted on examining the dominant development paradigm and its analytical assumptions and, for example, calling for a context-based and multidimensional analysis of the living situation of women in the Third World. The aim was to highlight all forms of oppression by gender, class, race, and nation, but at the same time, point out power differences that exist not only between the genders but also between the women themselves. DAWN also addressed the global political and socioeconomic following more colonial and post-colonial power relations as well as the patriarchal oppressive relations, which, in their opinion, are among the most important causes of the powerlessness of women. The Southern Women's Network counteracts this with, among other things, civil society and grassroots commitment. Women play a key role in this empowerment process, which is participation and conflict-oriented: they are the political and social actors in the empowerment processes. DAWN describes one Transformation strategy, a vision in which women's self-empowerment is the key concept of an emancipatory development model that goes beyond the conditions of oppression.

Hence, this once far-reaching term "empowerment" is now an essential element of development cooperation. The new GAD approach, which has been popular since the 1990s and differs from the integration approach, continues to focus not only on the analysis of gender relationships but also on development policy intervention in these relationships to empower women.

ACKNOWLEDGMENT

I want to thank Gulzhan Baibetova, Director of the Zhenskaya Demokratichyskaya Set Kyrgyzstana—ZDS Women's Democracy Network in the Kyrgyz Republic, for her encouragement and suggestions in writing this chapter.

REFERENCES

Andriamahery, A., & Qamruzzaman, M. (2022). Do access to finance, technical know-how, and financial literacy offer women empowerment through women's entrepreneurial development? *Frontiers in Psychology*, *12*, 776844. doi:10.3389/fpsyg.2021.776844 PMID:35058847

Batliwala, S. (1994). *Women's empowerment in South Asia: Concepts and practices*. Asian South Pacific Bureau of Adult Education.

Batliwala, S. (2007). Putting power back into empowerment. *Democracy (New York, N.Y.)*, *50*(3), 61–80.

Batliwala, S. (2007). Taking the power out of empowerment–an experiential account. *Development in Practice*, *17*(4-5), 557–565. doi:10.1080/09614520701469559

Batliwala, S. (2012). *Changing Their World*. Concepts and Practices of Women's.

Boserup, E., Kanji, N., Tan, S. F., & Toulmin, C. (2013). *Woman's role in economic development*. Routledge. doi:10.4324/9781315065892

Cardona, M. S., & Hamel-Roy, L. (2023). Popular education and learning as the bridge between activism and knowledge production. *Globalisation, Societies and Education*, *21*(5), 664–676. doi:10.1080/14767724.2023.2175644

Cornwall, A., & Brock, K. (2005). What do buzzwords do for development policy? A critical look at 'participation', 'empowerment' and 'poverty reduction'. *Third World Quarterly*, *26*(7), 1043–1060. doi:10.1080/01436590500235603

Denmark, F. L. (1993). Women, leadership, and empowerment. *Psychology of Women Quarterly*, *17*(3), 343–356. doi:10.1111/j.1471-6402.1993.tb00491.x

Duflo, E. (2012). Women empowerment and economic development. *Journal of Economic Literature*, *50*(4), 1051–1079. doi:10.1257/jel.50.4.1051

Fernández-Aballí Altamirano, A. (2016). Where is Paulo Freire? *The International Communication Gazette*, *78*(7), 677–683. doi:10.1177/1748048516655722

Huis, M. A., Hansen, N., Otten, S., & Lensink, R. (2017). A three-dimensional model of women's empowerment: Implications in the field of microfinance and future directions. *Frontiers in Psychology*, *8*, 283877. doi:10.3389/fpsyg.2017.01678 PMID:29033873

Jeanes, R. (2013). Educating through sport? Examining HIV/AIDS education and sport-for-development through the perspectives of Zambian young people. *Sport Education and Society*, *18*(3), 388–406. doi:10.1080/13573322.2011.579093

Kabeer, N. (1997). tactics and trade-offs: Revisiting the links between gender and poverty. *IDS Bulletin*, *28*(3), 1–13. doi:10.1111/j.1759-5436.1997.mp28003001.x

Kabeer, N. (1999). Resources, agency, achievements: Reflections on the measurement of women's empowerment. *Development and Change*, *30*(3), 435–464. doi:10.1111/1467-7660.00125

Kabeer, N. (2015). Tracking the gender politics of the Millennium Development Goals: Struggles for interpretive power in the international development agenda. *Third World Quarterly*, *36*(2), 377–395. doi:10.1080/01436597.2015.1016656

Kabeer, N. (2017). Economic pathways to women's empowerment and active citizenship: What does the evidence from Bangladesh tell us? *The Journal of Development Studies*, *53*(5), 649–663. doi:10.1080/00220388.2016.1205730

Kelsen, H. (1951). Science and politics. *The American Political Science Review*, *45*(3), 641–661. doi:10.2307/1951155

Koczberski, G. (1998). Women in development: A critical analysis. *Third World Quarterly, 19*(3), 395–410. doi:10.1080/01436599814316

Le, K., & Nguyen, M. (2021). How education empowers women in developing countries. *The B.E. Journal of Economic Analysis & Policy, 21*(2), 511–536. doi:10.1515/bejeap-2020-0046

Lukes, S. (2021). Power and rational choice. *Journal of Political Power, 14*(2), 281–287. doi:10.1080/2158379X.2021.1900494

Mandal, K. C. (2013, May). Concept and Types of Women Empowerment. In *International Forum of Teaching & Studies, 9*(2).

Mohanty, C. (1988). Under Western eyes: Feminist scholarship and colonial discourses. *Feminist Review, 30*(1), 61–88. doi:10.1057/fr.1988.42

Molyneux, M. (1979). Beyond the domestic labour debate. *New Left Review, 116*(3), 27.

Molyneux, M. (2000). Twentieth-century state formations in Latin America. *Hidden histories of gender and the State in Latin America*, 33-81.

Molyneux, M. (2002). Gender and the silences of social capital: Lessons from Latin America. *Development and Change, 33*(2), 167–188. doi:10.1111/1467-7660.00246

Molyneux, M. (2005). Analysing women's movements. In *Feminist Visions of Development* (pp. 74–97). Routledge.

Molyneux, M., & Molyneux, M. (2001). Mobilisation without emancipation? Women's interests, the state and revolution in Nicaragua (pp. 38-59). Palgrave Macmillan UK.

Moser, C. (2005). Has gender mainstreaming failed? A comment on international development agency experiences in the South. *International Feminist Journal of Politics, 7*(4), 576–590. doi:10.1080/14616740500284573

Moser, C. O. (2021). From gender planning to gender transformation: Positionality, theory and practice in cities of the global South. *International Development Planning Review, 43*(2), 205–229. doi:10.3828/idpr.2020.9

Radtke, H. L., & Stam, H. J. (2016). A history of psychology's complicated relationship to feminism: Theorizing difference. *Centrality of history for theory construction in psychology*, 167-185.

Rowlands, J. (1995). Empowerment examined. *Development in Practice, 5*(2), 101–107. doi:10.1080/0961452951000157074 PMID:12346153

Rowlands, J. (1997). *Questioning empowerment: Working with women in Honduras*. Oxfam. doi:10.3362/9780855988364

Rowlands, J. (1998). A word of the times, but what does it mean? Empowerment in the discourse and practice of development. In *Women and empowerment: Illustrations from the Third World* (pp. 11–34). Palgrave Macmillan UK. doi:10.1007/978-1-349-26265-6_2

Rowlands, J. (2016). Power in practice: Bringing Understandings and Analysis of power into Development Action in Oxfam. *IDS Bulletin*, *47*(5), 119–130. doi:10.19088/1968-2016.171

Sen, G., & Grown, C. (2013). *Development crises and alternative visions: Third world women's perspectives*. Routledge. doi:10.4324/9781315070179

Tambe, A., & Trotz, A. (2010). Historical reflections on DAWN: An interview with Gita Sen. *Comparative Studies of South Asia, Africa and the Middle East*, *30*(2), 214–217. doi:10.1215/1089201X-2010-006

Visvanathan, N. (1997). *Introduction to part 1*. The women, gender and development reader, 17-32.

Wong, S. (2014). A power game of multi-stakeholder initiatives. *Journal of Corporate Citizenship*, *2014*(55), 26–39. doi:10.9774/GLEAF.4700.2014.se.00006

Yigit, S. (2021). The Concept of Citizenship and the Democratic State. *Electronic Journal of Social and Strategic Studies*, *2*, 5–25.

Yigit, S. (2023). Multi-Dimensional Understandings of Migration: Threats or Opportunities? In Handbook of Research on the Regulation of the Modern Global Migration and Economic Crisis (pp. 239-256). IGI Global.

Zuo, J., & Zuo, J. (2016). Women's Triple Burden. *Work and Family in Urban China: Women's Changing Experience since Mao*, 67-76.

Chapter 5
Moving From Refugee to Entrepreneur in the US:
A Feminine Perspective

M. Gail Hickey
https://orcid.org/0000-0002-2858-8673
Purdue University, Fort Wayne, USA (Emerita)

ABSTRACT

The US refugee population has grown exponentially. More migrants than native-born US residents decide to become entrepreneurs. More than one-third US entrepreneurs are women, yet the scholarship on women entrepreneurs is scarce. This chapter explores the pre- and post-migration experiences and perspectives of a Southeast Asian female refugee entrepreneur residing in the Midwestern United States. The interviewee owns and manages a hair salon. Collected data include recorded oral history interview and transcript, participant observation at the entrepreneur's business, field notes, and a variety of social media sources. Data analysis yielded four emergent themes: memories of growing up/ethnic culture, importance of family and family support, learning the business, and resiliency.

INTRODUCTION

Global conflict continues to result in forced displacement of individuals and populations. Conflict, violence, persecution, and human rights violations resulted in the forced displacement of more than 114 million people worldwide by late 2023 (United Nations Office for the Coordination of Humanitarian Affairs, 2023). Historically, the United States of America (US) has resettled more displaced persons seeking asylum than any other country (Ward & Batalova, 2023).

The US refugee population has grown exponentially in the past 50 years. About 3 million refugees have been settled in the United States since the creation of the federal resettlement program in 1980, and about half of them are women (Budiman, 2020). Nearly 30 percent of US small businesses owe their beginnings to migrant individuals and their families (Kulkarni, 2014). Data reveal an increasing number of these small businesses are owned by migrant women (Pearce, 2005). The professional literature on

DOI: 10.4018/979-8-3693-2806-4.ch005

entrepreneurship, however, tends to focus on men with a lack of emphasis on migrant business owners and an even greater dearth of research on migrant women small business owners (Collins & Low, 2010; Surangi, 2016) despite the fact women represent about half the US refugee population (Jesuthasan, Witte, & Oert-Prigione, 2019). Furthermore, available data do not distinguish migrant business owners in the US into immigrant versus refugee categories. Thus, there is a definite need for current research related to female entrepreneurship among refugees now residing in the United States (Al-Dajani 2022).

This chapter seeks to redress the gap in the professional literature and, in the process, add to the information on migrant women entrepreneurs by focusing on a Laotian female refugee entrepreneur's perspectives and experiences in the Midwestern United States. The study also adds to the literature on entrepreneurship through the author's exploration of a female refugee entrepreneur's experiences with and perspectives about the importance of formal and non-formal education to development of one's own business.

More than 31 million US entrepreneur-based businesses existed in 2019; only 12.3 million are owned by women (LegalZoom, 2020). Scholarly research on female entrepreneurs, however, continues to be in an "embryonic stage" (Gradim & Daniel, 2023, 1). Female entrepreneurs, compared with their male counterparts, face challenges and barriers including, among others, less access to resources and mentorship (Figueiredo, Patricio, & Ferreira, 2023).

US refugees become entrepreneurs at rates exceeding those of voluntary US immigrants — 13 percent compared with 11 percent (Chanoff, 2016). It is not known how many of those 13 percent refugee-owned businesses are owned by women. More than one-third of US entrepreneurs are women, yet their voices largely are absent from the professional literature. Research that examines and explores feminine perspectives of refugee business ownership in the US is needed (Marlow & Al-Dajani, 2017).

The study of entrepreneurship from a gendered perspective not only is a topic of growing scholarly interest, it also is a topic germane to policy consideration (Link & Strong, 2016). Policy makers interested in bolstering economic impact of businesses owned by women entrepreneurs need greater understandings of characteristics and factors that contribute to the growth and financial success of these businesses (Adema et al., 2015). Research that focuses on female entrepreneurs' personal experiences, such as the instrumental case study detailed and analyzed in this chapter, is needed.

BACKGROUND

Southeast Asian Refugees in the United States

The United Nations High Commission for Refugees (UNHCR) defines "refugee" as "any person who is outside his or her country of nationality and is unable or unwilling to return to that country because of persecution or a well-founded fear of persecution that may be based on race, religion, nationality, membership in a particular social group, or political opinion" (US Department of State, 2023). The largest group of refugees resettled in the US to date is composed of Southeast Asians from Vietnam, Laos, and Cambodia. These refugees were forcibly displaced from their homelands in the 1970s due to what has come to be known as the Vietnam Conflict (Southeast Asian Resource Action Center, 2024). The withdrawal of US military troops from Vietnam in 1975, combined with the collapse of Laotian and Cambodian governments, resulted in more than two million refugees fleeing for their lives while fearing reprisals from the newly formed Communist government (Southeast Asian Archive, 1999).

The first wave of Southeast Asian refugees resettled in the US during the 1970s vastly outnumbered the small number of voluntary Southeast Asian immigrants (Gordon, 1987). The second wave of Southeast Asian refugees began to resettle in the US in about 1980 (Alperin & Batalova, 2018). The first wave of refugees in the 1970s was less likely than either those in the second wave or the small number of voluntary Southeast Asian migrants to have access to family or other social networks already living in the US (Alperin & Batalova, 2018). Multiple decades of war experiences and related trauma, combined with the most horrific genocides of the 20th century, meant the Southeast Asian refugees resettled in the US in the 1970s experienced many challenges. Moreover, the absence of family/social networks combined with the lack of available government resettlement resources often left these refugees feeling very alone in a location where both mainstream culture and language were alien to them (Southeast Asian Resource Action Center, 2018). Newly arrived Southeast Asian families were likely to experience post-traumatic stress disorder, high rates of poverty, and high drop-out rates. Southeast Asian adolescents growing up in poverty-stricken communities and/or attending failing schools sometimes turned to criminal gangs in order to survive (Southeast Asian Resource Action Center, 2018). Lack of access to English language training further complicated these refugees' resettlement efforts (Wright & Boun, 2011). Resettlement challenges for refugees are further exacerbated by social isolation, a phenomenon found to be more pronounced in refugee populations than in either voluntary migrant or members of the host populations (Lobel, Kroger & Tibubos, 2022).

Refugees/Immigrants as US Entrepreneurs

Early research on Southeast Asian refugees in the US focused on refugee entry into the local economy and potential economic burdens posed by the US refugee experience (Finnan, 1982; Chakroff & Lidsker, 1981). While early studies often concluded many native-born US citizens believe refugees to be a burden on their adopted society, growing evidence now exists demonstrating refugees contribute significantly to their host societies (Newman, Macaulay, & Dunwoodie, 2023). Interestingly, a recent report illustrates that US refugees are more likely than voluntary migrants to hold a job (Clemens, 2022). In addition, US refugees are more likely than native-born citizens to become entrepreneurs (Kosten, 2018). Entrepreneurship is defined as "the capacity and willingness to develop, organize and manage a business venture along with any of its risks in order to earn profit" (Matharu et al., 2016). Fourteen percent of US refugees, compared with 11.5 percent of US immigrants and 9 percent of native-born individuals, own their own business (Kosten, 2018).

Women as US Entrepreneurs

Long viewed by the general public as a dynamic, risk-laden business experiment, entrepreneurism has been associated more often with men than with women (Vasoya, 2023). Recent statistics on US small businesses, however, show 43.4 percent are owned by women (Main, 2024), up by 114 percent since the turn of the 21st century (Lafont, 2023). Some research indicates women entrepreneurship in the United States grew more quickly since the COVID-19 pandemic than in the years preceding 2020 (Pardue, 2023), from 28 percent to almost half (Masterson, 2022). Societal changes mean women are more readily accepted in positions of authority such as business ownership than in previous decades (Global Entrepreneurship Report, 2023).

In the US, women are more likely than men to start a new business later in life, when they feel better able to balance family and work responsibilities. Women entrepreneurs in the US also are more likely than men to classify themselves as "happy" in their work (Slade, 2014). Women business owners tend to employ 20 or fewer employees and are more likely than men to start a new business as a solo venture (Global Entrepreneurship Report, 2023).

METHODOLOGY

This chapter explores the experiences and perspectives of a Southeast Asian female refugee entrepreneur through oral history methodology. The study is qualitative in nature, drawing upon Minister's (1991) feminist oral history framework to develop an instrumental case study (Stake, 2008). The study also is informed by Mishler's (1996) model of narrative inquiry for case study research.

The goal of the study is to understand and explore the experience of entrepreneurship as it is "felt, understood and made sense of" (Schwandt, 2001, p. 84) by a Southeast Asian (Laotian) female refugee entrepreneur living and working in the Midwestern United States via personal narrative. Life history interviews and personal narrative, such as those captured in oral histories, are recommended methodologies for refugee research (Powles, 2004). Oral history interviews of refugees offer advantages to researchers in that they allow for direct communication of refugees' voices, permit researchers to capture the richness and complexity of refugees' experiences, tend to restore refugees' sense of agency, reveal the personal impact of trauma, and illuminate refugees' deepest concerns and challenge researchers as well as policymakers "to think creatively about ways to address them" (Powles, 2004, 1).

In this oral history study, the author also employs an instrumental case study approach. The case study model is a procedure of inquiry (Merriam & Tisdell, 2015) defined by "an analytic focus on an individual event, activity, episode, or other specific phenomenon" (Schram 2006, p. 104). A case study is an in-depth exploration of a bounded system (time, circumstance, process) selected because it "has merit in and of itself" (Creswell, 2009, p. 440). An instrumental case study is used when a particular case is analyzed to "provide insight into an issue or to redraw a generalization" (Stake, 2008, p. 121). The instrumental case study explored in this chapter is that of Ellie, a female entrepreneur from a refugee family.

The author developed a semi-structured questionnaire and used purposeful sampling to identify potential interviewees for a larger oral history study on migrant entrepreneurship. The interviewee upon whom the instrumental case study is based voluntarily participated in multiple oral history interviews. The interviews were digitally recorded at the interviewee's place of business at her request, and later transcribed.

Minister's (1991) feminist interviewing technique was employed during the actual interview process. Minister's technique uses a conversational format to interview migrants in their own homes or places of business and, when requested, in the interviewee's own language (Gluck & Patai, 1991). Multiple data collection techniques, including a semi-structured questionnaire, digital recordings and transcripts, participant observation, media sources, and informal conversations both before and after the interviews, were used to develop the study and to analyze findings. Media sources included both local newspaper articles and social media postings about the interviewee's business. Throughout the chapter, the interviewee is referred to by a pseudonym due to the sensitive nature of refugee family connections in the birth country.

A female entrepreneur from Laos voluntarily participated in semi-structured oral history interviews totaling about three hours. The interview was audio-recorded, transcribed, analyzed for patterns and coded using the constant comparative method (Creswell, 2017). The author obtained proper approvals from a university institutional review board prior to conducting the interview and provided the interviewee with a copy of the transcript. Data sources include an audiotaped oral history interview, permission form containing demographic information, field notes based on observation at place of business, information from social media including newspaper articles and Facebook posts, and family photographs.

The study was informed by the phenomenological research framework. In phenomenological studies, researchers focus on participants' "lived experiences within the world" (Neubauer, et al., 2019, p. 90) and attempt to facilitate participants' return to experience in an effort to gather deep description. This deep description, then, provides a basis for "reflective structural analysis that portrays the essences of the experience" (Moustakas, 1994, p. 13). Oral history methodology provides a vehicle by which the interviewee "return[s] to experience" (Moustakas, 1994, p. 13) and serves to facilitate the gathering and organization of "deep descriptions" (Lewis, 2015, p. 561).

Theoretical frameworks also include the biographical approach to studying entrepreneurs (Young et al., 2021; Bernard & Barbosa, 2016); inclusion of refugee experiences as a challenge to presumed notions of homogeneity in entrepreneurial research (Marlow & Al-Dajani, 2017); intersectionality and positionality in entrepreneurial research featuring women (Martinez & Marlow, 2017; Poggesi et al., 2016); and the exploration of resilience as a "contextual embedded dynamic process" in the lives of entrepreneurs (Korber & McNaughton, 2017).

Data were continually subjected to a filtering system from which units of information, categories, and recurring themes were identified (Stake, 2005). The transcribed narrative was coded for main themes and sub-categories that intersect with those main themes, as well as being analyzed for code, concept, and category (Miles & Huberman, 2020).

FINDINGS

Constant-comparative analysis yielded four emergent themes: memories of growing up/ethnic culture, importance of family and family support, learning the business, and resiliency. Each of these themes is examined in the following subsections.

The interviewee, Ellie, cited both non-formal and formal educational experiences as essential to her ability to develop and maintain her small business. Her family's emphasis on education, the interviewee believed, was a major contributor to her motivation to learn and to succeed. Family connections within and outside the United States were cited as primary factors in the interviewee's successful business experience. Ellie also emphasized the importance of developing and maintaining networks to the success of her business, including and perhaps dependent upon *guanxi*, or cultivation of long-term relationships involving the giving and receiving of gifts or favors based upon friendship (Light & Gold, 2000). The context of Ellie's memories, she emphasized, must be considered within the perspective of her Southeast Asian cultural immersion and family upbringing.

Memories of Growing Up/Ethnic Culture

Ellie's mother is Vietnamese, and her father is Laotian. Ellie's parents met, married, and started their family while living in Laos. With the possible exception of her knowledge of and respect for ethnic Chinese ancestors in Laos, Ellie identifies with Laotian culture. Singh's (2017) study of Laotian ethnic

Moving From Refugee to Entrepreneur in the US

identity stresses the fluidity of Laotian identity and its strong connections with cultural traditions from bordering countries such as Vietnam and Cambodia.

Laos, the only land-locked country in Southeast Asia, has over 91,000 square miles and an estimated population of 7,658,000. Officially known as the Lao People's Democratic Republic, its major ethnic groups include the valley people (about 50 percent), the highland tribal people, the Mon-Khmer, and the Lao-Soung group which includes the Hmong. The official language is Lao with smatterings of English, Vietnamese, and French. Buddhism is the major religion and traditional beliefs associated with Buddhism predominate (Britannica, 2024a). Laos borders China in the north, Vietnam in the east, Thailand and Myanmar in the west, and Cambodia in the south. This geographic situation means at different historical eras Laos has experienced many population movements across borders. The mass displacement of Laotian refugees in the 1970s, however, represents the largest population movement in the nation's history (Lee, 2020).

The first Laotians are believed to have arrived from South China in the 13th century A.D. and settled on the Laos-Thailand border near the Mekong and Me Nam rivers. This early settlement eventually was invaded by Thai, Burmese and Vietnamese soldiers. The French attempted to colonize Laos in the mid-19th century on the pretense of protecting French missionaries. French occupation of Laos lasted until 1940, when France fell to Germany and agreed to the occupation of Japanese troops in Laos. In 1947 the Laotian constitution gave the country a parliamentary system of government. In 1954 Laos became an independent state. The years 1955-1975 saw much political upheaval and civil unrest, including war crimes and bombings, in the Indo-Chinese countries of Laos, Cambodia and Vietnam. On December 2, 1975, the Laotian monarchy was abolished, a Communist government prevailed, and many Laotians began to flee for their lives across national borders (Lee, 2020).

Ellie's mother's family escaped to South Vietnam in 1954 when North Vietnam became Communist (Elkind, 2014). Ellie's parents met in Laos and escaped with their children to Thailand when Laos became Communist. "My father had his own business in Laos. He was a tailor, and my mom was a seamstress," Ellie explains while noting entrepreneurism seems to run in her family:

So after they met and married, my parents owned a business. They owned their own tailoring shop. Before my dad opened the shop, he made military clothing and had his own store in a strip mall in Laos. He made custom-made suits and clothing.

Ellie's US schooling experiences were quite different from schooling experiences when she lived in Laos and later, during her family's Thai residency. "I started preschool at a French school [in Laos] and we were taught by a nun," Ellie states. "There was a public school but, in our family, education is Number One — they want us to work hard [at school] and get the best of it," she continues. "So that's why the [French] preschool … my aunt and uncle were employed by the French [officials occupying Laos at the time], the French bank or French embassy, and they thought only the best education for us." Ellie's aunt and uncle were fluent in French and English, as well as Laotian. Their language facility as well as their jobs working for French government administrators enabled the aunt and uncle to serve as social capital for Ellie's family in Laos (Yetim, 2008; Morrice, 2007).

Ellie's position as the first-born in her family comes up several times during her interview. "Since I was the oldest grandchild, the first-born in the family, that's why my aunt suggested [I attend the best private school] in Laos at the time," she reports.

The family spent a little over a year in Thailand before being resettled in the US in 1976. "It wasn't a refugee camp," Ellie explains. "My dad's family lived in Thailand, so we were able to go to the village where they lived. I had one year of Thai school," she recalls, then admits, "which I totally don't remember now. Even my Chinese [language] is sketchy to me now."

Ellie's family was Buddhist prior to resettlement in the US. Their resettlement process was aided by a Lutheran religious associate (Borja, 2018). Gratitude and respect toward the local Lutheran church and congregation that helped them during resettlement led Ellie's parents to send their three children to a Lutheran school. Ellie was 12 when she came to the US. She and her younger sister both were placed in fifth grade because it was considered good practice at the time to enroll refugee siblings in the same classroom when possible (Hickey, 2005). "And they were the best years of my life!" she exclaims.

Aside from how Ellie describes her family's emphasis on getting a good education and going to the best schools, she also mentions the importance of maintaining ethnic language skills when she says:

Here in America, in the house we speak Laotian and outside we speak English. The reason I learned [to speak] Chinese at the private school in Laos is, since our ancestors are from China, at home in Laos we spoke Chinese and outside we spoke Laotian.

Ellie's memories of trying to learn to speak, understand, read, and write English are very vivid. "I was 12 and could not speak a lick of English. My sister is 18 months younger than me and they put us in the same grade." Ellie continues with this anecdote:

We are grateful to a retired teacher at the [Lutheran] school ... she couldn't speak Laotian and we couldn't speak English. And [yet] she took all three of us when we started school [in the US], my brother and sister and me. During English class she took us in every day for our English lesson. She started us [learning English] from like, basically, a picture — like preschoolers starting out [even though I was in fifth grade]. No words. Just a picture. That is how she taught us [to speak English]. There was a picture of a boy — I still remember his name. His name was 'Nelson.' He had a yellow shirt on and blue jeans. She would start us with, 'This is a boy. What color is his shirt?' And she would teach us from there. In another picture, Nelson was on a bike and she would say, 'Nelson is on a bike and he is wearing a yellow shirt and blue jeans.' That's how we started to learn English.

Ellie's respect and admiration for the retired teacher's efforts at English language instruction are apparent as she continues to describe the instruction she and her siblings received from this dedicated educator:

Monday through Friday this teacher took us to her little room [during our usual Language Arts instruction time]. We looked at the pictures and that is how she taught us. She went from the letter to the alphabet: A for apple, B for book.... We would take regular classes like math, science, art, choir in school but [our] English instruction was strictly with her. We came [to the US] in July and started school in September. By December English sounded familiar to me. It didn't sound like a foreign language, and I could speak to my classmates by then.

She was a retired teacher ... and all this [English instruction] was volunteer, without pay, and she was amazing! She'd never married and came from a large family. For her, education was everything, her

Moving From Refugee to Entrepreneur in the US

joy, her passion. We could not speak English, we did not know, we had no idea [where to start learning English and the school had no formal program at the time]. And she did all this as a volunteer. What she did was from her heart, and she had a good heart to help us the way she did. When she passed away, I went to her funeral.

As vital to her US educational experience as the English language classes were, Ellie and her siblings continued to struggle with everyday communication issues. For example:

We were going to lunch at 11:30am [at school] and we would say a prayer before we go to lunch because we went to a Lutheran school, so I got the basics [of communication through personal experience]. But let's say I got my period, and I didn't know the word for that, or the proper word for [sanitary] pads ... I had to learn. Personal stuff like that I had to learn myself. I would ask a friend, "Every month I have blood — what is that called [in English]?" Stuff like that.

Becoming an adolescent in the US, with its attendant emphasis on male-female relationships and differing cultural expectations about courtship and marriage (Yeung et al., 2018) created even more challenges for Ellie:

And boys. Okay ... the boys would tease me. They would try to talk to me but [my sister and I] couldn't speak English so they would talk so loud! I would think 'I can hear you, but I can't understand what you are saying.' So the boys would tease me. And by the end of 8th grade, that's when the crushes started. There was this boy — I had such a big crush on him — he was the star of [the football and basketball teams]. In 5th grade I hated him because he always teased me. In 8th grade, I had a big crush on him. We wrote notes to each other. My sister and my girlfriend knew, but not my parents [because my parents expected me to have an arranged marriage].

Ellie continues to reflect on her formal schooling experiences in the US while also commenting on her sense of being sheltered by her family as an unmarried Southeast Asian female:

Our [US schooling] was amazing; it was the best experience. At that time, I did not know to be thankful or grateful for the church that took us in [for resettlement and education, because] we kind of lived in our own box and it was kind of perfect.

Non-formal learning, as well as her formal education, helped prepare Ellie for her future as an entrepreneur. Talking about the importance of non-formal learning in her early years, Ellie recalls spending her 16th summer working as a server in her aunt's restaurant in a small town about 45 miles away from her parents' house. This also is the moment in her interview that Ellie realizes another family member besides her father is an entrepreneur. "It was a Chinese restaurant," Ellie explains, then adds, "It was the best experience working with the customers ... working in customer service. I think that is where I developed [the driving focus of my hair salon]. I learned [that summer] the connection with the customer is what I like."

Ellie goes on talking about lessons learned while working in her aunt's restaurant:

People give you a chance if you are nice. Even if you did not do the best service or bring the food [to their table], even if you took a lot of time to bring the food, or forgot the catsup, people will give you many chances if you are nice. I remember that. Pay attention to the customer. I did not realize I was doing this. When a family of four came in, I would talk to the children and compliment the children. The parents were really happy about that. When a retired couple came in, I would ask to see pictures of their grandchildren. I did not know I [was gaining skills in customer service]. I did not plan it. I just asked.

Following the summer Ellie worked in her aunt's restaurant, she began to think about how she could contribute to her family's support once she graduated high school. Since the US Lutheran school placed 12-year-old Ellie in the 5th grade, she was 20 rather than 18 when she completed high school. Ellie's parents wanted her to go on to college but, showing her strong sense of self even then, Ellie respectfully convinced them she could do well styling hair. Ellie explains:

I did not want to do hair at first. I had always wanted to go into nursing. At that time, in the early 1980s, all I knew of was women in college who were going to be a secretary or a teacher. Of those two, I don't have enough patience to sit behind a desk or teach, because my personality is all over the place. And when it came to nursing, my friend was hit in a car accident and when I went [to the hospital] to see her, I couldn't even get close to her. I just froze. I knew nursing wasn't for me. So I asked myself in my senior year of high school, What do I do? A girl who was a year ahead of me already had graduated [high school] and was enrolled in a course that was not a college course. I asked her, "Why did you not go to college?" She told me, "I want to do hair."

Well, do you know what? If I do hair, that means [I can complete my training and get a job to help support our family sooner than if I went to college] and my mother's hair will always look nice! When I told my dad I wanted to do hair, he was very disappointed because hair wasn't a college degree, wasn't a bachelor's degree. He was really disappointed, but he told me, "Okay. If you are going to do hair you pay attention — you work hard at it and you stay with it and ... someday ... you WILL own a shop! It was almost like a threat and I didn't take him seriously but, then I did because he was encouraging me. He said, "This is America. We are living the American dream." He said he wanted the best for his children. And he did an amazing job [with us], he and my mom. Amazing.

Purchasing and running her own hair salon, then, was a lifelong dream for Ellie and represented the accomplishment of a family goal. Initially, Ellie began working in as an employee in a hair salon owned by someone else. Ten years later, now married and with children of her own, Ellie began to imagine how she might purchase the hair salon where she worked as an employee. She discussed her plans with her father, who continued to encourage her.

Ellie's father passed away less than a year later. In keeping with her responsibility as first-born grandchild and eldest sibling, Ellie and her husband brought her mother to live with them. The relationship was reciprocal since Ellie's mother took on the role of housekeeper and chief cook. Ellie's mother's assistance was integral to Ellie's entrepreneurial success and, in later years, was essential following both Ellie's own stroke and her college-aged daughter's health long-term challenges. Ellie says:

When my dad died, we moved my mom in with us because that's what Asians do. She's wonderful! She keeps the house, does the cooking and [when both my daughter and I had health challenges] was essential to my keeping the shop open.

Importance of Family and Family Support

Ellie often spoke of perceived differences between Western (US) and Eastern (Southeast Asian) perspectives and practices related to family, especially familial interactions and behavioral expectations. As relates to Ellie's business, she stresses family support — emotional, financial, and through personal assistance — is perceived by Southeast Asian families as vital to the success of any business venture. The next several interview excerpts illustrate these viewpoints.

Our family is there for each other. [If one of us] is going to purchase a business or buy a house [the other relatives always] ask, 'Do you need some money? I have 10 thousand or 20 thousand, take it, pay me back whenever.' That is how it was. It was very supportive.

Ellie explains that her statement 'Our family is there for each other' was evident when extended family members (another aunt and uncle) initially came to the US:

My aunts and uncles and grandparents were already here in America [when our family arrived in 1976]. I had two uncles that came in the 1960s; one came in 1965 to go to school and one came in 1968 to go to school also. One of those uncles married an American citizen — she was a teacher, and she is the one that did the paperwork to get us to America. Lutheran Social Services were the ones that called her and told her they wanted our family [to resettle in this Midwestern city].

Elsewhere Ellie describes the summer she spent working in her aunt's restaurant. When she thinks about how 'Our family is there for each other,' Ellie realizes the extended family pulled together to help her aunt get ready to open the restaurant. She says:

Oh, yes. Everyone helped with that restaurant. When they first opened the restaurant, the whole family was involved in it. They were so proud of my aunt for opening a restaurant! It made [the whole family] look good. My dad was so proud, he was like bragging, 'My brother-in-law and sister just opened a restaurant.' I remember my mom took two weeks off from her job at the hospital where she worked in linen service — just to help with the restaurant opening. My aunt and uncle from Texas came and helped. Everyone in the family came [to town] to help them get started with their new business. My grandfather helped in the kitchen, and my youngest uncle would get off work at 2pm and work in the restaurant from 5 until 9.

So it was a big family involvement. I tell you, it's family. Our family is there for each other. I am not sure about other Asian families, but ours is very supportive. I want to do the same with my family. You see it and you learn from it. I have two children, a boy and a girl. My son will help my daughter if she needs some help, or she will help him if my son needs some help. It is generational.

Learning the Business

Entrepreneurs as a group do not consider the formal education conferred by college or university experience to be important to their success (Entrepreneur Statistics, 2023). Compared with high school graduates in the general US population at 91 percent, for example, about 30 percent of entrepreneurs graduate from high school. Seventeen percent of US entrepreneurs have a bachelor's degree, 18 percent have earned a master's degree, and only four percent have a Ph.D. (US Census Bureau, 2022).

Morrice's (2007) study of successful UK refugees suggests social capital is essential to economic success for resettled refugees. Ellie's experiences of and perspectives about learning the business of running a hair salon echo Waldinger's (1995) conclusion that, among migrant entrepreneurs, non-formal learning and social support from family are more important than formal education, technical skills, or financial support.

When Ellie considers her early work experiences — especially as a teenager helping her aunt's restaurant business get off the ground — she realizes those early experiences combined with her personality and interpersonal strengths enabled her later to view her salon clients as individuals with family lives, issues, and reasons to celebrate rather than simply as "customers." This practice, Ellie believes, is at the heart of her entrepreneurial success.

Ellie credits her late father, who owned his own business in Laos before she was born, with providing the business advice and personal encouragement she needed to become an entrepreneur in the US. "My dad has been gone for 10 years now and I still repeat a lot of what he said," she reminisces. "He always taught me, 'No matter what you do, get to know the people [clients, customers]. They are the ones that make you look good.'"

"When this shop went up for sale," she says," I told my dad I didn't think I could manage a shop. He encouraged me to try and — look! We've been in business for over 10 years now! And we're still growing!" Her father also taught Ellie 'It's not who you are, it's who you know.' Ellie took this advice to heart by becoming her own Public Relations agent. "When I tell people I do a [university] professor's hair, or do their [family doctor's] hair, they want to come here, too."

Another strategy Ellie employs to attract and maintain clients is to help potential and existing clients feel special. "I tell everybody," she announces, "only Beautiful People come to [my hair salon]!" She begins to elaborate on the concept of wanting her clients to feel they receive special treatment when they visit her hair salon. At the same time, Ellie explains that these practices embody the Asian tradition of giving and receiving gifts, or *guanxi* (Light & Gold, 2000):

I'll do whatever I need to do [to help clients feel special, including] ... bring them a home-cooked meal, take them to lunch, invite them to [holiday events in the ethnic community], you name it, I'll do it. And [our family economizes to keep the shop open] ... I buy clothes at Goodwill.

Resiliency

Resilience is defined as "the psychological ability of an individual to rebound from adversity, uncertainty, conflict, failure or increased responsibility" (Adeeko, 2019). Recently researchers have begun to focus on efforts to understand the psychological characteristics of entrepreneurs' resiliency (Hartmann et al., 2022). Studies featuring "sustainably successful" entrepreneurs reveal these individuals have a resilience that allows them to experience failures and crises yet emerge stronger than before (Duchek, 2018, 430). Such failures or crises may include financial setbacks or lack of ability to garner sufficient finances to begin a business; marginalization of migrant or refugee business managers by clients, customers, and/or other business managers; or difficulties finding or keeping employees (Pidduck & Clark, 2021). Research that sheds light on individual entrepreneur's response to these and similar issues is needed (Newman et al., 2018), in particular research illuminating female entrepreneurial experiences (Stephens et al., 2022).

Due to the inherent challenges faced by refugee women entrepreneurs during escape from their native countries, residence in refugee camps, resettlement, gender/ethnic bias, and setting up a business, resilience among these female refugee entrepreneurs may be considered an integral personality construct (Youssef & Luthans, 2007). Female refugee entrepreneurs also face particular barriers entering the workforce in their adopted country compared with males that relate to one or more of the following: "language, culture, gender and family, and employer attitudes and practices" (van Kooy, 2016).

In their study of female entrepreneurs during the COVID-19 pandemic, Stephens and colleagues (2022) learned when their businesses were shut down and/or threatened with closure, female entrepreneurs evidenced aspects of resilience that differed qualitatively from their male counterparts. Women entrepreneurs during the COVID-19 pandemic turned their attention and energy toward contributing to community organizations or charities. In addition, female entrepreneurs during COVID-19 were more likely than male entrepreneurs to turn to their peers for psychological support (Stephens et al., 2022). A study of female entrepreneurs in Pakistan supported these findings (Muhammad et al., 2022). Each of these studies demonstrates female entrepreneurs' use of "positive externality", or benefits received by charitable and/or community organizations through the actions of a female entrepreneur without the exchange of money or other compensation (Britannica, 2024b).

Ellie was invited by Junior Achievement to speak with secondary school students about her experiences as an entrepreneur. Initially, Ellie felt uncertain about agreeing to the community service. Her uncertainty had nothing to do with the fact she would receive no honoraria for her efforts. Rather, Ellie perceived the Junior Achievement event as recognition of "successful businesspeople" and did not visualize herself as belonging to such a group. Through multiple conversations with her clients, however, Ellie came to realize sharing her experiences setting up and maintaining a local business could be of great interest to adolescents considering a career as an entrepreneur. Her talk at the Junior Achievement event was featured in the local newspaper along with a group photo of local entrepreneurs. Ultimately Ellie began to perceive her voluntary contribution to the community event as "positive externality" and as an informal way to bring recognition to her hair salon. When Junior Achievement repeated their invitation for Ellie to speak the following year, she did not hesitate to accept.

Ellie also evidenced resiliency during her post-secondary training as a hair stylist. "I was the only Asian in … the whole beauty school," she states, noting the head supervisor marginalized her. "It was like he was a little prejudiced against me," she confesses. "In my mind," Ellie recalls, "I said, 'I'm going to make this man like me — you watch!' That is my personality, [believing] I *will* win with this guy!" Ellie says her relationship with the head supervisor took a 180-degree turn. "And we still keep in touch," she concludes.

Major family health challenges created crises for Ellie's business, both her own and her college-aged daughter's health. Yet she showed resiliency in both instances. "When I had my stroke," she confirms, "I was back doing hair as soon as I got out of rehab." Furthermore, Ellie continued to keep her business open during her daughter's serious health issues:

When [my daughter] … was in a coma, couldn't speak or eat by herself or take herself to the bathroom and we didn't have any more insurance, I didn't know how we were going to make it. When she was in the nursing home and [my husband lost his job], I was supporting my family, running this shop, and still going to see her every day, encouraging her to get better.

DISCUSSION AND CONCLUSION

The importance of children's education to Southeast Asian parents, refugees' difficulties learning English, use of native language and traditions within the home, social isolation of both refugee individuals and families, non-formal versus formal education, and Ellie's father's background as an entrepreneur in Laos are strong motifs in her recorded interview. Field notes show these motifs persist in informal conversations with the interviewee.

Ellie's position as eldest child and later as primary financial support for her own family facilitates her development of both responsibility and agency. Ellie's post-migration positions as an Asian woman and as a refugee present potential stumbling blocks to entrepreneurial success as well as resiliency to overcome and/or persist despite difficulties.

The traditional Southeast Asian family values that imbue Ellie's upbringing and extended family experience provide her both with financial and social capital support systems that, in turn, benefit entrepreneurial success. Among the varied strategies Ellie employs to keep her hair salon business open, the "positive externality" she exhibits is unique in that she both gives of her time and expertise to the Junior Achievement organization and later reaped free advertising for her business. In this way, Ellie both inspired confidence in adolescent women who may become future entrepreneurs and became more confident in her personal identity as a successful entrepreneur.

Research that examines women entrepreneurs from a variety of refugee and immigrant backgrounds is needed to better inform entrepreneurial training. This chapter adds to needed research through an instrumental case study of a Laotian female refugee entrepreneur in the American Midwest.

REFERENCES

Adeeko, K. (2019). *Resilient identities: Refugee women defining their entrepreneurial selves.* Unpublished paper. Nottingham, England: Institute of Small Business and Entrepreneurship Conference.

Adema, W., Clarke, C., & Frey, V. (2015). Paid parental leave: Lessons from OECD countries and selected US states. *OECD social, employment and migration working paper No. 172.* Paris. Organization for Economic Cooperation and Development. doi:10.1111/issr.12134

Al-Dajani, H. (2022). Refugee women's entrepreneurship: Where from and where next? *International Journal of Gender and Entrepreneurship, 14*(4), 489–498. doi:10.1108/IJGE-06-2022-0090

Alperin, E., & Batalova, J. (2018). *Vietnamese immigrants in the United States.* Migration Policy Institute. https://www.migrationpolicy.org/article/vietnamese-immigrants-united-states-5

Asia Society. (n.d.) *Introduction to Southeast Asia.* Asia Society. https://asiasociety.org/education/introduction-southeast-asia

Bernard, M. J., & Barbosa, S. D. (2016). Resilience and entrepreneurship: A dynamic and biographical approach to the entrepreneurial act. *Management, 19*(2), 89–121.

Borja, M. (2018). Not all rosy: Religion and refugee resettlement in the US. *Harvard Divinity Bulletin.* https://bulletin.hds.harvard.edu/not-all-rosy-religion-and-refugee-resettlement-in-the-u-s/

Budiman, A. (2020). *Key findings about U.S. immigrants*. Washington, DC: Pew Research Center. https://www.pewresearch.org/fact-tank/2020/08/20/key-findings-about-u-s-immigrants/

Chakroff, R. P., & Lidsker, C. (1981). A look at Vietnamese refugee fishermen: Five years on the Gulf Coast. *The Coastal Society Bulletin, 5*(3).

Chanoff, S. (2016). Refugees revitalize American cities. *Boston Globe*. https://www.bostonglobe.com/opinion/2016/11/25/refugees-revitalize-american-cities/7Xe7PX6JbRq4sfE8D4pNyJ/story.html

Clemens, M. (2022). *The economic and fiscal effects on the United States from reduced numbers of refugees and asylum seekers. Center for Global Development Working Paper 610*. Center for Global Development., https://www.cgdev.org/publication/economic-and-fiscal-effects-united-states-reduced-numbers-refugees-and-asylum-seekers

Creswell, J. W. (2009). *Educational research: Planning, conducting and evaluating quantitative and qualitative research* (3rd ed.). Merrill Prentice Hall.

Creswell, J. W., & Creswell, J. D. (2017). *Research design: Qualitative, quantitative, and mixed methods approaches* (5th ed.). Sage Pub.

Duchek, S. (2019). Entrepreneurial resilience: A biographical analysis of successful entrepreneurs. *The International Entrepreneurship and Management Journal, 141*(2), 429–455. doi:10.1007/s11365-017-0467-2

Elkind, J. (2014). 'The Virgin Mary is going south': Refugee resettlement in South Vietnam. *Diplomatic History, 35*(5), 987–1016. https://www.jstor.org/stable/26376620. doi:10.1093/dh/dht119

Figueiredo, N., Patricio, L. D., & Ferreira, J. J. (2023). Female entrepreneurship drivers: Entrepreneurial intention, performance, and outcomes. In A. D. Daniel & Cristina Fernandes (Eds.), Female entrepreneurship as a driving force of economic growth and social change, 16-38. IGI Global.

Finnan, C. R. (1982). Community influences on the occupational adaptation of Vietnamese refugees. *Anthropological Quarterly, 55*(3), 161–169. doi:10.2307/3318025

Global Entrepreneurship Report. (2023). Global Entrepreneurship Monitor. https://www.gemconsortium.org/reports/womens-entrepreneurship

Gluck, S., & Patai, D. (1991). *Women's words: The feminist practice of oral history*. Routledge.

Gordon, L. W. (1987). Southeast Asian refugee migration to the United States. *Center for Migration Studies Special Issues, 5*(3), 153–173. doi:10.1111/j.2050-411X.1987.tb00959.x

Gradim, A. C., & Daniel, A. D. (2023). Female entrepreneurship in the age of social media: A research agenda. In A. D. Daniel & Cristina Fernandes (Eds.), Female entrepreneurship as a driving force of economic growth and social change, 1-15. IGI Global. doi:10.4018/978-1-6684-7669-7.ch001

Hartman, S., Backmann, J., Newman, A., Brykman, K. M., & Pidduck, R. J. (2022). Psychological resilience of entrepreneurs: A review and agenda for future research. *Journal of Small Business Management, 60*(5), 1041–1079. doi:10.1080/00472778.2021.2024216

Hickey, G. (2005). 'This is American get punished': Unpacking narratives of Southeast Asian refugees in the US. *Intercultural Education, 16*(1), 25–40. doi:10.1080/14636310500061656

Jesuthasan, J., Witte, Z., & Oert-Prigione, S. (2019). Health-related needs and barriers for forcibly displaced women: A systematic Review. *Gender and the Genome, 3*, 1–8. doi:10.1177/2470289719895283

Korber, S., & McNaughron, R. B. (2018). Resilience and entrepreneurship: A systematic literature review. *International Journal of Entrepreneurial Behaviour & Research, 24*(7), 112–1154. doi:10.1108/IJEBR-10-2016-0356

Kosten, D. (2018). *Immigrants as economic contributors: Immigrant entrepreneurs*. National Immigration Forum., https://immigrationforum.org/article/immigrants-as-economic-contributors-immigrant-entrepreneurs/

Kulkami, S. (2014). RISE to the challenge: Immigrant entrepreneurship in Louisville. *Bridges*, 5-7.

Lafont, G. (2023). *Women in business*. LinkedIn. https://www.linkedin.com/pulse/women-business-gloria-lafont/

Lee, G. Y. (2020). *Refugees from Laos*. Gary Yia Lee. https://www.garyyialee.com/history-refugees-from-laos

LegalZoom. (2020). *86 key entrepreneur statistics for 2020 and beyond*. Legal Zoom. https://www.legalzoom.com/articles/entrepreneur-statistics

Light, I., & Gold, S. J. (2000). *Ethnic economies*. Academic Press.

Link, A. N., & Strong, D. R. (2016). Gender and entrepreneurship: An annotated bibliography. *Foundations and Trends in Entrepreneurship, 12*(4-5), 287–441. doi:10.1561/0300000068

Lobel, L.-M., Kroger, H., & Tibubos, A. N. (2022). How migration strategies shape susceptibility of individuals' loneliness to social isolation. *International Journal of Public Health, 67*, 1604576. doi:10.3389/ijph.2022.1604576 PMID:36561278

Main, K. (2024). Small business statistics of 2024. *Forbes Advisor*. https://www.forbes.com/advisor/business/small-business-statistics/

Marlow, S., & Al-Dajani, H. (2017). Critically evaluating contemporary entrepreneurship from a feminist perspective. In C. Essers, P. Dey, D. Tedmanson, & K. Verduyn (Eds.), *Critical perspectives on entrepreneurship: Challenging dominant discourses* (p. 179). Taylor & Francis. doi:10.4324/9781315675381-11

Martinez, D. A., & Marlow, S. (2017). Women entrepreneurs and their ventures: Complicating categories and contextualizing gender. In C. Henry, T. Nelson, & K. V. Lewis (Eds.), *The Rutledge Companion to Global Female Entrepreneurship*. Routledge. doi:10.4324/9781315794570-2

Masterson, V. (2022). *Here's what women's entrepreneurship looks like around the world*. The World Economic Forum. https://www.weforum.org/agenda/2022/07/women-entrepreneurs-gusto-gender/

Matharu, S. K., Changle, R., & Chowdhury, A. (2016). A study of motivational factors of women entrepreneurs. *The IUP Journal of Entrepreneurship Development, 13*(1), 33–46.

Merriam, S. B., & Tisdell, E. J. (2015). *Qualitative research: A guide to design and implementation* (4th ed.). Wiley.

Minister, K. (1991). A feminist frame for the oral history interview. In S. Gluck & D. Patai (Eds.), *Women's words: The feminist practice of oral history* (pp. 27–41). Routledge.

Mishler, E. G. (1996). *Research interviewing: Context and narrative*. Harvard University Press.

Morrice, L. (2007). Lifelong learning and the social integration of refugees in the UK: The significance of social capital. *International Journal of Lifelong Education*, 26(2), 155–172. doi:10.1080/02601370701219467

Moustakas, C. E. (1994). *Phenomenological research methods*. Sage Pub. doi:10.4135/9781412995658

Muhammad, S., Ximei, K., Saquib, S. E., & Foss, L. (2022). *Positive externality matters in the COVID-19 pandemic: The case of women informal businesses in District Mardan*. Pandemic Risk, Response, and Resilience., doi:10.1016/B978-0-323-99277-0.00009-7

Newman, A., Macaulay, L., & Dunwoodie, K. (2023). Refugee Entrepreneurship: A Systematic Review of Prior Research and Agenda for Future Research. *The International Migration Review*, 0(0), 01979183231182669. Advance online publication. doi:10.1177/01979183231182669

Newman, A., Mole, K. F., Ucbasaran, D., Subramanian, N., & Lockett, A. (2018). Can your network make you happy? Entrepreneurs' business network utilization and subjective well-being. *British Journal of Management*, 29(4), 613–633. doi:10.1111/1467-8551.12270

Pardue, L. (2023). *The rise of women entrepreneurs*. Gusto. https://gusto.com/company-news/the-rise-of-women-entrepreneurs

Pearce, S. C. (2005). Today's immigrant woman entrepreneur. *Immigration Policy in Focus*, 4(1), 1–20.

Pidduck, R. J., & Clari, D. R. (2021). Transitional entrepreneurship: Elevating research into marginalized entrepreneurs. *Journal of Small Business Management*, 59(6), 1081–1096. doi:10.1080/00472778.2021.1928149

Poggesi, S., Mari, M., & DeVita, L. (2016). What's new in female entrepreneurship research? Answers from the literature. *The International Entrepreneurship and Management Journal*, 12(3), 735–764. doi:10.1007/s11365-015-0364-5

Powles, J. (2004). *Life history and personal narrative: Theoretical and methodological issues relevant to research and evaluation in refugee contexts*. UNHCR.

Schram, T. H. (2006). *Conceptualizing and proposing qualitative research* (2nd ed.). Pearson.

Singh, S. (2017). Identities beyond ethnic-based subordination or conflict in the Southeast Asian borderlands: A case study of Lao villagers in northeast Cambodia. *Asian Ethnicity*, 18(1), 117–138. doi:10.1080/14631369.2015.1120053

Slade, H. (2014). Women entrepreneurs are happier than male entrepreneurs. *Forbes*. https://www.forbes.com/sites/hollieslade/2014/07/30/women-are-the-happiest-entrepreneurs-in-america-says-study/?sh=3a0883a84aae

Southeast Asian Archive. (1999). *Documenting the Southeast Asian refugee experience.* University of California Irvine. https://seaa.lib.uci.edu/sites/all/publications/exhibits/seaexhibit/firstpage.html

Southeast Asian Resource Action Center. (2018). *The devastating impact of deportation on Southeast Asian Americans.* SARAC. https://www.searac.org/wp-content/uploads/2018/04/the-devastating-impact-of-deportation-on-southeast-asian-americans.pdf

Southeast Asian Resource Action Center. (2024). *Immigration.* Southeast Asian Resource Action Center. https://www.searac.org/programming/national-state-policy-advocacy/immigration/

Stake, R. E. (2008). Qualitative case studies. In N. K. Denzin & Y. S. Lincoln (Eds.), *Strategies of qualitative inquiry* (3rd ed., pp. 119–149). Sage.

Stephens, S., Cunningham, I., & Kabir, Y. (2021). Female entrepreneurs in a time of crisis: Evidence from Ireland. *International Journal of Gender and Entrepreneurship, 13*(2), 106–120. doi:10.1108/IJGE-09-2020-0135

Surangi, H. A. K. N. S. (2016). The role of female entrepreneurial networks and small business development: A pilot study based on Sri Lankan migrant entrepreneurs of tourism industry in London. *International Journal of Business & Economic Development, 4*(1), 56–70.

United Nations Office for the Coordination of Humanitarian Affairs. (2023). *Global humanitarian overview 2024.* UN. https://humanitarianaction.info/document/global-humanitarian-overview-2024/article/forced-displacement-record-levels-cause-and-consequence-increased-need

US Census Bureau. (2022). *Educational attainment.* US Census Bureau. https://www.census.gov/data/tables/2021/demo/educational-attainment/cps-detailed-tables.html

US Department of State. (2023). *What is a refugee? What is an asylee?* USDoS. https://fam.state.gov/FAM/09FAM/09FAM020302.html#:~:text=In%20General%3A%20A%20refugee%20is,social%20group%2C%20or%20political%20opinion

Van Kooy, J. (2016). Refugee women as entrepreneurs in Australia. *Forced Migration Review, 53.* https://www.fmreview.org/community-protection/vankooy

Vasoya, N. H. (2023). Women entrepreneurship: An instinctive approach or stroke of luck? *South Asian Journal of Social Studies and Economics, 20*(2), 36-44. https://doi.org/ doi:10.9734/sajsse/2023/v20i2696

Waldinger, R. (1995). The 'other side' of embeddness: A case study of the interplay between economy and ethnicity. *Ethnic and Racial Studies, 18*(3), 555–558. doi:10.1080/01419870.1995.9993879

Ward, N., & Batalova, J. (2023). Refugees and asylees in the United States. *Migration Policy Institute.* https://www.migrationpolicy.org/sites/default/files/publications/frs-print-2023.pdf

Wright, W. E., & Boun, S. (2011). Southeast Asian American education 35 years after initial resettlement: Research report and policy recommendations. *Journal of Southeast Asian American Education & Advancement, 6*(1), 1. doi:10.7771/2153-8999.1017

Yetim, N. (2008). Social capital in female entrepreneurship. *International Sociology, 23*(6), 864–885. doi:10.1177/0268580908095913

Yeung, W.-J. J., Desai, S., & Jones, G. W. (2018). Families in Southeast Asia. *Annual Review of Sociology*, *44*(1), 469–495. doi:10.1146/annurev-soc-073117-041124

Young, V., Korinek, K., & Minh, N. H. (2021). A lifecourse perspective on the wartime migrations of northern Vietnamese war survivors. *Asian Population Studies*, *17*(3), 308–331. Advance online publication. doi:10.1080/17441730.2021.1956722 PMID:35529055

Youssef, C. M., & Luthans, F. (2007). Positive organizational behavior in the workplace:

KEY TERMS AND DEFINITIONS

Laos: Laos is a country located in Southeast Asia. Laos borders China in the north, Vietnam in the east, Thailand and Myanmar in the west, and Cambodia in the south.

Refugee Entrepreneur: When one enters the country as a refugee and after arrival in the adopted country starts and maintains a business, that person may be referred to as a "refugee entrepreneur."

Chapter 6
The Impact of Climate-Induced Livelihood, Health, and Migration on Women and Girls:
A Review

Laxmi Kant Bhardwaj
https://orcid.org/0000-0001-7518-4199
Amity University, Noida, India

Prangya Rath
https://orcid.org/0000-0002-6764-1625
Amity University, Noida, India

Harshita Jain
https://orcid.org/0000-0002-9544-2869
Amity University, Noida, India

Sanju Purohit
https://orcid.org/0009-0004-8951-7520
Akamai University, USA

Poornima Yadav
Fair Quality Institute, India

Vartika Singh
https://orcid.org/0000-0003-4400-8664
Amity University, Noida, India

ABSTRACT

Climate change is among the most well-known issues that the world's communities are currently dealing with in the 21st century. It calls into question basic assumptions about what objectives are suitable for socioeconomic policy, including the relationship between equity, growth, prosperity, and sustainable development. Globally, there is a general perception that the long-term resilience of societies and communities is threatened by climate change. The Earth's climate is changing as a result of greenhouse gas emissions brought on by human activity. Particularly impacted are women and girls, who eventually migrate as a result of food scarcity and social gender division. There are few studies on gender and migration brought on by climate change. An overview of the induced effects of climate change on women and girls' migration, health, and means of subsistence is given in this study. The objective of this article would greatly contribute to our comprehension of the existing connections between migration, patterns of displacement, and the effects of climate change.

DOI: 10.4018/979-8-3693-2806-4.ch006

The Impact of Climate-Induced Livelihood, Health, and Migration on Women and Girls

INTRODUCTION

Stressed-out resource systems as well as uncertainties associated with socio-economic factors lead to migration and forcible displacements. It has been used as an adaptation strategy in numerous marginal and disadvantaged communities for a long time. This has frequently been connected to weather and water-related events. The Dust Bowl in the United States during the 1930s forced large-scale migration and disproportionately affected the rural poor, including women and children. Currently, more than 60% of total forced displacements have been related to factors associated with climate and water. The World Bank's updated groundswell report emphasizes that climate change could prompt 216 million people to migrate within their own countries by 2050. After 2050 these climate-related migrations could intensify after 2050 with extreme heat events, declining water availability, and sea level rise being major drivers. The ability to effectively manage migration at different levels such as local, national, regional, and global, is severely constrained by a significant lack of quantitative knowledge and understanding of the direct as well as indirect determinants of migration connected to water and climate.

A comparative examination of climate-induced migration patterns, gender-specific consequences, and adaptation approaches across various geographical areas is presented in Table 1. Through a comprehensive analysis of various geographical contexts, policymakers and stakeholders can acquire valuable knowledge regarding prevalent patterns, obstacles, and inventive strategies to tackle the intricate interrelation among migration, climate change, and gender dynamics. The distinctive attributes and experiences of each region are emphasized, providing significant insights for the creation of interventions tailored to specific contexts and the promotion of international collaboration in endeavors to adapt to climate change. Displacement occurs in Sub-Saharan Africa as a result of drought, desertification, and conflict. In this region, women are primarily involved in domestic resilience and agricultural endeavors, with community initiatives and empowerment programs providing additional support (De Haan et al., 2002). In contrast, South Asia is confronted with migration dynamics that are exacerbated by cyclones, glacial melting, and flooding. These factors contribute to the vulnerability of women to violence and exploitation, underscoring the need for gender-responsive policies in conjunction with efforts to reduce disaster risk and diversify livelihoods (World Bank, 2021). Latin America is currently facing challenges related to rural-to-urban migration and the land rights struggles of indigenous women in the face of deforestation. These women are advocating for water access, forest preservation, and empowerment via environmental movements (IDB, 2019). In the interim, sea-level rise poses a threat of displacement to the Pacific Islands, which has detrimental effects on gendered livelihoods and cultural practices. As a result, climate-resilient infrastructure, the preservation of traditional knowledge, and regional cooperation initiatives are imperative (SPREP, 2020). This investigation reveals the intricate regional dynamics that influence reactions to challenges caused by climate change and emphasizes the critical need for interventions that are tailored to specific contexts and are informed by multidimensional analyses.

Table 1. Comparative analysis of climate-induced migration and gender dynamics across regions

Region	Climate-Induced Migration Patterns	Gender-Specific Impacts	Adaptation Strategies	Reference
Sub-Saharan Africa	Displacement due to drought, desertification, and conflict	Women's roles in agriculture, water collection, and household resilience	Community-based initiatives. Sustainable agriculture practices. Women's empowerment programs	De Haan et al., 2002
South Asia	Migration dynamics driven by flooding, cyclones, and glacial melting	Women's increased risk of exploitation and violence	Disaster risk reduction measures. Livelihood diversification. Gender-responsive policies	World Bank, 2021
Latin America	Rural-to-urban migration, displacement due to deforestation, and land degradation	Indigenous women's struggles for land rights	Access to water. Forest conservation. Indigenous women's leadership in environmental movements	IDB, 2019
Pacific Islands	Displacement and relocation in low-lying atolls threatened by sea-level rise	Gendered impacts on livelihoods and cultural practices	Climate-resilient infrastructure. Traditional knowledge preservation. Regional cooperation initiatives	SPREP, 2020

At the global level, data on migration due to water and climate factors is limited. Some crucial examples of climate-related migration can be discussed here. The arctic-melting ice and traditional livelihood, Latin American deforestation and land degradation, pacific islands facing sea level rise, South Asian cyclones and flooding, drought, and agriculture impact on Sub-Saharan Africa. These examples provide theoretical information, but the data relating to gender disaggregation is often missing from migration assessment, although migration adds to the burden and uncertainties in terms of conventional gender-based roles and duties. Therefore, one of the main research and development problems is expanding the outreach and participation of various stakeholders in the assessment of how water and climate influence migration, as well as gender-sensitive water management systems and adaptation planning associated with global climate change.

Such challenges as gender equality, proper water and sanitation requirements, inclusive policies, and effective institutions for timely implementations are on the priority list of the United Nations on Sustainable Development Goals (SDGs). Researchers highlight the use of nanotechnology for a sustainable solution to obtain water, food, and energy (Bhardwaj et al., 2023; Rath et al., 2023; Tokas et al., 2024). They also discussed the SDGs in their study. The poorest and most marginalized communities are disproportionately affected by climate change as it intensifies already-existing vulnerabilities and inequality and leaves them with fewer resources to adapt to and deal with its effects. Because many poor people in developing nations depend primarily on natural resources for their livelihoods, they are especially vulnerable to environmental degradation and climate-related disasters. Due to their involvement in food production, water collecting, and caregiving, studies have indicated that women and girls in these communities are disproportionately affected by the effects of climate change.

According to a study by Schuemer-Cross & Taylor (2009), for instance, women in rural poor nations are disproportionately impacted by climate-related disasters like floods and droughts, which jeopardize their access to food, means of subsistence, and general well-being. According to the Fund and United Nations Development Programme-United Nations Environment Programme (UNDP-UNEP) poverty-environment initiative (Fund, 2015), women and girls are more likely to experience poverty, starvation, and relocation following climatic shocks as a result of climate change. This is similar to how gender

The Impact of Climate-Induced Livelihood, Health, and Migration on Women and Girls

inequality is already exacerbated. The Intergovernmental Panel on Climate Change (IPCC) (2019) also emphasizes how poverty, gender inequality, and resource access are all closely related to climate change. Climate-related disasters have the potential to ruin local economies, worsen food insecurity, and raise the incidence of waterborne illnesses. Women and girls are disproportionately affected since they are frequently in charge of providing healthcare and food security for their households. Research focusing on the effects of migration brought on by climate change on gender is still scarce, despite increased awareness of the gendered aspects of climate change. Even while the amount of research on migration brought on by climate change has grown recently, a large portion of it falls short of accurately capturing the differences in experiences between men and women, especially in poor nations. Ferris & Martin (2019) discovered in their analysis of the literature that gender issues are frequently disregarded in migration studies in favour of aggregate trends and macro-level analyses. The gendered aspects of climate-induced migration also require further study, according to Adger et al., (2018), especially in susceptible areas like South Asia and sub-Saharan Africa.

Furthermore, studies that have already been done have a tendency to ignore the various ways that gender interacts with other social identities, such as age, class, and ethnicity, to shape people's vulnerabilities and capacity for adaptation. According to McLeman & Hunter's (2010) research, for instance, women and girls from marginalized groups may experience increased risks and adaption difficulties. This highlights the significance of taking intersectional perspectives into account in studies on climate-induced migration. As a result, climate change presents a serious threat to global development, with disproportionate effects on the poorest residents of emerging nations, especially women and girls. Studies that explicitly address the gender-specific effects of migration brought on by climate change are still rare, despite increased awareness of the gendered aspects of climate change. To create gender-responsive policies and interventions that address the particular needs and vulnerabilities of women and girls in vulnerable areas, as well as to better understand the various experiences that men and women have in the context of climate-induced migration, further research is required. This study aimed to provide an overview of the induced impact of climate change on the livelihood, health, and migration of women and girls.

FACTORS AFFECTING THE MIGRATION OF WOMEN AND GIRLS

Several factors influence the migration of women and girls directly or indirectly. Factors related to water and climate change have been observed to differ from region to region due to differences in the use of water and land and environmental conditions. Figure 1 shows some of the factors and consequences of climate change directly or indirectly impacting women and girls' populations.

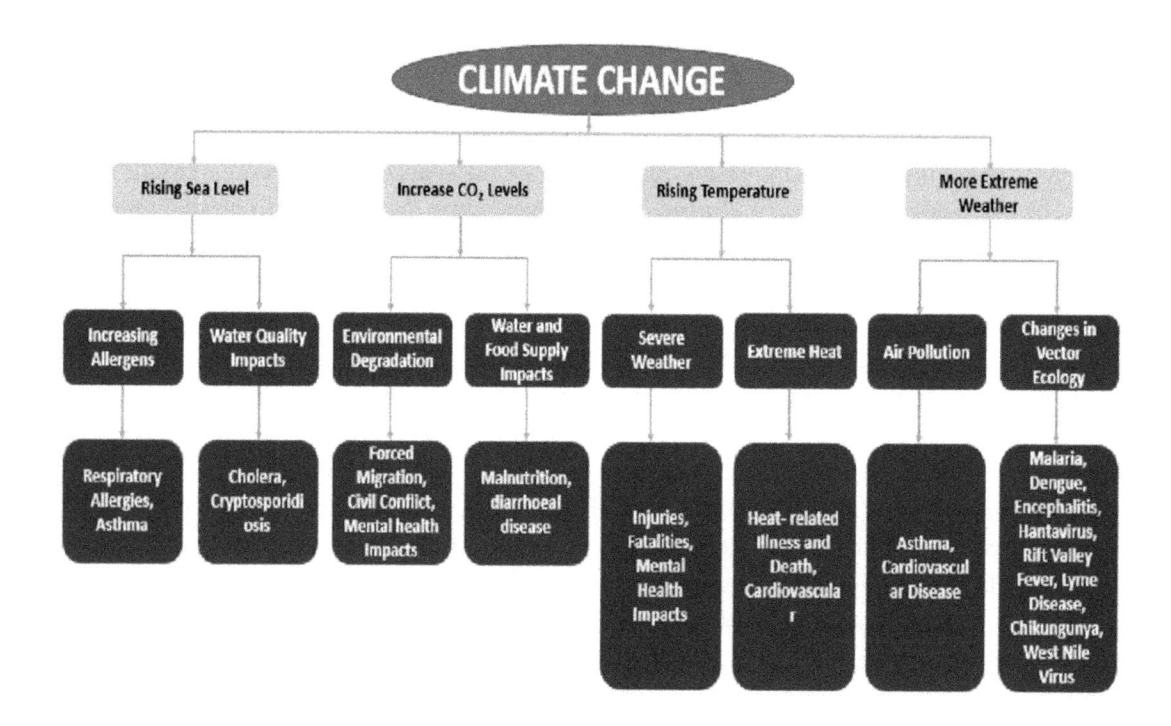

Figure 1. Impact of climate change on women and girl's migrants

[Flowchart: CLIMATE CHANGE branching into four categories:

- **Rising Sea Level** → Increasing Allergens (Respiratory Allergies, Asthma); Water Quality Impacts (Cholera, Cryptosporidiosis)
- **Increase CO_2 Levels** → Environmental Degradation (Forced Migration, Civil Conflict, Mental health Impacts); Water and Food Supply Impacts (Malnutrition, diarrhoeal disease)
- **Rising Temperature** → Severe Weather (Injuries, Fatalities, Mental Health Impacts); Extreme Heat (Heat-related Illness and Death, Cardiovascular)
- **More Extreme Weather** → Air Pollution (Asthma, Cardiovascular Disease); Changes in Vector Ecology (Malaria, Dengue, Encephalitis, Hantavirus, Rift Valley Fever, Lyme Disease, Chikungunya, West Nile Virus)]

Climate Change

The origins and outcomes of climate change are intricately linked to pervasive global inequalities. Climate change functions as an amplifier of pre-existing vulnerabilities in a world that has already been undergoing warming and transformation. The impacts of climate change amplify pre-existing gender vulnerabilities that are associated with cultural, religious, geographic, traditional, and socio-economic factors and practices. In rural areas, women are mostly dependent on natural resources, such as firewood, water and farming. These resources become scarce due to environmental degradation and climate change. In many southern hemisphere countries, girls and women travel long distances to get the water. This daily practice reduces their output in terms of female income-generating activities or education while increasing the workload on them. As per the study by Hunter & David (2009), climate change adversely impacts the vulnerable and poor sections of the population, especially women. Rising sea levels and escalating global temperatures caused by climate change not only have a direct impact on girls and women but also amplify their vulnerability when combined with socio-cultural factors (Harper, 2011). According to Masika's (2002) assertion, disparities in gender relations and resource access can heighten women's susceptibility to the effects of climate change in comparison to men.

Demetriades & Esplen (2010) described that individuals depend on their sources of income, pursuing education, health factors and accessibility to natural resources. As compared to men, girls and women are less educated, have no income, and have lesser direct accessibility to natural resources and hence they would be disproportionately affected due to climatic changes. The population of the countries situated in the southern hemisphere is most affected by climate change, despite contributing least to the climate change problems. Climate change has been reported to affect agricultural production and natural resources like water. Climate change could exacerbate conflict-driven migration, particularly in areas where climate-related changes contribute to disputes over natural resources, such as in Darfur. Climate shocks, like droughts in regions of Sahel or floods in the areas of Volta, Okavango, as well as Niger deltas, are likely to increase temporary and short-distance distress migration. However, the number of affected individuals might be lower provided anticipatory migration takes place in response to heightened climatic vulnerability.

Vulnerability associated with climate change is not solely determined by the climate stressors themselves, but also by underlying inequalities in resource access and poverty. Consequently, individuals in different social positions make divergent choices regarding mobility. For instance, the potential for natural disasters to trigger migration varies greatly. While migration of labours often intensifies as a response to climate-related hazards, patterns of migration driven by distress are influenced by factors such as asset ownership, social networks, as well as available assistance. It is also important to recognize that migration prompted by variability in climate is generally internal and of short duration, with limited connection to conflict risks. The effects of climate change have manifested in various ways, influencing human settlements by adversely impacting the health of humans, compromising food security, as well as diminishing the sustainability of economic activities reliant on natural resources (Bhardwaj, 2023). In 2010 and 2011, the United Nations Framework Convention on Climate Change (UNFCCC) incorporated displacement, migration, as well as planned relocation caused due to climate changes into its agenda (Chindarkar, 2012).

Gender Specificities

The population migration due to climate change is not gender-neutral. Due to the low levels of education, girls and women have no access to decision-making in their communities and households. They do not have access to information related to disasters. Moreover, in some instances, disaster management systems may not actively include women and girls. Several other systems like early warning systems (EWS) and emergency systems for disasters are usually designed by men and are used by them. These are the gender specificities that eventually lead to increased vulnerability and marginalization of women. For example, the messages for EWS are sent by the government to the senior most male person of the house who is also the only representative member of the entire family. In such practices, it is presumed that the male head of the household would deliver the messages to other family members. This highlights an example of gender inequality that has been carried forward since ancient times. Lau et al., (2019) stated that gender-unaware approaches have a likelihood of perpetuating and compounding gender inequality. All these factors restrict females from knowing and preparing for disaster management.

Migration is also a more challenging task for females because they have usually household responsibilities including taking care of their children and dependent elderly relatives. It is more difficult for them to choose to leave and organize their departure. As a result, they face major gender-based pressure during migration. Due to gender inequalities, the injustice is exacerbated for girls and women because their participation is minimized in decision-making, education, etc. As a result, they uptake options of migration. The condition of females in developing countries is worse due to the social gender division and scarcity of food. In many villages girls and women are considered responsible for collecting water for household purposes and this responsibility might also increase the domestic workload/burden on females. The current discourse on climate change often overlooks the substantial impact it has on gender-specific adaptation strategies and actions. Women's vulnerability to changes in climatic conditions is commonly influenced by economic disadvantages, limited resource access, dependency on male members of the family, and a lack of decision-making power.

Gendered social exclusion further compounds the vulnerability of girls and women to climate change. A striking example of this disparity is the disproportionate number of women, outnumbering men by a 14 to 1 ratio, who lose their lives in natural disasters (Aguilar et al., 2007). Cultural and behavioural restrictions, such as restrictive dress codes, may impede women's mobility during floods, leading to fatal consequences. Moreover, in many societies, essential survival skills like climbing trees and swimming are predominantly taught to males. This further exacerbates the gender gap in disaster resilience. Women's socially defined roles and duties, such as water and fuel collection, often result in a greater direct reliance on natural resources, thus rendering them disproportionately prone to the impacts of climate change.

Gender-Based Violence

Although girls and women have access to relief resources such as food, water, and shelter, they don't get the specific requirements like sexual, sanitation, and reproductive health needs. They are more likely to endure gender-based violence such as forced marriage, sexual violence, exposure to trafficking, etc. Due to these violent cases, their emotional, mental, and physical health also deteriorates. Their social support networks may be lost and due to heavy caregiving burdens, anxiety levels, post-traumatic stress, and other illnesses also occur.

Challenges of Livelihood Security

In developing countries, individuals living in poverty rely mainly on climate-sensitive sectors like agriculture, fishing, and forestry for their sustenance. Consequently, they have been observed to be more exposed to the adverse effects of climate change compared to those residing in developed countries. Moreover, populations in developing countries generally operate close to the threshold of its tolerance when it comes to changing patterns. The impacts of heightened climate variability and extreme weather events are disproportionately observed among underdeveloped or developing nations, exacerbating the challenges to livelihood security faced by the most vulnerable communities worldwide. Women in rural parts, who prominently rely on agriculture and natural resources for their livelihoods, are increasingly vulnerable to gradual impacts caused because of climate change. Consequently, they might be compelled to migrate into urban areas, particularly settlements of an informal nature, where they face heightened exposure to conflicts, crimes, violence, and inadequate social support structures. Figure 2 shows the previous data on causes of death amongst migrant females (IOM, 2013).

Figure 2. Data representing the causes of death among migrant females

Causes of death among migrant women, 2014–2022

- DROWNING — 3,025
- MIXED OR UNKNOWN — 1,098
- DEATH LINKED TO HAZARDOUS TRANSPORT — 597
- HARSH ENVIRONMENTAL CONDITIONS / LACK OF ADEQUATE SHELTER, FOOD, WATER — 368
- SICKNESS AND LACK OF ACCESS TO ADEQUATE HEALTHCARE — 288

Source: IOM's Missing Migrants Project, 2023. © IOM GMDAC 2023

Lack of Capabilities and Opportunities

According to a report by the United Nations Population Fund (UNPF), migration necessitates economic and physical resources that are not accessible to all individuals (Engelman, 2009). In situations of environmental crises, such as climate change, women, children, as well as elderly individuals are often left behind, lacking the necessary capabilities, opportunities and security. Some migration flows are driven because of economic opportunities and might also be influenced by climatic changes, such as decreased availability of seasonal work in the regions of Eastern Sudan or Central Ghana, alongside expanding employment prospects in the agriculture sector outside of Africa. Coastal and lower-lying regions would face vulnerability due to rising sea levels and increased flood hazards. Coupled with urban overcrowding, this could lead to secondary migration risks.

Other Factors

Additionally, factors like inadequate nutrition patterns as well as weak healthcare infrastructure have been observed to contribute to more human losses in developing countries as a consequence of climate change (Bhardwaj et al., 2024). Women face heightened vulnerability and challenges as compared to men during natural disasters due to factors such as lack of assets, proper shelter, availability of resources, as well as accessibility to information. Concerns about losing their family, children, as well as household assets often discourage women from seeking refuge in safe shelters during disasters. Additionally, women might not receive information regarding warnings that are primarily transmitted to males in public spaces. This disparity was evident in the aftermath of the 1991 cyclones and floods in Bangladesh, where the death rate among women aged between 20-24 years was 71 per 1000, compared to 15 per 1000 amongst men (Aguilar et al., 2007). Research indicates that these gender-based differences in death rates attributed to natural calamities are directly connected to the economic as well as social rights of women (Neumayer & Plumper, 2007). In general terms, the primary climate change trends that impact migration are anticipated to involve rising temperatures and decreased rainfall. These changes give rise to water scarcity, droughts, and shorter growing periods in drylands of tropical as well as subtropical regions, such as the Sahel. Additionally, the rise in sea level, more frequent storms and tropical cyclones, and flooding pose challenges to low-lying coastal areas. Conversely, increasing temperatures extend the growing season in temperate regions like northern Europe and Siberia.

GIRLS AND WOMEN CAN PLAY THE LEAD ROLE IN THE CHANGE

Several Non-Governmental Organizations (NGOs) are working with communities in nearly 100 countries. As per their studies, girls and women may play the lead role in the change. They can develop innovative ideas and successfully implement such ideas in their society. They can accelerate household and community-level resilience building. Similar to indigenous peoples, females are not only mere victims of climate change but also possess agency as a powerful scope of change and play active roles in managing the common pool as well as household resources. Their involvement is crucial because of their triple roles present in productive, reproductive, as well as community management activities. It is essential to prioritize the utilization of female leadership skills as well as their experiences in the revitalization of communities and natural resources management when designing and implementing adaptations related to climate change and risk-reduction strategies.

THE IMPACT OF MIGRATION DUE TO WATER AND CLIMATE CHANGE

The impact of migration due to water and climate change on different groups of genders may vary. Moreover, within the framework of the water and climate crisis, social turmoil and political instability have a direct impact on gender disparities in migration environments. The analysis of the interconnectedness between water, climate, migration, and conflict often fails to address or acknowledge the significance of gender-related factors adequately. In response to climatic change impacts, internal as well as cross-border movements are more probable as compared to international migrations with long-distance; this has been observed to be associated with economic losses due to climatic change and might hinder people's ability to invest in overseas relocation, compelling them to seek opportunities locally. During the droughts periods of the 1970s as well as the 1980s in the Sahel, for instance, international labor migration occurred due to resource limitations (Mearns, 2008).

The magnitude of climate change effects is likely to be more significant in areas that have the drivers of migration coinciding with higher vulnerability due to climatic changes and limited adaptive capacity. For instance, regions like the Sahel as well as the highlands of Ethiopia are expected to face growing pressure for migration. Assessing the potential impact caused because of climate change on the mobility of humans poses significant challenges. The conventional approach to linking climatic changes with migration involves identifying climate-affected areas, estimating the population residing in those regions, and using this information to predict future migration patterns. However, this method is insufficient as migration is influenced by multiple factors, and isolating the specific effects of variability in climate is complex. Moreover, secondary impacts play a role in shaping migration patterns. For instance, coping strategies adopted in response to climate challenges, such as withdrawing children from school or reducing food consumption, may undermine the long-term livelihoods of vulnerable individuals. This, in turn, may further incentivize labor migration.

STRATEGIES FOR THE PREVENTION OF MIGRATION

Social policies that promote gender inclusion and civic engagement, along with unrestricted access to information and justice, have demonstrated improvements in environmental outcomes. Preliminary evidence also indicates a similar correlation between mortality rates from extreme weather events and the implementation of such policies (Foa, 2009). Further advancement of approaches for the planned relocation of populations facing insecure livelihoods as well as settlements is imperative. Although the immediate need for population relocation may be limited, it is crucial to develop a best-practice strategy to address the most challenging scenarios in the future, such as those faced by small islands, developing states, as well as urban coastal regions. To mitigate the need for extensive emigration, current strategies could involve safeguarding coastal infrastructure and implementing restrictions on construction in vulnerable coastal areas. Additionally, it is essential to establish regional agreements in preparation for post-disaster recovery, ensuring prompt and effective response mechanisms are in place when the need arises. The inherent injustice of a world where those least responsible for causing climate change to suffer the most from its consequences highlights the urgent need to prioritize equality and social justice in climate policies and initiatives.

Human mobility has been considered as a complex social phenomenon, making it challenging to identify as well as isolate specific causal factors. When examining the connections between climate change and migration, the task becomes even more intricate. While climate change might influence migration decisions, it is usually not the primary cause, except in cases where migration has long been employed as an adaptation strategy to cope with climate variability. It is important to understand the various roles of women and men and how these roles influence vulnerability caused due to climate change as well as climate-related migration. There is also an urgent need to scale up gender-trans formative adaptations related to climate change. Such measures have to be beyond mere gender sensitivity and guide towards supporting more gender equality and building more resilient communities. Unfortunately, females have not been provided with equal opportunities to participate in the process of decision-making concerning climate adaptations and mitigation policies, both at the national as well as international levels. Gender considerations have been notably absent from discussions within the UNFCCC. The current policy discourse neglects to address the practical requirements as well as strategic needs of females.

MIGRATION PATTERNS IN DEVELOPING WORLD

Another approach involves examining existing patterns of migration and analyzing how the demographic trends as well as climate changes together might influence the drivers of such particular migrations. By integrating projected demographic as well as climate trends with existing patterns of migration, it is possible to anticipate a range of impacts.

Due to Climate Change

Anticipated alterations in migration patterns across the developing world are expected due to climate change. The connection between environmental changes as well as migration is complex, with limited evidence supporting direct causation. Vulnerability serves as a concept for describing the relative risk individuals, households and communities face when confronted with adverse environmental changes. It encompasses the capacity to anticipate, mitigate, resist, as well as recover from disasters. We argue that understanding the vulnerability of individuals and communities in developing countries regarding sustaining their livelihoods amid climate change and variability is best achieved through a scalar approach. This approach takes into account everyday concerns such as livelihoods as well as marginalized social statuses that can contribute to ineffective practices of land management, resource pressure, and heightened dependence on resources driven by demand.

Being vulnerable to climate change does not automatically imply being a prospective climate migrant. The presence of recurring ecological hazards affects how individuals integrate such risks into their means of sustaining their livelihoods (McLeman & Smit, 2006). Those residing in marginalized regions have devised a wide range of strategies to enhance their capacity for dealing with gradual climate shifts and severe climatic incidents. Communities facing persistent environmental hazards often employ risk mitigation measures through diversifying their livelihoods. Rural livelihoods typically involve a combinatorial form of three main strategies, i.e. agropastoral-associated activities, diversification of income sources, as well as migration (De Haan et al., 2002). Labor migration plays a crucial role in rural livelihoods as migrant wages serve as investment capitals that would be used for the production of rural commodities, while migration experiences facilitate the exchange of new social practices and ideas within rural areas. When confronted with severe stressors like drought, the significance of diverse sources of income and adaptive coping strategies becomes evident (Eriksen et al., 2005). The level of vulnerability largely depends on individuals' capacity to specialize effectively. International migration serves as a significant household strategy for reducing risks since remittances have been proven to substantially decrease vulnerability during post-disaster recovery (Suleri & Savage, 2006). Migration is just one among several survival strategies that are pursued by such families, either concurrently or consecutively along with other coping mechanisms (McLeman & Smit, 2006).

Due to Water Management

At a global scale, there is a scarcity of quantitative data that examines the interconnections between water and migration, with existing data often being incomplete or lacking in disaggregation. Additionally, studies focusing on migration assessments frequently overlook the importance of gender-disaggregated data. As a result, there is a need to enhance collaboration and involvement among diverse stakeholders to address the assessment of water as well as climate-related migration and promote gender-sensitive approaches to water management and adaptation planning associated with climate change. These challenges are prominent in the United Nations' efforts to achieve SDGs, particularly SDG 5 associated with gender equality, SDG 6 associated with water and sanitation, and SDG 16 associated with inclusive policies and institutions. Advancing research as well as development in these areas remains crucial in addressing these challenges.

Accelerating the Implementation of Water-Related SDGs

Reaching the target of SDG 6 by 2030 is anticipated to mark a significant milestone in the effective management of water and sanitation, serving as a fundamental basis for achieving various water-related SDGs. However, numerous countries face challenges in meeting SDG 6, as there is a lack of comprehensive evidence and relevant data that can inform policy-making and decision-making processes related to SDG 6. Addressing this data gap remains crucial in advancing progress toward SDG 6 and its associated water-related goals. Given this context, it is crucial to enhance and align the supportive framework for SDG 6, to effectively implement policies that contribute to its success. Reliable evidence plays a key role in enabling countries to adopt a systematic approach towards achieving SDG 6. Making informed policy decisions within the context of SDG 6 can be complex, requiring collaboration among organizations across different sectors to assess and integrate evidence related to targets and indicators. Therefore, countries must assess their strengths, weaknesses, data gaps, and opportunities to strive towards attaining SDG 6 by 2030.

Promoting Unconventional Water Resources and Technologies for Water Scare Areas

Water scarcity represents a crucial hurdle to achieving sustainable development and can potentially lead to social unrest and conflicts among nations. Moreover, it has a profound influence on well-established migration routes and causes a shift in migration patterns. The undeniable reality is that conventional methods of water provision, which heavily rely on snowfall, rainfall, river runoff, and easily accessible groundwater, are inadequate to meet the escalating demand for freshwater in arid and semi-arid regions. Water-scarce nations must undergo a fundamental re-evaluation of their approaches to water resource planning and management. This entails exploring innovative ways to utilize unconventional water sources for agriculture, food production, livelihoods, ecosystems, climate change adaptation, and sustainable development and conservation. Unconventional water resources refer to secondary water sources that require specific treatment and on-farm management before being utilized for irrigation or are obtained through specialized techniques for water collection and access. Certain global initiatives focused on unconventional water resources have contributed to raising awareness and expanding our understanding of these alternative water sources.

Increasing Resilience to Water-Related Risks and Operationalizing Water Security

Climate change has significant repercussions on the availability, quantity, and quality of water resources, posing a threat to sustainable and secure livelihoods. The impacts of climate change, including storms, floods, and droughts, have severe consequences for ecosystems, human societies, and economies. In 2019, the world witnessed nearly 325 water-related disasters, leading to approximately 8,500 fatalities and economic losses exceeding USD 100 billion. Floods accounted for a significant portion of these casualties and losses. Among the existing resources for risk reduction, the implementation of flood early warning systems and drought early warning systems is of utmost importance in mitigating adverse impacts. However, the successful operation of such systems requires substantial financial investments and extensive human effort. It is crucial to enhance their effectiveness significantly to ensure they serve as effective tools for disaster risk reduction.

Data and Technology for Strategic Water Planning and Management

The utilization of emerging technologies and applications such as big data, Artificial Intelligence (AI), Internet of Things (IoT), cloud computing, blockchain, and others is steadily increasing across various sectors of development. In the fields of water management, engineering, policymaking, and research, these technologies hold great potential for numerous water-related applications. They can contribute to optimizing water systems planning, identifying ecosystem changes using remote sensing as well as geographical information systems, predicting and detecting natural as well as human-induced disasters, managing irrigation schedules, mitigating environmental pollution, and studying the impacts of climate change, among other areas. These technologies are now gaining importance in water management systems for:

Historical Flood Mapping and Prediction of Future Flood Risk Tool

This tool comprises two modules aimed at addressing the data gap and improving flood risk management. The first module focuses on flood mapping, providing historical flood maps to fill the existing data void. The second module focuses on predicting future flood risks, enabling better-informed decision-making, and supporting preparedness and contingency planning. Utilizing AI models, the tool predicts the likelihood of future flood risks in specific areas. These AI models are trained using historical flood maps and various open temporal datasets that include temperature, land usage/cover, infrastructure, population, precipitation, as well as socioeconomic data disaggregated by sex and age. By leveraging this module, it becomes possible to identify areas that are most susceptible to future flood risks.

Surface Water Change Detection Tool

The tools to detect surface water change utilize the vast collection of Landsat and Sentinel 2 data stored in archives of the Google-Earth engine, along with Google's powerful cloud processing capabilities, to rapidly analyze historical patterns of surface water extent. By analyzing different layers of Landsat and Sentinel 2 imagery, this tool calculates changes in surface water over time. In its initial implementation, the tool focuses on the Indus River in Pakistan and generates a high-definition map that identifies areas of erosion as well as deposition after each monsoon season from 1984 to 2020. Future iterations of the tool will be tailored to provide similar analytical capabilities for other river systems at both national as well as regional levels.

Water Quality Monitoring With IoT Sensors

The objective of this toolkit is to facilitate real-time or near-real-time water quality monitoring in refugee camps. The toolkit would be designed to replace existing water monitoring systems by employing a network of inter-connected sensors that could transmit data without interventions of humans, utilizing IoT technology. Communication between the sensors will be facilitated through a Wi-Fi-based medium. The collected data from the sensors would be made available to refugees as well as camp managers us-

The Impact of Climate-Induced Livelihood, Health, and Migration on Women and Girls

ing hosted dashboards on micro-servers, ensuring easy access and dissemination of information. The availability of near real-time water quality data as well as information would enable camp managers to make timely decisions. For instance, they could proactively schedule the emptying of septic tanks to prevent overflow and the potential spread of disease. Additionally, identifying contaminated water sources before the majority of refugees consume the water would be possible. Real-time monitoring of the water supply to the camp would allow for adjustments in water release on an hourly basis, ensuring efficient management. These capabilities would contribute to the overall safety and well-being of the camp population. Remote sensing and Geographical information systems also aid in identifying areas at risk of becoming water-scarce and those affected by climate change. By applying cloud computing and blockchain, water management can become more efficient, transparent, and secure. These technologies offer tools for predictive analysis, and remote monitoring, and ensure the integrity of data related to water distribution and usage.

Capacity Development of Future Water Leaders, Communities, and Citizens

The United Nations University Institute for Water, Environment, and Health (UNUINWEH) aims to enhance the capabilities of water sector stakeholders in developing and emerging economies. Their efforts focus on fostering collaboration between scientific research and policymaking to address knowledge gaps and promote water literacy. UNU-INWEH's capacity development initiatives are practical and solution-oriented, utilizing case-based learning approaches. These initiatives are designed to provide participants with a comprehensive understanding of water challenges, encompassing the interconnected environmental, social, and political factors at play. Some successful examples of cross-border collaboration are also here, which can lead to show improved outcomes. The Great Green Wall initiative in Africa is a good example of cross-border collaboration. This initiative aims to combat desertification, enhance food security, and strengthen resilience against climate change impacts. By bringing together nations, NGOs, and international agencies, the project demonstrates the power of cooperative efforts in addressing climate change and its effects on vulnerable populations, including women and girls.

The Water Management Agreements for the Mekong River Basin, involving Laos, Cambodia, Thailand, and Vietnam, highlight how countries can collaborate to manage and protect water resources, crucial for preventing forced migration due to water scarcity. These agreements are prime examples of handling water issues in a way that also considers the impact on women, who are often the most affected in situations where communities must relocate because of a lack of water. The South Asia Women's Resilience Index, created with help from the Economist Intelligence Unit and support from global groups like the United Nations Development Programme (UNDP), aims to make women stronger in facing disasters and climate change. It promotes policies that make sure men and women are treated equally in planning for disasters. This team effort highlights how countries working together can come up with plans that pay special attention to the needs of women when adapting to changes in the climate.

COMPARING THE EFFECTS OF GENDER: A CLOSER LOOK AT MEN AND WOMEN

Given the growing threat that climate change poses to communities globally, it is critical to comprehend the subtle disparities in the experiences of women and men in order to develop policies and interventions that are successful. While the effects of environmental degradation are felt by both sexes equally, socioeconomic differences and deeply ingrained gender stereotypes frequently result in divergent effects. This section explores the gender-specific effects of climate change, looking at the ways in which men and women perceive and react to environmental issues. The experiences of men and women in the face of climate change are significantly shaped by socio-cultural norms and conventional gender roles. Gender inequality can make it difficult for women, especially in patriarchal settings, to obtain resources, participate in decision-making processes, and develop adaptive skills.

Women are often the primary carers, domestic workers, and food producers, which puts them at the forefront of the vulnerability caused by climate change (Kabeer, 2005). On the other hand, males are more likely to be in positions of power and control over resources, which gives them more freedom to make decisions and access to possibilities for personal growth. But men may also be constrained by traditional gender conventions, which might hinder their ability to communicate their emotions and deter them from asking for assistance or working together in times of need (Resurrección et al., 2019). One of the most important factors in determining susceptibility and resistance to climate change is access to resources. Inequalities in land, credit, education, and technology between men and women can worsen already-existing gender gaps. Women's capacity to adjust to shifting environmental conditions is hampered by limited access to resources, which prolongs cycles of vulnerability and poverty (Denton, 2002).

Men, on the other hand, might have easier access to formal work possibilities and financial resources, which would allow them to invest in diversified livelihoods and adaptable methods. But males may also be more vulnerable to the negative health effects and dangers associated with climate change if they rely too much on traditionally masculine activities and occupations like farming and fishing (Lama et al., 2021). Human health is impacted by climate change in many different ways, with varying effects on men and women. Due to their caregiving and reproductive obligations, women are frequently more vulnerable to health issues during environmental catastrophes. These issues can include increased susceptibility to hunger, waterborne infections, and maternal mortality (Pearse, 2017). Conversely, men may have mental health issues and occupational health risks related to job loss and relocation. Under some circumstances, the need to carry out the traditional duties of protector and provider can increase stress and worry, which can have a negative impact on one's health (Goughet al., 2016).

Migration brought on by climate change is a complicated issue that is influenced by environmental, gender-specific, and socioeconomic factors. Men and women may migrate for different reasons and encounter different difficulties along the way. Because of their limited mobility, reliance on the economy, and social marginalization, women are frequently more susceptible to being forced to relocate (Gioli & Milan, 2018). Men, on the other hand, might relocate for economic reasons in order to pursue job prospects abroad. They might, however, also experience particular difficulties with social support systems, integration, and mental health problems. Individuals' vulnerabilities and capabilities for adaptation may be shaped by gender norms and stereotypes, which may have an impact on migration decisions and experiences (McLeman & Smit, 2006). Therefore, developing fair and successful adaptation solutions requires an awareness of the gender-specific effects of climate change. Because of migratory patterns, sociocultural norms, resource accessibility, and health risks, men and women experience climate change in distinct ways. Men also face special hazards and obstacles related to environmental degradation, even though women typically bear the brunt of it. A comprehensive strategy that takes into account the various needs and vulnerabilities of both men and women is needed to address gender gaps in climate change responses.

CONCLUSION AND FUTURE RECOMMENDATIONS

Both at the federal and provincial levels are the effects on migratory patterns that were previously discussed being assessed. Policymakers can benefit greatly from this study's practical solutions to handle the complex interactions between gender issues, water dynamics, migration, and climate change. It also emphasizes how crucial it is to build alliances and relationships with professionals and organizations throughout the world in order to create and carry out knowledge-dissemination initiatives. These programs seek to provide a broad awareness of gender-sensitive approaches, migration, water management, and conflicts to a variety of stakeholders. Comprehensive and longitudinal data on internal migration and displacement are desperately needed, generally speaking. Such information would support the evaluation of local resilience and adaptation programs by enabling a fuller understanding of the disparate ways that catastrophes impact diverse development environments. Since vulnerability levels can differ greatly among impacted groups, information that is localized and context-specific is frequently more trustworthy than data that is collected at the national level.

Therefore, more study is crucial in regions with precarious livelihoods and small disaster margins. As a result, this analysis emphasizes how critical it is to treat environmentally induced migration as a developmental issue as opposed to just a potential security risk. To investigate the gender factors influencing women's vulnerability in climate-induced migration, more research is needed. It is necessary to conduct more thorough research, which should include looking at the temporal and spatial patterns of global climate change, conflicts related to water, and related migrations. Evaluating the gaps and current obstacles in gender-focused adaptations to climate change is essential. Furthermore, for well-informed policymaking and focused interventions, it is crucial to examine how new patterns of migration and conflict may affect human development, particularly for women and girls and in vulnerable situations. In addition, it is critical to stress how education and capacity building enable women and girls to become change agents in their own communities. Education not only improves their knowledge and abilities but also makes them more resilient to dangers associated with climate change and encourages them to participate in decision-making processes. Policymakers may enable women and girls to actively participate in efforts to adapt to climate change by funding education and capacity-building programs. This will eventually support resilience and sustainable development at the local level.

ACKNOWLEDGEMENTS

The authors thank Amity University, Noida, India for providing the platform to do this study.

REFERENCES

Adger, W. N., De Campos, R. S., & Mortreux, C. (2018). Mobility, displacement and migration, and their interactions with vulnerability and adaptation to environmental risks. In *Routledge handbook of environmental displacement and migration* (pp. 29–41). Routledge. doi:10.4324/9781315638843-3

Aguilar, L., Araujo, A., & Quesada-Aguilar, A. (2007). *Gender and climate change*. IUCN (International Union for the Conservation of Nature) Fact Sheet. http://www. Gender and environment. org/admin/admin_biblioteca/documentos/Fact sheet% 20ClimateChange. pdf.

BhardwajL. K. (2023). A Comprehensive Review on the Climate Change and Its Impact on Health. doi:10.20944/preprints202305.0159.v1

Bhardwaj, L. K., Rath, P., Bajpai, S., Upadhyay, D., Jain, H., Kumar, N., & Sinha, S. (2024). COVID-19 and the Interplay with Antibacterial Drug Resistance. In Frontiers in Combating Antibacterial Resistance: Current Perspectives and Future Horizons (pp. 246-273). IGI Global.

Bhardwaj, L. K., Rath, P., & Choudhury, M. (2023). A comprehensive review on the classification, uses, sources of nanoparticles (NPs) and their toxicity on health. *Aerosol Science and Engineering*, 7(1), 69–86. doi:10.1007/s41810-022-00163-4

Chindarkar, N. (2012). Gender and climate change-induced migration: Proposing a framework for analysis. *Environmental Research Letters*, 7(2), 025601. doi:10.1088/1748-9326/7/2/025601

De Haan, A., Brock, K., & Coulibaly, N. (2002). Migration, livelihoods and institutions: Contrasting patterns of migration in Mali. *The Journal of Development Studies*, 38(5), 37–58. doi:10.1080/00220380412331322501

De Haan, A., Brock, K., & Coulibaly, N. (2002). Migration, livelihoods and institutions: Contrasting patterns of migration in Mali. *The Journal of Development Studies*, 38(5), 37–58. doi:10.1080/00220380412331322501

Demetriades, J., & Esplen, E. (2010). The gender dimensions of poverty and climate change adaptation. *Social dimensions of climate change: Equity and vulnerability in a warming world*, 133-143.

Denton, F. (2002). Climate change vulnerability, impacts, and adaptation: Why does gender matter? *Gender and Development*, 10(2), 10–20. doi:10.1080/13552070215903

Engelman, R. (2009). The state of world population 2009. Facing a changing world: Women, population and climate. In The state of world population 2009. Facing a changing world: Women, population and climate (pp. 104-104).

Eriksen, S. H., Brown, K., & Kelly, P. M. (2005). The dynamics of vulnerability: Locating coping strategies in Kenya and Tanzania. *The Geographical Journal*, 171(4), 287–305. doi:10.1111/j.1475-4959.2005.00174.x

Ferris, E. E., & Martin, S. F. (2019). The global compacts on refugees and for safe, orderly and regular migration: Introduction to the special issue. *International Migration (Geneva, Switzerland)*, 57(6), 5–18. doi:10.1111/imig.12668

Foa, R. (2009). Social and governance dimensions of climate change: implications for policy. *World Bank Policy Research Working Paper*, (4939).

Fund, G. G., & UNDP-UNEP Poverty Environment Initiative. (2015). Gender and climate change: evidence and experience. *Gender Climate Brief*.

Gioli, G., & Milan, A. (2018). Gender, migration and (global) environmental change. In *Routledge handbook of environmental displacement and migration* (pp. 135–150). Routledge. doi:10.4324/9781315638843-11

Gough, B., Robertson, S., & Robinson, M. (2016). Men, 'masculinity' and mental health: Critical reflections. In *Handbook on gender and health* (pp. 134–147). Edward Elgar Publishing. doi:10.4337/9781784710866.00018

Harper, S. (2011). Migration and global environmental change. *PD7: Environment, migration and the demographic deficit.*

Hunter, L. M., & David, E. (2009). *Climate change and migration: Considering the gender dimensions.* University of Colorado, Institute of Behavioral Science.

IDB (2019). *Development in the Americas: Laying the Groundwork for a Sustainable Future.* IDB.

Intergovernmental Panel on Climate Change (IPCC). (2019). *Special Report on Climate Change and Land.* IPCC.

Kabeer, N. (2005). Gender equality and women's empowerment: A critical analysis of the third millennium development goal 1. *Gender and Development, 13*(1), 13–24. doi:10.1080/13552070512331332273

Lama, P., Hamza, M., & Wester, M. (2021). Gendered dimensions of migration in relation to climate change. *Climate and Development, 13*(4), 326–336. doi:10.1080/17565529.2020.1772708

Lau, D., Brown, S., Budimir, M., Sneddon, A., Upadhyay, S., & Shakya, P. (2019). *Gender transformative early warning systems: Experiences from Nepal and Peru.*

Masika, R. (Ed.). (2002). *Gender, development, and climate change.* Oxfam.

McLeman, R., & Smit, B. (2006). Migration as an adaptation to climate change. *Climatic Change, 76*(1), 31–53. doi:10.1007/s10584-005-9000-7

McLeman, R. A., & Hunter, L. M. (2010). Migration in the context of vulnerability and adaptation to climate change: Insights from analogues. *Wiley Interdisciplinary Reviews: Climate Change, 1*(3), 450–461. doi:10.1002/wcc.51 PMID:22022342

Mearns, R. (2008). *Social dimensions of climate change: workshop report 2008.*

Neumayer, E., & Plümper, T. (2007). The gendered nature of natural disasters: The impact of catastrophic events on the gender gap in life expectancy, 1981–2002. *Annals of the Association of American Geographers, 97*(3), 551–566. doi:10.1111/j.1467-8306.2007.00563.x

Pearse, R. (2017). Gender and climate change. *Wiley Interdisciplinary Reviews: Climate Change, 8*(2), e451. doi:10.1002/wcc.451

RathP.BhardwajL. K.YadavP.BhardwajA. (2023). A Synthesis of Biogenic Nanoparticles (NPs) for the Treatment of Wastewater and Its Application: A Review. https://doi.org/ doi:10.20944/preprints202311.1629.v1

Resurrección, B. P., Bee, B. A., Dankelman, I., Park, C. M. Y., Haldar, M., & McMullen, C. P. (2019). *Gender-transformative climate change adaptation: advancing social equity. Paper commissioned by the Global Commission on Adaptation*. GCA.

Schuemer-Cross, T., & Taylor, B. H. (2009). *The right to survive: the humanitarian challenge for the twenty-first century*. Oxfam.

SPREP. (2020). *State of Environment and Conservation in the Pacific Islands: 2020 Regional Report*. SPREP.

Suleri, A. Q., & Savage, K. (2006). *Remittances in crises: a case study from Pakistan*. Sustainable Development Policy Institute.

Tokas, R., Bhardwaj, L. K., Kumar, N., & Jindal, T. (2024). Nanotechnology for sustainable development and future: a review. *Green and Sustainable Approaches Using Wastes for the Production of Multifunctional Nanomaterials*, 221-233.

World Bank (2021). *South Asia's Hotspots: The Impact of Temperature and Precipitation Changes on Living Standards*. World Bank.

Chapter 7
An In-Depth Analysis of Women's Social Capital in Abu-Shouk Camp:
A Quantitative Assessment

Mawa Abdelbagi Osman Mohamed
https://orcid.org/0000-0002-9977-0798
University of Milano-Bicocca, Italy

Eslam ElBahlawan
https://orcid.org/0000-0002-5298-0018
University of Milano-Bicocca, Italy

Leila Omer Adam Ahmed
Independent Researcher, Sudan

ABSTRACT

This study explores the complex social bonds among women in the Abu-Shouk camp, an internally displaced person camp in Darfur, Western Sudan, against the backdrop of the prolonged Darfur conflict. Social bonds are essential for women in the Abu-Shouk camp as they provide emotional support, practical assistance, and a sense of community amidst the hardships of displacement. These bonds help them collectively guide daily challenges, fostering resilience and solidarity in the face of adversity. To examine these bonds, a robust research design was employed, including surveys to comprehensively assess various aspects of women's lives, including demographics, trust, solidarity, and women's empowerment. Findings reveal that trust plays a pivotal role, in influencing social relationships within the camp, as women show caution in various relationships. Moreover, education and age impact gift-giving behaviors, indicating potential avenues for stabilizing social ties. The study contributes valuable insights into the lives of women amidst conflict and displacement, emphasizing the centrality of trust and social bonds, and offering important implications for targeted interventions aimed at empowering women and promoting equitable decision-making within challenging contexts.

DOI: 10.4018/979-8-3693-2806-4.ch007

INTRODUCTION

Wars and conflicts have far-reaching and devastating effects that impact everyone, whether these effects are tangible or not. While the direct consequences of conflict and war are evident, there are also intangible repercussions that people endure. Following the cessation of hostilities, those affected not only have to come to terms with the immediate consequences and the physical damage to their lives – such as loss of family members, jobs, homes, and land – but they also have to struggle with continuing ramifications that can sometimes be permanent. It has been over two decades since the conflict in Darfur began, yet the region in western Sudan continues to struggle with the pressing aftermath of this war. Abu Al-Shouq camp stands as a striking reminder of the enduring scars of this conflict, established to provide shelter for refugees displaced by the violence.

Since February 2003, Sudan's westernmost region, Darfur, has become a battleground for relentless warfare between various militant groups and the central government. This ongoing conflict has tragically revealed the use of rape against women and girls as a deliberate and systematic weapon of war. The Arab Janjaweed militia, alongside the Sudanese government, is reported to have employed sexual violence as a means of ethnic cleansing and to suppress the population's will (Khadka, 2017). Moreover, many women had lost their husbands, homes, communities and belongings; The conflict left many women and girls to shoulder the burden of caring for their families alone. This significantly increased their vulnerability and piled on responsibilities and workload. Meanwhile, many men and boys, traditionally the primary source of household income, tragically lost their lives protecting their loved ones.

Conflict and violence in Darfur have led to the breakdown of communities. Lives have been tragically lost, infrastructure lies in ruins, and essential health and education services have crumbled; in addition to the huge damage that has affected the environment (Mohamed, 2023). The newly formed political tensions have fractured social bonds, severing the ties that once held communities together. This, coupled with the destruction wrought by the conflict, has significantly delayed socio-economic development in the region (Murithi, 2006). The armed conflict in Darfur stands as one of the most horrific in recent history. Both the United States and the United Nations have labelled it a "genocide" and the "world's worst humanitarian crisis" (Quach, 2004).

Despite the harsh realities of Darfur, women have built a powerful social network. This network acts as a crucial safety net for those facing domestic violence or assault. Within Darfur's close-knit communities, women often seek help from immediate family members to address social issues and improve their lives. However, some women extend their support system beyond family, seeking assistance from government organizations and NGOs. This willingness to explore options beyond traditional support networks highlights the women's adaptability and determination to build a better life. Women in Abu-Shouck camp, Western Sudan, spoke of the network's profound impact on their daily lives. Amna one of the women camp leaders stated: *"Many women in Darfur build a huge social network that helps women who are subject to domestic violence or rape."* Asia another camp leader collaborates to this; *"In Darfur, many women turn to their closely related family members for help or assistance to solve social problems or improve their social and economic situation. In contrast, others turn to the government and NGOs."*

Asia's and Amna's words underscore the efficacy of social structures and underlying attitudes in facilitating collective action. These examples illuminate the pivotal role of social trust, interaction, and reciprocity as wellsprings of social capital, shaping collective outcomes, both constructive and detrimental.

In recent years, the concept of "social capital" has garnered widespread attention across diverse disciplines. Originating from sociological foundations (Bourdieu, 1986; Coleman, 1990), the idea of social capital has transcended disciplinary boundaries, finding applications in economics (Sobel, 2002; Dasgupta & Serageldin, 2000), and notably in political science (Putnam, 2000).

The famous aphorism *"It's not what you know, it's who you know."* can summarize the conventional idea of social capital. Membership in exclusive circles often hinges on internal contacts. Likewise, when people go through a difficult time, they know that their family and friends are their first safety net. Similarly, people spend some of their happiest hours talking to neighbours, sharing meals with friends, and volunteering in community projects. Parents invest substantial time in community engagement, knowing full well that their children's intelligence and motivation are not enough to ensure a bright future for them. These principles extend beyond individuals to communities, where diverse social networks and civic associations empower collective problem-solving (Sanginga et.al, 2007), resilience in the face of poverty and vulnerability (Abdul-Hakim et.al, 2010), and seize new opportunities (Dudwick et.al, 2006).

Conversely, the absence of social ties can be equally impactful. Office workers fear exclusion from crucial decisions, and ambitious professionals acknowledge the necessity of active networking for advancement in a new company. Poverty, in this context, is characterized not only by economic lack but also by the absence of specific social networks and institutions crucial for securing housing and employment (Dudwick et.al, 2006).

Social capital, as a concept, embodies both benefits and costs. Intuition and everyday language reflect its dual nature—social ties can be an asset or a liability. Parents fear the influence of peer pressure on their teenagers, recognizing the potential for harmful habits. Additionally, close relatives, while a source of support, may overstay their welcome, prompting countries and organizations to establish nepotism laws addressing discriminatory practices.

Empirical evidence consistently supports these characteristics of social capital, emphasizing its crucial role in economic development and poverty alleviation (Grootaert, 2004). In a formal definition, social capital encompasses the norms and networks enabling collective action. Broadly, it refers to the internal social and cultural coherence of society, encompassing the norms and values governing interactions among people and the institutions in which they are embedded. Described as the glue holding societies together, social capital is indispensable for economic growth and human well-being. The seminal work of Robert D. Putnam in "Making Democracy Work" (1993) catapulted social capital into policy studies, business administration, economics, and sociology, underlining its profound implications for societal performance.

At the core of this exploration lies the recognition that social bonds are not merely relational intricacies but powerful agents of resilience. Women in Darfur, despite the adversities they face, have created a net of support, solidarity, and shared strength. These social bonds become a source of solace, a network for resource-sharing, and a collective force challenging the narratives of victimhood (Rabele, 2024).

This chapter explores the lives of women within the Abu-Shouk camp. The socio-cultural analysis in this chapter seeks to unravel the layers of social bonds shaped by conflict, shedding light on the transformative potential of community amidst adversity. The application of a social-cultural analysis of gender adds depth to our understanding, showing how specific cultural nuances shape the multifaceted aspects of women's lives in this internally displaced person camp.

The primary objective is to provide a comprehensive portrayal of women's social bonds within the Abu-Shouk camp. To achieve this, the study examines the dynamics of bridging and bonding social ties through the components of social capital, namely trust and solidarity, resource exchange, and participation in associations. These components serve as the threads weaving the fabric of social interactions, shedding light on the nature of relationships within the camp.

In the context of social capital, bonding social ties signify connections within the same group or community, while bridging social ties traverse boundaries between different social groups, classes, races, or other socio-demographic and socio-economic characteristics. Through women's perspectives, this study aims to delineate what lies within and outside these groups, elucidating the social cohesion prevalent among women inside the camp. A high level of cohesion becomes indicative of robust social solidarity, both between and within groups.

The secondary goal of this research is to scrutinize women's autonomy in household decision-making, a pivotal aspect of their agency. Autonomy, defined as the ability to make decisions about one's concerns, extends to healthcare decision-making, playing a crucial role in shaping maternal and child health outcomes and serving as a tangible indicator of women's empowerment.

In this study, data was primarily collected through surveys conducted by trained data collectors. The questionnaire was thoughtfully developed to assess various aspects of women's lives, encompassing demographics, family bonds, trust, solidarity, resource exchange, women's empowerment, and participation in associations. The data collection process involved reaching out to ever-married women aged 18 and above within the Abu-Shouk camp, with the data collection taking place from February 2021 to April 2021. By merging sociocultural analysis with a focus on social bonds and autonomy, this investigation aspires to amplify the voices of women in Darfur.

SUDAN CONTEXT

Sudan, the third-largest country in Africa with an area of 1,861,484 sq. km, is situated along the Red Sea south of Egypt. In 2019, its estimated population was 42.51 million, consisting of Arab and African groups. While Arabic is the predominant language, the country boasts over 70 ethnic and linguistic groups, showcasing its rich diversity. Sudan is endowed with abundant natural resources, including silver, gold, natural gas, asbestos, chromite, gypsum, manganese, lead, zinc, and Arabic gum. It also features a thriving livestock sector, fertile lands, and a dynamic manufacturing industry. However, the nation faces environmental challenges related to desertification, climate change, and recurrent droughts and floods.

Over three decades of famine and civil war have left a profound impact on Sudan. Many medical facilities were destroyed, resulting in personnel shortages, a weakened health system, and imbalances in access to quality medical services between rural and urban areas. The prevalence of diseases such as sleeping sickness, malaria, tuberculosis, snail fever, gastrointestinal disorders, and AIDS is high, contributing to elevated infant mortality rates. Additionally, Sudan grapples with high poverty levels, with a reported global poverty prevalence of 36.1% in 2014 (Etang Ndip, 2020).

Amidst these challenges, conflicts have displaced numerous Sudanese people. Since gaining independence in 1956, Sudan experienced two prolonged civil wars (1955-1972 and 1983-2005) rooted in northern dominance over mostly non-Muslim, non-Arab southern Sudanese. The Comprehensive Peace Agreement (CPA) in 2005 granted autonomy to the southern region, leading to South Sudan's independence in 2011. However, conflicts persisted, particularly in Southern Kordofan and Blue Nile states, resulting in 1.1 million Internally Displaced Persons (IDP) requiring urgent humanitarian assistance.

In 2003, another conflict erupted in Darfur in the Western region of Sudan, leading to the destruction of over 400 villages and approximately 2.2 million people, being internally displaced. The severity of violence and displacement prompted the United States and the United Nations to label it as "genocide" and "the world's worst humanitarian crisis" (Quach, 2004).

The History of the Darfur Conflict

The conflict in the Westernmost Region of Sudan can be traced back to the beginning of the 19th century. Darfur was an independent state for hundreds of years till 1916 when it became incorporated into Sudan by the Anglo-Egyptian forces. Since that time, the Western region has faced many years of tension overgrazing and land rights between farmers from indigenous communities and nomadic Arabs. Darfur is currently divided into five states, Central, Western, North, East, and South Darfur.

Since their incorporation into Sudan, the Darfuri[1] people have been marginalized politically, economically, and socially. The situation worsened when former President Omar al-Bashir declared sharia as the law of the land after he took over power in 1989. This created hatred and resentment among the Darfurian people, who, in turn, took up arms against al-Bashir's government. In 2003, two rebel groups of Darfurians, the Justice and Equality Movement (JEM), and the Sudan Liberation Army (SLA), started attacking government installations. They were blaming Khartoum for oppressing black Africans in favor of Arabs. In return, the Sudanese government supported raids and indistinctive military attacks by its Arab-backed militia, the Janjaweed. Hence, the current crisis in Darfur is the consequence of a long-standing civil war between government forces and different rebel groups who demand equal opportunity for the people of Darfur (Sikainga, 2009).

The Consequences of the Conflict

In the Darfur conflict, the Internally Displaced Persons (IDPs) bear the brunt of victimization, losing loved ones and being compelled to abandon rural homes for camps in urban centers or on the outskirts of towns, seeking protection from violence and necessities. According to UNAMID (2017), in 2016, 2.6 million IDPs were residing in 174 locations, including 33 gathering sites, 75 host communities, and 66 IDP camps.

Life in IDP camps is challenging, with security concerns persisting, posing risks of gender-based violence, extortion, arbitrary arrest, and looting from security forces or armed militias (UNAMID, 2017). The movement of IDPs is severely restricted due to insecurity, limiting their access to essential services, utilities, and sources of livelihood.

Inside camps, IDPs face several challenges, including limited housing size and plots, inadequate fuel sources for cooking, difficulties accessing water and land resources, as well as health facilities. Finding employment is also challenging due to under-qualification for urban jobs. The increase in living costs alters consumption patterns, leading to a reduction in the number of meals per day. Rao (2023) exemplifies this shift in the Don Bosco camp in South Sudan. Before the war, women's lives revolved around domestic duties like farming, cleaning, and cooking. However, the conflict forced them to take on the mantle of family head, a stark contrast to her pre-war experiences. Tragically, this empowerment came at a heavy cost, as they also endured abuse during the war, a trauma witnessed by the children.

Women and children, constituting the majority of IDPs, are most affected. The conflict has exposed them to high levels of sexual and gender-based violence, with rape being used as a systematic weapon of war. Between January 2014 and December 2016, rape constituted 82% of total cases of sexual gender-based violence, involving 533 victims, 3 boys, and 530 women. The ages of the victims ranged from 2 to 70 years. Many victims face severe physical injuries, HIV/AIDS, depression, phobic and panic attacks. Social stigma, lack of trust in authorities, and fear of reprisals hinder reporting, and even with evidence, formal prosecution is often neglected, leading communities to resort to traditional justice.

Women in the camps are also exposed to domestic violence by their Husbands. Domestic violence is frequently the result of gender role. The enforced idleness and loss of status experienced by many men in the camps can lead to feelings of humiliation and frustration, which may manifest as violence against their wives. When the vulnerability of men remains unaddressed in times of war and conflict, it often displays in alcoholism and domestic violence. Shifting gender norms exacerbate violence against women, stemming from this vulnerability (Akala, 2024, p.142). It's noteworthy that men also endure sexual abuse in times of conflict, yet societal norms and the complexity of identity and masculinity often silence their voices, preventing meaningful discourse on the subject. Consequently, discussions surrounding war narratives and identity tend to overshadow these painful experiences. Disrupted identities and the upheaval of traditional gender roles during conflict often result in profound frustration. As a coping mechanism, men may resort to heavy drinking and domestic violence to grapple with their altered realities (Esuruku, 2011). Thus, the stress, deprivation, and uncertainty may cause men to take out their frustrations through violence on their wives (Ibreck, 2023). Figure 1. Shows two displaced women working in brick-baking kilns in the camp.

Figure 1. Shows two displaced women working in brick-baking kilns in the camp

Paradoxically, crises like the Darfur conflict can create space for unintended social change within Internally Displaced Persons (IDP) camps. While conflict undoubtedly brings hardship, it can also disrupt traditional gender roles, compelling women to assume new responsibilities for which they may be unprepared, thereby challenging prevailing stereotypes and creating opportunities for transformative change. This shift in gender dynamics presents an 'opportunity for change,' breaking traditional molds and allowing women to enter decision-making spaces and participate in activities that were once exclusively reserved for men. The crisis becomes a catalyst for marginalized groups, providing a platform to challenge societal norms and embrace new roles.

An In-Depth Analysis of Women's Social Capital in Abu-Shouk Camp

As Brouder and Sweetman (2015) suggest, the crisis allows for a significant increase in women's roles, not only in contributing to household livelihoods but also in various capacities beyond the domestic sphere. This includes active participation in decision-making within community organizations and bodies, fostering increased visibility of women in leadership positions. The upheaval of conflict becomes a conduit for fostering new opportunities for leadership among women. Mansab (2023) highlights the misconception that women are not significant contributors to conflict resolution and peacebuilding. Contrary to this belief, women have demonstrated their strength in these areas when allowed to participate. Central to feminist peace concepts is the principle of gender equality at all levels and aspects of peace processes. This includes integrating gender perspectives into policies related to security, peace, and development.

Examples from the experiences of Palestinian, Northern Irish, Algerian, and Zimbabwean women underscore the vital role women play in post-conflict negotiations. These instances emphasize that women are indispensable in navigating the complexities of conflict aftermath and in laying the foundation for a more sustainable and inclusive peace (Karam 2010).

Crucially, social capital plays a pivotal role in enabling women to navigate and capitalize on opportunities for change. The accumulation of social capital within IDP camps fosters a sense of shared humanity, where women collectively prioritize each other's well-being and welfare. This shared concern results in cooperative efforts, effectively dividing tasks to reduce vulnerability. Women actively contribute to each other's support during the settlement process in camps, and some take on the role of caring for children who may have lost their families. In essence, the stock of social capital becomes a powerful force that not only helps women cope with the challenges brought about by conflict but also facilitates their active engagement in reshaping societal roles and structures. Akala (2024, p. 143) emphasizes the concept of agency and resilience, which positions social actors as active participants in shaping their realities within social contexts. This framework challenges the portrayal of individuals solely as passive victims, particularly vulnerable populations like women in conflict zones. Instead, it acknowledges their capacity to adapt and reconstruct their lives in the face of adversity. Consequently, the limited narrative of women as powerless victims during war and conflict requires critical reevaluation.

Nevertheless, the resilience and survival instincts of Darfurian women are not a recent phenomenon. In the eighteenth century, women in Darfur have a historical legacy as leaders. An exemplar of this leadership is Miram (Princess) Zamzam, whose unique qualities allowed her to almost rule the entire country. Defined by outsiders like men, she successfully held all the lands acquired from defeated kings and controlled the region (O'Fahey, 2008). However, contemporary times have witnessed a transformation in these established patterns (Puente, 2011).

OVERVIEW OF THE CONCEPT OF SOCIAL CAPITAL

Social capital, rooted in sociology, naturally emerges from a discipline that prioritizes methodological collectivism and structure over the individualism and agency emphasized in economic theory. Pierre Bourdieu (1985) is credited with the first modern use of the term, defining social capital as *"the aggregate of potential or actual resources linked to the possession of a durable network of more or less institutionalized relationships of mutual acquaintance or recognition"*. Bourdieu's analysis is considered one of the most theoretically refined among those who introduced the concept in contemporary sociological discourse (Portes, 1998). His treatment emphasizes the gains individuals accrue by participating in groups and intentionally constructing sociability to create this resource. Bourdieu contends that the benefits obtained from group participation form the basis of the solidarity that makes such groups possible, identifying two key elements: the social relationships that allow access to resources and the quantity and quality of those resources.

Another significant contribution comes from economist Glen Loury (1987), who, in criticizing neoclassical theories on racial income inequality, introduces social capital as the impact of one's social position on the acquisition of human capital. Loury argues that individuals start life with "social capital," nontransferable advantages conveyed by parental behaviors, leading to differential access to opportunities for minority and nonminority youth. Loury's work sets the stage for Coleman, who further refines the concept, emphasizing the "role of social capital in generating human capital." Coleman views social capital as an accumulated history in the form of a social structure usable for productive purposes by individuals pursuing their interests (Sandefur & Laumann, 1998). Social structures, whether in the form of organizations or communities, consist of relationships that shape the productivity of social capital. Coleman's definition paves the way for relabeling various processes as social capital, encompassing mechanisms, consequences, and the "appropriable" social organization facilitating its manifestation.

It is important to distinguish between recipients' motivations and donors in social capital exchange processes. Recipients seek access to assets, while donors, without immediate returns, have plural motivations that form the root processes social capital aims to capture. Coleman emphasizes the significance of closure in social relations for effective norms, where closure, or a lack thereof, influences the trustworthiness of social structures. Closed structures allow the proliferation of expectations and obligations, fostering trustworthiness. Coleman identifies factors such as obligation, expectation, trustworthiness, information channels, norms, and effective sanctions as components of social capital.

Beyond Bourdieu, Loury, and Coleman, many theoretical studies of social capital have emerged. Wayne Baker (1990) defines social capital as a resource derived from specific social structures and used to pursue individual interests. Maurice Schiff (1992) defines it as elements of the social structure affecting relations among people. Ronald Burt's (1992) structural hole theory offers a concrete interpretation, highlighting social capital as opportunities derived from network brokerage. Political scientist Robert Putnam (2000) emphasizes the importance of involvement in informal networks and civic organizations, distinguishing bonding and bridging social capital in homogenous and heterogeneous communities, respectively. Putnam's work, notably "Bowling Alone," underscores the impact of diminishing social capital on various aspects of American life.

Norris (2002) notes that Putnam's theory addresses both cultural (social norms) and structural (social networks) dimensions of social capital. Fukuyama (1995) broadens the discussion, defining social capital as shared informal values or norms fostering cooperation. Trust, a key dimension of social capital, is rationalized as a calculation, while Piotr Sztompka (2007) deems trust the most precious type of social capital, classifying it into various types.

RESEARCH DESIGN

This study adopts a descriptive approach to thoroughly explore and analyze the social bonds and dynamics within the Abu-Shouk camp. The primary objective is to provide a comprehensive depiction, unraveling the intricacies of relationships molded by the Darfur conflict. The central focus is on understanding how social capital plays a pivotal role in shaping the experiences of women within the camp. Through detailed descriptions, the study aims to illuminate the multifaceted interplay of social elements, shedding

An In-Depth Analysis of Women's Social Capital in Abu-Shouk Camp

light on the transformative impact of the Darfur conflict on community dynamics within the Abu-Shouk camp, with a particular emphasis on the role of social capital in the lives of women.

The selection of Darfur as the fieldwork location is grounded in the unique circumstances it presents for analyzing and understanding the plight of IDPs affected by a large-scale armed conflict. Darfur serves as a particularly poignant case study due to the massive displacement of people amid a backdrop of government reluctance to provide support, intricately connected to the conflict itself.

The tragic conditions in Darfur, marked by widespread violence and the reported rape of women and children, underscore the urgency and significance of studying women's social bonds in this context. The extreme nature of the challenges faced by the IDPs in Darfur offers a valuable lens through which to explore the dynamics of social bonds during adversity.

Five major camps were established in North Darfur State in 2004: Abu Shouk, Halloof, Zamzam, Fatta Barno, and Kassab. Our fieldwork focused on the Abu Shouk camp. This selection was based on several key factors. Firstly, Abu Shouk is the oldest established camp, offering a longer perspective on the situation. Secondly, it boasts the most diverse population among the camps, allowing for a broader range of experiences to be explored. Finally, Abu Shouk's accessibility facilitated our research endeavors. This strategic choice allows for a more in-depth and representative exploration of women's social bonds within the complex context of displacement and conflict in Darfur.

Quantitative Study Design

Designing the Questionnaire

A comprehensive self-reported questionnaire was carefully developed to systematically assess the intricate web of women's social bonds within the confines of the Abu-Shouk camp. This questionnaire was particularly crafted, from both the researcher's extensive ethnographic fieldwork conducted from August 2021 to November 2021 and a thorough review of relevant literature on social bonds and community dynamics. This approach ensures the questionnaire encapsulates dimensions of women's social bonds.

The questionnaire was strategically designed to target ever-married women aged 18 and above residing in the Abu-Shouk camp, with a particular focus on those who arrived in 2004 when the camp was closed. This demographic focus was chosen to capture a representative sample of women who have experienced the complexities of marital life, thereby providing a deeper understanding of the factors influencing social bonds within the camp.

Questionnaire Content

The questionnaires covered a wide range of topics ranging from women demographics, family bonds, trust and solidarity, resource exchange, women's autonomy, and participation in the association.

- *Demographic characteristics*: in this part, women were asked nine different questions. Questions were about their age, education level, material status, and occupations.

To indicate the women's age, two questions were posed: the year of birth and the current age. Both questions were posed to determine their actual age. To measure the level of education, a set of dummy variables was generated: Illiterate, literate, *khalwa*[2], primary, secondary, university degree, and postgraduate.

Likewise, a set of dummy variables were represented to measure women's current occupation. Eight categories were distinguished based on women's interviews in August 2021. The categories are housewife, government employee, private sector employee, worker, freelance (working at any jobs that she can find), trader (selling different products), farmer, and student. Similarly, there was a set of three dummy variables that indicated a woman's marital status: married, widowed, and divorced.

Since many women don't live with their husbands, an additional survey question was included. Respondents were asked whether their husbands lived with them (all dichotomous; 0 = no, 1 = yes). If the answer is yes, the woman will be asked about the reason and the length of his absence.

Women were also asked, "*In which year they come to the*. As we mentioned before, the Abu-Shouk camp was closed in 2004; and after that, there were no new IDPs. This question aimed to distinguish between the internally displaced women and other women who arrived as wives or with their families. Additionally, two measures of heterogeneity were incorporated in this section: the place of displacement and ethnicity.

- *Household characteristics:* this section contains nine questions about the individual in the household.
- *Trust, solidarity, and resource exchange*: These parts were developed according to a logical model proposed by Dudwick et.al (2006) and Milczarek et al., (2015). It consists of 37 items relating to various aspects of cognitive and social capital, including four about interpersonal relations, eight about community solidarity, 11 about trust, and 14 about reciprocity.
    I. <u>Solidarity instruments:</u> The assessment of social capital involved two sections. The first section is about personal relationships. Four statements were used to measure this part: "*Real friends are hard to find in the camp,*" "*Almost everyone inside the camp is polite and courteous to you,*" "*Everyone here tries to take advantage of you,*" and "*People around here show good judgment on you.*" The second section measures community solidarity through seven statements. These questions allow for an exploration of both personal and communal dimensions of social capital within the Abu-Shouk camp.
    II. <u>Trust instruments</u>: measure the level of trust. The study used four questions. The first question is the change in the levels of trust since women came to the camp. The second question is about the level of safety that the women feel inside the camp. In this section, women were asked if they trust different types of people such as closely related families, neighbors, people from the same or different ethnic groups, people from the same or different living conditions, and people from the same or other political groups[3] (Calvo et.al, 2020). The last question group is to whom you turn for help or assistance – your family, relatives, neighbors, religious organizations, community leaders, NGOs, and government institutions (Kuehnast & Dudwick, 2004).
    III. <u>Resource exchange</u>: The study used a resource exchange matrix to look at what goods and services are exchanged in specific networks and the objective of such exchanges (Kuehnast & Dudwick, 2004). Kuehnast and Dudwick's matrix offers a valuable tool to investigate social trust. The matrix addresses questions: "*What do you give, and to whom?*" and "*What do you receive, and from whom?*"
- **Women's autonomy:** The questionnaire comprehensively explored four dimensions of women's autonomy in decision-making. Participants were queried about their autonomy in women's health care, making major household purchase decisions, deciding about family money, and visiting their

family or friends. Each question had three responses. Additionally, the survey included a question assessing the extent of a woman's ability to make life-altering decisions, with five response options.
- ***Structural social capital (participation in an association):*** Participants were asked about their membership in various associations to measure structural social capital. Assessing participation in associations is crucial as it serves as a tangible indicator of social capital. Involvement in such groups reflects the extent to which individuals are connected within their community, fostering networks that contribute to shared resources, mutual support, and collaborative problem-solving.

Data Collection Process

To uphold the accuracy and reliability of the gathered data, the questionnaires were administered within the comfort of participants' homes, facilitated by a team of four trained data collectors carefully selected and prepared by the researcher. The training covered technical aspects of data collection and underscored the importance of cultural sensitivity, ensuring participants felt at ease throughout the survey. This commitment to cultural sensitivity, as emphasized by Dudwick et al. (2006), guided the crafting of survey questions and instruments, ensuring appropriateness and respect for diverse cultural contexts.

Moreover, the survey comprehensively addresses both structural and cognitive dimensions of social capital, incorporating assessments of norms and networks. This dual focus aims to provide an understanding of the collective potential for mutually beneficial action. Importantly, the survey aligns with local perceptions by incorporating activities that the community deems suitable for collective action, thereby capturing context-specific insights. Emphasis on simplicity, including minimal skips, straightforward language, and clear coding instructions, facilitates ease of integration and participant engagement. Ideally, the survey is implemented through random sampling within the community of interest, enhancing representativeness and yielding broader insights into social capital dynamics.

In ensuring high ethical standards and research rigor, the study took several measures, including obtaining an official letter from the University of Al-Fāshr, securing verbal approval from the head of the camp administration, obtaining full verbal consent from participants, implementing confidentiality protocols, and conducting prolonged fieldwork, among other considerations.

Sample Design

In establishing the sample size, a careful approach was adopted, considering the unique nature and demographics of the camp. Additionally, figure 2 was employed to conduct a spatial distribution analysis. The figure facilitated the segmentation of the camp into discernible sections: the Westside, characterized by eight squares and 11 blocks, and the Eastside, distinguished by 28 blocks and nine squares. Within each square, a configuration of 23 houses and two public bathrooms was observed.

Figure 2. Abu-Shouk camp aerial view

Considering this information, the calculated sample size was 407 women, with 88 houses on the Westside and 223 houses on the Eastside. To streamline the interview process, a random house was selected from each block and square, ensuring a representative distribution across the camp (e.g., Square One, Block One; Square One, Block Two; Square One, Block Three, and so forth). An observation during the ethnographic fieldwork detected similarities in responses among women from the same block and square, indicating shared locality, familial connections, or relational ties. This insight validated the chosen sampling method, affirming its representativeness.

To mitigate data collection errors and enhance the precision of confidence intervals, the initial sample size was increased by 10%, resulting in a total of 455 respondents (see Table 1).

Table 1. The number of participants based on location

location	Freq.	Percent
East camp	355	78.02%
West camp	100	21.98%
Total	455	100%

Before the commencement of the actual data collection, a pilot study was conducted to assess respondents' interaction with the survey. The pilot study revealed valuable insights:

- Difficulty Understanding the Questionnaire: Some women encountered challenges comprehending certain aspects of the questionnaire, prompting the need for adjustments to enhance clarity.

An In-Depth Analysis of Women's Social Capital in Abu-Shouk Camp

- Reluctance in Addressing Political and Trust Questions: Respondents exhibited reluctance in responding to questions pertaining to trust in political groups. This prompted a reevaluation of the questionnaire's sensitivity to cultural and contextual nuances.

Recognizing the inherent challenges in fieldwork, a proactive approach was adopted to address limitations encountered during data collection. A comprehensive risk and contingency plan were implemented to navigate unforeseen challenges, ensuring the reliability and validity of the study. While limitations emerged, the research team diligently sought optimal solutions, demonstrating a commitment to robust data collection methodologies.

THE OUTCOME OF THE SURVEY

Prior to analyzing data, the reliability of the collected data was carefully assessed using Cronbach's alpha, yielding a robust measure of interitem correlations (see Table 2). This widely recognized measure is employed to evaluate the internal consistency and reliability of a set of scale or test items (Chelsea Goforth, 2015).

Table 2. Reliability results

Section	Cronbach Alpha
Solidarity, Trust instruments, and Participation in association	0.82
Resource exchange	0.90
Women empowerment	0.71

Following the confirmation of data reliability, a comprehensive analysis was conducted utilizing descriptive statistics and cross-section analysis on Stata/MP 17.0.

Socio-Demographic Variables

A foundational step in data analysis involves presenting key information about variables in the researcher's dataset. This includes percentages, averages, and variances, all of which are presented in a clear and interpretable manner. Table 3 serves as a valuable resource, offering descriptive statistics for demographic characteristics variables concerning 455 women currently married, divorced, or widowed in the Abu-Shouk camp.

To facilitate a more streamlined presentation, certain variables, such as age and family size of women participants, were condensed into ranges. Noteworthy patterns emerged from the data, shedding light on key aspects of the demographic landscape within the Abu-Shouk camp:

Based on the data, it is notable that among housewives in the Abu-Shouk camp, 25% are illiterate, while 30% have attained primary education. Additionally, findings show that 32% of married women experience separation from their husbands, with 69% of these husbands working outside the camp and 14% being deserted. A significant portion, 26%, has been absent for more than three years.

Table 3. Summary statistics

Marital status (%)	
Married	*87*
Widowed	7
Divorced/separate	6
Age categories	
16- 24	24
25- 32	26
33-40	25
>40	25
Family size	
1 - 7	77
>=8	23
Education level	
Illiterate	19
Basic education	17
Primary	29
Secondary	21
University degree	13
Current occupation	
Housewife	70
A government employee	3
Private sector employee	0.66
Worker (Freelance & trader)	13
Farmer	8
Student	6
Other	0.44

The data also uncovers a diverse range of geographical origins among women in the camp, with the majority hailing from Jebel Si (33%), Tawila (22%), and Korma (20%). This distribution highlights the camp's significant ethnic diversity, as residents belong to 25 distinct ethnic groups. Predominant ethnicities include Fur (59.34%), Tanjur (15.16%), Zaghawa (9.45%), and Barti (3.08%).

The survey outcomes reveal a striking trend in the subjective well-being of women within the Abu-Shouk camp. A significant portion of respondents do not consider themselves happy. Notably, the level of happiness varies across different age groups, as depicted in Figure 3. How happy do you consider yourself to be? Women between the ages of 28-40 and 41-53 express lower levels of happiness compared to their counterparts aged 16-27 and those aged 54 and above. These sentiments are rooted in the perceived limitations of life within the camp, hindering women from realizing their aspirations and life goals.

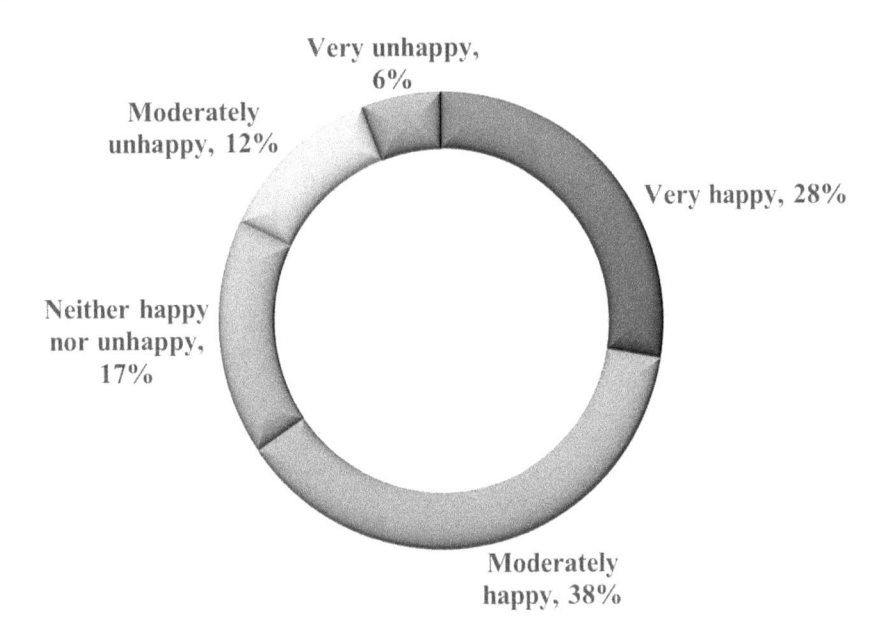

Figure 3. In general, how happy do you consider yourself to be

- Very unhappy, 6%
- Moderately unhappy, 12%
- Neither happy nor unhappy, 17%
- Moderately happy, 38%
- Very happy, 28%

Women's Autonomy

Women's empowerment, as defined by the UNFPA (1994) and Kabeer (2010), revolves around fostering women's self-worth, autonomy in decision-making, and the right to influence societal changes. These definitions underscore two critical aspects of women's empowerment: the ability to make decisions impacting their own lives and exerting significant influence at the household and societal levels.

In the Abu-Shouk camp, 52% of women assert their ability to change their lives, with the majority falling within the age range of 16 to 40. This affirmation aligns with the essence of empowerment, where individuals perceive agency in shaping their destinies.

To assess the impact on others' lives, household decision-making serves as a pivotal dimension. Kabeer emphasizes that empowerment entails deserving control over resources and decisions. Despite the belief in their capacity to effect personal change, the data detects a contrast: only 18% of women in the Abu-Shouk camp can unilaterally decide how family money is utilized (see Figure 4. Intra-household power and decision making). Furthermore, decisions regarding health status are seldom made independently, requiring involvement from others.

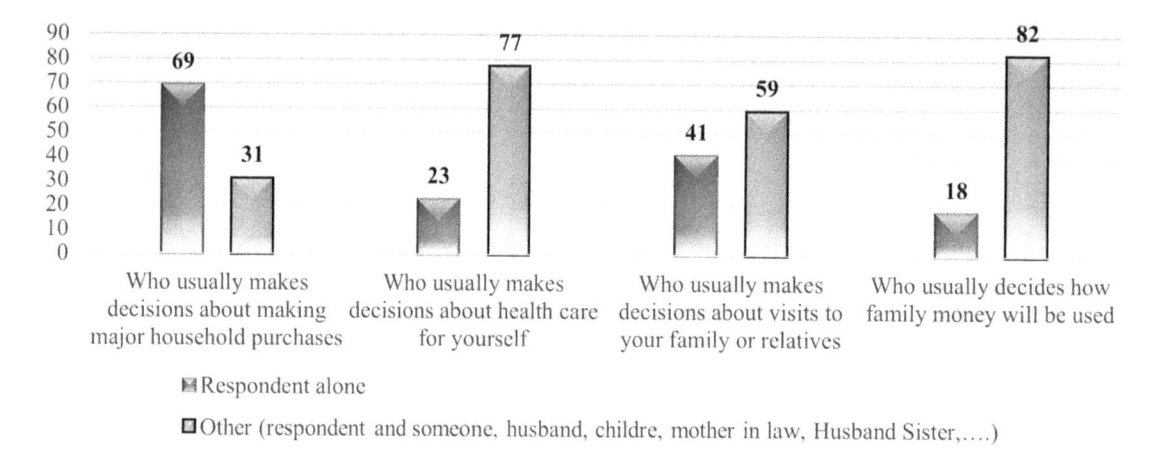

Figure 4. Intra-household power and decision-making

[Bar chart showing:
- Who usually makes decisions about making major household purchases: Respondent alone 69, Other 31
- Who usually makes decisions about health care for yourself: Respondent alone 23, Other 77
- Who usually makes decisions about visits to your family or relatives: Respondent alone 41, Other 59
- Who usually decides how family money will be used: Respondent alone 18, Other 82

Legend: ■ Respondent alone; □ Other (respondent and someone, husband, childre, mother in law, Husband Sister,....)]

Examining the distribution among total respondents, almost half (47.25%) of ever-married women decide how family money is used, either autonomously or jointly with their husbands or others. This proportion contrasts with higher percentages in other decision-making dominions: 63.52% for personal healthcare decisions, 76.65% for family visits, and 80% for major household purchases.

Cross-tabulation results underscore significant associations between socio-background characteristics and the four types of women's decision-making:

- *Age-Related Decision-Making:* Participation in health care decisions increases with age, from 62% among women aged 16-27 to 66% in middle-aged women (28-40 and 41-50) and decreases to 51% among women aged 54 and above. Similar age-related patterns are observed for main household purchases (28%-32%-36%-32%), money spent (10%-21%-25%-24%), and family and friend visits (40%-45%-41%-27%).
- *Occupation and Household Size Influence:* Women in paid employment exhibit greater decision-making influence. Similarly, those with smaller family sizes (1-7) actively participate in decision-making across all outcomes.

These findings illuminate the interplay of age, occupation, and family size in shaping women's decision-making dynamics within the Abu-Shouk camp, providing valuable insights into the multifaceted nature of empowerment in this context.

Community Bonds: Trust, Relations, and Resource Exchange

This section explores the intricate web of trust and solidarity at the community level within the Abu-Shouk camp. It offers a deep analysis of the social relations among women, shedding light on the communal bonds that shape daily life.

An In-Depth Analysis of Women's Social Capital in Abu-Shouk Camp

Trust and Solidarity: Navigating Community Dynamics

At the core of community dynamics within the Abu-Shouk camp lies the interplay of trust and solidarity among women. Trust, defined as reliance on the integrity and character of others, is a foundational element of community relationships. Solidarity, extending beyond trust, encapsulates a collective commitment to shared values and mutual support Durkheim (2014, [1893]). This section aims to unravel these vital elements, explaining their contributions to the resilience and cohesion of the Abu-Shouk community. The analysis of this section aims to explain individual, public, and occupation-related trust and women's solidarity, and then compare these dynamics based on the camp's geographical divisions (East and West).

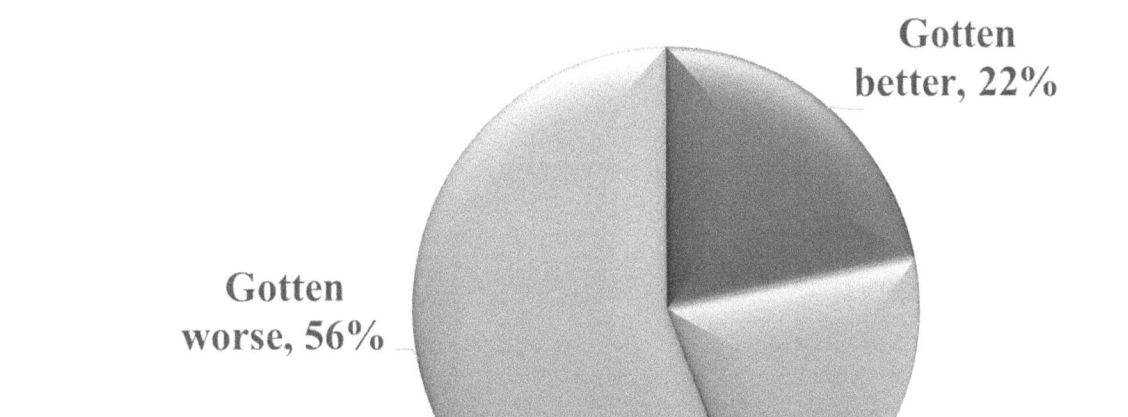

Figure 5. The change in trust levels within the camp since 2004

Figure 5. illustrates the change in trust levels within the camp since 2004, reflecting a belief among respondents that the level of trust has changed. This temporal shift is likely influenced by the economic and political landscape, as noted by Mohamed (2023). The dynamic nature of trust, responsive to economic fluctuations and political variations, has played a pivotal role in shaping the intricate fabric of relationships within the camp. As economic and political forces have induced shifts in alliances and affiliations, the contours of trust have adapted, showing the complex interplay of external influences on the internal dynamics of the community. Political divisions, in particular, have acted as a catalyst, segregating individuals into distinct groups and thereby influencing the ebb and flow of trust within the Abu-Shouk camp.

It is widely acknowledged that personal relationships are often idealized, with individuals holding distinct opinions on what constitutes a 'good person,' a 'good parent,' or a 'true friend.' While these idealized conceptions can foster judgment, real-life personal relations may deviate from these ideals, triggering diverse reactions. Notably, data uncovers a reality within the Abu-Shouk camp—where politeness and good judgment prevail (61%), yet a significant percentage of women find it challenging to establish genuine friendships (53%), and there's a perceived risk of others taking advantage (52%).

The examination in this section extends to community solidarity, unearthing revealing statistics (see Figure 6. Personal relations and community solidarity). A notable 58% express skepticism about trusting fellow camp residents, while 69% believe mutual trust is lacking in lending matters, and 46% emphasize the need to be alert against potential exploitation. The political dimension further influences community solidarity, with 60% asserting a lack of unity among camp residents when dealing with rule of law institutions.

The level of general trust is significantly diverse in terms of education level. The vast majority of women with basic education (primary, secondary, and university degrees) say that people in the camp cannot be trusted (65%, 68%, and 70%, respectively). On the other hand, the majority of the women with no education or informal education have agreed that people in the camp can be trusted (59% and 52%, respectively).

An In-Depth Analysis of Women's Social Capital in Abu-Shouk Camp

Figure 6. Personal relations and community solidarity

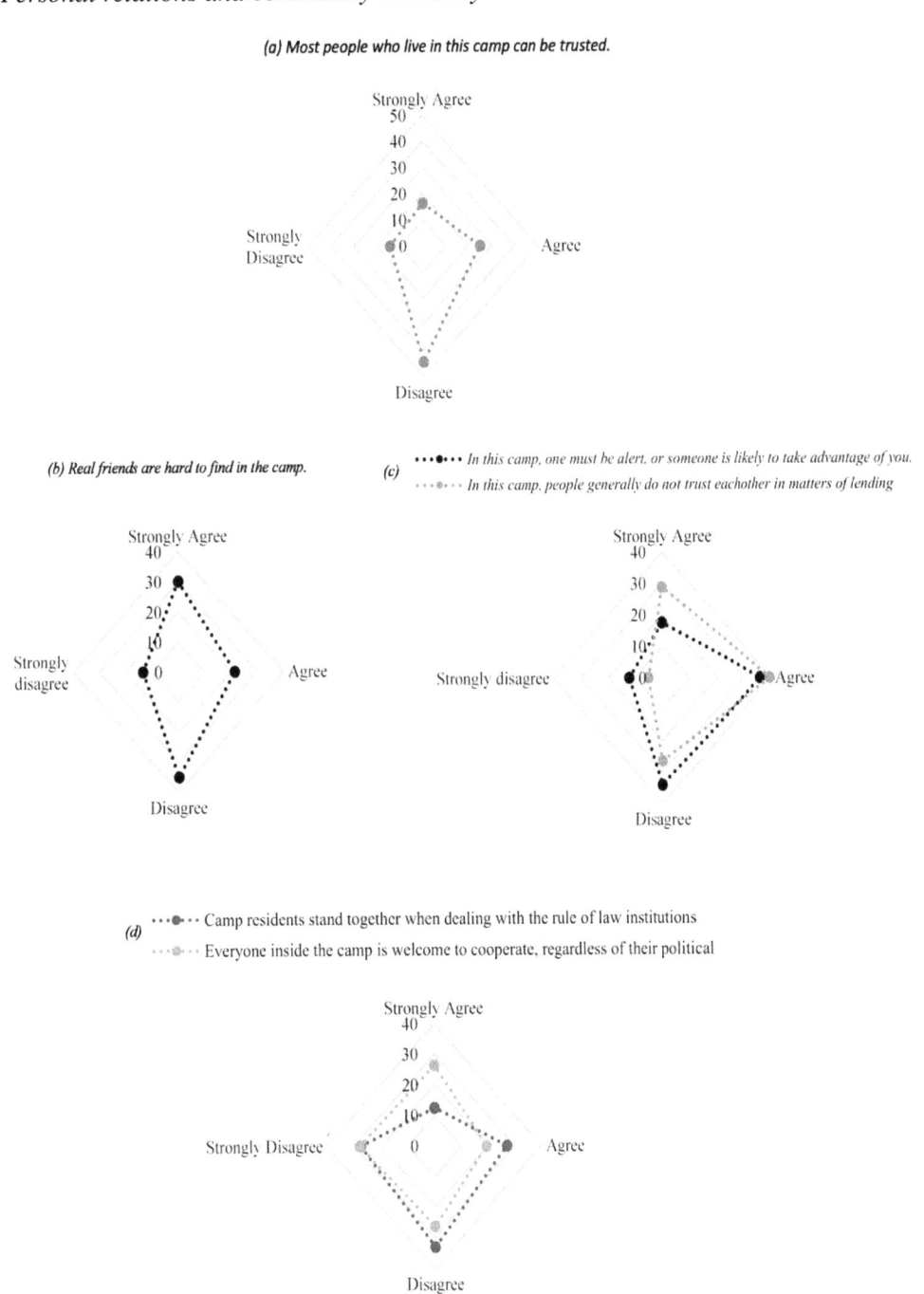

(a) Most people who live in this camp can be trusted.

(b) Real friends are hard to find in the camp.

(c) ••••• In this camp, one must be alert, or someone is likely to take advantage of you.
••••• In this camp, people generally do not trust eachother in matters of lending

(d) ••••• Camp residents stand together when dealing with the rule of law institutions
••••• Everyone inside the camp is welcome to cooperate, regardless of their political

Figure 7 explores the social trust and coping strategies employed by women in the Abu Shouk camp. The survey results reveal a strong sense of trust within close family circles, with 83% of women reporting complete trust towards their immediate relatives. This trust diminishes when considering broader social circles. Only 41% of women trust extended family members (relatives) and trust towards neighbors' dips even further to 36%. Interestingly, trust levels are relatively similar towards people from the same versus different ethnic and living conditions. However, political affiliation appears to be a significant dividing factor. A striking 63% of women reported distrusting others from the same political group, and this distrust intensifies further towards those from different political groups, with a staggering 70% expressing a lack of trust.

Figure 7. Women's general trust in both sides of the camp

East camp

- Strongly agree: 19.44
- Agree: 25.92
- Disagree: 38.31
- Strongly disagree: 16.34

West camp

- Strongly agree: 5
- Agree: 22
- Disagree: 66
- Strongly disagree: 7

While women exhibit a notable level of trust toward their relatives, an intriguing pattern emerges as they tend not to turn to them when dealing with social issues such as relationship challenges, neighborhood concerns, or economic hardships. Surprisingly, women often turn to their closely related family or neighbor in these situations, indicating a unique perspective on the concept of family within the Abu-Shouk camp.

The rationale behind this phenomenon becomes clearer when we examine the perspective that women hold regarding their neighbors. For these women, the definition of family transcends mere blood relations. Instead, family is perceived as a community of individuals who coexist within the same physical space, share a common religion, and collectively endure life's challenges (Mohamed, 2023). This more inclusive definition shapes their support networks, leading them to seek assistance from those who share their immediate living environment and common experiences.

Additionally, figure 7 sheds light on another intriguing aspect of women's coping strategies. The data illustrates that women in the camp never turn to community leaders when faced with social problems. The loss of trust in community leaders, exacerbated by incidents such as the loss of aid cards and perceptions of corruption, has contributed to a reluctance among women to seek guidance or support from these community leaders. This reluctance stems from a perceived bias in the community leaders' assistance, seemingly directed primarily towards family and friends. The findings underscore the importance of understanding the dynamics of trust and support networks within the camp's social fabric.

In the forthcoming section, the paper provides a comparative analysis, examining trust and solidarity levels between the East and West sides of the Abu-Shouk camp. The rationale behind this exploration is rooted in the characteristics of each side: the West, marked by remarkable homogeneity with a predominant Fur population (92%), and the East, distinguished by its diverse ethnic makeup. This comparative

An In-Depth Analysis of Women's Social Capital in Abu-Shouk Camp

lens aims to unravel the potential influence of ethnic diversity on the dynamics of trust among women within the camp.

By juxtaposing these two camp sections, the study seeks to answer pivotal questions: Does the high homogeneity of the West foster greater trust and solidarity? Conversely, does the ethnic diversity of the East introduce unique challenges to trust dynamics among women?

This analysis shed light on the interplay between ethnic composition and social cohesion within the Abu-Shouk camp, contributing to understanding the factors shaping trust and solidarity among women in this distinctive community.

General Trust and Solidarity Based on the Location of the Camp

In exploring the fabric of trust within the Abu-Shouk camp, a distinct pattern emerges when comparing the East and West sides. Notably, over half of the women on the Eastside (55%) believe that most people who live in this camp cannot be trusted at all. Simultaneously, their Westside counterparts exhibit a similar cautiousness, with 73% of respondents admitting a hesitancy to place trust in others.

This interesting parallel suggests an interplay of factors influencing trust dynamics within the camp. The diverse ethnic composition on the Eastside may introduce complexities in interpersonal relations, potentially impacting trust formation. In contrast, the Westside, characterized by a higher degree of homogeneity with the dominance of the Fur ethnic group, might foster a more cohesive social fabric that influences trust dynamics positively.

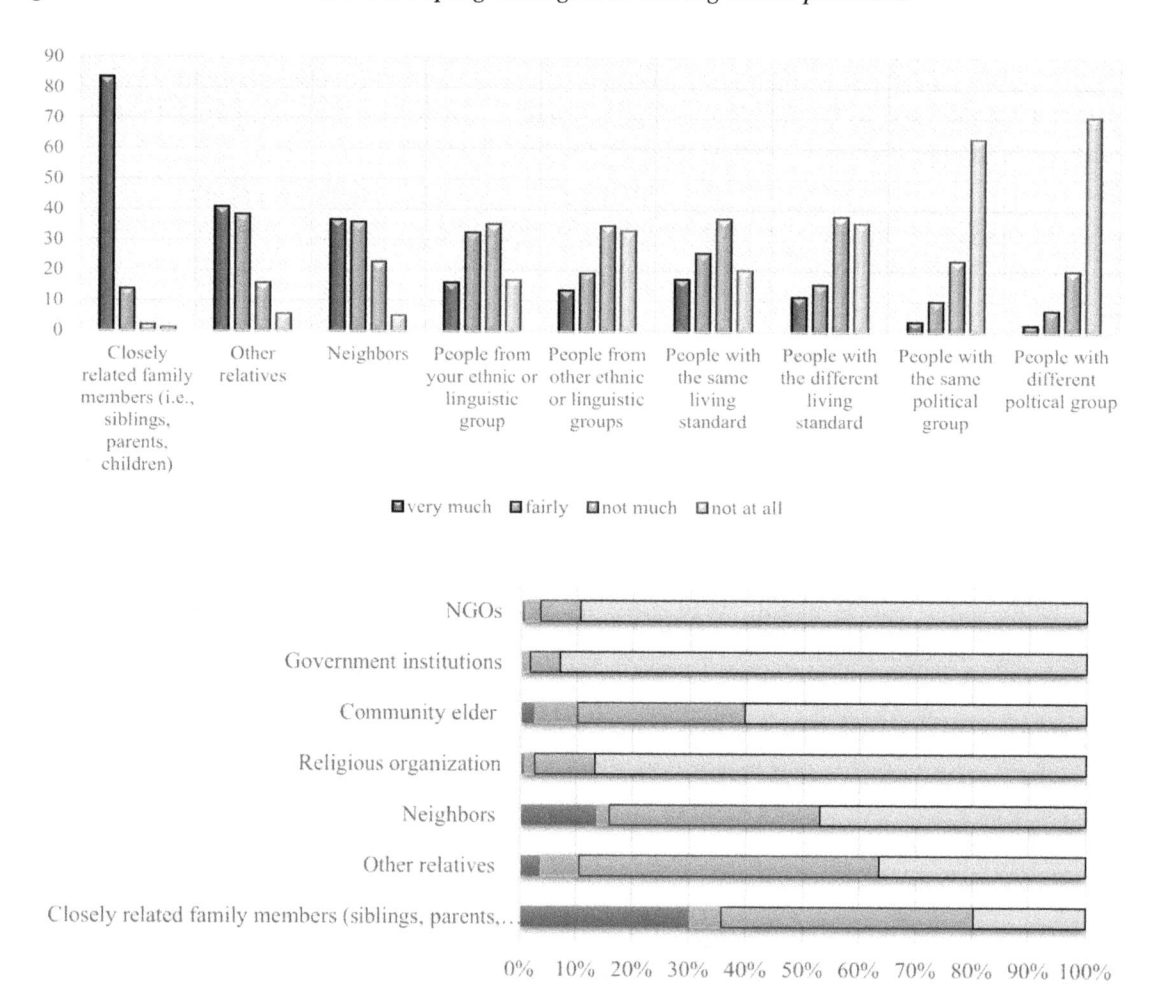

Figure 8. Women's social trust and coping strategies in solving social problems

Examining deeper the intricacies of trust declarations, a nuanced narrative unfolds. Women on the Eastside, despite their initial skepticism, exhibit a more frequent inclination to declare trust in other people compared to their Westside peers (see Figure 8. Women general trust of the East and the West side of the camp). This suggests a complex interplay of trust dynamics, where the Eastside, despite harboring reservations, engages more actively in verbalizing trust compared to the seemingly more cautious Westside residents. Figures 9. Shows interpersonal relations and community solidarity. The figure provides a lens into the intricate tapestry of interpersonal relationships, exposing the divergent trust perceptions between the East and West sides of the Abu-Shouk camp.

On the Eastside, where the majority (57%) of women find it challenging to find genuine friendships within the camp, a paradoxical landscape emerges. While a substantial 74% acknowledge the prevalence of politeness among residents, and 68% attest to the community's collective good judgment, a notable 58% harbor a belief that everyone within the camp seeks to take advantage of them. These findings

An In-Depth Analysis of Women's Social Capital in Abu-Shouk Camp

unveil a complex blend of positive and skeptical sentiments, reflecting the nature of trust dynamics among Eastside women.

Contrastingly, the Westside paints a different portrait. A mere 27% believe that everyone within the camp aims to take advantage, and only 38% perceive a widespread display of good judgment among residents. Yet, a striking 88% of Westside women assert that genuine friendships are easily forged within the camp, indicating a contrasting perception of social bonds.

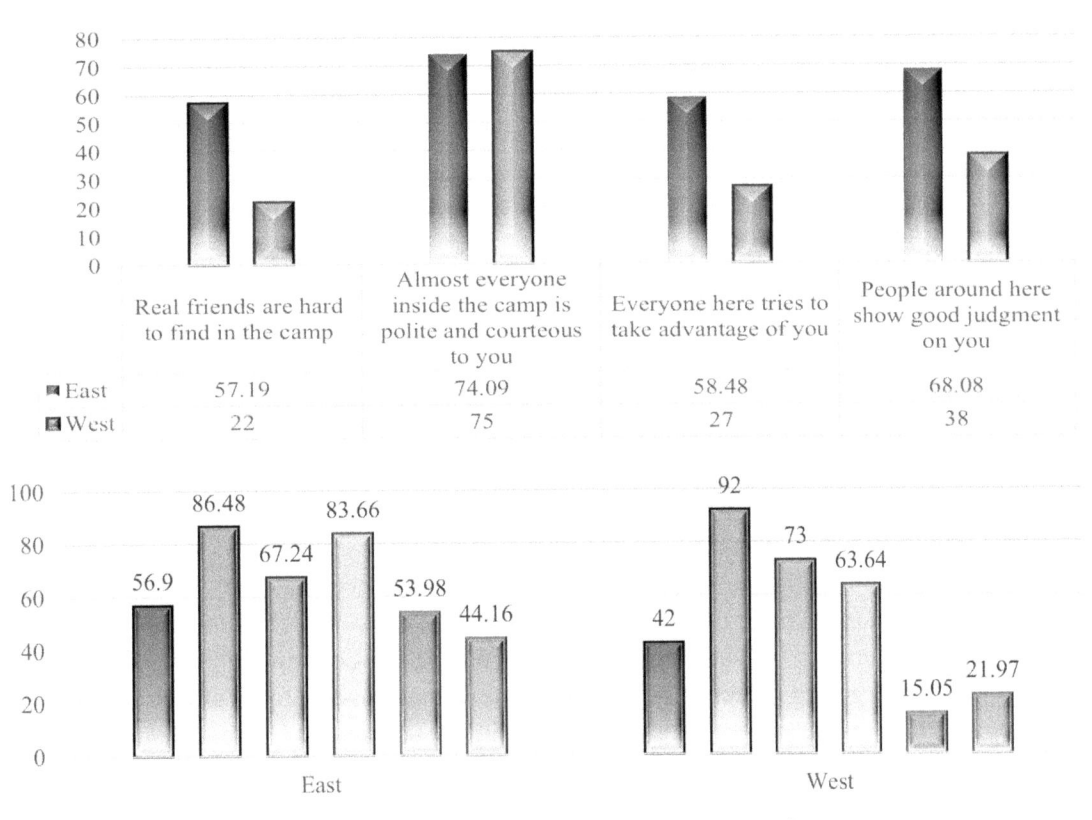

Figure 9. Interpersonal relations and community solidarity

	Real friends are hard to find in the camp	Almost everyone inside the camp is polite and courteous to you	Everyone here tries to take advantage of you	People around here show good judgment on you
East	57.19	74.09	58.48	68.08
West	22	75	27	38

East values: 56.9, 86.48, 67.24, 83.66, 53.98, 44.16
West values: 42, 92, 73, 63.64, 15.05, 21.97

- In this camp, one must be alert, or someone is likely to take advantage of you.
- Most people in this camp are willing to help if you need it.
- In this camp, people generally do not trust each other in matters of lending and borrowing money
- Everyone is welcome to collaborate with anyone regardless of their religious or ethnic background
- Everyone inside the camp is welcome to cooperate, regardless of their political background
- Camp residents stand together when dealing with the rule of law institutions

As we set our focus on community solidarity, a shared perspective emerges on both the East and West sides of the Abu-Shouk camp. Women from both sides unanimously affirm a collective willingness to assist others when asked for help, fostering an atmosphere of shared support within the community. Additionally, there is a resounding consensus that collaboration is open to everyone, transcending religious or ethnic backgrounds, as depicted in Figure 9.

However, amidst this shared sense of solidarity, a notable divergence surfaces when it comes to trust in financial matters. Women on both sides acknowledge a prevailing lack of trust among community members in lending and borrowing money. This insight suggests that, despite the communal spirit, financial transactions carry an undercurrent of skepticism and caution.

The impact of the political dimension on community dynamics becomes more pronounced on the Westside. A substantial majority of Westside women show a perceived lack of unity among camp residents when dealing with rule-of-law institutions. Furthermore, not everyone is considered welcome to cooperate in community endeavors, as illustrated in Figure 9.

Crucially, the data uncovers a compelling narrative about the influence of ethnic diversity on social trust among women. Contrary to expectations, women on the Westside, characterized by higher homogeneity, exhibit stronger social bonds than their counterparts on the Eastside. This revelation prompts a deeper exploration into the intricate interplay of ethnic diversity and community cohesion, showing the factors that contribute to the divergent trust dynamics within the Abu-Shouk camp.

Resource Exchange: The Gift Giving

Although there are almost no psychological studies on gift-giving, the related disciplines of social psychology and sociology present some interesting research findings. In general, reciprocity is assumed to be the rule in gift-giving, but this rule does not apply to specific gifts, like blood or organ donation. If at all, in these cases, reciprocity is experienced in a very abstract and indirect way. Reciprocity is, as if it were, delayed: if in the future, we could come to need organs or blood ourselves, we hope that other people will be as willing to give as we were (Komter, 2005).

This study used the respondents' definition of what they experience as gifts. The study is mainly interested in the sociological patterns of gift-giving and in the psychological motives underlying these patterns, and not primarily in the subjective definitions of "gifts" as opposed to "non-gifts," the study distinguished different giving objects, material and nonmaterial: money, food, clothes, presents, care/help, and stay (letting people stay in one's house). Despite the differences between them, practices like a ritual or spontaneous gift-giving, offering help/care, or staying have one vital element in common: *all these types of gifts are imbued by the subjective experience of being given out of a free well* (Komter, 2005. p.39). They are not being dictated by any economic rule like barter or a fair exchange. The data show that more than three-quarters of the women appeared to have given some of these gifts, and more than half of the women report having received one or more of these gifts from others (see Table 4. Resource exchange).

An In-Depth Analysis of Women's Social Capital in Abu-Shouk Camp

Table 4. Resource exchange

	Do you give........ people who have THE same as you			
	give		receive	
	Yes	No	Yes	No
Money	**61.5**	**38.5**	**62.97**	**37.03**
Food	90.14	9.86	79.91	20.09
Stay	58.45	41.55	56.64	43.36
Cloth	66.9	33.1	61.68	38.32
Help/care	86.38	13.62	82.2	17.8
Present	77.23	22.77	78.64	21.36

Table 4 shows a strong relationship between giving and receiving. Those who gave more were also the greatest recipients. Doing well has its reward. The table also shows that women received more than they gave. Suppose that this result reflects a factual truth and not some perceptual bias. In that case, the most plausible explanation is that an important category of gift recipients, men, and youth, is not included in the sample. But other interpretations are possible as well, for instance, the role of memory. Perhaps women have a greater consciousness of what other people give them than what they give to others.

Furthermore, there could be a perceptional bias: because women want to leave a great impression of themselves to the interviewer, one is inclined to exaggerate one's liberality. Contrariwise, women's discontent about what they have received from others leads to underestimating it. Possibly they make conscious or unconscious comparisons between other people's resources and their own, which can explain their experience of discontent. In other words, some types of giving are not recognized as such by their recipients; for instance, some forms of received care may be overlooked because they are so "normal." A final classification can be what Pahl has called *"the general concern of people not to appear too dependent on others"* (1984, p 250). He found that people claim to do more for others than they receive. Thus, this corresponds with our results concerning the experienced imbalance between receiving and giving.

Participation in Association

One of the most outstanding elements of the crisis is people's renewed interest in associations. The survey shows that 80% of the surveyed women reported taking part in associations. The primary goal of these regroupings is to create social solidarity between women's group members. Moreover, they are based on collaboration and tightening of the bonds among people sharing the same culture and sometimes the same political vision (Keho, 2009).

Table 5. Women's participation in different associations

Participation in association	Yes	No
At least one association	**79.55**	**20.45**
Neighborhood/ Village committee	62.61	37.39
The religious or spiritual group	47.03	52.97
Cultural group or association	30.97	69.03
Finance, credit, or savings group	28.25	71.75
Education Group	31.73	68.27
NGO or civic group	13.79	31.73
Political group or movement	3.53	96.47

Table 5 paints an interesting picture of who is and is not likely to participate in associations. As this table demonstrates, most women (62.61%) participate in neighborhood/village committees, while fewer participate in political groups or movements (3.53%).

Figure 10. Women's participation rate in camp associations (East vs. West)

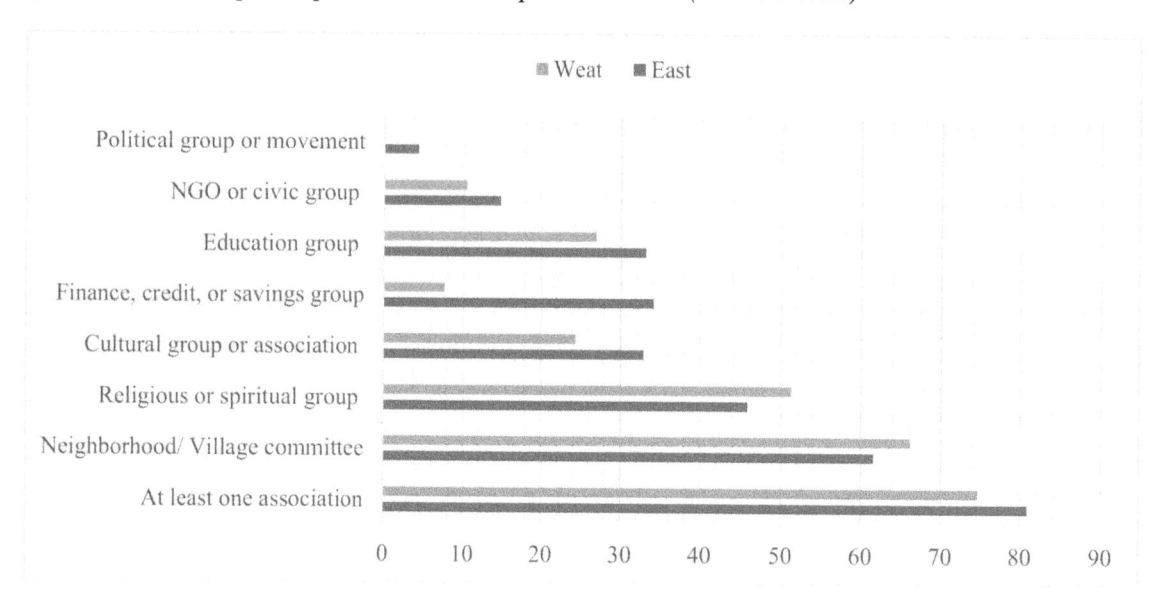

Comparison based on the women's location highlights some significant differences. Women in the Eastside of the camp are more likely to participate in associations. A lower level of social involvement is noted among women from the west side of the camp (see Figure 10. Women's participation in associations based on the camp location).

An In-Depth Analysis of Women's Social Capital in Abu-Shouk Camp

SOCIAL CAPITAL DYNAMICS: ASSESSING SOLIDARITY AND COHESION IN ABU-SHOUK CAMP

The concept of social capital, encompassing bonding, bridging, and linking elements, plays a crucial role in shaping relationships within a society. However, the mere existence of social capital does not guarantee inclusive relations. Various factors such as wealth inequality, ethnic tensions, and weak civic engagement can contribute to a lack of social cohesion, impacting both horizontal (bonding and bridging) and vertical (linking) social capital.

Figure 11. The level of women's social cohesion inside the camp

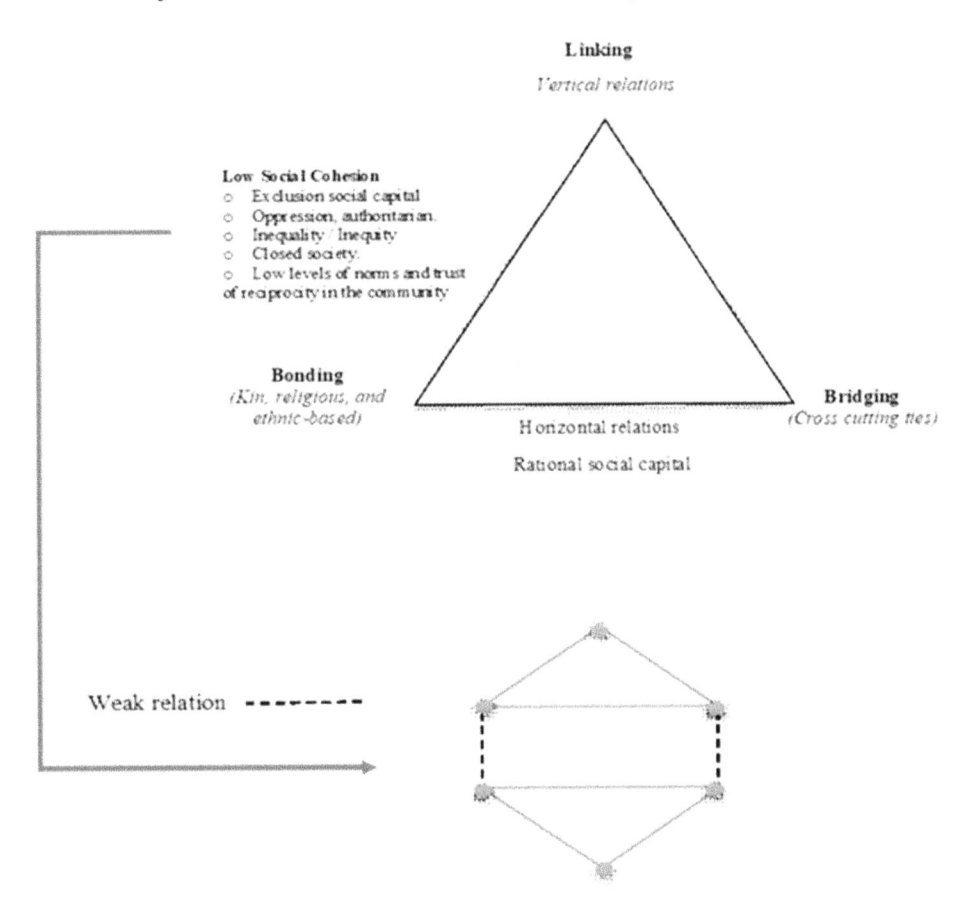

Our findings, supported by Mohamed's (2023) research and the quantitative data, suggest that women in Abu Shouk Camp primarily rely on collaboration within their close social support groups. This limited interaction with those outside their immediate circles is reflected in the lower social cohesion evident within the camp, as shown in Figure 11. The figure itself illustrates robust solidarity within these social support groups, evidenced by the high rates of collaboration reported in the survey. However, the survey data also reveals a decline in trust levels as social circles expand beyond close family, suggesting weaker connections with individuals outside this close-knit network.

Within the social support group, women exhibit high cohesion and structural unity. Members share strong, enduring, and direct relationships, indicating a high level of connectivity and unity. This finding emphasizes the importance of understanding not only the presence of social capital but also its specific manifestations and impact on social cohesion within the camp.

CONCLUSION

This study aims to offer a comprehensive understanding of the social bonds among women and within their communities in the Abu-Shouk camp, an internally displaced person camp in Darfur, Western Sudan. Among these women, the study explores the intricate dynamics of social relationships shaped by the Darfur conflict. By exploring the role of social capital in influencing these relationships, we aim to understand how social capital shapes the experiences of these women within the camp. In doing so, the study employed a carefully crafted research design, utilizing surveys conducted by trained data collectors. The questionnaire, thoughtfully developed, assessed various aspects of women's lives, including demographics, trust, solidarity, resource exchange, women's empowerment, and participation in associations. The data collection process involved engaging ever-married women aged 18 and above within the Abu-Shouk camp, with the surveys conducted in April 2021.

Analysis of the data shows that trust is a fundamental element of social relationships within the camp, alongside established networks and social norms. This emphasis on trust is not surprising, as it demonstrably influences the cohesion of groups, families, and communities. Stronger social bonds, built on a foundation of trust, can contribute to enhanced socio-economic development by facilitating cooperation and resource sharing.

The survey further uncovers those women in the camp exhibit caution in relationships, possibly stemming from the high level of diversity within. Specific barriers to trust were observed, potentially impacting the formation of social bonds. Interestingly, there is no significant difference between women on both sides of the camp regarding the "radius of trust," aligning with Fukuyama's findings that greater trust is often confined to family circles.

Educational and age disparities surfaced in the data, influencing gift-giving behaviors. Highly educated and younger women tend to give more, possibly linked to greater financial resources and evolving relational patterns. Additionally, the study sheds light on women's participation in household decision-making, emphasizing the need for intervention programs aligned with Sustainable Development Goals (SDGs 5). Older and younger women, with the least decision-making power, may benefit from involvement in decent employment and education, reducing dependency and promoting gender equality.

The Sustainable Development Goals (SDGs 5) emphasize increasing financial resources to accelerate women and girls' equal benefits and empowerment. Various intervention programs exist to enhance women's household position in the Abu-Shouk camp, yet their situation still appears bleak. Older and younger women have the least decision-making power, which suggests involving them in decent employment and education to lessen their dependency on their family members and husbands. Employment and education have always empowered women and positively affected decision-making, including reducing the inequalities among men and women. Attention must be given to those women who do not attend school through non-formal education.

In conclusion, this study significantly enhances our comprehension of the intricacies within the Abu-Shouk camp, offering valuable insights into the lives of women grappling with conflict and displacement.

An In-Depth Analysis of Women's Social Capital in Abu-Shouk Camp

It emphasizes the critical roles of trust, social bonds, and targeted interventions as crucial elements for empowering women and fostering equitable decision-making within this challenging context. In closing, this study contributes meaningfully to the scholarly discourse on conflict, displacement, and social dynamics. By illuminating the resilience of women and the vital role of their social bonds in the face of adversity, the research offers valuable insights into the complex interaction between these factors within an internally displaced persons camp setting.

REFERENCES

Abdul-Hakim, R., Ismail, R., & Abdul-Razak, N. A. (2010). The relationship between social capital and quality of life among rural households in Terengganu, Malaysia. *OIDA International Journal of Sustainable Development*, *1*(05), 99–106.

Akala, B. M. (2024). Gender and the conflict in South Sudan. In N. Alusala, E. A. Liaga, & M. R. Rupiya (Eds.), *Conflict Management and Resolution in South Sudan* (pp. 133–152). Routledge., doi:10.4324/9781003410249

Baker, W. E. (1990). Market networks and corporate behavior. *American Journal of Sociology*, *96*(3), 589–625. doi:10.1086/229573

Bourdieu, P. (1986). The Forms of Capital. In J. Richardson (Ed.), *Handbook of theory and research for the sociology of education* (pp. 241–258). Greenwood.

Bourdieu, P. (2018). The forms of capital. In *The sociology of economic life* (pp. 78–92). Routledge. doi:10.4324/9780429494338-6

Brouder, A., & Sweetman, C. (2015). Introduction: Working on gender issues in urban areas. *Gender and Development*, *23*(1), 1–12. doi:10.1080/13552074.2015.1026642

Coleman, J. (1986). *Individual Interests and Collective Action*. Cambridge University Press.

Coleman, J. S., & Fararo, Th. (1992). *Rational Choice Theory: Advocacy and Critique*. Sage.

Dasgupta, P., & Serageldin, I. (Eds.). (2000). *Social capital: a multifaceted perspective*. World Bank Publications.

De Beer, P., Berg, M., Koster, F., & Lepianka, D. (2017). Towards an interdisciplinary theory of solidarity. In P. de Beer & F. Koster (Eds.), *Ethnic Diversity and Solidarity: A Study of their Complex Relationship* (pp. 13–42). Cambridge Scholars Publishing.

De La Puente, D.De La Puente. (2011). Women's leadership in camps for internally displaced people in Darfur, western Sudan. *Community Development Journal: An International Forum*, *46*(3), 365–377. doi:10.1093/cdj/bsr036

Dudwick, N., Kuehnast, K., Jones, V. N., & Woolcock, M. (2006). Analyzing social capital in context. *A guide to using qualitative methods and data*, 1-46.

Durkheim, E. (1995). *[1915]. The elementary forms of the religious life*. Free Press.

Durkheim, E. (2014). *[1893]. The division of labor in society*. Free Press.

Esuruku, R. S. (2011). Beyond masculinity: Gender, conflict and post-conflict reconstruction in Northern Uganda. *Journal of Science and Sustainable Development, 4*(1), 25–40. doi:10.4314/jssd.v4i1.3

Etang Ndip, A. (2020). *Poverty & Equity Brief*. World Bank., https://databankfiles.worldbank.org/public/ddpext_download/poverty/33EF03BB-9722-4AE2-ABC7-AA2972D68AFE/Global_POVEQ_SSA.pdf

Fukuyama, F. (1995). Social Capital and the Global Economy. *Foreign Affairs, 74*(5), 89-103.

Gouldner, A. (1960). The Norm of Reciprocity: A Preliminary Statement. *American Sociological Review, 25*(2), 161–178. doi:10.2307/2092623

Ibreck, R. (2023). Protecting Women from Violence in the United Nations Protection of Civilians Sites, South Sudan? *Journal of Intervention and Statebuilding, 18*(1), 61–80. doi:10.1080/17502977.2023.2215604

Kabeer, N. (1999). Resources, agency, achievements: Reflections on the measurement of women's empowerment. *Development and Change, 30*(3), 435–464. doi:10.1111/1467-7660.00125

Kabeer, N. (2005). Gender equality and women's empowerment: A critical analysis of the third millennium development goal 1. *Gender and Development, 13*(1), 13–24. doi:10.1080/13552070512331332273

Kabeer, N. (2010). Women's empowerment, development interventions and the management of information flows. *ids. Bulletin, 41*(6), 105–113.

Karam, A. (2010). Women in War and Peacebuilding: The Roads Traversed the Challenges Ahead. *International Feminist Journal of Politics, 3*(1), 2–25. doi:10.1080/14616740010019820

Keho, Y. (2009). Social Capital in Situations of Conflict: A Case Study from Côte d'Ivoire (Pp. 158-180). *African Research Review, 3*(3), 158–180. doi:10.4314/afrrev.v3i3.47522

Khadka, M. (2017). *Darfur crisis: analyzing the issues of internally displaced persons (IDPs) in Darfur* [Doctoral dissertation].

Komter, A. E. (2005). *Social solidarity and the gift*. Cambridge University Press.

Kuehnast, K. R., & Dudwick, N. (2004). Better a hundred friends than a hundred rubles?: social networks in transition--the Kyrgyz Republic, 41181(4). World Bank Publications.

Loury, G. C. (1987). Why should we care about group inequality? *Social Philosophy & Policy, 5*(1), 249–271. doi:10.1017/S0265052500001345

Mansab, M. (2023). Nurturing Sustainable Peace: Unveiling the Integral Role of Women in Rwanda's Peacebuilding Endeavors. *NUST Journal of International Peace and Stability, 6*(2), 31–45. doi:10.37540/njips.v6i2.150

Mohamed, M. (2023). Solidarity in Time of Armed Conflict. Women's Patterns of Solidarity in Internally Displaced Person (IDP) Camps in Darfur, Western Sudan. *The Journal of Social Encounters, 7*(2), 5–23.

Murithi, T. (2006). African approaches to building peace and social solidarity. *African Journal on Conflict Resolution, 6*(2), 9–33.

Norris, P. (2002). *Democratic phoenix: Reinventing political activism*. Cambridge University Pres. doi:10.1017/CBO9780511610073

O'Fahey, R. S. (2008). *The Darfur sultanate: A history*. Hurst.

Pahl, R. E. (1984). *Divisions of Labour*. Basil Blackwell.

Portes, A. (1998). Social capital: Its origins and applications in modern sociology. *Annual Review of Sociology*, *24*(1), 1–24. doi:10.1146/annurev.soc.24.1.1

Putnam, R. D. (2000). Bowling alone: America's declining social capital. In Culture and politics (pp. 223-234). Palgrave Macmillan.

Putnam, R. D. (2007). E pluribus unum: Diversity and community in the twenty-first century the 2006 Johan Skytte Prize Lecture. *Scandinavian Political Studies*, *30*(2), 137–174. doi:10.1111/j.1467-9477.2007.00176.x

Quach, T. (2004). *The crisis in Darfur: an analysis of its origins and storylines* [Doctoral dissertation', Virginia Polytechnic Institute and State University].

Rabele, L. (2024). Women, mediation, and leadership in South Sudan. In N. Alusala, E. A. Liaga, & M. R. Rupiya (Eds.), *Conflict Management and Resolution in South Sudan* (pp. 153–162). Routledge., doi:10.4324/9781003410249

Rao, T. S. (2023, June). Crisis as displacement and opportunity: Reflections on the way South Sudanese women cope with war in refugee camps. In *International Academy of Practical Theology. Conference Series* (Vol. 3).

Sandefur, R. L., & Laumann, E. O. (1998). A paradigm for social capital. *Rationality and Society*, *10*(4), 481–501. doi:10.1177/104346398010004005

Sanginga, P. C., Kamugisha, R. N., & Martin, A. M. (2007). The dynamics of social capital and conflict management in multiple resource regimes: A case of the southwestern highlands of Uganda. *Ecology and Society*, *12*(1), 6. doi:10.5751/ES-01847-120106

Suryanti, D., Selly, M., Muttaqin, M. Z., & Makmun, S. (2023). Unfolding the Landscape of Conflict. *Journal of Southeast Asian Human Rights*, *7*(1), 21–21. doi:10.19184/jseahr.v7i1.30517

Sztompka, P. (2007). Trust in science: Robert K. Merton's inspirations. *Journal of Classical Sociology*, *7*(2), 211–220. doi:10.1177/1468795X07078038

UN Office of the High Commissioner for Human Rights (OHCHR), & the African Union-UN Hybrid Operation in Darfur (UNAMID). (2016). *The Human Rights Situation of Internally Displaced Persons in Darfur 2014 - 2016 - Sudan*. ReliefWeb. https://reliefweb.int/report/sudan/human-rights-situation-internally-displaced-persons-darfur-2014-2016

United Nations Population Fund (UNFPA). (2015). *Issue 7: Women Empowerment*. Unfpa.org. https://www.unfpa.org/resources/issue-7-women-empowerment

ENDNOTES

[1] Refer to people from Darfur Region.
[2] Traditional Sudanese school (study Quran, Arabic and Islamic jurisprudence).
[3] The living condition and the political group had been added to the questionnaire based on the results from then second phase of the data collection.

Chapter 8
Empowering Moroccan Women Through Social Entrepreneurship:
An Inclusive Approach

Malika Haoucha
https://orcid.org/0000-0003-1077-204X
University Hassan II of Casablanca, Morocco

Fadila Jehhad
University Hassan II of Casablanca, Morocco

ABSTRACT

This chapter explores how social entrepreneurship empowers women in Morocco through an inclusive approach towards disabled women by advancing their economic, social, and political empowerment. The chapter moves progressively by providing a historical context of women's status in Morocco, conceptual frameworks, and impact assessments, with a view to depicting the significant role of social entrepreneurship in driving women empowerment, with a special focus on including women with disabilities. The chapter underscores the importance of collaborative efforts and supportive policies in fostering an enabling environment for sustainable change. It focuses on the significant impact of social entrepreneurship on women's empowerment and calls for continued support and investment in women-led initiatives to create a more inclusive, equitable, and empowered future.

DOI: 10.4018/979-8-3693-2806-4.ch008

INTRODUCTION

Social entrepreneurship (SE) has emerged as a powerful tool for promoting women's empowerment and addressing social and economic challenges. Women empowerment through social entrepreneurship involves creating and supporting social enterprises that prioritize women's rights and economic development. These enterprises provide opportunities for women as customers, employees, and business owners, thereby increasing their agency, trust, and self-confidence.

Women empowerment through social entrepreneurship has a wide range of social and economic benefits, including but not limited to promoting gender equality, addressing social and environmental challenges, and driving economic growth. Social enterprises often aim to address social and environmental challenges, such as poverty, inequality, and environmental degradation, and women's empowerment initiatives can help to address these challenges in a more targeted and effective way.

Women entrepreneurs face challenges such as bias and discrimination, which reflect gender stereotypes that are common in the larger economy. To overcome these challenges and advance women empowerment, a supportive ecosystem with cooperation, partnerships, and inclusive policies is necessary.

In this chapter, we will explore how Moroccan women, namely those with disabilities are empowered through social entrepreneurship by looking into their economic empowerment, including income generation, financial inclusion, and access to resources. We will also discuss the challenges women entrepreneurs face and show that only by providing support and resources to women entrepreneurs, could an inclusive and equitable society be created.

HISTORICAL CONTEXT OF WOMEN'S STATUS IN MOROCCO

Historical Overview of Women's Roles and Rights in the Moroccan Society

In Morocco, women's roles and rights evolved since the country's independence from French rule in 1956. They have progressively moved from traditional occupations to an active participation in different aspects of society (Zirari, 2021).

The first demand made for equal rights for Moroccan women was fundamentally centered on reconstructing personal status regulations and family laws. In 1958, women's legal statement was officially formalized in the family structure through the passage of the personal status code in the family code. It is important to know that the view of gender role at this time was still hierarchical. Up to the year 2000, gender equality issues were still being addressed (Naciri,1998).

In Morocco, women's rights were heavily influenced by multiple factors in the socio-demographic field such as urbanization, access to education, increase in the average age of marriage, which led to a transformation in the economic, political and social landscape of the country requiring the need of granting equal gender rights for the sake of development (Manal, 2020).

Struggling to advocate for women's rights in Morocco is an inevitable part of the journey, hence the creation of women's associations such as the Democratic Association of Women in Morocco and the Union of Feminine Action, which played an essential role in promoting gender equality and opposing to biased practices. Women activists managed to make a pronounced effect in multiple fields including but not limited to politics, development and advocating against violence targeting women. (Elliot,2014)

The establishment of legal forms such as the 2004 family code enhances Moroccan women's rights by raising the minimum age for marriage and restricting polygamy. However, women in Morocco are still discriminated when it comes to accessing education, employment especially leadership roles which reflects the continuing struggle to achieve gender equality.

Legal and Policy Frameworks Related to Gender Equality

The Moroccan legal framework is known for the establishment of multiple reforms aiming to promote gender equality and women's rights.

The revision of the Personal Status Code (Mudawana) made in 2004 is considered one of the most impactful legal actions towards defending women's rights due to the expansion of its impact to areas such as children guardianship, child custody, and filing for divorce which empower women to make decisions to their own benefit without being restricted and stripped from their entitlements. Moreover, the 2011 constitutional revision focused on gender parity and ordered government-mandated organizations to advance gender equality by encouraging active involvement in all aspects of political, economic, social, and cultural spheres (world bank, 2015)

Gender equality can also be seen as a derivative of key laws in Morocco, mainly the revised 2003 labor code and law on Nationality of 2008. In 2009, Women's political representation was successfully increased by establishing the concept of a quota system in local elections. Additionally, in 2011 the country removed the restrictions and limitation it had previously set upon the implementation of the Convention on the Elimination of All Forms of Discrimination against Women (CEDAW), which reflects the Strengthened devotion to the principals of the convention. (Manal, 2020)

Regardless of the progress in the legal sphere, the effective application of gender equality laws in Morocco remains a challenge as women are still facing hindrances in accessing core necessities such as education and economic assets, limiting their economic opportunities. The need to furthermore work on the enforcement of existing laws is the employment disparities caused by gender, women are largely working in Slow-growth industries and are struggling with gender pay disparities. (UN,2020)

Challenges Faced by Women in Accessing Education, Employment, and Leadership Positions

Moroccan women confront major barriers when it comes to accessing education, employment, and leadership positions.

Education

When it comes to academic performance, research have found that women outperform men however they have a hard time transitioning from their educational success to employment. (Mouline,2022) (Canuto,2023). Even though women's access to education increased, their inclusion in the labor force is limited. This is heavily showcased in the high paying jobs of the service sector with only 8.1% of working women employed in the service sector (Canuto, 2023) (Bargain and Bue, 2021).

Employment

As previously stated, women hold occupations in low productivity sectors with low income which leads to gender disparities in the employment sectors mostly in the urban areas (Canuto,2023).

According to the distribution of labor market by sectors, women are mostly employed in the agricultural sector as opposed to men who are assertively present in the service sector which limits women to access high paying jobs with leadership roles (Canuto,2023).

Moreover, women only represent 7% of business owners in Morocco, within this proportion only 1% are leaders of these companies, as opposed to 37% and 18% worldwide, respectively (Berahab, Bouba & Agénor, 2017).

Leadership Positions

In 2019, female leaders in businesses led by women reached 13% which is still considered low (Mouline, 2022).

In 2021, the World Economic Forum's Gender Gap Index for economic participation and opportunity ranked Morocco 148th out of 156 countries emphasizing the notable gender gaps (Mouline, 2022).

Regardless of the favorable alterations made to the legal forms among them the adoption of the required quotas for women amid the boards of publicly traded companies, Women still struggle with gender disparities within corporate governance and leadership positions (Mouline, 2022).

INITIATIVES AND REFORMS AIMED AT IMPROVING WOMEN'S RIGHTS AND STATUS

Land Ownership and Inheritance Reforms

The MCC – Morocco Land and Employability Compact established legal forms to foster women's empowerment by providing just access to economic opportunities through land inheritance reforms that was in accordance with Morocco's Family Code (Thompson, 2024).

Female title holders went from 1% to 34% due to the results of the The pilot program created by MCC and Moroccan partners covering 56,000 hectares to produce a model for land privatization and titling (Thompson, 2024).

Moreover, actions were made to raise awareness, grant legal aid and train leaders to strengthen women's inheritance rights to ensure that women are able to maneuver through the administrative process and gain from land titling (Thompson, 2024).

Moudawana Reform

Socialist parties, feminist organizations, human activists, and feminists supported the Moudawana reform in Morocco to revitalize family law and campaign for gender equality regardless of the opposing preservationists endorsing the return to Sharia law (Wijetunge, 2023).

The reform showcased the stark separation between traditionalists and reformers regarding family law. the conflict lies in the demand of reformers to develop social reforms and empower women withing the everchanging economic demands (Wijetunge, 2023).

Women's Leadership Representation

Morocco is the first country in the MENA region to seek to achieve a 30% female representation by the year 2024 and 40% by the year 2027 through the employment of the reform mandating quotas for women on the boards of publicly traded companies (Mouline, 2022). Its aim is to enhance the belief in women's abilities and skills, support the progression of their professional careers, boost the economy's expansion. It's based on the previous successful experiences of other countries in promoting gender diversity in the corporate governance through the quota-based approach (Mouline, 2022)

The results of this reform are positive, and it is reflected by the selection of Moroccan women in leadership roles in major Moroccan cities (Mouline, 2022)

CONCEPTUAL FRAMEWORK OF WOMEN'S EMPOWERMENT

Theoretical Foundations of Women Empowerment

The present passage presents a brief explanation of processes and dimensions involved in empowering women within the theoretical framework.

Empowerment Process: Women's empowerment means acquiring the ability and power to make deliberate life decisions that were previously withheld from them, hence enabling women to practice autonomy and control over their own lives (Mahbub, 2021).

Three-Dimensional Model: Suggests that empowerment can transpire on three distinct levels: personal, relational, and societal, each level impacts women's agency and power in its own way (Huis, 2017).

Cultural Influence: Culture contributes significantly in molding women's empowerment, the latter is perceived differently from the perspective of different cultures, these differences need to be taken into consideration when launching empowerment initiatives (Huis, 2017).

- **Time as a Factor**: Besides culture, empowerment is also influenced by time, it is important to understand the temporal aspects of empowerment initiatives, what was considered empowering to women at certain time in a set cultural setting might not be as empowering to them nowadays (Huis, 2017).

- **Theory of Change:** Is described as a roadmap that explains the effects of actions and programs on women's empowerment. In a nutshell, it defines the needed resources and support to create and launch interventions suitable for empowering women. (according to the report titled theory of change done by Oxfam Novib)

Key Dimensions of Empowerment (Economic, Social, Political)

The key dimensions of empowerment include economic, social, and political aspects.

Economic empowerment encourages the advancement of one's economic capacity, opportunities, and resources to achieve financial prosperity and independence through access to economic resources, jo opportunities, financial training programs and entrepreneurship support (Bodner, 2003)

Social empowerment aims to enhance the social status of individuals, relationships, and their contribution to society. It entails advocating for social integration community engagement, access to social services and the ability to express one's viewpoint within a social setting (Ridde et al., 2007).

Political empowerment: relates to the individual's capability to contribute to political processes, impact decision making, and fight for their rights and preferences when it comes to the political sphere, the political dimension includes political representation, civil engagement, contributing to changes in policies and governance structures (Wiggins, 2021).

Role of Social Entrepreneurship in Advancing Women's Empowerment

Social entrepreneurship plays a crucial role in advancing women's empowerment by providing innovative solutions and opportunities that address economic, social, and political challenges faced by women. The search results highlight several key points regarding the role of social entrepreneurship in advancing women's empowerment:

Economic Empowerment: Women are empowered through social enterprises by gaining access to job opportunities, benefiting from training programs and generating revenues (Richardson et al, 2017; Holmes, 2017)

Social Impact: Social enterprises often offer access to education, health services, skill development and community engagement to their workers which contributes to social inclusion and empowerment (Holmes, 2017)

Social enterprises have to incorporate innovation in order to stay in the market, and this is usually done by practicing inclusive and collective leadership which enrich women's experiences and help close the gender disparity gap within the leadership roles (Holmes, 2017).

Women social entrepreneurs are more likely to include their communities in the thought process prior to making decisions which serves as an inspiration to other women to take leadership roles and promote inclusive and participatory approach to empowerment (Holmes, 2017).

Social enterprises offer important advantages benefiting women's empowerment however they're heavily tied down by the market constraints which reflects the strengths of the existing systemic hinderances. (Richardson et al, 2017)

Frameworks for Assessing Women's Empowerment Outcomes in the Context of Social Entrepreneurship

The framework of the assessment of women's empowerment in the context of social entrepreneurship relies on four power dimensions: power within, power to, power over, and power with. Their goal is to measure how much social enterprises change women's lives. It focuses on the importance of recognizing the relation between entrepreneurial practices and their impact on women while shedding the light on the need to remove barriers hindering women from making their own decisions and achieving financial autonomy (Miles, 2024) (Shin, 2022) (Barooah, 2022)

OVERVIEW OF SOCIAL ENTREPRENEURSHIP IN MOROCCO

Definition and Characteristics of Social Entrepreneurship

According to Hansman (1980), social businesses were considered nonprofit organizations prior to 2000 that aimed to achieve financial independence through the provision of goods and services or the management of successful programs (Dees, Anderson, & Emerson, 2002). In the past, a survey research by Predo and McLean (2006) found that most respondents concurred that the nonprofit sector is home to social entrepreneurship.

Since the nature of SE was still unknown at the start of the new century, many academics and practitioners became interested in it (Dees, 1998). Austin, Stevenson, and Wei-Skillern (2006) questioned the latter regarding the parallels and discrepancies between traditional and social entrepreneurs. The debate on SEs' organizational structure has cooled over the last ten years.

The idea of organizational form is no longer relevant because some profit companies are commonly recognized as SEs (Peredo & McLean, 2006; Santos, 2012).

Grassl (2012) asserts that hybridity dominates the structure of SEs in several dimensions.

During the 1980s and 90s, businesses in the nonprofit sector gained widespread recognition as a group of coordinated projects and programs aimed at achieving strategic goals. These organizations received financial support from philanthropic donors who did not receive any profit. Due to the convergence of business and non-profit organizations' practices over the past 20 years (Austin et al., 2007), SEs have increased their financial autonomy and strengthened the efficacy of their goals (Saebi et al., 2019).

Concepts like positioning, price, cost, and competition became more prominent in the SE literature the closer SEs went to the commercial market and the idea of enterprise (SEKN, 2006). Salamon et al.'s (2012) analysis revealed that a growing percentage of SEs had become less reliant on charitable donors to support their social initiatives through sales of products and services. Although the one-way value flow was altered by the progressive conversion of NPOs to SEs, wherein beneficiaries are now viewed as clients engaging in a transaction with the firm, SEs still struggle with finance.

Innovation is the answer to SEs' financial reliance, according to Bugg-Levine, Kogut, & Kulatilaka (2012, p. 4), since it "allows small firms to tap a considerably deeper pool of finance than was previously available to them, allowing them to greatly extend their social grasp." Entrepreneurship has always been associated with financial assets, economic expansion, and innovation (Schumpeter, 1934; Van Stel et al., 2005; Wennekers et al., 2005; Wong et al., 2005).

Social entrepreneurship (SE) is a new business concept that combines the creation of social and commercial values. The phrase "social entrepreneurship" was first used in academia by Young (1983), and it has since acquired pedagogical attention across several fields (Kraus et al., 2014). The only trait of SE, according to Tracey and Philips (2007), is striking a balance between turning a profit and achieving the enterprise's social mission. The capacity of entrepreneurs to recognize business possibilities is the only way to achieve the balance.

Make effective use of resources to gain funding (Abu-Saifan, 2012; Austin et al., 2006; Wei Skillern et al., 2007). Since prior research included several components from various perspectives, it is thought to be challenging to come to a consensus on a single definition of SE (Kraus et al., 2014; Wry & York, 2017).

But after conducting an extensive and integrative content analysis of 87 published definitions of SE, Kruse (2019) came to the following three important conclusions regarding SE:

(1) It has a business plan; (2) It combines the goal of making money with a social mission. (3) It's daring and inventive.

When the notion of social entrepreneurship was examined across multiple fields, the definitions attributed had a strong connection to the research' setting.

Peter Drucker asserts that social entrepreneurs have an effect on society's "performance capacity" (Gendron, 1996, p. 37). Heton et al. (1997) contend, however, that civic entrepreneurs represent a new class of leaders attempting to entwine the ties between industry, the public sector, education, and the community. In contrast, Schuler (1998) examines social entrepreneurs, those who have the financial means to pursue their ideas for social change, who not only possess the abilities of prosperous businesspeople but also have a strong commitment to social change activism. According to Thompson et al. (2000), social entrepreneurs are individuals who recognize needs that the state welfare system is unable to address and seek to raise the funds required to implement the required adjustments.

In addition to the various definitions assigned to social entrepreneurship, the use of other terms social purpose venture, community wealth venture, non-profit enterprise (Roberts Enterprise Development Fund, no date); venture philanthropy, caring capitalism, social enterprise (Cannon, 2000) and civic entrepreneurship tends to further muddy the definition of the term (Henton et al., 1997). A recurring characteristic in many depictions of social entrepreneurs and associated jargon is their "nature of problem solving," which materializes as founding institutions that yield notable advancements in social transformation. In summary, the discussion revolves around the focusing on definitions of social entrepreneurship, the first wave characterizes SE as applying business knowledge and the necessary abilities to thrive in the non-profit sector (reis, 1999). The latter claim is corroborated by McLeod (1996), which also names two categories of organizations that fit under this group. The first group consists of non-profit organizations that operate profitable enterprises and donate the proceeds to further their charitable objectives. The second category consists of nonprofits that use private sector management strategies to make the most of their current assets.

According to the second wave, social companies can function in the public, private, or nonprofit sectors. This is a broader interpretation of social entrepreneurship. Social entrepreneurs have embraced a diverse strategy that brings together profitable, non-profit, and cross-sectoral operations, rather than adhering to a particular paradigm.

The "entrepreneurial side" of the activities, which includes the inventive and creative tactics of social entrepreneurs who frequently concentrate on solving social problems, was highlighted rather than the market type or the company model.

In contrast to traditional businesses, which prioritize maximizing profits that will eventually be divided among shareholders, social enterprises seek to accomplish social goals such preserving the environment, assisting marginalized communities in their reintegration, and aged, or advocating for women's empowerment and gender equality in addition to making revenues that will be reinvested to advance the relevant social cause.

Growth of Social Entrepreneurship Ecosystem in Morocco

Multiple programs and initiatives have been implemented to reinforce the ecosystem and support social entrepreneurs in Morocco. For example, the Danish-Arab Partnership Program (DAPP II) was created for building partnerships to expand economic opportunities, especially for youth and women, in Morocco, Tunisia, Egypt, and Jordan. The Youth Inclusion and Employment Project (YIEP) in Morocco, under the

DAPP, aims to provide the younger generation with the right skills for employment and entrepreneurship, which is seen as a future oriented approach for sustainable growth in the said sector.

The British council conducted a study to identify issues that Moroccan social entrepreneurs are dealing with and to suggest possible tailored solutions. For instance, organizing capacity-building programs to raise awareness and provide technical support, promoting the creation and development of incubation hubs and startup accelerators, and creating co-working spaces in different regions of Morocco (Gregory et al., 2017)

Examples of Successful Social Enterprises in Morocco

"Sanady" is a social enterprise that offers education for the children of factory workers. It was established in 2006 with less than 50 students, and is now assisting more than 3,500 students, the company does not charge a huge amount for its activities, and it receives funding from the contributions of local enterprises. Sanady's goal is to innovatively address social needs, which are in this case improving education for children at disadvantage.

"Mayamin" focuses on allowing startups to access established distribution networks in Morocco through the creation of a platform where startups can showcase and sell their products.it increases the products and the company's visibility by exposing it to a much larger audience.

"Wuluj" is the first presale platform in the MENA region, and it tackles the biggest issue social entrepreneurs face which is lack of funding. Many people come up with brilliant concepts but do not have the financial resources to make it happen, Wuluj gives them the opportunity to generate early revenue and presell the service or product before it's ready and use the gains to make their concept a reality. (According to Moroccan Center for Innovation and Social Entrepreneurship)

These examples are living proof of the multiple ways in which Moroccan social entrepreneurs are positively influencing their country, all while sustainably addressing social issues,

Challenges and Opportunities for Social Entrepreneurs in The Country

According to the existing literature, there is a lack of research on the role of stakeholders in developing the ecosystem of social enterprises. Which translates in entrepreneurs finding difficulties in accessing the needed resources and support. As we previously brought up, funding a social enterprise Is considered to be the biggest challenge, especially for women who need to prove the value of their projects and convince investors with its potential (Elamrani, 2014) However, In the last decade, the country has shown its support for the growth of social enterprises mainly be implementing legal and tac reforms supporting entrepreneurship and contributing to the creation of job opportunities especially for females (Elamrani, 2014)

Key stakeholders involved in fostering social entrepreneurship in Morocco are focused on providing support in the early stages of the company's creation, for instance raising awareness and educating people about social entrepreneurship, offering mentorship programs, and establishing collaborative spaces. It's important to mention that these initiatives are usually organized in big cities and typically conducted in French or English which leaves out a significant number of people in rural areas who use mainly Arabic dialect, from benefiting from these programs (Gregory, 2017). Social entrepreneurs are also struggling with being recognized legally as independent workers (Gregory, 2017).

IMPACT OF WOMEN EMPOWERMENT THROUGH SOCIAL ENTREPRENEURSHIP

Social Enterprise and Empowerment

Social entrepreneurs empower vulnerable populations, including women and young people without expertise, and offer long-term solutions to societal problems (Levander, 2010). When people are able to make choices and take actions that will ultimately bring them to their desired outcomes (World Bank, 2011). Compared to other forms of entrepreneurship, empowerment is more likely to occur in the setting of social business because the goal of social entrepreneurship is to empower members both inside and outside the organization (Maguirre et al., 2016).

There is a connection between the two ideas because social innovations empower women and encourage them to give back to their organizations. The resources created by the expansion are redirected into the empowerment dimensions listed below, as noted by Foley (1997):

Democratic: the involvement of the whole public in the formulation and execution of public policy.

Economic: Possessing complete control and a steady income.

Developing and reiterating cultural values; obtaining the freedom to operate in their living environment; Gaining the ability to have an effect on a certain topic; and obtaining political power. A case study was done on the Ixtlán Group, a social enterprise in Mexico that effectively exemplified the accomplishment of the qualities. The benefits of a formal work strengthened the Ixtlán Group's women economically. Bonuses, paid time off, housing credit, social security, and pensions.

By advocating for equal opportunity for marginalized groups, political empowerment was observed.

Women played a significant role in planning environmental initiatives including river cleanups and reforestation, which led to environmental empowerment. Finally, the community's testimonies were used to attain cultural empowerment, which primarily focused on increasing women's roles within the community and encouraging their active participation in political and economic activities. A culture that is gradually transitioning from gender-neutral to male-dominated (Carrasco, 2019).

Social Enterprise and "Bounded Empowerment"

The community's belief that women will lead the organization in the future was made clear in this case study of the Ixtlán Group. Despite group empowerment, women continued to endure social, legal, and political limitations. This phenomenon was dubbed "bounded empowerment" by Gill and Ganesh (2017), who explained that it results from the simultaneous sense of empowerment and conditional constraints, which in turn creates a different kind of empowerment. Al-Dajani and Marlow (2013) agree and reiterate that empowering marginalized people in patriarchal societies has no effect on the pervasive patriarchal structure.

Empowerment and emancipation were distinguished by Rindova, Barry, and Ketchen (2009).

Many contend that the only way to strengthen one party is to weaken the other (Gandz and Bird 1996; Koggel, 2013). By eliminating limitations, emancipation brings about transformations.

Inglis (1997) chose to examine the two ideas under the prism of power to clarify their differences. When individuals can thrive inside. While the goal of emancipation is to challenge the existing power structures, Inglis contends that social movements do not have as much of an impact on "the agency of social change" as individuals do.

Since collaborative entrepreneurship allows for the opportunity of maintaining a work-life balance, most women tend to choose it.

This indicates that they follow the unspoken social and cultural norms to achieve.

Therefore, the lack of a better alternative may be the reason why women turn to cooperatives for flexibility, the accomplishment of social goals, and a sense of empowerment (Carrasco, 2019). By identifying gaps that enable them to be reframed, the systems that uphold gender-based inequality should be challenged and collaboratively altered. (Rao and others, 2016)

Evidence of the Impact of Social Entrepreneurship on Women's Empowerment in Morocco

The positive effect of social entrepreneurship on the empowerment of Moroccan women can be clearly seen through a range of initiatives and programs. For instance, the She Trades project aims to support female entrepreneurs in Morocco by offering them training in quality management and expanding their visibility by exposing them to potential markets. This initiative has enabled women entrepreneurs to learn new skills, grow their businesses, and tap into new market opportunities, ultimately leading to their economic empowerment.

An excellent instance of the impact of social entrepreneurship on women's empowerment is the work of Lamia Bazir, a 26-year-old Moroccan woman who decided to return to her country after obtaining a strong educational background abroad. She currently works for the Government of Morocco, on the development of the second compact of Millennium Challenge Corporation, she established a social venture named Empowering Women in the Atlas with the goal of breaking social barriers that hinder women from being perceived as the entrepreneurs that they are (Hekking, 2019)

Her initiative has been recognized for supplying a fresh perspective for social entrepreneurship in Morocco.

Economic Empowerment: Income Generation, Financial Inclusion, Access to Resources

The influence of women's empowerment through social entrepreneurship is considerable in enhancing economic empowerment, income generation, financial inclusion, and access to resources for women. Social enterprises play a significant role in advancing women's empowerment by offering chances for women to be customers, employees, and business owners, which eventually boost their sense of control, confidence, and self-assurance. These businesses provide women with reasonably priced products and services, training, job opportunities, and assistance in micro-entrepreneurship, all of which contribute to their economic empowerment.

Furthermore, female social entrepreneurs are often inspired benevolence and societal awareness, which make their social enterprises solutions for concrete issues of their communities. Within these enterprises, women are empowered through the support they get from each other and the close engagement that they have with the invested parties (Chandak, 2024)

CHALLENGES AND OPPORTUNITIES FOR SCALING WOMEN'S EMPOWERMENT INITIATIVES

Barriers to Scaling Women's Empowerment Through Social Entrepreneurship

Many limitations exist when it comes to growing women's empowerment through social entrepreneurship for instance social mobility hinders women to grow their businesses due to their incapability of hiring other people in this can be a result of social biases, limited access to resources and qualified candidates (Camdessus, 1997).Moreover, women social entrepreneurs find it challenging to access funding, to network, and to overcome legislative and regulatory obstacles, psychological challenges generated from societal norms and stereotypes are also detrimentally influential (Billen, 2024).

To confront these concerns, initiative providing tailored financial support and mentorship programs can ease access to capital and develop networking for women entrepreneurs.

As for the legal obstacle, it's mandatory to advocate for the establishment and the implementation of legislative frameworks promoting gender inclusivity (Billen, 2024).

Societal norms which hinder the achievement of an inclusive entrepreneurial environment can only be changed through the collaboration of both the public and private sectors (Billen,2024).

Policy Recommendations for Fostering an Enabling Environment

To foster an enabling environment for women's empowerment through social entrepreneurship, several policy recommendations can be made, firstly, promoting empowerment and equality through questioning existing social norms, offering targeted financial support and mentorship opportunities, and leaning toward a more gender inclusive legal framework (Lecoutere et al., 2023) .Secondly, easing the networking process between women's organization on the national and the international spectrum and social entrepreneurs to ensure that the latter learn from the implements successful business models and best practices (Lecoutere et al., 2023). Thirdly, recognizing the crucial role that social enterprises play in the Social and Solidarity Economy and the importance of their social mission.

By implementing these policy recommendations, governments, international organizations, and the private sector can create a more inclusive and supportive environment for women's empowerment through social entrepreneurship, fostering lasting transformative change in agri-food systems and wider societal benefits.

THE CASE OF THE SOCIAL ENTERPRISE "AL NOUR" MARRAKECH

In this section, we delve into a comprehensive examination of the impact of Al Nour Marrakech, a social enterprise dedicated to empowering marginalized individuals, particularly disabled women, through traditional Moroccan embroidery.

Context

This study explores the role of social enterprises in empowering Moroccan women through individual, relational, and financial means. The focus is on "Al Nour" Marrakech, founded by Patricia Kahane in

2013. Al Nour aims to provide disadvantaged individuals with dignified and independent livelihoods through traditional Moroccan embroidery. The company employs 40 individuals, predominantly women, 32 of whom have disabilities.

Al Nour's activities include the creation of hand embroidery for various products, sold online and through other channels. The company prioritizes the financial independence of its employees and offers numerous benefits to ensure their well-being, including health insurance, retirement pensions, childcare facilities, and accessible transportation.

Preparations for the study involved contacting Al Nour manager, confirming the visit, and preparing interview questions aimed at understanding the impact of Al Nour on its members' empowerment. Data collection was conducted through interviews with ten participants, focusing on their reasons for joining Al Nour, job experiences, and earnings management.

Data Collection

At the workshop of Al Nour Marrakech, ten members agreed to participate in the interviews. They were asked about their motivations for joining Al Nour, their job experiences, and how they managed their earnings. Data collection was facilitated through the use of a questionnaire created using Google Forms, with the interviewer filling in the responses during the interviews.

Recognizing the cultural context, the data collection process was conducted by female interviewers, who were directly involved in the data collection process. The visit was arranged with a key informant, the administrative assistant of Al Nour Marrakech, with a focus on understanding how the enterprise impacted its intended beneficiaries. We have included the complete questionnaire used in this study as an appendix for reference. The interview questions were written in French but they were also asked using Moroccan Arabic in cases where the interviewees could speak French.

Results

The case study of Al Nour Marrakech illustrates significant economic empowerment among its female employees. Financial independence is evident, with 90% of participants affirming the sufficiency of their salaries. Al Nour provides employment opportunities to 40 individuals, predominantly women with disabilities, many of whom consider it their first professional experience. The company offers comprehensive benefits, including health insurance, pensions, childcare, and transportation assistance, ensuring financial inclusion and access to essential resources.

Table 1. Economic empowerment at Al Nour Marrakech: Evidence from the case study

Aspects of Economic Empowerment	Evidence from the Case Study
Financial Empowerment	■ 90% of the participants confirm the sufficiency of their salary for financial independence. In fact, one of the participants stated, *"At Al Nour, my salary is enough for me to support myself financially"*. However, women who must take care of their children or elderly parents do not agree. The earnings are allocated towards essential expenses, namely, food, clothing, and housing. ■ 30% of respondents mentioned taking out loans, primarily for purchasing a house.
Income Generation	■ Al Nour provides employment opportunities to 40 individuals, 38 of whom are women and 32 have disabilities. ■ 40% of participants state that their job at Al Nour represents their first professional experience and their first resource of a stable income, one of the participants stated: *"Working at Al Nour has given me the opportunity to earn a stable income for the first time in my life"*.
Financial Inclusion and Access to Resources	■ Al Nour offers benefits, such as, health insurance, retirement pensions, free childcare, meals, and transportation assistance. Provides housing for those unable to afford rent. Ensures access to basic needs and essential resources for employees. ■ *"Al Nour not only pays us well but also provides us with health insurance and other benefits, which makes us feel secure and included"*, shared one participant.

The findings of this case study are consistent with existing theories on empowerment. The interviews confirmed the presence of individual, relational, and financial empowerment among the women of Al Nour. Beyond its role as a social enterprise, Al Nour emerged as a supportive community where members share values and support each other's growth.

Through their involvement with Al Nour, women gained new skills, increased their self-esteem, and improved their financial independence. The company's inclusive practices, such as disability-friendly facilities and supportive services, contributed to the overall well-being of its members.

Limitations to the Study

This study serves as an exploratory investigation to pilot some of the interview questions and gather preliminary insights. The findings presented in this chapter are intended to provide a foundation for further research and preparation for a main study. Therefore, it's important to note that the results of this work cannot be generalized beyond the specific context of Al Nour Marrakech and its employees. Further research with a larger sample size and broader scope is needed to validate and extend the findings of this preliminary study. While efforts were made to minimize bias and ensure the reliability of data collection, the subjective nature of interviews and potential respondent bias may impact the interpretation of the results.

CONCLUSION

To conclude, achieving women empowerment within social enterprises in Morocco sheds light on the potential positive impact and the continuous development that could take place by giving women more power across economic, social, and political dimensions.

Throughout history, we were able to see the significant progress of women's status when it comes to legal reforms affecting gender equality. However, challenges in education, employment, and leadership opportunities still exist.

To understand the concept of women empowerment, it's necessary to discuss the multiple facets that empowerment holds by nature which includes economic, social, and political dimensions. Social entrepreneurship offers innovative solutions to the struggles that women face in the previously mentioned dimensions.

The influence of women empowerment through social entrepreneurship can be powerful if the following points which are revenue generation, financial inclusion, and access to resources are considered. Social empowerment is evident in increased self-esteem, agency, and expanded social networks.

Challenges and opportunities to advance women empowerment initiatives require further collaborative efforts, supportive policies, and a conducive environment for growth. By addressing barriers and conducting partnerships between government, NGOs, and the private sector, the potential for replication and scaling of successful models becomes a reality.

The journey of women empowerment in Morocco through social entrepreneurship shows a combination of resilience, innovation, and empowerment. Continued efforts, and collaboration are necessary for the sustainability and the expanding of the effect of women-led initiatives, driving progress towards a more inclusive, equitable, and empowered society.

REFERENCES

Abderebbi, M., & Sanny, J. A.-N. (2023). *AD702: Moroccans endorse women's political participation but not equal access to jobs, land.*

Barooah, B., Banerjee, S., Dang, A., Kejriwal, K., & Aggarwal, R. (2022). A framework for examining women's economic empowerment in collective enterprises.

Billen, A. (2024). *Unlocking Potential: Addressing Challenges in Women Entrepreneurship Policy for a Sustainable Future.* Maastricht University.

Bodner, S. L. (2003). *Dimensional assessment of empowerment in organizations.* University of North Texas.

Camdessus, M. (1997). *Fostering an Enabling Environment for Development.* Address presented at the High-Level Meeting of the UN Economic and Social Council, Geneva, Switzerland.

Canuto, O., & Kabbach, H. (2023). *Gender inequality in the labor market: the case of Morocco.*

Chandak, P. (2024). *Social Entrepreneurship and Women.*

Elamrani, J., & Lemtaoui, M. (2014). *Social entrepreneurship funding in Morocco: Practices, constraints and prospects.*

Gregory, D. (2017). *Social Enterprise Landscape In Morocco.* British Council. https://www.britishcouncil.org/sites/default/files/social_enterprise_landscape_in_morocco.pdf

Hekking, M. (2019). Two Moroccan [Most Influential Young Africans Ranking. Morocco World News.]. *Women*, 100.

Huis, M. A., Hansen, N., Otten, S., & Lensink, R. (2017). A Three-Dimensional Model of Women's Empowerment: Implications in the Field of Microfinance and Future Directions. *Frontiers in Psychology, 1678*, 1678. doi:10.3389/fpsyg.2017.01678

Jehhad, F., & Haoucha, M. (2023). Women empowerment through social entrepreneurship in Morocco: A case study of Al Nour Marrakech. *International Journal of Trade and Management, 1*(2). https://ricg-encgt.ma/

Kabbaj, M. (2020). *Women's Rights in Post-2011 Morocco: The Divergences Between Institutions and Values [Policy Paper]*. Konrad-Adenauer-Stiftung (KAS). https://www.kas.de/documents/276068/8307005/KAS%2BMaroc%2BPolicy%2BPaper%2BNov%2B2020%2B-Women%E2%80%99s%2BRights%2Bin%2BPost-2011%2BMorocco%2BThe%2BDivergences%2BBetween%2BInstitutions%2Band%2BValues.pdf/9aacf4ba-a1ea-3e66-b70b-787498b50d12?t=1607504069145&version=1.0

Kraus, S., Filser, M., O'Dwyer, M. et al. (2014). Social Entrepreneurship: An exploratory citation analysis. *Rev Manag Sci, 8*(2), 275–292. doi:10.1007/s11846-013-0104-6

Lecoutere, E., Achandi, E. L., Ampaire, L., Fischer, G., Gumucio, T., Najjar, D., & Singaraju, N. (2023). Fostering an Enabling Environment for Equality and Empowerment in Agri-food Systems. *Global Food Security, 40*(2). doi:10.1016/j.gfs.2023.100735

Mahbub, M. (2021, June). *Women Empowerment: Theory, Practice, Process, and Importance*. University of Dhaka.

Manal, D. S. (2020). *Women's Rights in Post-2011 Morocco: The Divergences Between Institutions and Values [Policy Paper]*. Konrad-Adenauer-Stiftung (KAS). https://www.kas.de/documents/276068/8307005/KAS%2BMaroc%2BPolicy%2BPaper%2BNov%2B2020%2B-Women%E2%80%99s%2BRights%2Bin%2BPost-2011%2BMorocco%2BThe%2BDivergences%2BBetween%2BInstitutions%2Band%2BValues.pdf/9aacf4ba-a1ea-3e66-b70b-787498b50d12?t=1607504069145&version=1.0

Miles, L., Granados, M. L., & Tweed, J. (2024, March 15). *Social Entrepreneurship, Empowerment of Women Experiencing Homelessness and Gender Equality*. Millennium Challenge Corporation; United States of America. Empowering Youth and Women in Morocco is Key to Development. https://www.mcc.gov/news-and-events/feature/feature-morocco-employability-and-land-compact-closeout/

Mouline, S., Ozlu, O., & Herzog, L. (2022, January 19). A big step forward for women's leadership in Morocco. *World Bank Blogs*. https://blogs.worldbank.org/en/arabvoices/big-step-forward-womens-leadership-morocco

Naciri, R. (1998). *The women's movement and political discourse in Morocco* (UNRISD Occasional Paper, No. 8). United Nations Research Institute for Social Development (UNRISD), Geneva. Retrieved from https://www.econstor.eu/bitstream/10419/148779/1/862525705.pdf

Rahhou, J. (2024, January 17). *Morocco Takes Strides Towards Gender Equality in Education, Employment*. Morocco World News. https://www.moroccoworldnews.com/2024/01/360175/morocco-takes-strides-towards-gender-equality-in-education-employment

Richardson, M., Sappal, B., Tsui, J., & Woodman, P. (2017). *Activist to entrepreneur: The role of social enterprise in supporting women's empowerment.* Social Impact Consulting & ODI. https://www.britishcouncil.org/sites/default/files/social_enterprise_and_womens_empowerment_july.pdf

Ridde, V., Delormier, T., & Gaudreau, L. (2007). Evaluation of empowerment and effectiveness: Universal concepts? Shin, M. B., Garcia, P. J., Dotson, M. E., Valderrama, M., Chiappe, M., Ramanujam, N., Krieger, M., Ásbjörnsdóttir, K., Barnabas, R. V., Iribarren, S. J., & Gimbel, S. (2022). Evaluation of Women's Empowerment in a Community-Based Human Papillomavirus Self-Sampling Social Entrepreneurship Program (Hope Project) in Peru: A Mixed-Method Study. *Frontiers in Public Health, 10,* 858552. doi:10.3389/fpubh.2022.858552

Thompson, A. (2024). *Advancing Women's Rights to Land Ownership in Morocco.* MCC. https://www.mcc.gov/blog/entry/blog-030724-womens-land-rights-morocco/

United Nations Entity for Gender Equality and the Empowerment of Women. (2020). *Report of the Working Group on the issue of discrimination against women in law and in practice: Addendum.* UN. https://www.unwomen.org/sites/default/files/Headquarters/Attachments/Sections/CSW/64/National-reviews/Morocco_en.pdf

United Nations Human Rights Council. (2012). *Report of the Working Group on the issue of discrimination against women in law and in practice: Addendum.* UN. https://www.ohchr.org/sites/default/files/Documents/HRBodies/HRCouncil/RegularSession/Session20/A-HRC-20-28-Add1_en.pdf

Wijetunge, M. (2023). *Moudawana Reform in Morocco: The Long Feminist Struggle.* IGG. https://igg-geo.org/?p=18280&lang=en

World Bank. (2015). *Morocco: Mind the Gap - Empowering Women for a More Open, Inclusive and Prosperous Society.* World Bank.

Zirari, H. (2021). *Women's Rights in Morocco: Assessment and Perspectives.* Institut Europeu de la Mediterrània (IEMed).

Žvan Elliott, K. (2014). Morocco and Its Women's Rights Struggle: A Failure to Live Up to Its Progressive Image. *Journal of Middle East Women's Studies, 10*(2), 1-30.

APPENDIX

Figures

Figure 1.

The following part contains the interview questions that were asked to 10 of the members of ALNOUR company on the 16/09/2022 from 3:00 PM to 7:00 PM. the answers were collected and will be analysed and used for an upcoming research article

ALNOUR MARRAKECH

CE QUESTIONNAIRE EST DESTINÉ AUX EMPLOYÉS DE L'ENTREPRISE ALNOUR MARRAKECH ET SERVIRA À L'ÉLABORATION D'UNE ÉTUDE DANS LE CADRE D'UN PROJET DE THÈSE DE DOCTORATINTITULÉ "SOCIAL ENTERPRISE AND ITS ROLE IN MOROCCAN WOMEN'S EMPOWERMENT".

1. QUEL ÂGE AVEZ-VOUS ?

- ENTRE 20 - 25 ANS
- ENTRE 25 - 30 ANS
- ENTRE 30 - 35 ANS
- ENTRE 35 - 40 ANS PLUS QUE 45 ANS

2. QUEL EST VOTRE NIVEAU D'INSTRUCTION ?

- ETUDES CORANIQUES
- PRIMAIRE
- SECONDAIRE
- SUPÉRIEUR
- NON SCOLARISÉE

3. QUELLE EST VOTRE SITUATION FAMILIALE ? *

- CÉLIBATAIRE
- MARIÉE
- DIVORCÉE
- VEUVE

4. COMBIEN D'ENFANTS AVEZ-VOUS ?
- AUCUN 1
- 2
- 3
- 4
- PLUS QUE 4

Figure 2.

5.Avez-vous travaillé auparavant ?
- Oui
- Non

6.Si Oui .Quel était votre métier précédent et pourquoi l'avez vous quitter ?
_____

7.Comment avez-vous connu l'entreprise ALNOUR ?
- Par un moteur de recherche.
- Par un organisme de conseil ou d'accompagnement. Par la presse.
- Par un ami ou un membre de famille.
- Autre :
_____

8.Depuis combien de temps travaillez-vous chez l'entreprise ALNOUR ?
- Moins d'un an Entre 1-4 ans
- Entre 4-7 ans
- Entre 7-9 ans
- Plus de 9 ans

9.Quel est précisément votre travail au sein de l'entreprise ALNOUR ?
- Textiles de maison
- Accessoires divers
- Vêtements pour femmes, hommes et enfants
- Autre:
_____

10.Vous travaillez combien d'heure par jour ?

- 2 heures
- 4 heures
- 6 heures
- 8 heures
- Autre:
_____

11.Quelles sont les contraintes que vous avez rencontrées suite à votre décision d'intégrer cette entreprise ?
- Epoux opposé
- Milieu culturel défavorisant
- Long trajet domicile-travail.
- Difficulté d'équilibrer entre le travail familial et professionnel
- Autre:
_____

Figure 3.

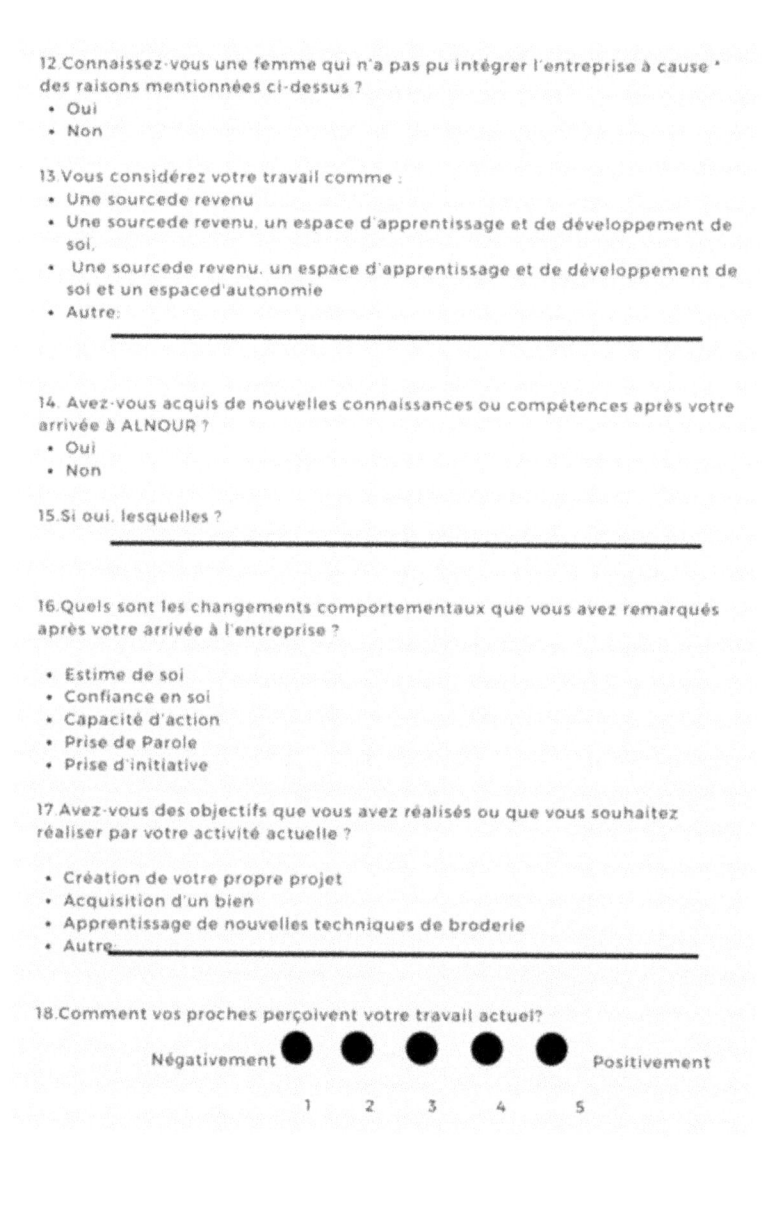

12. Connaissez-vous une femme qui n'a pas pu intégrer l'entreprise à cause des raisons mentionnées ci-dessus ?
- Oui
- Non

13. Vous considérez votre travail comme :
- Une source de revenu
- Une source de revenu, un espace d'apprentissage et de développement de soi.
- Une source de revenu, un espace d'apprentissage et de développement de soi et un espace d'autonomie
- Autre: _____

14. Avez-vous acquis de nouvelles connaissances ou compétences après votre arrivée à ALNOUR ?
- Oui
- Non

15. Si oui, lesquelles ? _____

16. Quels sont les changements comportementaux que vous avez remarqués après votre arrivée à l'entreprise ?
- Estime de soi
- Confiance en soi
- Capacité d'action
- Prise de Parole
- Prise d'initiative

17. Avez-vous des objectifs que vous avez réalisés ou que vous souhaitez réaliser par votre activité actuelle ?
- Création de votre propre projet
- Acquisition d'un bien
- Apprentissage de nouvelles techniques de broderie
- Autre: _____

18. Comment vos proches perçoivent votre travail actuel?

Négativement ● ● ● ● ● Positivement
           1 2 3 4 5

Figure 4.

19. Quels sont les changements comportementaux de votre voisinage que vous avez remarqués ?

- Ils sollicitent votre aide avant la prise d'une décision
- Ils accordent plus d'attention à votre opinion
- Ils partagent les taches ménagères avec vous
- Autre : _____

20. Quel type de relation avez-vous avec vos collègues ?

- Aucune
- Connaissances
- Amitié

21. Est ce que les conversations personnelles que vous avez avec vos collegues ont un impact positif sur vous ?

Pas du tout d'accord ● ● ● ● ● Tout à fait d'accord
              1 2 3 4 5

22. Pensez-vous que le revenu généré est suffisant pour être financièrement indépendante ?

- Oui
- Non

23. Est-ce que vous utilisez votre revenu pour financer

- Nourriture
- Vêtement
- Fournitures scolaires
- Frais médicaux
- Loyer
- Autre : _____

24. Avez-vous demandez un crédit ?

- Oui
- Non

Figure 5.

25. Si oui, pourquoi ?
- Pour acheter un bien
- Pour financer les études d'un membre de famille
- Pour lancer un projet personnel
- Autre :

26. Avez vous bénéficier des avantages suivants ?
- Les moyens de transport offerts par l'entreprise
- Le petit déjeuner et le déjeuner offerts par l'entreprise
- Les formations de langues et du développement des compétences professionnelles
- Les services à la petite enfance
- Autre:

27. les avantages ci-dessus ont eu un impact positif sur l'équilibre entre votre vie professionnelle et vie privé :

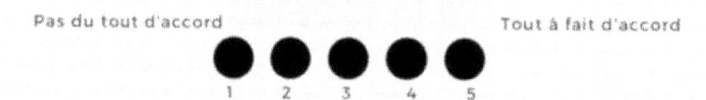

Pas du tout d'accord ● ● ● ● ● Tout à fait d'accord
                      1 2 3 4 5

28. Après votre intégration à l'entreprise ALNOUR, votre qualité de vie s'est améliorée :

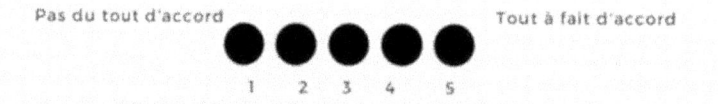

Pas du tout d'accord ● ● ● ● ● Tout à fait d'accord
                      1 2 3 4 5

Chapter 9
Women's Land Ownership in Morocco:
An Empowerment Initiative

Malika Haoucha
https://orcid.org/0000-0003-1077-204X
University Hassan II of Casablanca, Morocco

Fadila Jehhad
University Hassan II of Casablanca, Morocco

Karima Ragouba
University Hassan II of Casablanca, Morocco

ABSTRACT

The present research endeavor consists of a preliminary documentary investigation which paves the way towards a larger future study focusing on Moroccan women who have benefited from government initiatives like the "Centre D'inclusion des Femmes au Foncier" (CIFF) and the Millennium Challenge Corporation (MCC) in empowering them, more specifically, through land ownership. Hence, this chapter provides background information in relation to women empowerment through land ownership and aims to highlight the achievements of the Moroccan government and CIFF in meeting predefined objectives. It's part of a broader vision to address legal, social, and customary barriers hindering women's access to land and to promote their active involvement in land governance.

INTRODUCTION

In recent years, discussions surrounding women's empowerment have evolved from mere rhetoric to a practical quest for tangible solutions to combat gender inequality. Among the myriad issues under scrutiny, the relationship between women's empowerment and land ownership stands out as a focal point, drawing attention from scholars, analysts, and activists alike. This chapter provides an insightful

DOI: 10.4018/979-8-3693-2806-4.ch009

overview of the multifaceted aspects surrounding the issue of Women's Empowerment through Land Ownership in Morocco.

The concept of land ownership has long been intertwined with notions of economic autonomy and social status. It is widely believed that women's empowerment hinges on their ability to access and control land. Ownership of wealth and property not only symbolizes personal freedom from external control but also positions individuals to exert influence within their communities. Thus, it becomes imperative to delve deeper into how land ownership serves as a catalyst for empowerment, impacting economic resilience, social standing, and gender justice.

Our current research endeavor consists of a preliminary exploration in preparation for a main study that we intend to undertake in the near future and which is going to cover a large representative sample of the category of Moroccan women who have directly benefited from the initiative of the Moroccan government and the "Centre D'inclusion des Femmes au Foncier" (CIFF) together with the Millennium Challenge Corporation (MCC). The present chapter will, therefore, report through the existing documentation the background information which is going to set the grounds for a large scale future study. The present work is aimed at spotlighting the achievements of the Moroccan government in collaboration with the "Centre D'inclusion des Femmes au Foncier" (CIFF), in alignment with predefined objectives. This endeavor marks a crucial milestone in a broader vision aimed at monitoring and advocating for initiatives designed to overcome legal, social, and customary barriers that impede Moroccan women's access to land. Moreover, it seeks to bolster their effective participation in the governance of land resources in all forms.

WOMEN'S LAND OWNERSHIP AND EMPOWERMENT

Women often face challenges regarding access and control of land resources which hinders their empowerment. In multiple countries, women are considered as guardians of land, in other words they are preserving it for their children, mainly their sons, which reflects gender inequalities in property rights (Kartik, 2000). The existence of laws concerning property rights and constitutional references related to gender equality does not guarantee equal positioning of men and women in terms of land ownership and control (Pallas, 2011).

In legal terminology, empowerment is often linked with protecting and ensuring women's land rights. It enables women to make choices confidently and independently in the political, economic, and social spheres. It is a multi-faceted operation involving the transformation of power relations mainly through allowing access to resources, shrinking social disparities, and modifying the institutional structures that reinforce existing power dynamics (Pallas, 2011).

Women's economic empowerment is significantly hindered by their unequal access to land. In the developing world, women contribute heavily to produce food, yet they usually lack ownership and control over the land they work on and their work goes unnoticed. This disparity emphasizes the importance of increasing awareness of gender related issues, through a combination of legal education and implementing effective strategies to alleviate poverty (Ghimire, 2024).

On the one hand, women's access to land is crucial for advocating for gender equality and sustainable development. On the other hand, land ownership guarantees for women a solid food base production, stable income source, loan collateral, possibility to have savings, and most importantly, it contributes to the defining of their cultural identity. Equal access to land is a huge milestone in human rights development but also it leads to the reduction of domestic violence, expansion of agricultural production and nutritional security (Handbook on the OECD-DAC Gender Equality Policy Marker, 2016).

In the end, owning land ties women's empowerment not only to the productive systems but also to social, political and economic domains. Overcoming the challenges that female faces in terms of acquiring and managing the land property is necessary to achieve gender equality and support socio-economic dynamics and states´ sustainability development.

STATUS OF WOMEN AND LAND SYSTEM IN MOROCCO

History of Challenges in Implementing Supportive Policies in Morocco

Colonial Morocco: Legal Framework for Land Dispossession

In 1912, France and Spain seized control of Morocco under the agreement called the treaty of Fez. Which led to forming the French Protectorate of Morocco.

In 1913, the land registration act was introduced by colonial authorities.

In 1914, a "Dahir" or Decree dissected the Moroccan land into inalienable and alienable property. The latter contains Melk and public domain lands.

In 1919, to further protect landholders, notably Moroccan tribes, another policy was created to widen the alienable land selection to make it also include collectively held tribal land. After that, the Director of Indigenous Affairs created an office of land assessment based on the tribes' needs; the lands that were considered not needed were sold to Europeans, it's worth mentioning that these lands were often more fertile and better irrigated ones.

The colonial authorities took away land of the colonized people through the unfair legal system.

Rural Disenfranchisement

The French colonial policies stripped rural Moroccans away from their rights through land consolidation and tax advantages. They were also excluded from the advantages that came with the modern agricultural sector due to the agricultural methods employed at that time, the arable lands decreased significantly which pushed Moroccan farmers to quit farming or become sharecroppers. The combination of the challenges created in the agricultural sector paired with the limitations of education and job market in rural arears, locals were forced to switch to urban employment which marked the beginning of urban migration hindering the country's development by creating a gap between urban and rural areas and the increase of informal settlements.

Postcolonial Morocco

Land ownership rules changed after the colonization, King Mohammed V introduced policies in favor of the less fortunate farmers in rural areas. After Morocco's independence, a government survey showed economic inequality emerging from existing land ownership system, 5 to 10% of the population owned most of the land and 40% had none. Naturally tensions were formed, and a political debate was launched about landownership reform. King Mohamed V's approach was focused on regaining balance in terms of landownership and the gap between rural and urban areas mainly by Operation Plow implemented in 1975, targeting traditional rural farmers, the goal was to tackle two main obstacles, the harsh climate that farmers had to endure because of the lack of new farming technologies and land fragmentation due to the complexity of the land tenure system. The operation marginally increased crop production and did not reach the results that the government had hoped for.

Morocco witnessed substantial shifts in land ownership patterns under Hassan II's rule (1961–1999), particularly with the acceleration of modernization and urbanization efforts. With differing degrees of success, the government enacted land reforms to redistribute land to rural farmers.

There were hopes for more reforms once King Mohammed VI came to the throne in 1999, especially in the areas of land tenure, rural development, and the fair allocation of land resources. Mohammed VI highlighted the importance of economic growth and social justice, which prompted the creation of programs such as the National Initiative for Human Development (INDH), which was introduced in 2005 with the goal of improving living conditions, infrastructure, and access to basic services in rural areas.

Furthermore, under the reign of Mohammed VI various reforms have been introduced whose aim is to consolidate property right, encourage foreign investors and ensure a sustainable land management. The 2011 constitution included these reforms and enhanced the right to property and the role of the state in protecting them.

WOMEN'S STATUS

Legislative Reforms Benefiting Women

In Morocco, two legislative reforms, in labor code and the family code, were created to support women. Dahir No. 1.03.194 of September 11, 2003, promulgating Law No. 65.99 relating to the labor code. Article 9 cherishes gender equality and forbids all forms of discrimination, in fact getting paid equally for holding the same positions as men became mandatory. The maternity leave was stretched from 12 weeks to 14 weeks. Sexual harassment at the workplace was finally addressed as a transgression of law. Dahir No. 1.04.22 of February 3, 2004, promulgating Law No. 70.03 relating to the family code constructs fundamentals of equality between spouses, protection of family balance and children's rights. The articles 4 and 51 clearly state that household responsibility is shared between the spouses and denies the obedience rule to the husband mentioned in the previous code.

According to article 19, both men and women can legally get married at the age of 18. Article 24 and 25 states that adult women can now marry without needing a consent from their guardian. Article 49 indicates that property separation between spouses should be conducted as prescribed by Islamic law while allowing for agreements on the management of assets acquired during marriage. Under the previous code, men had the unilateral right to divorce without judicial intervention, while women were required to seek judicial recourse for divorce, which often took time and financial resources. Furthermore, the Moroccan government introduced major changes to the family code. The feminist associations requested major changes such as: the end of marriage of minors, equality in matters of inheritance, the right of guardianship of children and the end of polygamy.

Even though the minimum age of marriage was fixed at 18 in the previous code, the law authorized marriage of minors with the condition of the judge's approval, what was supposed to be an exception became the norm as 320 000 minor marriage requests were approved by Moroccan courts between 2009 and 2018.

Laws from different codes were revised or created to benefit women' rights:

Children born to Moroccan mothers and fathers are granted the Moroccan nationality as per the revision of the nationality code by Law No. 62.06 promulgated by Dahir No. 1.07.80 of March 23, 2007

Recognizing sexual harassment as a crime as per the revision of Dahir No. 1.59.415 of November 26, 1962, the penal code.

Policies Promoting Women's Rights

The government is committed to promoting women's rights by implementing mechanisms to ease the introduction execution of the above reforms:

In 2007 gender issues were considered a part of the mandate of the ministerial department for social development, family, and solidarity.

The year 2001 was marked by the creation of an independent body called Diwan al Madhalim, its objective is to investigate complaints from citizens who believe that they were mistreated by the government by requesting more information, making recommendations to the government and publishing reports on its findings.

The institutionalization of a gender-based approach to the state budget means that the government is ensuring that the budget distribution is fair regardless of gender.

In 2002, the Moroccan government created a comprehensive plan to address the issue of violence against women.

The implementation of a national strategy for equality and equity between men and women through a circular from the Prime Minister dated March 2007.

The 2008 Electoral Code in Morocco introduced a 12% quota for women's representation in both national and local elections. This quota aimed to address the historical underrepresentation of women in elected positions. The code also implemented the "Support Fund for the Encouragement of Women's Representation." Which covers campaign expenses in hopes of reducing financial barriers to their participation.

The 12% quota was not satisfying to some feminist organizations such as Association Démocratique des Femmes du Maroc (ADFM) and the Union de l'Action Féminine (UAF), which resulted in them forming "Mouvement pour le tiers vers la parité" (Movement for One-Third Towards Parity) to advocate for a more ambitious goal: 33% women's representation in national and local assemblies.

Increasing the participation of civil society in the Human Rights Consultative Council to promote human rights.

Establishment of the National Initiative for Human Development (INDH) to reduce poverty and precariousness, particularly among women.

Moroccan Land System

Dual Legal Regimes

The land tenure system in Morocco is distinguished by the coexistence of regimes: the traditional system and the "Immatriculation Foncière" (land registration) system. The traditional land tenure system is based on customary law and Maliki Islamic jurisprudence, focusing on community-based land rights and collective ownership. Muslim notaries known as "Adoul" are responsible for ensuring agreements authenticity of all transactions made under this system. In 1913 the "Immatriculation Foncière" system was introduced to facilitate acquiring land for the French colonists. After Morocco gained its independence in 1956, both systems were retained. However, the Immatriculation Foncière system was more common in urban areas due to its enhanced security and efficiency.

Diversity of Land Statuses

In Morocco, there are two main groups and the land tenure systems traditional and modern frameworks.

Traditional Land Tenure Systems

- **Melk:** in Arabic means to fully own land and it is primarily ruled by Maliki Islamic jurisprudence.
- **Collective Lands:** owned by tribes, collective land became inalienable community property under government control in 1919. Women were excluded from having usufruct rights based on custom, Women in Kenitra are fighting for their rightful access to this land with the help of NGOs.
- **Guich Lands:** are gifted from the sultan to soldiers as a reward for their military service, women were excluded since they couldn't serve as soldiers, they lived on the lands as wives or daughters of the soldiers.

Modern Land Tenure Systems

- **State Domain:** includes properties owned by the government, such as lands recovered from alienations, colonization, and confiscation. The state domain encompasses a wide range of land types, including forests, mines, and urban areas.
- **"Habous":** Lands dedicated to charitable or religious purposes, governed by specific regulations. Habous lands are often managed by religious institutions or foundations, with income generated from their use dedicated to charitable or religious causes.
- **"Habous" are regulated by articles** 73 to 75 of the decree of June 2, 1915 which defines them as immovable properties immobilized by the Muslim founder, the enjoyment of which benefits the categories of beneficiaries he designates. We can distinguish three types of Habous in Morocco:
    - Public "Habous," are managed by the ministry of Habous and Islamic affairs, they are characterized by their immovable properties with the state as the direct beneficiary
    - "Habous" belonging to Zaouias (religious brotherhoods), are properties that benefit their beneficiaries and they turn into public Habous upon the extinction of the last beneficiary.
    - Private family "Habous.": are established for the benefit of the descendants of the constituent until the lineage is extinguished, at which point they revert to the state and become public "Habous". It has often been used to avoid Islamic inheritance rules and keep the real estate within the male family line.
- **Immatriculated Lands:** These are ruled by the Immatriculation Foncière system. Inspired by the Torrens Act of 1858 from Australia, this system was introduced in Morocco during the early years of the French protectorate. Its objective is to introduce a clear land ownership structure by provid-

ing titles to each property. The immatriculation guarantees a clean legal title also known as the legal purge by eliminating any claims that previously existed on the properties. It also facilitates investments since this category of land can be used as collateral for loans.
- **Customary Muslim Rights:** Customary Muslim rights, known as "Menfaâ" in Arabic, represent usufruct rights granted to individuals over immovable property. These rights effectively divide ownership into two parts: bare ownership and usufruct. Customary Muslim rights are primarily associated with Habous state domain lands, but they can also apply to private property (Decroux, 1977). they're characterized by grating the holder the right to use the property without owning it, the holders usually pay rent to the landowner.

VARIOUS LAND AND ENVIRONMENTAL POLICIES IN MOROCCO

National Agency for Land Conservation, "Cadastre," and Cartography (ANCFCC) Policy

The National Agency for Land Conservation, Cadastre, and Cartography (ANCFCC) focuses on transitioning Morocco's land tenure system from the predominant informal Melk land regime to a fully immatriculated (registered) land system by offering free registration for agricultural and ensuring that their policies are applied without gender-based discrimination. Moreover, the agency is working towards simplifying the registration process and reducing delays in between the registration stages. To easily access information, a national database is being established and finally to educate and reach the public campaigns are organized to bring awareness about benefits of land registration.

Green Morocco Plan

The Green Morocco Plan is a national strategy aimed at propelling the agriculture sector into the forefront of Morocco's economic growth. Recognizing agriculture's longstanding significance, the plan consists of two pillars; firstly, it remodels agriculture to achieve market driven growth by attracting private investments to support up to 900 projects annually and focusing on supporting agricultural practices that produce high value goods that are highly demanded and consumed. Secondly, it uses solidarity to empower small holder agriculture by investing in up to 400 social projects per region and easing the transition of vulnerable farmers to high value-added agricultural activities.

Urban Planning Code

Since the late 60s, people started to move out from rural areas, which created a need for a more detailed approach to urban planning. In response, Morocco adopted a new Urban Planning Code in 2007. It aims to create cities with good infrastructure to meet the needs of the growing population, preserve the unique character for each city by attributing colors to certain cities as well as architectural structures which eventually boosts the tourism potential.it guarantees fair treatment to citizens when land is used for development purposes, and it updates urban plans regularly to adjust to the changing needs of the population.

INEQUALITY IN WOMEN'S ACCESS TO LAND RIGHTS

Inequalities Due to Legislation and Customary Practices

Moroccan women face significant challenges in accessing and owning land and properties, through inheritance and through contracts. This is largely due to legal and customary barriers. When it comes to inheritance, women are usually excluded from inheriting collective land and when they inherit Melk lands their shares are considerably smaller than those of the men of the family. As a result of culture and traditions lands owned by women are usually handled and controlled by male relatives through the placement of the said land under their custody. As for contracts between living person, women suffer from unfavorable terms in these land related contracts due to their financial vulnerability. (Agronomic and Veterinary Institute Hassan II, 1987).

Inequality in Inheritance Rights Exacerbated by Customs

The Moroccan inheritance law is based on Maliki Sunni Islamic law. there is a huge debate on the unequal inheritance distribution between men and women, some advocate to change it while others believe it should not be changed since it is derived from the Islamic religion. The issue is that the roles have changed, men used to be the main if not the sole bread winner and the providers for the family, but nowadays, due to the shift in social landscape, women are now making significant contributions to household income, and in some cases, they are even the sole breadwinners. This shift has highlighted the inadequacy of inheritance rules to modern life (Daoudi, 2017).

In addition to the unequal distribution of inheritance between men and women, there are several other factors that prevent women from accessing their inheritance rights in Morocco, such as, the institution of private Habous which often excludes women from the inheritance. In some cases, families do not declare female heirs to authorities after a death, to prevent women from inheriting their property. Women who are descendants of collective lands also known as "Sulaliyat" are often prevented from inheriting their share of the land because customs believe that only the men of the families should benefit, it's worth mentioning that the 1915 Dahir that rules collective lands does not support gender-specific favoritism (Daoudi, 2017).

The Difficulties in Passing Contracts Between Living Persons

Women's access to land and property through contracts between living persons, whether it's purchase, sale or rental is restricted due to their economic and financial situation. Women are by tradition forced into a limited position when it comes to financial autonomy. They are also at a disadvantage in the division of property acquired during marriage after a divorce, particularly when it comes to land.

Despite reforms introduced by the new family code, women may find themselves without land or housing after a long-term marriage if they cannot prove their contribution to the purchase of the property (article 49 of the family code). This is especially challenging since women's unpaid domestic work is not considered as a contribution to property acquisition.

Difficulties in Accessing and Securing Housing

In Morocco, access to land can be achieved either by renting or owning land, the latter holds the most significance to Moroccans depending on existing social groups.

- Low-income households rely on state aid granted for social housing. 100 000 social housing was set as a target to be built each year by the Ministry of Housing and Urban Planning.
- **Middle- and upper-income households access housing through their own resources or through bank loans.** People with informal jobs or low-income jobs find it difficult to obtain loans therefore it hinders their access to land. To remedy this issue, the Guarantee Fund for Irregular and Modest Incomes (FOGARIM) was launched in 2004.
- **Housing Security** in Morocco house security generally concerns divorced or widowed women with no children, The 2004 family code interferes only when children are involved. (High Commission for Planning, 2004)

EFFORTS TO PROMOTE AND STRENGTHEN WOMEN'S LAND RIGHTS

Women's Outreach Cells in Rural Areas

Women animation centers of the Moroccan Ministry of Agriculture and Fisheries used to educate women in rural areas about family planning and hygiene. After their reconstruction, they are now able to support the development of early-stage businesses by providing resources, mentorship, and networking opportunities for women.

Role of The Ministry of Interior in Advancing Collective Women's Rights

Collective Women known also as "Sulaliyat" in Kenitra were being stripped of their rights to own land due to gender based discrimination, in 2009, the minister of Interior recognized the unfairness and interfered by writing a letter to the local leader of the city, in which they highlighted that existing laws do not discriminate against women, hence the said unfair practices were taking place illegally and purely out of unfair customary rules (Daoudi, 2011).

Policies Impacting Women's Land Rights

Gender-Responsive Budgeting

In 2002, the ministry of economy and finance began a gender-oriented budgeting process, each a report about gender development, discussing mainly the government contribution to achieving gender equality is issued and presented to the parliament (Ministry of Economy and Finance, 2005).

National Strategy for Gender Equality and Equity

The national strategy for gender equality and equity is based on the circular from the Prime Minister dated March 8, 2007. It encourages the governmental departments to incorporate a gender-oriented approach into their policies and programs to guarantee that the needs of each gender are being met, especially, for women since they have been historically discriminated against. Since 2009, an annual evaluation has been added to the national strategy for gender equality to analyze and control the integration of gender dimension in national plans. (Circular from the prime minister, 2007)

« CENTRE D'INCLUSION DES FEMMES AU FONCIER (CIFF) » & MILLENNIUM CHALLENGE CORPORATION (MCC) INITIATIVE

Millennium Challenge Corporation (MCC)

In 2004, The Millennium Challenge Corporation, an independent U.S. foreign aid agency was established to provide effective foreign assistance. The MCC works with developing countries that demonstrate good governance through 20 policy indicators to create development aid programs. The US treasury funds these projects by directly paying the involved companies. The budget reached $800 million in the year 2020. (Millennium Challenge Corporation, 2016)

Main Objectives of "Centre d'Inclusion des Femmes au Foncier" CIFF

The Moroccan government partnered with the MCC to launch "Centre d'Inclusion des Femmes au Foncier" (The Center for Women's Inclusion in Land Rights), its goal is to promote women's land rights and ensure fair access to land ownership and management in Morocco through three main strategies:

Establishing a Land Data Observatory: The CIFF is working on creating a centralized platform to collect and analyze gender related land data. Mainly focusing on women's land access, their participation in land governance, and the status of land rights for women in Morocco.

Supporting Women in Exercising Their Land Rights: The CIFF directly supports women in understanding, claiming, and defending their land rights by raising awareness through campaigns, providing legal assistance, and building the capacity of women to navigate land-related legal and administrative procedures.

Advocating for Gender-Sensitive Land Policies: The CIFF engages in policy advocacy efforts to influence the development of land-related policies that are more equitable and inclusive for women. This may involve conducting research, providing recommendations to policymakers, and collaborating with other stakeholders to promote gender-sensitive land reforms. (Millennium Challenge Corporation, 2022)

The creation of the CIFF in the Ministry of Agriculture is an important step and can be a means for the promotion of women's land right in the future. The main objective of this center is to acquire gender specific land information, popularize women's land rights, support women to take part in land recognition and documentations, and propose policy reforms that take a gender perspective through research and analysis[1]. The CIFF's mission encompassed the following – protecting women in decision-making, especially in relation to different forms of land, which constitute a critical step to increase women's access to and control over land resources (Sharon, 2022).

The Main Achievements of the CIFF and the MILLENNIUM CHALLENGE CORPORATION (MCC)

1. CIFF Achievements:
   - CIFF has worked to increase women's access to land by providing legal assistance and advocacy to address discriminatory practices and laws related to land ownership.
   - The organization has conducted awareness campaigns and training programs to educate women about their land rights and empower them to assert their rights effectively.
   - CIFF has collaborated with local communities, government agencies, and other stakeholders to develop and implement policies and programs that promote gender equality in land ownership and management.
   - Through research and data collection, CIFF has contributed to a better understanding of the challenges faced by women in accessing and owning land in Morocco, which has informed the design of targeted interventions.
2. MCC Initiative Achievements:
   - The MCC Initiative in Morocco has included specific components aimed at promoting gender equality in land access and ownership as part of its broader development programs.
   - This initiative has supported legal reforms and policy changes to remove barriers to women's land ownership and ensure equal rights to land and property.
   - MCC has invested in capacity building and training programs to strengthen the skills and knowledge of women, especially in rural areas, to participate in land-related decision-making processes and manage land resources effectively.
   - The initiative has funded infrastructure projects that have benefited women, such as irrigation systems and rural roads, which can enhance women's access to and control over land.

By focusing on legal reforms, capacity building, awareness raising, and infrastructure development, both CIFF and the MCC Initiative have made significant strides in empowering Moroccan women through landownership. Their efforts have contributed to improving gender equality, enhancing women's economic empowerment, and promoting sustainable development in Morocco.

3. Financial Inclusion:
   - Both CIFF and the MCC Initiative has supported initiatives to increase women's access to financial resources for land acquisition and investment, such as through microfinance programs or access to credit.
4. Women's Land Rights Documentation:
   - These organizations in collaboration with the Moroccan government have supported efforts to formalize women's land rights through documentation and registration processes, ensuring that women have legal proof of their ownership and can protect their rights more effectively.
5. Partnerships and Collaboration:
   - CIFF and the MCC Initiative engaged in partnerships and collaborations with local NGOs, government agencies, community-based organizations, and international development partners to leverage resources, expertise, and networks for greater impact.
6. Monitoring and Evaluation:

- Both organizations conducted monitoring and evaluation activities to assess the effectiveness and impact of their interventions, ensuring that programs are achieving their intended outcomes and making necessary adjustments based on feedback and lessons learned.
7. Policy Advocacy:
    - CIFF and the MCC Initiative have engaged in policy advocacy efforts to influence national and local policies related to land tenure, property rights, and gender equality, advocating for legal reforms and institutional changes that promote women's land rights.
8. Sustainable Development Goals (SDGs):
    - Their initiatives align with the United Nations Sustainable Development Goals (SDGs), particularly Goal 5 (Gender Equality) and Goal 1 (No Poverty), contributing to broader efforts to achieve gender equality and eradicate poverty in Morocco.

By addressing these additional points, we can further highlight the comprehensive approach taken by CIFF and the MCC Initiative to empower Moroccan women through landownership, encompassing legal, financial, institutional, and policy dimensions to create lasting change and advance gender equality.

LIMITATIONS AND CONCLUSION

Acknowledging the significance of this preliminary exploration, it's important to recognize its inherent limitations, primarily stemming from its reliance on documentary analysis rather than fieldwork research. Here are some key limitations and constraints to consider:

1. Lack of Direct Engagement: Without direct fieldwork, the research may lack firsthand insights from individuals and communities directly affected by women's land rights issues. Fieldwork allows researchers to gather nuanced perspectives, experiences, and contextual understanding that may not be fully captured through document analysis alone.
2. Limited Contextual Understanding: Document-based research may provide a broad overview of global situations, but it may lack depth in understanding specific cultural, social, and economic contexts within which women's land rights are situated. Fieldwork enables researchers to immerse themselves in local environments, gaining deeper insights into the complexities of land tenure systems and gender dynamics.
3. Potential Bias in Document Selection: The selection of documents for analysis may introduce bias, as researchers may inadvertently prioritize certain sources over others, leading to incomplete or skewed representations of the issue. Fieldwork allows researchers to mitigate this bias by directly engaging with diverse stakeholders and sources of information.
4. Inability to Capture Dynamic Processes: Document-based research provides snapshots of information at specific points in time, but it may overlook the dynamic nature of women's land rights struggles and the evolving socio-political contexts in which they unfold. Fieldwork allows researchers to observe and document changes over time, capturing the fluidity and complexity of the issue.
5. Difficulty in Verifying Information: Information obtained from documents may be subject to inaccuracies, omissions, or misinterpretations, without the opportunity for verification through direct observation or interviews. Fieldwork enables researchers to corroborate and validate information through multiple sources and perspectives.

6. Limited Scope of Analysis: Document-based research may be constrained by the availability and scope of existing documents, potentially limiting the depth and breadth of the analysis. Fieldwork allows researchers to explore a wider range of issues and factors that may influence women's land rights, including local power dynamics, customary practices, and community perceptions.

While recognizing these limitations, it's important to acknowledge the valuable insights and contributions that document-based research can offer in advancing our understanding of women's empowerment through land ownership. However, future research efforts should strive to complement document analysis with fieldwork-based approaches to provide a more comprehensive and nuanced understanding of the complexities surrounding women's land rights.

REFERENCES

Adnane, S. (2018). Women's Land Ownership In Morocco: Current State & Challenges. OICRF. https://www.oicrf.org/-/women-s-land-ownership-in-morocco-current-state-challenges

Association for Women's Rights in Development (AWID). (2004). *Intersectionality: A Tool for Gender and Economic Justice*. AWID. https://www.awid.org/sites/default/files/atoms/files/intersectionality_a_tool_for_gender_and_economic_justice.pdf

Bouderbala, N. (1999). Les systèmes de propriété foncière au Maghreb: le cas du Maroc. Cahiers options méditerranéennes, 36.

Decroux, P. (1977). *Droit foncier marocain*. Editions La Porte.

Doss, C., & Meinzen-Dick, R. (2020). Land tenure security for women: A conceptual framework. *Land Use Policy*, 99, 105080. doi:10.1016/j.landusepol.2020.105080

Ghimire, P. R., Devkota, N., Marasini, T., Khanal, G., Deuja, J., & Khadka, U. (2024). Does joint land ownership empower rural women socio-economically? Evidence from Eastern Nepal. *Land Use Policy*, 138, 107052. doi:10.1016/j.landusepol.2024.107052

Global Land Tool Network (GLTN). (2023). *Land, Women Empowerment and Socioeconomic Development in the Arab Region. Evidence-based Perspectives*. GLTN. https://gltn.net/download/land-women-empowerment-and-socioeconomic-development-in-the-arab-region-evidence-based-perspectives/

Grabe, S., Grose, R. G., & Dutt, A. (2015). Women's land ownership and relationship power: A mixed methods approach to understanding structural inequities and violence against women. *Psychology of Women Quarterly*, 39(1), 7–19. doi:10.1177/0361684314533485

Kandeel, A. (2020). *Let justice be done: Respect for female land rights in the Middle East and North Africa*. MEI. https://www.mei.edu/publications/let-justice-be-done-respect-female-land-rights-middle-east-and-north-africa

Knapman, C., & Sutz, P. (2015). Reconsidering approaches to women's land rights in sub-Saharan Africa. *IIED Briefing Paper-International Institute for Environment and Development*, (17310).

Kolovich, L., & Ndoye, A. (2023). Implications of Gender Inequality for Growth in Morocco. *Morocco's Quest for Stronger and Inclusive Growth, 167.*

Land Portal. (2000). *Land Ownership and Women's Empowerment: A Comprehensive Review.* Land Portal. https://landportal.org/node/55028

Lastarria-Cornhiel, S., & García-Frías, Z. (2005). *Gender and land rights: Findings and lessons from country studies.*

Ministère de l'Agriculture et de la Réforme agraire. Office régional de la mise en valeur agricole du Gharb, 1987. Etude sur la législation et les structures agraires dans la zone d'action de l'ORMVAG, dossier IX: *Femme et propriété foncière.* Etude réalisée par l'Institut agronomique et vétérinaire Hassan II.

Mishra, K., & Sam, A. G. (2016). Does women's land ownership promote their empowerment? Empirical evidence from Nepal. *World Development, 78,* 360–371. doi:10.1016/j.worlddev.2015.10.003

Office of the United Nations High Commissioner for Human Rights (OHCHR). (2017). *Women's Land Rights: A Transformative Approach to Gender Justice.* OHCHR. https://www.ohchr.org/sites/default/files/Documents/Issues/Women/WG/Womenslandright pdf.

Organisation for Economic Co-operation and Development (OECD). (2016). *Handbook on the OECD-DAC Gender Equality Policy Marker.* OECD. https://www.oecd.org/dac/gender-development/Handbook-OECD-DAC-Gender-Equality-Policy-Marker.pdf

Organisation for Economic Co-operation and Development (OECD). (2020). OECD iLibrary Document. OECD. https://www.oecd-ilibrary.org/sites/13b65c6a-en/index.html?itemId=%2Fcontent%2Fcomponent%2F13b65c6a-en

Pallas, S. (2011). Women's land rights and women's empowerment: one and the same. C. Verschuur (Hg.): Du grain à moudre. Genre, dévelopment rural et alimentation. Genève.

Pradhan, R., Meinzen-Dick, R., & Theis, S. (2019). Property rights, intersectionality, and women's empowerment in Nepal. *Journal of Rural Studies, 70,* 26–35. doi:10.1016/j.jrurstud.2019.05.003

Rawal, D. S., & Agrawal, K. (2016). *Barriers to women's land and property access and ownership in Nepal.* International Organization for Migration.

Rogers, S. (2022). *Center for Women's Inclusion in Land Rights Launched in Morocco.* MCC. https://www.mcc.gov/blog/entry/blog-070722-center-womens-land-rights/

Slavchevska, V., Doss, C. R., de la O Campos, A. P., & Brunelli, C. (2021). Beyond ownership: Women's and men's land rights in Sub-Saharan Africa. *Oxford Development Studies, 49*(1), 2–22. doi:10.1080/13600818.2020.1818714

Swearingen, W. D. (2016) *Moroccan Mirages: Agrarian Dreams and Deceptions, 1912-1986. Princeton Legacy Library SWEDISH INTERNATIONAL DEVELOPMENT COOPERATION AGENCY(SIDCA). Quick Guide to What and How: increasing women's access to land.* OECD. https://www.oecd.org/dac/gender-development/47566053.pdf

Thompson, A. (2024). *Advancing Women's Rights to Land Ownership in Morocco*. MCC. https://www.mcc.gov/blog/entry/blog-030724-womens-land-rights-morocco/

Women U. N. (2013). *In Morocco, encouraged by success, Sulaliyyate women make strides in land rights*. Women UN. https://www.unwomen.org/en/news/stories/2013/2/in-morocco-encouraged-by-success-soulalyates-women-make-strides-in-land-rights

World Economic Forum. (2016). *This Is What Women's Land Rights Look Like Around the World*. World Economic Forum. https://www.weforum.org/agenda/2016/03/this-is-what-womens-land-rights-look-like-around-the-world/

Zartman, W. (1963). Farming and land ownership in Morocco. *Land Economics*, *39*(2), 187–198. doi:10.2307/3144754

ENDNOTE

[1] https://womeninbusiness.ma/2023/01/30/centre-dinclusion-des-femmes-au-foncier-une-rencontre-sur-le-dispositif-partenarial/

Chapter 10
Empresses of Legacy:
Unveiling the Tapestry of Historical Triumphs in Indian Women's Empowerment

Aparna Rao Yerramilli
https://orcid.org/0009-0005-0262-9712
GVP College of Engineering, India

ABSTRACT

The proposed chapter aims to shed light on Indian Stories of Historical Women's extraordinary courage and achievements which contributed to the empowerment of women in India. Examples of iconic women like Rani Padmini, Rani Lakshmibai, and Savitribai Phule will be discussed so as to illustrate their iconic roles in shaping India's socio-political and educational landscapes. The chapter will also delve into the contributions of these women in giving a direction to the movement of women empowerment in India. Hence, the focus on the women who played a pivotal role in social reforms, revolutionary movements, and political pioneers, freedom fighters, educationists who paved the way for inspiring the future generations to come, in a diverse and vast landscape as India.

INTRODUCTION

" I raise up my voice—not so I can shout, but so that those without a voice can be heard... we cannot succeed when half of us are held back." Malala Yousafzai

"Peace cannot exist without justice, justice cannot exist without fairness, fairness cannot exist without development, development cannot exist without democracy, democracy cannot exist without respect for the identity and worth of cultures and peoples." - Rigoberta Menchú

India, a land of diverse cultures, traditions, and histories, has been the crucible for countless movements and revolutions. Among these, the journey towards women's empowerment[1] stands as a testament to the

DOI: 10.4018/979-8-3693-2806-4.ch010

Empresses of Legacy

resilience and determination of the past generations. From the ancient scriptures that praise the virtues of women to the modern-day struggles for gender equality, Indian women have continuously fought against deeply entrenched patriarchal norms to claim their rightful place in society.

In the intricate tapestry of Indian history, resplendent with stories of Indian Emperors and their grand triumphs, lies a narrative of the remarkable yet untold contributions of Indian empresses and their legacies[2]. From the ancient times to the modern era, these empresses have wielded power, defied conventions, and left indelible marks on the fabric of Indian society especially with regards to empowerment and emancipation of women[3].

In this chapter, we delve into the lives and legacies of some of the most prominent women social reformers in Indian history, illuminating their contributions, struggles, and enduring impact on society. Through their stories, we gain insights into the challenges faced by Indian women and the resilience displayed in the face of adversity. From the regal courts of ancient dynasties to the tumultuous days of colonial rule, we delve into the lives of empresses and women social reformers who defied the constraints of their time and carved their places in history.

METHODOLOGY

The methodology of the present study involves several key approaches. The study involves extensive historical research to explore the lives and contributions of brave empresses throughout Indian history. The study is an amalgamation of biographies, and chronicles, for insights into the roles, actions, and influence of empresses in various Indian historical contexts. The study include \s a comprehensive literature review to understand the role and status of Indian women's history, empowerment, leadership, and socio-cultural contexts.

Biographical studies of individual empresses, delving into their life stories, achievements, challenges, and the broader historical significance of their actions has been undertaken at a multidisciplinary level so as to showcase the multifaceted nature of women's empowerment in the Indian context.

Narrative analysis technique has been employed to understand how the lives and times of these empresses have influenced women's empowerment in the Indian context while showcasing the differences and commonalities, the challenges and triumphs of these brave Indian women.

Empowerment of Women: An International Perspective

History is replete with examples of women who have transcended the invisible shackles and barriers of systemic discrimination, patriarchal societal norms and have emerged as harbingers of change in the domain of women empowerment. Empress Wu Zetian of China was known for her political astuteness and leadership, Empress Wu Zetian's legacy as the only female emperor in Chinese history challenged gender norms and stereotypes.

Wangari Maathai of Kenya was an environmentalist and activist who founded the Green Belt Movement, for women's empowerment through environmental conservation and sustainable development. She worked in empowering rural women by teaching them about tree planting, land rights, and environmental stewardship, leading to improved livelihoods and community resilience.

Rigoberta Menchú is a Nobel Peace Prize laureate known for her advocacy for indigenous rights and social justice. Her experiences as a Maya K'iche' woman[4] shaped her activism, highlighting the intersectionality of gender, ethnicity, and human rights in the struggle for empowerment and equality.

Audre Lorde was a poet, writer, and civil rights activist who advocated for intersectional feminism and the empowerment of marginalized communities, including women of color and LGBTQ+ individuals. Her work emphasized the importance of embracing differences and building solidarity across diverse backgrounds to achieve collective empowerment.

Empowerment of women is a global issue that transcends borders and cultures. From the suffragette movements in Europe to the feminist waves in the United States, there has been a rich tapestry of international movements, policies, and collaborations for the cause. the struggle for gender equality has been a resonating topic of concern not only in the developing third world countries, but also in well developed and progressive countries worldwide. The international perspective on women's empowerment, especially in the Indian context, has been shaped by global frameworks such as the Beijing Declaration and Platform for Action[5] which has underlined the importance of women's rights as human rights. This framework has been instrumental in affirming the fundamental rights of women and girls, including the right to education, health, and freedom from violence and discrimination. In addition, it has also been instrumental in advocating for increased participation of women in decision-making processes at all levels of society, including in political, economic, and social spheres.

International organizations like UN Women are also instrumental in advocating for gender equality to empower women globally. HeForShe campaign[6] and the Global Acceleration Plan for Women's Economic Empowerment[7] of the UN Women aim to promote gender-responsive policies to address the systemic barriers to women's empowerment.

National Perspective

In India, the pioneering efforts of social reformers like Raja Ram Mohan Roy and Jyotirao Phule to brave women warriors and reformers like Rani Lakshmi Bai and Sarojini Naidu, there are exemplary men and women who have defied societal norms and championed the cause of women's rights. In the modern day India, initiatives like women's self-help groups empower women economically and socially by providing financial literacy, entrepreneurship training, and collective decision-making opportunities.

At the national level, there are several policies and programs aimed at women's empowerment have evolved over time, like the National Mission for Empowerment of Women, Beti Bachao Beti Padhao[8], and the Mahila Shakti Kendras[9] aim at working towards attaining gender equality and women's empowerment. The National Commission for Women (NCW) serves as a supervisory body for women's rights and addresses issues of gender-based violence, discrimination, and empowerment.

Regional Perspective

Within India, states like Kerala, with high literacy rates and strong social indicators and have been at the forefront of gender equality initiatives, including women's education, healthcare, and political representation. Regional collaborations and initiatives within India, such as the Northeast Women Entrepreneurship Program[10] and the South India Women's Conference[11], highlight localized efforts to empower women and address region-specific challenges. The journey of women's empowerment in India is enriched by international perspectives, national policies, and regional dynamics. By embracing a multi-dimensional

Empresses of Legacy

approach that integrates global frameworks, national strategies, and regional innovations, India continues to advance the cause of women's empowerment.

Review of Literature

1. A. H. Mir and A. A. Dar, in the book, "Unveiling the Legacy: The History and Triumphs of 1. termined Queens in Ancient Kashmir" discuss about the influential queens who shaped ancient Kashmir's socio-political landscape. The study brings to the forefront, the pivotal roles played by female leaders in shaping the destiny of Kashmir. The narrative talks about the valour of Queen Yasovati, Queen Sugandha, Queen Didda, and how these queens proved that gender was not a barrier to effective leadership and good governance. In a patriarchal society, these queens traversed challenges with skill and determination and shaped Kashmir's destiny.

2. Benjamin G. Brawley's "Women of Achievement" praises African American women for their successes in various areas. He talks about their progress in forming clubs, educating children, and joining the workforce. Brawley especially highlights their contributions in medicine, law, literature, and music. Brawley talks about Harriet Tubman, who helped over 300 slaves escape to freedom; Nora Gordon, a missionary worker in Africa, stressing the importance of women in Christian missions; Meta Warrick Fuller, an artist whose later work focused more on social issues; Mary McLeod Bethune, an educator who started a school and hospital; Mary Church Terrell, an educated speaker and writer on African American issues, promoting anti-lynching efforts; and Joanna P. Moore, who founded Fireside Schools to educate African Americans and promote values like prayer, family duties, reading, and community support.

3. "The Freedom to Remember" by M. S. Maity and P. Shukla, published in 2023, explores how Black women authors use storytelling to discuss slavery, freedom, and gender in their modern fiction. The book analyzes how narrative techniques like storytelling, memory, and intergenerational narratives can be used to delve into themes of slavery's impact, gender roles, and identity. It also examines how these works challenge stereotypes and patriarchal views while reclaiming history and asserting agency. The book sheds light on the significance of storytelling in shaping discussions around race, gender, trauma, and liberation.

4. The research paper by Saiswaroopa Iyer, "Exploring Agency, Empowerment, And Identity In'Rukmini: 'Krishna's Wife" focuses on the portrayal of Rukmini, as Lord Krishna's Wife (2021). Rukmini is shown as a redoubtable and unyielding woman who challenges the prevailing societal norms and patriarchal constraints of her era. Rukmini, through thoughts, her deeds and choices becomes a symbol of women empowerment. transcending the boundaries set by a patriarchal society. This research paper digs deep into themes of women empowerment, self-discovery, and the breaking of societal norms.

5. The study, "A Portraiture Study: Women Leaders Advocating Religious Freedom in India" by Matney, A. E. (2022), focuses on the roles and experiences of women leaders advocating for religious freedom in India. It explores their activism, challenges, strategies, and impact on promoting religious pluralism and tolerance in a diverse society.

6. The Dissertation, "Neither Memsahibs nor Missionaries: Western Women Who Supported the Indian Independence Movement" by MacDonald, S. M. (2010), examines the contributions of Western women who supported the Indian independence movement. It sheds

light on their roles, motivations, alliances, and the complexities of their commitment in anti-colonial struggles in India.
7. The book, "Women, Peace and Welfare: A Suppressed History of Social Reform, 1880-1920" by Oakley, A. (2018) discusses the suppressed history of women's contributions to social reform, peace advocacy, and welfare initiatives during the late 19th and early 20th centuries. It highlights the activism, networks, and achievements of women in promoting social justice and welfare reforms.
8. "Empowered Presence: Theorizing an Afrocentric Performance of Leadership by African American Women" by Wamble-King, S. (2023) is a doctoral dissertation which explores how cultural identity, gender, and historical legacies shape leadership styles and strategies among African American women leaders.
9. The book, "Women in Power: World Leaders since 1960" by Hoogensen, G., & Solheim, B. O. (2006), provides an all-inclusive overview of women's political leadership globally since 1960. It profiles female world leaders, examines their impact on politics and society, and discusses challenges and opportunities for women in positions of power.

The Empresses of India

Indian empresses throughout history have wielded power and influence, contributing to women's empowerment. Their legacies inspire progress of today's modern women towards gender equality, challenging norms and shaping the narrative of empowerment in India.

Rani Durgavathi

Rani Durgavati, was a prominent ruler of the Gondwana Kingdom in the 16th century. She was born in 1524 and ruled from 1550 until her death in 1564. Durgavati was married to Dalpat Shah, the king of the Gondwana Kingdom, and upon his death, she ascended to the throne. Queen Durgavati is remembered for her bravery, resilience, and leadership, In 1564, when Akbar's forces invaded the Gondwana Kingdom, Durgavati led her army into battle against them. Despite being outnumbered and facing superior forces, she fought courageously to defend her kingdom. Her sacrifice and bravery in defending her kingdom against the Mughal invasion have made her a symbol of courage and resistance in Indian history. Queen Durgavati also worked greatly to promote the welfare of her subjects, including initiatives to improve education and empower women within her kingdom. As a ruler, she recognized the inherent potential of women and actively worked to uplift their status within her kingdom. Durgavati understood that education was key to empowerment, and she established schools and institutions specifically for girls, ensuring that they had access to knowledge and learning opportunities. By promoting education, Durgavati challenged societal norms and empowered women to pursue their aspirations beyond traditional gender roles. Queen Durgavati was also a trailblazer in advocating for women's economic independence. She implemented policies to encourage women's participation in trade, agriculture, and other economic activities, providing them with avenues for financial autonomy and self-sufficiency. Through initiatives such as granting women access to land and resources, Durgavati enabled them to contribute meaningfully to the economy and assert their agency in decision-making processes.

Asandhimitra Devi

Asandhimitra Devi, the wife of Emperor Ashoka, was a significant figure in ancient Indian history, during the reign of the Mauryan Empire. Under the reign of Emperor Ashoka and Empress Asandhimitra, several initiatives were undertaken to uplift the status of women in Mauryan society. Empress Asandhimitra was an advocate for women's rights and welfare, championing causes that aimed to improve their lives and opportunities. She passionately worked towards women's empowerment and her support for education and literacy among women was at the forefront. She sponsored the establishment of schools and educational institutions specifically for girls, ensuring that they had access to knowledge and intellectual development. She was also instrumental in promoting economic opportunities for women. She encouraged entrepreneurship and supported initiatives that enabled women to engage in trade, agriculture, and other economic activities. The empress felt that by fostering economic independence, women gained greater autonomy and agency in decision-making processes, contributing to their overall empowerment and societal advancement.

Didda of Kashmir

Empress Didda, also known as Didda of Kashmir, was a prominent ruler in the Kashmir region during the 10th and 11th centuries CE. She rose to power as a regent and later became the sovereign ruler of Kashmir. Her husband was King Kshemagupta, the ruler of the Kashmiri kingdom. Despite societal expectations and physical challenges, despite being a hunchback, Empress Didda exhibited remarkable political acumen and leadership. She wielded significant influence over the affairs of state, effectively governing Kashmir during a period of political instability. Didda's story embodies women's empowerment as she defied conventional gender roles to assert her authority and leave a lasting impact on her kingdom. Her reign was characterized by stability and prosperity, as she implemented policies to promote the welfare of her subjects and ensure justice and security for all citizens. Empress Didda's legacy as a powerful and capable ruler challenges traditional notions of female leadership and inspires future generations to recognize the potential of women in positions of authority. Her story serves as a reminder of the resilience and determination of women throughout history to overcome obstacles and effect positive change in society.

Rani Padmini

Rani Padmini, a legendary figure in Indian history, was the queen consort of King Ratan Sen, ruler of Chittor in the 13th century. Padmini's story embodies elements of women's empowerment through her courage, resilience, and unwavering commitment to her principles. When the Sultan of Delhi, Alauddin Khilji, coveted Padmini after hearing tales of her beauty, she refused to submit to his advances. Instead, she, along with other women of the court, made a valiant stand to protect their honor and dignity. Despite facing overwhelming odds, Padmini's unwavering resolve and sacrifice became symbols of resistance against oppression and tyranny. Her story highlights the agency of women in challenging patriarchal norms and defending their autonomy and integrity. Even today, Rani Padmini continues to inspire generations, underscoring the importance of courage, integrity, and empowerment in the face of adversity. Her legacy serves as a reminder of the enduring strength and resilience of women throughout history.

Rani Karnavati

Rani Karnavati, the Queen of Chittor, emerged as a symbol of courage and resilience during a tumultuous period in Indian history. In the face of imminent danger posed by Emperor Humayun's Mughal forces, Karnavati displayed remarkable leadership by appealing to fellow Rajput rulers for assistance in defending her kingdom. Karnavati's story exemplifies women's empowerment through her decisive actions and unwavering determination to protect her people and heritage. Despite the societal norms of her time that often marginalized women from political affairs, Karnavati boldly took matters into her own hands to safeguard Chittor. Her appeal to other Rajput rulers demonstrated her strategic acumen and diplomatic prowess, as she recognized the importance of unity and solidarity in the face of external threats. Though her efforts were ultimately unsuccessful in repelling the Mughal invasion, Karnavati's defiance and courage left an indelible mark on Indian history. Rani Karnavati's legacy serves as a powerful reminder of the significant contributions of women in shaping the course of events, even in male-dominated spheres. Her story continues to inspire generations, underscoring the importance of women's agency, leadership, and resilience in the face of adversity.

Nur Jahan

Nur Jahan, the Empress of the Mughal Empire during the 17th century, stands as an iconic figure in Indian history. She was renowned for her exceptional political acumen, administrative skills, and cultural patronage. Nur Jahan wielded significant influence and power, leaving an indelible mark on the Mughal court. As a woman in a male-dominated society, Nur Jahan's rise to prominence exemplifies women's empowerment. She navigated the intricate politics of the Mughal court with finesse, earning the trust and respect of Emperor Jahangir and becoming his trusted advisor and confidante. Nur Jahan's leadership was characterized by her astute decision-making and strategic vision, which contributed to the stability and prosperity of the empire during her tenure. She was also a patron of arts and culture and showcased her commitment to promoting women's creativity and expression. She supported poets, artists, and musicians, fostering a vibrant cultural milieu that celebrated diversity and innovation.

Rani Lakshmibai

Rani Lakshmibai, the valiant Queen of the princely state of Jhansi, remains an iconic figure in Indian history for her unwavering courage and leadership during the Indian Rebellion of 1857 against British rule. Her story epitomizes women's empowerment as she defied societal norms and took up arms to defend her kingdom and freedom from the Britishers. Rani Lakshmibai led her troops into battle, displaying strategic prowess and fearlessness, earning the admiration and respect of her followers and adversaries alike. Her leadership during the rebellion inspired countless men and women to join the fight for independence, breaking barriers and challenging stereotypes about women's roles in society. Rani Lakshmibai's commitment to her people and her unwavering dedication to the cause of independence serve as a powerful example of women's agency and empowerment. Her bravery and sacrifice symbolize the indomitable spirit of women throughout history who have fought for equality, justice, and freedom.

Empresses of Legacy

Razia Sultana

Razia Sultana, known as the Sultana of Substance, was a trailblazing ruler in the history of Delhi Sultanate. She was the one who shattered gender norms and championed progressive governance. She ascended the throne as the Sultana of Delhi in the 13th century and defied societal expectations by wielding power with wisdom and compassion. She challenged several stereotypes about women's capabilities in positions of authority. Her reign was marked by a commitment to gender equality and inclusive governance. She appointed officials based on merit rather than gender, thus prioritizing competency and expertise in administration. Razia also implemented policies to promote social justice, religious tolerance, and economic prosperity, thereby earning her the respect and admiration of her subjects. She remained steadfast in her pursuit of justice and equality irrespective of facing many odds. She led military expeditions, governed with transparency and accountability, and fostered cultural and intellectual advancements during her rule. She paved a way to create a more equitable and inclusive society.

Kittur Chennamma

Chennamma was hailed as the Resilient Rebel, a fearless leader and queen regnant of the princely state of Kittur in Karnataka, India, during the early 19th century. Chennamma's journey towards empowerment began when she ascended the throne after the death of her husband, King Mallasarja. Determined to protect her kingdom from British annexation, she led her forces in a fierce rebellion against the East India Company's expansionist policies. Despite facing overwhelming odds, she displayed unwavering courage and strategic wisdom on the battlefield. Her leadership inspired men and women alike to join the fight for independence, challenging gender norms and stereotypes about women's roles in society. Although she was suppressed by the British, she left a lasting legacy of courage and defiance. Chennamma's story continues to inspire women to stand up for their rights and fight against injustice, echoing her call for empowerment and liberation.

Rani Abbakka Chowta

Rani Abbakka Chowta, was the courageous queen of Ullal, in Karnataka during the 16th century. When the Portuguese sought to expand their influence along the coastal regions of Karnataka, Rani Abbakka fiercely defended her kingdom and heritage. She led her forces into battle, employing guerrilla tactics and strategic maneuvers to thwart Portuguese advances. Despite facing overwhelming odds, Abbakka's unwavering resolve and indomitable spirit earned her the admiration of her allies and the respect of her adversaries. She stands as a shining example of women's empowerment through her fearless resistance against Portuguese colonization. Her defiance of colonial oppression showcases the power of women in defending their territories and preserving their cultural heritage. Her bravery serves as a symbol of hope of empowerment, inspiring women to assert their agency and challenge oppressive forces. Abbakka's legacy is a testimony of courage, resilience, and the enduring strength of women in the face of adversity.

Indian Women Social Reformers

Women social reformers in India have been instrumental in advancing women's empowerment. Through advocacy for education, suffrage, and social equality, they have challenged norms and paved the way for progress, shaping the trajectory of women's empowerment in Indian society.

Rukhmabai Raut

Born in 1864 in Bombay, Rukhmabai was married off at the tender age of eleven to Dadaji Bhikaji, a man considerably older than her. This forced marriage not only disrupted her childhood but also threatened her dreams of education and independence. Refusing to accept her fate passively, Rukhmabai took a bold step and chose to contest the marriage in court. In 1885, Dadaji Bhikaji filed a lawsuit demanding conjugal rights, catapulting Rukhmabai into the legal limelight. Despite societal pressure and criticism, she stood firm in her resolve to assert her autonomy and right to self-determination. In 1888, the Bombay High Court delivered a historic verdict, granting Rukhmabai's petition for divorce on the grounds of her refusal to cohabit with her husband. This landmark decision marked the first divorce granted under the Indian legal system, setting a precedent for future cases and signaling a significant shift in societal attitudes towards women's rights and autonomy. Rukhmabai's courageous stance and unwavering determination paved the way for legislative reforms aimed at protecting women from the injustices of child marriage and marital coercion. Rukhmabai Raut's journey to empowerment with her historic divorce was a landmark event in Indian legal and social history.

Savitribai Phule

Savitribai Phule was a pioneer of women's education in 19th-century India. She had embarked on a remarkable journey of empowerment despite facing numerous obstacles. Born in 1831, Savitribai was married off at a very young age to Jyotirao Phule, who was a social reformer. Despite her lack of formal education, Savitribai's thirst for knowledge remained unquenchable. Along with her husband, Savitribai defied societal norms by establishing the first school for girls in Pune in 1848. Savitribai remained undeterred in her mission to educate and empower women inspite of facing several threats and challenges. She tasted success when the first batch of female students graduated from the school. This marked a significant milestone in the history of women's education in India. After this, the country witnessed a widespread establishment of schools for girls across the country. She was one of the pioneers who laid the foundation for women's empowerment through education. Savitribai's story is a testament to the transformative power of education in empowering individuals and communities, and her contributions to the cause of women's empowerment remain unparalleled in Indian history.

Kamaladevi Chattopadhyay

Kamaladevi Chattopadhyay, dedicated her life to breaking barriers and fostering social change. Born in 1903, Kamaladevi defied societal expectations by pursuing education and independence, becoming one of the first Indian women to study abroad. After returning to India, Kamaladevi became a prominent figure in the Indian independence movement. She advocated for gender equality and social justice. She played a pivotal role in the founding of several women's organizations, including the All India Women's

Conference, which fought for women's rights and empowerment. She championed the revival of traditional Indian arts and crafts, she also worked towards empowering rural artisans, especially women, by providing them with economic opportunities and recognition for their skills. She was awarded with the Padma Bhushan, India's third-highest civilian award. Her indomitable spirit and unwavering commitment to women's empowerment continue to inspire generations, serving as a guiding light for those dedicated to creating a more equitable and inclusive society in India and beyond.

Anandibai Joshi

Anandibai Joshi, a trailblazing figure in the annals of Indian history, shattered gender barriers to become the first Indian woman to earn a degree in Western medicine. She was born in 1865 in Maharashtra, and faced numerous obstacles in her pursuit of education and empowerment. With unwavering determination, she pursued her dream of becoming a doctor, earning admission to the Women's Medical College of Pennsylvania in the United States in 1883. Her journey was fraught with numerous challenges, from navigating cultural differences to battling health issues. Yet, she persevered, graduating with honors in 1886. After her return to India, Anandibai became a beacon of hope and inspiration for Indian women aspiring to break free from the confines of tradition. Tragically, her life was cut short at the age of 21 due to illness, but Anandibai's remarkable achievements paved the way for future generations of Indian women in the field of medicine and served as a catalyst for societal change.

Begum Rokeya Sakhawat Hossain

Begum Rokeya Sakhawat Hossain was a pioneering feminist and social reformer who dedicated her life to advancing women's rights and empowerment. Born in 1880 in British India (now Bangladesh), Rokeya faced the constraints of patriarchal society from a very early age but she refused to be silenced. Rokeya founded the first Muslim girls' school in Kolkata in 1911, advocating for education as a means of empowerment for women. She also established the Anjuman-e-Khawateen-e-Islam, an organization dedicated to promoting women's education and social reform. Her activism extended to her writing, where she penned powerful essays and stories advocating for women's rights and gender equality. Despite facing criticism and opposition, Rokeya remained steadfast in her commitment to women's empowerment until her passing in 1932.

Muthulakshmi Reddi

Muthulakshmi Reddi was a vanguard in the realm of women's empowerment in India. Born in 1886 in Tamil Nadu, Muthulakshmi faced severe discrimination and restrictions on her education due to her gender. She, however, refused to be deterred and broke many a barrier. She became the first female student to enroll in the prestigious Madras Medical College in 1907. Her passion for medicine extended beyond healing patients. She used her knowledge to address pressing social issues, more importantly those which affected women and children.

In 1926, Muthulakshmi created history by becoming the first woman legislator in British India's legislative council. Her tenure was marked by relentless efforts to advance women's rights. She was highly instrumental in advocating for the abolition of the devadasi system and she championed for the legislation to protect women and children. Her contributions also included founding institutions such as the Adyar Cancer Institute and the Avvai Home, providing healthcare and shelter to marginalized women and children. Her life is a reminder of the transformative power of resilience, determination in the fight for women's empowerment and social justice.

Begum Hazrat Mahal

Begum Hazrat Mahal was a symbol of resilience and leadership in India's struggle against the British colonialism. She played a pivotal role in empowering women during the Indian Rebellion of 1857. Born in 1820 in Faizabad, she rose to prominence as the wife of Nawab Wajid Ali Shah of Awadh. In 1856, when British forces annexed Awadh in 1856, she emerged as a formidable leader, rallying soldiers and civilians alike to resist colonial oppression. In spite of facing enormous challenges, together with the loss of her husband's throne, Begum Hazrat Mahal refused to surrender to British rule.

She led her troops into battle, with immense courage and determination, demonstrating outstanding strategic acumen and inspirational loyalty among her followers. In addition, she also championed the cause of women's empowerment. She advocated for their participation in the resistance movement and also provided support to widows and orphans affected by the conflict.

Begum Hazrat Mahal's legacy endured as a symbol of resistance and empowerment despite a defeat in the rebellion against the British. Her fearless disobedience of colonial authority and commitment to the welfare of her people remind us of the indomitable spirit of women in the face of adversity.

Kadambini Ganguly

Kadambini Ganguly's journey as one of the first female graduates and physicians in India, was one of grit and determination. She defied societal norms and paved the way for women's education and empowerment. Ganguly pursued her academic and professional aspirations, breaking barriers and thus inspired future generations of women to pursue their dreams. Her pioneering achievements in the field of medicine not only contributed to advancements in healthcare, also challenged traditional gender roles. She was the best example of the immense potential of women in traditionally male-dominated fields. Kadambini Ganguly's legacy serves as a testimony to the transformative power of education and perseverance in overcoming societal barriers and achieving empowerment.

Aruna Asaf Ali

Aruna Asaf Ali's story is one of courage and indomitable spirit in the pursuit of freedom and women empowerment. As a prominent figure in the Indian independence movement, she fearlessly fought against colonial oppression and injustice. Her heroic act of hoisting the Indian National Congress flag during the Quit India Movement symbolized the resilience and determination of Indian women in the struggle for independence. Aruna Asaf Ali was also a vocal advocate for women's rights and social reforms. She inspired many women across the nation to break free from the restraints of patriarchy and in shaping their destinies. She always fought for equality and empowerment of women.

Empresses of Legacy

Captain Lakshmi Sahgal

Captain Lakshmi Sahgal's life is a true testament to courage, resilience, and dedication to the cause of women's empowerment in India. She was a leader in the Indian National Army (INA) during the struggle for independence, and shattered gender stereotypes by leading the Rani of Jhansi Regiment, which was an all-female unit. She played a crucial role in the fight against the British colonial rule. Sahgal's leadership and bravery inspired women from all walks of life to join the freedom struggle. Even after independence, she advocated for social justice and women's empowerment. Her remarkable achievements and unwavering commitment to the cause makes Captain Lakshmi Sahgal an enduring symbol of empowerment and a source of inspiration for women across the globe.

Social Reformers and Models of the 21st Century India: Overcoming Barriers and Prioritizing Women's Empowerment

In the 21st century, several prominent women emerged as agents of change, challenging barriers and advocating for gender equality. They faced several barriers and obstacles and yet stood steadfast in their journey of paving a way of empowerment to the future generations of women.

History is replete with examples of how women in leadership positions encountered numerous barriers, like societal expectations, gender biases, discrimination and limited opportunities. Women leaders like Sucheta Kriplani and Indira Gandhi faced immense challenges in a predominantly male-dominated political landscape. Their authority and capabilities were questioned and undermined. Societal norms and cultural stereotypes of those days constrained their roles, relegating women to traditional spheres of influence rather than positions of power and decision-making. Despite these challenges and systemic barriers, the social reformers of the 21st century showcased resilience, determination, and strategic acumen in navigating complex socio-political environments.

Indira Gandhi's was propelled to become India's first female Prime Minister due to her assertive leadership style and strategic policymaking. Challenging gender norms and inspiring generations of women leaders, women like Sushma Swaraj and Sonia Gandhi demonstrated undaunted political prowess and advocated for women's rights, thereby breaking through the seemingly unbreakable barriers and emerged as influential voices in national and international arenas. The Indian women reformers of the 21st century pioneered in prioritizing women's empowerment through policy initiatives, legislative reforms, and advocacy campaigns. Line Sheila Dikshit's emphasis on education and healthcare for women in Delhi, Late J Jayalalitha's welfare schemes for marginalized communities in Tamil Nadu, and Mamata Banerjee's focus on inclusive development in West Bengal, Mayawati's leadership in Uttar Pradesh highlighted issues of social justice and empowerment for marginalized communities, including women from Dalit backgrounds.

Women leaders like Vasundhara Raje Scindia, Ambika Soni, Nirmala Sitharaman, Mahua Moitra, and others championed legislative changes, economic opportunities, and social reforms. For example, Raje's initiatives for women's entrepreneurship in Rajasthan, Sitharaman's gender responsive economic policies promoting financial inclusion, and Moitra's advocacy for gender equality and human rights in Parliament reflect the ever evolving priorities and strategies, championing the cause of women. Despite facing formidable challenges, these leaders have demonstrated resilience, vision, and commitment to creating a more equitable and inclusive world

The #MeToo movement[12] and has catalyzed conversations around gender equality, challenging patriarchal structures and promoting a more inclusive society. The contributions of social reformers and models of the 21st century India have been vital in furthering women's empowerment, breaking barriers, and reshaping societal norms. Moving forward, continued efforts in policy reforms, institutional support, and cultural shifts are essential to sustain progress and ensure meaningful empowerment for women across diverse sectors and communities.

Challenges Faced by Indian Women Social Reformers

Indian women social reformers face a range of unique challenges that stem from cultural, social, and economic factors.

1. Patriarchal Norms: Deep-seated patriarchal norms and traditional gender roles which restrict women's participation in public life, limiting their decision-making power, and hindering their ability to advocate for social change.
2. Social Stigma: Women who challenge societal norms and advocate for progressive reforms many a times face social stigma, backlash, and resistance from conservative elements within society.
3. Resource Constraints: women still have limited access to resources such as education, funding, networks, and platforms for advocacy which pose significant barriers for women social reformers.
4. Intersectional Discrimination: Women from marginalized communities, including Dalits, tribal groups, religious minorities, and LGBTQ+ individuals, experience intersecting forms of discrimination that exponentially compound their challenges in social reform efforts.
5. Political and Institutional Barriers: Women often encounter barriers within political and institutional structures, including gender bias, lack of representation, and exclusion from decision-making processes.

Indian women social reformers have however been successful in demonstrating resilience, creativity, and determination. They have been consistently overcoming obstacles and are also emerging as drivers of meaningful change.

However, some strategies and interventions are vital and imperative to address their specific needs and strengthen policy initiatives for women's empowerment. Tailoring empowerment programs to reflect cultural norms, values, and contexts, ensuring that interventions are culturally sensitive and resonate with local communities is the foremost. Also training, mentorship, and skills development programs to build the capacity of women social reformers in advocacy, leadership, communication, and networking can improve the visibility of the policies for women empowerment. Prioritizing education and literacy initiatives for women, including awareness campaigns, scholarships, and access to quality education, should be implemented at a large scale, as education is a key driver of empowerment.

Creating platforms, networks, and coalitions to enable women social reformers to amplify their voices, share experiences, collaborate on initiatives, and advocate for policy changes collectively. Also, promoting financial literacy, entrepreneurship training, microfinance opportunities, and access to credit and capital for women social reformers to support their initiatives and economic empowerment, will help fasten the velocity of empowerment of women.

In addition, legal Protections, addressing women's health issues, including reproductive health care, maternal health, mental health support, and access to healthcare services, as health and well-being is vital to achieving the goals of empowerment.

Recognizing and addressing the various forms of discrimination faced by women from marginalized communities, and ensuring that empowerment efforts are inclusive and equitable for all women are vital elements for sustained empowerment of women.

Challenges Faced by Marginalized Populations for Women's Empowerment: Insights and Recommendations

Marginalized populations, more specifically, women from low-income backgrounds or with limited access to empowerment opportunities, face multifaceted challenges that hinder their socio-economic progress and overall well-being. Women from low-income backgrounds often face barriers to accessing quality education due to financial constraints, lack of infrastructure, and societal norms that prioritize male education. Marginalized women also struggle with limited economic opportunities, unequal pay, and lack of access to financial resources and entrepreneurship support. Limited access to healthcare services, including reproductive health care, contributes to health disparities and impedes women's overall well-being. In addition, marginalized women are also affected by gender-based violence, like domestic violence, sexual assault, and exploitation, and other social evils which hinders their empowerment and growth. The prevailing Social norms and patriarchal structures of their societies essentially limit marginalized women's participation in decision-making processes at home, in communities, and in broader societal contexts.

As such, it becomes imperative to address these challenges by the following measures.

1. Enhancing Educational Opportunities: Implementing targeted programs and initiatives to improve access to quality education for marginalized women, like scholarships, mentorship programs, and vocational training.
2. Economic Empowerment: Promoting women's entrepreneurship through training, access to credit, and business development support. And by implementing policies that ensure equal pay, workplace rights, and opportunities for career advancement.
3. Healthcare Access: Expanding access to affordable and comprehensive healthcare services, with a specific focus on reproductive health care, maternal health, and mental health support for marginalized women.
4. Combatting Gender-Based Violence: Strengthening legal frameworks, support services, and community-based interventions to prevent and respond to gender-based violence effectively. Also promoting gender-sensitive education and awareness campaigns for a greater and sustainable benefit.
5. Empowering Decision-Making: Advocating for policies and initiatives to promote women's participation in decision-making processes at all levels, including political representation, leadership roles, and community governance.

Emerging Trends and Controversies

In the global context, there is a resurgence of global feminist movements rooting for women's rights, gender equality, and social justice on a transnational scale. Many countries and international organizations are adopting gender-responsive policy frameworks and action plans to advance women's empowerment and gender equality. This includes commitments to the Sustainable Development Goals (SDGs), gender mainstreaming in development programs, and legal reforms to address gender-based discrimination.

Controversies however arise in implementing and monitoring these policies, ensuring accountability, and addressing gaps in resources and capacity. Challenges still persist in overcoming cultural biases, systemic barriers, and deeply rooted gender norms that limit women's advancement and leadership opportunities.

The digital revolution is a boon and also a bane. On one hand, it is creating opportunities for women's empowerment, with initiatives focusing on digital literacy, access to technology. Yet we encounter issues of online safety. While technology is enhancing women's economic opportunities, deep concerns exist about online harassment, privacy risks, and biases that can reinforce gender stereotypes and inequalities.

The fight for women's reproductive rights, access to healthcare, and sexual and reproductive health rights (SRHR) remains a significant aspect of women's empowerment the world across. y. Debates on abortion rights, sex education, maternal health care, contraceptive access, still have found no solutions.

Irrespective of widespread knowhow on the interconnectivity between climate change and women's health, challenges still exist in addressing gender disparities in climate impacts, resource allocation, and decision-making processes related to environmental governance.

Irrespective of all these issues, social reformers and activists have made significant strides in advancing women's rights and empowerment. This has lead to increased awareness, visibility, representation, and policy changes. However several controversies and setbacks still plague the empowerment and emancipation of women. There are still persistent gender inequalities, backlash against feminist movements, and challenges in implementing and sustaining empowerment initiatives. Sustainable policies and efforts at international, national, regional and grassroots level, will however yield progressive results.

CONCLUSION

The stories of Indian empresses and women social reformers offer profound insights into the journey towards women's empowerment in India. From ancient times to the present day, these remarkable women have challenged patriarchal norms, defied conventions, and paved the way for progress. Their resilience, determination, and unwavering commitment to the cause of women's empowerment serve as beacons of inspiration for future generations.

REFERENCES

Bose, S., & Jalal, A. (2004). *Modern South Asia: History, Culture, Political Economy*. Routledge. doi:10.4324/9780203712535

Brawley, B. G. (2022). *Women of Achievement: Written for the Fireside Schools*. DigiCat.

Chatterjee, P. (1993). *The Nation and Its Fragments: Colonial and Postcolonial Histories*. Princeton University Press.

Forbes, G. (1999). *Women in Modern India*. Cambridge University Press.

Gandhi, M. (1993). *The Story of My Experiments with Truth*. Beacon Press.

Government of India. (1955). *Report of the Committee on the Status of Women in India*. Retrieved from. [URL]

Hoogensen, G., & Solheim, B. O. (2006). *Women in power: World leaders since 1960*. Bloomsbury Publishing USA.

Khan, R. W. (2009). *Women in Ancient India*. Goodword Books.

Kumar, R. (1993). *The History of Doing: An Illustrated Account of Movements for Women's Rights and Feminism in India, 1800-1990*. Zubaan.

Kumar, R. (2009). Mapping the Terrain of Indian Feminism: Colonial Legacies. [DOI]. *Signs (Chicago, Ill.), 35*(3), 559–561.

MacDonald, S. M. (2010). *Neither memsahibs nor missionaries: Western women who supported the Indian independence movement* (Doctoral dissertation, University of New Brunswick, Department of History).

Maity, M. S., & Shukla, P. (2023). Exploring Agency, Empowerment, And Identity In 'Rukmini: Krishna's Wife' By Saiswaroopa Iyer. *Journal of Namibian Studies: History Politics Culture, 33*, 2940–2963.

Matney, A. E. (2022). *A Portraiture Study: Women Leaders Advocating Religious Freedom in India*. Johnson University.

Menon, N., & Bhasin, K. (1998). *Borders and Boundaries: Women in India's Partition*. Rutgers University Press.

Mir, A. H., & Dar, A. A. (Year). *Unveiling the Legacy: The History and Triumphs of Determined Queens in Ancient Kashmir*. Publisher.

Mitchell, A. (2002). *The Freedom to Remember: Narrative, Slavery, and Gender in Contemporary Black Women's Fiction*. Rutgers University Press.

Mukherjee, M. (2004). *Peasants in India's Non-Violent Revolution: Practice and Theory*. Sage Publications.

Nanda, B. (2000). *The Changing Position of Women in Bengal, 1849-1905*. Routledge.

Oakley, A. (2018). *Women, Peace and Welfare: a suppressed history of social reform, 1880-1920*. Policy Press.

Roy, M. (2012). *The Rani of Jhansi: Gender, History, and Fable in India*. Cambridge University Press India.

Sarkar, T. (2001). *Hindu Wife, Hindu Nation: Community, Religion, and Cultural Nationalism*. Permanent Black.

Sarkar, T. (2008). *Women and Social Reform in Modern India: A Reader*. Indiana University Press.

Sen, A. P. (1993). *Hindu Revivalism in Bengal, 1872-1905: Some Essays in Interpretation*. Oxford University Press.

Thapar, R. (1990). *A History of India* (Vol. 1). Penguin Books.

Wamble-King, S. (2023). *Empowered Presence: Theorizing an Afrocentric Performance of Leadership by African American Women* [Doctoral dissertation, Antioch University].

ENDNOTES

[1] The empowerment of women is a multifaceted concept that encompasses economic, social, political, and cultural dimensions. It involves ensuring that women have equal opportunities, rights, and access to resources, and that they can actively participate in decision-making processes that affect their lives.

[2] The legacy of empresses refers to the lasting impact and influence left by powerful female rulers in history. For example, Empress Nur Jahan of the Mughal Empire in India is remembered for her political acumen and cultural patronage, leaving a legacy of women's leadership and empowerment,

[3] The emancipation of women refers to the process of liberating women from social, economic, political, and cultural constraints that limit their opportunities, rights, and autonomy. Emancipation aims to achieve gender equality by challenging and dismantling systems of oppression, discrimination, and inequality that have historically marginalized women.

[4] The Maya K'iche' people are an indigenous group in Guatemala, known for their rich cultural heritage, language, and traditions. Maya K'iche' women play significant roles within their communities, often preserving and passing down traditional knowledge, including weaving techniques, medicinal practices, and oral history. They are also active participants in community decision-making and cultural events, contributing to the preservation and promotion of Maya K'iche' identity.

[5] The Beijing Declaration and Platform for Action serve as a guiding framework for governments, civil society organizations, and international bodies to work towards achieving gender equality and women's empowerment. It is a significant document in the domain of women's rights and gender equality. It was adopted at the Fourth World Conference on Women held in Beijing, China, in 1995.

[6] The HeForShe campaign is an initiative launched by UN Women in 2014 with the goal of engaging men and boys as advocates for gender equality and women's rights. The campaign seeks to mobilize men and boys to take action against gender stereotypes, discrimination, and violence, and to promote a more inclusive and equal society.

[7] The Global Acceleration Plan for Women's Economic Empowerment (GAP) is an initiative launched by UN Women and the International Labour Organization (ILO) in 2017. The GAP aims to accelerate progress towards achieving women's economic empowerment globally by addressing key barriers and promoting inclusive economic policies and practices.

[8] "Beti Bachao Beti Padhao" (Save the Daughter, Educate the Daughter) is a flagship initiative of the Government of India launched in 2015. It aims to address the declining trend in the Child Sex Ratio (CSR) and promote the education and empowerment of girls.

[9] Mahila Shakti Kendras (MSKs) are one of the key components of the Government of India's Mahila Shakti Kendra Scheme, which was launched in 2017 under the Ministry of Women and Child Development. The primary goal of MSKs is to empower women by providing them with access to various support services and opportunities for skill development and capacity building.

[10] The Northeast Women Entrepreneurship Program (NE-WEP) is an initiative focused on promoting and supporting women entrepreneurs in the northeastern region of India. This program is designed

to empower women economically, foster entrepreneurship, and contribute to the overall development of the region.

11 The South India Women's Conference is an annual event that brings together women from various states in southern India to discuss and address issues related to women's empowerment, gender equality, and social justice. The conference serves as a platform for women to share experiences, knowledge, and ideas, and to advocate for policies and initiatives that promote women's rights and well-being.

12 The #MeToo movement is a global social movement that emerged in 2017, initially within the entertainment industry but quickly spreading to various sectors and countries. It focuses on raising awareness about sexual harassment, assault, and misconduct, particularly in the workplace. The movement gained momentum through social media platforms, where individuals, predominantly women, shared their experiences of harassment and abuse using the hashtag #MeToo.

Chapter 11
Statistical Analysis of the Empowerment of Women In India

Jothi Sagar Patil
Shahaji Law College, Kolhapur, India

Sagar Dnyandev Patil
https://orcid.org/0000-0003-0283-4853
Sharad Institute of Technology College of Engineering, Yadrav, India

Moula C. Sheikh
Shahaji Law College, Kolhapur, India

ABSTRACT

In this study, various metrics derived from secondary data are used to assess the extent of women's empowerment in India. As evidenced by the survey, women in India continue to have less status and influence than men, despite multiple government attempts. The number of people who can obtain jobs and education varies based on gender. Depending on factors like age, education level, and employment, women's freedom of movement and decision-making power in the home differ significantly. Women are still accepting gender norms that are not equitable in society, it has been found. The final say in how they are paid has gotten less for women. Women receive less media attention than males do as well. It is more common for rural women than urban ones to experience domestic abuse. The gender gap in political participation is also very noticeable. According to the study's conclusion, achieving the goal of empowerment mostly depends on people's views towards gender equality, even though access to employment and education are only enabling factors.

DOI: 10.4018/979-8-3693-2806-4.ch011

Statistical Analysis of the Empowerment of Women In India

INTRODUCTION

The idea of women's empowerment has experienced a fundamental transformation over the past fifty years, moving from a welfare-focused methodology to an egalitarian methodology. It has been perceived as the procedure by which the helpless acquire more power over the events that affect their life. Having authority over resources and ideology is specifically necessary for empowerment. In accordance with Sen and Batliwala (2000), it advances to an inner shift of awareness, a developing internal capability, and a gain in self-confidence, all of which enable one to get over obstacles from the outside world. This perspective of view primarily highlights two important elements. It is first and foremost a power of accomplishment rather than a power over individuals. Second, regardless of gender, caste, class, or other demographic, the idea of empowerment is better suited for individuals who lack authority. While not exclusive to women, the idea of empowerment transcends all social groups and castes, as well as domestic relationships (Malhotra et al., 2002). Another way to define women's empowerment is as a change in a woman's surroundings that makes it possible for her to live a full life. [Mathew (2003) cites Human Development in South Asia, 2000] It shows up in both internal (like self-awareness and self-confidence) and external (like health, mobility, education, awareness, family status, engagement in decision-making, and level of material security) aspects.

The UNDP (1990) initially unveiled the Human Development Index (HDI). It was first developed as a broader measure of a nation's socioeconomic progress, but it soon became well-known as a standard for the typical progress of human development for people of both sexes. In stark contrast to the popular perception that progress is gender-neutral, data indicates that women globally—including those in India—fall short of men in nearly every sphere of life. For this reason, the focus on human development since 1995 (UNDP 1995) has been on emphasizing the gender component and the persistence of discrimination against women. According to the report, humans can't flourish fully without empowering women. It was underlined once more how dangerous it is to discourage advancement. To illustrate the data and facts related to women's suffering, two indices were created: Gender-Related Development Index (GDI) and the Gender Empowerment Measure (GEM). Despite using the same dimensions and variables as the HDI, the GDI takes gender variations in attainment into account (Anand and Sen, 1995). The gender gap in human development widens but the difference between a nation's GDI and HDI narrows. The HDI that has been adjusted for gender disparity is called the GDI. GEM, on the other hand, reveals if women can fully participate in political and economic life. The index might theoretically have any value between 0 and ∞, with unity representing complete equality between male and female achievement. A value greater than unity would suggest that women are more accomplished than men.

Development of GDI and EDI

As everyone knows, the Human Development Index (HDI) is a concise measure of development. The GDP per capita in PPP terms in US dollars, known as the Income Index, measures the standard of living. Life expectancy at birth, measured by the Health Index, measures longevity. Knowledge, determined by the adult proficiency rate and associated total enrolment ratio in elementary, secondary, and tertiary education, measured by the Education Index, measures average progress in the three fundamental areas of human development. Applying the following formulas, performance in each dimension is given as a number between 0 and 1:

I_1 (Education Index), I_2 (Health Index) are constructed by (1) & I_3 (Income Index) by (2)

$$I_j = \frac{X_{ij} - Min(X)}{Max(X_i) - Min(X_i)} \qquad (1)$$

$$I_3 = \frac{Log(X_{ij}) - Log\{Min(X_i)\}}{Log\{Max(X_i)\} - Log\{Min(X_i)\}} \qquad (2)$$

Where Xij denotes the actual value concerning the relevant variables that were utilized to create the aforementioned indices. Then, the dimension indices are simply averaged to provide the HDI. While the HDI measures average attainment, the GDI modifies it to account for gender disparities in the same dimensions as those used in the HDI. The three procedures listed below are used to build GDI:

Step-I: Dimension indices are created for each literacy and health dimension for men and women individually using formula (1), and for the income index using formula (2);

Step II: Using the formula (3), the Equally Distributed Index (EDI) is created for each dimension as follows:

EDI = (Male population Share / Dimension Index for Male) + (Female Population Share / Dimension Index for Female)[-1]

Step III: Using the formula (4), the three equally dispersed indices are averaged to produce the GDI.

$$GDI_j = \frac{1}{3}(EDI_1 + EDI_2 + EDI_3) \qquad (4)$$

Development of GEM

To the best of our knowledge, gender empowerment initiatives prioritize the opportunities available to women over their qualifications. It measures gender inequality in three important areas: (a) power over the economy; (b) economic participation and decision-making power as measured by the percentages of women and men who hold positions as legislators, senior officials, and managers; and (c) political participation and legislative seat percentages for men and women indicate decision-making authority.

The general formula (5) is used to determine an Equally Distributed Equivalent Percentage (EDEP) for each of these three dimensions as a population-weighted average.

EDEP = [(Female Popn. Share / Female Index) + (Male Popn. Share / Male Index)][-1] (5)

The EDEPs for economic and political involvement are each multiplied by 50 to create the corresponding indexed EDEPs, while the simple EDEP for economic resources is taken into account. To create the GEM, these three indexes are averaged.

Statistical Analysis of the Empowerment of Women In India

The Planning Commission (G.O.I., 2002) employed a third statistic, the Gender Equality Index (GEI), in the National Human Development Report. The HDI and GEI construction processes are identical. The index's starting point entails expressing it as a ratio of female to male attainment levels. Second, unlike the HDI, which uses per-capita monthly expenditure, the index's estimation of the economic levels of males and females has taken into account their respective worker-population ratios. This was mainly done to avoid falling back on norms that could never be reached when distributing income or consumption between men and women at the family or individual level. The same set of metrics used for the HDI have been used to record health and educational attainments. In addition to these three indices, other socioeconomic and political factors are commonly used to evaluate women's empowerment (G.O.I., 2005–2006).

LITERATURE SURVEY

Numerous researches on women's empowerment have been conducted both internationally and in India. Studies have covered a variety of topics, including methodological concerns, empirical analysis, and empowerment instruments and metrics. In this section, we've listed some of the significant studies that were conducted on a global scale first, followed by studies done in India.

Moser (1993) concentrated on how gender and development interact, how gender policy is created, and how gender planning and practices are put into practice. Shields' (1995) work offered an exploratory framework for comprehending and developing the idea of empowerment from both a theoretical and practical standpoint, with a focus on women's perceptions of what empowerment meant in their own lives. In 1995, Anand and Sen attempted to create a measurement of gender disparity. Pillarisetti and Gillivray (1998) placed a strong emphasis on the GEM's construction technique, constituents, and determinants. In response to their suggestions, UNDP modified its GDI calculation methodology, which took effect in 1999 but was not explicitly announced as such (Bardhan and Klasen, 2000).

The concept of GDI was evaluated similarly by Dijkstra and Hanmer (2000), who noted its flaws. They contend that the Global Development Index (GDI) conflates relative gender equality with absolute levels of human development and provides no information on the comparative gender gap across nations. They went on to create a Relative Status of Women (RSW) index using the GDI and acknowledged that RSW isn't the best indicator of gender disparity. To establish the foundation for an alternative measurement of gender disparity, the paper's conclusion offered a conceptual framework.

Barkat (2008) expressed her opinion on the state of women in Bangladesh, saying that although moms are valued for who they are, empowerment—a process of raising awareness and ability that gives a woman more control over her own life—is not well understood.

In addition to offering specific recommendations for the two gender-related indicators, Klasen and Schüler (2009) expanded on their earlier research by providing examples of the outcomes of the suggested measures. The two most significant suggestions were the creation of a gender gap index (GGI) to replace the GDI and the computation of a male and female HDI. The earned income component of the GEM was proposed to be handled in various ways, and it was also suggested that it be replaced with a simpler calculation method. He discovered different rankings for countries compared to those of GDI and GEM using the methodologies he had suggested. In their 2007 article, Desai and Thakkar highlighted the role of education, legal rights, and political participation in empowering women. By using self-assessed points on a ten-step power and rights ladder, where the bottom rung represented those who had no power or rights at all and the top rung represented those who had a lot of power and rights, Deepa Narayan (2007) attempted to measure women's empowerment for various countries and regions. In her research on the impact of female representation in state legislatures on public goods, policy, and expenditure in the setting of India, Figueras (2008) concluded that a politician's gender and social standing have an impact on policy.

As a result, it is clear from the literature analysis above that several studies on women's empowerment and related topics have already been conducted. Overarching themes across the entire corpus of work have been conceptualization, quantification, and obstacles to women's empowerment. Accordingly, using data from multiple sources, the current study analyses the state of women's empowerment in India by considering several factors, including women's freedom of movement, financial independence, acceptance of unequal gender roles, political participation, access to education, experience of domestic violence, media exposure, etc.

According to earlier studies, women's empowerment can change the demographics and result in better reproductive health outcomes (Mason, 1995). Economic empowerment of women is linked to increased levels of economic security, independent decision-making, exposure to violence, and political and legal awareness and engagement (Schuler and

Ashemi (1994). According to several studies (Hindin, 2000; Mabsout, 2011; Basu and Koolwal, 2005; Upadhyay et al. 2014;Yount et al., 2019), women's empowerment has also been related to self-confidence, financial confidence, attitude towards gender norms, autonomous decision-making, household communication, partner relationships, and participation in social groups.

THE FACTS IN INDIA

Enumerated in the Preamble, Fundamental Rights, Fundamental Duties, and Directive Principles, the Indian Constitution makes clear reference to the significance of gender equality. The Constitution not only guarantees women's equality but also grants the States the power to pass laws that discriminate positively against men and women. Indian women's status has always been influenced by their cultural background. There is proof that throughout the Vedic era, women held the highest positions in society (Seth, 2001). They were free to pursue their education, remain single, and spend the rest of their lives learning and realizing who they were. Equally as their husbands, married women shared in all the tasks and sacrifices.

According to the UNDP, India has a very low level of development when it comes to the status of women in terms of a variety of indicators, including adult literacy, gross enrollment, the proportion of women in parliament, and the technical and professional positions held by them (as shown in Table - 1). Although data for the GEM indicator beyond 1995 are not published, analysis of GDI values suggests that women continue to lag. India was ranked 113th with a GDI value of 0.600, whereas a small neighboring country like Sri Lanka was ranked 89th with a GDI value of 0.753 (UNDP, 2007-08). Additionally, India's ranking has decreased from 99 in 1995 to 113 in 2007-2008, changing from year to year.

Statistical Analysis of the Empowerment of Women In India

Table 1. Status of women based on variety of indicators

Indicators	1990 W	1990 M	1995 W	1995 M	2000 W	2000 M	2005 W	2005 M	2007-08 W	2007-08 M
Lifespan Estimate	NA	NA	61.4	61.3	62.3	61.5	64.0	62.8	64.3	63.3
Adult Education	28	58	34.2	64.7	43.5	67.1	47.8	73.4	47.8	73.4
Total Enrollment	NA	NA	44.8	64.8	45.0	62.0	57.0	63.0	61.0	69.0
Parliamentary Seat Distribution	NA	NA	6.3	93.7	9.9	90.1	8.3	91.7	8.8	91.2
Proportion of Technical and Professional Personnel	NA	NA	21.5	78.5	21.5	78.5	NA	NA	NA	NA
Development Index pertaining to Gender	NA		0.411 (R-98)		0.555 (R-107)		0.576 (R-97)		0.598 (R-112)	
Measure of Gender Empowerment	NA		0.216 (R- 100)		NA		NA		NA	

Source: UNDP

Information on GDI and GEM indexes was included in the National Human Development Report (G.O.I, 2002). In the 1980s, GDI exhibited a slight improvement. From 62 percent in the early 1980s to 67.6 percent in the early 1990s, GEI rose. This suggests that on average, women's achievements on human development indices were only two-thirds as high as men's. The State with the most gender equality in the 1980s was Kerala, followed by Nagaland, Meghalaya, Manipur, and Himachal Pradesh. Gender equality was greater than the national average in Goa and the Union Territories, with the exception of Delhi. Himachal Pradesh had the most equality in the 1990s, while Bihar was at the bottom and had decreased in absolute terms from the previous period.

Decision Making Power

One of the key signs of women's empowerment is the ability of women to make decisions in their homes. Merely 37% of married women take part in choosing their own or their husbands' health care, major household purchases, purchases for everyday household necessities, and visits to family and relatives. 43% of people participate in some decisions but not all of them, and 21% don't participate at all. As many as 32.4% of the time, respondents make the majority of decisions regarding the purchase of everyday household necessities, whereas husbands or partners typically make the majority of decisions involving visits to the wife's relatives.

Freedom of Movement

Another sign of women's empowerment is their freedom of movement. According to the data, around half of women are permitted to visit the market or a medical facility by themselves. Only 38% of people are permitted to travel alone outside of their village or town. Only a small percentage of women are prohibited from visiting these locations, not all are not permitted to go alone. Rural women are less mobile than metropolitan women. Age, education, marital status, kind of household, and other background characteristics have an impact on women's mobility. Table 4 shows that while freedom of mobility does not change linearly with education, it does rise with age. Compared to 49% of women with no education, 70% of women in the highest education category are permitted to enter the market on their own.

Acceptance of Unequal Gender Role

Another sign of women's empowerment is how women rebel against unfavorable gender roles, such as choosing sons over wives or abusing them. According to the findings, 54% of Indian women agree that beatings by their husbands are acceptable for any of the above justifications. Similarly, 35% of women think it's OK to neglect their homes or kids. Though it does not significantly change with a woman's age or home structure, support for wife-beating declines sharply with education. It should be highlighted that even among women with the highest levels of education, at least one in three support one or more defenses of wife abuse.

Access to Education

Women's access to education, one of the main sources of empowerment, can be measured by looking at the gender differences in literacy rates and enrollment in different school levels. In 2001, the literacy gap between women and men reached a peak of 21.7%. The difference fluctuated between 18.3% in 1951 and 23.9% in 1971, but it has been trending somewhat downward since 1981.

Access to Employment

Only 43% of married women in the 15–49 age range are working, compared to 99% of married men in the same age range, according to statistics from the National Family Health Survey issued by the Indian government. It also demonstrates the existence of gender disparity in the workplace. The similar figure for men is as high as 72.5%, compared to married women who are employed for cash only at 51%. Comparatively few men (3.4%) are hired for just kind purposes compared to women (11.6%).

Domestic Violence

It has been noted that aging does not reduce the severity of violence. In India, 22.5% of women aged 15 to 19 reported having suffered physical or sexual abuse, compared to 39% of women aged 40 to 49. When compared to never-married women, ever-married women experience higher rates of both types of violence. Compared to 16.9% of never-married women, nearly 40% of women who have ever been married had experienced physical or sexual assault.

Political Participation

One of the key issues in the framework of empowerment is women's political engagement. According to traditional analysis, this refers to electoral politics-related activities like voting, campaigning, holding party office, and running for office. But in a larger sense, it includes all volunteer efforts meant to affect public policy making, public relations management, and the selection of political leaders at all levels of government. The political activism of Indian women now ranges from the promotion of peace and good government to protests against dowry, rape, domestic abuse, tainted food, rising prices, and other issues. (2007) [Desai et al.]

WOMEN EMPOWERMENT MODELS

Model With Three-Dimensional Aspect

According to Lee-Rife (2010), women's empowerment is viewed as a gradual process that turns them become agents who manage resources, make decisions, and make calculated life choices. She focused on the strategic life decisions—choice of career, marriage, and having children—which are regarded as first-order decisions and how these affect less consequential second-order decisions—raising children, making daily decisions for the home, and overseeing the family's well-being.

Figure 1. Kabeer's three dimensional model

The researcher underlined that, since resources expand one's capacity for choice, having access to resources—material, human, and social—is a necessary prerequisite for empowerment (Kabeer, 1999). According to Malhotra, Schuler, and Boender (2002), Kabeer highlighted (fig.01) that women need to be able to recognise and make use of the resources they have access to. According to Kabeer, empowerment is both a goal in and of itself. For instance, achieving education is one status, obtaining meaningful employment is another, and the result of empowerment may include having authority over decisions pertaining to oneself or one's family.

Conceptual Framework by Commission of Women and Development

Figure 2. The commission on women and development's conceptual framework

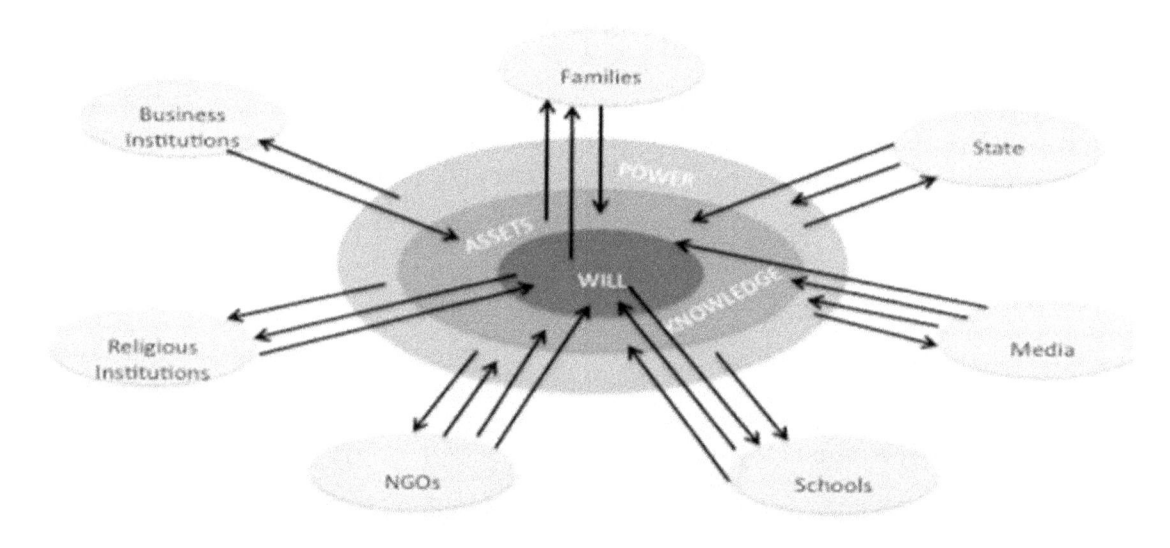

The DAWN women's movement, Kabeer, Longwez, Rowlands, and Leon, as well as the Belgian government and the Commission for Women and Development, an international aid agency, all had an influence on the framework and technique for empowerment. According to the commission, there are two levels of empowerment.

The individual and group.

However, the previous model defined the four fundamental elements of empowerment—assets, knowledge, will, and capacity—and focused mostly on the individual aspects of empowerment.

According to this paradigm, resources are divided into knowledge (which gives people access to procedures, training, literacy, and critical analysis abilities) and assets (material items that increase one's economic power). The ability to employ resources (assets, knowledge, and will), make decisions, and assume responsibilities is referred to as capacity. Will is defined as the psychological strength or power within to make one's own choices.

Summary and Findings

When examining women's current position in India, many markers of women's empowerment are examined utilizing data from various sources. Metrics like the degree of decision-making power women have in the house, their financial independence, their mobility, their acceptance of gender roles that are not equal, their exposure to the media, their access to education, their experiences with domestic abuse, etc. are the main focus. Indicators like the percentage of female MPs and female voters are used to analyze the political participation of women. After analyzing the data, it was shown that women's decision-making authority in the home and their freedom to roam about differ significantly with age, education, and job. Women who are married or have never been married have more freedom than ever to roam around. Similarly, it has been found that women still accept the unfair gender stereotypes that society perpetuates. When one or more of the following specific offenses are committed—such as bad cooking, disregard for the in-laws, hiding sex with the spouse, or neglecting the home and children—more than half of women believe that slapping a spouse is justified. This attitude, however, does not significantly change with age or household composition, although it does drastically change with education and place of residence. There is a gender difference in both the career and educational opportunities available to women, according to research.

REFERENCES

Anand, S., & Sen, A. (1995). Gender Inequality in Human Development: Theories and Measurement. In F. Parr & A. K. Shiv Kumar (Eds.), *Readings in Human Development*. OUP.

Bardhan, K., & Klasen, S. (1999). UNDP's Gender Related Indices: A Critical Review. *World Development*, 27(6), 985–1010. doi:10.1016/S0305-750X(99)00035-2

Bardhan, K., & Klasen, S. (2000). On UNDP's Revisions to the Gender- Related Development Index. *Journal of Human Development*, 1(2), 191–195. doi:10.1080/713678044

Barkat, A. (2008). *Women Empowerment: A Key to Human Development*. Good Governance. http://www.goodgovernance.org

Beteta, K. C. (2006). What is Missing in Measures of Women's Empowerment? *Journal of Human Development*, 7(2), 221–241. doi:10.1080/14649880600768553

Blumberg, R.L. (2005). *"Women's Economic Empowerment as the Magic Potion of Development?"* Paper presented at the 100th annual meeting of the American Sociological Association, Philadelphia.

Census of India. (2001). Govt. of India.

Chattopadhyay, R. & Duflo, E. (2001). *Women's Leadership and Policy Decisions: Evidence from a Nationwide Randomized Experiment in India*. Indian Institute of Management, Calcutta and Department of Economics, MIT, and NBER.

Desai, N., & Thakkar, U. (2007). *"Women and Political Participation in India", Women in Indian Society*. National Book Trust.

Dijkstra, G. (2002). Revisiting UNDP's GDI and GEM: Towards an Alternative. *Social Indicators Research*, 57(3), 301–338. doi:10.1023/A:1014726207604

Dijkstra, G. (2006). Towards a Fresh Start in Measuring Gender Equality: A Contribution to the Debate. *Journal of Human Development*, 7(2), 275–284. doi:10.1080/14649880600768660

Dijkstra, G., & Hanmer, L. C. (2000). Measuring Socio-economic Gender Inequality: Towards an Alternative to the UNDP- Gender-related Development Index. *Feminist Economics*, 6(2), 41–75. doi:10.1080/13545700050076106

Figueras, I.C. (2008). *Women in Politics: Evidence from the Indian States*. Department of Economics, Universidad Carlos III de Madrid.

G.O.I. (2000). *National Population Policy*. Ministry of Health & Family Welfare.

G.O.I. (2001). *Census Report*. Office of the Registrar General and Census Commissioner.

G.O.I. (2002). *National Human Development Report, 2001*. Planning Commission.

G.O.I. (2009). *Gendering Human Development Indices: Recasting the Gender Development Index and Gender Empowerment Measure for India: A Summary Report*. Ministry of Woman and Child Welfare.

G.O.I. (2005). *National Family Health Survey – III*. Ministry of Health and Family Welfare, New Delhi.

Upadhyay, U., Gipson, J., Withers, M., Lewis, S., Ciaraldi, E., Fraser, A., Huchko, M., & Prata, N. (2014). Women"s empowerment and fertility: A review of Literature. *Social Science & Medicine, 115*, 111–120. doi:10.1016/j.socscimed.2014.06.014 PMID:24955875

Yount, K., Cheong, Y., Maxwell, L., Heckert, J., Martinez, E., & And Seymour, G. (2019). Measurement properties of the project level Women Empowerment in Agriculture Index. *World Development, 124*, 1–19. doi:10.1016/j.worlddev.2019.104639 PMID:31798204

Chapter 12
The Relationship Between Premenstrual Syndrome and Menstrual Attitude:
Women's Life Quality in Deharadun City

S. Srinivasan

https://orcid.org/0009-0002-0179-9849

Department of Humanities and Social Sciences, Graphic Era University (deemed), Dehradun, India

Somya Rawat

Department of Humanities and Social Sciences, Graphic Era University (deemed), Dehradun, India

Kanchan Yadav

Department of Humanities and Social Sciences, Graphic Era University (deemed), Dehradun, India

ABSTRACT

The lives of women are characterized by honor and numerous responsibilities, including navigating biological complexities and cultural dynamics. Adjusting daily routines to accommodate menstruation is crucial. This study examines premenstrual syndrome (PMS), menstrual attitude (MA), and quality of life (QoL) for women, aiming to understand their experiences and perspectives on the menstrual cycle. Conducted with 124 female participants aged 18 to 35 in Dehradun, it highlights the significant challenges posed by PMS and MA, particularly for working women and college students, compared to men. Addressing these challenges empowers women and enhances their community. The research underscores the importance of socioeconomic background, revealing greater difficulties faced by women of lower economic status during menstruation. Overall, the study contributes valuable insights into the multidimensional impact of PMS on women's lives and emphasizes the need for supportive attitudes and behaviors towards menstruation.

DOI: 10.4018/979-8-3693-2806-4.ch012

INTRODUCTION

Women's lives are distinguished by honour and an abundance of duties and obstacles ranging from biological complexity to cultural dynamics. Changing one's daily schedule to accommodate women's menstruation is an important part of their lives. The study deals with three variables that are Premenstrual Syndrome, Menstrual Attitude and Quality of Life for the women. This research is to investigate the relationships between these characteristics and offer insight into women's menstrual cycle experiences and perspectives. The study aims to contribute to our understanding of the multidimensional impact of PMS on women's general quality of life and the part that menstrual attitude plays in detail in these practices, by studying these relationships. This study includes 124 female participants (Unmarried=64 & Married=60) with an age range of 18 to 35 years from Dehradun. Menstrual Syndrome, along with Menstrual Attitude, poses numerous challenges for adolescent girls and women, especially for working women and college students, compared to men. They deal with, cope with, overcome, and empower the women's community.

This research study mainly focuses on Premenstrual Syndrome (PMS), menstrual attitudes, behaviours, and enhancing the women's community, challenging, overcoming, and empowering the model of the nation. The book chapter exhibits strengths in the research findings, mainly focused on PMS, MA, and QoL. Socioeconomic background women face many problems during menstruation. Normal and quiet settled people fare better compared to those with low economic status among the respondents. To examine the relationship between PMS with the menstrual attitude and quality of life in females. The honour of being a woman is great in itself. Holding different roles and facing various issues from biological to societal, is extraordinary. Scheduling her daily activities every month whether it is to go outside or do indoor work because of her menstruation period. Her monthly and regular plan concentrates on it (Gittelsohn, 1994a; Joshi et al., 1998). In rural India, several restrictions are enforced on women during menstruation. Many daily domestic duties that are deemed sacred are forbidden (Gittelsohn, 1994b).

According to one study, the topic of menstruation in India focuses on the concept of filth, taboos, and limits in different aspects of women's lives (Garg et al., 2001). Premenstrual Syndrome One of the common health problems that women face is PMS. PMS or Premenstrual Syndrome is a comprehensive phrase that refers to a set of emotional, behavioural, and physical symptoms that occur a few days to several weeks before menstruation and then disappear. These symptoms can range from moderate to severe. It impacts their everyday life. When the symptoms of PMS first appear and begin to affect a woman's daily activities (American College of Obstetricians and Gynecologists, 2000). Symptoms irritability, depression, breast tenderness, bloating, and behavioural changes (Rees, 1953; Dalton, 1984). According to Walker (1995a), theorists think that there are three steps in self-diagnosis of PMS: the appearance of physical and/or emotional sensations, and interpreting them as dysfunctional and requiring treatment.

This is what the biopsychosocial model claims that these stages interact with psychological, biological and social factors (Walker, 1995b). The root cause of PMS is nonetheless undetermined. Biological causes (Rapkin & Akopians, 2012) and Psychosocial causes include (e.g., menstruation perception or Stressing out and having an attitude) (Lee & Yang, 2020) or health-related behaviours (e.g., eating sleep cycle, dieting, drinking or smoking, nutrition intake) may all contribute to the root of the problem (Kim, H.Y., Kim, S.N., 2018). Types of PMS (Luck, 2023) There are four types of PMS: PMS-A(Anxiety), PMS-D (Depression), PMS-H (Hydration/Water Retention), and PMS-C (Cravings).

PMS-A(Anxiety): The main symptoms are feeling overwhelmed, getting irritated and being sensitive to certain issues or everything.

PMS-D (Depression): The main symptoms are feeling depressed, lethargic and confused, and less involvement with everyday activities.

PMS-H (Hydration/Water Retention): The person may gain weight, and bloated abdominal or breast tenderness.

PMS- C (Cravings): The person may binge eat, junk food intake increases, and decrease in appetite.

There were three questionnaires used to evaluate various features. The Premenstrual Symptoms Screening Tool (PSST) (Steiner et al., 2003a) has 14 items, The Quality of Life Scale (Flanagan, 1978a) has 16 items and the Menstrual Attitude Questionnaire (Chandra et al., 1989a) has 22 items were employed as data analysis tools. Participants reported moderate PMS symptoms, excellent Quality of Life QOL, and favourable views towards menstruation. The data demonstrated a negative relationship between PMS and QOL, indicating that when PMS symptoms develop, QOL drops. However, there was no significant link between PMS symptoms and MA, suggesting that PMS had minimal influence on women's attitudes towards menstruation. Married women had somewhat higher MA than unmarried women. Overall, the study emphasizes the necessity of managing PMS symptoms to improve women's well-being and relationships throughout their menstrual cycle.

Causal theories of PMS Clare's (1985) theories discussed the idea of causal factors of PMS. There are two types of theories with subdivision: (1) Constitutional: (a) Genetic and (b) Hormonal, and (2) Environmental: (a) Social stress, (b) Social support and (c) Sex roles. Under the first type, it discusses genetic and hormonal causes. In genetics, the tension caused by PMS may have value for survival (Rosseinsky & Hall, 1974) and also how the menstrual cycle tension and the occurrence of menstruation might be synchronized among the blood relation like between a mother and daughters or sisters (Kantero, 1971). In hormonal, the imbalance between progesterone and estrogen is the causal factor for PMS. The decrease in the level of estrogen (Steiner & Carroll, 1977) and progesterone (Bäckström & Carstensen, 1974) can cause the symptoms of PMS to arise. The second type discusses social stress, social support and sex roles. In social stress, there is evidence that women have more severe social stress than men (Radloff & Rae, 1979) and how certain change in our lives impacts the level of PMS (Siegel et al., 1979).

Social support, tells about the support a human needs from family, friends and even work colleagues. In sex roles, the female roles in society have led to the internal conflicts inside them. The pain that carries with menstruation has invoked undesirable actions among themselves. This was seen in one of the British murder trials (1980-1981) where two women were charged with manslaughter by claiming that they couldn't control their actions because they were having severe PMS (Rittenhouse, 1991). The effects of PMS symptoms impact daily activities. It incorporates Quality of Life (QOL), which includes acts of a person's existence. When a woman had PMS and experienced an erratic menstrual cycle, her QOL was lower than when she had a balanced menstrual cycle (Khalid & Naqvi, 2022). One of the common conditions that adversely affects women of reproductive age and hurts their emotions and activities is PMS (Zendehdel & Elyasi, 2018). Premenstrual syndrome (PMS) affects about 5-8% of women, with most severe cases meeting the criteria for premenstrual dysphoric disorder (PMDD) (Yonkers et al., 2008a). Various theoretical frameworks have been proposed to understand and address PMS. Cognitive-behavioral therapy (CBT) has been highlighted as a key approach in treating emotional and physical symptoms associated with PMS, such as pain and anxiety (Babajani et al., 2017a). Studies have systematically reviewed the effectiveness of CBT for PMS and PMDD, emphasizing its potential in managing these conditions (Lustyk et al., 2009). Additionally, social learning and stress theory have been used to explain why some women experience PMS symptoms, suggesting that environmental factors play a role in symptom patterns (Woods et al., 1995). Furthermore, research has explored the impact of premenstrual embodiment on women's distress, highlighting the role of negative self-constructions in exacerbating PMS symptoms (Ussher & Perz, 2020a). Studies have also investigated the quality of life among university students with PMS, shedding light on the challenges faced by this population (Victor et al., 2019a). Moreover, the heritability of PMS has been examined, indicating a genetic component to the disorder (Jahanfar et al., 2011).

Quality of Life

QOL is characterized as a sense of physical, material, social, and emotional well-being that includes objective and subjective assessments, all of which contribute to a person's growth and completion of tasks, all of which are weighted by a personal set of values (Teoli & Bhardwaj, 2022). According to the WHO, Quality of Life is a subjective concept which deals with how a person perceives their life and tries to reach goals that are observed through the lens of the culture and value system. When it comes to QOL, there are four broad health domains to consider (Aaronson, 1988). (1) Physical health (somatic sensations, disease symptoms, treatment side effects), (2) Mental health (ranges from positive sense of well-being to identifiable psychological disorder), (3) Social health (qualitative as well as quantitative components of social interactions), (4) Functional health (physical and social role functioning). QOL is considered "The overall enjoyment of life" (NCI Dictionary of Cancer Terms). Borthwick-Duffy (2000) has defined QOL from three different perspectives that it can be defined:

life condition's quality, (b) satisfaction with life condition and (c) combining the condition and satisfaction with life. Flanagan (1978b) described five domains of QOL: physical and material well-being; relations with other people; social, community, and civic activities; personal development and fulfilment; and recreation (Felce & Perry, 1995a). It is shown that there is interaction between the three elements which results in good QOL. These elements are independent and can also be influenced by environmental factors. If there are certain changes in some aspects, it can change one's values. Baker and Intagliata (1982) proposed the conceptualized model of QOL. They described that four elements interact with each other: (1) External environment (focus on qol's objective indicators), (2) Individual experience (individual perception differs with different experiences), (3) Health status (includes psychological and physical aspect of an individual), (4) QOL responses (assess the outcome of behaviour with the help of assessments). The QOL model proposed by Andrews and Withey (2012) widely accepted framework for assessing and evaluating individuals' subjective well-being and life satisfaction. Shi et al. (2023a) examined the outcome of the study Global School-based Student Health Survey the data was reported that 1 in 3 adolescents had lifestyle-related risk factors. The most prominent lifestyle risk factors are non-communicable diseases where the fruit-vegetable intake is very low and physical activities are inadequate.

According to the concept, several domains or aspects that contribute to Quality of life are determined by an individual's well-being. These factors are as follows:

Physical: includes factors such as health, energy levels, physical fitness, and the absence of disease or discomfort.

Material: it relates to a person's economic situation, which includes income, wealth, and access to basic requirements like food, housing, and clothes.

Social: It refers to the quality of an individual's relationships with family, friends, and the community as well as the quality of their social support networks.

Emotional: it refers to a person's emotional condition, which includes their capacity to experience happy emotions, regulate negative emotions, and maintain overall emotional stability.

Personal growth, self-actualization, and participation in meaningful activities such as jobs, hobbies, and personal interests are all addressed in this domain. It includes an individual's impression of their civil rights, political liberties, and sense of autonomy and control over their own life choices.

Personal beliefs: This category encompasses an individual's spiritual and religious views, values, and the degree to which they find purpose and meaning in their lives.

Women's thoughts and attitudes regarding menstruation, which include societal taboos, cultural beliefs, and personal experiences, might have an impact on their psychological well-being and QOL during menstruation (Santhya & Jejeebhoy, 2015a).

Figure 1. Quality of life model
Note. *The quality of life model is adopted by Felce and Perry (1995b).*

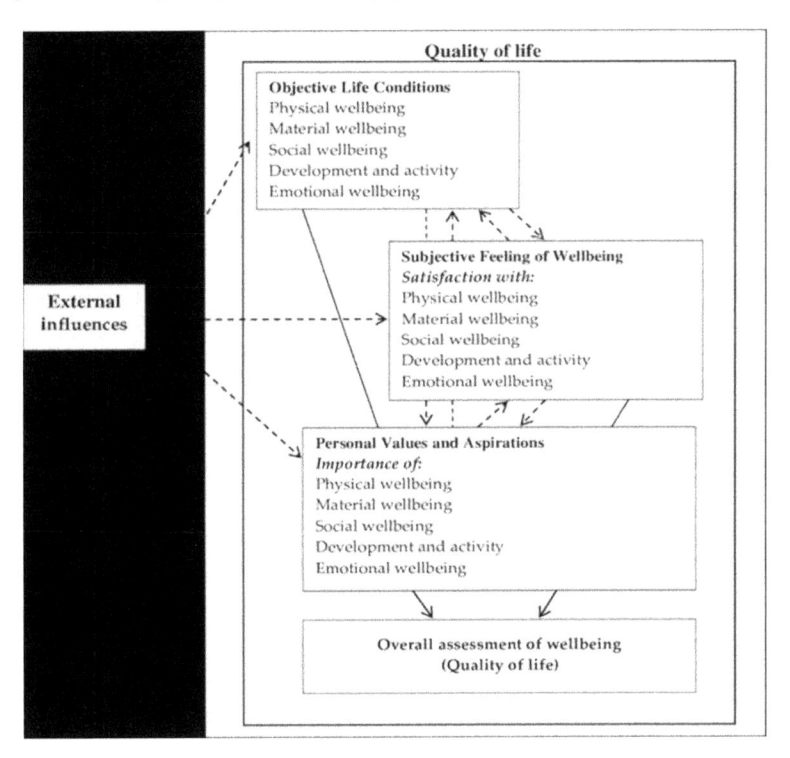

QOL not only covers the psychological but also the physical, behavioural cognitive etc. aspects of human beings. These aspects can also be covered in the symptoms of PMS. As we know PMS can also impact the attitude towards menstruation (Chang & Chen, 2009a; Chayachinda et al., 2008a).

Menstrual Attitude

"Attitude refers to a learned tendency to evaluate some object, person, or issue in a particular way," according to the American Psychological Association (APA). It consists of cognitive, emotional, and behavioural elements". According to Hogg and Vaughan (2014), attitude is People, objects, or ideas are evaluated enduringly - positively or negatively. "Attitudes are beliefs with cognitive, affective, and behavioural components".

There Are Different Types of Attitudes

Cognitive Attitude: According to Eagly and Chaiken (1993), cognitive attitudes are the opinions and thoughts that people have about an item, person, or topic. This dimension is concerned with cognitive assessment and information processing.

Affective Attitude: The affective component of attitudes relates to individuals' emotional or affective responses to an item, person, or topic. Feelings, emotions, likes, dislikes, and emotional reactions related to the attitude object are all included in this dimension (Petty & Krosnick, 1995).

Implicit Attitude: Implicit attitudes are automatic or unconscious attitudes that people may have without being aware of them. They can impact behaviour and judgements even when persons are not deliberately aware of their incidence. There are implicit attitudes often assessed using implicit association tests (Greenwald & Banaji, 1995).

Explicit Attitude: Explicit attitudes are conscious and purposeful attitudes that persons are aware of and may express or report. They are frequently assessed using self-report measures such as questionnaires or surveys (Fazio & Olson, 2003).

Behavioural Attitude: Sarver (1975) presents the Theory of Reasoned Action, which proposes that attitudes impact an individual's behavioural intentions and inclinations. This component examines how attitudes influence an individual's behaviour and proclivity to act or respond in a particular way.

MA Does Change or be Influenced by Different Factors

Cultural Differences: Cultural beliefs and practices influence menstrual perception. Some cultures, for example, consider menstruation to be dirty or forbidden, whilst others welcome it as a symbol of fertility or womanhood. Cultural attitudes about menstruation can influence how women view and feel their menstrual periods (Chrisler, 2008a). Health Education and Awareness: Menstruation education and awareness can impact women's attitudes. Menstrual health education programmes, as well as open talks about menstruation, can help debunk myths, decrease stigma, and encourage positive perspectives (Sommer et al., 2015).

Personal Experiences: Women's particular menstrual experiences, such as pain, discomfort, or irregular cycles, can also influence their views. Personal experiences, both positive and unpleasant, might influence how women perceive their menstrual periods and their general attitude towards menstruation (Ussher, 2003).

Social Stigma: Menstruation is frequently connected with social stigma, leading to unfavourable opinions and attitudes. Because of cultural taboos and the reinforcement of menstrual myths and stereotypes, women may feel embarrassed, humiliated, or uncomfortable discussing menstruation (Santhya & Jejeebhoy, 2015b).

PMS, QOL and MA have different impacts on a woman's life. Many research studies were conducted on the relationship between PMS and QOL, and the findings show that women who have severe PMS symptoms frequently have worse overall well-being and a lower quality of life than those who have moderate or no symptoms. PMS can interfere with everyday activities, social interactions, and work performance, influencing many facets of a woman's life. The physical symptoms, menstrual attitude or perspective influence how women perceive and manage menstruation. Social taboos, cultural beliefs, and personal experiences can all influence a woman's MA. Addressing PMS symptoms and modifying menstrual attitudes can improve a woman's QOL. This might include a variety of interventions such as lifestyle changes, hormonal therapies, and education regarding menstrual health and cleanliness.

Effects of QoL and MA

Quality of life is a multidimensional concept that encompasses various aspects of an individual's well-being. Several studies have been conducted to explore the factors influencing quality of life in different populations. For instance, research has shown that there is a significant association between age and quality of life impairment in patients with acne, with females experiencing more impairment than males (Ismail & Mohammed-Ali, 2012). Additionally, studies on infertile couples have highlighted the impact of infertility on health-related quality of life, with women often experiencing more distress due to societal stigma and blame associated with infertility (Rashidi et al., 2008; Amiri et al., 2017). Furthermore, the quality of life of caregivers has been investigated, with some studies suggesting a relationship between education level and quality of life, although this relationship has not been consistently found across all studies (Ovayolu et al., 2013).

In patients with conditions like oral lichen planus and vitiligo, research has demonstrated a high prevalence of impaired quality of life, emphasizing the importance of addressing psychological and social aspects in patient care (López-Jornet & Camacho-Alonso, 2010; Sawant et al., 2015a; Poudyal et al., 2020). Moreover, studies have explored the impact of chronic conditions such as alcoholic chronic pancreatitis and onychomycosis on quality of life, highlighting the need for holistic approaches to patient management that consider both physical and psychosocial well-being (Benincá et al., 2016; Bunyaratavej et al., 2015). Overall, these studies underscore the complexity of factors influencing quality of life across different populations and health conditions. By examining various dimensions such as mental health, social support, and disease-specific factors, researchers can gain insights into how to improve quality of life outcomes for individuals facing diverse challenges.

Understanding attitudes towards menstruation involves examining various psychological, sociological, and health behaviour models to grasp individuals' perceptions and beliefs regarding menstruation. The Menstrual Attitude Questionnaire, developed by (Brooks-Gunn & Ruble, 1980), offers a structured approach to assess attitudes towards menstruation and its effects on behaviour and symptomatology. Grose and Grabe (2014) studied sociocultural attitudes surrounding menstruation, connecting self-objectification to attitudes towards menstrual products, and highlighting the impact of societal norms on individual perceptions. Goldstein-Ferber and Granot (2006) emphasized the significance of personality factors and attitudes in understanding dysmenorrhea, shedding light on the psychological aspects of menstrual experiences. Furthermore, Frank (2020) explored the intersection of menstruation discourse and gender identity, broadening the discussion beyond cisgender women. These studies collectively underscore the importance of psychological theories, sociocultural influences, and individual attitudes in shaping perceptions and experiences related to menstruation.

An Analysis of the Relationship Between Three Variables: PMS, MA, and QOL

The study done by Ussher and Perz (2020b) can be utilized to explore how negative constructions of premenstrual embodiment contribute to women's distress during PMS. This framework emphasizes the role of societal norms and beliefs in shaping women's experiences of PMS, shedding light on how menstrual attitudes may influence symptom perception and quality of life. Moreover, the study by Victor et al. (2019b) on the quality of life among university students with PMS can provide insights into the impact of PMS on daily functioning and well-being. By integrating this research with the feminist theoretical lens, it becomes apparent that societal attitudes towards menstruation and PMS can significantly affect women's quality of life. Negative perceptions and stigmas surrounding menstruation may exacerbate the psychological and physical symptoms experienced during PMS, thereby influencing overall quality of life.

Additionally, the study by Narvel et al. (2018) on the association between attitudes towards menstruation and PMS symptoms among nursing staff highlights the need to explore how individual beliefs and cultural norms regarding menstruation intersect with the experience of PMS. Understanding the interplay between menstrual attitudes, symptom perception, and quality of life can provide a comprehensive framework for addressing the holistic impact of PMS on women's well-being. Premenstrual syndrome (PMS) is a complex condition characterized by a range of physical, cognitive, affective, and behavioural symptoms that occur cyclically during the luteal phase of the menstrual cycle (Balaha et al., 2010). Understanding PMS involves exploring coping mechanisms, such as Avoiding Harm, Awareness and Acceptance of Premenstrual Change, Adjusting Energy, Self-Care, and Communicating (Read et al., 2014). The Health Belief Model has been applied effectively to promote preventive behaviours related to PMS, emphasizing the importance of education in adopting preventive measures (Qalawa et al., 2022).

Additionally, cognitive-behavioral therapy has shown promise in managing emotional and physical symptoms associated with PMS (Babajani et al., 2017b). The impact of PMS extends beyond the individual, affecting interpersonal relationships, daily activities, and work productivity (Rezaee et al., 2015; Chougule & Behere, 2017). Moreover, PMS has been linked to a reduction in health-related quality of life, emphasizing the need for effective interventions (Enuka & Ukamaka, 2022). Sociologically, PMS is recognized as a public health issue that influences not only women but also families, societies, and nations at large (Zeleke et al., 2023). By considering the biopsychosocial aetiology of PMS, which encompasses biological, psychological, and social factors, a more comprehensive understanding of this condition can be achieved (Zendehdel & Elyasi, 2018). Ultimately, addressing PMS requires a multidimensional approach that integrates psychological, sociological, and health behaviour models to enhance the quality of life for individuals experiencing this syndrome.

REVIEW OF THE STUDY

PMS develops during the luteal phase of the menstrual cycle and disappears in coming menstruation days, and is considered by persistent, moderate-to-severe affective, physical and behavioural symptoms (Ryu & Kim, 2015). PMS is the term for distressing physical, and psychological, and It is common for behavioural symptoms to occur during the same phase of the menstrual cycle and gradually diminish over time or go away for the balance of the cycle but are not associated with an organic disease (Cronje & Hawkins, 2003). A collection of symptoms that are chronologically related to the menstrual cycle characterizes premenstrual syndrome (PMS). The signs and symptoms of PMS include physical and emotional changes that peak before menstruation and may disappear soon after the onset of menstrual flow (Kessel, 2000).

Greene and Dalton (1953a) invented the term "premenstrual syndrome" to describe an amalgamation that includes both physiological and psychological symptoms. PMS is also characterized by psychological and physical symptoms occurring before menses. It is a collection of symptoms among women that makes its impact not only physical but also psychological, behavioural and social (Siahbazi et al., 2018a). During most of the menstrual months, women experience these symptoms. Various factors influence the PMS symptom severity, like age, culture, physical health, and also, mental health status (Guvenc et al., 2012a). The prevalence of PMS among women is the average of 80% around the world. It is a common health issue among women of reproductive age (Ussher & Perz, 2013). There is some evidence that early stage of life emotional and physical abuse can affect the prevalence of PMS (Bertone-Johnson et., 2014). The level of severity of PMS symptoms is increasing, which results in decreasing mental health status and vitality (Arbabi et al., 2008a).

PMS prevalence was found at 36.4% and the rate was between 48% to 90% (Guvenc et al., 2012b); in India, it was found the prevalence of PMS between 14.3% to 74.4% (Bharathi et al., 2022). For example, the prevalence was found in the research on PMS (Gantela & Choppara, 2015; Bansal et al., 2019; Shamnani et al., 2018; Ravindran, 2007). Menstruation does interfere with the day-to-day life of PMS. In the study of women veterans, 17% were found to have irregular, abnormal, heavy periods; 37% were having dysmenorrhea; 55% were having PMS. These issues were interfering with their usual activities (Barnard et al., 2003). Some studies claim that women do consider menstruation as a natural event (Guvenc et al., 2012c).

The awareness of PMS is important. If a person wouldn't know of it then they won't be able to tackle their symptoms and may consider it something else. In the research, 20% of Pakistani females (Perveen et al., 2022), 90.5% of Nepali females (Shrestha & Giri, 2020) from the 18 articles of 2008-2019 found 50% of Indian females (Katjiukua et al., 2020), to have a lack of knowledge about PMS. Because many women don't know who they should meet, they go to the doctor, who overlooks their symptoms and focuses on something else. Only the 220 Women who had been medically diagnosed with PMS were unable to identify, classify or treat their symptoms (Lete et al., 2011). Women also experience moderate to severe levels of dysmenorrhea (painful menstruation cramps) which affects their day-to-day life. This is found in Thai nurses (Chayachinda et al., 2008b). They are more likely to get PMS. The prevalence of dysmenorrhea was found around 58% to 55% in Turkish females and the reason for the differences can be due to sociocultural and ethnic factors (Ozerdogan et al., 2009). There was a 31% presence of dysmenorrhea in the menstrual cycle (Guvencet al., 2012d).

Women with PMS find it difficult to their emotional reactions, relationships, and mood changes (Ussher, 2003) They don't know the severity of these symptoms. The severe conditions of PMS can lead to premenstrual dysphoric disorder (PMDD). It is a subset of PMS. The symptoms tend to worsen than the ones in PMS. People experience extreme mood shifts. DSM-IV has its diagnostic criteria for PMDD but the clinicians are called upon to make the diagnosis based on personal interviews regardless of what the diagnostic criteria are stating (Steiner et al., 2003b). In reality, the majority of women who initially complain of PMS are not discovered to have it, and the PMS calendar is essential in making this conclusion. Some factors were excluded in one investigation of patients reporting suspected PMS: monthly irregularities (16.6%), and menopausal or perimenopausal status (10.2%), The provided text appears to be concise and well-structured, with no apparent grammatical errors. It effectively conveys information about the absence of a symptoms-free window in the follicular phase (20.5%) and other psychiatric diagnoses (20.1%). If you have any specific concerns or if there's more context you'd like to provide, feel free to share and I'll be happy to assist with further monthly irregularities (16.6%), menopause or perimenopause (8.4%), and other medical illnesses (8.4%) (Mortola, 1993) there is no recognized pathophysiology for PMS. Uncertainty exists regarding the proportional contributions of social and genetic influences. Significant heredity for premenstrual symptoms has been indicated by twin studies (Kendler et al., 1998).

The premenstrual symptoms of a woman are probably influenced by social factors as well as her expectations. Premenstrual discomfort, including PMS and PMDD, is still poorly understood, but research is beginning to shed light on its complex etiopathogenesis, or the way that progesterone and estrogen, two hormones produced by the ovaries, fluctuate throughout the menstrual cycle and cleverly interact with the immune, endocrine, and nervous systems (Janiger et al., 1972). This mysterious combination has an impact on a variety of functions, including physiological, emotional, stress reactivity, sensory processing problems and neurocognitive function (Matsumoto et al., 2013).

About 5% of the women in are reproductive age group consistently report having severe PMS (Yonkers et al., 2008b). Taking a biological aspect, menstrual cycles lasting more than six days were more typical in females with PMS, with prevalence rates of 19.0% and 6.8% for cycles lasting more than six days and those lasting six days or less, respectively. However, there was no difference between the prevalence of PMS among women who had previously given birth (8.1%) and women who had not (7.2%) (Deuster et al., 1999). The effects of PMS symptoms impact daily activities. It incorporates QOL, which includes all facets of a person's existence. When a woman had PMS and experienced an erratic menstrual cycle, her QOL was lower than when she had a balanced menstrual cycle (Khalid & Naqvi, 2022). Females with PMS had a highly disturbed quality of life (Irshad et al., 2022). The QOL is reduced during PMS and women do not feel good about it (Siahbazi et al., 2018b). The high level of PMS lowers the level of quality of life (Ziba et al., 2008). A large percentage of women who start ovulating routinely experience a variety of symptoms that signal the beginning of their menstruation; Usually minor, these alterations don't interfere with their capacity to perform daily tasks (Yuk et al., 1991). The impact may differ as PMS may not severely affect women's quality of life (Goker et al., 2015).

Life Quality and Premenstrual Syndrome

The concept of "quality of life" or QOL refers to a person's total state of welfare, which encompasses both objective and subjective measures of their physical, material, social, emotional, and mental health as well as their level of individual development and meaningful activities, all of which are weighted according to one's own set of values (Felce & Perry, 1995c). Women only report their limitations who have signs of PMS or PMDD rather than with no indication of PMS in QOL (Yang et al., 2010). It is shown that women who have high PMS levels have poorer QOL in comparison to those with low PMS levels (Lustyk et al., 2004a). It is shown that the QOL was higher no matter what the level of PMS is (Delara et al., 2012). The difference in QOL may be due to the culture, ethnicity, and living style (Arbabi et al., 2008b; Lustyk et al., 2004b; Delara et al., 2012).

Women should increase their understanding of the QOL in varied PMS symptoms (Lustyk et al., 2004c). Even young women who are still in school are affected, in addition to the home and the job. To ascertain the occurrence, severity and QoL effects of PMS, an observational study including 172 medical college students was carried out. According to DSM-IV criteria, it was discovered that 51% of women matched the requirements for PMS and 5.8% had PMDD. The productivity of the student's academic work and social life were both significantly hampered. The authors concluded that PMS is a prevalent issue among young women that negatively impacts both their academic performance and emotional well-being (Nisar et al., 2008). It has become essential to research the effects that PMS can have on young women's social and academic lives due to the multifaceted nature of life quality, the extensive variety of diagnostic criteria and the significant frequency of PMS (Halbreich, 2003).

In one study it was found that women believed that premenstrual symptoms mostly affected their social, psychological, and physical health. It was discovered that their QOL was negatively impacted by PMS. Women with PMS showed worse physical role functioning, emotional role functioning, mental health, vitality status, and general health views (Kırcan et al., 2012). Conflicting findings were identified in the literature addressing the influence of PMS behavioural and physical symptoms on QOL related to health (Rapkin & Winer, 2009). Women who had PMS and PMDD were considerably more likely to experience poorer QOL, greater amounts of sick leave from work, lower levels of productivity, strained interpersonal relationships, and higher rates of visits to medical professionals (Thakrar et al., 2021). Women with PMS perform worse at work, in their social and personal lives, and overall (Ekholm & Backstrom, 1994). Women's quality of life and productivity at work are dramatically decreased by PMS symptoms (Borenstein et al., 2003; Borenstein et al., 2007).

Compared to women without menstruation issues, women with menstrual disorders experience poorer QOL and mental health issues. To improve QOL, it is imperative to address this group's mental health difficulties (Sarwar & Rauf, 2021). Students with PMS have lower levels of satisfaction, feel worse, experience greater pressure at work, do worse academically, are more prone to anxiety and conflict, and ultimately, these symptoms affect how well nursing students function and live their lives in terms of health (Cheng et al., 2015).

PMS impacts the QOL of an individual. Additionally, a study found that it contributes to distress, anxiety, and impairment of functioning, which lowers job productivity (Tkachenko et al., 2010). These physical and emotional symptoms of PMS have an impact on women's everyday activities, interpersonal connections, and employment (Teixeira et al., 2013). PMS patients are more likely to experience impairments in their physical and mental health, which can result in significantly lower QOL, higher absenteeism rates from work, decreased productivity at work, deteriorated social and interpersonal relationships, and more frequent hospital visits. Ten per cent of the women said their symptoms were serious enough to require medical attention, and about 20% of the women said they were unable to go about their normal activities because of these symptoms. (Bertone-Johnson et al., 2007). No matter how severe or numerous the premenstrual symptoms, having them was linked to a considerable decline in QOL (Dean et al. 2006). Women with PMS are more likely to experience job productivity impairment than women without PMS, and PMS is linked to a decrease in health-related quality of life frequently experience PMS, which has the potential to lower their QOL and their productivity at work (Zaka & Mahmood, 2012). Researchers discovered that the occurrence of PMS was significantly correlated with a decline in health-related QOL in the sample of 436 women. Five to ten per cent of women of childbearing age may experience severe symptoms that must be treated, this may negatively affect one's social life and career (WHO report, 2000).

A female's understanding of her menstrual cycles can be affected by the physiological phenomena of menstruation, which also has several psychosocial features. Females' opinions and ideas regarding menstruation are influenced by their cultural, social, and family settings (Chang & Chen, 2009b; Firat et al., 2009). When researchers looked at the connection between attitudes and PMS, they discovered that suffering throughout the menstrual cycle was significantly associated with negative attitudes regarding menstruation (Chang & Chen, 2009c; Chayachinda et al., 2008c). The impression of menstrual distress may be significantly influenced by attitudes towards menstruation (Anjum et al., 2010). Numerous research studies have shown how social context and culture affect perceptions regarding menstruation (Hoerster et al., 2003; Sveinsdottir, 1993a). Shi et al. (2023b) examined the research study emphasis on physical activities, sedentary behaviour and premenstrual syndrome among college students affect behaviour, cognitive issues, mental health issues, and academic problems they faced in college students during the premenstrual issues are the major findings of the gaps the researcher identified the gap socio-economic condition of the family level and living conditions, genetic issues are associated with PMS. Even lifestyle factors main reason for the increase in the risk of PMS such as poor diet, overweight, obesity, junk food, smoking, and inactive PA is to improve and address the issues in the high emphasis on the research study.

Premenstrual Syndrome and Menstrual Attitude

There have been reports of striking cross-cultural variations in the frequency of menstruation symptoms (Monagle et al., 1993). The relevance of fostering positive attitudes and ideas around menstruation is supported by research that reveals a favourable relationship between the onset of menstrual symptoms and attitudes regarding menstruation (Lu, 2001a). Women's attitudes about and experiences with their menstrual cycles are influenced by their status in a given society as well as the cultural ideals that society has regarding women's bodies (Chrisler, 2008b). Menstrual attitude also depends upon the cultural context. This was seen in the research studies where Compared to American women, Indian women exhibit more optimistic views. Americans have more negative perceptions regarding menstruation (Katherine et al., 2003a). There was a positive relationship between menstrual attitude and premenstrual attitude among Korean women (Hwang & Sung, 2016). The way people view menstruation has a significant impact on the idea of menstrual problems and the agony they experience, which are multifaceted (Philip et al., 2022).

The most acute monthly discomfort was reported by absolutely devout Roman Catholic women and Orthodox Jewish women. This demonstrated the connection between religiosity, adherence to the stereotypical feminine gender role, and menstruation pain (Paige, 1973). Menstrual symptoms tended to be more frequent and more severe in women who had the least positive attitudes towards their periods (Levitt & Lubin, 1967). Menstruation is not typically seen as particularly painful or troublesome by Indian women, but due to taboos or conventions, 13.5 per cent of them choose to skip work or school during their menstrual cycle. Christians reported their symptoms as being more severe than Hindus. (Rao et al., 1982). In some parts of India, there are still menstrual taboos and myths that continue to exist and these issues could influence how young people are taught about menstruation (Ullrich, 1992). Although Indians frequently see the menstrual cycle from a positive or neutral perspective, they are likely less interested in negative information than Americans are. Access to a lot of unpleasant information is widespread among Americans. This unfavourable information comes from a variety of sources, including stereotypes about how women behave throughout certain menstrual cycle periods (Katherine et al., 2003b).

Even though they were aware of the negative effects of menstruation, women tended to view it as a natural, that wasn't particularly predictable or debilitating (Sveinsdottir, 1993b). According to the study's findings, the majority of Indians gave their educational sources positive ratings; yet, it's likely that they were both positive and inadequate at the same time. Indeed, this must be the case, at least in part, because despite receiving accurate and positive information from these sources, they were unable to provide adequate responses to many straightforward inquiries about the menstrual cycle. They would rank their sources favourably because they were the only ones available (Katherine et al., 2003c). QOL not only covers psychological but also physical, behavioral cognitive, etc. aspects of human beings. These aspects can also be covered in the symptoms of PMS. As we know PMS can also impact the attitude towards menstruation (Chang & Chen, 2009d; Chayachinda et al., 2008d). Here we can see that in PMS there can be a link between QOL and menstrual attitude.

Quality of Life and Menstrual Attitude

There is little research done on the QOL and menstrual to explain their relations. We can see a link between QOL and Menstrual attitude through the PMS symptoms and aspects of Quality of life. One of the research studies discussed that physical, cognitive, behavioural, and psychological components of women's views towards their periods were impacted by premenstrual and menstrual symptoms (Lu, 2001b). Women who believed they lacked appropriate understanding about menstruation and who had a compared to a negative attitude towards menstruation were more likely to develop PMS (Kısa et al., 2012).

As PMS severity increases, so does the level of hostility towards menstruation (Lu et al., 2001; Sönmezer & Yosmaoğlu, 2014). The above studies showed how these variables (PMS, QOL and Menstrual Attitude) have some link with each other whether it is direct or indirect. In Indian culture, there are few studies done on these three variables altogether. The Indian social system is viewed as collectivist (Hofstede, 1980). Having the mindset that they are a vital component of one or more internal communities (Triandis, 1989), menstrual-related taboos hinder women and girls from participating in many facets of social and cultural life (Garg & Anand, 2015). India being a developing country still has a taboo regarding menstruation. Also, PMS still impacts QOL and menstrual attitudes of women unfavourably in this country. This study aims to explore the idea of menstruation, PMS and MA of women and how it impacts the women residing in Dehradun city.

METHODOLOGY

To explore whether the menstrual attitude has an impact on premenstrual syndrome.

To investigate the relationship between premenstrual syndrome and quality of life.

To predict the relationship between Menstrual Attitude, Premenstrual Syndrome and Quality of Life.

There were a total of 124 young female participants from 18 to 35 years old in Dehradun city and it was a purposive sampling method used for this research. A quantitative research method was used. There were three variables used for this research - Premenstrual syndrome, Quality of Life and Menstrual Attitude. Independent variable: PMS, Dependent variable: Attitude and QOL. Description of the tool, Pearson r is used to determine the correlation of coefficient between two variables. Student's t-test was used to determine the difference between the two variables. Regression analysis was used to predict the relationship between QOL, MA and PMS. In this research purposive sampling method was used to collect data. The target sample was female. The participants belonged from different areas of Dehradun varying from age 18 to 35 years old. The researcher visited different areas of Dehradun like Prem Nagar, Shubash Nagar, Vasant Vihar, Rishi Vihar, and Rajpur to collect data. The participants were briefed regarding the purpose of the research and took informed consent from them. Few people refused to be a part of this research as they did not feel comfortable with the topic. The collected data then was stored in SPSS to calculate it. After collecting the data, it was organized in SPSS, summarized using tables and graphs, and subjected to statistical analysis. Mean, SD, t-test, and correlation were calculated to test the hypotheses.

The Quality of Life Scale (Flanagan, 1978c): The scale consists of 16 items with 7 Likert point scales ranging from Delighted (7) to Terrible (1).

Reliability: Over 3 weeks in stable chronic disease groups, the scale was internally consistent (=.82 to .92) and exhibited strong test-retest reliability (r = 0.78 to r = 0.84) (Burckhardt et al., 1989). Other studies have reported comparable estimations of reliability for the 16-item measurements (Burckhardt et al., 1992; Anderson, 1995; Neumann & Buskila, 1997; Wahl et al., 1998).

Validity: The QOLS have undergone content and construct validity testing, and several translations have been completed (Burckhardt & Anderson, 2003).

Menstrual Attitude Questionnaire (Chandra et al., 1989b): The questionnaire is the Indian Adaptation which consists of 22 items with 7 Likert point scales ranging from Disagree Strongly (1) to Agree Strongly (7).

Reliability: The test-retest was used and it was found to be good with concordance for each item and overall scores which ranged from 82% to 96% (Chandra, et al., 1989c).

Validity: The MAQ Indian Adaptation was standardized and the validity was found good to be used for the Indian setup (Chandra & Chaturvedi, 1992).

The Premenstrual Symptoms Screening Tool(PSST) (Steiner et al., 2003c): The tool consists of 14 items and 5 additional items to check whether the symptoms interfere with others. It has 4 Likert-point scales ranging from Not at All to Severe.

Reliability: The reliability requirements were good (Cronbach's alpha=0.9 and intra-class correlation=0.8) (Siahbazi et al., 2011).

Validity: The acquired Content Validity Ratio (CVR) and Content Validity Index (CVI) were 0.7 and 0.8, which were higher than our chosen norms (0.62 and 0.79, respectively) (Shiva et al., 2011).

Premenstrual syndrome (PMS) is commonly faced by following physical, emotional and behavioural symptoms. It is occurring cyclically in PMS in the menstrual cycle. These symptoms have very important roles to play woman's quality of life, they affect various aspects such as physical health, mental well-being and social functioning. PMS affects the quality of life it is influenced by individual attitudes and behaviour during menstruation. The relationship between PMS, menstrual attitudes and QoL involves theoretical frameworks such as psychological, social, cultural, and biological features.

Theoretical Framework Approach

Biopsychosocial Model: Bio-Psychosocial framework reflects health and illness interaction between biological, psychological and social factors. PMS and QoL biological factors such as hormonal fluctuations, psychological factors including attitudes towards menstruation, it is a social factor even cultural, and social behavioural role play a crucial role.

Cognitive-Behavioural Theory: CBT reflects various aspects individual's thoughts, attitudes and behavioural beliefs that influence their emotional aspects. MA is always between negative attitudes and thoughts during menstruation much of the time feels like stigma and shame. PMS has faced various symptoms that reduce overall QoL. Coping strategies may indicate the impact of PMS on QoL.

Feminist Theory: Feminist theory indicates the impact of gender roles, responsibility, power, and societal rules on women's experience. In these aspects of menstruation, societal taboos and stereotypes societal aspects menstruation can contribute to negative menstrual attitudes and stigmatize PMS. The inequalities among menstruation time major challenges faced by menstrual stigma, feminist perspectives can increase the positive menstrual thoughts to improve the QoL individual experience during the PMS.

Health Belief Model: Individual health as well as behaviours perceived susceptibility to a health condition. During the MA negative thoughts and behaviour symptoms as more severe and they faced lots of barriers to seeking help and even to implementing coping strategies, which are impacting their quality of life

A transactional approach to bringing stress and coping strategy: Stress levels increase during menstruation time the transactional model will utilize interaction between individual coping strategies PMS symptoms can be perceived as stressors. The positive coping strategies, social support and engaging in self-care activities are the negative impacts of PMS on QoL. The Theoretical framework approach indicates the relationship between PMS, MA, and QoL. It considers biological, psychological, social, cultural and gender-based approaches to the research view of the point to develop comprehensive interventions aimed at improving the well-being of affected people by PMS. Women Empowering and facing many challenges negative MA, and promoting positive coping strategies it is based on the systematic problem during menstrual health can contribute to enhanced QoL and menstrual well-being.

Figure 2.

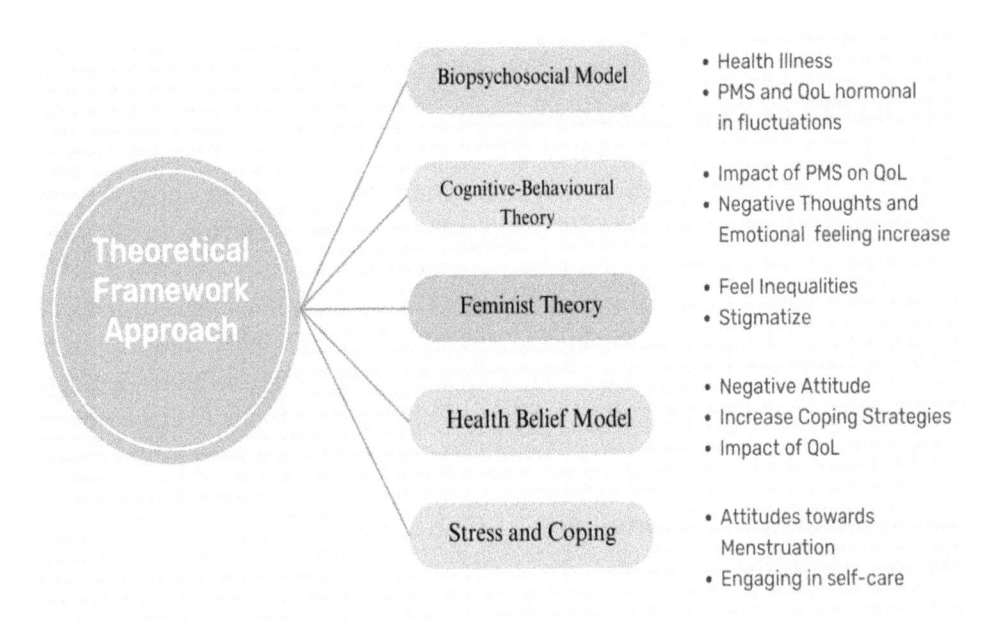

Premenstrual Syndrome (PMS): PMS refers to a combination of physical, emotional and behavioural symptoms it is cycling the menstrual period. It is typically in the leading up to menstruation.

Operational Definition: PMS is operationally defined using standardized diagnostic criteria such as those in the Diagnostic and Statistical Manual of Mental Disorders (DSM-5) and the International Classification of Diseases (ICD-10). It includes physical and psychological symptoms luteal phase and during the menstrual cycle. Daily functioning is absent during the follicular stage.

Menstrual Attitudes

Definition: MA includes individual beliefs, myths, perceptions and emotional well-being during menstruation the physiological process of shedding the uterus occurs every month in an individual during the menstrual cyclical period.

Operational Definition: MA individual attitudes and beliefs towards menstruation, including their level of acceptance, comfort, stigma, and control of the menstrual perceived. These attitudes validate and measure the Menstrual Attitude Questionnaire (MAQ) and conduct the focus group discussion to capture the range of viewpoints of their life.

Quality of Life

Definition: QoL individual's subjective perception of overall life satisfaction in various aspects of their lives. It is physical health, mental health and emotional well-being, social relationships, environmental factors and personal fulfilment.

Operational Definition: In this research chapter QoL will be defined as standardized assessment tools in the World Health Organization Quality of Life (WHOQOL) Questionnaire or specific domains of quality of life scales relevant to the PMS context. Life satisfaction provides a comprehensive evaluation of an individual's quality of life about PMS. In this PMS will follow physical symptoms, emotional distress and social functioning of life.

The Impact of PMS on Female Adolescents

Victor et al. (2019c) examined the research study as focusing on young adolescent groups aged between 18 to 24 living with parents and unemployed it is similar to Brazilian studies. In this research study, half of them were active, with many using combined oral contraceptives (COC) which is the impact of PMS. Alcohol consumption was prevalent even though it is evident that linking chocolate, caffeine, and alcohol to PMS is lacking. To improve the physical activity role of PMS in the studies even though PMS dominance is 49.9% similar for other countries it is stem for the diagnostic criteria for demographics. The quality of lime was leading for daily activities in terms of relational conflicts. To create education awareness among PMS-affected young women to increase their quality of life was an increase in a better way.

Women With Pre-Existing Mental Health Conditions and Premenstrual Syndrome

Hardy and Hunter (2021) author contribute to the PMS syndrome women face in the workplace. This study revealed that 40% of the women experienced severe symptoms and impairing normal functioning. There are 35% of them experienced PMS Premenstrual Dysphoric Disorder (PMDD) is affected by severe complex work-related finding presenteeism, tardiness, and absenteeism. Working women their many work-related problems were associated such as health, alcohol consumption, quality of sleep, anxiety, depression, and hormonal contraception problems and it is including coping strategies. To recommendation for the study those who are working women to create awareness and increase communication to implement the policies and provide the sources. There is a significant number of women in the UK workforce potentially affected by PMS, and to address this issue in the workplace it is very difficult to handle. Even though this study supports and importance of reproductive health in the context of women's economic participation to increase the workplace as well as the PMS health issue to handle.

The Prevalence of Premenstrual Syndrome in Marginalized Communities

Yonkers et al. (2008c) examined for the research study suppression cuts of PMS. The long-term use of bone density problems and the Oophorectomy is the last resort. Transdermal estrogen stops PMS without menopause. It protects and prevents the symptoms. Oral contraceptive has a limited efficacy. Regular exercise to protect and CBT help but limit and prevent the PMS syndrome. Many times support for non-medical treatment also supports. To advise to meet Gynaecologists to manage and handle the severe cases.

Logue and Moos (1986) examined consistent diagnostic criteria to identify them effectively. To explore the positive experiences during the menstrual cycle during the arousal and elation for the impact of the study. It is essential for the treatment approach and even the life context of nutrition. The feature research study could concentrate on various aspects of life context and nutritional aspects. Further research made a biopsychosocial perspective to understand the diverse factors influencing premenstrual syndromes thoroughly. The research study mainly collaboration among the researchers for biomedical, psychological and social sciences is crucial for comprehensive progress in this field.

Unique Challenge Faced by Women and Adolescent

Premenstrual symptoms can be challenging in certain populations it is including physiological, healthcare, cultural myths, and socioeconomic conditions. Certain populations face unique challenges and manage during premenstrual symptoms. Adolescents are a young age group lack of compressive attitudes during the menstrual time it is associated with symptoms it is lead to confusion and distress. Even though the young age group people and their families or societal communities follow cultural taboos during menstruation it may prevent open discussion and seeking for the premenstrual symptoms it is cause of the stigma. Adolescents face irregular menstrual cycles and hormonal fluctuations even abnormal changes during the premenstrual symptoms. To access the health care system adolescents, face many barriers due to financial support and lack of family support.

Women with disabilities express their premenstrual symptoms to accessing the appropriate care due to communication barriers. Physical disabilities can make it challenging to manage menstrual hygiene to access healthcare facilities for symptom management. They are managed quite effectively during the PMS. PMS may exclude dysphoria in transgender who experience distress related to their assigned sex at birth. Healthcare providers are knowledgeable about transgender to provide affirming care for managing PMS symptoms. Therapy associated with menstruation and hormone therapy can lead to identifying the symptoms and require specialized management. Vulnerable and Homeless Women Poor women and vulnerable women are facing plenty of hygiene products as they don't have affordable menstrual hygiene products and they face discomfort due the health-seeking behaviour and associated PMS. They don't have proper financial support and medical care unable to purchase. Homeless their unstable housing condition it is difficult to handle PMS in a safe and sanitary environment. Women in rural or remote areas in the rural area very difficult handling the PMS issues leading to challenges to diagnosis and treatment for PMS. In rural places unable to get proper transportation facilities to reach health care centres. In the local area their cultural practices and beliefs are followed in the rural communities it is women are affected during the PMS and they follow local homemade remedies for precaution. The holistic approach to considering the specific needs and each population it is includes education, access the resources, care and support during the PMS time. To improve affordable healthcare support for vulnerable communities.

Different Types of Approaches PMS, Pharmacological intervention, Lifestyle Modification

Steiner (2000) noticed that most reproductive-age women face PMS which can be physical or affective. It is 5% endure severe symptoms significantly impacting daily life. The accurate diagnosis is to require over two menstrual cycles. This criterion for PMS or PMDD and other experiences worsened existing conditions or unrelated cyclic symptoms. Treatment starts in the various ways PMS or PMDD and others experience worsened existing conditions or unrelated cyclic symptoms. Pharmacological intervention. The treatment may be effective for daily use. Menstrual cycle modification is considered only after other options fail.

Campagne and Campagne (2007) opinioned that PMS is viewed as a complex socio-psychosomatic condition with biological cyclists. Treatment should address all contributing factors, not just physiological or mood symptoms, emphasizing the importance of psychological and social interventions alongside medical approaches. Various studies highlight the significance of psychological factors, stress levels, and cognitive effects during the premenstrual phase, advocating for comprehensive multidisciplinary therapy. CBT has shown effectiveness in treating psychological aspects of PMS, with some studies suggesting it as preferable to medication. However, further research is needed to establish its efficacy conclusively. Non-pharmacologic treatments, including socio-psychologic therapies, are recommended initially for all PMS patients, according to the American Academy of Family Physicians (AAFP) and the American College of Obstetricians and Gynecologists (ACOG). Despite ongoing debates about PMS definition, diagnostic criteria, and treatment recommendations, integrating socio-psychologic therapies into management strategies is crucial.

Empowering Women Through Specific Mechanisms or Strategies

Robinson and de Bessa (2002) provided an overview of the study on poor nutrition followed by an improper diet and its use in explaining PMS. Many Western medical healers advise taking certain nutritional aspects, such as vitamins, minerals, and magnesium supplements, as a precaution for women experiencing PMS syndrome. However, in opposition to the study, the University of Sydney rejected the idea that vitamin scarcity causes PMS. Austrian scholars aim to inform about the PMS problem, emphasizing deficiencies in vitamins and minerals. The research study found that PMS syndrome is often associated with insufficient magnesium, zinc, vitamin A, vitamin E, or B six.

The present research study advocates following a Indian traditional diet rich in magnesium to regulate serotonin, which plays a vital role in mood fluctuation and pain sensitivity, significantly influencing PMS. Foods rich in magnesium include brown rice, lentils, whole grain bread, sunflower seeds, spinach leaves and stems, beans, and cashews. Additionally, foods with a high vitamin B content, such as bananas, chicken breast, sweet potatoes, whole grains, and beans, are recommended. Potassium is also necessary, so adding a fresh fruit salad with oranges and apples is advisable.

To increase water content food intake, foods like watermelon and cucumber are suggested. Drinking milk to provide vitamin D helps reduce irritability during PMS. Vitamin A-rich foods such as carrots, eggs, melons, and mangoes, along with vitamin E sources like wheat germ oil and fish, as well as other nutritional supplements, can protect against PMS symptoms. School-level education should provide information about PMS and raise awareness in schools, colleges, and workplaces. With increased awareness and the ability to overcome related problems, individuals can work in various places and concentrate on their jobs, thus empowering women to achieve equality with men in various fields.

ENSURE THAT WOMEN'S EMPOWERMENT IS A BROADER THEME

Initiative to Promoting Education

Chau and Chang (1999a) adopted a study to promote educational programs that were more crucial in playing a biological and psychosocial role related to PMS, contributing more effectively to reducing symptoms such as anxiety, fear, water retention, and thirst. The initiative to promote education significantly improved adolescents' knowledge of PMS and self-care. Post-test knowledge assessment indicates a need for further improvement in promoting education. Providing information on menstruation, PMS, and self-care measures as a regular subject in the school education curriculum should start from the primary school itself and early education to support young girls in developing a better understanding of health-related issues and coping with situations to adopt positive mental attitudes towards PMS and menstruation self-care.

Access to Healthcare

Chau and Chang (1999b), healthcare promotion is achieved through various means, such as nurses being identified and promoting health and facilitating self-care among adolescents. Healthcare education will provide the following ways: teachers will have a knowledge base in health education, enabling them to effectively implement educational programs (Molugulu et al., 2016). Research studies examine the identification of PMS through a collection of physical, psychological, and behavioural assessments of adolescents and women during the late luteal phase of each menstrual cycle, occurring 7-14 days before menstruation.

This healthcare access support is provided at the school, college, workplace, and family levels. At the home level, issues and difficulties faced by women during PMS or menstruation can be addressed by accessing nearby primary health centres or through village health nurses or Anganwadi staff. School and college-level educational institutions provide health centre facilities to support access during this time. Working women also face many problems during this time, whether in government or private sectors, so necessary support should be provided to women during PMS or menstruation. Even if they seek leave due to these conditions, strong policy recommendations should be made to address their situation.

Awareness Campaigns Related Menstrual Hygiene and Well-Being

Banerjee et al. (2021) discussed the awareness campaigns related to Menstrual Hygiene and well-being through Accredited Social Health Activists (ASHAs) and Community Health Workers (CHWs). People must create mass-level, regular campaigns to raise awareness among adolescents and women receiving Antenatal Care (ANC) and Postnatal Care (PNC) by attending to their household needs and addressing local-level immediate health issues for support. At the village level, regular awareness campaigns should be conducted, and health teams along with health practitioners should provide menstrual hygiene and well-being programs in schools and nearby colleges.

RESULTS

The result benefits an individual by presenting the study's findings, offering evidence and supporting the research aims, and contributing to overall knowledge and comprehension of the issue. It also enables the examination and analysis of obtained data, which aids in the development of relevant findings and implications for future study or practical applications. Here are some of the results that were found in this research study.

Table 1. Socio demographics

	No	Percentage
Age		
18-25	59	47.58%
26-35	65	52.41%
Marital Status		
Married	60	48.38%
Unmarried	64	51.61%
Education Qualification		
Undergraduate	62	50%
Post-Graduate	57	45.96%
PhD	5	4.03%
Socioeconomic Background		
Upper Middle	10	8.06%
Middle	101	81.45%
Lower Middle	13	10.48%
Lower	0	0

Note. Socio-demographics are shown in the table like age range, marital status, education qualifications and socioeconomic background.
N= Total number out of 124 participants.
N= Total number out of 124 participants.

Table 2. Total numbers and mean of all variables

Variables	N	Mean
PMS	124	21.71
QOL	124	80.41
MA	124	99.51

Note. The mean and total number of the variables (Premenstrual syndrome, quality of life and menstrual attitude) are shown.

Table 3. Correlation between three variables

Variables	1	2	3
1. PMS	-	-0.3648	0.0280
2. QOL	-0.3648	-	-0.0895
3. MA	0.0280	-0.0895	-

Note. The Pearson correlation was used to check the correlation between the variables (PMS, QOL and MA).

Figure 3. Percentage of females with PMS felt its interference in their life
Note. The figure shows how the PMS impacts participant's other aspects of their lives by categorizing them into five domains (work efficiency or productivity, relationship with coworkers, relationships with family, social life activities, and home responsibilities).

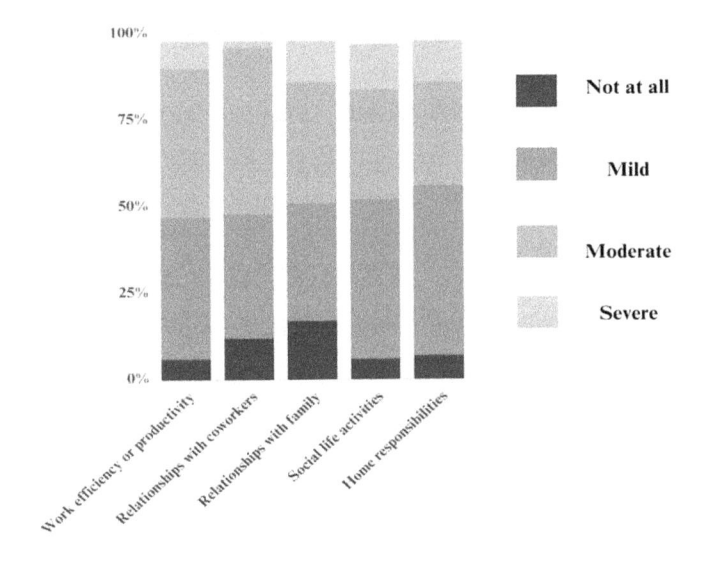

Figure 4. Number of females with different attitude towards menstruation
Note. From each domain of 124 participants, women who take menstruation as a debilitating event are 93.5%, natural events are 93.5%, bothersome events are 78.2% and denial of effects are 61.2%.

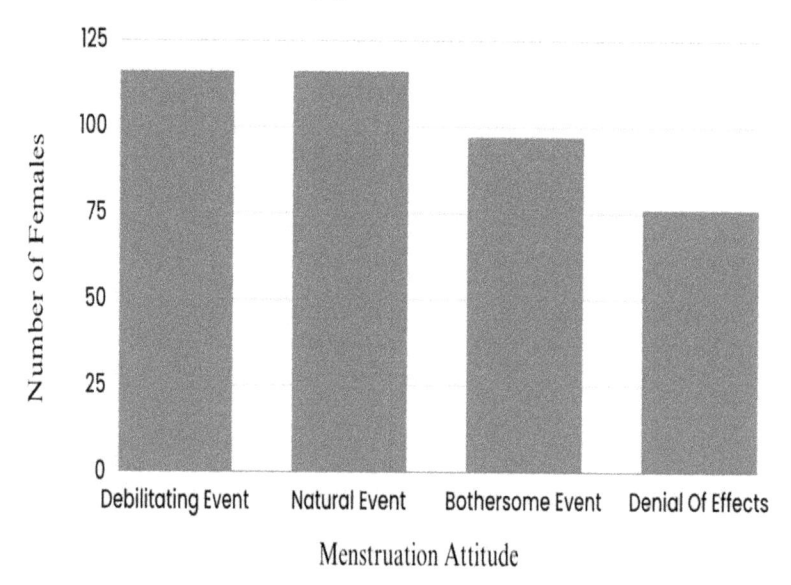

Table 4. The mean, standard deviation, significance level and t-value of marital status of all variables

Variables	N	Mean	SD	t-value	Significance level
PMS					
Unmarried	64	22.18	11.2	1.98	>0.05
Married	60	21.21	11.3		
QOL					
Unmarried	64	79.12	14.61	1.97	>0.05
Married	60	81.8	14.6		
MA					
Unmarried	64	98.25	15.16	1.98	>0.05
Married	60	100.86	15.02		

Note. The table displays the total number of participants, mean, standard deviation(SD), t-value and significance level of 0.05 of all the variables by comparing unmarried and married women.

Table 5. Correlation between PMS, QOL and MA for unmarried women

	Coefficients	SE	t Stat	P-value	95% CI LL	95% CI UL
Intercept	52.75	15.66	3.368	<0.01	21.43	84.08
QOL	-0.26	0.099	-2.68	<0.01	-0.46	-0.067
MA	-0.09	0.124	-0.77	>0.01	-0.34	0.152

Note. The table displays the coefficients, standard errors(SE), t-stat, p-value and the confidence interval of 95% with lower limit(LL) and upper limit(UL) for unmarried women.

Table 6. Correlation between PMS, QOL and MA for married women

	Coefficients	SE	t Stat	P-value	95% CI LL	95% CI UL
Intercept	42.47	10.11	4.200	<0.01	22.22	62.72
QOL	-0.318	0.086	-3.679	<0.01	-0.49	-0.14
MA	0.047	0.067	0.706	>0.01	-0.087	0.182

Note. The table displays the coefficients, standard errors(SE), t-stat, p-value and the confidence interval of 95% with lower limit(LL) and upper limit(UL) for married women.

Table 7. The mean, standard deviation, significance level and t-value of women with no and with PMS of MA and QOL

Variables	N	Mean	SD	t-value	Significance level
QOL					
With PMS	79	76.21	13.76	1.98	>0.05
No/Mild PMS	45	87.8			
MA					
With PMS	79	100.27	13.86	1.99	>0.05
No/Mild PMS	45	98.17	16.96		

Note. The table displays the total number of participants, mean, standard deviation(SD), t-value and significance level of 0.05 of quality of life and menstrual attitude by comparing women with no/mild PMS and women with moderate to severe PMS.

DISCUSSION

The primary objective of this study was to investigate the relationships between PMS and Marital Status, QOL and MA, shedding light on the experiences and insights of women during their menstrual cycle. By addressing this objective, we sought to contribute to the understanding of the multifaceted impact that PMS has on women's overall QOL and the role that MA plays in shaping these experiences. The total sample size of females was 124. As we can see in Table 2, with a mean score of PMS of 21.71, the results indicate that, on average, participants reported experiencing moderate levels of premenstrual symptoms. The mean score of QOL is 80.41 indicating that, on average, participants reported relatively high levels of QOL. The mean score of MA is 99.51 which suggests that, on average, participants exhibited a positive attitude towards menstruation.

Table 1 displays data on many characteristics such as age range, marital status, education qualification, and socio-demographics. In terms of age, those aged 18 to 25 account for 47.58% of participants, while those aged 26 to 35 account for 52.41%. In terms of marital status, married people make up 48.38% of the total, while unmarried people make up 51.61%. Undergraduates account for 50% of the workforce, while postgraduates account for 45.96% and PhDs account for 4.03%. The socio-economic background distribution is as follows: upper-middle class at 8.06%, middle class at 81.45%, lower-middle class at 10.48%, and no participation from the lowest class. Overall, the findings show that the participants in the research had a broad representation in terms of age, marital status, academic qualification, and socio-economic background.

Hypothesis 1 states that "There will be no significant relationship between PMS, QOL and MA in young women". PMS and QOL have a -0.3648 correlation coefficient. This points to a moderately unfavourable association. Table 2 explains the correlations. It implies that as the intensity of PMS symptoms grows, the QOL decreases. Similar results were also found by Jang and Sung (2018). PMS and MA have a correlation value of 0.0280. This points to a very faint positive association. It implies that there is a practically weak positive correlation between PMS symptoms and menstrual attitude. PMS symptoms have little effect on how women perceive or feel about menstruation. In the study of Bae et al. (2013), similar results found a weak correlation between MA and PMS. QOL and MA have a correlation value of -0.0895.

This suggests a weakly negative association. It implies that there is a slight negative association between MA and QOL. Lower levels of QOL are linked to somewhat more unfavourable attitudes regarding menstruation. PMS has a somewhat negative correlation with QOL, implying that more severe PMS symptoms are associated with lower levels of well-being. However, there is little to no correlation between PMS symptoms and MA. Furthermore, there is a modest negative association between QOL and MA, showing that lower levels of QOL are correlated with somewhat more unfavourable views towards menstruation. Hypothesis 1 is rejected at a 5% level of significance and there is some significant relationship (correlation) between PMS, MA and QOL. These variables have an impact on each other.

Hypothesis 2 states that "Married and unmarried women will not differ significantly on PMS, QOL and MA". The mean value for both, married (n=60) was 21.2166 and unmarried women(n=64) was 22.1875 (Table 3); and the t value was found to be 1.98. This implies that there is a low statistically significant difference in PMS levels between unmarried and married women. The mean value of MA was found to be, in married 100.86 and unmarried 98.25; and t-value was found to be 1.98 (significance of 0.05). This implies that there is a statistically significant difference in the MA between unmarried and married women. The unmarried women's mean score of 98.25 indicates that, on average, the unmarried women in the sample had a lower score or a less favourable MA. The mean value of 100.866 for married women, on the other hand, implies that the married women in the sample had a little higher score or a more favourable MA. The mean value of QOL was found to be, in married 81.8 and unmarried 79.125; and t-value was found to be 1.98 (significance of 0.05). This implies that there is a low statistically significant difference in QOL levels between unmarried and married women. This concludes that hypothesis 2 is rejected at a 5% level of significance as there is some difference in the PMS, QOL and MA levels in both marital statuses.

Hypothesis 3 states that "There is no significant relationship between PMS, QOL and MA in married women". The predicted value of the PMS when all predictors are zero is indicated by the intercept coefficient, which is 52.75(table 6). The intercept is statistically significant, as shown by the t-statistic of 3.368 and the p-value of less than 0.01. The QOL has a coefficient of o-0.26, indicating that a drop in the PMS is connected to a drop in QOL by one unit. QOL is a statistically significant predictor, as shown by its t-statistic of -2.68 and p-value of less than 0.01. The MA has a coefficient of -0.09, meaning that a one-unit change in MA results in a comparable change in the response variable. However, it has a t-statistic of -0.77 and a p-value greater than 0.01, showing that MA is not a statistically significant predictor. The findings imply that QOL has a major influence on PMS, with lower QOL related to a decrease in reaction. However, MA has no impact on PMS. Therefore, hypothesis 3 is rejected at a 5% level of significance as there is some significant relationship between PMS, QOL and MA in married women.

Hypothesis 4 states that "There is no significant relationship between PMS, QOL and MA in unmarried women''. In Table 5, the predicted value of the response variable when all predictors are zero is shown by the intercept's coefficient, which is 52.75. The intercept appears to be statistically significant, as indicated by the t-statistic of 3.368 and a p-value below 0.01. The coefficient for QOL is -0.26, which represents the shift in the response variable brought on by a one-unit change in QOL. According to the negative coefficient, the response variable should also decline as QOL does. The QOL is statistically significant, as shown by the t-statistic of -2.68 and the p-value of less than 0.01. The coefficient for the MA is -0.09, indicating that a one-unit change in the MA causes an equivalent change in the PMS. The MA is less statistically significant, according to the t-statistic of -0.77 and the p-value, which is bigger than 0.01.

The findings reveal that QOL has a significant and detrimental impact on PMS, indicating that as QOL declines, so does PMS. However, the MA does not significantly change PMS. Therefore, hypothesis 4 is rejected at a 5% level of significance as there is a significant relationship between PMS, QOL and MA in unmarried women. Hypotheses 5 and 6 state that "There's no significant relationship between MA and QOL women with PMS" and "There's no significant relationship between MA and QOL in women without PMS", respectively which have been shown in Table 6. Both correlations reveal a modest negative correlation between QOL and MA in both categories. Individuals with moderate-severe PMS had a mean QOL score of 80.04 and a mean MA score of 99.46. Individuals with moderate or no PMS had a mean QOL score of 80.27 and a mean MA score of 99.38. These are the average QOL and MA scores for each group. Overall, evidence implies that regardless of PMS severity, there is a modest negative correlation between QOL and MA. Hypothesis 5 and 6 are rejected at a 5% level of significance as there is a significant relationship between MA and QOL in women with and without PMS.

Hypothesis 7 states that "Women with and without PMS will not differ significantly on MA and QOL". Table 7 shows that the mean QOL score for women with PMS is 76.21, whereas it is 87.8 for women without PMS. The standard deviation (SD) for women with PMS is 1.98, while it is 13.10 for women without PMS. At a significance level larger than 0.05, the t-value of 13.76 indicates a significant difference between the two groups. The mean MA score for women with PMS is 100.27, whereas it is 98.17 for women without PMS. Women with PMS have an SD of 1.99, while women without PMS have an SD of 13.86. At a significance level larger than 0.05, the t-value of 1.99 shows that there is no significant difference between the two groups. The findings indicate that women with PMS had lower QOL ratings than those without PMS. Therefore, hypothesis 7 is rejected at a 5% level of significance as there is a significant difference in MA and QOL in women with and without PMS. Figure 2, shows different impacts of PMS.

Due to PMS, Approximately 6% indicated no impact, 41% mild impact, 43% moderate impact, and 8% severe impact on job efficiency or production as a result of PMS; around 12% had no impact, 36% reported mild impact, 48% reported moderate impact, and 2% indicated severe damage on their relationships with coworkers; around 17% had no impact, 34% reported mild impact, 35% reported moderate impact, and 12% reported severe impact on their relationships with family members; about 6% indicated no impact, 46% reported mild impact, 32% reported moderate impact, and 13% reported severe impact on their social life activities.; about 7% had no impact, 49% reported mild impact, 30% reported moderate impact, and 12% indicated severe impact on their household obligation. These data suggest that PMS can have differing degrees of influence on various parts of women's lives. It has varying degrees of influence on job efficiency or production, connections with coworkers, family relationships, social life activities, and home obligations, with a sizable number reporting moderate to severe effects. These findings emphasize the necessity of recognizing and controlling PMS symptoms to reduce their harmful impact on women's everyday functioning and relationships.

For Figure 3, Menstruation is perceived as a devastating occurrence by the vast majority of women, roughly 93.5%. This implies that people regard it as a physically and emotionally demanding event that has a substantial influence on their everyday lives. Similarly, 93.5% of women perceive menstruation to be a natural phenomenon. This demonstrates a comprehension of its biological and physiological origin, as well as an understanding that it is a normal process that occurs in their bodies. A significant portion, around 78.2%, consider menstruation to be an unpleasant event. This implies that they feel some inconveniences or pain as a result of menstruation, but not to the level that they consider it debilitating. Approximately 61.2% of women are in denial about the impact of menstruation. This suggests that individuals may minimize or dismiss the influence of menstruation on their lives to cope with any unfavourable beliefs or experiences related to it.

Overall, these data illustrate the various perspectives on menstruation among the women polled. While the majority sees it as both debilitating and normal, a sizable number finds it irritating. Furthermore, a sizable proportion rejects or minimizes its impact. These disparities illustrate the complexities and subjectivity of how women perceive and experience menstruation. encourage them to seek medical help (Lancastle et al., 2023). In this study, the problem of women being delayed in receiving medical aid during treatment for menstrual issues is examined. Mostly, illiterate women or women with low levels of education are the reason for this. When people have a good educational background, their quality of life improves. Akin and Erbil (2023) author explained that during menstruation, women are affected with symptoms, and their effectiveness may differ between cultures and ethnic groups. It is aimed at encouraging women to take medication, seek social support, and adopt social and cultural beliefs. In the current study, we look at how women can empower themselves during menstruation time and how to plan and overcome some of the issues that arise during this time.

Daronco et al. (2024) the result of the study on menstruation in school students between the ages of 11 and 13. A period of 3 to 5 days during which menstruation occurs. 40.4% of respondents reported using hormonal contraceptive methods, while 37.7% stated that they did not use any type of contraceptive method. The majority (61.4%) frequently experienced PMS issues, with 93.9% reporting regular feelings of anger, 91.2% experiencing continual irritation, and 88.6% facing increased sensitivity. Additionally, 86.8% of respondents reported experiencing anxiety and tension, resulting in a high level of decreased participation in social activities. The study demonstrated that women faced challenges in empowerment due to these issues. The current study highlights the importance of providing support and coping strategies during menstruation to address these challenges.

Talib Hassan et al. (2023) the current study aims to explore the relationship between premenstrual tension and symptoms, particularly about low education background and poor interpersonal relationships. It seeks to address this gap in knowledge for a better future. The study is designed to analyze and assess the causes of premenstrual tension symptoms and evaluate therapeutic interventions. Emphasizing the quality of life, attitudes, and behaviours related to premenstrual symptoms, the research aims to empower young women and foster leadership qualities to help them cope with their lifestyles more effectively.

Suner-Keklik and Bargi (2023) identified the relationship between the level of physical activity and symptoms of menstruation in healthy women. It explores how the duration of menstruation affects women's experiences of pain and their engagement in physical domestic activities, particularly noting an increase in symptoms and severity for women with regular menstruation. The current research aims to address these issues by empowering women during menstruation and providing strategies to cope with the challenges they face during this time. By integrating these strategies and addressing the issues, the study also aims to develop leadership qualities and foster improvement in women's empowerment. Van Niekerk et al. (2023) focused on the health-related quality of life (HRQoL) and its influences on women diagnosed with these conditions. It examines aspects such as physical well-being, emotional well-being, bodily pain, fatigue, and social engagement during the menstruation period, as well as the general HRQoL experienced by women. The study adopts various interventions, including psychological interventions and therapies aimed at improving body compassion to alleviate stress, anxiety, and aggressiveness.

FUTURE DIRECTIONS AND IMPLICATIONS

Future research with bigger and more varied samples, including women from a broader range of socio-economic backgrounds, could help to overcome these limitations and provide a deeper comprehension of the phenomena being studied.

Women's Empowerment Within the Context of Menstrual Health Could Be Directly Addressed in Future Research to Bridge This Gap

The proposed research study aimed to explore the relationships between PMS and Marital Status, QOL, and MA, shedding light on women's experiences during their menstrual cycle. For this objective, to contribute to the understanding of the multifaceted impact that PMS has on women's overall Quality of Life and the role that Menstrual Attitude plays a crucial role in these aspects. The sample size of females was 124. The above table 2 indicates a mean PMS score of 21.71 respondents reported that experience moderate levels of PMS on average. The mean QoL score of 80.41 indicated relatively high levels of QoL, while the mean MA score of 99.51 suggested a positive attitude towards menstruation. The above table 1 indicates that various data such as age range, marital status, education status, and socio-demographics. Respondents were broadly represented across age groups, marital status, education, and socio-economic status.

Hypothesis 1, stating that "There will be no significant relationship between PMS, QOL, and MA in young women," was rejected, as correlations revealed some significant relationships among these variables. Specifically, PMS was moderately negatively correlated with QOL, indicating that higher PMS symptoms were associated with lower QOL. However, there was only a weak positive correlation between PMS and MA, suggesting minimal influence of PMS symptoms on menstrual attitude. Additionally, a weak negative association was observed between QOL and MA. Hypothesis 2, which posited that "Married and unmarried women will not differ significantly on PMS, QOL, and MA," was partially rejected. While there was no significant difference in PMS and QOL levels between married and unmarried women, a statistically significant difference was found in MA levels, with married women exhibiting a slightly more favourable attitude towards menstruation. Hypothesis 3, focusing on married women, was rejected as well, indicating some significant relationship between PMS, QOL, and MA in this group.

QOL emerged as a significant predictor of PMS, while MA showed no significant impact. Similarly, Hypothesis 4, concerning unmarried women, was rejected, revealing a significant relationship between PMS, QOL, and MA. QOL emerged as a significant predictor of PMS, while MA showed no significant impact. Hypotheses 5 and 6 were rejected, indicating a significant relationship between MA and QOL in women with and without PMS. Hypothesis 7, asserting that "Women with and without PMS will not differ significantly on MA and QOL," was partially rejected, as a significant difference was found in QOL between women with and without PMS, but no significant difference was observed in MA. Figure 2 illustrates the varying impacts of PMS across different aspects of women's lives, emphasizing the need to address PMS symptoms to mitigate their adverse effects. Figure 3 highlights different perspectives on menstruation among women, illustrating its complex and subjective nature. In conclusion, the study provides insights into the relationships between PMS, QOL, and MA, emphasizing the need for tailored interventions to address women's menstrual health and empower them to cope effectively with menstrual challenges. Additional research is warranted to further explore these relationships and develop targeted interventions to improve women's well-being during their menstrual cycles.

Limitations

One of the limitations encountered is that the small sample size limited the study's statistical power, potentially restricting the capacity to discover significant impacts or correlations. Small sample findings may be more sensitive to random fluctuation and may not correctly reflect the wider population of interest. Furthermore, the lack of data from low socio-economic women limited the range and depth of insights that could be obtained from the study. These limitations may have an impact on the study's generalizability and representation.

SUMMARY AND CONCLUSION

Finally, the purpose of this study was to investigate the associations between premenstrual symptoms (PMS), quality of life (QOL), and menstrual attitude (MA) in women. On average, participants reported modest PMS symptoms, good QOL, and a favourable attitude towards menstruation. The findings validated the hypothesis of a negative relationship between PMS and QOL, demonstrating that as PMS symptoms worsen, QOL deteriorates. There was no significant link between PMS symptoms and MA, indicating that PMS had little influence on women's views regarding menstruation. The study also looked at the differences between married and unmarried women and discovered no significant changes in PMS levels or QOL between the two groups. However, there was a substantial variation in MA, with married women having slightly more favourable attitudes regarding menstruation than unmarried women.

Furthermore, when married and unmarried women were studied individually, the study found that PMS had a substantial influence on QOL in both groups, with greater PMS levels linked with poorer QOL. However, the effect of PMS on MA was quite minimal, showing that PMS has a lower influence on views regarding menstruation. Furthermore, irrespective of PMS severity, the study discovered a minor negative connection between MA and QOL in women.

This implies that lower QOL is linked to somewhat more unfavourable attitudes regarding menstruation. Finally, the study showed the numerous effects of PMS on many parts of women's lives. Participants reported varied degrees of effect on job productivity, colleague connections, family relationships, social life activities, and domestic responsibilities. The findings emphasized the need to recognize and control PMS symptoms to reduce their harmful influence on women's everyday functioning and relationships. In conclusion, this study adds to our understanding of the links between PMS, QOL, and MA in women. It emphasises the need for interventions and assistance in addressing PMS difficulties and improving women's general well-being throughout their menstrual cycle.

Abbreviations

AAFP American Academy of Family Physicians
ACOG American College of Obstetricians and Gynecologists
APA American Psychological Association
ASHAs Accredited Social Health Activists
CBT Cognitive-Behavioral Theory
CHWs Community Health Workers
COC Combined Oral Contraceptives
CVI Content Validity Index
CVR Content Validity Ratio
DSM-5 Diagnostic and Statistical Manual of Mental Disorders Fifth edition
HRQoL Health Related Quality of Life
LL Lower Limit
MA Menstrual Attitude
MAQ Menstrual Attitude Questionnaire
PA Physical Activity
PMS Premenstrual Syndrome
PMSA Premenstrual Syndrome Menstrual Attitude
PMSA Premenstrual Syndrome Menstrual Anxiety
PMSC Premenstrual Syndrome Menstrual Cravings
PMSD Premenstrual Syndrome Menstrual Depression
PMDD Premenstrual Dysphoric Disorder
PMSH Premenstrual Syndrome Menstrual Hydration
PSST Premenstrual Symptoms Screening Tool
QoL Quality of Life
SPSS Statistical Package of Social Sciences
SD Standard Deviation
SE Standard Errors
UL Upper Limit

UK United Kingdom

WHOQOL World Health Organization Quality of Life

Author Contribution

It is confirmed by all authors that Srinivasan is the author. In collaboration with all authors, contributed to the writing and analysis of the article. The study was conceived by Soumya and Kanchan Yadav. Direction and planning were handled by Srinivasan, S. Results were discussed, the article was reviewed, and the final draft was approved.

Funding

This study does not have a funding opportunity.

Data Availability

Although the corresponding author can provide the datasets upon reasonable request, they are not publically accessible due to participant privacy issues, having been generated and/or analyzed during the current study.

Declarations

Ethics approval and consent to participate, Participants, gave their informed consent, and the experimental protocol was developed by the Srinivasan S Declaration's ethical criteria and approved by the Graphic Era (Deemed to be University) ethics committee.

ACKNOWLEDGEMENTS

Soumya, Kanchan Yadav, and other fieldworkers contributed greatly to the data collection, and we are grateful to them.

REFERENCES

Aaronson, N. K. (1988). Quantitative issues in health-related quality of life assessment. *Health Policy (Amsterdam)*, *10*(3), 217–230. doi:10.1016/0168-8510(88)90058-9 PMID:10291115

Akın, Ö., & Erbil, N. (2024). Investigation of coping behaviors and premenstrual syndrome among university students. *Current Psychology (New Brunswick, N.J.)*, *43*(2), 1685–1695. doi:10.1007/s12144-023-04419-1 PMID:37359568

Amiri, M., Chaman, R., Sadeghi, Z., Khatibi, M., Ranjbar, M., & Khosravi, A. (2017). Quality of life among fertile and infertile women. *Iranian Journal of Psychiatry and Behavioral Sciences*, *11*(1), 1–5. doi:10.5812/ijpbs.5641

Anderson, K. L. (1995). The effect of chronic obstructive pulmonary disease on quality of life. *Research in Nursing & Health*, *18*(6), 547–556. doi:10.1002/nur.4770180610 PMID:7480855

Andrews, F. M., & Withey, S. B. (2012). *Social indicators of well-being: Americans' perceptions of life quality*. Springer Science & Business Media. https://books.google.co.in/books?hl=en&lr=&id=4g7rBwAAQBAJ&oi=fnd&pg=PA1&dq=Andrews,+F.+M.,+%26+Withey,+S.+B.+(2012).+Social+indicators+of+well-being:+Americans%27+perceptions+of+life+quality.+Springer+Science+%26+Business+Media.&ots=chSmZ7r7kV&sig=x4QUIWO_HWUTVPBByhe_N-iQ_uk&redir_esc=y#v=onepage&q&f=false

Anjum, F., Zehra, N., Haider, G., Rani, S., Siddique, A. A., & Munir, A. A. (2010). Attitudes towards menstruation among young women. *Pakistan Journal of Medical Sciences*, *26*(3), 619–622.

Arbabi, M., Shirmohammadi, M., Taghizadeh, Z., & Mehran, A. (2008). The effect of premenstrual syndrome on quality of life in adolescent girls. *Iranian Journal of Psychiatry*, *3*(3), 105–109.

Babajani, S., Asgari, K., Orayzi, H., & Ghasemi, N. (2017). Effectiveness of cognitive-behavioral therapy on premenstrual syndrome through compliance to treatment in an iranian sample. *Zahedan Journal of Researches in Medical Sciences*, *19*(6). doi:10.5812/zjrms.12537

Bäckström, T., & Carstensen, H. (1974). Estrogen and progesterone in plasma in relation to premenstrual tension. *Journal of Steroid Biochemistry*, *5*(3), 257–260. doi:10.1016/0022-4731(74)90139-3 PMID:4859320

Baker, F., & Intagliata, J. (1982). Quality of life in the evaluation of community support systems. *Evaluation and Program Planning*, *5*(1), 69–79. doi:10.1016/0149-7189(82)90059-3 PMID:10257372

Balaha, M., Amr, M., Moghannum, M., & Muhaidab, N. (2010). The phenomenology of premenstrual syndrome in female medical students: A cross sectional study. *The Pan African Medical Journal*, *5*(1), 1–14. doi:10.4314/pamj.v5i1.56194 PMID:21120003

Banerjee, S., Chowdhury, A., & Srivastava, A. (2021). Creating awareness about health and hygiene during menstrual cycle among Indian adolescent girls using virtual reality. In *Advanced Manufacturing Systems and Innovative Product Design: Select Proceedings of IPDIMS 2020*. Springer. 10.1007/978-981-15-9853-1_27

Bansal, D., Raman, R., & Rao, T. S. (2019). Premenstrual dysphoric disorder: ranking the symptoms and severity in Indian college students. *Journal of Psychosexual Health*, *1*(2), 159-163. doi:10.1177/2631831819827

Barnard, K., Frayne, S. M., Skinner, K. M., & Sullivan, L. M. (2003). Health status among women with menstrual symptoms. *Journal of Women's Health*, *12*(9), 911–919. doi:10.1089/154099903770948140 PMID:14670171

Benincá, S., Melhem, A., Martins, R., & Libera, E. (2016). Alcoholic chronic pancreatitis: A quality of life study. *Revista de Nutrição*, *29*(1), 23–31. doi:10.1590/1678-98652016000100003

Bertone-Johnson, E. R., Hankinson, S. E., Johnson, S. R., & Manson, J. E. (2007). A simple method of assessing premenstrual syndrome in large prospective studies. *Journal of Reproductive Medicine-Chicago, 52*(9), 779. PMID:17939593

Bertone-Johnson, E. R., Whitcomb, B. W., Missmer, S. A., Manson, J. E., Hankinson, S. E., & Rich-Edwards, J. W. (2014). Early life emotional, physical, and sexual abuse and the development of premenstrual syndrome: A longitudinal study. *Journal of Women's Health, 23*(9), 729–739. doi:10.1089/jwh.2013.4674 PMID:25098348

Bharathi, N. S., Kayalvizhi, E., & Sylvia, J. (2022). Premenstrual syndrome-An overview. *International Journal of Nursing Education and Research, 10*(4), 395–398. doi:10.52711/2454-2660.2022.00089

Borenstein, J. E., Dean, B. B., Endicott, J., Wong, J., Brown, C., Dickerson, V., & Yonkers, K. A. (2003). Health and economic impact of the premenstrual syndrome. *The Journal of Reproductive Medicine, 48*(7), 515–524. PMID:12953326

Borenstein, J. E., Dean, B. B., Leifke, E., Korner, P., & Yonkers, K. A. (2007). Differences in symptom scores and health outcomes in premenstrual syndrome. *Journal of Women's Health, 16*(8), 1139–1144. doi:10.1089/jwh.2006.0230 PMID:17937566

Borthwick-Duffy, S. A. (2000). Quality of life and quality of care in mental retardation. *Mental Retardation, 4*, 52–66. doi:10.1007/978-1-4613-9115-9_4

Brooks-Gunn, J., & Ruble, D. (1980). The menstrual attitude questionnaire. *Psychosomatic Medicine, 42*(5), 503–512. doi:10.1097/00006842-198009000-00005 PMID:7465737

Bunyaratavej, S., Pattanaprichakul, P., Leeyaphan, C., Chayangsu, O., Bunyaratavej, S., & Kulthanan, K. (2015). Onychomycosis: A study of self-recognition by patients and quality of life. *Indian Journal of Dermatology, Venereology and Leprology, 81*(3), 270. doi:10.4103/0378-6323.154796 PMID:25851764

Burckhardt, C. S., & Anderson, K. L. (2003). The Quality of Life Scale (QOLS): Reliability, validity, and utilization. *Health and Quality of Life Outcomes, 1*(1), 1–7. doi:10.1186/1477-7525-1-1 PMID:14613562

Burckhardt, C. S., Archenholtz, B., & Bjelle, A. (1992). Measuring the quality of life of women with rheumatoid arthritis or systemic lupus erythematosus: A Swedish version of the Quality of Life Scale (QOLS). *Scandinavian Journal of Rheumatology, 21*(4), 190–195. doi:10.3109/03009749209099220 PMID:1529286

Burckhardt, C. S., Woods, S. L., Schultz, A. A., & Ziebarth, D. M. (1989). Quality of life of adults with chronic illness: A psychometric study. *Research in Nursing & Health, 12*(6), 347–354. doi:10.1002/nur.4770120604 PMID:2602575

Campagne, D. M., & Campagne, G. (2007). The premenstrual syndrome revisited. *European Journal of Obstetrics, Gynecology, and Reproductive Biology, 130*(1), 4–17. doi:10.1016/j.ejogrb.2006.06.020 PMID:16916572

Chandra, P. S., & Chaturvedi, S. K. (1992). Cultural variations in attitudes toward menstruation. *Canadian Journal of Psychiatry, 37*(3), 196–198. doi:10.1177/070674379203700310 PMID:1591671

Chandra, P. S., Chaturvedi, S. K., & Isaac, M. K. (1989). Measurement of menstrual attitudes in Indian women: A cultural perspective. *Journal of Psychosomatic Obstetrics and Gynaecology, 10*(3), 247–253. doi:10.3109/01674828909016698

Chang, Y. T., & Chen, Y. C. (2009). Study of menstrual attitudes and distress among postmenarcheal female students in Hualien County. *The Journal of Nursing Research, 17*(1), 20–29. doi:10.1097/JNR.0b013e3181999d25 PMID:19352226

Chau, J. P., & Chang, A. M. (1999). Effects of an educational programme on adolescents with premenstrual syndrome. *Health Education Research, 14*(6), 817–830. doi:10.1093/her/14.6.817 PMID:10585388

Chayachinda, C., Rattanachaiyanont, M., Phattharayuttawat, S., & Kooptiwoot, S. (2008). Premenstrual syndrome in Thai nurses. *Journal of Psychosomatic Obstetrics and Gynaecology, 29*(3), 203–209. doi:10.1080/01674820801970306 PMID:18608818

Cheng, S., Sun, Z. J., Lee, I., Shih, C. C., Chen, K., Lin, S. H., Lu, F. H., Yang, Y. C., & Yang, Y. (2015). Perception of premenstrual syndrome and attitude of evaluations of work performance among incoming university female students. *Biomedical Journal, 38*(2), 167–172. doi:10.4103/2319-4170.138319 PMID:25179727

Chougule, K. (2017). A phenomenological study of premenstrual symptoms in medical and nursing students. *Journal of Evolution of Medical and Dental Sciences, 6*(46), 3576–3581. doi:10.14260/Jemds/2017/771

Chrisler, J. C. (2008). PMS as a culture-bound syndrome. In J. C. Chrisler, C. Golden, & P. D. Rozee (Eds.), Lectures on the psychology of women (4), 155–171.

Clare, A. W. (1985). Premenstrual syndrome: Single or multiple causes? *Canadian Journal of Psychiatry, 30*(7), 474–482. doi:10.1177/070674378503000704 PMID:3907815

Cronje, W., & Hawkins, A. P. (2003). Premenstrual symptoms. In J. Studd (Ed.), *Progress in. Obstetrics and Gynaecolology* (pp. 169–183). Elsevier Science. doi:10.1016/S0095-4543(03)00070-8

Dalton, K. D. (1984). *Premenstrual syndrome and progesterone therapy.* https://cir.nii.ac.jp/crid/1130000796254365952

Daronco, K. F., Muller, L. A., & Arruda, E. H. P. D. (2024). Prevalence of premenstrual syndrome in female nursing students at a public university: Cross-sectional study. *British Journal of Pain, 7*. doi:10.5935/2595-0118.20240006-en

Dean, B. B., Borenstein, J. E., Knight, K., & Yonkers, K. (2006). Evaluating the criteria used for identification of PMS. *Journal of Women's Health, 15*(5), 546–555. doi:10.1089/jwh.2006.15.546 PMID:16796482

Delara, M., Ghofranipour, F., Azadfallah, P., Tavafian, S. S., Kazemnejad, A., & Montazeri, A. (2012). Health related quality of life among adolescents with premenstrual disorders: A cross sectional study. *Health and Quality of Life Outcomes, 10*(1), 1–5. doi:10.1186/1477-7525-10-1 PMID:22208808

Deuster, P. A., Adera, T., & South-Paul, J. (1999). Biological, social, and behavioral factors associated with premenstrual syndrome. *Archives of Family Medicine, 8*(2), 122–128. doi:10.1001/archfami.8.2.122 PMID:10101982

Eagly, A. H., & Chaiken, S. (1993). *The psychology of attitudes*. Harcourt brace Jovanovich college publishers. https://psycnet.apa.org/record/1992-98849-000

Ekholm, U. B., & Bäckström, T. (1994). Influence of premenstrual syndrome on family, social life, and work performance. *International Journal of Health Services*, 24(4), 629–647. doi:10.2190/P0Y8-J7UF-K2MG-LBL4 PMID:7896466

Enuka, C., & Nwankwo, C. U. (2022). Assessment of Premenstrual Syndrome and Coping Strategies among Female Students of the School of Basic Medical Sciences, University of Benin, Benin City, Nigeria. *Bayero Journal of Nursing and Healthcare*, 4(1), 927–938. doi:10.4314/bjnhc.v4i1.2

Fazio, R. H., & Olson, M. A. (2003). Implicit measures in social cognition research: Their meaning and use. *Annual review of psychology*, 54(1), 297-327. doi: s10.1146/annurev.psych.54.101601.145225

Felce, D., & Perry, J. (1995). Quality of life: Its definition and measurement. *Research in Developmental Disabilities*, 16(1), 51–74. doi:10.1016/0891-4222(94)00028-8 PMID:7701092

Firat, M. Z., Kulakaç, Ö., Öncel, S., & Akcan, A. (2009). Menstrual Attitude Questionnaire: Confirmatory and exploratory factor analysis with Turkish samples. *Journal of Advanced Nursing*, 65(3), 652–662. doi:10.1111/j.1365-2648.2008.04919.x PMID:19222663

Flanagan, J. C. (1978). A research approach to improving our quality of life. *The American Psychologist*, 33(2), 138–147. doi:10.1037/0003-066X.33.2.138

Frank, S. E. (2020). Queering menstruation: Trans and non-binary identity and body politics. *Sociological Inquiry*, 90(2), 371–404. doi:10.1111/soin.12355

Gantela, S., & Choppara, S. (2015). Severity and frequency of premenstrual syndrome in college girls aged 18-25 years. *Journal of Evolution of Medical and Dental Sciences*, 4(87), 15228–15233. doi:10.14260/jemds/2015/2164

Garg, S., & Anand, T. (2015). Menstruation related myths in India: Strategies for combating it. *Journal of Family Medicine and Primary Care*, 4(2), 184–186. doi:10.4103/2249-4863.154627 PMID:25949964

Garg, S., Sharma, N., & Sahay, R. (2001). Socio-cultural aspects of menstruation in an urban slum in Delhi, India. *Reproductive Health Matters*, 9(17), 16–25. doi:10.1016/S0968-8080(01)90004-7 PMID:11468832

Gittelsohn, J. (Ed.). (1994). *Listening to women talk about their health: Issues and evidence from India*. Har-Anand Publications., doi:10.1080/13691058.2011.644065

Goker, A., Artunc-Ulkumen, B., Aktenk, F., & Ikiz, N. (2015). Premenstrual syndrome in Turkish medical students and their quality of life. *Journal of Obstetrics & Gynaecology*, 35(3), 275–278. doi:10.3109/01443615.2014.948820 PMID:25140580

Goldstein-Ferber, S., & Granot, M. (2006). The association between somatization and perceived ability: Roles in dysmenorrhea among Israeli Arab adolescents. *Psychosomatic Medicine*, 68(1), 136–142. doi:10.1097/01.psy.0000197644.95292.00 PMID:16449424

Greene, R., & Dalton, K. (1953). The premenstrual syndrome. *British Medical Journal*, 1(4818), 1007–1014. doi:10.1136/bmj.1.4818.1007 PMID:13032605

Greenwald, A. G., & Banaji, M. R. (1995). Implicit social cognition: Attitudes, self-esteem, and stereotypes. *Psychological Review*, *102*(1), 4–27. doi:10.1037/0033-295X.102.1.4 PMID:7878162

Grose, R. G., & Grabe, S. (2014). Sociocultural attitudes surrounding menstruation and alternative menstrual products: The explanatory role of self-objectification. *Health Care for Women International*, *35*(6), 677–694. doi:10.1080/07399332.2014.888721 PMID:24527840

Guvenc, G., Kilic, A., Akyuz, A., & Ustunsoz, A. (2012). Premenstrual syndrome and attitudes toward menstruation in a sample of nursing students. *Journal of Psychosomatic Obstetrics and Gynaecology*, *33*(3), 106–111. doi:10.3109/0167482X.2012.685906 PMID:22901294

Halbreich, U. (2003). The etiology, biology, and evolving pathology of premenstrual syndromes. *Psychoneuroendocrinology*, *28*, 55–99. doi:10.1016/S0306-4530(03)00097-0 PMID:12892990

Hardy, C., & Hunter, M. S. (2021). Premenstrual symptoms and work: Exploring female staff experiences and recommendations for workplaces. *International Journal of Environmental Research and Public Health*, *18*(7), 3647. doi:10.3390/ijerph18073647 PMID:33807463

Hoerster, K. D., Chrisler, J. C., & Rose, J. G. (2003). Attitudes toward and experience with menstruation in the US and India. *Women & Health*, *38*(3), 77–95. doi:10.1300/J013v38n03_06 PMID:14664306

Hofstede, G. (1980). Motivation, leadership, and organization: Do American theories apply abroad? *Organizational Dynamics*, *9*(1), 42–63. doi:10.1016/0090-2616(80)90013-3

Hogg, M. A., & Vaughan, G. M. (2014). Social Psychology 7th Eds. *Harlow: Pearson Education Limited.* 12 (10), https://www.scirp.org/reference/referencespapers?referenceid=3097274

Hwang, J. H., & Sung, M. H. (2016). Impacts of menstrual attitudes, premenstrual syndrome and stress on burnout among clinical nurses. *Korean Journal of Women Health Nursing*, *22*(4), 233–240. doi:10.4069/kjwhn.2016.22.4.233 PMID:37684872

Irshad, A., Mehmood, S., Noor, R., Mumtaz, S., Saleem, M., & Laique, T. (2022). Frequency of Premenstrual Syndrome and Its Association with Quality of Life among University Students. *Pakistan Journal of Medical & Health Sciences*, *16*(02), 521–521. doi:10.53350/pjmhs22162521

Ismail, K. H., & Mohammed-Ali, K. B. (2012). Quality of life in patients with acne in Erbil city. *Health and Quality of Life Outcomes*, *10*(1), 1–4. doi:10.1186/1477-7525-10-60 PMID:22672256

Jahanfar, S., Lye, M. S., & Krishnarajah, I. S. (2011). The heritability of premenstrual syndrome. *Twin Research and Human Genetics*, *14*(5), 433–436. doi:10.1375/twin.14.5.433 PMID:21962135

Jang, H. J., & Sung, M. H. (2018). Impact of menstrual attitudes, premenstrual syndrome, and stress response on quality of life among nursing students. *Korean Journal of Women Health Nursing*, *24*(4), 346–354. doi:10.4069/kjwhn.2018.24.4.346 PMID:37684941

Janiger, O., Riffenburgh, R., & Kersh, R. (1972). Cross cultural study of premenstrual symptoms. *Psychosomatics*, *13*(4), 226–235. doi:10.1016/S0033-3182(72)71414-0 PMID:4677677

Joshi, A., Kurien, E., Misra, A., Rajeshwari, M., & Biswas, S. (1998). *Socio-cultural implications of menstruation and menstrual problems on rural women's lives and treatment seeking behaviour*. Operations Research Group, Baroda. (Unpublished Ford Foundation supported study).

Kantero, R. (1971). A statistical analysis of the menstrual patterns of 8,000 Finish girls and their mothers. The age of menarche in Finish girls in 1969. *Acta Obstetricia et Gynecologica Scandinavica, 14*, 1–36.

Katherine, D., Chrisler, J. C., & Rose, J. S. (2003c). Attitudes Toward and Experience with Menstruation in the US and India. *Women & Health, 38*(3), 77–95. doi:10.1300/J013v38n03_06 PMID:14664306

Katjiukua, C. R., Simon, N., Chatterjee, A., & Akinola, A. (2020). Prevalence and knowledge of premenstrual syndrome among adolescent girls in India. *International Journal of Community Medicine and Public Health, 7*(12), 5169–5181. doi:10.18203/2394-6040.ijcmph20205202

Kendler, K. S., Karkowski, L. M., Corey, L. A., & Neale, M. C. (1998). Longitudinal population-based twin study of retrospectively reported premenstrual symptoms and lifetime major depression. *The American Journal of Psychiatry, 155*(9), 1234–1240. doi:10.1176/ajp.155.9.1234 PMID:9734548

Kessel, B. (2000). Premenstrual syndrome: Advances in diagnosis and treatment. *Obstetrics and Gynecology Clinics of North America, 27*(3), 625–639. doi:10.1016/S0889-8545(05)70160-1 PMID:10958008

Khalid, Z., & Naqvi, I. (2022). *Premenstrual Syndrome and Quality of Life Among Adolescent Girls: Exploration of Prevalent Home Remedies*.

Kırcan, N., Ergin, F., Adana, F., & Arslantaş, H. (2012). The Prevalance of Premenstrual Syndrome in Nursery Students and its Relationship with Quality of Life. *Meandros Medical and Dental Journal, 13*(1), 19–25.

Kısa, S., Zeyneloğlu, S., & Güler, N. (2012). Prevalence of premenstrual syndrome among university students and affecting factors. *Gümüşhane University Journal of Health Sciences, 1*(4), 284–297.

Lancastle, D., Kopp Kallner, H., Hale, G., Wood, B., Ashcroft, L., & Driscoll, H. (2023). Development of a brief menstrual quality of life measure for women with heavy menstrual bleeding. *BMC Women's Health, 23*(1), 105. doi:10.1186/s12905-023-02235-0 PMID:36918914

Lee, E., & Yang, S. (2020). Do depression, fatigue, and body esteem influence premenstrual symptoms in nursing students? *Korean Journal of Women Health Nursing, 26*(3), 231–239. doi:10.4069/kjwhn.2020.09.10 PMID:36313171

Lete, I., Dueñas, J. L., Serrano, I., Doval, J. L., Martínez-Salmeán, J., Coll, C., Pérez-Campos, E., & Arbat, A. (2011). Attitudes of Spanish women toward premenstrual symptoms, premenstrual syndrome and premenstrual dysphoric disorder: Results of a nationwide survey. *European Journal of Obstetrics, Gynecology, and Reproductive Biology, 159*(1), 115–118. doi:10.1016/j.ejogrb.2011.06.041 PMID:21775045

Levitt, E. E., & Lubin, B. (1967). Some personality factors associated with menstrual complaints and menstrual attitude. *Journal of Psychosomatic Research, 11*(3), 267–270. doi:10.1016/0022-3999(67)90020-7 PMID:6076919

Logue, C. M., & Moos, R. H. (1986). Perimenstrual symptoms: Prevalence and risk factors. *Psychosomatic Medicine, 48*(6), 388–414. doi:10.1097/00006842-198607000-00002 PMID:3529156

López-Jornet, P., & Camacho-Alonso, F. (2010). Quality of life in patients with oral lichen planus. *Journal of Evaluation in Clinical Practice*, *16*(1), 111–113. doi:10.1111/j.1365-2753.2009.01124.x PMID:20367822

Lu, Z. J. (2001). The relationship between menstrual attitudes and menstrual symptoms among Taiwanese women. *Journal of Advanced Nursing*, *33*(5), 621–628. doi:10.1046/j.1365-2648.2001.01705.x PMID:11298198

Lustyk, M. K. B., Gerrish, W. G., Shaver, S., & Keys, S. L. (2009). Cognitive-behavioral therapy for premenstrual syndrome and premenstrual dysphoric disorder: A systematic review. *Archives of Women's Mental Health*, *12*(2), 85–96. doi:10.1007/s00737-009-0052-y PMID:19247573

Lustyk, M. K. B., Widman, L., Paschane, A., & Ecker, E. (2004). Stress, quality of life and physical activity in women with varying degrees of premenstrual symptomatology. *Women & Health*, *39*(3), 35–44. doi:10.1300/J013v39n03_03 PMID:15256354

Matsumoto, T., Asakura, H., & Hayashi, T. (2013). Biopsychosocial aspects of premenstrual syndrome and premenstrual dysphoric disorder. *Gynecological Endocrinology*, *29*(1), 67–73. doi:10.3109/09513590.2012.705383 PMID:22809066

Molugulu, N., Tumkur, A. N. I. L., & Nilugal, K. C. (2016). Study of premenstrual syndrome among future healthcare professionals in Masterskill Global College. *International Journal of Pharmacy and Pharmaceutical Sciences*, *8*(2), 66–71.

Monagle, L., Dan, A., Krogh, V., Jossa, F., Fannaro, E., & Trevisan, M. (1993). Perimenstrual symptom prevalence rates: An Italian-American comparison. *American Journal of Epidemiology*, *138*(12), 1070–1081. doi:10.1093/oxfordjournals.aje.a116825 PMID:8266909

Mortola, J. F. (1993). Applications of gonadotropin-releasing hormone analogues in the treatment of premenstrual syndrome. *Clinical Obstetrics and Gynecology*, *36*(3), 753–763. doi:10.1097/00003081-199309000-00032 PMID:8403622

Narvel, H., Merchant, H., Kore, G., Nayak, A., & De Sousa, A. (2018). A Study on Premenstrual Syndrome symptoms and their association with the Attitudes towards Menstruation in Nursing Staff. *Indian Journal of Mental Health*, *5*(4), 481. doi:10.30877/IJMH.5.4.2018.481-485

Neumann, L., & Buskila, D. (1997). Measuring the quality of life of women with fibromyalgia: A Hebrew version of the quality of life scale. *Journal of Musculoskeletal Pain*, *5*(1), 5–16. doi:10.1300/J094v05n01_02

Nisar, N., Zehra, N., Haider, G., Munir, A. A., & Sohoo, N. A. (2008). Frequency, intensity and impact of premenstrual syndrome in medical students. *Journal of the College of Physicians and Surgeons—Pakistan*, *18*(8), 481–484. PMID:18798584

Ovayolu, Ö., Ovayolu, N., Tuna, D., Serçe, S., Sevinç, A., & Pirbudak Çöçelli, L. (2014). Quality of life of caregivers: A cross-sectional study. *International Journal of Nursing Practice*, *20*(4), 424–432. doi:10.1111/ijn.12147 PMID:25157944

Özerdoğan, N., Sayiner, D., Ayranci, U., Ünsal, A., & Giray, S. (2009). Prevalence and predictors of dysmenorrhea among students at a university in Turkey. *International Journal of Gynaecology and Obstetrics: the Official Organ of the International Federation of Gynaecology and Obstetrics*, *107*(1), 39–43. doi:10.1016/j.ijgo.2009.05.010 PMID:19539288

Paige, K. E. (1973). Women learn to sing menstrual blues. *Psychology Today*, *7*(4), 41.

Perveen, S., Mairaj, N., Maqbool, M., Bilal, A., & Munir, S. (2022). Prevalence the Premenstrual Syndrome (PMS) in Pakistani Women. *Pakistan Journal of Medical & Health Sciences*, *16*(09), 433–433. doi:10.53350/pjmhs22169433

Petty, R. E., & Krosnick, J. A. (2014). *Attitude strength: Antecedents and consequences.* Psychology Press. https://www.researchgate.net/profile/Russell-Fazio/publication/232544154_Attitudes_as_object-evaluation_associations_Determinants_consequences_and_correlates_of_attitude_accessibility/links/02e7e52f38247646e8000000/Attitudes-as-object-evaluation-associations-Determinants-consequences-and-correlates-of-attitude-accessibility.pdf

Philip, S. M., & Suresh, A., priyadharshini Dhanasekaran, G., Sivasankaran, P., AP, R., & Nagendra, V. H. (2022). Assessment of menstrual attitudes and predictors for premenstrual syndrome in university students of Ooty, South India. *Journal of Positive School Psychology*, *6*(6), 3736–3746.

Poudyal, Y., Parajuli, N., Dahal, S. C., & Jha, C. B. (2020). The Study of Quality of Life in Patient with Vitiligo. *Birat Journal of Health Sciences*, *5*(3), 1206–1209. doi:10.3126/bjhs.v5i3.33699

Qalawa, S. A. A., Alsuhaibani, H. O., Alluhaydan, A. A., & Alghaidani, A. A. (2022). Health beliefs and coping strategies regarding premenstrual syndrome among health college students at Qassim University. *International Journal of Health Sciences*, *6*, 4264–4277. doi:10.53730/ijhs.v6nS8.13145

Radloff, L. S., & Rae, D. S. (1979). Susceptibility and precipitating factors in depression: Sex differences and similarities. *Journal of Abnormal Psychology*, *88*(2), 174–181. doi:10.1037/0021-843X.88.2.174 PMID:447900

Rao, S., Jaiprakash, I., & Murthy, V. N. (1982). Prevalence of menstrual symptoms in a college population. *Indian Journal of Clinical Psychology*, *9*(2), 89–94.

Rapkin, A. J., & Akopians, A. L. (2012). Pathophysiology of premenstrual syndrome and premenstrual dysphoric disorder. *Menopause International*, *18*(2), 52–59. doi:10.1258/mi.2012.012014 PMID:22611222

Rapkin, A. J., & Winer, S. A. (2009). Premenstrual syndrome and premenstrual dysphoric disorder: Quality of life and burden of illness. *Expert Review of Pharmacoeconomics & Outcomes Research*, *9*(2), 157–170. doi:10.1586/erp.09.14 PMID:19402804

Rashidi, B., Montazeri, A., Ramezanzadeh, F., Shariat, M., Abedinia, N., & Ashrafi, M. (2008). Health-related quality of life in infertile couples receiving IVF or ICSI treatment. *BMC Health Services Research*, *8*(1), 1–6. doi:10.1186/1472-6963-8-186 PMID:18803838

Read, J. R., Perz, J., & Ussher, J. M. (2014). Ways of coping with premenstrual change: Development and validation of a premenstrual coping measure. *BMC Women's Health*, *14*(1), 1–15. doi:10.1186/1472-6874-14-1 PMID:24383580

Rees, L. (1953). Psychosomatic aspects of the premenstrual tension syndrome. *The Journal of Mental Science*, *99*(414), 62–73. doi:10.1192/bjp.99.414.62 PMID:13023368

Rezaee, H., Mahamed, F., & Mazaheri, M. A. (2016). Does spousal support can decrease women's premenstrual syndrome symptoms? *Global Journal of Health Science*, *8*(5), 19. doi:10.5539/gjhs.v8n5p19 PMID:26652081

Rittenhouse, C. A. (1991). The emergence of premenstrual syndrome as a social problem. *Social Problems*, *38*(3), 412–425. doi:10.2307/800607

Robinson, A., & de Bessa, G. H. (2002). Forms and functions of premenstrual syndrome. *Senior Thesis, Dep. of Sociology & Anthropology, Illinois State University, lilt. ilstu. edu/soa/html/anthrothesis/amrobin.* 1-27.

Rosseinsky, D. R., & Hall, P. G. (1974). An evolutionary theory of premenstrual tension. *Lancet*, *304*(7887), 1024. doi:10.1016/S0140-6736(74)92132-1 PMID:4138262

Ryu, A., & Kim, T. H. (2015). Premenstrual syndrome: A mini review. *Maturitas*, *82*(4), 436–440. doi:10.1016/j.maturitas.2015.08.010 PMID:26351143

Santhya, K. G., & Jejeebhoy, S. J. (2015). Sexual and reproductive health and rights of adolescent girls: Evidence from low-and middle-income countries. *Global Public Health: An International Journal for Research, Policy and Practice*, *10*(2), 189–221. doi:10.1080/17441692.2014.986169 PMID:25554828

Sarver, V. T. (1983). *Ajzen and Fishbein's" theory of reasoned action: A critical assessment*. Wiley. https://doi:10.1111/j.1468-5914.1983.tb00469.x

Sarwar, U., & Rauf, U. (2021). Social support, quality of life and mental health problems among females with and without menstruation problems: A comparative study. *Khyber Medical University Journal*, *13*(4), 206–210. doi:10.35845/kmuj.2021.21373

Sawant, N. S., Vanjari, N. A., & Khopkar, U. (2019). Gender differences in depression, coping, stigma, and quality of life in patients of vitiligo. *Dermatology Research and Practice*, *2019*, 1–11. doi:10.1155/2019/6879412 PMID:31065260

Shamnani, G., Gupta, V., Jiwane, R., Singh, S., Tiwari, S., & Bhartiy, S. S. (2018). Prevalence of premenstrual syndrome and premenstrual dysphoric disorder among medical students and its impact on their academic and social performance. *National Journal of Physiology, Pharmacy and Pharmacology*, *8*(8), 1205–1208. doi:10.5455/njppp.2018.8.0415728042018

Shi, Y., Shi, M., Liu, C., Sui, L., Zhao, Y., & Fan, X. (2023). Associations with physical activity, sedentary behavior, and premenstrual syndrome among Chinese female college students. *BMC Women's Health*, *23*(1), 173. doi:10.1186/s12905-023-02262-x PMID:37041480

Shrestha, I., & Giri, R. (2020). Knowledge and prevalence regarding premenstrual syndrome among adolescents in Morang District, Nepal. *Current Women's Health Reviews*, *16*(3), 214–219. doi:10.2174/1573404816999200421100011

Siahbazi, S., Hariri, F. Z., Montazeri, A., & Moghaddam, B. L. (2011). Translation and psychometric properties of the Iranian version of the Premenstrual Symptoms Screening Tool (PSST). *10*(4), 421-427.

Siahbazi, S., Montazeri, A., Taghizadeh, Z., & Masoomie, R. (2018). The consequences of premenstrual syndrome on the quality of life from the perspective of affected women: A qualitative study. *Journal of Research in Medical and Dental Science*, 6(2), 284–292.

Siegel, J. M., Johnson, J. H., & Sarason, I. G. (1979). Life changes and menstrual discomfort. *Journal of Human Stress*, 5(1), 41–46. doi:10.1080/0097840X.1979.9935001 PMID:422838

Sommer, M., Hirsch, J. S., Nathanson, C., & Parker, R. G. (2015). Comfortably, safely, and without shame: Defining menstrual hygiene management as a public health issue. *American Journal of Public Health*, 105(7), 1302–1311. doi:10.2105/AJPH.2014.302525 PMID:25973831

SönmezerSönmezer. E., & Yosmaoılu, H. (2014). *Changes of menstrual attitude and stress perception in Women with dysmenorrhea*. ResearchGate. https://www.researchgate.net/publication/287236200_Changes_of_menstrual_attitude_an d_stress_perception_in_women_with_dysmenorrhea

Steiner, M. (2000). Premenstrual syndrome and premenstrual dysphoric disorder: Guidelines for management. *Journal of Psychiatry & Neuroscience*, 25(5), 459–468. PMID:11109297

Steiner, M., & Carroll, B. J. (1977). The psychobiology of premenstrual dysphoria: Review of theories and treatments. *Psychoneuroendocrinology*, 2(4), 321–335. doi:10.1016/0306-4530(77)90002-6 PMID:202982

Steiner, M., Macdougall, M., & Brown, E. (2003). The premenstrual symptoms screening tool (PSST) for clinicians. *Archives of Women's Mental Health*, 6(3), 203–209. doi:10.1007/s00737-003-0018-4 PMID:12920618

Suner-Keklik, S., & Barği, G. (2023). Investigation of the Relationship between Physical Activity Levels and Menstrual Symptoms in Healthy Women. *Online Türk Sağlık Bilimleri Dergisi*, 8(2), 192–199. doi:10.26453/otjhs.1193870

Sveinsdottir, H. (1993). The Attitudes towards Menstruation among Icelandic Nursing Students -Their Relationship with Menstrual Preparation and Menstrual Characteristics. *Scandinavian Journal of Caring Sciences*, 7(1), 37–41. doi:10.1111/j.1471-6712.1993.tb00159.x PMID:8502853

Talib Hassan, I., Saadi Issa, H., Hussein, E. A., & Ali Haddad, R. (2023). The effect of premenstrual tension on academic performance and social interactions among Iraqi medical students. *Cellular. Molecular and Biomedical Reports*, 3(4), 205–211. doi:10.55705/cmbr.2023.390101.1113

Teixeira, A. L. D. S., Oliveira, É. C. M., & Dias, M. R. C. (2013). Relationship between the level of physical activity and premenstrual syndrome incidence. *Revista Brasileira de Ginecologia e Obstetrícia*, 35, 210–214. doi:10.1590/S0100-72032013000500004 PMID:23843118

Teoli, D., & Bhardwaj, A. (2022). Quality of Life Quality of Life. *StatPearls, editor*. https://www.ncbi.nlm.nih.gov/books/NBK536962/

Thakrar, P. D., Bhukar, K., & Oswal, R. (2021). Premenstrual dysphoric disorder: Prevalence, quality of life and disability due to illness among medical and paramedical students. *Journal of Affective Disorders Reports*, 4, 100112. doi:10.1016/j.jadr.2021.100112

Tkachenko, L. V., Kurushina, O. V., & Atagadzhieva, M. S. (2010). The quality of life in women suffering from premenstrual syndrome. *Problemy Sotsial'noi Gigieny. Zdravookhraneniia i Istorii Meditsiny*, (2), 13–16.

Triandis, H. C. (1989). The self and social behavior in differing cultural contexts. *Psychological Review*, 96(3), 506–520. doi:10.1037/0033-295X.96.3.506

Ullrich, H. E. (1992). Menstrual taboos among Havik Brahmin women: A study of ritual change. *Sex Roles*, 26(1), 19–40. doi:10.1007/BF00290123 PMID:12317387

Ussher, J. M. (2003). The ongoing silencing of women in families: An analysis and rethinking of premenstrual syndrome and therapy. *Journal of Family Therapy*, 25(4), 388–405. doi:10.1111/1467-6427.00257

Ussher, J. M., & Perz, J. (2013). PMS as a process of negotiation: Women's experience and management of premenstrual distress. *Psychology & Health*, 28(8), 909–927. doi:10.1080/08870446.2013.765004 PMID:23383644

Ussher, J. M., & Perz, J. (2020). "I feel fat and ugly and hate myself": Self-objectification through negative constructions of premenstrual embodiment. *Feminism & Psychology*, 30(2), 185–205. doi:10.1177/0959353519900196

Van Niekerk, L. M., Dell, B., Johnstone, L., Matthewson, M., & Quinn, M. (2023). Examining the associations between self and body compassion and health related quality of life in people diagnosed with endometriosis. *Journal of Psychosomatic Research*, 167, 111202. doi:10.1016/j.jpsychores.2023.111202 PMID:36812662

Victor, F. F., Souza, A. I., Barreiros, C. D. T., Barros, J. L. N. D., Silva, F. A. C. D., & Ferreira, A. L. C. G. (2019). Quality of life among university students with premenstrual syndrome. *Revista Brasileira de Ginecologia e Obstetrícia*, 41(5), 312–317. doi:10.1055/s-0039-1688709 PMID:31181584

Wahl, A., Burckhardt, C., Wiklund, I., & Hanestad, B. R. (1998). The Norwegian Version of the Quality of Life Scale (QOLS-N) A Validation and Reliability Study in Patients Suffering from Psoriasis. *Scandinavian Journal of Caring Sciences*, 12(4), 215–222. doi:10.1080/02839319850162823 PMID:10067647

Walker, A. (1995). Theory and methodology in premenstrual syndrome research. *Social Science & Medicine*, 41(6), 793–800. doi:10.1016/0277-9536(95)00046-A PMID:8571150

Woods, N. F., Mitchell, E. S., & Lentz, M. J. (1995). Social pathways to premenstrual symptoms. *Research in Nursing & Health*, 18(3), 225–237. doi:10.1002/nur.4770180306 PMID:7754093

World Health Organization. (2000). *Obesity: preventing and managing the global epidemic: report of a WHO consultation*. WHO.

Yang, M., Gricar, J. A., Maruish, M. E., Hagan, M. A., Kornstein, S. G., & Wallenstein, G. V. (2010). Interpreting Premenstrual Symptoms Impact Survey scores using outcomes in health-related quality of life and sexual drive impact. *The Journal of Reproductive Medicine*, 55(1-2), 41–48. PMID:20337207

Yonkers, K. A., O'Brien, P. S., & Eriksson, E. (2008). Premenstrual syndrome. *Lancet*, 371(9619), 1200–1210. doi:10.1016/S0140-6736(08)60527-9 PMID:18395582

Yuk, V. J., Cumming, C. E., Fox, E. E., & Cumming, D. C. (1991). Frequency and Severity of Premenstrual Symptoms in Women Taking Birth Control Pills. *Gynecologic and Obstetric Investigation*, *31*(1), 42–45. doi:10.1159/000293098 PMID:2010113

Zaka, M., & Mahmood, K. T. (2012). Pre-menstrual syndrome-a review. *Journal of Pharmaceutical Sciences and Research*, *4*(1), 1684.

Zeleke B. Workineh Y. Melese A. Semachew A. Yigizaw M. (2023). Premenstrual syndrome, life style & behavioral coping mechanisms and associated factors among public high school regular female students at Bahir Dar City, Northwest, Ethiopia. doi:10.21203/rs.3.rs-2418487/v1

Zendehdel, M., & Elyasi, F. (2018). Biopsychosocial etiology of premenstrual syndrome: A narrative review. *Journal of Family Medicine and Primary Care*, *7*(2), 346–356. doi:10.4103/jfmpc.jfmpc_336_17 PMID:30090776

Ziba, T., Mohammadi, M. S., Mohammad, A., & Abas, M. (2008). The Effect of Premenstrual Syndrome on Quality of Life in Adolescent Girls. *Iranian Journal of Psychiatry*, *3*(3), 105–109. https://ijps.tums.ac.ir/index.php/ijps/article/download/480/504

Chapter 13
The 360-Degree Gender Sphere and the Six Strategies to Create Resilience

Dawn Adams-Harmon
https://orcid.org/0000-0002-6916-253X
Kean University, USA

ABSTRACT

Women in the bioscience sector continue to be under-represented at higher organizational levels. Only ten percent of the biopharmaceutical industry has female CEOs, and only one company had a board where women outnumbered men. Further, one female CEO exists within the largest pharmaceutical companies: Emma Walmsley of GlaxoSmithKline, and Reshma Kewelramani of Vertex joined in 2020. The bioscience sector is extremely lucrative, where the average female CEO pay is $5.2 million versus the average male earnings of $5.7 million. Diversity at high organizational levels within the bioscience sector is essential. Having women represented at higher organizational levels brings customer perspectives to the strategic decision-making process, provides mentors and sponsors for other women in the organization, and contributes to innovation and creativity. This chapter includes findings from previous research, which showed the barriers encountered "360-Degree Gender Sphere" and the strategies used "Six Strategies to Create Resilience" during career progression by women. There are three modules of this work. The first is an awareness program of the barriers women encounter while ascending in the bioscience sector the 360-degee gender sphere. The second section assesses and accentuates which barriers are most troublesome; and the last segment is "The Six Strategies to Create Resilience Action Plans". These programs assist females in understanding the barriers they may encounter and the necessary strategies one must take to overcome the peripheral "360-Degree Gender Sphere" and create resilience. The 360-degree gender sphere and the six strategies to create resilience conveys decades of knowledge from successful executives in the healthcare industry.

DOI: 10.4018/979-8-3693-2806-4.ch013

INTRODUCTION

Women in the bioscience sector continue to be under-represented at higher organizational levels. Ten percent of the biopharmaceutical industry has female CEOs and only one company had a board where women outnumbered men (Biopharmadive, 2019). Further, one female CEO exists within the largest pharmaceutical companies: Emma Walmsley of GlaxoSmithKline, and Reshma Kewelramani of Vertex joined in 2020 (BIOPHARMADIVE, 2019). The bioscience sector is extremely lucrative where the average female CEO pay is $5.2 million versus the average male earnings of $5.7 million (Dunn, & Pagliarulo, 2018).

Diversity at high organizational levels within the bioscience sector, is essential. Having women represented at higher organizational levels brings customer perspectives to the strategic decision making process, provides mentors and sponsors for other women in the organization, and contributes to innovation and creativity (Stratford, 2023).

This chapter includes findings from previous research, which showed the barriers encountered *"360-Degree Gender Sphere"* and the strategies used *"Six Strategies to Create Resilience"* during career progression by women. There are three modules of this work. The first is an awareness program of the barriers women encounter while ascending in the bioscience sector the *"360-Degee Gender Sphere"*. The second section are *assessments* that accentuate which barriers are most troublesome; and the last segment is *"The Six Strategies to Create Resilience Action Plans"*. These programs assist females in understanding the barriers they may encounter and the necessary strategies one must take to overcome the peripheral *"360-Degree Gender Sphere"* and create resilience.

Data from the Biosciences' Sector

Worldwide data from companies' websites, annual, DEI, sustainability, and ESG reports, show that there are close ratios of male and female representation in the biosciences. Looking at the specific numbers within the pharmaceutical sector the secondary analysis showed that 51% were females versus 49% men see Table (1). However, there are outliers in this analysis where Pfizer has a ratio of 43% females to 57% males and Abbvie has 56% females and 44% males. Within specialty companies the data shows 40% females versus 60% males; however the outliers are Viatris with 36% females and 64% males and Neurocrine represents 53% female and 47% male Table (1). The data from diagnostics and research show that women represent 51% and men represent 49% of workers in this sector, with outliers of Waters Corporation having 32% of women and 68% men in their organization, with Medpace Holdings 67% females and 33% males in their organizations Table (1). Delving into Biotech, the percentages of women are greater with an average of women represented by 53% and men 47%, with outliers of Regeneron and Moderna at 50% for men and women and Veracyte 59% for women and 41% for men Table (1). Medical Instruments and Supplies have 46% of women and 54% men with outliers from Intuitive and Repligan having 34% women to 66% men and Teleflex has 59% females to 41% men Table (1). Lastly, for medical devices, the amount of women in these organizations represents 47% and men at 53% of that sector's workforce with outliers of Zimmer Biomet at 36% for females and 64% of men; and Artivian with 60% of their workforce represented by women and 40% by men Table 1.

Table 1. Status of women based on variety of indicators

Indicators	1990 W	1990 M	1995 W	1995 M	2000 W	2000 M	2005 W	2005 M	2007-08 W	2007-08 M
Lifespan Estimate	NA	NA	61.4	61.3	62.3	61.5	64.0	62.8	64.3	63.3
Adult Education	28	58	34.2	64.7	43.5	67.1	47.8	73.4	47.8	73.4
Total Enrollment	NA	NA	44.8	64.8	45.0	62.0	57.0	63.0	61.0	69.0
Parliamentary Seat Distribution	NA	NA	6.3	93.7	9.9	90.1	8.3	91.7	8.8	91.2
Proportion of Technical and Professional Personnel	NA	NA	21.5	78.5	21.5	78.5	NA	NA	NA	NA
Development Index pertaining to Gender	NA		0.411 (R-98)		0.555 (R-107)		0.576 (R-97)		0.598 (R-112)	
Measure of Gender Empowerment	NA		0.216 (R- 100)		NA		NA		NA	

Source: UNDP

On the surface, it looks as though the bioscience sector is a favorable sector for women. However, women in the bioscience sector continue to be under-represented at higher organizational levels and over-represented at lower organizational levels. Ten percent of the biopharmaceutical industry has female CEOs and only one company had a board where women outnumbered men (Biopharmadive, 2019). Further, one female CEO exists within the largest pharmaceutical companies: Emma Walmsley of GlaxoSmithKline, and Reshma Kewelramani recently joined Vertex in 2020 (Biopharmadive, 2019). The bioscience sector is extremely lucrative where the average female CEO pay is $5.2 million versus the average male earnings of $5.7 million (Dunn, & Pagliarulo, 2018).

Diversity at high organizational levels within the bioscience sector is essential. Having women represented at higher organizational levels brings customer perspectives to the strategic decision making process, provides mentors and sponsors for other women in the organization, contributes to innovation and creativity, and financially firms that have women at the helm outperform other companies in the sector by 30% (Stratford, 2023). The following 360-Degree Gender Sphere and Six Strategies to Create Resilience program was derived from previous research in the biopharmaceutical sector, and was presented to local, national and international audiences in bioscience associations and corporations to support females in their quest for self-actualization.

PART ONE: THE 360-DEGREE GENDER SPHERE AWARENESS PROGRAM

Qualitative research of 12 female executives in the healthcare sector revealed that a new theory called the 360-Degree Gender Sphere was stifling women in their attempts to progress in their careers (Adams-Harmon & Greer-Williams, 2021). Understanding each of the six barriers that encapsulates women, is the first step towards actualization. The 360-Degree Gender Sphere has displaced the glass ceiling metaphor as a description of how each of the components encapsulates women with barriers that stem from the acculturation of cis-gender females.

The primary theme that evolved in this research was the Barriers Encountered and the subtheme results of Adams-Harmon and Greer-Williams (2021)'s research found that "92% of participants mentioned that Gendered Structures posed a barrier; 75% mentioned Self as a barrier; Peers evolved with 67% mentioning this subtheme; Direct Managers, Family, and Societal Norms all had 50% of respondents stating these as barriers" (pg. 12).

Some examples of gendered structures were that women in this research felt there was an old-boys club that excludes women from formal and informal networks. It also included the thought that Human Resource policies such as FMLA do not protect women when downsizing occurs. Since men were at the helm during H/R policy development, policies are inherently biased (Adams-Harmon & Greer-Williams, 2021).

The second most dominant subtheme that was revealed was self as a barrier. The statement by participants said that they felt insecure if they didn't have one hundred percent of the job knowledge to be considered for the next step promotion. Yet other participants felt that they could not relocate because they held themselves back due to not being the sole wage earner in the family (Adams-Harmon & Greer-Williams, 2021).

Thirdly, peers presented as the third barrier at 67% to these research subjects. Here women expressed being in meetings with male counterparts and when the female executive spoke up they were completely ignored, but then a few minutes later a male said the same thing and everyone was attentively listening and engaged in the conversation. Further, when women were promoted, male peers made derogatory statements about how they were promoted and did not attribute the promotion based on competencies but to fulfill a quota (Adams-Harmon & Greer-Williams, 2021).

Statements from 50% of the participants showed that Direct Managers were a barrier. One woman responded that her boss said a women's place was in the home taking care of children and all the house responsibilities, in front of all of her male peers. While another respondent said they did not get a promotion and was told that the male counterpart got the job because the leadership team knew him (Adams-Harmon & Greer-Williams, 2021).

Next, family was mentioned by 50% of the contributors as a barrier. Due to family obligations, the executives did not pursue promotions because they had children and familial obligations that weighed heavily on them. They said they intentionally did not pursue promotions specifically for this reason and their male counterparts had wives that stayed home so they could relocate easily and thus they received the promotions (Adams-Harmon & Greer-Williams, 2021).

Lastly, societal norms were divulged by 50% of the respondents as a challenge. Society has different expectations of women and men. Career conversations are not welcomed from women but they are expected by men (Adams-Harmon & Greer-Williams, 2021). These factors all contributed to an outer sphere that encapsulates women and thwarts their attempts to rise up the corporate rungs seamlessly.

PART TWO: THE 360-DEGREE GENDER SPHERE ASSESSMENT

The following 360-Degree Gender Sphere Assessment will hone in on the components of the Sphere that are most challenging for you. By creating self-awareness and understanding your barriers, you will be more equipped to use the Six Strategies to Create Resilience action plans to ascend.

PART THREE: THE SIX STRATEGIES TO CREATE RESILIENCE

The aforementioned research conducted in the biosciences sector, showed that the executive females experienced the 360-Degree Gender Sphere that challenged their ascendance (Adams-Harmon & Greer-Williams, 2021). The Six Strategies to Create Resilience emerged as an overarching theme with several subthemes that the women leveraged to successfully climb the corporate ladder. The executives created resilience and were able to ascend in their organizations by leveraging "Sponsorship (100%); Mentoring (100%); Leadership Development (100%); Flexibility (100%); Self-Branding (100%); and Networked (83%)" (Adams-Harmon & Greer-Williams, 2021, pg. 14).

Sponsorship

Although many misconstrue sponsorship with mentorship, sponsorship has been found to be more influential to promotional success (Helms et al., 2016). Sponsorship assists top talent in ascending the corporate ladder by providing their protégé with access to professional relationships and highly visible assignments. Griffeth et al. (2021) found that women were over- mentored and under-sponsored and this could be a contributing factor of their lower executive presence. Men, as compared to women leverage sponsorship to a greater degree (Griffeth et al., 2021). Having a sponsor gives intentionality to career aspirations (Griffeth et al., 2021; Mate et al., 2018). In male-dominated corporate cultures, where many women experience micro aggressions, career advancement can occur if a sponsor endorses and supports a female's candidacy and pulls them up in the organization (Mate et al., 2018) and provides necessary encouragement when faced with obstacles (Searby et al., 2015).

Mentorship

Personal challenges such as work-life balance and professional isolation for women require additional support to overcome them, and mentoring programs have been shown to increase resilience for females in organizations (Palmer & Jones, 2018)

Helms et al. (2016) shared that women tend to select mentors that are similar to themselves, whereas men select mentors that will help them achieve their goals, which helps men progress more rapidly in their careers. Palmer and Jones (2019) suggested that due to women being socially isolated and the need to achieve work-life balance, females benefit to a greater degree when they have women-to-women mentoring, where they are given advice for career advancement.

There are two types of mentorships, internal and external mentoring. Often, companies do not have formal mentoring programs available to employees. Although, external associations do offer them. Associations may provide paid mentoring programs where members can select a mentor and the mentor will provide career and professional development advice as part of the fee.

Organizations that have qualified personnel with strong capabilities, can create formal mentoring programs that mentor high performing, top talent in their organizations, as part of their Employer Resource Groups (ERG) programs and Leadership Development training. Ideally, a database of previously trained mentors is made available to mentees via technology. A summary of the mentors' qualifications, interests and goals for the mentoring relationship are videotaped and saved in a Mentoring Excellence database.

The mentee is provided the Mentee Qualification Form and a code to enter a mentoring program, after receiving their direct manager's approval. The mentee records their responses to the Mentee Form and then saves it in the Mentoring Excellence database. The mentee enters search criteria then a list of potential internal mentors with their taped-recorded videos appears. The mentee reviews the videos, ascertains whether the mentor is available, selects a potential mentor, and clicks a request for mentor button. Once the mentor accepts the invite, they arrange a live meeting or a meeting through the use of webinar technology. Both the mentor and mentee fill out their respective forms prior to the meeting and arrange a first meeting.

Leadership Development

Preparing women for the next level includes development in the area of leadership. There are a plethora of leadership development programs if your organization does not have its own internal leadership development department. Leadership effectiveness can be learned in executive development seminars and MBA programs across the United States. The foundational programs include emotional intelligence, situational leadership, and learning your personality style and the styles of others in your work group.

Emotional Intelligence

Certain leadership skill sets may not be innate; however, women can learn the necessary skills to become compelling, visionary leaders. The foundational attributes of successful leaders stem from the ability to acknowledge and manage your own emotions and the emotions of others, known as Emotional Intelligence. To increase the likelihood of achieving organizational objectives and reducing attrition, author Dan Goleman (1998) found that emotional competence and interpersonal skills are critical skills for leaders. Conversely, in a study reviewing top executives' competencies, it showed that those that derailed were very rigid and did not have good relationships, lacked empathy, had no self-control (Goleman, 1998). Further studies showed that high emotional intelligence was far more important than high IQ in career success (Doe et al., 2015; Goleman, 1998). Edelman and van Knippenberg (2018), found that responses by leaders when more predictable, foster trust and accelerate leader effectiveness thus they recommend emotional intelligence training to develop these essential capabilities.

The elements of emotional intelligence that also contribute to followership trust are self-awareness, self-management, and empathy (Gomez-Leal et al., 2021) and conflict resolution skills are appropriately developed as emotional intelligence evolves (Chen et al. 2019). Emotional intelligence is basically having the right response with the right person at the right time. Those with emotional intelligence use: self-awareness (being aware of your strengths and weaknesses and triggers); self-management (the ability to process your thoughts and have a thoughtful and appropriate reaction); social awareness (knowing what other's needs are and knowing other's triggers); and social skills' techniques (such as showing concern and empathy for others) (Goleman, 1998).

Situational Leadership

Having confidence, understanding how to lead others and the capability to be adaptable, are cornerstones of leadership effectiveness. Kahn et al., (2016) explained that leadership is a flexible and dynamic process and Hersey and Blanchard's situational leadership model includes that type of flexibility. With the situational leadership approach, the leader provides a combination of support and direction based on a follower's task proficiency (The Center for Leadership Studies).

The 360-Degree Gender Sphere and the Six Strategies to Create Resilience

When a follower is new to a task, the situational leadership model states to provide high levels of direction and low levels of support (The Center for Leadership Studies). As task capabilities improve, the leader decreases the focus on providing direction and increases the levels of support, especially when a follower exhibits frustration (The Center for Leadership Studies). When the follower demonstrates task mastery, the leader provides low levels of support and low levels of direction, and delegates that person as a task mentor, helping to coach others learning that particular task (The Center for Leadership Studies).

Personality Styles

In the workforce, personality styles may differ from our own. To navigate while working with others, understanding one's own personality style and that of others is crucial to identify and resolve conflict and to motivate others, thereby leading to professional and organizational success (Pierre & Okstad, 2021). Further, there are many personality theories and assessments, and all have their merits. Preferentially, the DISC personality theory is simple and easy to understand and apply as it has been around for many decades and has been modified over time (Pierre & Okstad, 2021).

Studies have shown that the DISC assessment is very accurate (81%) in identifying a person's behavioral and personality patterns (Jones & Hartley, 2013). Gordon et al., (2019) shared that DISC assists in understanding others and when used effectively, is a highly influential tool. The DISC assessment contains four different quadrants of Dominance (D), Influence (I), Steadiness (S), or Conscientiousness (C) (DISC profiles). D styles are direct, pessimistic, and interested in the bottom line; I styles are outgoing, optimistic, expressive and enthusiastic; S styles move at a slow and steady pace, are accepting of others, and are even keeled; and lastly C personality styles are analytical, like details, are cautious, and question things (DISC profiles). After you take the assessment recommended in the leadership development action plan to understand your personality style and create self- awareness, it is beneficial to have all members of each team that you work with, take the assessment to identify their personality styles and identify potential personality conflicts. If others have dichotomous personality styles, an effective leader flexes to the other person's style so that a synergistic relationship can develop.

Flexibility

Resilience is created by having both flexible organizations and a flexible and adaptable personality (van Gool et al., 2022). Moreover, resilience and flexibility are tightly coupled (van Gool et al., 2022). Being flexible for individuals means the ability to pivot and change direction when encountering challenges or obstacles and resilience refers to tenacity and persistence when faced with challenges and obstacles. In the biotech field which maintains interorganizational networks, there is more flexibility for upwardly mobile women as compared to hierarchical organizations that are rigid with more systems in place that reinforce the old boys network, such as in the pharmaceutical industry (Smith-Doerr, 2004). Moreover, women are 60% less likely to be in a supervisory position in the hierarchical, pharmaceutical industry (Smith-Doerr, 2004). Female leaders were found to be represented at eight times higher numbers in biotech versus the pharmaceutical sector (Smith-Doerr, 2004). Flatter, networked biotech organizations offer greater flexibility options for women during their corporate ascent.

For women working in the bioscience sector, personally approaching careers with flexibility is crucial to upward mobility. Early in women's careers, relocation for promotions assists in ascending the corporate ladder. Women would benefit from taking promotable positions that require relocation when additional home-life responsibilities are encountered. However, once married, relocation requirements create a major barrier as married women often have spouses that also have careers, so relocation is very challenging at that point. If a female employee desires to move up in her organization and is facing severe barriers, then leaving their hierarchical organization and moving to a different geographical area of the country where there is more diversity support, may assist in their ascendance.

Flexibility for women also requires taking on new job assignments, projects, and learning new skills, that will differentiate themselves from others. Joining a learning organization will stretch a female employee's capabilities making them more valuable to the company and help the organization attain organizational objectives. Lastly, having a flexible support system that can assist with home-life obligations is essential to achieve work-life balance. If a woman is working outside of the home, all members of her family should engage and assist in home responsibilities, so as to achieve successful work-life balance. Flexibility is required by everyone in the household and delegation of home tasks helps relieve stress and contributes to well-being, work-life balance and creates resilience.

Self-Branding

The fifth strategy leveraged by female executives in the healthcare industry was self-branding. This success strategy helps women project an image of themselves (Hu, 2021), that is crafted, well thought out, professional and consistent. Self-branding commodifies an image of a person and attention is placed onto women of this branded image, which in turn leads to fulfillment of career goals (Hu, 2021). In essence, the brand is the person and the image they portray (Hu, 2021). Skills, motivations and career interests are the foundation of self-branding, however, self-branding takes those elements a step further, and packages them into a polished image that is shown to the world (Lair et al., 2005).

Executive coaches can assist women by coaching them towards projecting a professional image and in creating a self-branding message. Executive coaches can provide guidance and support through addressing public speaking deficiencies; analyzing a professional's wardrobe; looking for complimentary color choices and suggest more powerful color choices and styles, evaluating communication and leadership styles; and analyzing peer and superior interactions and conflict resolution skills. Stylists can also assist in wardrobe and color selection and are typically free when purchasing clothes from their department stores. Executive coaches, however, are costly, and organizations will not invest significant resources unless the person is on the fast track and headed toward the upper echelons of the organization.

In today's digital age and with the advent of social media, women have a free platform to engage followership and convey their professional, branded image effectively. This aspect supplements their corporate image and consistently conveys their image in and outside of their corporations. Marketing publicists and social media experts can assist women in creating this online branded image for a fee, or if an executive has social media expertise, they can create and manage the branding themselves.

Creating an elevator pitch that is thoughtful, planned out and one that reveals your strengths, accomplishments, and career aspirations is necessary. Imagine you are on an elevator with the CEO or someone from the top management team and you have 20 floors to convey to them who you are. The following self-branding action plan will assist you in planning that elevator conversation so you are prepared in the event a chance meetings occurs.

Networking

Networking with professional associations and networking within an organization, contributes to career success for women (Cross & Thomas, 2008). The majority of females in the previously mentioned qualitative study leveraged networking to assist them in forging professional relationships that enabled them to gain access to high profile assignments, gain connections for promotional support, and gain external contacts for positions external to their existing organizations. Professional associations also provide access to resources and opportunities for capability development (Bapna & Funk, 2021). The ability to leverage both professional networks and internal corporate networks (employer resource groups-ERG) is essential for women as they are less connected and have few opportunities than men (Bapna & Funk, 2021).

Bapna and Funk (2021)'s research, found that reducing social barriers by giving women a list of people to network with, resulted in increased contacts, increased time speaking with new contacts and improvement in job changes. Further, when search barriers improved at professional conferences, more time was spent with new contacts (Bapna & Funk, 2021). The benefits of joining professional networks does not end there. When women in top organizational positions joined professional networks, increases in economic efficiencies were realized (Manello, et al., 2020). Thus, there are benefits to women in organizations and the organizations themselves by having women involved in both internal and external network associations.

CONCLUSION

Women in the biosciences sector have a tremendous opportunity to move up in their organizations, but it takes a thoughtful and strategic approach. Understanding the 360-Degree Gender Sphere as a multi-dimensional barrier that encapsulate women in this sector, is the first step in the journey of ascendance. Females in this sector have shown upward mobility by implementing the Six Strategies to Create Resilience. The tools provided in this chapter will support you in your quest for self-actualization and have been proven over decades to be highly effective.

ACKNOWLEDGEMENT

I would like to acknowledge my wonderful husband, my children, nephews, my mother, my grandmother, my cousins and all of my wonderful and supportive friends, mentors, and colleagues, for all of the encouragement and support they have provided to me over my lifetime. I am truly blessed.

I also want to acknowledge that it has been a very difficult and long journey while climbing the ladder in the biosciences sector, and this work is also dedicated to all of my research participants that have contributed to this body of knowledge.

To all readers, I am thrilled to have you benefit from this chapter with the intent to help you not only gain knowledge but to ascend as high as you are able to. I dedicate this chapter to all women that will not stop increasing their skills and capabilities, and continue to keep pushing forward to rise.

REFERENCES

Adams-Harmon, D., & Greer-Williams, N. (2021). Successful ascent of female leaders in the pharmaceutical industry: A qualitative, transcendental, and phenomenological study. *Equality, Diversity and Inclusion*, *40*(7), 819–837. doi:10.1108/EDI-01-2019-0031

Bapna, S., & Funk, R. J. (2021). Interventions for improving professional networking for women: Experimental evidence from the IT sector. *Management Information Systems Quarterly*, *45*(2), 593–636. doi:10.25300/MISQ/2021/15620

Biopharmadive. (2019). *Number of female biotech CEOs remains 'shockingly low,' putting spotlight on BIO*. BioPharmDrive. https://www.biopharmadive.com/news/female-biotech-ceos-bio-efforts-diversity-goals/558604/

Chen, H. X., Xu, X., & Phillips, P. (2019). Emotional intelligence and conflict management styles. *The International Journal of Organizational Analysis*, *27*(3), 458–470. doi:10.1108/IJOA-11-2017-1272

Cross, R., & Thomas, R. J. (2008). How top talent uses networks and where rising stars get trapped. *Organizational Dynamics*, *37*(2), 165–180. doi:10.1016/j.orgdyn.2008.02.001

Doe, R., Ndinguri, E., & Phipps, S. T. (2015). Emotional intelligence: The link to success and failure of leadership. *Academy of Educational Leadership Journal*, 105–114.

Dunn, A., & Pagliarulo, N. (2018). *Follow the money: How biopharma CEOs and workers get paid in 2018*. BioPharmDrive. https://www.biopharmadive.com/news/biotech-pharma-ceo-employee-pay/554283/#:~:text=BioPharma%20Dive%20looked%20at%20nearly,stock%20performance%20and%20gender%20representation

Edelman, P., & van Knippenberg, D. (2018). Emotional intelligence, management of subordinate's emotions, and leadership effectiveness. *Leadership and Organization Development Journal*, *39*(5), 592–607. doi:10.1108/LODJ-04-2018-0154

Goleman, D. (1998). *Working with Emotional Intelligence*. Random House.

Gómez-Leal, R., Holzer, A. A., Bradley, C., Fernández-Berrocal, P., & Patti, J. (2021). The relationship between emotional intelligence and leadership in school leaders: A systematic review. *Cambridge Journal of Education*, 1–21.

Gordon, K., Auten, J. N., Gordon, D., & Rook, A. (2019). *Linking behavioral styles of leaders to organizational success: Using the DISC model to Grow Behavioral Awareness. International Journal of Adult Vocational Education and Technology (IJAVET), 10(1)*. IGI Global. doi:10.4018/IJAVET.2019010104

Griffeth, L. L., Malik, R. F., Charas, S., & Randall, N. (2021). Sponsorship: An intervention to accelerate women's career velocity. *The IUP Journal of Soft Skills*, *15*(3), 7–22.

Hu, L. (2021). Self as brand and brand as self: A 2x2 dimension conceptual model of self-branding in a digital economy. *Journal of Internet Commerce*, *20*(3), 355–370. doi:10.1080/15332861.2021.1907170

Jones, C. S., & Hartley, N. T. (2013). Comparing correlations between four-quadrant and five-factor personality assessments. *American Journal of Business Education*, *6*(4), 459–470. doi:10.19030/ajbe.v6i4.7945

Khan, Z., Nawaz, A., & Khan, I. (2016). Leadership Theories and Styles: A Literature Review. *Journal of Resources Development and Management*, 1-7.

Lair, D. J., Sullivan, K., & Cheney, G. (2005). Marketization and the recasting of the professional self: The rhetoric and ethics of personal branding. *Management Communication Quarterly*, *18*(3), 307–343. doi:10.1177/0893318904270744

Manello, A., Cisi, M., Devincienti, F., & Vannoni, D. (2020). Networking: A business for women. *Small Business Economics*, *55*(2), 329–348. doi:10.1007/s11187-019-00300-3

Mate, S. E., McDonald, M., & Do, T. (2018). The barriers and enablers to career and leadership development: An exploration of women's stories in two work cultures. *The International Journal of Organizational Analysis*, 857–874.

Pierre, D. E., & Okstad, J. (2021). Utilizing leadership assessment tools in graduate education. *New Directions for Student Leadership*, *2021*(170), 87–95. doi:10.1002/yd.20445 PMID:34487623

Searby, L., Ballenger, J., & Tripses, J. (2015). Climbing the ladder, holding the ladder: The mentoring experiences of higher education females. *Advancing Women in Leadership*, 98-107.

Smith-Doerr, L. (2004). Flexibility and Fairness: Effects of the network form of organizationa on gender equity in life science careers. *Sociological Perspectives*, *47*(1), 25–54. doi:10.1525/sop.2004.47.1.25

Stratford, L. (2023). *Gender Disparities Within Life Sciences and the Need to Increase Female Representation in the Industry*. CSG Talent. https://www.csgtalent.com/insights/blog/gender-disparities-within-life-sciences-and-the-need-to-increase-female-representation-in-the-industry/

van Gool, F., Bongers, I., Bierbooms, J., & Janssen, R. (2022). Whether and how top management create flexibility in mental healthcare organizations: COVID-19 as a rest case. *Journal of Health Organization and Management*, *36*(5), 604–616. doi:10.1108/JHOM-07-2021-0258 PMID:35238189

KEY TERMS AND DEFINITIONS

Emotional Intelligence: A four-quadrant model that is the cornerstone of leadership and interpersonal effectiveness. The premise is that everything stems from a person knowing themselves and their ability to manage and control their emotions and emotional triggers. Once that is accomplished, a person must know what other's triggers are to effectively interact and motivate others.

ERG Groups: Internal employer resource groups that exist in larger organizations. The intention is to provide networking opportunities for people that have similar demographic characteristics and to provide support and developmental opportunities to those groups. For example there may be groups for women, African Americans, Hispanic Groups, Asian Groups, Muslim Groups, LGBTQ+ groups in organizations.

Glass Ceiling: A metaphor that describes an invisible barrier that women encounter as they attempt to ascend the corporate ladder.

Mentoring: Mentoring can be informal or formal and is a process where a mentor provides career guidance to a mentee.

Self-Branding: An ability to consistently convey your strengths, career successes and goals for career advancement.

Situational Leadership: The flexible ability of a leader to give various combinations of support and direction, depending on the task proficiency of a follower.

Sponsorship: A process where a sponsor who is higher up in an organization exposes an employee that is lower in the organization, to their networks, gives them stretch assignments, and vouches for them when going for a promotion.

The 360-Degree Gender Sphere: A theory that displaces the glass ceiling metaphor, in which states that women are encapsulated by barriers such as themselves, peers, direct managers, gendered structures, gendered norms and family.

Compilation of References

Menon, N., & Bhasin, K. (1998). *Borders and Boundaries: Women in India's Partition*. Rutgers University Press.

Aaronson, N. K. (1988). Quantitative issues in health-related quality of life assessment. *Health Policy (Amsterdam)*, *10*(3), 217–230. doi:10.1016/0168-8510(88)90058-9 PMID:10291115

Abderebbi, M., & Sanny, J. A.-N. (2023). *AD702: Moroccans endorse women's political participation but not equal access to jobs, land.*

Abdul-Hakim, R., Ismail, R., & Abdul-Razak, N. A. (2010). The relationship between social capital and quality of life among rural households in Terengganu, Malaysia. *OIDA International Journal of Sustainable Development*, *1*(05), 99–106.

Adamovic, M., & Leibbrandt, A. (2023). Is there a glass ceiling for ethnic minorities to enter leadership positions? Evidence from a field experiment with over 12,000 job applications. *The Leadership Quarterly*, *34*(2), 101655. doi:10.1016/j.leaqua.2022.101655

Adams-Harmon, D., & Greer-Williams, N. (2021). Successful ascent of female leaders in the pharmaceutical industry: A qualitative, transcendental, and phenomenological study. *Equality, Diversity and Inclusion*, *40*(7), 819–837. doi:10.1108/EDI-01-2019-0031

Adeeko, K. (2019). *Resilient identities: Refugee women defining their entrepreneurial selves*. Unpublished paper. Nottingham, England: Institute of Small Business and Entrepreneurship Conference.

Adema, W., Clarke, C., & Frey, V. (2015). Paid parental leave: Lessons from OECD countries and selected US states. *OECD social, employment and migration working paper No. 172*. Paris. Organization for Economic Cooperation and Development. doi:10.1111/issr.12134

Adger, W. N., De Campos, R. S., & Mortreux, C. (2018). Mobility, displacement and migration, and their interactions with vulnerability and adaptation to environmental risks. In *Routledge handbook of environmental displacement and migration* (pp. 29–41). Routledge. doi:10.4324/9781315638843-3

Adisa, T., Cooke, F. L., & Iwowo, V. (2019). Mind Your Attitude: The Impact of Patriarchy on Women's Workplace Behaviour. *Career Development International*, *25*(2), 146–164. doi:10.1108/CDI-07-2019-0183

Adnane, S. (2018). Women's Land Ownership In Morocco: Current State & Challenges. OICRF. https://www.oicrf.org/-/women-s-land-ownership-in-morocco-current-state-challenges

Africa Partnership Forum. (2007). *Gender and economic empowerment in Africa*. 8th Meeting of the Africa Partnership Forum, Berlin, Germany. https://www.oecd.org/dac/gender-development/38829148.pdf

AgierI.SzafarzA. (2010). Credit to women entrepreneurs: The curse of the trustworthier sex. *Available at SSRN 1718574*. doi:10.2139/ssrn.1718574

Agrawal, A., Gandhi, P., & Khare, P. (2023). Women empowerment through entrepreneurship: Case study of a social entrepreneurial intervention in rural India. *The International Journal of Organizational Analysis*, *31*(4), 1122–1142. doi:10.1108/IJOA-03-2021-2659

Aguilar, L., Araujo, A., & Quesada-Aguilar, A. (2007). *Gender and climate change.* IUCN (International Union for the Conservation of Nature) Fact Sheet. http://www. Gender and environment. org/admin/admin_biblioteca/documentos/ Fact sheet% 20ClimateChange. pdf.

Ahl, H., & Nelson, T. (2015). How policy positions women entrepreneurs: A comparative analysis of state discourse in Sweden and the United States. *Journal of Business Venturing*, *30*(2), 273–291. doi:10.1016/j.jbusvent.2014.08.002

Akala, B. M. (2024). Gender and the conflict in South Sudan. In N. Alusala, E. A. Liaga, & M. R. Rupiya (Eds.), *Conflict Management and Resolution in South Sudan* (pp. 133–152). Routledge., doi:10.4324/9781003410249

Akın, Ö., & Erbil, N. (2024). Investigation of coping behaviors and premenstrual syndrome among university students. *Current Psychology (New Brunswick, N.J.)*, *43*(2), 1685–1695. doi:10.1007/s12144-023-04419-1 PMID:37359568

Al-Dajani, H. (2022). Refugee women's entrepreneurship: Where from and where next? *International Journal of Gender and Entrepreneurship*, *14*(4), 489–498. doi:10.1108/IJGE-06-2022-0090

Alderman, H., Behrman, J. R., Ross, D. R., & Sabot, R. (1996). Decomposing the gender gap in cognitive skills in a poor rural economy. *The Journal of Human Resources*, *31*(1), 229–254. doi:10.2307/146049

Ali, P., Anderson, M. E., McRae, C. H., & Ramsay, I. (2014). The financial literacy of young Australians: An empirical study and implications for consumer protection and ASIC's National Financial Literacy Strategy. *Company and Securities Law Journal*, *32*(5), 334–352.

Allen, T. D., Eby, L. T., Poteet, M. L., Lentz, E., & Lima, L. (2004). Career benefits associated with mentoring for protégés: A meta-analysis. *The Journal of Applied Psychology*, *89*(1), 127–136. doi:10.1037/0021-9010.89.1.127 PMID:14769125

Alperin, E., & Batalova, J. (2018). *Vietnamese immigrants in the United States.* Migration Policy Institute. https://www.migrationpolicy.org/article/vietnamese-immigrants-united-states-5

Amiri, M., Chaman, R., Sadeghi, Z., Khatibi, M., Ranjbar, M., & Khosravi, A. (2017). Quality of life among fertile and infertile women. *Iranian Journal of Psychiatry and Behavioral Sciences*, *11*(1), 1–5. doi:10.5812/ijpbs.5641

Anand, S., & Sen, A. (1995). Gender Inequality in Human Development: Theories and Measurement. In F. Parr & A. K. Shiv Kumar (Eds.), *Readings in Human Development*. OUP.

Anderson, K. L. (1995). The effect of chronic obstructive pulmonary disease on quality of life. *Research in Nursing & Health*, *18*(6), 547–556. doi:10.1002/nur.4770180610 PMID:7480855

Andrews, F. M., & Withey, S. B. (2012). *Social indicators of well-being: Americans' perceptions of life quality.* Springer Science & Business Media. https://books.google.co.in/books?hl=en&lr=&id=4g7rBwAAQBAJ&oi=fnd&pg=PA1&dq=Andrews,+F.+M.,+%26+Withey,+S.+B.+(2012).+Social+indicators+of+well-being:+Americans%27+perceptions+of+life+quality.+Springer+Science+%26+Business+Media.&ots=chSmZ7r7kV&sig=x4QUIWO_HWUTVPBByhe_N-iQ_uk&redir_esc=y#v=onepage&q&f=false

Andriamahery, A., & Qamruzzaman, M. (2022). Do access to finance, technical know-how, and financial literacy offer women empowerment through women's entrepreneurial development? *Frontiers in Psychology*, *12*, 776844. doi:10.3389/fpsyg.2021.776844 PMID:35058847

Anjum, F., Zehra, N., Haider, G., Rani, S., Siddique, A. A., & Munir, A. A. (2010). Attitudes towards menstruation among young women. *Pakistan Journal of Medical Sciences*, *26*(3), 619–622.

Compilation of References

Arbabi, M., Shirmohammadi, M., Taghizadeh, Z., & Mehran, A. (2008). The effect of premenstrual syndrome on quality of life in adolescent girls. *Iranian Journal of Psychiatry*, *3*(3), 105–109.

Arini, F. D. (2018, March). Financial Literacy in Women Empowerment. In *2018 Annual Conference of Asian Association for Public Administration:" Reinventing Public Administration in a Globalized World: A Non-Western Perspective" (AAPA 2018)* (pp. 635-643). Atlantis Press.

Asia Society. (2022). *Women Leaders of New Asia*. Asia Society. https://asiasociety.org/women-leaders

Asia Society. (n.d.) *Introduction to Southeast Asia*. Asia Society. https://asiasociety.org/education/introduction-southeast-asia

Association for Women's Rights in Development (AWID). (2004). *Intersectionality: A Tool for Gender and Economic Justice*. AWID. https://www.awid.org/sites/default/files/atoms/files/intersectionality_a_tool_for_gender_and_economic_justice.pdf

Babajani, S., Asgari, K., Orayzi, H., & Ghasemi, N. (2017). Effectiveness of cognitive-behavioral therapy on premenstrual syndrome through compliance to treatment in an iranian sample. *Zahedan Journal of Researches in Medical Sciences*, *19*(6). doi:10.5812/zjrms.12537

Bäckström, T., & Carstensen, H. (1974). Estrogen and progesterone in plasma in relation to premenstrual tension. *Journal of Steroid Biochemistry*, *5*(3), 257–260. doi:10.1016/0022-4731(74)90139-3 PMID:4859320

Baker, F., & Intagliata, J. (1982). Quality of life in the evaluation of community support systems. *Evaluation and Program Planning*, *5*(1), 69–79. doi:10.1016/0149-7189(82)90059-3 PMID:10257372

Baker, W. E. (1990). Market networks and corporate behavior. *American Journal of Sociology*, *96*(3), 589–625. doi:10.1086/229573

Balaha, M., Amr, M., Moghannum, M., & Muhaidab, N. (2010). The phenomenology of premenstrual syndrome in female medical students: A cross sectional study. *The Pan African Medical Journal*, *5*(1), 1–14. doi:10.4314/pamj.v5i1.56194 PMID:21120003

Ballenger, J. (2010). *Women's access to higher education leadership: Cultural and structural barriers*. Forum on Public Policy. https://files.eric.ed.gov/fulltext/EJ913023.pdf

Bandura, A. (1977). Self-efficacy: Toward a unifying theory of behavioral change. *Psychological Review*, *84*(2), 191–215. doi:10.1037/0033-295X.84.2.191 PMID:847061

Banerjee, S., Chowdhury, A., & Srivastava, A. (2021). Creating awareness about health and hygiene during menstrual cycle among Indian adolescent girls using virtual reality. In *Advanced Manufacturing Systems and Innovative Product Design: Select Proceedings of IPDIMS 2020*. Springer. 10.1007/978-981-15-9853-1_27

Bansal, D., Raman, R., & Rao, T. S. (2019). Premenstrual dysphoric disorder: ranking the symptoms and severity in Indian college students. *Journal of Psychosexual Health, 1*(2), 159-163. doi:10.1177/2631831819827

Bapna, S., & Funk, R. J. (2021). Interventions for improving professional networking for women: Experimental evidence from the IT sector. *Management Information Systems Quarterly*, *45*(2), 593–636. doi:10.25300/MISQ/2021/15620

Bardhan, K., & Klasen, S. (1999). UNDP's Gender Related Indices: A Critical Review. *World Development*, *27*(6), 985–1010. doi:10.1016/S0305-750X(99)00035-2

Bardhan, K., & Klasen, S. (2000). On UNDP's Revisions to the Gender- Related Development Index. *Journal of Human Development*, *1*(2), 191–195. doi:10.1080/713678044

Barkat, A. (2008). *Women Empowerment: A Key to Human Development.* Good Governance. http://www.goodgovernance.org

Barnard, K., Frayne, S. M., Skinner, K. M., & Sullivan, L. M. (2003). Health status among women with menstrual symptoms. *Journal of Women's Health, 12*(9), 911–919. doi:10.1089/154099903770948140 PMID:14670171

Barooah, B., Banerjee, S., Dang, A., Kejriwal, K., & Aggarwal, R. (2022). A framework for examining women's economic empowerment in collective enterprises.

Batliwala, S. (1994). *Women's empowerment in South Asia: Concepts and practices.* Asian South Pacific Bureau of Adult Education.

Batliwala, S. (2007). Putting power back into empowerment. *Democracy (New York, N.Y.), 50*(3), 61–80.

Batliwala, S. (2007). Taking the power out of empowerment–an experiential account. *Development in Practice, 17*(4-5), 557–565. doi:10.1080/09614520701469559

Batliwala, S. (2012). *Changing Their World.* Concepts and Practices of Women's.

Baughn, C. C., Chua, B. L., & Neupert, K. E. (2006). The normative context for women's participation in entrepreneruship: A multicountry study. *Entrepreneurship Theory and Practice, 30*(5), 687–708. doi:10.1111/j.1540-6520.2006.00142.x

Bea, M. D., & Yi, Y. (2019). Leaving the financial nest: Connecting young adults' financial independence to financial security. *Journal of Marriage and Family, 81*(2), 397–414. doi:10.1111/jomf.12553

Benincá, S., Melhem, A., Martins, R., & Libera, E. (2016). Alcoholic chronic pancreatitis: A quality of life study. *Revista de Nutrição, 29*(1), 23–31. doi:10.1590/1678-98652016000100003

Berg, A., Ostry, J. D., Tsangarides, C. G., & Yakhshilikov, Y. (2018). Redistribution, inequality, and growth: New evidence. *Journal of Economic Growth, 23*(3), 259–305. doi:10.1007/s10887-017-9150-2

Bernard, M. J., & Barbosa, S. D. (2016). Resilience and entrepreneurship: A dynamic and biographical approach to the entrepreneurial act. *Management, 19*(2), 89–121.

Bertone-Johnson, E. R., Hankinson, S. E., Johnson, S. R., & Manson, J. E. (2007). A simple method of assessing premenstrual syndrome in large prospective studies. *Journal of Reproductive Medicine-Chicago, 52*(9), 779. PMID:17939593

Bertone-Johnson, E. R., Whitcomb, B. W., Missmer, S. A., Manson, J. E., Hankinson, S. E., & Rich-Edwards, J. W. (2014). Early life emotional, physical, and sexual abuse and the development of premenstrual syndrome: A longitudinal study. *Journal of Women's Health, 23*(9), 729–739. doi:10.1089/jwh.2013.4674 PMID:25098348

Beteta, K. C. (2006). What is Missing in Measures of Women's Empowerment? *Journal of Human Development, 7*(2), 221–241. doi:10.1080/14649880600768553

Bharathi, N. S., Kayalvizhi, E., & Sylvia, J. (2022). Premenstrual syndrome-An overview. *International Journal of Nursing Education and Research, 10*(4), 395–398. doi:10.52711/2454-2660.2022.00089

Bhardwaj, L. K., Rath, P., Bajpai, S., Upadhyay, D., Jain, H., Kumar, N., & Sinha, S. (2024). COVID-19 and the Interplay with Antibacterial Drug Resistance. In Frontiers in Combating Antibacterial Resistance: Current Perspectives and Future Horizons (pp. 246-273). IGI Global.

BhardwajL. K. (2023). A Comprehensive Review on the Climate Change and Its Impact on Health. doi:10.20944/preprints202305.0159.v1

Compilation of References

Bhardwaj, L. K., Rath, P., & Choudhury, M. (2023). A comprehensive review on the classification, uses, sources of nanoparticles (NPs) and their toxicity on health. *Aerosol Science and Engineering*, 7(1), 69–86. doi:10.1007/s41810-022-00163-4

Billen, A. (2024). *Unlocking Potential: Addressing Challenges in Women Entrepreneurship Policy for a Sustainable Future*. Maastricht University.

Biopharmadive. (2019). *Number of female biotech CEOs remains 'shockingly low,' putting spotlight on BIO*. BioPharmDrive. https://www.biopharmadive.com/news/female-biotech-ceos-bio-efforts-diversity-goals/558604/

Blau, F., & DeVaro, J. (2006). New evidence on gender difference in promotion rates: An empirical analysis of a sample of new hires. *Industrial Relations*, 46(3), 511–550. doi:10.1111/j.1468-232X.2007.00479.x

Blumberg, R.L. (2005). *"Women's Economic Empowerment as the Magic Potion of Development?"* Paper presented at the 100th annual meeting of the American Sociological Association, Philadelphia.

Boatwright, K. J., & Egidio, R. K. (2003). Psychological predictors of college women's leadership aspirations. *Journal of College Student Development*, 44(5), 653–669. doi:10.1353/csd.2003.0048

Boddy, J. (2009). Challenging gender role stereotypes and creating pathways for goal achievement. *Qualitative Social Work: Research and Practice*, 8(4), 489–508. doi:10.1177/1473325009346527

Bodner, S. L. (2003). *Dimensional assessment of empowerment in organizations*. University of North Texas.

Borenstein, J. E., Dean, B. B., Endicott, J., Wong, J., Brown, C., Dickerson, V., & Yonkers, K. A. (2003). Health and economic impact of the premenstrual syndrome. *The Journal of Reproductive Medicine*, 48(7), 515–524. PMID:12953326

Borenstein, J. E., Dean, B. B., Leifke, E., Korner, P., & Yonkers, K. A. (2007). Differences in symptom scores and health outcomes in premenstrual syndrome. *Journal of Women's Health*, 16(8), 1139–1144. doi:10.1089/jwh.2006.0230 PMID:17937566

Borja, M. (2018). Not all rosy: Religion and refugee resettlement in the US. *Harvard Divinity Bulletin*. https://bulletin.hds.harvard.edu/not-all-rosy-religion-and-refugee-resettlement-in-the-u-s/

Borthwick-Duffy, S. A. (2000). Quality of life and quality of care in mental retardation. *Mental Retardation*, 4, 52–66. doi:10.1007/978-1-4613-9115-9_4

Boserup, E., Kanji, N., Tan, S. F., & Toulmin, C. (2013). *Woman's role in economic development*. Routledge. doi:10.4324/9781315065892

Bose, S., & Jalal, A. (2004). *Modern South Asia: History, Culture, Political Economy*. Routledge. doi:10.4324/9780203712535

Bouderbala, N. (1999). Les systèmes de propriété foncière au Maghreb: le cas du Maroc. Cahiers options méditerranéennes, 36.

Bourdieu, P. (1986). The Forms of Capital. In J. Richardson (Ed.), *Handbook of theory and research for the sociology of education* (pp. 241–258). Greenwood.

Bourdieu, P. (2018). The forms of capital. In *The sociology of economic life* (pp. 78–92). Routledge. doi:10.4324/9780429494338-6

Braddy, P. W., Sturm, R. E., Atwater, L., Taylor, S. N., & McKee, R. A. (2020). Gender bias still plagues the workplace: Looking at derailment risk and performance with self–other ratings. *Group & Organization Management*, 45(3), 315–350. doi:10.1177/1059601119867780

Brawley, B. G. (2022). *Women of Achievement: Written for the Fireside Schools*. DigiCat.

Brooks-Gunn, J., & Ruble, D. (1980). The menstrual attitude questionnaire. *Psychosomatic Medicine*, *42*(5), 503–512. doi:10.1097/00006842-198009000-00005 PMID:7465737

Brouder, A., & Sweetman, C. (2015). Introduction: Working on gender issues in urban areas. *Gender and Development*, *23*(1), 1–12. doi:10.1080/13552074.2015.1026642

Brush, C., de Bruin, A., & Welter, F. (2009). A gender-aware framework for women's entrepreneurship. *International Journal of Gender and Entrepreneurship*, *1*(1), 8–24. doi:10.1108/17566260910942318

Brush, C., de Bruin, A., & Welter, F. (2014). Advancing theory development in venture creation: Signposts for scholars. In A. C. Corbett, J. A. Katz, & A. McKenzie (Eds.), *Entrepreneurial Resourcefulness: Competing with Constraints* (pp. 111–132). Emerald Group Publishing Limited.

Brush, C., Edelman, L. F., Manolova, T., & Welter, F. (2019). A gendered look at entrepreneurship ecosystems. *Small Business Economics*, *53*(2), 393–408. doi:10.1007/s11187-018-9992-9

Brush, C., Greene, P., Balachandra, L., & Davis, A. (2018). The gender gap in venture capital: Progress, problems, and perspectives. *Venture Capital*, *20*(2), 115–136. doi:10.1080/13691066.2017.1349266

Budiman, A. (2020). *Key findings about U.S. immigrants*. Washington, DC: Pew Research Center. https://www.pewresearch.org/fact-tank/2020/08/20/key-findings-about-u-s-immigrants/

Bunyaratavej, S., Pattanaprichakul, P., Leeyaphan, C., Chayangsu, O., Bunyaratavej, S., & Kulthanan, K. (2015). Onychomycosis: A study of self-recognition by patients and quality of life. *Indian Journal of Dermatology, Venereology and Leprology*, *81*(3), 270. doi:10.4103/0378-6323.154796 PMID:25851764

Burckhardt, C. S., & Anderson, K. L. (2003). The Quality of Life Scale (QOLS): Reliability, validity, and utilization. *Health and Quality of Life Outcomes*, *1*(1), 1–7. doi:10.1186/1477-7525-1-1 PMID:14613562

Burckhardt, C. S., Archenholtz, B., & Bjelle, A. (1992). Measuring the quality of life of women with rheumatoid arthritis or systemic lupus erythematosus: A Swedish version of the Quality of Life Scale (QOLS). *Scandinavian Journal of Rheumatology*, *21*(4), 190–195. doi:10.3109/03009749209099220 PMID:1529286

Burckhardt, C. S., Woods, S. L., Schultz, A. A., & Ziebarth, D. M. (1989). Quality of life of adults with chronic illness: A psychometric study. *Research in Nursing & Health*, *12*(6), 347–354. doi:10.1002/nur.4770120604 PMID:2602575

Bureau, C. F. P. (2015). *Financial Well-Being: The Goal of Financial Education*. Consumer Financial Protection Bureau.

Cahyati, D., & Hariri, H. Sowiyah, & Karwan, D. H. (2021). Women's leadership in higher education: Barriers and opportunities in Indonesia. *International Journal of Education Policy & Leadership, 17*(9). https://files.eric.ed.gov/fulltext/EJ1319884.pdf

Camdessus, M. (1997). *Fostering an Enabling Environment for Development*. Address presented at the High-Level Meeting of the UN Economic and Social Council, Geneva, Switzerland.

Campagne, D. M., & Campagne, G. (2007). The premenstrual syndrome revisited. *European Journal of Obstetrics, Gynecology, and Reproductive Biology*, *130*(1), 4–17. doi:10.1016/j.ejogrb.2006.06.020 PMID:16916572

Canuto, O., & Kabbach, H. (2023). *Gender inequality in the labor market: the case of Morocco*.

Cardona, M. S., & Hamel-Roy, L. (2023). Popular education and learning as the bridge between activism and knowledge production. *Globalisation, Societies and Education*, *21*(5), 664–676. doi:10.1080/14767724.2023.2175644

Compilation of References

Carpena, F., Cole, S. A., Shapiro, J., & Zia, B. (2011). *Unpacking the causal chain of financial literacy.* (World Bank Policy Research Working Paper, (5798)).

Cartwright, A., Hussey, I., Roche, B., Dunne, J., & Muphy, C. (2017). An investigation into the relationship between the gender binary and occupational discrimination using the implicit relational assessment procedure. *The Psychological Record*, *67*(1), 121–130. doi:10.1007/s40732-016-0212-1

Catalyst, inc. (2004). *Advancing African-American women in the workplace: What managers need to know.* Catalyst.

Catherine Ehrich, L. (1995). Professional mentorship for women educators in government schools. *Journal of Educational Administration*, *33*(2), 69–83. doi:10.1108/09578239510081318

Ceci, S. J., Ginther, D. K., Kahn, S., & Williams, W. M. (2014). Women in academic science: A changing landscape. *Psychological Science in the Public Interest*, *15*(3), 75–141. doi:10.1177/1529100614541236 PMID:26172066

Census of India. (2001). Govt. of India.

Center, P. R. (2023). *Views of having a woman president.* Pew Research Center's Social & Demographic Trends Project. https://www.pewresearch.org/social-trends/2023/09/27/views-of-having-a-woman-president/#:~:text=Women%20 (21%25)%20are%20more

Chakroff, R. P., & Lidsker, C. (1981). A look at Vietnamese refugee fishermen: Five years on the Gulf Coast. *The Coastal Society Bulletin, 5*(3).

Chandak, P. (2024). *Social Entrepreneurship and Women.*

Chandra, P. S., & Chaturvedi, S. K. (1992). Cultural variations in attitudes toward menstruation. *Canadian Journal of Psychiatry*, *37*(3), 196–198. doi:10.1177/070674379203700310 PMID:1591671

Chandra, P. S., Chaturvedi, S. K., & Isaac, M. K. (1989). Measurement of menstrual attitudes in Indian women: A cultural perspective. *Journal of Psychosomatic Obstetrics and Gynaecology*, *10*(3), 247–253. doi:10.3109/01674828909016698

Chang, Y. T., & Chen, Y. C. (2009). Study of menstrual attitudes and distress among postmenarcheal female students in Hualien County. *The Journal of Nursing Research*, *17*(1), 20–29. doi:10.1097/JNR.0b013e3181999d25 PMID:19352226

Chanoff, S. (2016). Refugees revitalize American cities. *Boston Globe*. https://www.bostonglobe.com/opinion/2016/11/25/refugees-revitalize-american-cities/7Xe7PX6JbRq4sfE8D4pNyJ/story.html

Chatterjee, P. (1993). *The Nation and Its Fragments: Colonial and Postcolonial Histories.* Princeton University Press.

Chattopadhyay, R. & Duflo, E. (2001). *Women's Leadership and Policy Decisions: Evidence from a Nationwide Randomized Experiment in India.* Indian Institute of Management, Calcutta and Department of Economics, MIT, and NBER.

Chau, J. P., & Chang, A. M. (1999). Effects of an educational programme on adolescents with premenstrual syndrome. *Health Education Research*, *14*(6), 817–830. doi:10.1093/her/14.6.817 PMID:10585388

Chayachinda, C., Rattanachaiyanont, M., Phattharayuttawat, S., & Kooptiwoot, S. (2008). Premenstrual syndrome in Thai nurses. *Journal of Psychosomatic Obstetrics and Gynaecology*, *29*(3), 203–209. doi:10.1080/01674820801970306 PMID:18608818

Chen, G., Kark, R., Shamir, B. (2003). *The Two Faces of Transformational Leadership: Empowerment and Dependency.* 246-254.

Cheng, S., Sun, Z. J., Lee, I., Shih, C. C., Chen, K., Lin, S. H., Lu, F. H., Yang, Y. C., & Yang, Y. (2015). Perception of premenstrual syndrome and attitude of evaluations of work performance among incoming university female students. *Biomedical Journal*, *38*(2), 167–172. doi:10.4103/2319-4170.138319 PMID:25179727

Chen, H. X., Xu, X., & Phillips, P. (2019). Emotional intelligence and conflict management styles. *The International Journal of Organizational Analysis*, *27*(3), 458–470. doi:10.1108/IJOA-11-2017-1272

Chindarkar, N. (2012). Gender and climate change-induced migration: Proposing a framework for analysis. *Environmental Research Letters*, *7*(2), 025601. doi:10.1088/1748-9326/7/2/025601

Chisamya, G., DeJaeghere, J., Kendall, N., & Khan, M. A. (2012). Gender and education for all: Progress and problems in achieving gender equity. *International Journal of Educational Development*, *32*(6), 743–755. doi:10.1016/j.ijedudev.2011.10.004

Chougule, K. (2017). A phenomenological study of premenstrual symptoms in medical and nursing students. *Journal of Evolution of Medical and Dental Sciences*, *6*(46), 3576–3581. doi:10.14260/Jemds/2017/771

Chrisler, J. C. (2008). PMS as a culture-bound syndrome. In J. C. Chrisler, C. Golden, & P. D. Rozee (Eds.), Lectures on the psychology of women (4), 155–171.

Clare, A. W. (1985). Premenstrual syndrome: Single or multiple causes? *Canadian Journal of Psychiatry*, *30*(7), 474–482. doi:10.1177/070674378503000704 PMID:3907815

Clemens, M. (2022). *The economic and fiscal effects on the United States from reduced numbers of refugees and asylum seekers. Center for Global Development Working Paper 610*. Center for Global Development., https://www.cgdev.org/publication/economic-and-fiscal-effects-united-states-reduced-numbers-refugees-and-asylum-seekers

Coleman, J. (1986). *Individual Interests and Collective Action*. Cambridge University Press.

Coleman, J. S., & Fararo, Th. (1992). *Rational Choice Theory: Advocacy and Critique*. Sage.

Cook, A., & Glass, C. (2014). Women and top leadership positions: Towards an institutional analysis. *Gender, Work and Organization*, *21*(1), 91–103. doi:10.1111/gwao.12018

Corbett, H. (2022). *Forbes. *How To #BreakTheBias At Work On International Women's Day*. And Every Day.

Cornwall, A., & Brock, K. (2005). What do buzzwords do for development policy? A critical look at 'participation', 'empowerment' and 'poverty reduction'. *Third World Quarterly*, *26*(7), 1043–1060. doi:10.1080/01436590500235603

Cornwall, A., & Rivas, A.-M. (2015). From 'gender equality and 'women's empowerment' to global justice: Reclaiming a transformative agenda for gender and development. *Third World Quarterly*, *36*(2), 396–415. doi:10.1080/01436597.2015.1013341

Corrêa, V. S., Brito, F. R. D. S., Lima, R. M. D., & Queiroz, M. M. (2022). Female entrepreneurship in emerging and developing countries: A systematic literature review. *International Journal of Gender and Entrepreneurship*, *14*(3), 300–322. doi:10.1108/IJGE-08-2021-0142

Creswell, J. W. (2009). *Educational research: Planning, conducting and evaluating quantitative and qualitative research* (3rd ed.). Merrill Prentice Hall.

Creswell, J. W., & Creswell, J. D. (2017). *Research design: Qualitative, quantitative, and mixed methods approaches* (5th ed.). Sage Pub.

Cronje, W., & Hawkins, A. P. (2003). Premenstrual symptoms. In J. Studd (Ed.), *Progress in. Obstetrics and Gynaecolology* (pp. 169–183). Elsevier Science. doi:10.1016/S0095-4543(03)00070-8

Compilation of References

Cross, R., & Thomas, R. J. (2008). How top talent uses networks and where rising stars get trapped. *Organizational Dynamics*, *37*(2), 165–180. doi:10.1016/j.orgdyn.2008.02.001

Cullen, C., Barnes-Holmes, D., Barnes-Holmes, Y., & Stewart, I. (2009). The Implicit Relational Assessment Procedure (IRAP) and the malleability of ageist attitudes. *The Psychological Record*, *59*(4), 591–620. doi:10.1007/BF03395683

Dalton, K. D. (1984). *Premenstrual syndrome and progesterone therapy*. https://cir.nii.ac.jp/crid/1130000796254365952

Daronco, K. F., Muller, L. A., & Arruda, E. H. P. D. (2024). Prevalence of premenstrual syndrome in female nursing students at a public university: Cross-sectional study. *British Journal of Pain*, *7*. doi:10.5935/2595-0118.20240006-en

Darwin, A., & Palmer, E. (2009). Mentoring circles in higher education. *Higher Education Research & Development*, *28*(2), 125–136. doi:10.1080/07294360902725017

Dasgupta, P., & Serageldin, I. (Eds.). (2000). *Social capital: a multifaceted perspective*. World Bank Publications.

De Beer, P., Berg, M., Koster, F., & Lepianka, D. (2017). Towards an interdisciplinary theory of solidarity. In P. de Beer & F. Koster (Eds.), *Ethnic Diversity and Solidarity: A Study of their Complex Relationship* (pp. 13–42). Cambridge Scholars Publishing.

De Clercq, D., & Brieger, S. A. (2022). When discrimination is worse, autonomy is key: How women entrepreneurs leverage job autonomy resources to find work–life balance. *Journal of Business Ethics*, *177*(3), 665–682. doi:10.1007/s10551-021-04735-1

De Haan, A., Brock, K., & Coulibaly, N. (2002). Migration, livelihoods and institutions: Contrasting patterns of migration in Mali. *The Journal of Development Studies*, *38*(5), 37–58. doi:10.1080/00220380412331322501

De La Puente, D.De La Puente. (2011). Women's leadership in camps for internally displaced people in Darfur, western Sudan. *Community Development Journal: An International Forum*, *46*(3), 365–377. doi:10.1093/cdj/bsr036

De Vita, L., Mari, M., & Poggesi, S. (2014). Women entrepreneurs in and from developing countries: Evidences from the literature. *European Management Journal*, *32*(3), 451–460. doi:10.1016/j.emj.2013.07.009

Dean, B. B., Borenstein, J. E., Knight, K., & Yonkers, K. (2006). Evaluating the criteria used for identification of PMS. *Journal of Women's Health*, *15*(5), 546–555. doi:10.1089/jwh.2006.15.546 PMID:16796482

Deci, E. L., & Ryan, R. M. (2013). *Intrinsic motivation and self-determination in human behavior*. Springer Science & Business Media.

Delara, M., Ghofranipour, F., Azadfallah, P., Tavafian, S. S., Kazemnejad, A., & Montazeri, A. (2012). Health related quality of life among adolescents with premenstrual disorders: A cross sectional study. *Health and Quality of Life Outcomes*, *10*(1), 1–5. doi:10.1186/1477-7525-10-1 PMID:22208808

Demetriades, J., & Esplen, E. (2010). The gender dimensions of poverty and climate change adaptation. *Social dimensions of climate change: Equity and vulnerability in a warming world*, 133-143.

Demirgüç-Kunt, A., Klapper, L., Singer, D., & Ansar, S. (2022). *The Global Findex Database 2021: Financial inclusion, digital payments, and resilience in the age of COVID-19*. World Bank Publications. doi:10.1596/978-1-4648-1897-4

Denmark, F. L. (1993). Women, leadership, and empowerment. *Psychology of Women Quarterly*, *17*(3), 343–356. doi:10.1111/j.1471-6402.1993.tb00491.x

Denton, F. (2002). Climate change vulnerability, impacts, and adaptation: Why does gender matter? *Gender and Development*, *10*(2), 10–20. doi:10.1080/13552070215903

Desai, N., & Thakkar, U. (2007). *"Women and Political Participation in India", Women in Indian Society*. National Book Trust.

Deuster, P. A., Adera, T., & South-Paul, J. (1999). Biological, social, and behavioral factors associated with premenstrual syndrome. *Archives of Family Medicine*, *8*(2), 122–128. doi:10.1001/archfami.8.2.122 PMID:10101982

Díaz-García, M. C., & Brush, C. G. (2012). Gender and business ownership: Questioning "what" and "why". *International Journal of Entrepreneurial Behaviour & Research*, *18*(1), 4–27. doi:10.1108/13552551211201358

Diehl, A. B., Stephenson, A. L., Dzubinski, L. M., & Wang, D. C. (2020). Measuring the invisible: Development and multi-industry validation of the Gender Bias Scale for Women Leaders. *Human Resource Development Quarterly*, *31*(3), 249–280. doi:10.1002/hrdq.21389

Dijkstra, G. (2002). Revisiting UNDP's GDI and GEM: Towards an Alternative. *Social Indicators Research*, *57*(3), 301–338. doi:10.1023/A:1014726207604

Dijkstra, G. (2006). Towards a Fresh Start in Measuring Gender Equality: A Contribution to the Debate. *Journal of Human Development*, *7*(2), 275–284. doi:10.1080/14649880600768660

Dijkstra, G., & Hanmer, L. C. (2000). Measuring Socio-economic Gender Inequality: Towards an Alternative to the UNDP- Gender-related Development Index. *Feminist Economics*, *6*(2), 41–75. doi:10.1080/13545700050076106

Doe, R., Ndinguri, E., & Phipps, S. T. (2015). Emotional intelligence: The link to success and failure of leadership. *Academy of Educational Leadership Journal*, 105–114.

Doss, C., & Meinzen-Dick, R. (2020). Land tenure security for women: A conceptual framework. *Land Use Policy*, *99*, 105080. doi:10.1016/j.landusepol.2020.105080

Duchek, S. (2019). Entrepreneurial resilience: A biographical analysis of successful entrepreneurs. *The International Entrepreneurship and Management Journal*, *141*(2), 429–455. doi:10.1007/s11365-017-0467-2

Dudwick, N., Kuehnast, K., Jones, V. N., & Woolcock, M. (2006). Analyzing social capital in context. *A guide to using qualitative methods and data*, 1-46.

Duflo, E. (2012). Women empowerment and economic development. *Journal of Economic Literature*, *50*(4), 1051–1079. doi:10.1257/jel.50.4.1051

Dunn, A., & Pagliarulo, N. (2018). *Follow the money: How biopharma CEOs and workers get paid in 2018*. BioPharmDrive. https://www.biopharmadive.com/news/biotech-pharma-ceo-employee-pay/554283/#:~:text=BioPharma%20Dive%20looked%20at%20nearly,stock%20performance%20and%20gender%20representation

Durkheim, E. (1995). *[1915]. The elementary forms of the religious life*. Free Press.

Durkheim, E. (2014). *[1893]. The division of labor in society*. Free Press.

Eagly, A. H., & Chaiken, S. (1993). *The psychology of attitudes*. Harcourt brace Jovanovich college publishers. https://psycnet.apa.org/record/1992-98849-000

Eagly, A. H., Gartzia, L. L., & Carli, L. (2014). Female advantage: revisited S. Kumra, R. Simpson, R. Burke (Eds.), The Oxford handbook of gender in organizations. Oxford University Press, New York.

Edelman, P., & van Knippenberg, D. (2018). Emotional intelligence, management of subordinate's emotions, and leadership effectiveness. *Leadership and Organization Development Journal*, *39*(5), 592–607. doi:10.1108/LODJ-04-2018-0154

Compilation of References

Ekholm, U. B., & Bäckström, T. (1994). Influence of premenstrual syndrome on family, social life, and work performance. *International Journal of Health Services*, 24(4), 629–647. doi:10.2190/P0Y8-J7UF-K2MG-LBL4 PMID:7896466

Elamrani, J., & Lemtaoui, M. (2014). *Social entrepreneurship funding in Morocco: Practices, constraints and prospects.*

Elkind, J. (2014). 'The Virgin Mary is going south': Refugee resettlement in South Vietnam. *Diplomatic History*, 35(5), 987–1016. https://www.jstor.org/stable/26376620. doi:10.1093/dh/dht119

Else-Quest, N. M., Hyde, J. S., & Linn, M. C. (2010). Cross-national patterns of gender differences in mathematics: A meta-analysis. *Psychological Bulletin*, 136(1), 103–127. doi:10.1037/a0018053 PMID:20063928

Engelman, R. (2009). The state of world population 2009. Facing a changing world: Women, population and climate. In The state of world population 2009. Facing a changing world: Women, population and climate (pp. 104-104).

Ensher, E. A., Grant-Vallone, E. J., & Donaldson, S. I. (2001). Effects of perceived discrimination on job satisfaction, organizational commitment, organizational citizenship behavior, and grievances. *Human Resource Development Quarterly*, 12(1), 53–72. doi:10.1002/1532-1096(200101/02)12:1<53::AID-HRDQ5>3.0.CO;2-G

Enuka, C., & Nwankwo, C. U. (2022). Assessment of Premenstrual Syndrome and Coping Strategies among Female Students of the School of Basic Medical Sciences, University of Benin, Benin City, Nigeria. *Bayero Journal of Nursing and Healthcare*, 4(1), 927–938. doi:10.4314/bjnhc.v4i1.2

Eriksen, S. H., Brown, K., & Kelly, P. M. (2005). The dynamics of vulnerability: Locating coping strategies in Kenya and Tanzania. *The Geographical Journal*, 171(4), 287–305. doi:10.1111/j.1475-4959.2005.00174.x

Erkal, N., Gangadharan, L., & Xiao, E. (2022). Leadership selection: Can changing the default break the glass ceiling? *The Leadership Quarterly*, 33(2), 101563. doi:10.1016/j.leaqua.2021.101563

Essers, C., Pio, E., Verduijn, K., & Bensliman, N. (2021). Navigating belonging as a Muslim Moroccan female entrepreneur. *Journal of Small Business Management*, 59(6), 1250–1278. doi:10.1080/00472778.2020.1769989

Esuruku, R. S. (2011). Beyond masculinity: Gender, conflict and post-conflict reconstruction in Northern Uganda. *Journal of Science and Sustainable Development*, 4(1), 25–40. doi:10.4314/jssd.v4i1.3

Etang Ndip, A. (2020). *Poverty & Equity Brief.* World Bank., https://databankfiles.worldbank.org/public/ddpext_download/poverty/33EF03BB-9722-4AE2-ABC7-AA2972D68AFE/Global_POVEQ_SSA.pdf

Fattoracci, E. S. M., & King, D. D. (2022). The need for understanding and addressing microaggressions in the workplace. *Perspectives on Psychological Science*, 18(4), 174569162211338. doi:10.1177/17456916221133825 PMID:36379041

Fauzi, M. A., Sapuan, N. M., & Zainudin, N. M. (2023). Women and female entrepreneurship: Past, present, and future trends in developing countries. *Entrepreneurial Business and Economics Review*, 11(3), 57–75. doi:10.15678/EBER.2023.110304

Fazio, R. H., & Olson, M. A. (2003). Implicit measures in social cognition research: Their meaning and use. *Annual review of psychology*, 54(1), 297-327. doi: s10.1146/annurev.psych.54.101601.145225

Felce, D., & Perry, J. (1995). Quality of life: Its definition and measurement. *Research in Developmental Disabilities*, 16(1), 51–74. doi:10.1016/0891-4222(94)00028-8 PMID:7701092

Female Wave of Change. (2022). *Female Wave of Change: Equality.* https://www.facebook.com/groups/femalewaveofchange

Fernández-Aballí Altamirano, A. (2016). Where is Paulo Freire? *The International Communication Gazette*, 78(7), 677–683. doi:10.1177/1748048516655722

Fernandez, M., & Menon, M. (2022). Media influences on gender stereotypes. *The International Journal of Social Sciences (Islamabad), 10*(2), 121–125.

Ferris, E. E., & Martin, S. F. (2019). The global compacts on refugees and for safe, orderly and regular migration: Introduction to the special issue. *International Migration (Geneva, Switzerland), 57*(6), 5–18. doi:10.1111/imig.12668

Figueiredo, N., Patricio, L. D., & Ferreira, J. J. (2023). Female entrepreneurship drivers: Entrepreneurial intention, performance, and outcomes. In A. D. Daniel & Cristina Fernandes (Eds.), Female entrepreneurship as a driving force of economic growth and social change, 16-38. IGI Global.

Figueras, I.C. (2008). *Women in Politics: Evidence from the Indian States*. Department of Economics, Universidad Carlos III de Madrid.

Finnan, C. R. (1982). Community influences on the occupational adaptation of Vietnamese refugees. *Anthropological Quarterly, 55*(3), 161–169. doi:10.2307/3318025

Firat, M. Z., Kulakaç, Ö., Öncel, S., & Akcan, A. (2009). Menstrual Attitude Questionnaire: Confirmatory and exploratory factor analysis with Turkish samples. *Journal of Advanced Nursing, 65*(3), 652–662. doi:10.1111/j.1365-2648.2008.04919.x PMID:19222663

Fiske, S. T., Bersoff, D. N., Borgida, E., Deaux, K., & Heilman, M. (1991). Social science research on trial: Use of sex stereotyping research in Price Waterhouse v. Hopkins. *The American Psychologist, 46*(10), 1049–1060. doi:10.1037/0003-066X.46.10.1049

Flanagan, J. C. (1978). A research approach to improving our quality of life. *The American Psychologist, 33*(2), 138–147. doi:10.1037/0003-066X.33.2.138

Fleming, K., Foody, M., & Murphy, C. (2020). Using the implicit relational assessment procedure (IRAP) to examine implicit gender stereotypes in science, technology, engineering and maths (STEM). *The Psychological Record, 70*(3), 459–469. doi:10.1007/s40732-020-00401-6

Foa, R. (2009). Social and governance dimensions of climate change: implications for policy. *World Bank Policy Research Working Paper*, (4939).

Fonseca, R., Mullen, K. J., Zamarro, G., & Zissimopoulos, J. (2012). What explains the gender gap in financial literacy? The role of household decision making. *The Journal of Consumer Affairs, 46*(1), 90–106. doi:10.1111/j.1745-6606.2011.01221.x PMID:23049140

Forbes. (2022). Bias Holds Women Back. *Forbes*. https://www.forbes.com/sites/andiekramer/2022/02/24/bias-holds-women-back/?sh=6d0f775d3f09

Forbes, G. (1999). *Women in Modern India*. Cambridge University Press.

Frank, S. E. (2020). Queering menstruation: Trans and non-binary identity and body politics. *Sociological Inquiry, 90*(2), 371–404. doi:10.1111/soin.12355

Frola, A., Delprato, M., & Chudgar, A. (2024). Lack of educational access, women's empowerment and spatial education inequality for the Eastern and Western Africa regions. *International Journal of Educational Development, 104*, 102939. doi:10.1016/j.ijedudev.2023.102939

Fukuyama, F. (1995). Social Capital and the Global Economy. *Foreign Affairs, 74*(5), 89-103.

Fund, G. G., & UNDP-UNEP Poverty Environment Initiative. (2015). Gender and climate change: evidence and experience. *Gender Climate Brief*.

Compilation of References

G.O.I. (2000). *National Population Policy*. Ministry of Health & Family Welfare.

G.O.I. (2001). *Census Report*. Office of the Registrar General and Census Commissioner.

G.O.I. (2002). *National Human Development Report, 2001*. Planning Commission.

G.O.I. (2005). *National Family Health Survey – III*. Ministry of Health and Family Welfare, New Delhi.

G.O.I. (2009). *Gendering Human Development Indices: Recasting the Gender Development Index and Gender Empowerment Measure for India: A Summary Report*. Ministry of Woman and Child Welfare.

Galsanjigmed, E., & Sekiguchi, T. (2023). Challenges Women Experience in Leadership Careers: An Integrative Review. *Merits*, *3*(2), 366–389. doi:10.3390/merits3020021

Gandhi, M. (1993). *The Story of My Experiments with Truth*. Beacon Press.

Gantela, S., & Choppara, S. (2015). Severity and frequency of premenstrual syndrome in college girls aged 18-25 years. *Journal of Evolution of Medical and Dental Sciences*, *4*(87), 15228–15233. doi:10.14260/jemds/2015/2164

Garg, S., & Anand, T. (2015). Menstruation related myths in India: Strategies for combating it. *Journal of Family Medicine and Primary Care*, *4*(2), 184–186. doi:10.4103/2249-4863.154627 PMID:25949964

Garg, S., Sharma, N., & Sahay, R. (2001). Socio-cultural aspects of menstruation in an urban slum in Delhi, India. *Reproductive Health Matters*, *9*(17), 16–25. doi:10.1016/S0968-8080(01)90004-7 PMID:11468832

Ghimire, P. R., Devkota, N., Marasini, T., Khanal, G., Deuja, J., & Khadka, U. (2024). Does joint land ownership empower rural women socio-economically? Evidence from Eastern Nepal. *Land Use Policy*, *138*, 107052. doi:10.1016/j.landusepol.2024.107052

Gioli, G., & Milan, A. (2018). Gender, migration and (global) environmental change. In *Routledge handbook of environmental displacement and migration* (pp. 135–150). Routledge. doi:10.4324/9781315638843-11

Gittelsohn, J. (Ed.). (1994). *Listening to women talk about their health: Issues and evidence from India*. Har-Anand Publications., doi:10.1080/13691058.2011.644065

Global Entrepreneurship Report . (2023). Global Entrepreneurship Monitor. https://www.gemconsortium.org/reports/womens-entrepreneurship

Global Land Tool Network (GLTN). (2023). *Land, Women Empowerment and Socioeconomic Development in the Arab Region. Evidence-based Perspectives*. GLTN. https://gltn.net/download/land-women-empowerment-and-socioeconomic-development-in-the-arab-region-evidence-based-perspectives/

Gluck, S., & Patai, D. (1991). *Women's words: The feminist practice of oral history*. Routledge.

Goker, A., Artunc-Ulkumen, B., Aktenk, F., & Ikiz, N. (2015). Premenstrual syndrome in Turkish medical students and their quality of life. *Journal of Obstetrics & Gynaecology*, *35*(3), 275–278. doi:10.3109/01443615.2014.948820 PMID:25140580

Goldstein-Ferber, S., & Granot, M. (2006). The association between somatization and perceived ability: Roles in dysmenorrhea among Israeli Arab adolescents. *Psychosomatic Medicine*, *68*(1), 136–142. doi:10.1097/01.psy.0000197644.95292.00 PMID:16449424

Goleman, D. (1998). *Working with Emotional Intelligence*. Random House.

Gómez-Leal, R., Holzer, A. A., Bradley, C., Fernández-Berrocal, P., & Patti, J. (2021). The relationship between emotional intelligence and leadership in school leaders: A systematic review. *Cambridge Journal of Education*, 1–21.

Gonçalves, V. N., Ponchio, M. C., & Basílio, R. G. (2021). Women's financial well-being: A systematic literature review and directions for future research. *International Journal of Consumer Studies*, *45*(4), 824–843. doi:10.1111/ijcs.12673

González, M. J., Cortina, C., & Rodríguez, J. (2019). The role of gender stereotypes in hiring: A field experiment. *European Sociological Review*, *35*(2), 187–204. doi:10.1093/esr/jcy055

Gordon, K., Auten, J. N., Gordon, D., & Rook, A. (2019). *Linking behavioral styles of leaders to organizational success: Using the DISC model to Grow Behavioral Awareness. International Journal of Adult Vocational Education and Technology (IJAVET), 10(1)*. IGI Global. doi:10.4018/IJAVET.2019010104

Gordon, L. W. (1987). Southeast Asian refugee migration to the United States. *Center for Migration Studies Special Issues*, *5*(3), 153–173. doi:10.1111/j.2050-411X.1987.tb00959.x

Gough, B., Robertson, S., & Robinson, M. (2016). Men, 'masculinity' and mental health: Critical reflections. In *Handbook on gender and health* (pp. 134–147). Edward Elgar Publishing. doi:10.4337/9781784710866.00018

Gouldner, A. (1960). The Norm of Reciprocity: A Preliminary Statement. *American Sociological Review*, *25*(2), 161–178. doi:10.2307/2092623

Government of India. (1955). *Report of the Committee on the Status of Women in India*. Retrieved from. [URL]

Grabe, S., Grose, R. G., & Dutt, A. (2015). Women's land ownership and relationship power: A mixed methods approach to understanding structural inequities and violence against women. *Psychology of Women Quarterly*, *39*(1), 7–19. doi:10.1177/0361684314533485

Gradim, A. C., & Daniel, A. D. (2023). Female entrepreneurship in the age of social media: A research agenda. In A. D. Daniel & Cristina Fernandes (Eds.), Female entrepreneurship as a driving force of economic growth and social change, 1-15. IGI Global. doi:10.4018/978-1-6684-7669-7.ch001

Greene, R., & Dalton, K. (1953). The premenstrual syndrome. *British Medical Journal*, *1*(4818), 1007–1014. doi:10.1136/bmj.1.4818.1007 PMID:13032605

Greenwald, A. G., & Banaji, M. R. (1995). Implicit social cognition: Attitudes, self-esteem, and stereotypes. *Psychological Review*, *102*(1), 4–27. doi:10.1037/0033-295X.102.1.4 PMID:7878162

Greenwald, A. G., Poehlman, T. A., Uhlmann, E. L., & Banaji, M. R. (2009). Understanding and using the Implicit Association Test: III. Meta-analysis of predictive validity. *Journal of Personality and Social Psychology*, *97*(1), 17–41. doi:10.1037/a0015575 PMID:19586237

Gregory, D. (2017). *Social Enterprise Landscape In Morocco*. British Council. https://www.britishcouncil.org/sites/default/files/social_enterprise_landscape_in_morocco.pdf

Griffeth, L. L., Malik, R. F., Charas, S., & Randall, N. (2021). Sponsorship: An intervention to accelerate women's career velocity. *The IUP Journal of Soft Skills*, *15*(3), 7–22.

Grose, R. G., & Grabe, S. (2014). Sociocultural attitudes surrounding menstruation and alternative menstrual products: The explanatory role of self-objectification. *Health Care for Women International*, *35*(6), 677–694. doi:10.1080/07399332.2014.888721 PMID:24527840

Gruneau, M. F. (2021). The persistence of social norms, family formation, and gender balance in politics. *Politics & Gender*, *18*(3), 1–33.

Gudjonsson, S., Kristinsson, K., & Minelgaite, I. (2022). Follow us, not? Gender differences in financial literacy within the global leader of gender equality. *Entrepreneurship and Sustainability Issues*, *10*(2), 351–361. doi:10.9770/jesi.2022.10.2(21)

Guvenc, G., Kilic, A., Akyuz, A., & Ustunsoz, A. (2012). Premenstrual syndrome and attitudes toward menstruation in a sample of nursing students. *Journal of Psychosomatic Obstetrics and Gynaecology*, *33*(3), 106–111. doi:10.3109/0167482X.2012.685906 PMID:22901294

Halbreich, U. (2003). The etiology, biology, and evolving pathology of premenstrual syndromes. *Psychoneuroendocrinology*, *28*, 55–99. doi:10.1016/S0306-4530(03)00097-0 PMID:12892990

Halonen, T. (2023). *Securing women's land rights for increased gender equality, food security and economic empowerment*. United Nations. https://www.un.org/en/un-chronicle/securing-women%E2%80%99s-land-rights-increased-gender-equality-food-security-and-economic

Haque, A., & Zulfiqar, M. (2016). Women's economic empowerment through financial literacy, financial attitude and financial wellbeing. *International Journal of Business and Social Science*, *7*(3), 78–88.

Hardy, C., & Hunter, M. S. (2021). Premenstrual symptoms and work: Exploring female staff experiences and recommendations for workplaces. *International Journal of Environmental Research and Public Health*, *18*(7), 3647. doi:10.3390/ijerph18073647 PMID:33807463

Harper, S. (2011). Migration and global environmental change. *PD7: Environment, migration and the demographic deficit*.

Hartman, S., Backmann, J., Newman, A., Brykman, K. M., & Pidduck, R. J. (2022). Psychological resilience of entrepreneurs: A review and agenda for future research. *Journal of Small Business Management*, *60*(5), 1041–1079. doi:10.1080/00472778.2021.2024216

Heilman, M. E., Caleo, S., & Manzi, F. (2024). Women at work: Pathways from gender stereotypes to gender bias and discrimination. *Annual Review of Organizational Psychology and Organizational Behavior*, *11*(1), 165–192. doi:10.1146/annurev-orgpsych-110721-034105

Hekking, M. (2019). Two Moroccan [Most Influential Young Africans Ranking. Morocco World News.]. *Women*, 100.

Hentschel, T., Heilman, M. E., & Peus, C. V. (2019). The multiple dimensions of gender stereotypes: A current look at men's and women's characterizations of others and themselves. *Frontiers in Psychology*, *10*(11), 11. doi:10.3389/fpsyg.2019.00011 PMID:30761032

Hickey, G. (2005). 'This is American get punished': Unpacking narratives of Southeast Asian refugees in the US. *Intercultural Education*, *16*(1), 25–40. doi:10.1080/14636310500061656

Hill, C., Miller, K., Benson, K., & Handley, G. (2016). *Barriers and Bias: The Status of Women in Leadership*. American Association of University Women.

Hoerster, K. D., Chrisler, J. C., & Rose, J. G. (2003). Attitudes toward and experience with menstruation in the US and India. *Women & Health*, *38*(3), 77–95. doi:10.1300/J013v38n03_06 PMID:14664306

Hofstede, G. (1980). Motivation, leadership, and organization: Do American theories apply abroad? *Organizational Dynamics*, *9*(1), 42–63. doi:10.1016/0090-2616(80)90013-3

Hogg, M. A., & Vaughan, G. M. (2014). Social Psychology 7th Eds. *Harlow: Pearson Education Limited*. *12* (10), https://www.scirp.org/reference/referencespapers?referenceid=3097274

Hoogensen, G., & Solheim, B. O. (2006). *Women in power: World leaders since 1960*. Bloomsbury Publishing USA.

Hoyt, C. L., & Simon, S. (2024). Social psychological approaches to women and leadership theory. In *Handbook of research on gender and leadership* (pp. 65–83). Edward Elgar Publishing. doi:10.4337/9781035306893.00015

Huis, M. A., Hansen, N., Otten, S., & Lensink, R. (2017). A three-dimensional model of women's empowerment: Implications in the field of microfinance and future directions. *Frontiers in Psychology*, 8, 1678. doi:10.3389/fpsyg.2017.01678 PMID:29033873

Hu, L. (2021). Self as brand and brand as self: A 2x2 dimension conceptual model of self-branding in a digital economy. *Journal of Internet Commerce*, 20(3), 355–370. doi:10.1080/15332861.2021.1907170

Hung, A., Yoong, J., & Brown, E. (2012). *Empowering women through financial awareness and education.*

Hunter, L. M., & David, E. (2009). *Climate change and migration: Considering the gender dimensions.* University of Colorado, Institute of Behavioral Science.

Hutchison, K. (2020). Four types of gender bias affecting women surgeons and their cumulative impact. *Journal of Medical Ethics*, 46(4), 236–241. doi:10.1136/medethics-2019-105552 PMID:32229595

Hwang, J. H., & Sung, M. H. (2016). Impacts of menstrual attitudes, premenstrual syndrome and stress on burnout among clinical nurses. *Korean Journal of Women Health Nursing*, 22(4), 233–240. doi:10.4069/kjwhn.2016.22.4.233 PMID:37684872

Ibarra, H., Ely, R., & Kolb, D. (2013). Women rising: The unseen barriers. *Harvard Business Review*. https://hbr.org/2013/09/women-rising-the-unseen-barriers

Ibreck, R. (2023). Protecting Women from Violence in the United Nations Protection of Civilians Sites, South Sudan? *Journal of Intervention and Statebuilding*, 18(1), 61–80. doi:10.1080/17502977.2023.2215604

IDB (2019). *Development in the Americas: Laying the Groundwork for a Sustainable Future.* IDB.

Intergovernmental Panel on Climate Change (IPCC). (2019). *Special Report on Climate Change and Land.* IPCC.

Inter-Parliamentary Union. (2022). *Women & Politics, 2022.* IPU. https://data.ipu.org/women-ranking?month=3&year=2022

Irshad, A., Mehmood, S., Noor, R., Mumtaz, S., Saleem, M., & Laique, T. (2022). Frequency of Premenstrual Syndrome and Its Association with Quality of Life among University Students. *Pakistan Journal of Medical & Health Sciences*, 16(02), 521–521. doi:10.53350/pjmhs22162521

Isaga, N. (2018). Start-up motives and challenges facing female entrepreneurs in Tanzania. *International Journal of Gender and Entrepreneurship*, 11(2), 102–119. doi:10.1108/IJGE-02-2018-0010

Ismail, K. H., & Mohammed-Ali, K. B. (2012). Quality of life in patients with acne in Erbil city. *Health and Quality of Life Outcomes*, 10(1), 1–4. doi:10.1186/1477-7525-10-60 PMID:22672256

Ito, A., & Bligh, M. (2024). Organizational processes and systems that affect women in leadership. In *Handbook of Research on Gender and Leadership* (pp. 292-311). Edward Elgar Publishing. doi:10.4337/9781035306893.00030

Jahanfar, S., Lye, M. S., & Krishnarajah, I. S. (2011). The heritability of premenstrual syndrome. *Twin Research and Human Genetics*, 14(5), 433–436. doi:10.1375/twin.14.5.433 PMID:21962135

Jang, H. J., & Sung, M. H. (2018). Impact of menstrual attitudes, premenstrual syndrome, and stress response on quality of life among nursing students. *Korean Journal of Women Health Nursing*, 24(4), 346–354. doi:10.4069/kjwhn.2018.24.4.346 PMID:37684941

Janiger, O., Riffenburgh, R., & Kersh, R. (1972). Cross cultural study of premenstrual symptoms. *Psychosomatics*, *13*(4), 226–235. doi:10.1016/S0033-3182(72)71414-0 PMID:4677677

Jayaweera, S. (1997). Higher education and the economic and social empowerment of women—The Asian experience. *Compare: A Journal of Comparative Education*, *27*(3), 245–261. doi:10.1080/0305792970270302 PMID:12348990

Jeanes, R. (2013). Educating through sport? Examining HIV/AIDS education and sport-for-development through the perspectives of Zambian young people. *Sport Education and Society*, *18*(3), 388–406. doi:10.1080/13573322.2011.579093

Jehhad, F., & Haoucha, M. (2023). Women empowerment through social entrepreneurship in Morocco: A case study of Al Nour Marrakech. *International Journal of Trade and Management, 1*(2). https://ricg-encgt.ma/

Jennings, J. E., & McDougald, M. S. (2007). Work-family interface experiences and coping strategies: Implications for entrepreneurship research and practice. *Academy of Management Review*, *32*(3), 747–760. doi:10.5465/amr.2007.25275510

Jesuthasan, J., Witte, Z., & Oert-Prigione, S. (2019). Health-related needs and barriers for forcibly displaced women: A systematic Review. *Gender and the Genome*, *3*, 1–8. doi:10.1177/2470289719895283

Jha, P., Makkad, M., & Mittal, S. (2018). Performance-oriented factors for women entrepreneurs–a scale development perspective. *Journal of Entrepreneurship in Emerging Economies*, *10*(2), 329–360. doi:10.1108/JEEE-08-2017-0053

Jones, C. S., & Hartley, N. T. (2013). Comparing correlations between four-quadrant and five-factor personality assessments. *American Journal of Business Education*, *6*(4), 459–470. doi:10.19030/ajbe.v6i4.7945

Joshi, A., Kurien, E., Misra, A., Rajeshwari, M., & Biswas, S. (1998). *Socio-cultural implications of menstruation and menstrual problems on rural women's lives and treatment seeking behaviour*. Operations Research Group, Baroda. (Unpublished Ford Foundation supported study).

Kabbaj, M. (2020). *Women's Rights in Post-2011 Morocco: The Divergences Between Institutions and Values [Policy Paper]*. Konrad-Adenauer-Stiftung (KAS). https://www.kas.de/documents/276068/8307005/KAS%2BMaroc%2BPolicy%2BPaper%2BNov%2B2020%2B-Women%E2%80%99s%2BRights%2Bin%2BPost-2011%2BMorocco%2BThe%2BDivergences%2BBetween%2BInstitutions%2Band%2BValues.pdf/9aacf4ba-a1ea-3e66-b70b-787498b50d12?t=1607504069145&version=1.0

Kabeer, N. (1997). tactics and trade-offs: Revisiting the links between gender and poverty. *IDS Bulletin*, *28*(3), 1–13. doi:10.1111/j.1759-5436.1997.mp28003001.x

Kabeer, N. (1999). Resources, agency, achievements: Reflections on the measurement of women's empowerment. *Development and Change*, *30*(3), 435–464. doi:10.1111/1467-7660.00125

Kabeer, N. (2003). *Gender Mainstreaming in Poverty Eradication and the Millennium Development Goals: A handbook for policy-makers and other stakeholders*. Commonwealth Secretariat. doi:10.14217/9781848598133-en

Kabeer, N. (2005). Gender equality and women's empowerment: A critical analysis of the third millennium development goal 1. *Gender and Development*, *13*(1), 13–24. doi:10.1080/13552070512331332273

Kabeer, N. (2010). Women's empowerment, development interventions and the management of information flows. *ids. Bulletin*, *41*(6), 105–113.

Kabeer, N. (2015). Tracking the gender politics of the Millennium Development Goals: Struggles for interpretive power in the international development agenda. *Third World Quarterly*, *36*(2), 377–395. doi:10.1080/01436597.2015.1016656

Kabeer, N. (2017). Economic pathways to women's empowerment and active citizenship: What does the evidence from Bangladesh tell us? *The Journal of Development Studies*, *53*(5), 649–663. doi:10.1080/00220388.2016.1205730

Kadoya, Y., & Khan, M. S. R. (2020). What determines financial literacy in Japan? *Journal of Pension Economics and Finance*, *19*(3), 353–371. doi:10.1017/S1474747218000379

Kandeel, A. (2020). *Let justice be done: Respect for female land rights in the Middle East and North Africa*. MEI. https://www.mei.edu/publications/let-justice-be-done-respect-female-land-rights-middle-east-and-north-africa

Kan, M. Y., Sullivan, O., & Gershuny, J. (2011). Gender convergence in domestic work: Discerning the effects of interactional and institutional barriers from large-scale data. *Sociology*, *45*(2), 234–251. doi:10.1177/0038038510394014

Kantero, R. (1971). A statistical analysis of the menstrual patterns of 8,000 Finish girls and their mothers. The age of menarche in Finish girls in 1969. *Acta Obstetricia et Gynecologica Scandinavica*, *14*, 1–36.

Karam, A. (2010). Women in War and Peacebuilding: The Roads Traversed the Challenges Ahead. *International Feminist Journal of Politics*, *3*(1), 2–25. doi:10.1080/14616740010019820

Katjiukua, C. R., Simon, N., Chatterjee, A., & Akinola, A. (2020). Prevalence and knowledge of premenstrual syndrome among adolescent girls in India. *International Journal of Community Medicine and Public Health*, *7*(12), 5169–5181. doi:10.18203/2394-6040.ijcmph20205202

Kebede, J., Selvanathan, S., & Naranpanawa, A. (2024). Financial inclusion and monetary policy effectiveness in a monetary union: Heterogenous panel approach. *Economics of Transition and Institutional Change*, ecot.12402. doi:10.1111/ecot.12402

Keho, Y. (2009). Social Capital in Situations of Conflict: A Case Study from Côte d'Ivoire (Pp. 158-180). *African Research Review*, *3*(3), 158–180. doi:10.4314/afrrev.v3i3.47522

Kelsen, H. (1951). Science and politics. *The American Political Science Review*, *45*(3), 641–661. doi:10.2307/1951155

Kendler, K. S., Karkowski, L. M., Corey, L. A., & Neale, M. C. (1998). Longitudinal population-based twin study of retrospectively reported premenstrual symptoms and lifetime major depression. *The American Journal of Psychiatry*, *155*(9), 1234–1240. doi:10.1176/ajp.155.9.1234 PMID:9734548

Kessel, B. (2000). Premenstrual syndrome: Advances in diagnosis and treatment. *Obstetrics and Gynecology Clinics of North America*, *27*(3), 625–639. doi:10.1016/S0889-8545(05)70160-1 PMID:10958008

Khadka, M. (2017). *Darfur crisis: analyzing the issues of internally displaced persons (IDPs) in Darfur* [Doctoral dissertation].

Khalid, Z., & Naqvi, I. (2022). *Premenstrual Syndrome and Quality of Life Among Adolescent Girls: Exploration of Prevalent Home Remedies*.

Khamis, Z. K. (2022). The Social Learning Theory and Gender Representations in Leadership Positions. A case of Health Sector in Tanzania. *Journal of Social and Development Sciences*, *13*(4 (S)), 24–33. doi:10.22610/jsds.v13i4(S).3318

Khan, Z., Nawaz, A., & Khan, I. (2016). Leadership Theories and Styles: A Literature Review. *Journal of Resources Development and Management*, 1-7.

Khan, R. W. (2009). *Women in Ancient India*. Goodword Books.

Khodijah, A. S., Pekerti, R. D., Wara, A. A., & Rahmayanti, A. J. M. H. (2024). Women's Perceptions of Glass Ceiling In The Accounting Profession In Indonesia. *Journal of accounting Science/jas. umsida. ac. id/index. php/jas January*, *8*(1), 58.

King, T. L., Scovelle, A. J., Meehl, A., Milner, A. J., & Priest, N. (2021). Gender stereotypes and biases in early childhood: A systematic review. *Australasian Journal of Early Childhood*, *46*(2), 112–125. doi:10.1177/1836939121999849

Kırcan, N., Ergin, F., Adana, F., & Arslantaş, H. (2012). The Prevalance of Premenstrual Syndrome in Nursery Students and its Relationship with Quality of Life. *Meandros Medical and Dental Journal*, *13*(1), 19–25.

Kısa, S., Zeyneloğlu, S., & Güler, N. (2012). Prevalence of premenstrual syndrome among university students and affecting factors. *Gümüşhane University Journal of Health Sciences*, *1*(4), 284–297.

Knapman, C., & Sutz, P. (2015). Reconsidering approaches to women's land rights in sub-Saharan Africa. *IIED Briefing Paper-International Institute for Environment and Development*, (17310).

Koczberski, G. (1998). Women in development: A critical analysis. *Third World Quarterly*, *19*(3), 395–410. doi:10.1080/01436599814316

Kolbe, K. (2009). Self-Efficacy Results from Exercising Control over Personal Conative Strengths. Wisdom of the Ages.

Kolovich, L., & Ndoye, A. (2023). Implications of Gender Inequality for Growth in Morocco. *Morocco's Quest for Stronger and Inclusive Growth*, 167.

Komter, A. E. (2005). *Social solidarity and the gift*. Cambridge University Press.

Kooser, A. (2021). Empowered women change the world. *Opportunity International*. https://opportunity.org/news/blog/2017/03/empowered-women-change-the-world

Korber, S., & McNaughron, R. B. (2018). Resilience and entrepreneurship: A systematic literature review. *International Journal of Entrepreneurial Behaviour & Research*, *24*(7), 112–1154. doi:10.1108/IJEBR-10-2016-0356

Kosten, D. (2018). *Immigrants as economic contributors: Immigrant entrepreneurs*. National Immigration Forum., https://immigrationforum.org/article/immigrants-as-economic-contributors-immigrant-entrepreneurs/

Kraus, S., Filser, M., O'Dwyer, M. et al. (2014). Social Entrepreneurship: An exploratory citation analysis. *Rev Manag Sci, 8*(2), 275–292. doi:10.1007/s11846-013-0104-6

Kuehnast, K. R., & Dudwick, N. (2004). Better a hundred friends than a hundred rubles?: social networks in transition--the Kyrgyz Republic, 41181(4). World Bank Publications.

Kulkami, S. (2014). RISE to the challenge: Immigrant entrepreneurship in Louisville. *Bridges*, 5-7.

Kumar, A., & Sahoo, S. (2024). Caste, gender, and intersectionality in stream choice: Evidence from higher secondary education in India. *Education Economics*, *32*(1), 20–46. doi:10.1080/09645292.2023.2170983

Kumar, R. (1993). *The History of Doing: An Illustrated Account of Movements for Women's Rights and Feminism in India, 1800-1990*. Zubaan.

Kumar, R. (2009). Mapping the Terrain of Indian Feminism: Colonial Legacies. [DOI]. *Signs (Chicago, Ill.)*, *35*(3), 559–561.

Kurtaran, A. T., Aydin, A., & Yeşildağ, A. Y. (2024). Glass Ceiling Syndrome: A Perspective of Women Working in Health Institutions. *Ege Academic Review*, *24*(1), 71–84.

Lafont, G. (2023). *Women in business*. LinkedIn. https://www.linkedin.com/pulse/women-business-gloria-lafont/

Lair, D. J., Sullivan, K., & Cheney, G. (2005). Marketization and the recasting of the professional self: The rhetoric and ethics of personal branding. *Management Communication Quarterly*, *18*(3), 307–343. doi:10.1177/0893318904270744

Lama, P., Hamza, M., & Wester, M. (2021). Gendered dimensions of migration in relation to climate change. *Climate and Development*, *13*(4), 326–336. doi:10.1080/17565529.2020.1772708

Lancastle, D., Kopp Kallner, H., Hale, G., Wood, B., Ashcroft, L., & Driscoll, H. (2023). Development of a brief menstrual quality of life measure for women with heavy menstrual bleeding. *BMC Women's Health, 23*(1), 105. doi:10.1186/s12905-023-02235-0 PMID:36918914

Land Portal. (2000). *Land Ownership and Women's Empowerment: A Comprehensive Review*. Land Portal. https://landportal.org/node/55028

Lastarria-Cornhiel, S., & García-Frías, Z. (2005). *Gender and land rights: Findings and lessons from country studies.*

Lau, D., Brown, S., Budimir, M., Sneddon, A., Upadhyay, S., & Shakya, P. (2019). *Gender transformative early warning systems: Experiences from Nepal and Peru.*

Lecoutere, E., Achandi, E. L., Ampaire, L., Fischer, G., Gumucio, T., Najjar, D., & Singaraju, N. (2023). Fostering an Enabling Environment for Equality and Empowerment in Agri-food Systems. *Global Food Security, 40*(2). doi:10.1016/j.gfs.2023.100735

Lee, G. Y. (2020). *Refugees from Laos*. Gary Yia Lee. https://www.garyyialee.com/history-refugees-from-laos

Lee, E., & Yang, S. (2020). Do depression, fatigue, and body esteem influence premenstrual symptoms in nursing students? *Korean Journal of Women Health Nursing, 26*(3), 231–239. doi:10.4069/kjwhn.2020.09.10 PMID:36313171

Lee, I.-C., Hu, F., & Li, W.-Q. (2020). Cultural factors facilitating or inhibiting the support for traditional household gender roles. *Journal of Cross-Cultural Psychology, 51*(5), 333–352. doi:10.1177/0022022120929089

LegalZoom. (2020). *86 key entrepreneur statistics for 2020 and beyond*. Legal Zoom. https://www.legalzoom.com/articles/entrepreneur-statistics

Le, K., & Nguyen, M. (2021). How education empowers women in developing countries. *The B.E. Journal of Economic Analysis & Policy, 21*(2), 511–536. doi:10.1515/bejeap-2020-0046

Lemmon, G. T., & Vogelstein, R. (2017). *Building inclusive economies: How women's economic advancement promotes sustainable growth*. Council On Foreign Relations, Inc. https://cdn.cfr.org/sites/default/files/report_pdf/Discussion_Paper_Lemmon_Vogelstein_Women_Economies_OR.pdf

Lete, I., Dueñas, J. L., Serrano, I., Doval, J. L., Martínez-Salmeán, J., Coll, C., Pérez-Campos, E., & Arbat, A. (2011). Attitudes of Spanish women toward premenstrual symptoms, premenstrual syndrome and premenstrual dysphoric disorder: Results of a nationwide survey. *European Journal of Obstetrics, Gynecology, and Reproductive Biology, 159*(1), 115–118. doi:10.1016/j.ejogrb.2011.06.041 PMID:21775045

Levitt, E. E., & Lubin, B. (1967). Some personality factors associated with menstrual complaints and menstrual attitude. *Journal of Psychosomatic Research, 11*(3), 267–270. doi:10.1016/0022-3999(67)90020-7 PMID:6076919

Light, I., & Gold, S. J. (2000). *Ethnic economies*. Academic Press.

Lilienfeld, S. O. (2017). Microaggressions: Strong claims, inadequate evidence. *Perspectives on Psychological Science, 12*(1), 138–169. doi:10.1177/1745691616659391 PMID:28073337

Link, A. N., & Strong, D. R. (2016). Gender and entrepreneurship: An annotated bibliography. *Foundations and Trends in Entrepreneurship, 12*(4-5), 287–441. doi:10.1561/0300000068

Lloyd, C. B., Mensch, B. S., & Clark, W. H. (2000). The effects of primary school quality on school dropout among Kenyan girls and boys. *Comparative Education Review, 44*(2), 113–147. doi:10.1086/447600

Lobel, L.-M., Kroger, H., & Tibubos, A. N. (2022). How migration strategies shape susceptibility of individuals' loneliness to social isolation. *International Journal of Public Health, 67*, 1604576. doi:10.3389/ijph.2022.1604576 PMID:36561278

Logue, C. M., & Moos, R. H. (1986). Perimenstrual symptoms: Prevalence and risk factors. *Psychosomatic Medicine*, *48*(6), 388–414. doi:10.1097/00006842-198607000-00002 PMID:3529156

López-Jornet, P., & Camacho-Alonso, F. (2010). Quality of life in patients with oral lichen planus. *Journal of Evaluation in Clinical Practice*, *16*(1), 111–113. doi:10.1111/j.1365-2753.2009.01124.x PMID:20367822

Losocco, K. A., & Robinson, J. (1991). Barriers to women's small-business success in the United States. *Gender & Society*, *5*(4). https://www.jstor.org/stable/190098

Loury, G. C. (1987). Why should we care about group inequality? *Social Philosophy & Policy*, *5*(1), 249–271. doi:10.1017/S0265052500001345

Lukes, S. (2021). Power and rational choice. *Journal of Political Power*, *14*(2), 281–287. doi:10.1080/2158379X.2021.1900494

Lunsford, L. G., Crisp, G., Dolan, E. L., & Wuetherick, B. (2017). Mentoring in higher education. The SAGE handbook of mentoring, 20, 316-334.

Lusardi, A., & Mitchell, O. S. (2008). Planning and financial literacy: How do women fare? *The American Economic Review*, *98*(2), 413–417. doi:10.1257/aer.98.2.413

Lusardi, A., & Mitchell, O. S. (2014). The economic importance of financial literacy: Theory and evidence. American Economic Journal. *Journal of Economic Literature*, *52*(1), 5–44. doi:10.1257/jel.52.1.5 PMID:28579637

Lustyk, M. K. B., Gerrish, W. G., Shaver, S., & Keys, S. L. (2009). Cognitive-behavioral therapy for premenstrual syndrome and premenstrual dysphoric disorder: A systematic review. *Archives of Women's Mental Health*, *12*(2), 85–96. doi:10.1007/s00737-009-0052-y PMID:19247573

Lustyk, M. K. B., Widman, L., Paschane, A., & Ecker, E. (2004). Stress, quality of life and physical activity in women with varying degrees of premenstrual symptomatology. *Women & Health*, *39*(3), 35–44. doi:10.1300/J013v39n03_03 PMID:15256354

Lutz, H. L., Re, T. C., Brandt, J. A. A., & Garcia, R. (2023). Gender Bias toward Supervisors' Empowering Leadership Behavior. *Behavior and Social Issues*, 1-16.

Lu, Z. J. (2001). The relationship between menstrual attitudes and menstrual symptoms among Taiwanese women. *Journal of Advanced Nursing*, *33*(5), 621–628. doi:10.1046/j.1365-2648.2001.01705.x PMID:11298198

MacDonald, S. M. (2010). *Neither memsahibs nor missionaries: Western women who supported the Indian independence movement* (Doctoral dissertation, University of New Brunswick, Department of History).

Madsen, S. R., & Andrade, M. S. (2018). Unconscious gender bias: Implications for women's leadership development. *Journal of Leadership Studies*, *12*(1), 62–67. doi:10.1002/jls.21566

MahajanP. (2019). Women in Leadership: Comparing Developed (The UK) and the Developing (India) Corporate Economy. SSRN 3444165. doi:10.2139/ssrn.3444165

Mahbub, M. (2021, June). *Women Empowerment: Theory, Practice, Process, and Importance*. University of Dhaka.

Main, K. (2024). Small business statistics of 2024. *Forbes Advisor*. https://www.forbes.com/advisor/business/small-business-statistics/

Maity, M. S., & Shukla, P. (2023). Exploring Agency, Empowerment, And Identity In 'Rukmini: Krishna's Wife' By Saiswaroopa Iyer. *Journal of Namibian Studies: History Politics Culture*, *33*, 2940–2963.

Malapit, H. J. L. (2012). Are women more likely to be credit constrained? Evidence from low-income urban households in the Philippines. *Feminist Economics*, *18*(3), 81–108. doi:10.1080/13545701.2012.716161

Manal, D. S. (2020). *Women's Rights in Post-2011 Morocco: The Divergences Between Institutions and Values [Policy Paper]*. Konrad-Adenauer-Stiftung (KAS). https://www.kas.de/documents/276068/8307005/KAS%2BMaroc%2BPolicy%2BPaper%2BNov%2B2020%2B-Women%E2%80%99s%2BRights%2Bin%2BPost-2011%2BMorocco%2BThe%2BDivergences%2BBetween%2BInstitutions%2Band%2BValues.pdf/9aacf4ba-a1ea-3e66-b70b-787498b50d12?t=1607504069145&version=1.0

Mandal, K. C. (2013, May). Concept and Types of Women Empowerment. In *International Forum of Teaching & Studies, 9*(2).

Manello, A., Cisi, M., Devincienti, F., & Vannoni, D. (2020). Networking: A business for women. *Small Business Economics*, *55*(2), 329–348. doi:10.1007/s11187-019-00300-3

Mansab, M. (2023). Nurturing Sustainable Peace: Unveiling the Integral Role of Women in Rwanda's Peacebuilding Endeavors. *NUST Journal of International Peace and Stability*, *6*(2), 31–45. doi:10.37540/njips.v6i2.150

Marlow, S., & Al-Dajani, H. (2017). Critically evaluating contemporary entrepreneurship from a feminist perspective. In C. Essers, P. Dey, D. Tedmanson, & K. Verduyn (Eds.), *Critical perspectives on entrepreneurship: Challenging dominant discourses* (p. 179). Taylor & Francis. doi:10.4324/9781315675381-11

Martinez, D. A., & Marlow, S. (2017). Women entrepreneurs and their ventures: Complicating categories and contextualizing gender. In C. Henry, T. Nelson, & K. V. Lewis (Eds.), *The Rutledge Companion to Global Female Entrepreneurship*. Routledge. doi:10.4324/9781315794570-2

Masika, R. (Ed.). (2002). *Gender, development, and climate change*. Oxfam.

Masterson, V. (2022). *Here's what women's entrepreneurship looks like around the world*. The World Economic Forum. https://www.weforum.org/agenda/2022/07/women-entrepreneurs-gusto-gender/

Mate, S. E., McDonald, M., & Do, T. (2018). The barriers and enablers to career and leadership development: An exploration of women's stories in two work cultures. *The International Journal of Organizational Analysis*, 857–874.

Matharu, S. K., Changle, R., & Chowdhury, A. (2016). A study of motivational factors of women entrepreneurs. *The IUP Journal of Entrepreneurship Development*, *13*(1), 33–46.

Matney, A. E. (2022). *A Portraiture Study: Women Leaders Advocating Religious Freedom in India*. Johnson University.

Matsumoto, T., Asakura, H., & Hayashi, T. (2013). Biopsychosocial aspects of premenstrual syndrome and premenstrual dysphoric disorder. *Gynecological Endocrinology*, *29*(1), 67–73. doi:10.3109/09513590.2012.705383 PMID:22809066

McLeman, R. A., & Hunter, L. M. (2010). Migration in the context of vulnerability and adaptation to climate change: Insights from analogues. *Wiley Interdisciplinary Reviews: Climate Change*, *1*(3), 450–461. doi:10.1002/wcc.51 PMID:22022342

McLeman, R., & Smit, B. (2006). Migration as an adaptation to climate change. *Climatic Change*, *76*(1), 31–53. doi:10.1007/s10584-005-9000-7

Mearns, R. (2008). *Social dimensions of climate change: workshop report 2008*.

Mensah, M. S. B., & Derera, E. (2023). "Analysis of Ghana's and South Africa's women's entrepreneurship policies." *Women's Entrepreneurship Policy: A Global Perspective*: 214.

Mensah, M. S. B., & Derera, E. (2023). Feminist Critique of Ghana's Women's Entrepreneurship Policies. *JWEE*, (1-2), 1–31. doi:10.28934/jwee23.12.pp1-31

Mentorcli, Q. (2022). *Women's Mentorship Program*. Mentor Clinic. https://mentorcliq.com/women-leadership-program

Merriam, S. B., & Tisdell, E. J. (2015). *Qualitative research: A guide to design and implementation* (4th ed.). Wiley.

Meyer, N., & Mostert, C. (2016). Perceived barriers and success factors of female entrepreneurs enrolled in an entrepreneurial programme. *International Journal of Social Sciences and Humanity Studies*, *8*(1).

Miles, L., Granados, M. L., & Tweed, J. (2024, March 15). *Social Entrepreneurship, Empowerment of Women Experiencing Homelessness and Gender Equality*. Millennium Challenge Corporation; United States of America. Empowering Youth and Women in Morocco is Key to Development. https://www.mcc.gov/news-and-events/feature/feature-morocco-employability-and-land-compact-closeout/

Ministère de l'Agriculture et de la Réforme agraire. Office régional de la mise en valeur agricole du Gharb, 1987. Etude sur la législation et les structures agraires dans la zone d'action de l'ORMVAG, dossier IX: *Femme et propriété foncière*. Etude réalisée par l'Institut agronomique et vétérinaire Hassan II.

Minister, K. (1991). A feminist frame for the oral history interview. In S. Gluck & D. Patai (Eds.), *Women's words: The feminist practice of oral history* (pp. 27–41). Routledge.

Mir, A. H., & Dar, A. A. (Year). *Unveiling the Legacy: The History and Triumphs of Determined Queens in Ancient Kashmir*. Publisher.

Mishler, E. G. (1996). *Research interviewing: Context and narrative*. Harvard University Press.

Mishra, K., & Sam, A. G. (2016). Does women's land ownership promote their empowerment? Empirical evidence from Nepal. *World Development*, *78*, 360–371. doi:10.1016/j.worlddev.2015.10.003

Mitchell, A. (2002). *The Freedom to Remember: Narrative, Slavery, and Gender in Contemporary Black Women's Fiction*. Rutgers University Press.

Mohamed, M. (2023). Solidarity in Time of Armed Conflict. Women's Patterns of Solidarity in Internally Displaced Person (IDP) Camps in Darfur, Western Sudan. *The Journal of Social Encounters*, *7*(2), 5–23.

Mohanty, C. (1988). Under Western eyes: Feminist scholarship and colonial discourses. *Feminist Review*, *30*(1), 61–88. doi:10.1057/fr.1988.42

Mollaeva, E. A. (2017). Gender stereotypes and the role of women in higher education (Azerbaijan case study). *Education and Urban Society*, *50*(8), 747–763. doi:10.1177/0013124517713613

Molugulu, N., Tumkur, A. N. I. L., & Nilugal, K. C. (2016). Study of premenstrual syndrome among future healthcare professionals in Masterskill Global College. *International Journal of Pharmacy and Pharmaceutical Sciences*, *8*(2), 66–71.

Molyneux, M. (2000). Twentieth-century state formations in Latin America. *Hidden histories of gender and the State in Latin America*, 33-81.

Molyneux, M., & Molyneux, M. (2001). Mobilisation without emancipation? Women's interests, the state and revolution in Nicaragua (pp. 38-59). Palgrave Macmillan UK.

Molyneux, M. (1979). Beyond the domestic labour debate. *New Left Review*, *116*(3), 27.

Molyneux, M. (2002). Gender and the silences of social capital: Lessons from Latin America. *Development and Change*, *33*(2), 167–188. doi:10.1111/1467-7660.00246

Molyneux, M. (2005). Analysing women's movements. In *Feminist Visions of Development* (pp. 74–97). Routledge.

Monagle, L., Dan, A., Krogh, V., Jossa, F., Fannaro, E., & Trevisan, M. (1993). Perimenstrual symptom prevalence rates: An Italian-American comparison. *American Journal of Epidemiology*, *138*(12), 1070–1081. doi:10.1093/oxfordjournals.aje.a116825 PMID:8266909

Morrice, L. (2007). Lifelong learning and the social integration of refugees in the UK: The significance of social capital. *International Journal of Lifelong Education*, *26*(2), 155–172. doi:10.1080/02601370701219467

Mortola, J. F. (1993). Applications of gonadotropin-releasing hormone analogues in the treatment of premenstrual syndrome. *Clinical Obstetrics and Gynecology*, *36*(3), 753–763. doi:10.1097/00003081-199309000-00032 PMID:8403622

Moser, C. (2005). Has gender mainstreaming failed? A comment on international development agency experiences in the South. *International Feminist Journal of Politics*, *7*(4), 576–590. doi:10.1080/14616740500284573

Moser, C. O. (2021). From gender planning to gender transformation: Positionality, theory and practice in cities of the global South. *International Development Planning Review*, *43*(2), 205–229. doi:10.3828/idpr.2020.9

Mouline, S., Ozlu, O., & Herzog, L. (2022, January 19). A big step forward for women's leadership in Morocco. *World Bank Blogs*. https://blogs.worldbank.org/en/arabvoices/big-step-forward-womens-leadership-morocco

Moustakas, C. E. (1994). *Phenomenological research methods*. Sage Pub. doi:10.4135/9781412995658

Muhammad, S., Ximei, K., Saquib, S. E., & Foss, L. (2022). *Positive externality matters in the COVID-19 pandemic: The case of women informal businesses in District Mardan*. Pandemic Risk, Response, and Resilience., doi:10.1016/B978-0-323-99277-0.00009-7

Mukherjee, M. (2004). *Peasants in India's Non-Violent Revolution: Practice and Theory*. Sage Publications.

Muralidharan, K., & Prakash, N. (2017). Cycling to school: Increasing secondary school enrollment for girls in India. *American Economic Journal. Applied Economics*, *9*(3), 321–350. doi:10.1257/app.20160004

Muravyev, A., Talavera, O., & Schäfer, D. (2009). Entrepreneurs' gender and financial constraints: Evidence from international data. *Journal of Comparative Economics*, *37*(2), 270–286. doi:10.1016/j.jce.2008.12.001

Murithi, T. (2006). African approaches to building peace and social solidarity. *African Journal on Conflict Resolution*, *6*(2), 9–33.

Naciri, R. (1998). *The women's movement and political discourse in Morocco* (UNRISD Occasional Paper, No. 8). United Nations Research Institute for Social Development (UNRISD), Geneva. Retrieved from https://www.econstor.eu/bitstream/10419/148779/1/862525705.pdf

Nanda, B. (2000). *The Changing Position of Women in Bengal, 1849-1905*. Routledge.

Narvel, H., Merchant, H., Kore, G., Nayak, A., & De Sousa, A. (2018). A Study on Premenstrual Syndrome symptoms and their association with the Attitudes towards Menstruation in Nursing Staff. *Indian Journal of Mental Health*, *5*(4), 481. doi:10.30877/IJMH.5.4.2018.481-485

National Science Foundation. (2021). *Women, Minorities and Persons with Disabilities in Science and Engineering*. NSF. https://ncses.nsf.gov/pubs/nsf21321

Neumann, L., & Buskila, D. (1997). Measuring the quality of life of women with fibromyalgia: A Hebrew version of the quality of life scale. *Journal of Musculoskeletal Pain*, *5*(1), 5–16. doi:10.1300/J094v05n01_02

Neumayer, E., & Plümper, T. (2007). The gendered nature of natural disasters: The impact of catastrophic events on the gender gap in life expectancy, 1981–2002. *Annals of the Association of American Geographers*, *97*(3), 551–566. doi:10.1111/j.1467-8306.2007.00563.x

Compilation of References

Newman, A., Macaulay, L., & Dunwoodie, K. (2023). Refugee Entrepreneurship: A Systematic Review of Prior Research and Agenda for Future Research. *The International Migration Review*, *0*(0), 01979183231182669. Advance online publication. doi:10.1177/01979183231182669

Newman, A., Mole, K. F., Ucbasaran, D., Subramanian, N., & Lockett, A. (2018). Can your network make you happy? Entrepreneurs' business network utilization and subjective well-being. *British Journal of Management*, *29*(4), 613–633. doi:10.1111/1467-8551.12270

Nikolaou, A. (2017). *Barriers and Biases: A case study of women's experiences of underrepresentation at senior management levels.*

Nisar, N., Zehra, N., Haider, G., Munir, A. A., & Sohoo, N. A. (2008). Frequency, intensity and impact of premenstrual syndrome in medical students. *Journal of the College of Physicians and Surgeons—Pakistan*, *18*(8), 481–484. PMID:18798584

Njanike, K., & Mpofu, R. T. (2024). Factors Influencing Financial Inclusion for Social Inclusion in Selected African Countries. *Insight on Africa*, *16*(1), 93–112. doi:10.1177/09750878231194558

Norris, P. (2002). *Democratic phoenix: Reinventing political activism*. Cambridge University Pres. doi:10.1017/CBO9780511610073

Novakovic, A., & Fouad, N. A. (2013). Background, personal, and environmental influences on the career planning of adolescent girls. *Journal of Career Development*, *40*(3), 223–244. doi:10.1177/0894845312449380

O'Fahey, R. S. (2008). *The Darfur sultanate: A history*. Hurst.

Oakley, A. (2018). *Women, Peace and Welfare: a suppressed history of social reform, 1880-1920*. Policy Press.

Office of the United Nations High Commissioner for Human Rights (OHCHR). (2017). *Women's Land Rights: A Transformative Approach to Gender Justice*. OHCHR. https://www.ohchr.org/sites/default/files/Documents/Issues/Women/WG/Womenslandright pdf.

Organisation for Economic Co-operation and Development (OECD). (2016). *Handbook on the OECD-DAC Gender Equality Policy Marker*. OECD. https://www.oecd.org/dac/gender-development/Handbook-OECD-DAC-Gender-Equality-Policy-Marker.pdf

Organisation for Economic Co-operation and Development (OECD). (2020). *OECD iLibrary Document*. OECD. https://www.oecd-ilibrary.org/sites/13b65c6a-en/index.html?itemId=%2Fcontent%2Fcomponent%2F13b65c6a-en

Ovayolu, Ö., Ovayolu, N., Tuna, D., Serçe, S., Sevinç, A., & Pirbudak Çöçelli, L. (2014). Quality of life of caregivers: A cross-sectional study. *International Journal of Nursing Practice*, *20*(4), 424–432. doi:10.1111/ijn.12147 PMID:25157944

Oxford University Press. (n.d.). Bias. In Oxford English Dictionary (3rd ed.). Oxford University Press.

Özerdoğan, N., Sayiner, D., Ayranci, U., Ünsal, A., & Giray, S. (2009). Prevalence and predictors of dysmenorrhea among students at a university in Turkey. *International Journal of Gynaecology and Obstetrics: the Official Organ of the International Federation of Gynaecology and Obstetrics*, *107*(1), 39–43. doi:10.1016/j.ijgo.2009.05.010 PMID:19539288

Pahl, R. E. (1984). *Divisions of Labour*. Basil Blackwell.

Paige, K. E. (1973). Women learn to sing menstrual blues. *Psychology Today*, *7*(4), 41.

Pallas, S. (2011). Women's land rights and women's empowerment: one and the same. C. Verschuur (Hg.): Du grain à moudre. Genre, développement rural et alimentation. Genève.

Panda, S. (2018). Constraints faced by women entrepreneurs in developing countries: Review and ranking. *Gender in Management*, *33*(4), 315–331. doi:10.1108/GM-01-2017-0003

Pardue, L. (2023). *The rise of women entrepreneurs*. Gusto. https://gusto.com/company-news/the-rise-of-women-entrepreneurs

Park, B., Smith, J. A., & Correll, J. (2008). "Having it all" or "doing it all"? Perceived trait attributes and behavioral obligations as a function of workload, parenthood, and gender. *European Journal of Social Psychology*, *38*(7), 1156–1164. doi:10.1002/ejsp.535

Paunesku, D., Walton, G. M., Romero, C., Smith, E. N., Yeager, D. S., & Dweck, C. S. (2015). Mind-set interventions are a scalable treatment for academic underachievement. *Psychological Science*, *26*(6), 784–793. doi:10.1177/0956797615571017 PMID:25862544

Pearce, S. C. (2005). Today's immigrant woman entrepreneur. *Immigration Policy in Focus*, *4*(1), 1–20.

Pearse, R. (2017). Gender and climate change. *Wiley Interdisciplinary Reviews: Climate Change*, *8*(2), e451. doi:10.1002/wcc.451

Perveen, S., Mairaj, N., Maqbool, M., Bilal, A., & Munir, S. (2022). Prevalence the Premenstrual Syndrome (PMS) in Pakistani Women. *Pakistan Journal of Medical & Health Sciences*, *16*(09), 433–433. doi:10.53350/pjmhs22169433

Petty, R. E., & Krosnick, J. A. (2014). *Attitude strength: Antecedents and consequences*. Psychology Press. https://www.researchgate.net/profile/Russell-Fazio/publication/232544154_Attitudes_as_object-evaluation_associations_Determinants_consequences_and_correlates_of_attitude_accessibility/links/02e7e52f38247646e8000000/Attitudes-as-object-evaluation-associations-Determinants-consequences-and-correlates-of-attitude-accessibility.pdf

Philip, S. M., & Suresh, A., priyadharshini Dhanasekaran, G., Sivasankaran, P., AP, R., & Nagendra, V. H. (2022). Assessment of menstrual attitudes and predictors for premenstrual syndrome in university students of Ooty, South India. *Journal of Positive School Psychology*, *6*(6), 3736–3746.

Pidduck, R. J., & Clari, D. R. (2021). Transitional entrepreneurship: Elevating research into marginalized entrepreneurs. *Journal of Small Business Management*, *59*(6), 1081–1096. doi:10.1080/00472778.2021.1928149

Pierre, D. E., & Okstad, J. (2021). Utilizing leadership assessment tools in graduate education. *New Directions for Student Leadership*, *2021*(170), 87–95. doi:10.1002/yd.20445 PMID:34487623

Poggesi, S., Mari, M., & DeVita, L. (2016). What's new in female entrepreneurship research? Answers from the literature. *The International Entrepreneurship and Management Journal*, *12*(3), 735–764. doi:10.1007/s11365-015-0364-5

Popal, F., & Langley, B. (2021). *Women's leadership & economic empowerment: A solution for the economies of the middle east & north africa*. GWB Center. http://gwbcenter.imgix.net/Publications/Resources/gwbi-_2021_CIPE_paper.pdf

Portes, A. (1998). Social capital: Its origins and applications in modern sociology. *Annual Review of Sociology*, *24*(1), 1–24. doi:10.1146/annurev.soc.24.1.1

Poudyal, Y., Parajuli, N., Dahal, S. C., & Jha, C. B. (2020). The Study of Quality of Life in Patient with Vitiligo. *Birat Journal of Health Sciences*, *5*(3), 1206–1209. doi:10.3126/bjhs.v5i3.33699

Powles, J. (2004). *Life history and personal narrative: Theoretical and methodological issues relevant to research and evaluation in refugee contexts*. UNHCR.

Pradhan, R., Meinzen-Dick, R., & Theis, S. (2019). Property rights, intersectionality, and women's empowerment in Nepal. *Journal of Rural Studies*, *70*, 26–35. doi:10.1016/j.jrurstud.2019.05.003

Psacharopoulos, G., & Patrinos, H. A. (2018). Returns to investment in education: A decennial review of the global literature. *Education Economics*, *26*(5), 445–458. doi:10.1080/09645292.2018.1484426

Putnam, R. D. (2000). Bowling alone: America's declining social capital. In Culture and politics (pp. 223-234). Palgrave Macmillan.

Putnam, R. D. (2007). E pluribus unum: Diversity and community in the twenty-first century the 2006 Johan Skytte Prize Lecture. *Scandinavian Political Studies*, *30*(2), 137–174. doi:10.1111/j.1467-9477.2007.00176.x

Pyramid: Women in the United States workforce [Infographic]. (2023, February 7). Catalyst

Qalawa, S. A. A., Alsuhaibani, H. O., Alluhaydan, A. A., & Alghaidani, A. A. (2022). Health beliefs and coping strategies regarding premenstrual syndrome among health college students at Qassim University. *International Journal of Health Sciences*, *6*, 4264–4277. doi:10.53730/ijhs.v6nS8.13145

Quach, T. (2004). *The crisis in Darfur: an analysis of its origins and storylines* [Doctoral dissertation', Virginia Polytechnic Institute and State University].

Radloff, L. S., & Rae, D. S. (1979). Susceptibility and precipitating factors in depression: Sex differences and similarities. *Journal of Abnormal Psychology*, *88*(2), 174–181. doi:10.1037/0021-843X.88.2.174 PMID:447900

Radtke, H. L., & Stam, H. J. (2016). A history of psychology's complicated relationship to feminism: Theorizing difference. *Centrality of history for theory construction in psychology*, 167-185.

Rahhou, J. (2024, January 17). *Morocco Takes Strides Towards Gender Equality in Education, Employment*. Morocco World News. https://www.moroccoworldnews.com/2024/01/360175/morocco-takes-strides-towards-gender-equality-in-education-employment

Rametse, N., Weerakoon, C., & Moremomg-Nganunu, T. (2021). Parental role models' influence on entrepreneurial aspirations of Botswana female students. *Journal of Developing Areas*, *55*(1). doi:10.1353/jda.2021.0000

Rao, T. S. (2023, June). Crisis as displacement and opportunity: Reflections on the way South Sudanese women cope with war in refugee camps. In *International Academy of Practical Theology. Conference Series* (Vol. 3).

Rao, S., Jaiprakash, I., & Murthy, V. N. (1982). Prevalence of menstrual symptoms in a college population. *Indian Journal of Clinical Psychology*, *9*(2), 89–94.

Rapkin, A. J., & Akopians, A. L. (2012). Pathophysiology of premenstrual syndrome and premenstrual dysphoric disorder. *Menopause International*, *18*(2), 52–59. doi:10.1258/mi.2012.012014 PMID:22611222

Rapkin, A. J., & Winer, S. A. (2009). Premenstrual syndrome and premenstrual dysphoric disorder: Quality of life and burden of illness. *Expert Review of Pharmacoeconomics & Outcomes Research*, *9*(2), 157–170. doi:10.1586/erp.09.14 PMID:19402804

Rashidi, B., Montazeri, A., Ramezanzadeh, F., Shariat, M., Abedinia, N., & Ashrafi, M. (2008). Health-related quality of life in infertile couples receiving IVF or ICSI treatment. *BMC Health Services Research*, *8*(1), 1–6. doi:10.1186/1472-6963-8-186 PMID:18803838

RathP.BhardwajL. K.YadavP.BhardwajA. (2023). A Synthesis of Biogenic Nanoparticles (NPs) for the Treatment of Wastewater and Its Application: A Review. https://doi.org/ doi:10.20944/preprints202311.1629.v1

Rawal, D. S., & Agrawal, K. (2016). *Barriers to women's land and property access and ownership in Nepal*. International Organization for Migration.

Read, J. R., Perz, J., & Ussher, J. M. (2014). Ways of coping with premenstrual change: Development and validation of a premenstrual coping measure. *BMC Women's Health*, *14*(1), 1–15. doi:10.1186/1472-6874-14-1 PMID:24383580

Redala - Red de Empresarias Latinoamericanas. (2022). *Quienes Somos*. ReDala. https://www.redala.org/nosotras

Rees, L. (1953). Psychosomatic aspects of the premenstrual tension syndrome. *The Journal of Mental Science*, *99*(414), 62–73. doi:10.1192/bjp.99.414.62 PMID:13023368

Resurrección, B. P., Bee, B. A., Dankelman, I., Park, C. M. Y., Haldar, M., & McMullen, C. P. (2019). *Gender-transformative climate change adaptation: advancing social equity. Paper commissioned by the Global Commission on Adaptation*. GCA.

Revel, B. (2020, June 5). *How to maximize Syrian refugee economic inclusion in Turkey*. Atlantic Council. https://www.atlanticcouncil.org/blogs/turkeysource/how-to-maximize-syrian-refugee-economic-inclusion-in-turkey/

Rezaee, H., Mahamed, F., & Mazaheri, M. A. (2016). Does spousal support can decrease women's premenstrual syndrome symptoms? *Global Journal of Health Science*, *8*(5), 19. doi:10.5539/gjhs.v8n5p19 PMID:26652081

Rice, L., & Barth, J. M. (2017). A tale of two gender roles: The effects of implicit and explicit gender role traditionalism and occupational stereotype on hiring decisions. *Gender Issues*, *34*(1), 86–102. doi:10.1007/s12147-016-9175-4

Richardson, M., Sappal, B., Tsui, J., & Woodman, P. (2017). *Activist to entrepreneur: The role of social enterprise in supporting women's empowerment*. Social Impact Consulting & ODI. https://www.britishcouncil.org/sites/default/files/social_enterprise_and_womens_empowerment_july.pdf

Ridde, V., Delormier, T., & Gaudreau, L. (2007). Evaluation of empowerment and effectiveness: Universal concepts? Shin, M. B., Garcia, P. J., Dotson, M. E., Valderrama, M., Chiappe, M., Ramanujam, N., Krieger, M., Ásbjörnsdóttir, K., Barnabas, R. V., Iribarren, S. J., & Gimbel, S. (2022). Evaluation of Women's Empowerment in a Community-Based Human Papillomavirus Self-Sampling Social Entrepreneurship Program (Hope Project) in Peru: A Mixed-Method Study. *Frontiers in Public Health*, *10*, 858552. doi:10.3389/fpubh.2022.858552

Risman, B. J., & Davis, G. (2013). From sex roles to gender structure. *Current Sociology*, *61*(5-6), 733–755. doi:10.1177/0011392113479315

Rittenhouse, C. A. (1991). The emergence of premenstrual syndrome as a social problem. *Social Problems*, *38*(3), 412–425. doi:10.2307/800607

Robinson, A., & de Bessa, G. H. (2002). Forms and functions of premenstrual syndrome. *Senior Thesis, Dep. of Sociology & Anthropology, Illinois State University, lilt. ilstu. edu/soa/html/anthrothesis/amrobin*. 1-27.

Rogers, S. (2022). *Center for Women's Inclusion in Land Rights Launched in Morocco*. MCC. https://www.mcc.gov/blog/entry/blog-070722-center-womens-land-rights/

Rosseinsky, D. R., & Hall, P. G. (1974). An evolutionary theory of premenstrual tension. *Lancet*, *304*(7887), 1024. doi:10.1016/S0140-6736(74)92132-1 PMID:4138262

Rowlands, J. (1995). Empowerment examined. *Development in Practice*, *5*(2), 101–107. doi:10.1080/0961452951000157074 PMID:12346153

Rowlands, J. (1997). *Questioning empowerment: Working with women in Honduras*. Oxfam. doi:10.3362/9780855988364

Rowlands, J. (1998). A word of the times, but what does it mean? Empowerment in the discourse and practice of development. In *Women and empowerment: Illustrations from the Third World* (pp. 11–34). Palgrave Macmillan UK. doi:10.1007/978-1-349-26265-6_2

Rowlands, J. (2016). Power in practice: Bringing Understandings and Analysis of power into Development Action in Oxfam. *IDS Bulletin*, *47*(5), 119–130. doi:10.19088/1968-2016.171

Roy, C. K., & Xiaoling, H. (2022). Achieving SDG 5, gender equality and empower all women and girls, in developing countries: How aid for trade can help? *International Journal of Social Economics*, *49*(6), 930–959. doi:10.1108/IJSE-12-2020-0813

Roy, M. (2012). *The Rani of Jhansi: Gender, History, and Fable in India*. Cambridge University Press India.

Rughoobur-Seetah, S., Hosanoo, Z., & Balla Soupramanien, L. D. (2023). Financial independence of women–the impact of social factors on women empowerment in small island developing states (SIDS). *The International Journal of Organizational Analysis*, *31*(6), 2383–2408. doi:10.1108/IJOA-10-2021-2980

Rutherford, S. (2011). *Women's work, men's cultures: overcoming resistance and changing organizational cultures*. Palgrave Macmillan. doi:10.1057/9780230307476

Ryan, R. M., & Deci, E. L. (2000). Self-determination theory and the facilitation of intrinsic motivation, social development, and well-being. *The American Psychologist*, *55*(1), 68–78. doi:10.1037/0003-066X.55.1.68 PMID:11392867

Ryan, R. M., & Deci, E. L. (2017). *Self-determination theory: Basic psychological needs in motivation, development, and wellness*. Guilford publications. doi:10.1521/978.14625/28806

Ryu, A., & Kim, T. H. (2015). Premenstrual syndrome: A mini review. *Maturitas*, *82*(4), 436–440. doi:10.1016/j.maturitas.2015.08.010 PMID:26351143

Saadin, I., Ramli, K., Johari, H., & Harin, N. A. (2016). Women and barriers for upward career advancement–a survey at Perak state secretariat, Ipoh, Perak. *Procedia Economics and Finance*, *35*, 574–581. doi:10.1016/S2212-5671(16)00070-8

Samie, S. F., Johnson, A. J., Huffman, A. M., & Hillyer, S. J. (2015). Voices of empowerment: Women from the Global South re/negotiating empowerment and the global sports mentoring programme. *Sport in Society*, *18*(8), 923–937. doi:10.1080/17430437.2014.997582

Sandefur, R. L., & Laumann, E. O. (1998). A paradigm for social capital. *Rationality and Society*, *10*(4), 481–501. doi:10.1177/104346398010004005

Sanginga, P. C., Kamugisha, R. N., & Martin, A. M. (2007). The dynamics of social capital and conflict management in multiple resource regimes: A case of the southwestern highlands of Uganda. *Ecology and Society*, *12*(1), 6. doi:10.5751/ES-01847-120106

Santhya, K. G., & Jejeebhoy, S. J. (2015). Sexual and reproductive health and rights of adolescent girls: Evidence from low-and middle-income countries. *Global Public Health: An International Journal for Research, Policy and Practice*, *10*(2), 189–221. doi:10.1080/17441692.2014.986169 PMID:25554828

Sarkar, T. (2001). *Hindu Wife, Hindu Nation: Community, Religion, and Cultural Nationalism*. Permanent Black.

Sarkar, T. (2008). *Women and Social Reform in Modern India: A Reader*. Indiana University Press.

Sarver, V. T. (1983). *Ajzen and Fishbein's" theory of reasoned action: A critical assessment*. Wiley. https://doi:10.1111/j.1468-5914.1983.tb00469.x

Sarwar, U., & Rauf, U. (2021). Social support, quality of life and mental health problems among females with and without menstruation problems: A comparative study. *Khyber Medical University Journal*, *13*(4), 206–210. doi:10.35845/kmuj.2021.21373

Sawant, N. S., Vanjari, N. A., & Khopkar, U. (2019). Gender differences in depression, coping, stigma, and quality of life in patients of vitiligo. *Dermatology Research and Practice*, *2019*, 1–11. doi:10.1155/2019/6879412 PMID:31065260

Schram, T. H. (2006). *Conceptualizing and proposing qualitative research* (2nd ed.). Pearson.

Schuemer-Cross, T., & Taylor, B. H. (2009). *The right to survive: the humanitarian challenge for the twenty-first century*. Oxfam.

Searby, L., Ballenger, J., & Tripses, J. (2015). Climbing the ladder, holding the ladder: The mentoring experiences of higher education females. *Advancing Women in Leadership*, 98-107.

Sen, A. P. (1993). *Hindu Revivalism in Bengal, 1872-1905: Some Essays in Interpretation*. Oxford University Press.

Sen, G., & Grown, C. (2013). *Development crises and alternative visions: Third world women's perspectives*. Routledge. doi:10.4324/9781315070179

Shamnani, G., Gupta, V., Jiwane, R., Singh, S., Tiwari, S., & Bhartiy, S. S. (2018). Prevalence of premenstrual syndrome and premenstrual dysphoric disorder among medical students and its impact on their academic and social performance. *National Journal of Physiology, Pharmacy and Pharmacology*, *8*(8), 1205–1208. doi:10.5455/njppp.2018.8.0415728042018

Sharma, A., & Johri, A. (2014). Learning and empowerment: Designing a financial literacy tool to teach long-term investing to illiterate women in rural India. *Learning, Culture and Social Interaction*, *3*(1), 21–33. doi:10.1016/j.lcsi.2013.10.003

Shi, Y., Shi, M., Liu, C., Sui, L., Zhao, Y., & Fan, X. (2023). Associations with physical activity, sedentary behavior, and premenstrual syndrome among Chinese female college students. *BMC Women's Health*, *23*(1), 173. doi:10.1186/s12905-023-02262-x PMID:37041480

Shrestha, I., & Giri, R. (2020). Knowledge and prevalence regarding premenstrual syndrome among adolescents in Morang District, Nepal. *Current Women's Health Reviews*, *16*(3), 214–219. doi:10.2174/1573404816999200421100011

Siahbazi, S., Hariri, F. Z., Montazeri, A., & Moghaddam, B. L. (2011). Translation and psychometric properties of the Iranian version of the Premenstrual Symptoms Screening Tool (PSST). *10*(4), 421-427.

Siahbazi, S., Montazeri, A., Taghizadeh, Z., & Masoomie, R. (2018). The consequences of premenstrual syndrome on the quality of life from the perspective of affected women: A qualitative study. *Journal of Research in Medical and Dental Science*, *6*(2), 284–292.

Siegel, J. M., Johnson, J. H., & Sarason, I. G. (1979). Life changes and menstrual discomfort. *Journal of Human Stress*, *5*(1), 41–46. doi:10.1080/0097840X.1979.9935001 PMID:422838

Singh, B., & Singh, M. (2023). Financial literacy and its determinants among the schedule tribes: Evidences from India. *International Journal of Social Economics*, *50*(12), 1804–1817. doi:10.1108/IJSE-01-2023-0008

Singh, S. (2017). Identities beyond ethnic-based subordination or conflict in the Southeast Asian borderlands: A case study of Lao villagers in northeast Cambodia. *Asian Ethnicity*, *18*(1), 117–138. doi:10.1080/14631369.2015.1120053

Slade, H. (2014). Women entrepreneurs are happier than male entrepreneurs. *Forbes*. https://www.forbes.com/sites/hollieslade/2014/07/30/women-are-the-happiest-entrepreneurs-in-america-says-study/?sh=3a0883a84aae

Slavchevska, V., Doss, C. R., de la O Campos, A. P., & Brunelli, C. (2021). Beyond ownership: Women's and men's land rights in Sub-Saharan Africa. *Oxford Development Studies*, *49*(1), 2–22. doi:10.1080/13600818.2020.1818714

Slim, H. (2018, March 15). *Masculinity and war–let's talk about it more*. Humanitarian Law & Policy Blog. https://blogs.icrc.org/law-and-policy/2018/03/15/masculinity-and-war-let-s-talk-about-it-more/

Compilation of References

Smith-Doerr, L. (2004). Flexibility and Fairness: Effects of the network form of organizationa on gender equity in life science careers. *Sociological Perspectives*, *47*(1), 25–54. doi:10.1525/sop.2004.47.1.25

Sommer, M., Hirsch, J. S., Nathanson, C., & Parker, R. G. (2015). Comfortably, safely, and without shame: Defining menstrual hygiene management as a public health issue. *American Journal of Public Health*, *105*(7), 1302–1311. doi:10.2105/AJPH.2014.302525 PMID:25973831

SönmezerSönmezer. E., & Yosmaoılu, H. (2014). *Changes of menstrual attitude and stress perception in Women with dysmenorrhea*. ResearchGate. https://www.researchgate.net/publication/287236200_Changes_of_menstrual_attitude_and_stress_perception_in_women_with_dysmenorrhea

Southeast Asian Archive. (1999). *Documenting the Southeast Asian refugee experience*. University of California Irvine. https://seaa.lib.uci.edu/sites/all/publications/exhibits/seaexhibit/firstpage.html

Southeast Asian Resource Action Center. (2018). *The devastating impact of deportation on Southeast Asian Americans*. SARAC. https://www.searac.org/wp-content/uploads/2018/04/the-devastating-impact-of-deportation-on-southeast-asian-americans.pdf

Southeast Asian Resource Action Center. (2024). *Immigration*. Southeast Asian Resource Action Center. https://www.searac.org/programming/national-state-policy-advocacy/immigration/

SpencerStuart. (2022). *2022 S&P 500 Board Diversity Snapshot*. Spencer Stuart. https://www.spencerstuart.com/-/media/2022/june/diversitysnapshot/sp500_board_diversity_snapshot_2022.pdf

SPREP. (2020). *State of Environment and Conservation in the Pacific Islands: 2020 Regional Report*. SPREP.

Stake, R. E. (2008). Qualitative case studies. In N. K. Denzin & Y. S. Lincoln (Eds.), *Strategies of qualitative inquiry* (3rd ed., pp. 119–149). Sage.

Stanfors, M., & Goldscheider, F. (2017). The forest and the trees: Industrialization, demographic change, and the ongoing gender revolution in Sweden and the United States, 1870-2010. *Demographic Research*, *36*, 173–226. doi:10.4054/DemRes.2017.36.6

Steiner, M. (2000). Premenstrual syndrome and premenstrual dysphoric disorder: Guidelines for management. *Journal of Psychiatry & Neuroscience*, *25*(5), 459–468. PMID:11109297

Steiner, M., & Carroll, B. J. (1977). The psychobiology of premenstrual dysphoria: Review of theories and treatments. *Psychoneuroendocrinology*, *2*(4), 321–335. doi:10.1016/0306-4530(77)90002-6 PMID:202982

Steiner, M., Macdougall, M., & Brown, E. (2003). The premenstrual symptoms screening tool (PSST) for clinicians. *Archives of Women's Mental Health*, *6*(3), 203–209. doi:10.1007/s00737-003-0018-4 PMID:12920618

Stein, J. A., Newcomb, M. D., & Bentler, P. M. (1992). The effect of agency and communality on self-esteem: Gender differences in longitudinal data. *Sex Roles*, *26*(11-12), 465–483. doi:10.1007/BF00289869

Stephens, S., Cunningham, I., & Kabir, Y. (2021). Female entrepreneurs in a time of crisis: Evidence from Ireland. *International Journal of Gender and Entrepreneurship*, *13*(2), 106–120. doi:10.1108/IJGE-09-2020-0135

Stratford, L. (2023). *Gender Disparities Within Life Sciences and the Need to Increase Female Representation in the Industry*. CSG Talent. https://www.csgtalent.com/insights/blog/gender-disparities-within-life-sciences-and-the-need-to-increase-female-representation-in-the-industry/

Stromquist, N. P. (2018). *The global status of teachers and the teaching profession*. Education International.

Sue, D. W., Capodilupo, C. M., Torino, G. C., Bucceri, J. M., Holder, A. M. B., Nadal, K. L., & Esquilin, M. (2007). Racial microaggressions in everyday life: Implications for clinical Practice. *The American Psychologist*, *62*(4), 271–286. doi:10.1037/0003-066X.62.4.271 PMID:17516773

Suleri, A. Q., & Savage, K. (2006). *Remittances in crises: a case study from Pakistan*. Sustainable Development Policy Institute.

Sultana, S., Guimbretière, F., Sengers, P., & Dell, N. (2018). Design within a patriarchal society: Opportunities and challenges in designing for rural women in bangladesh. In *Proceedings of the 2018 CHI Conference on Human Factors in Computing Systems*, (pp. 1-13). ACM. 10.1145/3173574.3174110

Suner-Keklik, S., & Barği, G. (2023). Investigation of the Relationship between Physical Activity Levels and Menstrual Symptoms in Healthy Women. *Online Türk Sağlık Bilimleri Dergisi*, *8*(2), 192–199. doi:10.26453/otjhs.1193870

Surangi, H. A. K. N. S. (2016). The role of female entrepreneurial networks and small business development: A pilot study based on Sri Lankan migrant entrepreneurs of tourism industry in London. *International Journal of Business & Economic Development*, *4*(1), 56–70.

Suryanti, D., Selly, M., Muttaqin, M. Z., & Makmun, S. (2023). Unfolding the Landscape of Conflict. *Journal of Southeast Asian Human Rights*, *7*(1), 21–21. doi:10.19184/jseahr.v7i1.30517

Sveinsdottir, H. (1993). The Attitudes towards Menstruation among Icelandic Nursing Students -Their Relationship with Menstrual Preparation and Menstrual Characteristics. *Scandinavian Journal of Caring Sciences*, *7*(1), 37–41. doi:10.1111/j.1471-6712.1993.tb00159.x PMID:8502853

Swearingen, W. D. (2016) *Moroccan Mirages: Agrarian Dreams and Deceptions, 1912-1986. Princeton Legacy Library SWEDISH INTERNATIONAL DEVELOPMENT COOPERATION AGENCY(SIDCA). Quick Guide to What and How: increasing women's access to land*. OECD. https://www.oecd.org/dac/gender-development/47566053.pdf

Sztompka, P. (2007). Trust in science: Robert K. Merton's inspirations. *Journal of Classical Sociology*, *7*(2), 211–220. doi:10.1177/1468795X07078038

Talib Hassan, I., Saadi Issa, H., Hussein, E. A., & Ali Haddad, R. (2023). The effect of premenstrual tension on academic performance and social interactions among Iraqi medical students. *Cellular. Molecular and Biomedical Reports*, *3*(4), 205–211. doi:10.55705/cmbr.2023.390101.1113

Tambe, A., & Trotz, A. (2010). Historical reflections on DAWN: An interview with Gita Sen. *Comparative Studies of South Asia, Africa and the Middle East*, *30*(2), 214–217. doi:10.1215/1089201X-2010-006

Teixeira, A. L. D. S., Oliveira, É. C. M., & Dias, M. R. C. (2013). Relationship between the level of physical activity and premenstrual syndrome incidence. *Revista Brasileira de Ginecologia e Obstetrícia*, *35*, 210–214. doi:10.1590/S0100-72032013000500004 PMID:23843118

Teoli, D., & Bhardwaj, A. (2022). Quality of Life Quality of Life. *StatPearls, editor*. https://www.ncbi.nlm.nih.gov/books/NBK536962/

Thakrar, P. D., Bhukar, K., & Oswal, R. (2021). Premenstrual dysphoric disorder: Prevalence, quality of life and disability due to illness among medical and paramedical students. *Journal of Affective Disorders Reports*, *4*, 100112. doi:10.1016/j.jadr.2021.100112

Thapar, R. (1990). *A History of India* (Vol. 1). Penguin Books.

Thompson, A. (2024). *Advancing Women's Rights to Land Ownership in Morocco*. MCC. https://www.mcc.gov/blog/entry/blog-030724-womens-land-rights-morocco/

Tkachenko, L. V., Kurushina, O. V., & Atagadzhieva, M. S. (2010). The quality of life in women suffering from premenstrual syndrome. *Problemy Sotsial'noi Gigieny. Zdravookhraneniia i Istorii Meditsiny*, (2), 13–16.

Tokas, R., Bhardwaj, L. K., Kumar, N., & Jindal, T. (2024). Nanotechnology for sustainable development and future: a review. *Green and Sustainable Approaches Using Wastes for the Production of Multifunctional Nanomaterials*, 221-233.

Triandis, H. C. (1989). The self and social behavior in differing cultural contexts. *Psychological Review*, 96(3), 506–520. doi:10.1037/0033-295X.96.3.506

Tyson, L. D., & Klugman, J. (2017). *Women's economic empowerment is the smart thing to do. What's stopping us?* World Economic Forum. https://www. weforum. org/agenda/2017/01/womens-economic-empowerment-is-the-smart-and-right-thing-to-do-whats-stopping-us/

Ullrich, H. E. (1992). Menstrual taboos among Havik Brahmin women: A study of ritual change. *Sex Roles*, 26(1), 19–40. doi:10.1007/BF00290123 PMID:12317387

UN Office of the High Commissioner for Human Rights (OHCHR), & the African Union-UN Hybrid Operation in Darfur (UNAMID). (2016). *The Human Rights Situation of Internally Displaced Persons in Darfur 2014 - 2016 - Sudan.* ReliefWeb. https://reliefweb.int/report/sudan/human-rights-situation-internally-displaced-persons-darfur-2014-2016

UNHR. (2014). *Gender stereotypes and Stereotyping and women's rights*. UNHR. https://www.ohchr.org/sites/default/files/Documents/Issues/Women/WRGS/OnePagers/Gender_stereotyping.pdf

UNIDO. (2021). *Women's Entrepreneurship Development Programme. United Nations Industrial Development Organization*. UNIDO. https://www.unido.org/our-focus-cross-cutting-services/women-and-youth/womens-entrepreneurship-development

United Nations Entity for Gender Equality and the Empowerment of Women. (2020). *Report of the Working Group on the issue of discrimination against women in law and in practice: Addendum*. UN. https://www.unwomen.org/sites/default/files/Headquarters/Attachments/Sections/CSW/64/National-reviews/Morocco_en.pdf

United Nations Human Rights Council. (2012). *Report of the Working Group on the issue of discrimination against women in law and in practice: Addendum*. UN. https://www.ohchr.org/sites/default/files/Documents/HRBodies/HRCouncil/RegularSession/Session20/A-HRC-20-28-Add1_en.pdf

United Nations Office for the Coordination of Humanitarian Affairs. (2023). *Global humanitarian overview 2024*. UN. https://humanitarianaction.info/document/global-humanitarian-overview-2024/article/forced-displacement-record-levels-cause-and-consequence-increased-need

United Nations Population Fund (UNFPA). (2015). *Issue 7: Women Empowerment*. Unfpa.org. https://www.unfpa.org/resources/issue-7-women-empowerment

United Nations. (2023). *Sustainable Development Goals. Goal 5: Achieve gender equality and empower all women and girls*. United Nations. https://sdgs.un.org/goals/goal5/

Unterhalter, E., North, A., Arnot, M., Lloyd, C., Moletsane, L., Murphy-Graham, E., & Saito, M. (2014). Girls Education and Gender Equality. *International Journal of Educational Development*.

Upadhyay, U., Gipson, J., Withers, M., Lewis, S., Ciaraldi, E., Fraser, A., Huchko, M., & Prata, N. (2014). Women"s empowerment and fertility: A review of Literature. *Social Science & Medicine*, 115, 111–120. doi:10.1016/j.socscimed.2014.06.014 PMID:24955875

US Census Bureau. (2022). *Educational attainment*. US Census Bureau. https://www.census.gov/data/tables/2021/demo/educational-attainment/cps-detailed-tables.html

US Department of State. (2023). *What is a refugee? What is an asylee?* USDoS. https://fam.state.gov/FAM/09FAM/09FAM020302.html#:~:text=In%20General%3A%20A%20refugee%20is,social%20group%2C%20or%20political%20opinion

Ussher, J. M. (2003). The ongoing silencing of women in families: An analysis and rethinking of premenstrual syndrome and therapy. *Journal of Family Therapy*, 25(4), 388–405. doi:10.1111/1467-6427.00257

Ussher, J. M., & Perz, J. (2013). PMS as a process of negotiation: Women's experience and management of premenstrual distress. *Psychology & Health*, 28(8), 909–927. doi:10.1080/08870446.2013.765004 PMID:23383644

Ussher, J. M., & Perz, J. (2020). "I feel fat and ugly and hate myself": Self-objectification through negative constructions of premenstrual embodiment. *Feminism & Psychology*, 30(2), 185–205. doi:10.1177/0959353519900196

van Gool, F., Bongers, I., Bierbooms, J., & Janssen, R. (2022). Whether and how top management create flexibility in mental healthcare organizations: COVID-19 as a rest case. *Journal of Health Organization and Management*, 36(5), 604–616. doi:10.1108/JHOM-07-2021-0258 PMID:35238189

Van Kooy, J. (2016). Refugee women as entrepreneurs in Australia. *Forced Migration Review*, 53. https://www.fmreview.org/community-protection/vankooy

Van Niekerk, L. M., Dell, B., Johnstone, L., Matthewson, M., & Quinn, M. (2023). Examining the associations between self and body compassion and health related quality of life in people diagnosed with endometriosis. *Journal of Psychosomatic Research*, 167, 111202. doi:10.1016/j.jpsychores.2023.111202 PMID:36812662

Vanderbilt University. (2021). *MOTIV: Fostering girls' interest in technology careers through robotics.* Vanderbilt University. https://my.vanderbilt.edu/motiv/

Vasoya, N. H. (2023). Women entrepreneurship: An instinctive approach or stroke of luck? *South Asian Journal of Social Studies and Economics*, 20(2), 36-44. https://doi.org/ doi:10.9734/sajsse/2023/v20i2696

Victor, F. F., Souza, A. I., Barreiros, C. D. T., Barros, J. L. N. D., Silva, F. A. C. D., & Ferreira, A. L. C. G. (2019). Quality of life among university students with premenstrual syndrome. *Revista Brasileira de Ginecologia e Obstetrícia*, 41(5), 312–317. doi:10.1055/s-0039-1688709 PMID:31181584

Visvanathan, N. (1997). *Introduction to part 1.* The women, gender and development reader, 17-32.

Vital Voices. (2022). *Our History.* Vital Voices. https://www.vitalvoices.org/about-us/our-history/

Vitores, A., & Gil-Juárez, A. (2016). The trouble with 'women in computing': A critical examination of the deployment of research on the gender gap in computer science. *Journal of Gender Studies*, 25(6), 666–680. doi:10.1080/09589236.2015.1087309

Wahl, A., Burckhardt, C., Wiklund, I., & Hanestad, B. R. (1998). The Norwegian Version of the Quality of Life Scale (QOLS-N) A Validation and Reliability Study in Patients Suffering from Psoriasis. *Scandinavian Journal of Caring Sciences*, 12(4), 215–222. doi:10.1080/02839319850162823 PMID:10067647

Waldinger, R. (1995). The 'other side' of embeddness: A case study of the interplay between economy and ethnicity. *Ethnic and Racial Studies*, 18(3), 555–558. doi:10.1080/01419870.1995.9993879

Walker, A. (1995). Theory and methodology in premenstrual syndrome research. *Social Science & Medicine*, 41(6), 793–800. doi:10.1016/0277-9536(95)00046-A PMID:8571150

Wamble-King, S. (2023). *Empowered Presence: Theorizing an Afrocentric Performance of Leadership by African American Women* [Doctoral dissertation, Antioch University].

Wang, M. T., & Degol, J. L. (2017). Gender gap in science, technology, engineering, and mathematics (STEM): Current knowledge, implications for practice, policy, and future directions. *Educational Psychology Review*, *29*(1), 119–140. doi:10.1007/s10648-015-9355-x PMID:28458499

Ward, N., & Batalova, J. (2023). Refugees and asylees in the United States. *Migration Policy Institute*. https://www.migrationpolicy.org/sites/default/files/publications/frs-print-2023.pdf

Ward, L. M., & Grower, P. (2020). Media and the development of gender role stereotypes. *Annual Review of Developmental Psychology*, *2*(1), 177–199. doi:10.1146/annurev-devpsych-051120-010630

Warner, J., & Corley, D. (2017). *The Women's Leadership Gap*. Centre for American Progress.

Webster, J., & Watson, R. T. (2002). Analyzing the past to prepare for the future: Writing 253 a literature review. *Management Information Systems Quarterly*, *26*(2).

Welsh, D. H., Kaciak, E., Trimi, S., & Mainardes, E. W. (2018). Women entrepreneurs and family firm heterogeneity: Evidence from an emerging economy. *Group Decision and Negotiation*, *27*(3), 445–465. doi:10.1007/s10726-017-9544-8

Wijetunge, M. (2023). *Moudawana Reform in Morocco: The Long Feminist Struggle*. IGG. https://igg-geo.org/?p=18280&lang=en

Women for Afghan Women. (2022). *Our Programs*. Women for Afghan Women. https://www.womenforafghanwomen.org/programs

Women U. N. (2013). *In Morocco, encouraged by success, Sulaliyyate women make strides in land rights*. Women UN. https://www.unwomen.org/en/news/stories/2013/2/in-morocco-encouraged-by-success-soulalyates-women-make-strides-in-land-rights

Women, U. N. (2020). The Power of Women Leading Change in the Americas and the Caribbean. https://lac.unwomen.org/en/digiteca/publicaciones/2020/12/el-poder-de-las-mujeres

Wong, S. (2014). A power game of multi-stakeholder initiatives. *Journal of Corporate Citizenship*, *2014*(55), 26–39. doi:10.9774/GLEAF.4700.2014.se.00006

Woods, N. F., Mitchell, E. S., & Lentz, M. J. (1995). Social pathways to premenstrual symptoms. *Research in Nursing & Health*, *18*(3), 225–237. doi:10.1002/nur.4770180306 PMID:7754093

World Bank (2021). *South Asia's Hotspots: The Impact of Temperature and Precipitation Changes on Living Standards*. World Bank.

World Bank. (2015). *Morocco: Mind the Gap - Empowering Women for a More Open, Inclusive and Prosperous Society*. World Bank.

World Bank. (2017). *What triggered the increase in girls' education in Mali in the 2000s?* World Bank. https://openknowledge.worldbank.org/handle/10986/28853

World Bank. (2022). *SEAES Providing Pathways for Bangladesh's Girls and Women*. World Bank. https://www.worldbank.org/en/news/feature/2022/03/08/seaes-providing-pathways-for-bangladesh-girls-and-women

World Economic Forum. (2016). *This Is What Women's Land Rights Look Like Around the World*. World Economic Forum. https://www.weforum.org/agenda/2016/03/this-is-what-womens-land-rights-look-like-around-the-world/

World Economic Forum. (2023). *Gender Equality: Global Annual Results Report 2022*. WEF.

World Health Organization. (2000). *Obesity: preventing and managing the global epidemic: report of a WHO consultation*. WHO.

Wright, W. E., & Boun, S. (2011). Southeast Asian American education 35 years after initial resettlement: Research report and policy recommendations. *Journal of Southeast Asian American Education & Advancement*, *6*(1), 1. doi:10.7771/2153-8999.1017

Wu, J., Richard, O. C., Triana, M. D. C., & Zhang, X. (2022). The performance impact of gender diversity in the top management team and board of directors: A multiteam systems approach. *Human Resource Management*, *61*(2), 157–180. doi:10.1002/hrm.22086

Xheneti, M., Karki, S. T., & Madden, A. (2021). Negotiating business and family demands within a patriarchal society–the case of women entrepreneurs in the Nepalese context. In *Understanding Women's Entrepreneurship in a Gendered Context* (pp. 93–112). Routledge. doi:10.4324/9781003139454-7

Yang, M., Gricar, J. A., Maruish, M. E., Hagan, M. A., Kornstein, S. G., & Wallenstein, G. V. (2010). Interpreting Premenstrual Symptoms Impact Survey scores using outcomes in health-related quality of life and sexual drive impact. *The Journal of Reproductive Medicine*, *55*(1-2), 41–48. PMID:20337207

Yap, R. J. C., Komalasari, F., & Hadiansah, I. (2018). The effect of financial literacy and attitude on financial management behavior and satisfaction. *BISNIS & BIROKRASI: Jurnal Ilmu Administrasi dan Organisasi*, *23*(3), 4.

Yetim, N. (2008). Social capital in female entrepreneurship. *International Sociology*, *23*(6), 864–885. doi:10.1177/0268580908095913

Yeung, W.-J. J., Desai, S., & Jones, G. W. (2018). Families in Southeast Asia. *Annual Review of Sociology*, *44*(1), 469–495. doi:10.1146/annurev-soc-073117-041124

Yigit, S. (2023). Multi-Dimensional Understandings of Migration: Threats or Opportunities? In Handbook of Research on the Regulation of the Modern Global Migration and Economic Crisis (pp. 239-256). IGI Global.

Yigit, S. (2021). The Concept of Citizenship and the Democratic State. *Electronic Journal of Social and Strategic Studies*, *2*, 5–25.

Yonkers, K. A., O'Brien, P. S., & Eriksson, E. (2008). Premenstrual syndrome. *Lancet*, *371*(9619), 1200–1210. doi:10.1016/S0140-6736(08)60527-9 PMID:18395582

Young, V., Korinek, K., & Minh, N. H. (2021). A lifecourse perspective on the wartime migrations of northern Vietnamese war survivors. *Asian Population Studies*, *17*(3), 308–331. Advance online publication. doi:10.1080/17441730.2021.1956722 PMID:35529055

Yount, K., Cheong, Y., Maxwell, L., Heckert, J., Martinez, E., & And Seymour, G. (2019). Measurement properties of the project level Women Empowerment in Agriculture Index. *World Development*, *124*, 1–19. doi:10.1016/j.worlddev.2019.104639 PMID:31798204

Yousafzai, S. Y., Saeed, S., & Muffatto, M. (2015). Institutional theory and contextual embeddedness of women's entrepreneurial leadership: Evidence from 92 countries. *Journal of Small Business Management*, *53*(3), 587–604. doi:10.1111/jsbm.12179

Youssef, C. M., & Luthans, F. (2007). Positive organizational behavior in the workplace:

Yuk, V. J., Cumming, C. E., Fox, E. E., & Cumming, D. C. (1991). Frequency and Severity of Premenstrual Symptoms in Women Taking Birth Control Pills. *Gynecologic and Obstetric Investigation*, *31*(1), 42–45. doi:10.1159/000293098 PMID:2010113

Compilation of References

Zaka, M., & Mahmood, K. T. (2012). Pre-menstrual syndrome-a review. *Journal of Pharmaceutical Sciences and Research*, *4*(1), 1684.

Zartman, W. (1963). Farming and land ownership in Morocco. *Land Economics*, *39*(2), 187–198. doi:10.2307/3144754

Zeb, A., & Ihsan, A. (2020, March). Innovation and the entrepreneurial performance in women-owned small and medium-sized enterprises in Pakistan. []. Pergamon.]. *Women's Studies International Forum*, *79*, 102342. doi:10.1016/j.wsif.2020.102342

ZelekeB.WorkinehY.MeleseA.SemachewA.YigizawM. (2023). Premenstrual syndrome, life style & behavioral coping mechanisms and associated factors among public high school regular female students at Bahir Dar City, Northwest, Ethiopia. doi:10.21203/rs.3.rs-2418487/v1

Zendehdel, M., & Elyasi, F. (2018). Biopsychosocial etiology of premenstrual syndrome: A narrative review. *Journal of Family Medicine and Primary Care*, *7*(2), 346–356. doi:10.4103/jfmpc.jfmpc_336_17 PMID:30090776

Zhang, C., & Basha, D. (2023). Women as leaders: The glass ceiling effect on women's leadership success in public bureaucracies. *Gender in Management*, *38*(4), 489–503. doi:10.1108/GM-09-2021-0283

Ziba, T., Mohammadi, M. S., Mohammad, A., & Abas, M. (2008). The Effect of Premenstrual Syndrome on Quality of Life in Adolescent Girls. *Iranian Journal of Psychiatry*, *3*(3), 105–109. https://ijps.tums.ac.ir/index.php/ijps/article/download/480/504

Zirari, H. (2021). *Women's Rights in Morocco: Assessment and Perspectives*. Institut Europeu de la Mediterrània (IEMed).

Zuo, J., & Zuo, J. (2016). Women's Triple Burden. *Work and Family in Urban China: Women's Changing Experience since Mao*, 67-76.

Žvan Elliott, K. (2014). Morocco and Its Women's Rights Struggle: A Failure to Live Up to Its Progressive Image. *Journal of Middle East Women's Studies, 10*(2), 1-30.

About the Contributors

Malika HAOUCHA, PhD in English Language Teacher Education from Warwick University, England, 2005; MA in ELT, Warwick University, England, 1995, is an associate professor at the Faculty of Law, Economics and Social Sciences, Hassan II University of Casablanca, Morocco. She teaches general English, English for Specific Purposes and coordinates a bachelor course in International Trade. Before joining the faculty, she had been a lecturer at Alakhawayn University in Ifrane; worked as a part-time English language teacher at the Centre for English Language Teacher Education (CELTE) at Warwick University, England. She also ran her private company and provided English Language training to Dell Corporation employees in Casablanca. The courses taught included both general English and English for Specific Purposes, Intercultural Management. Her research areas of interest include, but are not limited to, academic writing, Higher education branding, innovation in the Moroccan tertiary education.

***

Mawa Mohamed holds a Ph.D. in Sociology and Social Research, with a strong foundation in postwar recovery studies and international relations. Her academic pursuits are complemented by hands-on experience in conflict analysis, providing her with a multifaceted understanding of conflict dynamics. As a researcher, she aims to extend the boundaries of understanding conflict mediation and analysis, examining unheard human stories. She seeks to utilize her skills and passion to contribute significantly to research related to gender, children, and education. She is committed to fostering a culture of excellence and collaboration, enriching the academic tapestry. She is a research fellow at the University of Milano-Bicocca, researching women's empowerment and reproductive health in Sub-Saharan Africa. She also teaches at the University of Khartoum. In the classroom, she ensures students actively engage in critical conversations, creating a collaborative environment that yields positive learning outcomes and a deeper understanding of the subject matter. Her main aim is to help her people through her research and contribute to developing a better Sudan for the next generation, where they can enjoy their lives and be happy and safe.

Dawn Adams-Harmon obtained an Undergraduate degree in Marketing and Psychology from Montclair State University, received an MBA in Management from Fairleigh Dickinson University, and has completed her Doctorate in Management/Organizational Leadership. Her doctoral dissertation topic: Successful Ascent of Female Executives in the Pharmaceutical Industry: A Qualitative, Transcendental, Phenomenological Study; was published in ProQuest in 2018, and published in the Equality, Diversity and Inclusion International Journal/Special Edition (EDI) in November, 2020. Her current research

About the Contributors

on the Intersectionality of Race and Female Gender on STEM career ascendance was presented at the Academy of Management (AOM) for the 83rd annual meeting in Boston, MA: 8/23 conference; has been published in the SocioEconomic Challenges Journal from the Academic Research and Publishing UG ; presented at the Kean Annual Faculty Research 2023; and presented at the Qualitative Research in Organizations (QROM), January 2023. The other research published this year is entitled: "Motivational Book Reading: The Changes in Self-efficacy and Locus of Control in Minority Students: A Mixed Method Study" which was also approved in the Scientific Bulletin. Her professional career has been dedicated to over 30 successful years in the healthcare industry. She spent the majority of her time as a sales leader launching five sales teams and launching products in the New York Metropolitan marketplace with Pfizer, Schering Plough, and Merck. She also held training management positions and was a Director of Leadership Development at Pfizer, and developed a mentoring program that was executed nationally at Schering Plough and Merck. Dr. Adams-Harmon developed the 360-Degree Gender Sphere Awareness, Assessment, and Action Planning workshops and the 6 Success Strategies that create resilience to enable minority and female ascent, in the healthcare sector. She has lectured for International and Domestic audiences on the 360-Degree Gender Sphere and the 6 Strategies to Create Resilience workshops. The International and Domestic audiences include the Healthcare Business Women's Association Mid-NJ; Northern HBA, Post-Doctoral Network (PDN), and IPharma. November, 2020 she spoke at the National Healthcare Businesswomen's Association, and the Association for Talent Development (ATD) in 11/21. She presented her collaborative mixed method study at DSI in 11/21 on increasing self-efficacy and locus of control through motivational book reading. Recently, Dr. Adams-Harmon collaborated with Biogen Biotech and rolled out the 360-Degree Gender Sphere and 6 Success Strategies to Create Resilience Awareness, Assessment, and Action Planning workshops in its entirety. As a full-time faculty member of Kean University, Dr. Dawn Adams-Harmon prepares and mentors diverse students to be the leaders of tomorrow. Her current interests include researching intersectional studies of women and minority leaders, LGBTQ challenges in organizations, self-esteem in minorities, geographical effects of healthcare access on female minority ascendance, research on programs to increase leadership in minorities, and the 360-Degree Intersectionality Sphere. Dr. Harmon has been married for over 31 years and has two children, who are talented in various academic, sports, and artistic disciplines. Her son is in his psychiatry residency after graduating from Rowan Medical School ('23) and her daughter is graduating high school in May '24 and will be attending Roger Williams University in Bristol RI to focus on obtaining her undergraduate and graduate degrees in elementary education and special education. Dr. Harmon has been able to balance an extremely successful career while being present and involved in her family and children's lives. Her interests include skiing, dance, art, music, and she is an outdoor enthusiast.

Melina Seedoyal Doargajudhur is the Programme Lead for the MBA Strategic Project Management Course in the Business School at Edinburgh Napier University. Prior to joining Edinburgh Napier University Business School, Melina was a senior lecturer at the Curtin Mauritius School of Information Technology, an establishment she joined in 2004. She holds a PhD in Information Systems, a Masters in International Business from Curtin University, Australia, and a Bachelor of Science in Information Systems from the University of South Africa. Her current research interests are Remote Working, Education 5.0, Project Management, Bring Your Own Device (BYOD), Mobile/Digital Technology, Information Systems, Structural Equation Modelling, Positive and negative Work Outcomes, Work Behaviour, Employees' well-being and burnout, Job Demands and Resources, Future Workforce and Gender Studies.

Eslam Alaa ELBAHLAWAN is a researcher with a PhD in Cultural and Social Anthropology from the University of Milano-Bicocca in Italy. His primary research focuses on the interchanges between migration studies, everyday life, and religious practices, particularly within Middle Eastern and European diaspora communities. His diverse academic background, enclosing prior master's degrees in economics and development economics, and an MPhil in economic sociology and labour studies, informs his research on these dynamics. Dr ElBahlawan's experience extends beyond academia, fostering a deep understanding of social realities, especially in the context of migration between the Middle East and Europe. His areas of expertise include cultural and social anthropology, migration studies, religious studies, development studies, and the application of mixed methods research.

Courtney Lyn Groenendyk is currently a second-year student in the Doctor of Psychology (PsyD) program at Adler University in Chicago, Illinois. Courtney graduated with a Bachelor of Arts degree in Psychology from Point Loma Nazarene University in San Diego, California. Her research interests include forensics, mindfulness practice, and trauma.

Malika Haoucha, PhD in Applied Linguistics and English Language Teacher Education from Warwick University, England, 2005; MA in ELT, Warwick University, England, 1995, is an associate professor at the Faculty of Law, Economics and Social Sciences, Hassan II University of Casablanca, Morocco. She teaches general English, English for Specific Purposes and coordinates a bachelor course in International Trade. Before joining the faculty, she had been a lecturer at Alakhawayn University in Ifrane; worked as a part-time English language teacher at the Centre for English Language Teacher Education (CELTE) at Warwick University, England. She also ran her private company and provided personal development coaching and English Language Courses to Dell Corporation employees in Casablanca. The courses taught included both general English and English for Specific Purposes, Intercultural Management. Her research areas of interest include, but are not limited to, academic writing, Higher education branding, innovation, and the use of ICTs in the Moroccan tertiary education. Malika Haoucha has a substantial number of publications in high indexed journals, such as Scopus and Web of Science, contributed book chapters and has been an active member in the editorial advisory committees of many renowned journals. In 2022, she edited an IGI published book entitled: Policies and Procedures for the Implementation of Safe and Healthy Educational Environments: Post-COVID-19 Perspectives.

M. Gail Hickey is Professor Emerita of Education at Purdue University Fort Wayne and a trained oral historian. Her research focuses on contemporary U.S. migration, with an emphasis on pre- and post-migration educational experiences and perspectives. Dr. Hickey is the author of four textbooks, more than 75 journal articles, dozens of textbook chapters, and more than 200 conference papers. She has served as Visiting Research Fellow at the Center for the Study of Ethnicity and Race in America (University of Colorado-Boulder), the Immigration History Research Center (University of Minnesota), and the Indiana University Institute for Advanced Study, among others. In addition, Dr. Hickey has been invited to present her research on contemporary U.S. migrants at Charles University (Prague, Czech Republic), the University of Wales (Bangor), Kings College (London), and the Sorbonne University (Paris, France).

Fadila Jehhad is specialising in women empowerment and social entrepreneurship, Fadila Jehhad is a dedicated PhD student at Hassan II University. With a focus on this vital research domain, Fadila has published two impactful articles, contributing to the intersection of economics and social sciences.

About the Contributors

Concurrently, while working as an accountant in the private sector, Fadila also shares expertise as a temporary English instructor at the Faculty of Law, Economics and Scocial Sciences, Ain Sebâa, University Hassan II of Casablanca.

Riley Kowalski is a doctoral clinical psychology student with an emphasis in traumatic stress. She currently attends Adler University in Chicago, Illinois. Riley graduated from The George Washington University in 2020 with a Bachelor's degree in psychological and brain sciences and a minor in criminal justice. Her research interests include trauma, forensics, and women's studies.

Kritika is a post graduate (Master of Technology(M.Tech)) in computer science and engineering and holds the position of an independent researcher, author and peer reviewer of reputed journals indexed in SCOPUS, Web of Science, etc. She is the recipient of Young Researcher Award 2023, Gold Medallist and Silver Medallist in International Olympiad of Mathematics and holds accolades from Government of India for obtaining distinction during high school and senior school. The author is serving as Lifetime Member of International Association of Engineers(IAENG), Member of Women In Cybersecurity(WiCys) India Affiliate and and professional member of InSc Institute of Scholars. The author has obtained certifications in cyber security and is a top scorer in examinations like NTSE(India). The area of research includes cyber security, digital forensics, neuroscience, women empowerment, governance, and code smells.

Maneesha Nagabandi is a rising scholar and clinician, currently in her second year of the Doctor of Psychology (PsyD) program in Clinical Psychology at Adler University. She earned her undergraduate degree in Cognitive Science with a focus on Machine Learning from the University of California, San Diego, where she demonstrated a keen interest in the intersection of cognitive processes and advanced technologies. Maneesha's clinical interests lie in neuropsychological assessment, particularly with diverse clinical populations. Her research background is characterized by an integration of machine learning techniques with psychological phenomena and cognition systems. Her multi-faceted experience positions her as a promising contributor in the evolving landscape of clinical psychology.

Kailey G. Pickhardt is a second-year doctoral student studying clinical psychology at Adler University in Chicago, Illinois. As an undergraduate, she attended the University of Miami in Coral Gables, Florida where she received a Bachelor of Arts in Psychology with a secondary major in Anthropology and a minor in Criminology. She has clinical experience working with adolescents and adults with severe mental impairment in inpatient settings as well as neuropsychological testing experience with adults in an out-patient private practice setting. Her research interests involve intimacy, sexual health, reproductive care, and the intersection of these factors for individuals within correctional systems.

Somya Rawat is from a small village called Tejam, Pithoragarh in Uttarakhand, India. Due to her father's job, she has lived in different cities of India such as Haldwani(Uttarakhand), Lucknow(UP), and Dehradun(Uttarakhand), where she has completed her graduation in BA (Hons.) Psychology from Graphic Era Deemed to be University. Having spent a larger part of her childhood in Haldwani she has been closer to her village roots on the paternal and maternal sides where she felt a lack of mental health awareness, thus she tries to spread awareness about it by engaging in talks with locals and elderly women. Her mother is a homemaker who has spent her youth in the treacherous mountains collecting firewood and hay for the cattle. This adaptability and resilience have been inherited and learned by Somya. Somya's unique experience with rural and urban parts of society made her realize that the stigma regarding mental health is rampant even amongst the educated classes which takes an even exaggerated form in the latter. Therefore, she intends to work in a bridging gap between common populace and mental health care across class, age and gender and contribute towards the betterment of society.

Srinivasan Vasan's three main areas of expertise are Ageing, Migration and Tuberculosis. I attended two international conferences: The 2nd International Social Work Conference 2015, where I presented a paper at the University of Sains Malasiya, and the 8th International Conference on Social Work in Health and Mental Health (ICSW 2016) at the National University of Singapore. In addition, he published 18 articles, six of which were in the field of ageing.

Kanchan Yadav is a PhD from Hemvanti Nandan Bahuguna Garhwal University, Srinagar. She has joined the department of Humanities and social sciences, Graphic era university as Assistant Professor in 2018. She has a teaching and research experience of 9 years and has qualified UGC – NET in 2015. She has worked as faculty member and has taught fair number of Psychology subjects to UG, PG and PhD students. At present she is supervising 4 internal and 1 external research scholars. Her research area includes cognitive behavior therapy, positive psychology, counselling psychology, mindfulness and Depression. She has published number of research papers in national and international journals. She has extensive experience in guidance and counselling to enable the clients (patients / students) to know himself, identify his/ her strengths and weaknesses, to know the facts about education and occupations and to interpret them in relation to each other for planning his own future and to remove unnecessary mental pressures & tension.

Sureyya Yigit is a Professor of Politics and International Relations at the School of Politics and Diplomacy at New Vision University in Tbilisi, Georgia. He has lectured at several universities in Scandinavia, Turkey, and Central Asia. His current research interests focus on the Ukraine crisis, British politics, Globalisation, Soft Power and foreign policy, African development and post-communist transition. He is a consultant at Aeropodium as well as senior consultant to ZDS Women's Democracy Network in the Kyrgyz Republic. He is also a member of the Editorial Board for the IGI Book Series on Conflict Management as well as an Associate Editor for the International Journal of Green Business and Editorial Board Member of AcademCraft - Open access journal of education research and case studies. His most recent books are "India-Mongolia Relations: Beyond Greater Central Asia", published in 2023, and "Africa at Crossroads: Society, Security and Geopolitics" published in 2024.

Index

360-Degree Gender Sphere 259-263, 267, 270

A

Abu-Shouk Camp 119, 121-122, 126-128, 130-135, 138-142, 145-146

B

Barriers 1-2, 6-11, 13-15, 17-18, 22, 25-26, 28-32, 38-40, 42-45, 50, 52-56, 83, 93, 96, 146, 153, 156, 161-162, 165, 173-174, 177, 180, 183, 186, 189-190, 194, 196-202, 204, 231, 233, 259-262, 266-267, 269-270
Biases 1-7, 11-13, 15, 17-18, 25, 28-30, 39, 54, 56, 76, 162, 199, 202
Biosciences 259-260, 263, 267

C

Career Growth 17-18, 25, 31
Climate change 100-118, 122, 202
Creating Resilience 259
Cultural influence 155

D

Darfur Conflict 119, 123-124, 126-127, 146
DEI 259-260
Disabled Women 151, 162

E

Economic empowerment 1, 7, 10, 14-16, 21, 27, 38, 41, 64, 152, 155-156, 161, 163-165, 174, 183, 190, 200-201, 204, 210, 215
Emotional Intelligence 264, 268-269
Empowerment 1-2, 4-8, 10-11, 13-18, 21, 23-25, 27-29, 31-32, 34-38, 40-41, 44-46, 52-54, 56-57, 59, 62, 64-66, 68, 70-80, 101, 117, 119, 122-123, 133-134, 146, 148-149, 151-152, 154-156, 158, 160-167, 173-175, 183, 185-186, 188-216, 235, 242-243
Empowerment narratives 188
Entrepreneur 37, 65, 82-83, 85, 89, 91-94, 96-97, 99, 167
Environmental Degradation 102, 104, 114, 151-152
Equality 2, 8-9, 11, 15, 18, 21-22, 30, 32-33, 36-37, 40-42, 44-45, 53-56, 59-60, 62-66, 68-69, 77, 100, 102, 109-110, 117, 123, 125, 146, 148, 151-154, 158, 162, 165-167, 173-177, 181-184, 186, 188-190, 192, 194-202, 204-207, 209-211, 215, 235, 268
ERG Groups 269

F

Fairness 22, 32, 62, 188, 269
Female Leaders 9, 29, 43, 47, 52, 64, 154, 191, 259, 265, 268
Feminist movements 71, 76, 201-202
Financial Independence 17-18, 25, 31, 34-35, 40, 157, 163-164, 210, 214

G

gender equality 11, 15, 18, 21-22, 30, 32-33, 36-37, 40-41, 44-45, 53-56, 60, 62, 64, 66, 69, 100, 102, 109-110, 117, 125, 146, 148, 151-154, 158, 165-167, 173-176, 181-184, 186, 188-190, 192, 195-197, 199-202, 204-206, 209-211, 215
gender gap 18-21, 26, 33-35, 37, 58, 60, 106, 117, 154, 206-207, 209
Gender justice 173-174, 186
Glass Ceiling 1, 8-9, 29-30, 35, 37, 39, 41, 259, 261, 269-270

H

Human activities 100

I

Implicit Bias 1, 6, 28
Inclusive Approach 151
Inequality 7, 11, 21, 34-35, 37, 53, 63-64, 67, 69, 77, 103, 105, 114, 126, 145, 148, 151-152, 161, 165, 173, 175, 180, 186, 204, 208, 215
Internalization 1, 6
Internally Displaced Persons (IDP) 119, 122, 124

J

Justice 28, 36, 53, 62-63, 109, 123, 173-174, 176, 185-186, 188, 190, 192-196, 198-199, 201, 205

L

Land reform Legal frameworks 173
Land tenure 173, 176-179, 184-185
Laos 82-83, 85-88, 92, 94, 96, 99, 113
Leadership 1-14, 16-25, 27-39, 41-43, 45-47, 51-57, 60, 62, 64, 67, 79, 108, 125, 147, 149, 153-156, 165-166, 189, 191-195, 198-202, 204, 215, 243, 251, 262-266, 268-270
leadership development 30, 39, 42, 45-46, 53, 55, 57, 263-265, 269

M

Menstrual Attitude 217-219, 221-223, 228-230, 232, 236, 239-240, 243-245, 248, 250, 252, 256
Mentoring 8-9, 30, 33, 40, 42-45, 47-55, 57-59, 263-264, 269-270
mentoring programs 42, 45, 263
Microaggressions 1, 5-7, 11, 13-16
Microassaults 5
Microinsults 5
Microinvalidations 5-6
Migration 81, 94-98, 100-103, 105, 107, 109-111, 113-117, 175, 186
Moroccan Women 152-153, 155, 161-162, 173-174, 180, 183-184

O

Opportunity 10, 13, 15, 18, 33-34, 46-47, 62-63, 123-124, 149, 154, 159-161, 184, 246, 267
Organisation 25, 30, 32, 34, 62, 66-67, 71, 75-76, 186

P

Politics 12, 19, 22, 37, 43, 51, 59, 62-65, 67, 70, 79-80, 148-149, 152, 192, 194, 203, 216, 250
Poverty 22, 38, 42-44, 54-55, 66, 70-71, 77, 79, 84, 102-103, 105-106, 114, 116, 121-122, 148, 152, 174, 177, 184
Premenstrual Syndrome 217-219, 224, 226, 228-233, 236, 245-258

Q

Quality of Life 62, 147, 217-224, 226-227, 229-232, 236, 239, 242-258

R

Refugee 16, 55, 82-86, 88, 92-95, 97-99, 112, 149
Refugee Entrepreneur 82-83, 85, 94, 99

S

Security 12, 15, 21, 35, 55, 69, 103, 105-107, 111, 113, 115, 123, 125, 160, 166, 175, 178, 181, 185, 193, 207, 210
Self-Branding 263, 266, 268, 270
Self-confidence 9, 24, 34, 45, 56, 75, 152, 207, 210
Situational Leadership 264-265, 270
Social Capital 80, 87, 92, 94, 97-98, 119, 121-122, 125-129, 145-149
Social Entrepreneurship 151-152, 156-162, 165-167
Social justice 28, 53, 109, 176, 190, 192, 195-196, 198-199, 201, 205
Social reformers 188-190, 196, 199-200, 202
Socio-economic development 120, 146
Southeast Asia 82, 87, 94, 99
Sponsorship 50, 52, 55, 263, 268, 270
statistical analysis 25, 206, 229, 252
STEM education 42, 46
Stereotypes 1-5, 7, 9, 11-16, 22, 24, 28-29, 31-32, 37-38, 41-42, 45-46, 56, 64, 114, 124, 152, 162, 189, 191, 194-195, 199, 202, 204, 215, 222, 228, 230, 251
Systemic Biases 17, 28

T

The 360-Degree Gender Sphere 259, 261-263, 267, 270

Index

Trust 48, 50, 119-123, 126-128, 131, 134-142, 145-147, 149, 152, 194, 215, 264

W

Women 1-5, 7-12, 14-28, 30-48, 51-73, 75-86, 90, 93-98, 100-109, 113-117, 119-128, 130-149, 152-156, 158-167, 173-178, 180-203, 205-225, 227-235, 238-270

Women and girls 11, 21, 40-42, 47, 54-55, 100, 102-103, 105, 113, 115, 120, 146, 190, 229

Women Autonomy 119

Women Empowerment 4, 13, 17-18, 23-25, 28, 31-32, 34-35, 40, 78-80, 149, 151-152, 155, 160, 164-166, 173, 185, 188-189, 191, 198, 200, 206, 213, 215-216

Women Empowerment Initiatives 165

Women leaders 24, 29, 33-34, 36, 45-46, 51-53, 58, 188, 191-192, 199, 203

Publishing Tomorrow's Research Today

IGI Global
Publishing Tomorrow's Research Today
www.igi-global.com

Uncover Current Insights and Future Trends in Education
with IGI Global's Cutting-Edge Recommended Books

Print Only, E-Book Only, or Print + E-Book.
Order direct through IGI Global's Online Bookstore at www.igi-global.com or through your preferred provider.

Artificial Intelligence Applications Using ChatGPT in Education: Case Studies and Practices
ISBN: 9781668493007
© 2023; 234 pp.
List Price: US$ 215

Generative AI in Teaching and Learning
ISBN: 9798369300749
© 2024; 383 pp.
List Price: US$ 230

Dynamic Curriculum Development and Design Strategies for Effective Online Learning in Higher Education
ISBN: 9781668486467
© 2023; 471 pp.
List Price: US$ 215

Illuminating and Advancing the Path for Mathematical Writing Research
ISBN: 9781668465387
© 2024; 389 pp.
List Price: US$ 215

Cases on Economics Education and Tools for Educators
ISBN: 9781668475836
© 2024; 359 pp.
List Price: US$ 215

Emerging Trends and Historical Perspectives Surrounding Digital Transformation in Education: Achieving Open and Blended Learning Environments
ISBN: 9781668444238
© 2023; 334 pp.
List Price: US$ 240

Do you want to stay current on the latest research trends, product announcements, news, and special offers?
Join IGI Global's mailing list to receive customized recommendations, exclusive discounts, and more.
Sign up at: www.igi-global.com/newsletters.

Scan the QR Code here to view more related titles in Education.

www.igi-global.com | Sign up at www.igi-global.com/newsletters | facebook.com/igiglobal | twitter.com/igiglobal | linkedin.com/igiglobal

Ensure Quality Research is Introduced to the Academic Community

Become a Reviewer for IGI Global Authored Book Projects

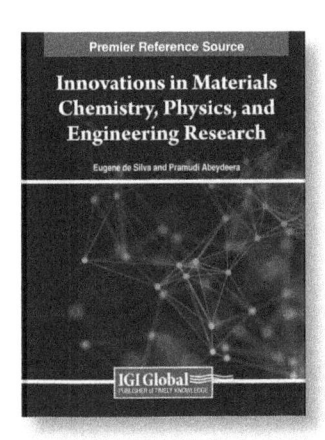

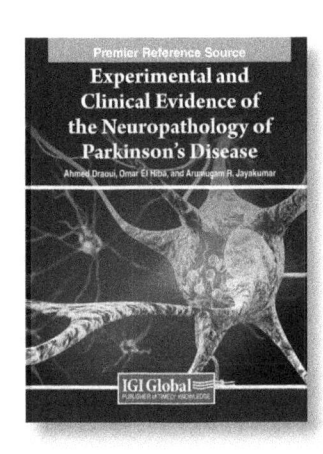

The overall success of an authored book project is dependent on quality and timely manuscript evaluations.

Applications and Inquiries may be sent to:
development@igi-global.com

Applicants must have a doctorate (or equivalent degree) as well as publishing, research, and reviewing experience. Authored Book Evaluators are appointed for one-year terms and are expected to complete at least three evaluations per term. Upon successful completion of this term, evaluators can be considered for an additional term.

If you have a colleague that may be interested in this opportunity, we encourage you to share this information with them.

IGI Global
Publishing Tomorrow's Research Today
www.igi-global.com

IGI Global Open Access Journal Program

Publishing Tomorrow's Research Today
IGI Global's Open Access Journal Program
Including Nearly 200 Peer-Reviewed, Gold (Full) Open Access Journals across IGI Global's Three Academic Subject Areas: Business & Management; Scientific, Technical, and Medical (STM); and Education

Consider Submitting Your Manuscript to One of These Nearly 200 Open Access Journals for to Increase Their Discoverability & Citation Impact

Web of Science Impact Factor **6.5**	Web of Science Impact Factor **4.7**	Web of Science Impact Factor **3.2**	Web of Science Impact Factor **2.6**
 JOURNAL OF **Organizational and End User Computing**	JOURNAL OF **Global Information Management**	INTERNATIONAL JOURNAL ON **Semantic Web and Information Systems**	JOURNAL OF **Database Management**

Choosing IGI Global's Open Access Journal Program Can Greatly Increase the Reach of Your Research

Higher Usage
Open access papers are 2-3 times more likely to be read than non-open access papers.

Higher Download Rates
Open access papers benefit from 89% higher download rates than non-open access papers.

Higher Citation Rates
Open access papers are 47% more likely to be cited than non-open access papers.

Submitting an article to a journal offers an invaluable opportunity for you to share your work with the broader academic community, fostering knowledge dissemination and constructive feedback.

Submit an Article and Browse the IGI Global Call for Papers Pages

We can work with you to find the journal most well-suited for your next research manuscript.
For open access publishing support, contact: journaleditor@igi-global.com

Publishing Tomorrow's Research Today
IGI Global
e-Book Collection

Including Essential Reference Books Within Three Fundamental Academic Areas

Business & Management
Scientific, Technical, & Medical (STM)
Education

- Acquisition options include Perpetual, Subscription, and Read & Publish
- No Additional Charge for Multi-User Licensing
- No Maintenance, Hosting, or Archiving Fees
- Continually Enhanced Accessibility Compliance Features (WCAG)

| Over 150,000+ Chapters | Contributions From 200,000+ Scholars Worldwide | More Than 1,000,000+ Citations | Majority of e-Books Indexed in Web of Science & Scopus | Consists of Tomorrow's Research Available Today! |

Recommended Titles from our e-Book Collection

Innovation Capabilities and Entrepreneurial Opportunities of Smart Working
ISBN: 9781799887973

Advanced Applications of Generative AI and Natural Language Processing Models
ISBN: 9798369305027

Using Influencer Marketing as a Digital Business Strategy
ISBN: 9798369305515

Human-Centered Approaches in Industry 5.0
ISBN: 9798369326473

Modeling and Monitoring Extreme Hydrometeorological Events
ISBN: 9781668487716

Data-Driven Intelligent Business Sustainability
ISBN: 9798369300497

Information Logistics for Organizational Empowerment and Effective Supply Chain Management
ISBN: 9798369301593

Data Envelopment Analysis (DEA) Methods for Maximizing Efficiency
ISBN: 9798369302552

Request More Information, or Recommend the IGI Global e-Book Collection to Your Institution's Librarian

For More Information or to Request a Free Trial, Contact IGI Global's e-Collections Team: eresources@igi-global.com | 1-866-342-6657 ext. 100 | 717-533-8845 ext. 100